AMBIGUOUS TRANSITIONS

# AMBIGUOUS TRANSITIONS
*Gender, the State, and Everyday Life in Socialist and Postsocialist Romania*

Jill Massino

berghahn
NEW YORK • OXFORD
www.berghahnbooks.com

Published in 2019 by

Berghahn Books

www.berghahnbooks.com

© 2019, 2025 Jill Massino
First paperback edition published in 2025

All rights reserved. Except for the quotation of short passages
for the purposes of criticism and review, no part of this book
may be reproduced in any form or by any means, electronic or
mechanical, including photocopying, recording, or any information
storage and retrieval system now known or to be invented,
without written permission of the publisher.

Library of Congress Cataloging-in-Publication Data

Names: Massino, Jill, author.
Title: Ambiguous transitions : gender, the state, and everyday life in
　socialist and postsocialist Romania / Jill Massino.
Description: 1st Edition. | New York : Berghahn Books, [2019] | Includes
　bibliographical references and index.
Identifiers: LCCN 2017052489 (print) | LCCN 2018000867 (ebook) | ISBN
　9781785335990 (eBook) | ISBN 9781785335983 (hardback : alk. paper)
Subjects: LCSH: Gender identity—Romania. | Women—Romania—
　Social conditions. | Women and communism—Romania—History. |
　Romania—History—1944–1989. | Romania—History—1989–
Classification: LCC HQ1075.5.R6 (ebook) | LCC HQ1075.5.R6 M37 2018
　(print) | DDC 305.309498—dc23
LC record available at https://lccn.loc.gov/2017052489

British Library Cataloguing in Publication Data

A catalogue record for this book is available from the British Library

EU GPSR Authorized Representative
LOGOS EUROPE, 9 rue Nicolas Poussin, 17000, LA ROCHELLE, France
Email: Contact@logoseurope.eu

ISBN 978-1-78533-598-3 hardback
ISBN 978-1-83695-070-7 paperback
ISBN 978-1-83695-205-3 epub
ISBN 978-1-78533-599-0 web pdf

https://doi.org/10.3167/9781785335983

*For my children, Sofia and Sebastian*

# Contents

| | |
|---|---|
| List of Illustrations | viii |
| Acknowledgments | ix |
| **Introduction.** Ambiguous Transitions: Gender, the State, and Everyday Life in Romania from Socialism to Postsocialism | 1 |
| **Chapter 1.** The Times, They Are A-Changin': Gender, Citizenship, and the Transition to Socialism | 31 |
| **Chapter 2.** Children of the Revolution: Gender and the (Ab)Normality of Growing Up Socialist | 86 |
| **Chapter 3.** Career Opportunities: Gender, Work, and Identity | 140 |
| **Chapter 4.** Love and Marriage: Gender and the Transformation of Marital Roles and Relations | 195 |
| **Chapter 5.** It's a Family Affair: Parenthood, Reproductive Politics, and State "Welfare" | 247 |
| **Chapter 6.** Good Times, Bad Times: Gender, Consumption, and Lifestyle | 311 |
| **Chapter 7.** Revolution Blues: Gender and the Transformation from Socialism to Pluralism | 364 |
| Bibliography | 419 |
| Index | 445 |

# Illustrations

**Figure 1.1.** "Knowing Our Rights," *Femeia*, March 1958 — 68

**Figure 1.2.** "Questions, Confessions, Experiences," *Femeia*, 1973 — 70

**Figure 2.1.** Cover of *Cutezătorii*, nos. 52–53, 1976 — 109

**Figure 3.1.** Women's Labor Force Participation Rates in Various Sectors of the Romanian Economy, 1948–89 — 152

**Figure 3.2.** Cover of *Femeia*, July 1969 — 154

**Figure 4.1.** "The First Year of Marriage," *Femeia*, June 1971 — 211

**Figure 4.2.** "Be a Man!" *Femia*, June 1971 — 218

**Figure 4.3.** "The Truth about Frigidity," *Femeia*, October 1968 — 221

**Figure 5.1.** "Those 280 Miraculous Days," *Femeia* 1972 — 263

**Figure 5.2.** Cover of *Femeia*, September 1980 — 268

**Figure 6.1.** Traveling in Style, *Moda*, Spring 1963 — 320

**Figure 6.2.** Advertisement for the Practic vacuum cleaner, *Moda* 97, Winter 1969–70 — 325

**Figure 6.3.** "Contemporary Woman: Principal Beneficiary," *Femeia*, February 1971 — 326

# Acknowledgments

This book was long in the making, the product of extended periods of solitary—albeit voluntary—confinement and the support of a range of individuals. My first academic debt goes to my doctoral adviser, Maria Bucur, who shepherded me through the initial stages of this project and served as my strongest advocate from the early days of graduate school through my arrival at that prized destination: a tenure track job. Maria has been a model of scholarly excellence and instrumental to my growth as a historian, and I am forever in her debt. Similarly inspirational is Mihaela Miroiu, whose insights on gender, the state, and Romania have fundamentally shaped my thinking, and with whom it is always a pleasure to spend time. Heartfelt thanks also go to Nancy Wingfield for her mentorship and moral support during my exciting, though often exhausting, journey from assistant to associate professor. At Indiana University, Jean Robinson tirelessly supported my work and got me hooked on feminist philosophy, while Laura Frader planted the seeds for my fascination with gender history years earlier at Northeastern University. Other faculty who enthusiastically supported me during the early part of this project include Christina Zarifopol-Illias, Jeff Wasserstrom, Marci Shore, and Jeffrey Veidlinger. At Bowdoin College, Jennifer Scanlon, as well as Kristen Ghodsee, served as a crucial professional and moral support as I muddled through my first year of college teaching while trying to finish my dissertation and navigate the choppy waters of the job market. Meanwhile, at Oberlin College, Carol Lasser and Len Smith, among other history faculty, provided a warm and welcoming environment for new professors. Last but not least, my colleagues at the University of North Carolina Charlotte have been a continuous source of inspiration and support, and I feel exceedingly fortunate to be part of such a talented, accomplished, and kind community of scholars. In particular, I would like to extend my gratitude to John David Smith, Christine Haynes, Jürgen Buchenau, John Cox, Ritika Prasad, Gregory Mixon, Amanda Pipkin, Sonya Ramsay,

Karen Flint, Carmen Soliz, Heather Perry, and Peter Thorsheim for their guidance and encouragement.

Early research for this book was made possible by a Fulbright IIE Fellowship and grants from Indiana University's Russian and East European Institute and the Association for Women in Slavic Studies. Completion of it was supported by generous funding from the University of North Carolina Charlotte in the form of a Faculty Research Grant and a Junior Faculty Development Grant.

I am very fortunate to have found an editor as attentive, patient, and understanding as Chris Chappell at Berghahn Books; I thank him for his tireless support of this project. I would also like to extend my gratitude to Amanda Horn, who has gracefully shepherded this book through various stages. Finally, I am greatly indebted to the two anonymous reviewers at Berghahn whose critical readings and insightful comments helped me refine my arguments and reframe various portions of the book.

A number of individuals have read all or portions of this book, including Maria Bucur, Mia Jinga, John David Smith, Malgorzata Fidelis, Bogdan Iacob, Nancy Wingfield, Muriel Blaive, Cynthia Paces, Alex Drace-Francis, Ioana Pătuleanu, and Oana Băluță. Their careful reading and valuable insights, for which I am greatly appreciative, have markedly enhanced the quality of the final product. M. Benjamin Thorne deserves particular thanks for his multiple readings and extensive (and rapid) feedback on this manuscript. Additionally, I am indebted to Clara Burghelea, who helped translate many a tricky idiom and expression, as well as Adrian Sorescu, Carmen Mihalache, Ionuț Iuria, Anca Coman, and Ioana Manoliu, who transcribed many of the interviews. I would also like to express my gratitude to Ulf Brunnbauer, Muriel Blaive, Jan Behrends, Sabrina Ramet, Cynthia Paces, Mara Lazda, Janet Johnson, Nancy Wingfield, and Benjamin Thorne, who provided opportunities to present my research at their institutions, where I received excellent feedback. Alongside these individuals, Melissa Feinberg and Chad Bryant deserve special acknowledgment for their ongoing encouragement and support. Over the years, I have developed friendships with many of the aforementioned individuals, for which I am deeply grateful.

For my first introduction to Romania, I must thank Anamaria Dutceac-Segesten who invited me to spend an unforgettable Christmas with her family and friends in Bucharest and Brașov in 1999. Special thanks also to her father for retrieving me late on Christmas Eve from Gara de Nord after my exceedingly long train journey from Munich. More generally, I am eternally grateful to friends in Romania who always make my visits more joyous and less stressful. Irina Hasnaș-Hubbard, who I met while interning at the Museum of the Romanian Peasant in 2000, was, along with her parents, a lifeline during my first months in Romania. At the museum I also met Carmen Mihalache, who has been a great friend and scholarly support to me over the years. Thanks also go to Ioana Popescu, the late Irina Nicolau, Șerban Angelescu, Cosmin Manolache, Ciprian Voicilă and many others in the museum community who made my first year in Romania both enlightening and entertaining. Camelia Sabau and Gianina Frunza (along with their families) also deserve special thanks for their hospitality and generosity during my first year in Romania. Finally, I am grateful for the friendship of Andreea Mottram, who introduced me to the beautiful Oltenian countryside, as well as excellent food and people, including her grandmother (the other) Elena Ceaușescu. It was during this time I met my good friends Clara and Iulian Burghelea, along with the Burghelea family, who ensured I had my fill of regional drinks and dishes.

In Brașov, I am ever grateful to Ionuț Iuria for connecting me with most of my 2003 respondents and who, along with Anca Coman and Ioana Manoliu, conducted a number of the interviews featured in this book. I would also like to thank the generous Iuria family, who treated me as one of their own. In addition, I offer a shoutout to the Coman and Manoliu families for their assistance and kindness. Clio Dumain deserves special recognition for her help with various matters (from securing lodging to ensuring my visa was in order) and for her scintillating conversation and love of good food and wine. Finally, thanks to Ștefan Ungerean and Mircea Ivanoiu for helping me make important contacts at the University of Transylvania and in the city more generally.

In Bucharest, a heartfelt thanks to the Pătuleanu family for putting me up not once, but twice, and for indulging me with great food, conversation, and visits to the symphony. Their home was a much-needed respite from the hubbub and heat of Bucharest, and I cherish my time with Anda, including watching episodes of *Inspector Morse*. I also would like to thank Vali for opening her home in Brănești to me and for her delectable dishes, as well as her daughter, Oana Sandu, a kind soul and first-rate journalist with whom I shared many engaging and entertaining exchanges during our trips from Brănești to Bucharest. Finally, a big thank you to Corina and Adrian Doboș for sharing their cozy flat with me as well as food, drink, and great conversation.

Conducting research in Romania can be challenging, and I am grateful that this process was eased by the helpful and friendly staff at the institutions where I spent most of my time. At the Library of the Romanian Academy, "The BAR," Mirel Berechet and Elena Ioniţa were especially generous with their time, ensuring that I had rapid access to resources and indulging me in coffee and pastry breaks. They bring cheer and warmth to what is usually a solitary and often monotonous task. I would also like to thank Oana, Roxana, Natalia, and Puiu for their assistance and engaging conversations over the years. At the National Archives, Doina Sima and Gabriela Dumitraşcu made sure I received files in an expeditious manner and maximized my time. Last but by no means least, I am deeply thankful to my respondents who generously opened their homes and lives to me and without whom this book would not have been possible. Learning about their experiences has fundamentally shaped how I do history and has been the source of much reflection about my own country, culture, and life.

My family has been supportive of me throughout this project, both morally and practically. Especially critical were their contributions as caregivers while I was conducting research abroad. I would also like to thank my parents for inspiring in me a love of travel and an enduring fascination with Europe; my paternal grandmother, Ginny, who nourished my love of reading and learning; and my maternal grandmother Eva, who nourished me (literally) with Austrian dishes and sparked my passion for preparing Central European cuisine. My mother, Christine, deserves special thanks for her generosity and the sacrifices she has made for her loved ones. Also, I'm blessed to have two wonderful siblings—Kerry and Danny—who have greatly enhanced my life. Finally, my greatest thanks go to my children, Sofia and Sebastian, whose love, kindness, and curiosity have enriched my life beyond measure, providing me with perspective and balance. I am grateful for them in so many ways from being quiet while "mommy works" to insisting that I take much-needed breaks from said work.

Parts of this manuscript appear in the *Journal of Women's History* and *Aspasia: The International Yearbook of Central, Eastern, and Southeastern European Women's and Gender History,* and in the books *Gender Politics and Everyday Life in Central and Eastern Europe* and *Communism Unwrapped: Consumption in Cold War Eastern Europe.* I thank John's Hopkins University Press, Palgrave, and Oxford University Press, respectively, for granting me permission to republish these herein.

INTRODUCTION

# Ambiguous Transitions

Gender, the State, and Everyday Life in Romania from Socialism to Postsocialism

How was our life then? The fact is, we found jobs, we were promoted, and we got raises ... it didn't seem difficult to me. During the communist period they guaranteed us a job, well-paid or not so well-paid, each person was important in their own way. We led a very industrious life. I came home from work, I washed, I ironed, I made food ... and after all that I embroidered and knit. I led a very active life. Now I feel awful because it's very difficult to pass from a period full of activity to a period where time is dead. Now I'm looking for work so that I won't go crazy.[1]
—Maria, unemployed electrician (b. 1955)

For someone raised in an era of alarmist rhetoric about the "evil empire" and made-for-TV movies depicting the aftereffects of nuclear war, excerpts such as the one quoted above seem highly unlikely, if not wholly implausible. While growing up in the United States, my visions of life "over there" were of crumbling apartment blocks, factories spewing pollutants, and empty store shelves and bread lines. Glimmers of hope did appear in the form of TV broadcasts of Lech Wałęsa and protesting workers, but being nine years old when Solidarity formed I was too young to appreciate the movement's significance—or the irony of its very existence. And, even if I had, such images reinforced rather than challenged existing perceptions of life east of the Brandenburg Gate as repressive. Moreover, while I understood that the United States was engaged in a Cold War with the Soviet Union, I really didn't think much about the countries that fell into the latter camp—one reason why I failed, in third grade, to place the word "West" in front of the word "Germany" on the envelope containing a letter to my transatlantic pen pal. Over the course of the 1980s, I developed an interest in history and the reality of this division had sunk in. By 1989 I simply took it for granted that a wall separated East and West Berlin—and would continue to do so for the majority, if not the entirety, of my lifetime.

When the Wall unexpectedly "fell" on 9 November 1989, I was in Austria, about to celebrate my birthday. I greeted the news with shock and excitement and even contemplated jumping on the next train to Berlin, which, much to my continued regret, I did not do. Shock and excitement were also sentiments felt by people in the region. So too was hope. Believing that liberal democracy had finally triumphed over communist tyranny, policymakers, intellectuals, and ordinary East Europeans hoped that pluralism would be a panacea for the stagnation, corruption, and malaise that had characterized the Eastern Bloc.[2]

Over a quarter of a century later, the effects of these transformations have been mixed. While most countries in the region have "returned to Europe" by joining NATO and the European Union, national and local particularities, as well as larger global processes, have shaped the character of economic and political change in the region.[3] As a result, for some the transition to postsocialism has been less than hoped for, and, indeed, outright disappointing. This is especially the case in Romania where corruption, high rates of inflation, rising income disparity, and the curtailment of social entitlements have, alongside more positive developments such as free speech, association, and travel, characterized the post-1989 period. This is not to claim that Maria, the woman quoted at the beginning of this chapter, desires a return to socialism. Rather she, like others I spoke with, desires the security and stability—or perceived security and stability—of the old system.

While repudiated as a political system, socialism, as a way of life, continues to shape how individuals think about their government, society, and themselves.[4] Rising inequality and downward mobility serve in part to explain people's positive appraisal of the socialist past. Perhaps had the transition been smoother, quicker, and more just, their assessment would be less generous? Although this is a plausible and, indeed, tempting interpretation, we must contend with reality, in this case what has come to pass since 1989. Thus, rather than simply writing off Maria's recollection as nostalgic, we must view it as a genuine and legitimate perspective on the past. We must also place it within the larger story of her life, in which positive memories mingle with negative ones. Alongside working third shift and desperately searching for baby formula in the dead of winter, Maria recalled weeklong holidays at the seaside and gatherings with friends and family. Her reflections reveal that there is no simple, coherent narrative of life under socialism, but rather multiple and, at times, contradictory ones. This underscores the importance of analyzing larger political and structural transformations alongside local and everyday practices. It also points to the complexities, contradictions, and ambiguities of socialist modernization and everyday life in Romania.

This book seeks to shed light on these complexities, contradictions, and ambiguities through an analysis of socialist policies, media representations, and women's life stories in Romania from the advent of socialist rule to the present. Although triumphalist narratives extolling the virtues of capitalism and liberal democracy have been subject to increased scrutiny since the global financial crisis of 2008, interpretations emphasizing the criminality, illegality, and inhumanity of former communist regimes remain salient.[5] In Romania, this is evident in the many autobiographies, journals, and memoirs that have been published by former political prisoners, peasants, intellectuals, and others who suffered marginalization or repression under socialism. Because victims of communist repression have dominated historical investigations and public discussions of the past, scholars studying individuals who remained comparatively free of repression or who managed to muddle through, in some cases even experiencing upward mobility, are faced with a particular moral dilemma since, "after one learns about so many broken lives, it actually seems insensitive to remember anything less tragic about the communist period."[6] Accordingly, stories such as Maria's are considered of unequal value, written off as nostalgic products of selective remembering rather than reflections of an authentic lived reality. However, privileging particular experiences over others, aside from being an exercise in historical cherry-picking, can yield simplistic narratives of the past that equate personal trauma with national trauma and obscure the polyvalent meanings of people's lived experiences. This approach also produces a dichotomous view of state and society that neglects the fluidity and interconnection between the two, while glossing over the complexity of human behaviors, beliefs, and relationships.

This book is premised on the belief that examining the oppressive alongside the emancipatory, the monotonous alongside the joyous, the ordinary alongside the extraordinary—and all that falls between these extremes—yields not only a fuller, more nuanced portrait of state socialism and everyday life, but is a historical necessity. This is particularly true of Romanian women whose lived experiences are often interpreted through the prism of pronatalist policies and are overshadowed by heroic narratives of (mainly men's) struggles against a brutal regime. As such, this book seeks to contribute to a small but growing body of work on gender and everyday life in socialist Romania that goes beyond totalitarian interpretations of state-society relations to analyze the complexities of the socialist project and women's lived experiences of it.[7]

While I do not regard the former communist government as legitimate, I do regard the memories of those who lived, worked, took holidays, and raised families during the period as legitimate. Thus, I aim to validate and historicize people's experiences while also recognizing that they occurred under a regime that was neither popularly elected nor popularly supported and that committed repressive acts, often of a violent nature, against its people. Weaving women's varied experiences into the broader political and social fabric of Romania, this book also contributes to scholarship on gender, state making, and modernization in the twentieth century. In so doing, it complicates conventional portraits of the socialist state as an all-powerful monolith ruling over an atomized and hapless populace.

A class-based ideology, socialism sought to fashion a new society, economy, and culture through new laws, institutions, and modes of representation. As in other periods of major transformation, women were essential to this process. Indeed, considering that women, the working class, and low-level peasants were among the most disempowered groups under capitalism, they ostensibly had the most to gain from the transition to socialism. Thus, this book illuminates the centrality of gender in the politics and practices of socialist state making, examining how ideas about women and men influenced policymaking and social organization, and how, through both persuasive and coercive means, the state mobilized women for the purpose of socialist modernization. Because this transformation entailed not only the reformulation of gender as a social construct but also women's and men's everyday lives, I analyze how this process shaped people's ideas about womanhood and manhood and how gender served as a lens through which people understood this transformation. Therefore, this book examines women as objects of state policy *and* agents who made choices, albeit under limited and at times highly restrictive circumstances. Yet, rather than viewing women and the state as oppositional forces, I consider how state socialism constrained *and* enabled agency, focusing on "not only what was repressed or prohibited but what was made possible or produced."[8] I do not, however, attempt to answer the long-debated question of whether socialism liberated women. Rather, I analyze how it sought to do so through state policies and programs and how women, in turn, experienced and reflected on these efforts. As such, this book does not offer a definitive narrative of women's lives in socialist Romania but instead seeks to explore the impact of socialist transformation by drawing on multiple stories and perspectives.

Scholars of women in the Eastern Bloc have examined the centrality of gender in state making and socialist modernization, particularly the ways these processes shaped women's roles, relationships, and self-identities.⁹ For instance, in her study of industrialization in Stalinist Poland, Malgorzata Fidelis analyzes how ideas about gender and the nation influenced labor and family policies, state commitment to gender equality, and women's occupational status. At the same time, Fidelis emphasizes women's agency in challenging state policies and asserting their rights as equal citizens. For the East German case, Donna Harsch similarly examines the interrelationship between work and family, exploring how state neglect of domestic concerns prompted women to lobby the government for policy change, specifically a relaxation in divorce laws, enhanced social welfare benefits, and increased access to consumer goods. Meanwhile, Lynne Haney's analysis of welfare regimes in socialist and postsocialist Hungary illustrates how ideas about gender, family, and need informed state approaches to benefit distribution—and how women strategically drew on their identities as mothers and workers to secure benefits. By analyzing how gender shaped policymaking and how women, in turn, responded to these policies, this body of scholarship illuminates the contradictions and limitations of the socialist project for women as well as its possibilities and opportunities. As a corollary, it explores how state socialism influenced (or not) gender relations in a range of spaces from the workplace to the household.

This book similarly examines gender in its various manifestations—from legislative measures and media depictions to family roles and workplace relations. Like Kathleen Canning, I regard gender as a "category of social analysis that denotes the relational character of social difference" as well as a "symbolic system or as a signifier of relations of power in which men and women are positioned differently."[10] Thus, as employed in this book, gender is both a methodological approach and a subject of study. I consider how gender served as an organizing principle of the state, used by policymakers to restructure various spheres and legitimate the socialist project. For example, in order to rapidly industrialize, the state employed gender-homogenizing strategies, mobilizing both women and men into the labor force. At the same time, the state used gender-differentiating strategies, defining women according to their reproductive capacities, for which they were also instrumentalized, especially after 1966.[11] As a corollary, despite state guarantees of equality between women and men, gender hierarchies and discrimination characterized certain sectors of the labor force. While some women criticized these practices, others ignored them (or were unaffected by them) and embraced the occupational opportunities available to them, regarding work as personally validating and fulfilling. Meanwhile, although pronatalist policies sharply curtailed women's bodily freedom, they also enabled women to draw on the officially vaunted role of mother to secure extended maternity leave or take sick leave. This demonstrates that women did not necessarily regard all aspects of socialism as coercive or oppressive, or that they were unable to assert agency. Indeed, women often strategized to secure certain resources and benefits, appealing to the state based on their social identities as workers or mothers.

I also examine how gender shaped people's beliefs, norms, and practices, serving as frames through which they made sense of their lives. Despite the emancipatory message of socialist rhetoric, in practice gender roles were often more rigid than socialist policymakers envisioned. Thus, traditional attitudes and modes of behavior remained powerful, at times working against women's equality. This was especially evident in male-dominated fields where the presence of women executing traditionally masculine jobs disrupted existing work cultures and men's conception of skill. It was also evident in men's reluctance to assist in the domestic sphere.

Women grappled with gender hierarchies and the tension between socialist ideology and practice in varying ways. While some grudgingly resigned themselves to their fates, others challenged their subordination or negotiated with state actors to improve their situation. For instance, women working in male-dominated areas might assert their legal status as "equal socialist workers and citizens" to call out the sexist behaviors of coworkers, while wives referenced slogans of equality between women and men to persuade husbands to assist with household chores. Moreover, in letters to the communist leadership, women mobilized their maternal roles to request larger dwellings for their families. Although women's savvy use of state rhetoric was strategic, intended to improve working and living conditions, it was also rooted in ideas of citizenship, equality, and social justice. Indeed, like Alexi Yurchak, I found that some of the values promoted by the state (e.g. social equality, community-mindedness, selflessness, diligence) resonated with my respondents, regardless of ideological affiliation.[12] Thus, while many individuals were anti-Ceaușescu, especially by the 1980s, they nonetheless identified with certain aspects of socialist rhetoric and policy (peace, public security, education, orderliness).[13]

While this book is fundamentally about women, rather than posit a "shared female experience," I place subjectivity at the heart of my analysis, exploring the wide-ranging meanings that women attributed to their experiences.[14] Thus, I examine women's varied roles and identities (as workers, mothers, wives, daughters, consumers, activists, dissidents), recognizing that they overlapped and intersected with one another to shape lived experience. I also recognize that their meanings shifted with respect to temporal and contextual factors. Although not a generational study per se, since women from certain age cohorts experienced common historical events and viewed particular periods as life-defining, my analysis, where relevant, generalizes about specific social groups and cohorts.

At the same time, I acknowledge that women did not always understand their experiences as gendered but rather as common to most people living in a one-party state. For example, suffering in a cold apartment due to heat rationing, as one of my respondents stressed, was something that men and women alike endured. Thus, while I believe that gender often *mattered*, I also emphasize cases where, according to my subjects, gender didn't matter. In the end, I did make choices about what issues to focus on, namely youth, work, marriage and the family, motherhood and reproduction, and consumption and leisure; however, I analyze these issues in reference to the meanings that both women and official discourses ascribed to them, recognizing that these meanings changed over time and with respect to context.

As the aforementioned examples illustrate, the interrelationship of not only gender and politics but everyday life and politics is essential for understanding the complexity of life under state socialism. To this end, *Alltagsgeschichte* (everyday life history) is a central site of analysis as well as a methodological approach of this book. A slippery concept, an everyday life approach, according to historian Maureen Healy, enables scholars "to write about politics and the workings of power in a given historical context … and emphasize human agency in the process."[15] Thus, everyday life history illuminates personal responses to policymaking and governance; the different ways individuals interpreted and responded to state power, be it through resistance, dissimulation, or mockery, or through toleration, accommodation, or even affirmation.[16] My analysis of individual agency, therefore, goes beyond the resistance-accommodation dichotomy, acknowledging that individuals could hold multiple, overlapping, and sometimes conflicting opinions of the regime.[17] Thus, they might be supportive of the regime's employment policies, while condemning its reproductive policies. Given the reach and invasiveness of the socialist state and its efforts to transform all aspects of life, an analysis of everyday life is not only useful but also necessary for understanding the dynamics of state power—and people's responses to it.

The everyday life approach has been used to great effect by scholars of Nazism and socialism to illuminate how individuals asserted agency within a system that undermined personal choice and freedom.[18] Through analyses of state (official) and personal (unofficial) sources, these studies have demonstrated that rather than coercion and repression, these regimes relied on a degree of concession and accommodation.[19] Drawing on letters to government officials and editorials, scholars have analyzed how individuals expressed their approval of, concern about, and resistance to state policies—sometimes using socialist parlance to do so.[20] They have also explored how, through connections and personal networks, people negotiated the system of shortage and privilege, securing promotions, scholarships, larger apartments, and a vast array of items from basic foodstuffs to luxury goods. These insights have been instrumental in challenging totalitarian interpretations of communist systems, which focus on their coercive, violent, and repressive aspects. As used in this book, everyday life considers how ordinary individuals engaged with power, including negotiating a range of different relationships to suit their needs. As such, it offers a nuanced portrait of how people resisted or flouted state policies, "worked" the system, enjoyed state services, or simply muddled through. For example, remunerating Romanian doctors with coveted Kent cigarettes and other "luxury" goods could help ensure better treatment in hospital or secure a longer maternity leave. Such an act, what Alf Lüdtke refers to as *Eigen-sinn* (self will), illuminates individual forms of self-preservation and self-assertion and is particularly useful for understanding operations of power on the everyday level. As employed here, however, *Eigen-sinn* need not involve asserting oneself against the state; rather it might entail asserting oneself against traditional beliefs, in some cases even using official discourse to do so. Accordingly, a woman might emphasize her role as an "equal socialist worker and citizen" as a weapon against prejudice in a male-dominated workspace.

An everyday life approach also offers insight into the private sphere or, more aptly, private life, which, in the socialist context, variously served as a retreat and refuge, a place for entertaining friends and family, a site for informal and illicit exchanges, and a space for opposition and honest living.[21] Both personal and social, private life allowed people to sustain traditions, fashion identities, and escape (or grouse about) the overly politicized public sphere or public life.[22] At the same time, everyday life investigations can shed light on morally questionable and ambiguous practices, offering a deeper understanding of how and why individuals supported, complied with, or simply tolerated communist policies. Seen in this light, falsifying statistics, buttressing the Ceaușescu cult, or turning a blind eye to surveillance of friends, neighbors, or coworkers was not necessarily rooted in ideological fidelity to communism, but in the acquisition of basic (or even luxury) goods and services or in the need to protect family members and oneself.[23]

More broadly, explorations of gender and everyday life enhance understandings of the relationship between state and citizen and how politics and ideology were felt by people in their daily lives. Drawing on historian Konrad Jarausch's notion of "welfare dictatorship" and Jan Palmowski's concept of "socialist citizenship," this book complicates conventional Cold War understandings of state-society relations in the Eastern Bloc.[24] In contrast to citizenship in liberal democracies, socialist citizenship was relatively passive: individuals did not genuinely participate in the political process and were prohibited from associating freely, though they did appeal, through letters, protests, and revolts, to the state for improved conditions. While lacking political rights, peoples of the Eastern Bloc did enjoy certain economic and social rights.[25] Although not substitutes for full rights, economic rights, such as guaranteed employment, and social rights, such as universal healthcare, education, and childcare were, for some individuals, as important as—if not more important than—political rights. This was especially the case for women in Romania who were denied a host of political rights during the interwar period.[26] As the country was overwhelmingly agrarian when the communists took power, social entitlements improved the lives of many, often serving as a basis upon which people's understanding of rights developed and their identities were expressed. Indeed, despite (or perhaps because of) the fact that people in the region lacked political rights, their identities developed with respect to social and economic rights. This suggests that some individuals regarded certain aspects of socialist rule, specifically its policies, as legitimate.

At the same time, the existence of social entitlements and people's positive identification with them does not override the fact that people lacked autonomy—though it should also be noted that even in liberal democracies autonomy is constrained by race, class, gender, and sexual orientation. Nor does it override censorship, barriers to travel, material want, repressive pronatalist policies, or other violations of people's civil and human rights. In sum, a broader conceptualization of citizenship allows for a more complex understanding of the state, not only as an instrument of coercion but also of possibilities. As such, it is particularly useful for understanding people's ambiguous relationship toward socialism, as well as state efforts to secure popular legitimacy."[27]

The promise of egalitarianism notwithstanding, socialist citizenship, like other types of citizenship, contained hierarchies and exclusions as some people enjoyed more rights and benefits than others.[28] Some of these exclusions were codified in law, while others were de facto; some were political forms of exclusion, others were social. For example, while social mobility was possible, it was often linked to social origin, job type, and political servility rather than merit. This was evident in the privileges enjoyed by the political elite and, to a lesser extent, heavy laborers. Moreover, access to welfare entitlements varied temporally and as a function of status and political expediency. For instance, during the early years of socialist rule, entitlements were used strategically as a form of social leveling and punishment. As such, poor peasants and laborers were the beneficiaries of "affirmative action" policies, with groups deemed essential to socialist modernization, such as heavy industrial laborers, being privileged for food and housing. As a corollary, while there was a good deal of educational mobility in the country, especially for children of workers and peasants, occupational mobility was limited. Meanwhile, homosexuals, those with "unhealthy social origins," such as interwar elites and alleged reactionaries and kulaks (well-off or landowning peasants), faced discrimination or persecution.

That said, because the state was not static and monolithic but a layered entity, composed of multiple institutions and agencies that relied on bureaucrats, journalists, social workers and the police, among others, to interpret, disseminate, and enforce (or not) its policies, socialist rule was by no means a seamless, transparent, and consistent practice. Indeed, given that connections, favoritism, and bribery became endemic to the system, how policies were enforced could vary depending on the situation and persons involved. The discrepancy between citizenship as legislated, implemented, and experienced thus demonstrates that rights—particularly the enjoyment of them—are never certain or guaranteed, but are often contingent on circumstance and personal relationships. Similarly, people's enjoyment and expression of their rights is often contingent on particular conditions.

Analyzing the nexus between gender, citizenship, and everyday life also illuminates the complexities of socialist modernization. As in the West, in Romania modernization (e.g. industrialization, urbanization, social intervention, welfare entitlements, and consumption) shaped various aspects of life, including gender relations, reproduction, culture, education, and public health. Moreover, in both East and West modernization was a process of assessing, categorizing, managing, and regulating society through institutions, laws, and policies.

It also involved reformulating and identifying need and distributing benefits.[29] Although the state alone defined need, it relied on a host of functionaries, such as physicians, social workers, and pedagogues to do so. By promoting particular practices and values (e.g. literacy, sobriety, punctuality, rational thinking and self-awareness, as well as proper hygiene and child-rearing practices), these "experts" sought to change people's behaviors—to civilize them by creating new men and women.[30]

While socialist policymakers were influenced by Enlightenment notions of progress, state policies were implemented in an illiberal, one-party state that subordinated individual needs to the collective. As such, Romania followed an "alternative path to modernity"—what some scholars refer to as "socialist modernity."[31] Accordingly, socialist leaders and policymakers were not necessarily trying to compete with Western versions of modernity but were following their own version, which they (or at least the true believers) regarded as superior. Indeed, "alternative modernity" became a means by which countries in the Eastern Bloc engaged in the Cold War struggle, with "equality between women and men" being one of the bases upon which they claimed superiority to the West. Thus, gender equality, like social equality, was not only part and parcel of the radiant future envisaged by the communists, but also assumed geopolitical significance. As such, socialist Romania serves as a compelling case study for illuminating different ways that modernization was imagined and implemented, making it a fruitful basis of comparison with noncommunist regimes and other societies in transition.

As in the West, modernization was characterized by tensions and contradictions and often had darker sides. Thus, my understanding of modernity takes into account its ambivalences, contradictions, uses of force, tragedies, and ironies.[32] For example, while the first decade of Gheorghe Gheorghiu-Dej's rule (1947–1965) is associated with repression, it was Dej who decriminalized abortion and made it available on demand in 1957. On the other hand, the early Nicolae Ceaușescu period (mid-1960s to early 1970s) is associated with cultural liberalization, increased consumption, engagement with the West, and the expansion of industry and technology. However, liberalization was also accompanied by the passage of repressive pronatalist policies and restrictive divorce laws. While women welcomed the consumer thaw, their sexual lives became a major source of concern for them. A focus on gender thus underscores the ambiguities of socialist modernization, bringing into sharp relief the tensions between political and economic policies on the one hand and family and reproductive policies on the other. Moreover, it illuminates how relaxations and liberalizations in certain spheres could serve as substitutes for genuine reform in others. As such, a gender analysis disrupts conventional periodizations of postwar Romania, providing a more complex understanding of state making and modernization.

Finally, although the party-state embraced modernity, as in other postwar societies (including liberal democracies), tradition did not wholly disappear but remained a potent force, which the state sought to variously eradicate, accommodate, and appropriate for larger economic and ideological goals.[33] Indeed, rather than being diametrically opposed, at times tradition and modernity operated in tandem with one another. As Jelena Batinić argues with respect to the Yugoslav Partisans, "the success of the party's rhetoric lay not in a mere invocation of traditions, but rather in a deft combination of the old and the new, of traditional symbols and revolutionary ideas."[34] Similarly, in socialist Romania traditional values and practices could prove highly useful for legitimating the socialist project.[35] For example, during the period of heightened nationalism, Ceaușescu relied on the Orthodox Church to promote national identity, an institution that had greater popular resonance than socialist propaganda. Similarly, in justifying restrictive divorce legislation, the state manipulated broader cultural stigmas surrounding divorce.

At the same time, tradition influenced people's daily lives be it in the form of religious beliefs and practices or patriarchal attitudes toward women and gender roles. As such, tradition could be a source of community, self-preservation, and resistance. Yet, it could also be disempowering or regressive, evident in the sexual double standard, gender discrimination in the workplace, and women's (often sole) responsibility for the household. Thus, traditional, cultural, and family practices could go against more progressive policies instituted by the state. As with other states that experienced political revolution (e.g. Nazi Germany, fascist Italy, the USSR), the advent of a new system was characterized by continuities with the prerevolutionary period.

## Historical Sources and Their Discontents

This book draws on numerous primary sources, both archival and human, that have become available since the collapse of socialism. It includes sources produced during the communist period, including legislation, statistics, print media, film, and social science research. Propaganda was invested with a great deal of importance for its capacity to transform mentalities and social practices. Accordingly, a wide range of print media—from the party daily, *Scânteia* (The Spark), to more specialized magazines on art, culture, science, youth, women and foreign policy—and radio and television programs were designed to educate or "enlighten" people about a range of events and issues. These publications aimed to create a new society and a "new person," to shape people's attitudes, values, and behaviors. For instance, the official communist women's monthly *Femeia* (Woman), with its advice columns, debates, and articles on health and hygiene, sought to inculcate certain values and construct a new socialist woman. In particular, the social scientists, medical professionals, and other "experts" featured in the magazine sought to modernize and moralize the population. As such, their research findings were not simply descriptive but also prescriptive. Although some pieces, especially advice columns and debates, were cautiously critical of socialist policy, in the final analysis they were orchestrated or "framed" discussions, designed to promote particular ideas and behaviors and to legitimate state policies and initiatives. Under the pretense of being open forums that sought popular input, these debates, discussions, and advice columns were therefore both safety valves and consensus builders.[36] Yet, while more scripted and ideologically inflected than media in societies with free presses, orchestrated discussions are not absent from those contexts either as women's magazines in the West also prescribed certain behaviors, values, and ideas about womanhood, albeit typically in more subtle and visually appealing ways.[37]

Although socialist media were ideologically driven, they are nonetheless rich sources for analyzing state constructions of a wide range of issues from work, marital relations, and morality to culture, international politics, and economic development. They also illuminate how the state sought to appeal to women and instill in them particular beliefs and practices. Though women certainly did not identify with all the stories in socialist women's magazines, given their lack of access to other women's magazines (except those that were smuggled across the border or sent in from relatives abroad) they cannot be dismissed as entirely meaningless. Indeed, women gleaned from them what they deemed useful or interesting—clothing patterns, recipes, and articles on infant and family health—while ignoring sections that focused on the communist leadership or party congresses.

In addition to socialist media and scholarship, I analyze documents from the archive of the Central Committee of the Romanian Communist Party (Comitetul Central al Partidul Comunist Român, PCR).[38] Ranging from meeting minutes, official reports, and debates to correspondence from foreign dignitaries and ordinary Romanians, these documents are products of both selective recording and selective archiving and, as such, offer particular and partial perspectives on the past. Nonetheless, certain information can be gleaned from them, which, when analyzed alongside other sources, provide a more nuanced understanding of the party leadership and the issues it deemed most pressing and worthy of policy response. Of particular relevance for everyday life is the wealth of correspondence between ordinary citizens and the communist leadership. From fawning letters requesting Ceauşescu's attendance at their child's baptism to desperate mothers pleading for increased rations to laborers highlighting workplace graft, these "letters to the leader" serve as windows onto popular opinion. They also offer insight into people's understandings of socialist citizenship and their willingness to speak "socialist" in order to acquire goods or seek redress for a particular problem or disservice. Although they did not assume the same level of significance as did East German *Eingaben* (petitions), which were voluminous, the fact that the regime chose to archive the letters at all—and, in some cases, respond to them—indicates that it was at least moderately concerned with the "mood of the people" and securing a modicum of popular legitimacy, if only to stave off dissent.[39] I also include letters transmitted by ordinary Romanians to Radio Free Europe, a news source that kept many Romanians informed about domestic and foreign events and showcased Romanian dissidents and various acts of resistance in the country.[40] In comparison with letters that ordinary Romanians sent to local and national leaders, these letters were less guarded in their criticism of the regime and, therefore, more evocative of the frustrations and sufferings felt by Romanians, especially during the final decade of communist rule.

I consider these official sources alongside the more than one hundred oral histories I have collected in Romania since 2003.[41] The interviews were conducted with women and men of varying socioeconomic, educational, ethnic, religious, and professional backgrounds who currently reside and spent most of their lives in two major urban areas: Braşov and Bucharest.[42] Thus, my study does not examine the everyday lives of rural women per se. However, because the country was over 75 percent rural at the time of the communist takeover and many of my respondents were born and raised in the countryside, I consider how their upbringing shaped their outlook and life trajectories.

Most of my respondents were ethnic Romanians, though I also interviewed ethnic Hungarian and ethnic German women. I did not, however, interview Roma women because I had no means of establishing a rapport (through an intermediary, for example) with individuals from a Roma community, and none of my respondents introduced me to women who identified as Roma. Although guided by a questionnaire, the interviews were conversational in style, following the life history approach wherein subjects narrate their lives from childhood to the present, though they also jumped about chronologically and thematically. The questionnaire focused on a range of issues: schooling, work, marriage, parenting, consumer culture and leisure, as well as major events such as the communist takeover, mass industrialization, Ceaușescu's rise to power, and the Romanian Revolution and transition to democracy. I was particularly interested in the diverse ways state policies affected women's lives and which facets of their lives they chose to emphasize (e.g. education, work, family, leisure).

Oral histories conducted after the collapse of state socialism benefit from the fact that people need not fear for their safety as a result of sharing their stories. Thus, unlike interviews conducted during the socialist period (as well as private journals kept during that time), which were, to varying degrees, products of self-censorship, oral histories conducted after 1989 provide (ostensibly) a more candid and in-depth portrait of individuals' lives. Additionally, oral histories offer people a medium for articulating their identities and reclaiming parts of the past.[43] Indeed, the very act of recollecting the past can serve as a form of catharsis—especially for those who spent the majority of their lives under socialism—imbuing their lives with coherence and meaning. Life stories also offer different layers of meaning, illustrating the complex and varied ways that people experience—and in turn remember—events, people, and ordinary practices. At the same time, life stories are not objective reflections of a lived reality but instead provide a particular view—or interpretation—of life experiences, which involve privileging some aspects, downplaying or obscuring others, and refashioning others.

Yet, memories are not only a product of personal engagement with the past, but shaped by relationships, social practices, and discourses. In Romania the regime controlled the construction and dissemination of knowledge, saturating the public sphere with socialist and nationalist rhetoric, which necessarily influenced how people understood and subsequently remembered their environment.[44] At the same time, official discourses existed alongside other, less ideologically freighted discourses. Thus, communist slogans such as the "struggle for peace," "equality between women and men," and "the construction of a multilaterally developed society" coexisted with family stories about the Iron Guard and World War II, while Orthodox prayers coexisted with lines from a Beatles song. In addition, people's experiences were constituted by various practices, from swimming in the Black Sea to participating in obligatory May Day festivals to attending religious celebrations. Thus, in my analysis I consider the different mediums and tropes that shaped people's experiences and memories, recognizing that, while individuals took care to keep certain aspects of their lives private, the official and unofficial often overlapped and informed one another to influence their understandings of the world.

People's memories of the past are also refracted through present-day experiences and discourses, while their experiences of the present (or post-1989 period) are framed through discourses and experiences of the past. Romania's transition to pluralism, entry into NATO and the European Union, and the growth of civil society are indicative of the country's progress over the past twenty-five years. However, progress has not been experienced by all. Indeed, the collapse of socialist industry, wide-scale corruption, and the global financial crisis have produced downward mobility and financial insecurity for many. Consequently, some express disillusionment with the transformation and Romania's "return to Europe." With respect to oral history, this presents challenges since dissatisfaction with the present can translate into veneration of or nostalgia for the past. However, it should not be assumed that people's experiences of the transformation have completely misshaped or colored their memories of the past—or that people yearn for all aspects of the socialist past. For example, women's frustration over the loss of what they consider basic rights (guaranteed work and state-subsidized vacations and childcare) is not so much evidence of nostalgia as it is an unsentimental response to a real sense of displacement and economic uncertainty.

In addition, public (or publically accessible) discourses about the past in the form of memoirs, films, television shows, museum exhibits, and discussions can also shape—and even trigger—memory, which, in turn, can affect how individuals narrate their lives. Moreover, people's narrations of the past are selective due to the passage of time and the choice to present their lives in a certain light (e.g. a sanitized or positive light) or to explain or justify actions with reference to a specific context. In some cases, selective remembering is rooted in self-preservation: a means whereby individuals who suffered repression or other tragedies minimize or reformulate their experiences, identifying themselves as survivors rather than victims. Conversely, selective remembering can conceal or obscure complicity in illicit, immoral, or socially unacceptable acts—and even enable individuals to claim the identity of victim. As a means of dealing with these challenges, I tried to be sensitive to the silences, lapses, and evasions in people's narratives, including their use of ambiguous language, not responding to a question or responding with another question, or simply changing the subject. That said, since remembering the past can be an emotionally taxing process, and some individuals, as a form of coping or survival, work to forgot or repress unpleasant episodes and events, I did not press individuals on particular issues if I sensed discomfort or reluctance on their part. These were, after all, life history interviews not interrogations or therapy sessions. In short, the relationship between experience and memory is complex, and oral histories, like official documents, necessarily represent particular constructions of the past.

While rich, these sources are nonetheless uneven; thus, I employ a triangulated approach in my analysis, juxtaposing official sources alongside unofficial ones, governmental sources alongside personal ones, socialist sources alongside postsocialist ones. In this manner, I highlight common and shared themes and experiences as well as less common or unique ones. As a corollary, since I seek to understand my informants' lives through local and everyday practices, as well as larger political, economic, and social transformations, I consider the degree to which current realities affect their attitudes toward the past. That is, how people have weathered the changes engendered by the transition and how this experience shapes their interpretation of the past. As such, this book is not about one but two major transitions. Exploring the interrelationship between these two periods is crucial, as many of the beliefs and social practices that framed individuals' lives during socialism remain salient today. Moreover, this interrelationship is important from a political perspective given efforts by some elites to condemn and distance themselves from the past and, thereby, obscure complex discussions about it.

Many of the people interviewed for this project led what they considered more or less ordinary lives during what many would consider extraordinary times—what some refer to as "socialist normality."[45] Not all were so fortunate, however. One of them faced outright persecution, two were sent to Soviet Ukraine as forced laborers, and another was jailed after the massive Steagul Roşu workers' strike in 1987; meanwhile, others suffered occupational and related forms of discrimination as a result of their "unhealthy social origins." None, however, suffered the type of persecution associated with Stalinism in the Soviet Union, in part because prolonged, arbitrary terror did not characterize socialist rule in Romania.[46] To be sure, tens of thousands of individuals were—largely unjustly—arrested, imprisoned, and forcibly exiled during the early Dej years. Moreover, individuals faced a range of repressions under Ceaușescu, from the women left to die after botched abortions to the dissidents relegated to psychiatric wards to the children with physical and cognitive disabilities who languished in the "houses for the irrecoverables." However, fear, uncertainty, and inhumanity by no means characterized all or even most aspects of my respondents' lives. Rather, respondents made reference to a range of experiences: the pleasures of work or purchasing a car or household goods, celebrations with family and trips to the seaside, frustrations in finding good childcare and healthy food, difficulties in dealing with sexist colleagues or spouses, fear of unwanted pregnancy. Similarly, discrimination on the basis of ethnic difference was not, according to my Hungarian and German respondents, a significant problem in socialist Romania. This is not to assert that ethnicity did not play a role in the formulation of socialist politics or that individuals of Hungarian, German, Roma, or Jewish descent did not experience discrimination under socialist rule, but rather that the women I interviewed did not encounter notable problems in their daily lives as a result of their ethnic background or confessional affiliation. By focusing on the good times as well as the bad, I am not trying to whitewash the socialist dictatorship or minimize the real injustice and suffering individuals experienced. Instead, I am trying to tell the history of the period through their voices, considering how they presented their lives: what they emphasized or excluded, enthused or remained silent about. By acknowledging that some women and men lived, according to them, a "normal life" does not negate the indignities and inhumanity faced by others, but instead reflects the complexity of socialist rule and the diversity of lived experience during it.

## Organization

This book is organized around experiences that typically structure individuals' lives: childhood and schooling, work, marriage, and family life, and leisure and consumption. Each chapter focuses on a particular topic (e.g. work), examining this topic through the lens of policy, propaganda, and women's recollections of their lived experiences. Inspired by Victoria De Grazia's work on women and gender in fascist Italy, I provide a general overview of the period and the changing nature of socialism while also illuminating the varied ways it shaped women's lives, connecting subjective experiences to larger events, processes, and social changes.[47] As such, each chapter does not offer a definitive examination of the topic, but rather seeks to illuminate the relationship between ideology, policy, and social practice. Consequently, some readers might find that certain topics have been unaddressed (or insufficiently addressed), or that the stories presented here don't reflect their understandings or experiences of the periods under investigation. However, it should be noted that the narrative has largely been structured around the events and episodes my respondents chose to share with me.

While my aim in utilizing the life history approach was to construct a complex portrait of women's lives under socialism, some questions were left unanswered and some issues unaddressed. One issue that receives little attention is sexual behavior. This is due to the fact that sexuality is a highly private matter in Romania, and I feared producing discomfort within—or even jeopardizing my rapport with—respondents if questions were too intimate. Instead, I used our discussions about sexual education, courtship practices, and reproductive policies to get at sexual attitudes and practices. Additionally, I do not examine the experiences of LGBT individuals, as none of my respondents identified themselves (or friends and family members) as such. Moreover, the dearth of source material on the topic for the socialist period presents challenges in contextualizing this history.[48] Another topic not thoroughly explored is intimate partner violence. Although I did ask respondents about the incidence of domestic violence during the socialist period, I did not inquire about this with respect to their own relationships out of consideration for privacy and concern that it could trigger traumatic memories. That said, in response to questions about their relationships with partners, one woman explicitly referenced physical abuse and two others did so obliquely. Given the high incidence—or increased reporting—of domestic violence since 1989, it can be inferred that it was by no means uncommon during the socialist period.[49] Moreover, as we shall see, *Femeia* occasionally took up the issue, illustrating that it was pervasive enough that it could not simply be ignored, but required media acknowledgment. As such, respondents' silences surrounding the topic are perhaps more revealing than concealing.

Chapter 1 provides context for the book, placing women's position in Romania from the latter half of the nineteenth century through the communist consolidation of power within the broader political, economic, and social history of Romania. I explore public engagement with the "woman question" and the contributions of women's organizations in expanding educational and employment opportunities for girls and women and lobbying for women's civic equality prior to World War II. This is followed by an analysis of state efforts to mobilize women for socialist modernization through policy and propaganda. The socialist women's organization The National Council of Women (Consiliul Național al Femeilor; CNF) and its affiliated magazine, *Femeia*, sought to broaden women's roles, valorizing their achievements inside and outside the home. Both descriptive and prescriptive, the articles featured in *Femeia* were designed to promote certain values and behaviors, offering women new ways of thinking about themselves, their relationships, and their place in society. Because women read these magazines, albeit selectively, they should not be written off as empty rhetoric, but instead be considered complex and polyvalent sources that offer important insight into state constructions of gender and women's roles in socialist society.

Chapter 2 examines youth, both as the social group most highly prized for building socialism and as a developmental stage experienced by individuals. With respect to gender, state policy was comparatively progressive: young people were typically treated as a general category, education was compulsory for boys and girls alike, and socialist youth organizations included both sexes. Moreover, both boys and girls were encouraged in the sciences and to participate in academic and sporting competitions. Consequently, female youth's opportunities and experiences expanded dramatically under socialism, indicating that state institutions and organizations served as potentially powerful sites for promoting gender equality. That said, not all families embraced the state's egalitarian approach to youth as cultural beliefs about gender roles remained strong, especially with respect to sexual behavior and socializing with the opposite sex.

While young people were invested with great hope, they were also regarded as potentially dangerous, particularly during the first years of socialist rule when "social origin" influenced access to and treatment within the educational system. Moreover, social origin affected youths' upbringing and standard of living, as families were torn asunder when parents were sent to prison. Thus, while official media represented the family as the bedrock of society, state policies at times undermined family cohesion. By the later 1960s, concern over youth arose again, this time with respect to "workshy" and "asocial" youth who were regarded as contaminating elements and a stain on the collective. Taken as a whole, state policies on youth were progressive, conservative and, for some, repressive, illustrating the larger ambiguities of socialist rule and everyday life in Romania. Yet, despite such restrictions and ambiguities, most of my respondents recalled their childhoods as "normal," as they engaged in a wide range of leisure and other activities with friends and family, which often enriched their lives. Indeed, it was only when they reached later childhood and early adolescence that they began to notice the abnormalities, contradictions, and repression that characterized the system.

In chapter 3, I analyze the impact of socialist modernization on the makeup of the labor force, labor relations, and women's experiences of work. Although codified as equal laborers and feted for their productive contributions, women's experiences of work often diverged from official representations. While women's advancement in industry and the sciences was indeed impressive, the socialist workforce reflected larger gender hierarchies, with women dominating light and service industries and medicine, culture, and education—jobs that garnered lower pay and status than those in heavy industry. The gendering of labor intensified under Ceaușescu with the introduction of promotional schemes that directed women into science and technology, but also channeled them into less physically demanding jobs. In addition to heavy industry, women were underrepresented in leadership positions, including in politics, undermining their ability to effect change. As such, the workplace offered opportunities for social advancement and empowerment, but could also institutionalize difference and reinforce gender hierarchies.

More generally, women were less likely to advance professionally due to male prejudice and family responsibilities, illustrating state inability to effectively transform patriarchal mentalities and incentivize women's dual roles as workers and mothers. Finally, women employed in male-dominated areas faced prejudice and, in some cases, harassment by male colleagues. That said, work was also a vehicle for social and personal transformation: while some women reflected upon their work experiences negatively, as burdensome and unfulfilling, others considered work empowering and personally validating, providing them with the opportunity to leave the family home, earn a living wage, and develop new relationships. Indeed, some even cited employment opportunities as evidence of their equality with men.

Chapter 4 examines continuities and changes in spousal roles and relationships. Socialist family codes reconfigured women's marital status from dependents to equal partners, and socialist propagandists promoted men's participation in household maintenance and childcare. These progressive constructions, however, existed alongside policies, such as maternity leave, that reinforced gendered caregiving and broader cultural ideas about gender and domestic labor. This translated into a double or even triple burden for women, which the state paid lip service to by promising labor-saving devices and one-stop grocery stores, yet generally failed to deliver on. More problematically, with the advent of pronatalist policies the state assumed a decidedly conservative approach to marriage, tightening divorce legislation and depicting it as immoral and detrimental to children's development. These realities, combined with housing shortages and cultural stigmas surrounding divorce, forced many women to remain in unhappy, unhealthy, and even dangerous partnerships.

Despite this, according to some of my respondents, marital roles did become more equal over the course of socialist rule. While in part related to men's increased sensitivity to women's challenges, this shift was mainly related to necessity as inadequate childcare facilities, relocation away from extended family, and the reintroduction of rationing in the 1980s required contributions of both spouses (and, indeed, all family members) in the maintenance of the household. Thus, state failure to substantially improve material realities in some cases inadvertently fostered more equitable partnerships.

Chapter 5 examines how civic and parental roles were reformulated as a result of state demographic goals and welfare policies, underscoring the interplay between the body, citizenship, and the nation. While Dej, for the most part, incentivized motherhood through positive measures such as child allowances and heroine mother awards, Ceaușescu, in response to the declining birth rate, introduced repressive measures, including the criminalization of abortion and the taxation of childless couples. Accordingly, motherhood was transformed from a cultural practice that was celebrated into a duty of all women of childbearing age. As such, it became a fundamental basis for defining and evaluating civic worth—as well as for policing and punishing women. Indeed, socialist Romania offers a rare example of women experiencing systematic violence by a state during peacetime in the name of promoting life.

As a corollary to policy analysis, I explore women's efforts to circumvent antiabortion legislation, along with the anxiety, fear, and tragedy surrounding it. Respondents stressed the inhumanity of pronatalist policies, particularly the way in which they undermined bodily autonomy and family well-being. While women did not resist these policies in the form of public protests, by procuring an abortion they were effectively opposing the state. Given the real physical dangers and legal risks involved in this practice, women of childbearing age were thus engaged in prolonged acts of resistance against the state under Ceaușescu.[50]

This chapter also examines family policies and the everyday experience of parenthood. For the vast majority of my respondents, family was the most rewarding aspect of their lives, revealing that even in the midst of material shortage and invasive pronatalist policies, motherhood could be highly rewarding. Still, mothers faced a host of challenges in reconciling the demands of work and family, particularly finding adequate childcare. In response, women devised clever strategies to maximize the time spent with their infants, drawing on maternalist discourse to persuade doctors to extend maternity leave.

In chapter 6, I examine the interplay between consumption, citizenship, and identity, exploring Romania's transformation from postwar austerity in the late 1940s and 1950s to cultural and consumer liberalization in the 1960s and 1970s to the return to austerity in the 1980s. Consumption served as a tool of political legitimacy and social control, a means of highlighting the modernity and seeming progressiveness of the regime and for asserting national autonomy. It was also a constitutive element of identity formation, a medium for constructing and reinforcing social hierarchies, and a central facet of everyday life, which could elicit pleasure but also anxiety. Increased access to consumer goods during the 1960s and 1970s markedly improved the lives of many—and helped garner popular support for the regime. In terms of gender specifically, new models of womanhood, often influenced by Western styles, emerged, and heretofore-personal issues, such as marital relations and sexuality, were featured topics in socialist media. At the same time, the "marketing" of modern fashions and furnishings was accompanied by draconian pronatalist policies, which conflicted with the progressive depictions featured in the magazines.

By the late 1970s, the state reversed consumer policies in an effort to pay off the foreign debt. The result was a desperate and disgruntled population that relied on the black market, connections, and barter as basic survival strategies. Shortage presented particular challenges for women as they struggled to procure infant formula, concoct nourishing and palatable meals, and complete essential tasks, at times without hot water or electricity. Such shortages compounded the stress and indignity women experienced as a result of the criminalization of abortion, which, when considered alongside official rhetoric about women's noble roles as mothers, further underscored the ideological bankruptcy of the regime. Ultimately, increased penury and repression, along with the waning of socialism elsewhere in the Bloc, compelled Romanians to topple the Ceaușescu regime, illustrating the centrality of consumption in regime legitimacy and longevity.

Chapter 7 examines another major transition in twentieth-century Romania: the transition from socialism to pluralism. It traces the lead-up to the revolution of 1989, the ensuing political and social turmoil, and the shift to pluralism. I argue that the postsocialist period, like the socialist period, has been characterized by ambiguity. As such,

David Kideckel's term "actually existing turbulence" aptly describes the flux and uncertainty that Romanians experienced during the 1990s and early 2000s.[51] In terms of my respondents, while some successfully retooled their skills and integrated into the competitive marketplace, others, due to structural transformations and factors outside of their control, were less successful in this endeavor. Consequently, some women praised the political freedoms and professional opportunities of the post-1989 period, while others were more measured and even critical in their assessments of the past twenty-five years, lamenting the loss of security, validation, and camaraderie they had enjoyed during the socialist period. At the same time, they universally praised the rights they have gained since 1989: freedom of speech, association, and travel, and, crucially for women, reproductive freedom. Indeed, many Romanians have availed themselves of these freedoms, participating in marches and protests and migrating to Western Europe for improved educational and employment opportunities.

Yet, continuities with the past also remain in the form of wide-scale corruption and political graft. Thus, this chapter problematizes triumphalist discourses that emerged after 1989, highlighting the complex effects of political and economic pluralism on Romanians' lives. As a corollary, it challenges the prevailing belief that people's positive recollections of the past are evidence of communist nostalgia, illustrating that, for some, socialism was not simply about security and economic stability but also identity formation and collective belonging. Whatever my respondents' views of the past, I conclude that socialism remains alive in the minds—and in some cases the hearts—of Romanians today, influencing how they make sense of both past and present.

## Notes

1. Maria, interview with author, Brașov, 15 June 2003.
2. For triumphalist narratives on the fall of communism, see Francis Fukuyama, *The End of History and the Last Man* (New York: Free Press, 1992); and François Furet, *The Passing of an Illusion: The Idea of Communism in the Twentieth Century* (Chicago: University of Chicago Press, 1995).
3. See Sorin Antohi and Vladimir Tismăneanu, eds., *Between Past and Future: The Revolutions of 1989 and Their Aftermath* (Budapest: Central European University Press, 2000).
4. Scholars of the Eastern Bloc use various terms to describe the regimes and societies they investigate (e.g. socialism, state-socialism, communism, and Communism) and, as of this writing, there is no consensus on what is the most appropriate or accurate term to use. Because party leaders, propagandists, and policymakers in Romania used the term "communist" to refer to the party and "socialist" to refer to the type of governmental system they had created—or were in the process of creating—I have chosen to use these terms as well. Thus, my use of the terms "communist" and "socialist" to refer to one-party rule by the Romanian Communist Party and the economic, social, and cultural system that was implemented by the state between 1947 and 1989 does not reflect a belief that either of these stages were realized. Rather, it reflects the designations employed by leaders and propagandists at the time as well as those used by my respondents.
5. According to this interpretation, communist politics in the East European satellites was orchestrated by the Soviet Union, and a self-interested ruling elite controlled all aspects of life through terror, coercion, and intimidation. For examples of the totalitarian model, see Hugh Seton-Watson, *The East European Revolutions* (Boulder, CO: Westview Press, 1983); and Carl Friedrich and Zbigniew Brzezinski, *Totalitarian Dictatorship and Autocracy* (Cambridge, MA: Harvard University Press, 1956).
6. Cristina Petrescu and Dragoș Petrescu, "The Cannon of Remembering Romanian Communism: From Autobiographical Recollections to Collective Representations," in *Remembering Communism: Private and Public Recollections of Lived Experience in Southeast Europe*, ed. Maria Todorova, Augusta Dimou, and Stefan Troebst (Budapest: Central European University Press, 2014), 49.
7. The most comprehensive analysis of gender policy and propaganda in socialist Romania is Luciana M. Jinga, *Gen și reprezentare în România comunistă, 1944–1989* (Iași: Polirom, 2015). Additionally, Gail Kligman's *The Politics of Duplicity: Controlling Reproduction in Ceausescu's Romania* (Berkeley: University of California Press, 1998) provides an extensive analysis of the policies and practices associated with Ceaușescu's pronatalist program. With respect to women's reflections on their experiences under socialism, a number of memoir collections have been published in Romania over the past decade, most notable among them Zoltán Rostás and Theodora Eliza Văcăresu, *Cealaltă jumătate a istoriei: Femei povestind* (Bucharest: Curtea Veche, 2008), which focuses on the lives of

rural women, and Radu Pavel Gheo and Dan Lungu, *Tovarăşe de drum: Experienţa feminină în comunism* (Iaşi: Polirom, 2008). For general oral histories of the period, see, for example, Zoltán Rostás and Sorin Stoica, eds., *Istorie la firul ierbii: Documente sociale orale* (Bucharest: Editura Tritonic, 2003); Smaranda Vultur, *Istorie trăită—Istorie povestită: Deportarea în Bărăgan (1951–1956)* (Timişoara: Editura Amarcord, 1997); and *Germanii din Banat prin povestirile lor* (Bucharest: Paideia, 2000). On social and everyday life histories of communism, see Adrian Neculau, ed., *Viaţa cotidiană în comunism* (Iaşi: Polirom, 2004); and Paul Cernat, Angelo Mitchievici, and Ioan Stanomir, eds., *Explorări în comunismul românesc*, vols. 1, 2, and 3 (Iaşi: Polirom, 2004, 2005, and 2008).
8. See Stephen Kotkin, *Magnetic Mountain: Stalinism as a Civilization* (Berkeley: University of California Press, 1995), 22.
9. For the Soviet Union, see Wendy Z. Goldman, *Women, the State and Revolution: Soviet Family Policy and Social Life, 1917–1936* (New York: Cambridge University Press, 1993); Wendy Goldman, *Women at the Gates: Gender and Industry in Stalin's Russia* (New York: Cambridge University Press, 2002); Elizabeth A. Wood, *The Baba and the Comrade: Gender and Politics in Revolutionary Russia* (Bloomington, IN: Indiana University Press, 1997); Lynne Attwood, *Creating the New Soviet Woman: Women's Magazines as Engineers of Female Identity, 1922–1953* (Basingstoke: Macmillan, 1999); Choi Chatterjee, *Celebrating Women: Gender, Festival Culture, and Bolshevik Ideology, 1910–1939* (Pittsburgh, PA: University of Pittsburgh Press, 2002); Melanie Ilić ed., *Women in the Stalin Era* (New York: Palgrave, 2001); and Melanie Ilić, Susan Reid, and Lynne Attwood, eds., *Women in the Khrushchev Era* (New York: Palgrave Macmillan, 2004). For Eastern Europe, see Lynne Haney, *Inventing the Needy: Gender and the Politics of Welfare in Hungary* (Berkeley: University of California Press, 2002); Donna Harsch, *Revenge of the Domestic: Women, the Family, and Communism in the German Democratic Republic* (Princeton, NJ: Princeton University Press, 2006); Kligman, *The Politics of Duplicity*; Malgorzata Fidelis, *Women, Communism, and Industrialization in Postwar Poland* (New York: Cambridge University Press, 2010); Shana Penn and Jill Massino, eds., *Gender Politics and Everyday Life in State Socialist Eastern and Central Europe* (New York: Palgrave, 2009); Catherine Baker, ed., *Gender in Twentieth-Century Europe and the USSR* (London: Palgrave Macmillan, 2017); and Joanna Goven, "Gender and Modernism in a Stalinist State," *Social Politics* 9, no. 1 (2002): 3–28.
10. Kathleen Canning, *Gender History in Practice: Historical Perspectives on Bodies, Class, and Citizenship* (Ithaca, NY: Cornell University Press, 2006), 4.
11. The conceptualization of gender-homogenizing and gender-differentiating strategies is taken from Goven, "Gender and Modernism."
12. Alexi Yurchak, *Everything Was Forever, until It Was No More: The Last Soviet Generation* (Princeton, NJ: Princeton University Press, 2005), 8.
13. State promotion of such issues, argues Thomas Lindenberger, provided a "tacit consensus" between the rulers and the ruled. See Thomas Lindenberger, "Tacit Minimal Consensus: The Always Precarious East German Dictatorship," in *Popular Opinion in Totalitarian Regimes: Fas-*

*cism, Nazism, Communism*, ed. Paul Corner (Oxford: Oxford University Press, 2009), 208–222. Also see Ulf Brunnbauer, *Die sozialistische Lebensweise: Ideologie, Gesellschaft, Familie und Politik in Bulgarien (1944–1989)* (Vienna: Böhlau Verlag, 2007).

14. In this capacity, I am influenced by oral historians of women and gender. See, for example, Sherna Berger Gluck and Daphne Patai, eds., *Women's Words: The Feminist Practice of Oral History* (New York: Routledge, 1991).
15. See Maria Bucur, Rayna Gavrilova, Wendy Goldman, Maureen Healy, Kate Lebow, and Mark Pittaway, "Six Historians in Search of Alltagsgeschichte," in *Aspasia: International Yearbook of Central, Eastern, and Southeastern European Women's and Gender History* 3 (2008): 189–212.
16. On making do, See Michel De Certeau, *The Practice of Everyday Life* (Berkeley: University of California Press, 2002).
17. On the importance of historicizing the various ways individuals expressed agency under socialism see Jan Plamper, "Beyond Binaries: Popular Opinion in Stalinism," in *Popular Opinion in Totalitarian Regimes*, 65–80.
18. See Alf Lüdtke, ed., *The History of Everyday Life: Reconnecting Historical Experience and Ways of Life* (Princeton, NJ: Princeton University Press, 1995); Sheila Fitzpatrick, *Everyday Stalinism: Ordinary Life in Extraordinary Times: Soviet Russia in the 1930s* (New York: Oxford, 1999); Thomas Lindenberger, ed., *Herrschaft und Eigen-sinn in der Diktatur: Studien zur Gesellschaftsgeschichte der DDR* (Cologne: Böhlau Verlag, 1999); and Donald J. Raleigh, *Soviet Baby Boomers: An Oral History of Russia's Cold War Generation* (Oxford: Oxford University Press, 2012).
19. See Kotkin, *Magnetic Mountain;* Padraic Kenney, *Rebuilding Poland: Workers and Communists, 1945–1950* (Ithaca, NY: Cornell University Press, 1997); Padraic Kenney, *A Carnival of Revolution: Central Europe 1989* (Princeton, NJ: Princeton University Press, 2002); Konrad Jarausch, ed., *Dictatorship as Experience: Towards a Socio-Cultural History of the GDR* (New York: Berghahn Books, 1999); Mark Pittaway, *The Workers' State: Industrial Labor and the Making of Socialist Hungary* (Pittsburgh, PA: University of Pittsburgh Press, 2012); and Josie McLellan, *Love in the Time of Communism: Intimacy and Sexuality in the GDR* (Cambridge: Cambridge University Press, 2011).
20. See Sarah Davies, *Popular Opinion in Stalin's Russia: Terror, Propaganda, and Dissent, 1934–1941* (Cambridge: Cambridge University Press, 1997); Sheila Fitzpatrick, "Supplicants and Citizens: Public Letter-Writing in Soviet Russia in the 1930s," *Slavic Review* 55, no. 1 (1966): 78–105; Paul Betts, *Within Walls: Private Life in the German Democratic Republic* (Oxford: Oxford University Press, 2011); Martin K. Dimitrov, "What the Party Wanted to Know: Citizen Complaints as a 'Barometer of Public Opinion' in Communist Bulgaria," *East European Politics and Societies* 28, no. 2 (2014): 271–295. Mioara Anton and Laurenţiu Constantiniu, ed., *Guvernaţi şi Guvernanţi: Scrisori către putere, 1945–1965* (Bucharest: IICCMER, 2013); Mioara Anton *"Ceauşescu şi poporul!" Scrisori către "iubitul conducător" (1965–1989)* (Târgovişte: Cetatea de Scaun, 2016); and Manuela Marin, *Între prezent şi trecut: cultul personalităţii lui Nicolae Ceauşescu şi opinia publica românească* (Cluj-Napoca: Editura MEGA, 2014).

21. See Betts, *Within Walls*.
22. By employing the terms private sphere/private life and public sphere/public life, I am not claiming that these were oppositional spaces or that one existed outside the other. Indeed, I fully recognize that private life was decisively compromised within the socialist context, particularly in Romania, and that there was a good deal of fluidity between the two. At the same time, people managed to find spaces (both physical and mental) where they could take refuge from the state and engage in pursuits that were outside of its purview.
23. On definitions of complicity under socialism, see Kligman, *Politics of Duplicity*, 14–15.
24. For a discussion of socialist citizenship in the GDR, see Konrad H. Jarausch, "Care and Coercion: The GDR as Welfare Dictatorship," in *Dictatorship as Experience*, 47–72; and Jan Palmowski, "Citizenship, Identity, and Community in the German Democratic Republic," in *Citizenship and National Identity in Twentieth-Century Germany*, ed. Geoff Eley and Jan Palmowski (Stanford, CA: Stanford University Press, 2008): 73–94.
25. On different types of citizenship in the modern state, see T. H. Marshall's classic, *Class, Citizenship, and Social Development* (New York: Doubleday, 1964).
26. On women and citizenship in Romania, see Enikő Magyari-Vincze, "Romanian Gender Regimes and Women's Citizenship," in *Women and Citizenship in Central and Eastern Europe*, ed. Jasmina Lukić, Joanna Regulska, and Darja Zaviršek (Aldershot: Ashgate, 2006), 26.
27. On legitimacy as a frame for analyzing socialist state-building efforts and the relationship between the regime and society in Hungary, see Pittaway, *The Workers' State*, 3–6.
28. On the exclusivity of socialist citizenship, see Golfo Alexopoulos, "Soviet Citizenship, More or Less: Rights, Emotions, and States of Civic Belonging," *Kritika: Explorations in Russian and Eurasian History* 7, no. 3 (2006): 487–528.
29. Lynne Haney refers to these as "architectures of need." Haney, *Inventing the Needy*, 7.
30. James Scott, *Seeing Like a State: How Certain Schemes to Improve the Human Condition Have Failed* (New Haven, CT: Yale University Press, 1999), 90–91.
31. On socialist modernity, see Kotkin, *Magnetic Mountain*; Jarausch, "Care and Coercion"; and Katherine Pence and Paul Betts, eds., *Socialist Modern: East German Everyday Culture and Politics* (Ann Arbor, MI: University of Michigan Press, 2008). On alternative modernity, see David Hoffmann, *Stalinist Values: The Cultural Norms of Soviet Modernity, 1917–1941* (Ithaca, NY: Cornell University Press, 2003).
32. Dipesh Chakrabarty, "Postcoloniality and the Artifice of History: Who Speaks for 'Indian' Pasts?," *Representations* 37 (1992), 21.
33. On the use of tradition for socialist purposes see Hoffmann, *Stalinist Values*, 9–10.

34. Jelena Batinić, *Women and Yugoslav Partisans: A History of World War II Resistance* (New York: Cambridge University Press, 2015), 75.
35. On the gendered dimensions and implications of nationalist discourse in socialist Romania, see Katherine Verdery, *What Was Socialism, and What Comes Next?* (Princeton, NJ: Princeton University Press, 1996), in particular chapter three, "From Parent-State to Family Patriarchs: Gender and Nation in Contemporary Eastern Europe."
36. See Marcin Kula, "Poland: The Silence of Those Deprived of Voice," in *Popular Opinion in Totalitarian Regimes*, 153.
37. See, for example, Jennifer Scanlon, *Inarticulate Longings: The Ladies' Home Journal, Gender, and the Promises of Consumer Culture* (New York: Routlege, 1995).
38. The Communist Party of Romania (PCdR), changed its name to the Romanian Workers Party (Partidul Muncitoresc Român; PMR) in 1948. In order to emphasize the historical continuity with the prewar, revolutionary movement, Ceaușescu changed its name back to the Communist Party of Romania in 1965.
39. See Betts, *Within Walls*, for an analysis of *Eingaben* in the GDR. In this respect, Romania was not a "participatory dictatorship" in the sense that the GDR was. See Mary Fulbrook, *The People's State: East Germany from Hitler to Honecker* (New Haven, CT: Yale University Press, 2008), 11–12. The letters were received and archived in the Department of Letters and Audiences, which was a section within the Central Committee of the Romanian Communist Party. Individuals typically appealed to high-ranking leaders at the Central Committee in Bucharest as a last resort, after having unsuccessfully sought redress of an issue through the Party at the local or regional level.
40. Although listening to Radio Free Europe broadcasts was illegal in Romania, its audience grew considerably under Ceaușescu, and by the final decade of communist rule most of the population—including members of the *miliția* and Securitate—tuned in. During the 1980s, prime listening time was between 6pm and 11pm. See Marin, *Între prezent și trecut*.
41. Respondents were identified through friends, colleagues, and the snowball method, which, while not scientific, helps foster trust since it involves an intermediary who is familiar with researcher and subject. All interviews were conducted in Romanian and digitally recorded and typically occurred in the respondents' homes. In the spring and summer of 2003, three sociology students from the University of Transylvania—Ioana Manoliu, Anca Coman, and Ionuț Iuria—conducted twenty-five interviews, while I conducted fifty interviews. Meanwhile, I conducted all interviews in 2009 and 2012.
42. While my respondents were born between 1924 and 1972, most were born in the 1940s and 1950s.
43. See Luisa Passerini, ed., *International Yearbook of Oral History and Life Stories: Volume I: Memory and Totalitarianism* (New York: Oxford University Press: 1992); and Rubie Watson, ed., *Memory, History, and Opposition under State Socialism* (Santa Fe, NM: School of American Research Press,

1994). For more general scholarship on oral history and agency, see Paul Thompson, *The Voice of the Past: Oral History* (Oxford: Oxford University Press, 2000); Berger and Patai, *Women's Words;* and Alessandro Portelli, *The Death of Luigi Trastulli and Other Stories: Form and Meaning in Oral History* (Albany, NY: State University of New York Press, 1991).

44. For a discussion of how official culture influenced people's understanding of state and society in socialist Romania, see the introduction in Gail Kligman and Katherine Verdery, *Peasants under Siege: The Collectivization of Romanian Agriculture, 1949–1962* (Princeton, NJ: Princeton University Press, 2011).
45. See Daniela Koleva, ed., *Negotiating Normality: Everyday Lives in Socialist Institutions* (New Brunswick, NJ: Transaction Publishers, 2012).
46. Like Vladimir Tismăneanu, I agree that from a political and economic perspective both Dej and Ceaușescu were committed Stalinists—albeit to differing degrees. However, because neither employed the same brutal and arbitrary methods of Stalin, the term neo-Stalinist or national Stalinist is more appropriate for the Romanian context. See Vladimir Tismăneanu, *Stalinism for All Seasons: A Political History of Romanian Communism* (Berkeley: University of California Press, 2003).
47. Victoria De Grazia, *How Fascism Ruled Women: Italy 1922–1945* (Berkeley: University of California Press, 1993).
48. The heteronormativity of socialist discourse and policy, state criminalization of homosexuality, and homophobic tendencies within Romanian society at large makes this a challenging topic. As such, Irina Costache's "Archiving Desire: Materiality, Sexuality, and the Secret Police in Romanian State Socialism (PhD diss., Central European University, 2014) is an impressive and welcome critical analysis of LGBT identities and practices in socialist Romania.
49. Studies of rural families and folklore reveal that domestic violence was commonplace and more or less accepted, both in pre-communist and communist Romania, by rural women as a part of being married, see Gail Kligman, *The Wedding of the Dead: Ritual, Poetics, and Popular Culture in Transylvania* (Berkeley: University of California Press, 1988), 132.
50. See Maria Bucur, "Gendering Dissent: Of Bodies and Minds, Survival and Opposition under Communism," in *Beyond Little Vera: Women's Bodies, Women's Welfare in Russia and Central/Eastern Europe*, ed. Angela Brintlinger and Natasha Kolchevska, *Ohio Slavic Papers*, vol. 7 (2008): 9–26.
51. As quoted in Daphne Berdahl, "Introduction: An Anthropology of Postsocialism," in *Altering States: Ethnographies of Transition in Eastern Europe and the Former Soviet Union*, ed. Daphne Berdahl, Matti Bunzl, and Martha Lampland (Ann Arbor, MI: University of Michigan Press, 2000), 2.

CHAPTER I

# The Times, They Are A-Changin'
Gender, Citizenship, and the Transition to Socialism

Woman can be emancipated only when she can take part on a large social scale in production and is engaged in domestic work only to an insignificant degree. And this has become possible only in the big industry of modern times, which not only admits of female labor on a grand scale but even formally demands it.
—Friedrich Engels, *The Origin of the Family, Private Property and the State*, 1884

The Party has given its full support to women; it has created conditions such that they will no longer be considered women ... but people, just like men.
—Elena Livezeanu, Executive Committee, National Council of Women, 1974

I don't think there were many women who wanted positions in leadership because women always put family in the balance.
—D., geologist (b. 1953)

As elaborated by Friedrich Engels in *The Origin of the Family, Private Property and the State*, patriarchy, in its modern form, was a product of private property and sustained through women's legal subordination and economic disempowerment.[1] Lacking basic rights, along with a living wage, women thus depended on family or a spouse for economic survival. Socialism, however, proposed to dramatically alter this situation. By abolishing private property and promoting women's wide-scale and equal participation in paid labor, socialism, Engels believed, would facilitate women's economic autonomy, emancipating them from patriarchal strictures. Upon demonstrating their competence in the workforce, women would, in turn, be recognized as equals by their male counterparts, resulting in a radical transformation of gender roles and relations.[2] No longer the domestic and sexual slaves of their husbands, women would thus become their confidantes, joined in an emotional union rather than a financial one.

Engels's program for women's liberation was highly progressive, if not wholly revolutionary, for its time. In connecting women's liberation to the larger struggle for social transformation, socialism proposed to fashion a new society based on the equality of all individuals. Moreover, by encouraging women's participation in all spheres of human activity, Engels challenged the notion of gender complementarity, which emphasized women's biological and psychological difference from men and their unique contributions as mothers, caregivers, and moral educators. By conceptualizing women's equality with respect to their contributions as workers, Engels thus departed from relational feminism—the prevailing approach to the woman question in the nineteenth and early twentieth century.[3] Instead of citizen-mothers dedicated to the moral education of their children, under socialism women's citizenship was to be based on their active and equal engagement in the public sphere.[4]

Engels's theorization of women's emancipation influenced a range of socialist feminists from Clara Zetkin, leader of the women's bureau of the German Social Democratic Party, to Aleksandra Kollontai, first director of the *Zhenotdel*, the Soviet women's organization. Moreover, it provided a blueprint for women's liberation that informed, to varying degrees, the policies of state socialist regimes around the globe. Although Engels's vision of gender equality was never fully realized in Romania or any other socialist states, socialist modernization and, more specifically, women's mass employment did dramatically affect many women's lives, often in positive ways. Thus, for women throughout the globe, Engels's notion of emancipation through work rang true.

This chapter provides historical context for subsequent chapters, placing women's position in Romania from the latter half of the nineteenth century through the period of communist consolidation within a broader political, social, and cultural framework. Beginning in the mid-nineteenth century, the "woman question" was debated among numerous individuals and groups throughout Europe. Like their Western counterparts, elite Romanian women engaged in philanthropic work, including supporting education and training for impoverished girls and women. They also advocated for women's equality under the law. Up to the early twentieth century, claims for equal citizenship were based on women's complementarity to men and their contributions to the nation as mothers, educators, and sponsors of charitable initiatives; however, by the twentieth century their claims broadened to include liberal and feminist conceptions of equality and human rights (e.g. economic, legal, and political rights). Although reflecting contemporaneous initiatives in other parts of Europe and the United States,

Romanian women's efforts to broaden women's educational opportunities and promote their legal and political rights were particularly impressive in light of the conservative culture and restrictive political and legal climate in which they were operating.

With the advent of socialist rule in Romania, Engels's approach to women's liberation was officially adopted by the party-state. Accordingly, women were granted full equality with men, and women's organizations worked actively to mobilize women for socialist modernization and reformulate their roles, responsibilities, and relationships. Both the National Council of Women (Consiliul Național al Femeilor; CNF) and its magazine, *Femeia* (Woman), presented women as equal socialist citizens, celebrating their productive achievements in industry and farming, glorifying their roles as mothers and educators of youth, and showcasing their efforts as activists. They also expressed, at least officially, concern with women's challenges in advancing professionally, dealing with insensitive or abusive spouses, and reconciling workplace and household duties. While strategic in its promotion of particular behaviors, values, and practices, the CNF's policies, along with *Femeia*, are essential for understanding how the state used gender to create a modern socialist society. Although the degree to which actual women were influenced by *Femeia's* messages and the CNF's programs cannot be known, as the only entities focused on women's issues, they affected women's lives in some capacity. Indeed, given *Femeia's* wide circulation, it can be safely assumed that many women (as well as some men) at least glanced at it—or even read it, albeit selectively and occasionally. As such, both the organization and the magazine cannot simply be written off as tools of the regime or instrumentalist propaganda, but should instead be considered complex and polyvalent sources, meriting analysis alongside women's recollections of their lived experiences.

## Gender, Society, and the Nation

National unity and sovereignty, rather than women's status and social equality, topped the agenda of Romanian policymakers and thinkers during the nineteenth and early twentieth century in the principal regions that would constitute modern-day Romania—Wallachia, Moldavia, and Transylvania. Although Romania had been the site of foreign invasion and domination for centuries, nationalism initially emerged as a cultural movement among Orthodox priests, who began using the Romanian language in their liturgies, and Uniate priests, who began documenting Romania's historical connection to Romanian history and culture.⁵ Opposition to foreign domination and the rising influence of national self-determination and liberalism facilitated the development of political nationalism in the Romanian Principalities (Wallachia and Moldavia) and in Transylvania in the mid-nineteenth century.⁶ As in other parts of Europe, the Principalities were sites of revolutionary tumult in 1848 as students, intellectuals, and liberal elites rose up against foreign rule, demanding national independence, freedom of the press and speech, and equal civil rights (for males).⁷ Although ultimately unsuccessful, their efforts laid the foundation for the union of Wallachia and Moldavia under one leader, Prince Alexandru Ioan Cuza, in 1859. While in power, Cuza instituted a number of progressive reforms, including extension of the franchise and land reform; however, he also passed legislation enabling him to rule by decree, therefore significantly undermining his progressive program.⁸ Threatened by his agrarian reform, which had caused production rates to plummet, a coalition of Liberals and Conservatives ousted Cuza in a coup, replacing him with a foreign ruler, Prince Charles of Hohenzollern-Sigmaringen (Carol I).

In 1878, Romania was internationally recognized as an independent state. Given its regional diversity and agrarian character, however, many individuals identified more with their locality or social group than the Romanian nation. Like other countries that became nation-states in the latter nineteenth century, national identity was thus constructed from "above" by intellectuals and cultural figures seeking to unify the people around what they believed to be a shared identity and historical experience. Meanwhile, Transylvania, a region with a large Romanian population that had been incorporated into the Habsburg Empire in the late seventeenth century (and had also experienced a failed revolution in 1848), fell under Hungarian rule as a result of the *Ausgleich* (Compromise) in 1867. Here Romanian nationalism developed in reaction to aggressive Magyarization policies that politically and socially marginalized ethnic Romanians.⁹

In 1866 a constitution for the Principalities had been drafted. Modeled on the Belgian Constitution of 1831, it was considered one of the most progressive in Europe for its embrace of liberal principles. Accordingly, Romania became a constitutional monarchy under which all citizens were, in principle, guaranteed legal equality and freedom of speech and association. However, like similar documents influenced by liberalism, the constitution was elitist and sexist in conception, granting political rights only to property-owning men of the boyar and bureaucratic classes. In addition to excluding Jews of foreign origin from citizenship and the right to own property (until 1879), the constitution restricted political rights of most men due to mandated property qualifications.[10] The peasantry, comprising over 80 percent of the population, thus remained politically impotent. Meanwhile, the two leading political parties, the Conservatives and the Liberals, although embracing different visions of national development, focused primarily on safeguarding their economic advantages. As such, governance was marred by corruption and favoritism as elites were generally concerned with increasing profits rather than the welfare of the people. Consequently, most peasants lived in dire poverty, suffering under the combined weight of an expanding population and crushing payments to landowners, leaseholders, and moneylenders.

Resistance to exploitation and increased taxation erupted in the 1907 peasant uprising, powerfully demonstrating the need for reform. During the rebellion—which assumed anti-Semitic overtones as some leaseholders were Jewish—peasants in Moldavia and Wallachia seized lands, burned estates, and killed landlords and leaseholders. The response of the authorities was brutal: approximately 11,000 peasants were killed in the quashing of the rebellion.[11] Modest reforms were eventually instituted, however, they did little to ameliorate peasant poverty.

While the situation of the peasantry remained precarious, the Roma were the most marginalized social group in Romania. Although technically emancipated in 1856, the Roma continued to live in dire poverty, often at the margins of villages and towns; their centuries of enslavement reinforcing popular perceptions of them as primitive, immoral, and even diabolical.[12]

Finally, women, along with children, criminals, and individuals with disabilities, were among the most disenfranchised groups in Romania, defined as passive citizens and "legal incompetents," wholly lacking political citizenship.[13] As such, the constitution reinforced and built upon the Civil Code of 1865, under which married women were subject to the authority of their husbands and were prohibited from participating in the justice system, keeping their earnings, withdrawing money from their own bank accounts, and receiving inheritance without spousal permission.[14] Moreover, the code bound adult women to their husbands, or, if unmarried, to a male family member or a legal guardian (e.g. "caretaker"). Collectively, then, both the constitution and Civil Code were setbacks for women who, under previous codes, had at least been allowed to control their dowries and personal earnings, as well as enjoy some parental rights.[15] By comparison, women in Transylvania and other areas of Austria-Hungary that would be integrated into Romania after World War I were able to control their assets, and married women could sign their own contracts, work freely, and relocate to other localities.[16]

Despite their political, legal, and social subordination, Romanian women were actively engaged in labor. By 1913, the number of women in agriculture reached 1,574,919, nearly the same as men.[17] This included not only subsistence farmers, but also those who produced goods, especially grains, for domestic and foreign markets.[18] Agricultural labor was often supplemented by cottage work, such as sewing, knitting, and weaving. With the gradual modernization of Romania during the second half of the nineteenth century, women also increasingly worked in industry. For example, in 1867, 23,000 women were employed in manufacturing (primarily food processing and textiles) in the Romanian Kingdom—a figure that reached 70,000 on the eve of World War I.[19] Similarly, in Transylvania women's participation in industry (mainly in wool, linen, paper, and tobacco production) increased during this period: from 12,277 in 1890 to 22,427 in 1910.[20] As in the West, most of these jobs were unskilled, poorly paid (especially in comparison with male laborers), and required working long hours. According to a survey with women laborers during the first decade of the twentieth century, workdays ranged from twelve to fourteen hours, though in some cases up to sixteen hours, and remuneration was so meager that women could often not afford basic necessities.[21] Moreover, conditions were abysmal as factories lacked proper ventilation, which seriously compromised workers' health and safety. For example, a study conducted with women laborers in Bucharest in the early 1900s found that they suffered the highest rates of tuberculosis of all workers in Europe.[22] Although legislation officially protected women and children from subterranean work in mineshafts, as historian Ștefania Mihăilescu notes, this law was only "on paper" and would not be respected until 1924 with the passage of a new labor code.[23] In addition to working in hazardous conditions, women were poorly paid, forcing many to marry or depend on family, charity, and, in some cases, prostitution for economic survival.

Outside of agriculture and industry, women were employed in white-collar jobs, particularly in the public sector (e.g. at post and telegraph offices), although they typically assumed auxiliary positions, which limited their salaries and opportunities for advancement. Meanwhile, increased access to post-secondary education during the late nineteenth and early twentieth century broadened women's professional opportunities, especially in fields such as social work, medicine, and law—though sexist legislation still hindered eligibility for certain positions. For example, although Ella Negruzzi earned a law degree in 1913, she was forbidden from taking the bar exam because she did not enjoy full political rights, rendering her degree essentially useless. Negruzzi attempted to appeal the decision in court; however, the opposing lawyer suggested that "it would be more useful if Ms. Negruzzi helped with the Romanian educational system" rather than practice as a lawyer.[24] Undaunted, Negruzzi finally took the bar exam in 1919, which she passed, becoming the first woman to practice law in Romania.[25]

Despite possessing the requisite qualifications, women were also barred from administrative and leadership positions in banks and corporations.[26] Furthermore, women could not advance to the post of university professor since teaching at the primary or secondary level was considered more in line with their "nature." Although some women did regard teaching as their calling, others became teachers due to lack of other viable career options. Yet, while elite women could at least turn to private tutors or attend the few private schools founded for girls in Romania during the latter half of the nineteenth century, the vast majority of girls were denied educational opportunities on par with boys. This was a function of both local budgetary decisions and family choice. For instance, although the Constitution of 1866 legislated free primary schooling for all Romanians, local officials (who allocated municipal funding) prioritized boys' schools over girls' schools, and rural parents tended to privilege a son's education over a daughter's."[27] Consequently, in 1899 the illiteracy rate for males was 67.2 percent, while for females it was 89.1 percent (with rates significantly higher in rural than urban areas), though these figures were not dissimilar from other countries in southeastern Europe.[28] Ideas about gender, then, influenced the organization of society and family life, contributing to women's legal subordination, along with their marginalization within or exclusion from schooling

Status intersected with gender in particular ways to shape women's everyday experiences. Because Romania was predominantly agrarian, the majority of women labored in the fields alongside men, engaging in backbreaking work and living in poverty. Yet, while peasant men were subordinate only to their boyar landlords, peasant women were also subordinate to their husbands and were expected to devote their energies to agricultural, cottage, and domestic labor.[29] Meanwhile, elite women were expected to assume the role of the charming, cultured, and at least moderately educated, yet subordinate, wife.[30] Although some elite marriages were more egalitarian than others, and while status could lighten the restrictiveness of patriarchal control, most elite women remained economically dependent on their husbands and were defined in relation to the family. More generally, although spousal relations varied from family to family, the husband was still regarded as "the master of the house," and domestic violence was not uncommon. In addition, the Orthodox Church, around which many people's lives were organized, defined women as weak and with respect to their familial and reproductive roles. Finally, nationalist discourse, promoted by literary and intellectual figures, reinforced traditional gender norms as natural and central to the integrity of the Romanian nation. Indeed, a number of physicians and leading thinkers invoked biology to explain women's subordination and unsuitability for university education and certain professions. According to philosopher Titu Maiorescu, for instance, men's domination of public and political life was justified on the basis of their comparatively heavier brain weight, which he claimed was associated with intellectual superiority.[31] While in retrospect comical in its absurdity, Mairoescu's pseudoscientific argument was not unique to the Romanian context. More generally, ill-founded beliefs about women's intellectual capacities had real bearing on women's lives, excluding or marginalizing them from certain spheres and professions.

Nevertheless, women persisted, increasingly attending university and demonstrating their capabilities in fields such as medicine, journalism, and social work. Moreover, elite women engaged in philanthropic, cultural, and humanitarian initiatives. These initiatives often occurred through women's organizations such as the Reunion of Romanian Women of Iaşi (Reuniunea femeilor române din Iaşi), which, in 1870, founded a trade school (şcoala de meserii) for impoverished girls with skills in arts, crafts, and dressmaking, as well as a studio where students' productions were sold. Similarly, the Reunion of Romanian Women for the Assistance of the Poorest Romanian Orphans (Reuniunea femeilor române pentru ajutoral creşterii fetiţelor orfane române mai sărace), founded in Braşov, Transylvania in 1850, subsidized the education of orphans and young impoverished girls and founded day and boarding schools in Sibiu, Blaj, and Braşov.[32] Meanwhile, the Women's Society of Bukovina (Societăţii doamnelor române din Bucovina), founded in 1891, offered courses in Romanian language and literature and established a boarding school for girls.

By creating opportunities for impoverished girls and women to attend school and improve their economic position, these elite women were enacting their identities as social mothers and de facto republican citizens. Denied the right to participate in politics, they, like their contemporaneous Western counterparts, demonstrated their commitment to the nation and women's empowerment by engaging in philanthropic activities and associational life and, in so doing, sought to prove their civic worth. Such experiences afforded these women access to public realms, enabling them to interact socially with other women and men. It also heightened their social and, in some cases, feminist awareness.[33]

In attempting to persuade other elite women to support philanthropic activities, women often emphasized the connection between women's education and national progress. For example, journalist Sofia Chrisoscoleu, in her 1859 "Letter to Romanian Ladies," drew a parallel between women's contributions as moral educators of the nation and men's contributions as soldiers, couching her claim for women's equality in republican conceptions of citizenship.[34] As a corollary, she presented women's continued legal subordination in Romania as barbaric, linking national progress to women's ability to serve as full members of the national community.

In addition to appealing to other women, activists appealed to political bodies. For instance, in 1863 Constanța Dunca, echoing Mary Wollstonecraft before her, petitioned the Romanian Chamber of Deputies (Parliament) to include girls' and women's education in the regular school system and to establish training programs for women teachers, justifying her claims on the basis of women's roles as moral educators of the nation.[35] According to historian Maria Bucur, Dunca's focus on educational reform, rather than the expansion of civil rights, did not mean she was uninterested in political citizenship, but that she regarded education as "a stepping stone towards future political empowerment."[36]

By the late nineteenth century, women became more vocal in advocating for increased rights. The journal *Femeia Română* (Romanian Woman), for instance, served as an important forum for debating the "woman question," challenging antiquated notions about women's roles, promoting suffrage, and highlighting women's movements abroad. Indeed, by this time major publications of the day, particularly leftist ones such as *Lumea Nouă* (New World), *Munca* (Work), *Drepturile Omului* (The Rights of Man), and the widely read *Contemporanul* (The Contemporary), engaged with the "woman question." Journalist and women's rights activist, Sofia Nădejde, who was influenced by John Stuart Mill, was especially prolific in this respect. Drawing on scientific evidence, in 1882 she challenged Titu Maiorescu's claim that men's larger brain size made them more suitable for political leadership, arguing instead that women's brain size was, like men's, proportionate to their overall body size. Indeed, Nădejde's impressive knowledge of science, politics, and a range of other subjects perfectly illustrated her acumen—as well as the fallaciousness of Maoirescu's claims. More generally, Nădejde called out elite men for abusing their power, comparing women's subordination to the subordination of workers, asserting, "men have power in their hands and do not want to share it with us [women], knowing that they would have to diminish their part; they do not give rights to women for the same reason they do not give rights to workers."[37] Yet, neither rational argumentation nor appeals to liberal ideals would convince Romanian policymakers to expand women's rights. For instance, in 1884, during a parliamentary debate on the revision of the Constitution, deputy C. A. Rosetti's proposal that married women who met financial requirements be allowed to vote was met by laughter from the other deputies.[38]

In light of women's continued lack of basic, civic rights, by the turn of the century women's groups became more forceful in arguing for equal rights and legal protections, stressing women's social contributions to the nation as well as their vulnerabilities as individuals. For example, the Iași-based Women's League of Romania (Liga femeilor din România, formed in 1894), which included Nădejde among its members, submitted petitions to the Romanian Parliament in 1896 and 1898, demanding women's equal civic and economic rights (e.g. right to self-representation in court and to keep their own earnings) and a law requiring fathers to support children born out of wedlock.[39] Meanwhile, Women's Rights (Drepturile Femeii; founded in Bucharest in 1911 under the name Women's Emancipation), embraced a decidedly liberal feminist approach to the "woman question." In addition to organizing public debates about women's rights, in spring 1914, the organization submitted a written statement to parliament demanding women's equal political and legal equality, admission of women into all professions, equal pay for equal work, married women's right to keep their own earnings, and women's right to determine paternity of their child.[40] Finally, on the eve of World War I, when the Romanian government was considering a law for universal male suffrage, the Women's League petitioned Parliament, albeit unsuccessfully, for women's inclusion in it.[41]

## Women, War, and Greater Romania

Although an ally of the Central Powers, after two years of neutrality Romania entered World War I on the side of the Entente in August 1916, ultimately mobilizing over one million men for the conflict. Initially the war went well for the Romanian Army with advances into Transylvania; however, by December 1916, the Central Powers occupied Bucharest and conquered the southern half of the country. Meanwhile, King Ferdinand and the Romanian government fled to Iași in the northeastern part of the country. During the war, most women's lives revolved around basic survival with many facing poverty, displacement, and the wrath of invading armies. As male heads of households were drafted for war—and some subsequently imprisoned in POW camps—many women struggled to support themselves and their families. Although married rural women had historically engaged in farming while their husbands were at war, this proved challenging in light of the 1856 Civil Code, which prohibited them from selling the harvest or working without written permission from their husbands.[42] With the exception of a minority of elite and middle-class women who could rely on the support of friends and family, women were thus in a precarious situation and many resorted to barter, begging, and domestic service to support themselves and their families. In addition to financial insecurity, women faced physical insecurity as the Civil Code impeded their freedom of movement, leaving them in potentially great peril as the Central Powers occupied ever-greater territory.[43] As in all wars, women were thus victims of sexual assault and other forms of violence from which they could not protect themselves.

Alongside these legal prohibitions, women were restricted by cultural mores, which deemed work in heavy industry and transport "unladylike."[44] Unlike their English and French counterparts, then, Romanian women did not work in munitions industries or as tram or train conductors during the war, with the result that by 1917 public transport was at a virtual standstill. Instead, women supported the war in a culturally acceptable manner through social mothering, idealized in the persona of Queen Marie, who volunteered for the Red Cross, raised funds for medical services, and toured military hospitals in Moldavia (though she never herself served as a nurse). Specifically, Romanian women volunteered as nurses, organized soup kitchens, and ran homes for orphaned and displaced children. One notable exception was Ecaterina Teodoroiu, who initially served as a nurse, but then decided to take up soldiering after the death of her brother at the front. Teodoroiu died in battle in September 1917, and was later decorated for her bravery and honored as "The Virgin of Jiu."[45]

On 10 November 1918, one day before Germany's surrender, Romania reentered the war and reconquered its lost territory. In return for its alliance with the Entente, Transylvania, Bukovina, the Banat and Bessarabia were integrated into the Romanian Kingdom, increasing the territorial size of the country twofold and its population by nearly nine million.[46] According to historian Irina Livezeanu, the creation of Greater Romania was a "national revolution" which "brought opportunities for national redefinition as well as profound social and cultural crisis."[47] After two years of war, which included subsidizing the German occupying forces, the recently enlarged country was beset by massive debt and widespread devastation. Accordingly, industrial and agricultural output remained low, as did personal consumption levels.[48] Moreover, as a result of war and disease, the country lost an estimated 250,000 soldiers and 430,000 civilians (in Wallachia and Moldavia), leaving many families without a male breadwinner.[49]

The postwar Romanian government thus faced a host of challenges, including rebuilding destroyed villages, towns, and infrastructure; spiraling inflation and social unrest; and staving off bankruptcy. Like other reconstituted states in Eastern Europe, it was also faced with modernizing ethnically, socially, and culturally diverse regions with large rural, illiterate, and impoverished populations. Fearing potential peasant unrest after the Bolshevik Revolution, the government, in the hands of the National Liberal Party, instituted the Agrarian Law of 1918–1921, the most extensive land reform in Europe with the exception of the USSR.[50] Although impressive in scope, distributing 9.6 million acres of land to 1.4 million peasants, holdings were typically too small (12.3 acres) to be economically viable, let alone efficient.[51] This, combined with lack of agricultural credit and modern farming equipment, anachronistic inheritance laws, and high export duties, did little to attenuate peasant poverty; indeed, productivity actually declined.[52] With respect to industry, the country fared better as state support of domestic entrepreneurs facilitated growth in leading sectors of the economy such as food processing and petroleum, as well as newer areas such as metallurgy and chemicals. At the same time, industrial development benefited the political and business elite rather than Romanian laborers. Consequently, Romanian society was characterized by a large, impoverished peasant population, a small wealthy elite, a modest though expanding middle class, and a fledgling working class, eking out a meager living in often grueling and unsafe working conditions.

Like other agrarian societies, Romania had a high fertility rate but also a high infant mortality rate—the second highest in Europe at 18.5 deaths (per 100 births) in 1932—primarily due to poor nutrition and hygiene, a rudimentary healthcare system, and arduous labor during pregnancy.[53] Moreover, life expectancy was the lowest in Europe at 40 years for men and 41 years for women.[54] Increased concern about public health prompted the establishment of mobile dispensaries, which supplied rural populations with checkups, medicine, and advice on pre- and postnatal health and hygiene, leading to a gradual decline in the infant mortality rate.[55] The expansion of public education was even more impressive, as thousands of new schools were constructed throughout the country.⁵⁶ Yet, while primary schooling was made compulsory and opportunities for secondary education increased, by the end of the 1930s the majority of the population claimed no more than a fourth grade education. Consequently, even by 1938 the illiteracy rate stood at 54.3 percent—one of the highest in Europe—with females and individuals in rural areas constituting the highest proportion of the illiterate.⁵⁷ Moreover, boys rather than girls tended to advance to secondary and technical school or university, though girls did attend primary school at nearly the same rate as boys.⁵⁸ Beyond this, the educational system served as an instrument of nationalism, with Romanian-language schools and universities being privileged for subsidies. Finally, jobs in state administration were typically filled by ethnic-Romanian elites, including positions in which minorities had once been employed. More generally, ethnic minorities faced discrimination and marginalization as the government followed a policy of Romanianization in Transylvania and other recently incorporated regions with large minority populations (e.g. Hungarians, Germans, and Jews).

While minorities, particularly Hungarians and Jews, experienced marginalization within the highly centralized Romanian state, so too did women. Although the 1923 Constitution codified equality between the sexes and the Socialist Party, the Romanian National Party, and a number of leading politicians had supported extension of the franchise, most policymakers were averse to granting women suffrage, and women remained politically disenfranchised (although suffrage was extended to all adult males). The prevailing sentiment had already been illustrated in 1917 when Women's Emancipation had petitioned the Romanian Senate for suffrage and was told that the notion of women voting was "unfeminine" and that their energies were best spent in the domestic sphere or in social mothering.⁵⁹ Being denied the franchise was a major disappointment for women's groups who had actively advocated for it and believed women would be granted equal political rights after the war.⁶⁰ However, in this regard Romania was by no means exceptional, as France, Italy, Switzerland and a host of other countries in the West did not extend the franchise to women until after World War II. Women's political and legal subordination not only prevented them from participating in the polity as active citizens, but, on a more basic level, left them economically vulnerable. For instance, widowed women were still prohibited from inheriting their husband's property, and ex-husbands were only required to support their ex-wives and children for a year after the divorce.⁶¹ Moreover, women were prohibited from "investigating paternity," freeing men of legal responsibility for offspring born out of wedlock.

With a rural population of 78 percent in 1939, the vast majority of Romanian women (as well as men) relied on agriculture for their livelihood. Thus, as they had prior to the war, women were responsible for sowing, harvesting, and animal husbandry, as well as home-based labor such as weaving, embroidery, and shoe and clothing manufacturing. Meanwhile, in 1930 approximately 18 percent of the population worked in commerce, banking, transportation, public services, and various other professions, and approximately 10 percent worked in industry.[62] Of this modest industrial working class, women constituted only 19 percent and were concentrated in low-paid areas such as food, textile, clothing, glass, and ceramic production.[63] However, with the expansion of education women made impressive inroads in fields such as commerce, public administration, healthcare, and teaching. Thus, a new generation of women with professional ambition and a desire for economic autonomy gradually emerged in Bucharest and other cities during the interwar period. Some of these women devoted their energies to improving women's status, advocating for equal political and civil rights, promoting safe working conditions, and protecting women from discrimination.

The writer and teacher Calypso Botez, perhaps the most dynamic and well-known feminist of the interwar period, was especially active in this capacity, founding the National Council of Romanian Women (Consiliul Național al Femeilor Române), which worked with other women's organizations to improve women's political and economic status and expand their educational opportunities.[64] Like other liberal feminists, Botez connected women's rights to democracy, claiming, "to live only in tradition means to wear the damaged clothing of prejudices."[65] In 1918, Botez, in conjunction with Ella Negruzzi, Romania's first practicing woman lawyer, founded the Association for the Political and Civic Emancipation of Romanian Women (Asociația pentru emanciparea civică și politică a femeilor române). This organization promoted female suffrage and women's occupational and educational advancement, which came under increasing attack as a result of the economic downturn after the Depression.[66] Botez and Negruzzi also established the first women's studies program in Romania and were strong advocates of rural women's economic empowerment through the founding of vocational schools.

Alongside Botez and Negruzzi, Alexandrina Cantacuzino was a prominent advocate for women's equality during the interwar period, though of the nationalist rather than the liberal variant. In 1910, Cantacuzino had founded the National Society for Romanian Orthodox Women (Societății Ortodoxe Naționale a Femeilor Române; SONFR), the most popular women's organization in interwar Romania, attracting women from a range of social and political backgrounds.⁶⁷ Arguing for women's full equality on the basis of their roles as mothers and moral educators, Cantacuzino believed women's contributions in both public and private spheres were critical to the development—and ultimate survival—of the Romanian nation. Indeed, she considered charity and social assistance (jobs typically taken up by women) as bases for the "spiritual revival" of the nation. To this end, in 1929 Cantacuzino opened the School for Social Assistance (Şcoala Asistenţei Auxiliare Sociale), which trained women social workers, while also inculcating them with decidedly eugenic ideas about health and hygiene.⁶⁸ She also founded schools, canteens for workers and students, and "Woman's House" ("Casa Femeii"), a shelter for unemployed women and female students and civil servants.

Outside of these individuals and organizations, women members of the Romanian Communist Party (PCdR), most notably Elena Filipovici and Ana Pauker, advocated on behalf of impoverished women and families.⁶⁹ In contrast to Botez and Cantacuzino, Filipovici envisaged women's liberation as part of the broader struggle for social liberation, which was dependent on overturning "capitalist tyranny." Thus, she asserted:

> The place of women workers in their struggle for emancipation is in worker's unions, in worker's parties, alongside male workers, fighting for the end of class exploitation and the dissolution of the current society, for the liberation of the working class. Only in this way will she also be fully emancipated.⁷⁰

At the same time, Filipovici recognized the importance of mobilizing women as a social group and thus began agitating, at the mere age of fifteen, in the factory where she worked. More generally, the PCdR recognized the importance of offering essential services to impoverished women and their families. To that end, in 1935 the PCdR founded the Society for the Protection of Mothers and Children (Societatea pentru protecţia mamei şi copilului), which established kindergartens and provided medical checkups and literacy courses to working-class families.⁷¹ The society also published a newspaper, *Drumul femeii* (Women's Path), and served as a basis for the Female Front, which brought together communist and social democratic women activists with the aim of uniting women in the struggle for social, cultural, and political equality. Although laudable, their efforts were risky given that the PCdR was banned in 1924 and under intense surveillance by the Siguranţa (the secret police) throughout the interwar period and during World War II. Consequently, many PCdR activists—including Ana Pauker, who was arrested multiple times before being sent to Moscow on a prisoner exchange—were limited in their ability to effect concrete change.[72]

With the advent of the National Peasant Party (NPP) to power in 1929—after the freest election Romania had seen—married women over 30 years of age who met certain requirements were granted the right to vote in municipal elections.[73] While only enfranchising a select group, women's issues nonetheless attracted increased visibility during this period and women engaged more actively in politics. For instance, Botez, Negruzzi, and Cantacuzino all served as representatives on the Bucharest city council.[74] Such progress notwithstanding, women continued to face subordination with respect to property rights, self-representation in court, child custody, and control over inheritance. Moreover, in 1936 abortion was criminalized in all instances except severe mental illness on the part of one or both of the parents and in the event the child would suffer from a mental illness.[75] In this respect, Romania did not differ from the United States and most countries in Europe where abortion was banned and women dealt with unwanted pregnancy through self-inducing, the use of midwives and back-alley abortionists, and, for the privileged few, private doctors.[76] Moreover, like women in other states with declining fertility rates, Romanian women—particularly feminist and middle-class and professional women—faced a backlash, becoming the object of criticism by eugenicists for not bearing enough children and not sufficiently contributing to the healthy growth of the Romanian nation.[77]

Over the course of the 1920s and 1930s, a variety of groups, including policymakers, medical professionals, and intellectuals, searched for solutions to Romania's manifold problems. While some promoted economic modernization along Western lines, others embraced a nationalist and even xenophobic approach, and others attempted to synthesize these two models. Meanwhile, eugenicists promoted a scientific view of modernization based on the "proper" breeding and nurturing of the professional class and the intelligentsia. Although the NPP government was invested with great hope for political and social change, once in power it toned down the more radical aspects of its program. Thus, although it abolished duties on agricultural exports and strengthened independent farmers, it only supported well-off peasants. Moreover, while reducing protectionism and opening up the country to foreign markets and loans, the NPP's loyalties were with the industrial elite rather than the workers, most visible in its bloody crackdown on the Jiu Valley protest in 1929.[78] More generally, the NPP failed to find solutions to the manifold problems facing Romania, and, once the Depression hit, its program was compromised by protracted economic challenges, in particular decreasing demands for exports and high rates of unemployment. This, combined with continued corruption and ethnic tension, increased the appeal of nationalism, right-wing extremism, and fascism, especially among unemployed youth.

The advent of King Charles II (Carol II) to power in 1930 set Romania on a decidedly authoritarian path, culminating, in 1938, with the suspension of the constitution and proclamation of a royal dictatorship under the Front of National Rebirth, which became the only legal political party in Romania. In this respect, Romania was by no means unique as Italy, Germany, Hungary, and Poland, among others, had already shifted radically to the right. Loss of Western markets as a result of the Depression had left Romania economically isolated, its peasants desperate, and its educated youth disaffected. Rather than pushing people toward social democracy and communism, uneven modernization led some to embrace anticapitalism, anti-Semitism, and nationalism (often of a xenophobic nature), as well as mysticism. Disillusioned by Romania's partial and halting democracy, as well as economic instability, a range of individuals from Orthodox clergy, peasants, and workers to youth, professionals, and prominent intellectuals, were increasingly drawn to the radical right, in particular the Iron Guard, the largest fascist movement in Eastern Europe.[79] The Guard's popular appeal was related not only to its embrace of traditional, religious, and ultranationalist (read ethnic-Romanian) values, but also its success in appealing to local communities through public works and cultural initiatives. Meanwhile, some intellectuals and professionals found the Guard's approach to politics the only viable alternative to the corruption that characterized existing political parties.

Although the PCdR attempted to mobilize the small, incipient proletariat to support a leftist solution to Romania's problems, its appeal was minimal as it was perceived as slavishly loyal to the USSR—and thus an enemy of the Romanian nation. Additionally, communism had little resonance for most workers, who, as recent peasant migrants, tended to view social conditions through a rural and traditional lens. Consequently, Communist Party membership never exceeded five thousand during the interwar period.[80]

Under Charles II's royal dictatorship, basic civic freedoms, particularly for Jews, were rescinded or restricted, reflecting similar legislation in Nazi Germany. These included the Romanianization of Jewish businesses, properties, and professions; prohibition of marriage between

Romanians and Jews; and restrictions on Jewish doctors. Moreover, a constitutional law in February 1938 defined Romanians according to "race" and "residence."[81] Meanwhile, in March 1939, Romania entered into a trade agreement with the Third Reich, drawing the country ever closer to the Axis orbit. While this gave the economy a modest boost, productivity rates still lagged behind most countries in Europe. In this intolerant climate, women were finally granted the right to vote in national elections—an essentially meaningless gesture given the dissolution of political parties.

## From World War II to Communist Takeover

Romania remained neutral during the first year of World War II, formally joining the Axis in November 1940 and officially entering the war in June 1941 with the Nazi invasion of the USSR. By this point, the country had experienced the humiliating losses of Bessarabia and northern Bukovina to the Soviet Union, northern Transylvania to Hungary, and southern Dobrudja to Bulgaria, which decreased Romania's territorial size by one-third, essentially reversing the acquisitions it had secured at the close of World War I. Romanians responded to the territorial cessions with protests against Charles II, while the Iron Guard overthrew him in a coup. Although the king was replaced by his nineteen-year-old son, Michael (Mihai), Ion Antonescu became the self-proclaimed *conducător* (leader) of a "National Legionary State," ruling the country as a military dictatorship.

Before Romania ventured onto a foreign battlefield, it was engaged in a war against internal "enemies" as the Iron Guard unleashed its wrath against those deemed enemies of the nation, particularly Jews and Roma, although conservative politician and historian Nicolae Iorga was also not spared their brutality. In January 1941, the Guard killed more than 120 Jews in the Bucharest Pogrom, destroying Jewish homes, businesses, and synagogues in the process. Antonescu, angered as much by the Guard's disregard for his authority as their wanton destruction, ordered the legionnaires arrested (during which approximately 200 were killed) and seized power for himself. However, violence against Jews did not end but intensified. Focusing his wrath upon those he believed to be communist sympathizers for their proximity to the USSR, Antonescu organized a pogrom in Iași in late June 1941, with the result that 13,266 Jews were killed, followed by another 150,000 to 160,000 who were shot by Romanian and German troops in June and July 1941.[82] An additional 105,000–120,000 Jews from Bukovina and Bessarabia were subsequently transported eastward to Transnistria (then under Romanian jurisdiction) where many succumbed to typhoid fever, which reached epidemic proportions, killing tens of thousands.[83] Jews in northern Transylvania (then a part of Hungary) were also not spared, being among the final group sent to Auschwitz in summer 1944, though in this case by the fascist-led Hungarian government, the Arrow Cross.

As an Axis power, Romania participated in the invasion of the USSR, which proved territorially beneficial with the reintegration of Bukovina and Bessarabia into Romania. At the same time, the Romanian Army suffered enormous losses, culminating in the Axis defeat at Stalingrad. For the civilian population, war produced instability and social dislocation as families were uprooted during the annexation of Bessarabia and cession of northern Transylvania to Hungary. Indeed, ethnic minorities (e.g. Hungarians and Romanians) in both halves of Transylvania suffered discrimination and persecution, including harassment for using their native language, requisition of foodstuffs and property, arrest for alleged slander, forced labor, and murder.[84] Although women were not mobilized en masse for wartime labor in Romania as they were elsewhere, some did work in munitions production in factories that had been militarized for the war.[85] The vast majority of women, however, lived in the countryside and were left to fend for themselves and their families, facing poverty, insecurity, and vulnerability at the hands of German and later Soviet soldiers, both of whom committed atrocities. At the same time, women were bystanders during persecutions and pogroms against ethnic minorities, in some cases profiting from them.

In February 1943 the Allies defeated the Axis at Stalingrad, and in the summer of 1944 the Red Army began its offensive against Romania. The war brought mass death, destruction, and displacement to Romanians: approximately 300,000 soldiers died at the front, over 100,000 languished as POWs in the USSR, and more than 469,000 civilians, most of them Jews and Roma, perished.[86] Meanwhile, thousands of others were driven from their homes. Additionally, civilians suffered the horrors of Axis and Allied bombing campaigns, which targeted Bucharest and other cities and towns as well as the Ploieşti oil fields. One of my oldest respondents, Maria F. (b. 1931), an ethnic Romanian, recalled the war as a "time of struggle and sadness" as her mother was left to look after the children while her father was conscripted into forced labor, loading supply trains for the Axis. Living in Mureş County in northern Transylvania, a region that had been ceded to Hungary in August 1940, Maria and her four siblings helped their mother with farm work and tended to the household. Even in 2003, the horrors of war loomed large in her memories of the period:

> It was a very difficult period. Father was interned. Mother was left with five children. Very difficult ... and with the harvest and animals. And she put us to work at a young age so she could run the household as she had before. In any case, we had to work, we all worked. ... I have many painful memories. Very painful. War only brings suffering. When the war began we were already occupied by the Hungarians, and we were occupied until 1944, when the Russians came. War and pain, and many victims. It was a disaster for us. ... The shells were Russian with large projectiles that exploded in the air, and when they fell they came down like a rain of shrapnel. They killed children and people and animals. You had to run and hide in a shelter somewhere.[87]

Maria's experiences were by no means exceptional as populations living in contested regions such as Transylvania, as well as places rich in resources such as Ploieşti, were subject to occupation and bombardment at the tail end of the war.

The Soviet advance left King Michael with little choice but to oust Antonescu in a coup, which he did on 23 August 1944. On that same day, the Red Army officially "liberated" Romania from the Nazis, and Romania broke its alliance with the Axis. Michael then reinstated the Constitution of 1923—and thus multi-party democracy—and appointed General Constantin Sănătescu prime minister of the National Democratic Bloc, a coalition government composed of the National Peasant, National Liberal, and Social Democratic parties, along with the Romanian Communist Party (Partidul Comunist din România; PCdR). In August, the Romanian Army joined the Red Army to push the Axis out of Romania, Hungary, and Czechoslovakia, suffering great losses in the process. The reconquest of northern Transylvania was accompanied by atrocities, in some cases committed by voluntary battalions of Romanians as revenge for earlier atrocities committed by the Hungarian Army in 1940.[88] At the same time, Romanian civilians experienced suffering at the hands of their Soviet "liberators" as destruction caused by ground and air campaigns left many homeless. Moreover, minorities in recently recovered regions, particularly Hungarians and Germans, were subject to internment, with many dying in camps.[89]

By October 1944, the PCdR was the smallest of its kind in Eastern Europe, claiming four to five thousand members—hardly enough for fomenting revolution.[90] Although part of the National Democratic Bloc, the PCdR vied with the historic parties, particularly the National Liberal and National Peasant parties, for popular support. Given its weakness, the PCdR allied, in October 1944, with the Social Democrats, the Ploughman's Front (the rural arm of the PCdR), and trade unions in a communist-dominated political bloc: the National Democratic Front. To curry favor with the peasants, the Front promoted agrarian reform, including the annulment of peasant debts. Moreover, it sought to attract the support of industrial workers, some of whom had already joined factory committees and trade unions and engaged in protests demanding increased wages and a new form of governance.[91] While not necessarily supportive of the PCdR or a communist system, these workers hoped for a more egalitarian approach to politics and workplace organization as an alternative to the corrupt and exploitative practices of the interwar period. In addition to agitation, the Front called for the purging of reactionaries and war criminals from the army and the government.

Although popular, King Michael was unable to effectively counterbalance the influence of the Front and the USSR on Romanian politics. In particular, his power was compromised by the presence of the Red Army on Romanian soil and the Allied Control Commission, a multinational body—which the Soviets effectively dominated—charged with supervising the armistice terms. For instance, when King Michael condemned the Soviet order to deport tens of thousands of ethnic-German Romanians to the USSR for forced labor (as a form of war reparations and punishment for alleged Nazi collaboration) his protests fell on deaf ears. Indeed, government efforts to halt the Front by quashing pro-communist demonstrations in February 1945 only added fuel to the fire, serving as pretext for the Red Army's occupation of Romanian Army Headquarters and Soviet demands for the appointment of Petru Groza as prime minister.[92] Although flouting the "Declaration on Liberated Europe" (i.e. self-determination for states liberated from the Axis) made by the big three at Yalta a few weeks earlier, with the Japanese theater still open, the U.S. and Britain only offered cautious criticism of Soviet heavy-handedness. Lacking Western support and faced with the threat of a full Soviet occupation, King Michael bowed to pressure and dismissed General Nicolae Rădescu (who had replaced Sănătescu the previous December), appointing Groza in his stead in March 1945. Force and coercion rather than free and fair electoral politics, thus determined Romania's postwar fate.

Upon King Michael's insistence, the new government included four members from the historical parties, which also provided it with a mantle of legitimacy; however, communists assumed important ministerial posts such as Interior, Justice, and Finance while also securing control over county and local councils, which had wide-ranging political and economic powers. At the same time, the Groza government promised to hold free elections, facilitating Allied recognition of it. Agrarian reform, particularly the expropriation of properties of real and alleged war criminals and collaborators—including ethnic Germans—and restrictions on land ownership to fifty hectares, increased the PCdR's popularity among segments of the peasantry.[93] Thus, the PCdR manipulated social tensions to its advantage, in the process attracting thousands of new members. By April 1945, the PCdR had swelled to over forty-two thousand members, and by October 1945 over two hundred thousand more were added to the ranks, many of them industrial workers, peasants, and, to a lesser degree, members the middle class.[94] Additionally, the PCdR appealed to ethnic minorities, particularly Hungarians and Jews who lived in areas riven by conflict and who had felt vulnerable under interwar (Romanian) nationalist parties.[95] Because no verification process was required for party membership, a range of individuals (including Iron Guardists), recognizing which way the wind was blowing, joined the PCdR during this time.[96] Thus, self-preservation and opportunism help explain the surge in party membership. At the same time, the corruption and general ineffectiveness of interwar governments, as well as the previous ethno-nationalist orientation of Romanian politics, attracted a range of individuals who viewed communism as the only viable engine for political, economic, and social change.

In November 1946, by way of intimidation, violence, and fraud, the PCdR further consolidated power with the Bloc claiming 70 percent of the vote and an overwhelming majority in parliament. Although it has been argued that, had the elections been fair, the National Peasant Party would have won, recent research has demonstrated that the country was politically divided, suggesting a less certain outcome.[97] The election was followed by the signing of the peace treaty, which included the reintegration, in August 1947, of northern Transylvania and southern Bukovina into Romania.[98] The economy was also revamped and the foundations for central planning laid with economic modernization following the Stalinist model (i.e. nationalization of industry, banking, transport, and healthcare). Meanwhile, *Sovroms* (joint Soviet-Romanian enterprises which had emerged already in March 1945) organized around rich resources such as oil, timber, petroleum, and coal, as well as transport, banking, and film, were officially established. The *Sovroms* constituted the effective pillaging of Romanian resources by the USSR—albeit legally justified as war reparations—and solidified the economic coordination of the two countries through the use of Soviet specialists in Romanian industries. In addition, a purging of real and alleged enemies ensued, or, more aptly, continued. Among them were Peasant Party leaders, Iuliu Maniu and Ion Mihalache, who were arrested in 1947 and found guilty of treason and imprisoned for life, along with Socialist Party leaders.

The final blow to the existing government occurred in December 1947 with the forced abdication of King Michael.

On 30 December 1947, Romania officially became a People's Republic (Republica Populară Română), a one-party state based on Marxist-Leninist principles, and the Social Democratic Party was absorbed into the PCdR to form the Romanian Workers Party (Partidul Muncitoresc Român; PMR).[99] The new constitution, adopted in March 1948, wholly reformulated civic identity: Article 16 granted all "citizens" full and equal political rights without reference to sex, nationality, race, religion, or creed.[100] Moreover, Article 18 entitled women to positions in national, regional, and local government, while Article 21 declared that "women have equal rights with men in all public domains: economic, social, cultural, political, and in private life," as well as the right to work the same jobs as men and receive equal pay for equal work.[101] Although on the surface progressive, these rights, especially that of work, were also presented as an obligation of all citizens.[102]

In 1948, a new criminal code was enacted with vaguely-defined infractions that could be used with flexibility. As a corollary, the Securitate (General Directorate of State Security), the communist political police, was established to "protect" citizens from "domestic and foreign enemies."[103] With the onset of the Cold War, Soviet ire shifted from fascism to capitalist-imperialism, and Gheorghe Gheorghiu-Dej unleashed a terror against tens of thousands of "class enemies," "capitalist spies," and "national deviationists," who were arrested, imprisoned, and sent to forced labor camps on a range of grounds, including "conspiracy against the social order" and "undermining the national economy."[104] Among those arrested were approximately 80,000 peasants and thousands of Romanian intellectuals and members of the bourgeois and elite class, many of whom ended up in prisons or work camps. Some of the most notorious camps were located on the planned canal route from the Danube River to the Black Sea, where tens of thousands were sent as "class enemies" between 1949 and 1953.[105] Tens of thousands also languished in prisons, where they endured brutal treatment and underwent various forms of "reeducation."[106] Finally, tens of thousands of ethnic minorities and interwar elites were forcibly relocated from Western Romania to the plains of Bărăgan, an inhospitable region in the southeastern part of the country, where they were left to fend for themselves.[107]

In an effort to purge Romanian culture of reactionary and bourgeois elements, prewar cultural organizations were disbanded, associational life was quashed, and censorship was imposed on the media and in education. Moreover, all nonstate organizations, including interwar workers unions and women's and youth organizations, were dissolved and replaced with communist variants. As in the USSR, Nazi Germany, and fascist Italy, these new organizations were designed to mobilize the population, serving as transmission belts for state policies and programs. Additionally, intellectuals and cultural figures that embraced Western styles and values were dubbed "cosmopolitans" and faced censorship, with all "nonconformists" eventually losing their jobs and, in some cases, being arrested. Meanwhile, professionals, as a form of punishment for their "unhealthy social origins," experienced economic marginalization, being forced into manual labor jobs or positions incommensurate with their training and expertise.

With respect to religion and religious institutions, the regime was more cautious and selective in meting out repression. While all confessional schools were closed, the regime, recognizing the cultural significance of the Orthodox Church, allowed it to survive, albeit as a subordinate of the state. Although some 2,500 non-cooperating Orthodox priests and nuns were arrested and more than one-half of all monasteries were closed during the Dej period, many Orthodox clergy proclaimed their loyalty to the state, supporting collectivization and the literacy program and engaging in social service efforts. Indeed, some even collaborated with the Securitate.[108] By contrast, the regime's treatment of the Greek Catholic (or Uniate) Church, because it refused collaboration, was decidedly repressive: in 1948 the church was completely dissolved, its properties nationalized, and much of its clergy arrested. A similar onslaught ensued against the Catholic Church.

As in other parts of Eastern Europe, then, the postwar period was not associated with peace, but with continued social, economic, and political tumult. The establishment of a communist state produced a climate of fear and uncertainty, prolonging and exacerbating the insecurity, poverty, and violence many Romanians had experienced during the war. Alongside damaged infrastructure and bombed-out homes, social dislocation, in the form of wandering refugees, fragmented families, and homeless orphans characterized the period. Yet, even for those who did not lose their homes or loved ones, everyday life remained precarious. Due to the combined effects of Soviet war reparations ($300 million) and a decline in agricultural output (as a result of the drought and land redistribution), prices for basic foods such as grain and potatoes soared. Desperate, people responded by participating in food riots and workplace strikes.[109] While many sank deeper into poverty as they struggled to feed their families, hundreds of thousands in northeastern Romania perished during the famine of 1946–1947—the worst in modern Romanian history.

Although not affected by famine, G., who was born in Constanţa in 1941, recalled the material desperation experienced by families in her community during the early postwar period:

> It was after the war, people were poor. Only now do I understand how my mom was able to handle the changes. She cried all the time because she didn't have the means to raise kids, powdered foods to raise the children—like we do today—powdered milk, tapioca, powdered rice, cereal. You couldn't find anything. Nothing. Nothing. [Only] cow's milk, if you could afford it.[110]

Even though G.'s father worked as a factory section manager, his earnings, along with low-rations, presented challenges in properly nourishing the family. Although Romania did not experience the same degree of physical and human devastation as Poland, Germany, Yugoslavia, and the USSR, it nonetheless faced massive food shortages. Austerity was felt throughout Europe, however, this was mitigated somewhat in Western countries through Marshall Plan funding. The Eastern Bloc, by contrast, could not benefit from such funding as Stalin prohibited these countries from accepting aid. Thus, economic uncertainty coexisted with political repression and the advent of illiberal governance in Romania and other parts of the region.

However, this was only part of the story. As Stefano Bottoni contends, communism in Romania, rather than being forcibly imposed by the Soviets upon a reluctant citizenry, had a degree of local support as the PMR "adeptly managed to build political consensus among a broad range of social strata" through its promotion of ethnic equality, land redistribution, and full employment.[111] Accordingly, communism was not only appealing to true believers, but also to those living on the edge of poverty, to groups who, because of their ethnicity, had been marginalized, persecuted, or targeted for expulsion or extermination, and to those who had lost faith in other parties' ability to govern responsibly and transparently. Alongside hopes for a more ethnically harmonious society, individuals were attracted by the possibility of guaranteed employment, a stable, albeit modest, income, educational opportunities, and the potential for fashioning a new identity and, indeed, a new life.

## Creating the New (Wo)man

Upon assuming power, the communist government faced a number of challenges, paramount among them mobilizing a predominantly agrarian population, wracked by five years of war, for the building of socialism. As such, it needed to make communism—a Soviet import—appealing to the people. As elsewhere in the Bloc, undermining social privilege and expanding opportunities for workers and peasants was done through brute force and more peaceful means. Alongside purging "enemies of the people," the party-state embarked on the construction of a new society, a radical and ambitious project that required forging new men, new women, and a new consciousness. Represented as *omul nou* (new man), this new person was to embody sacrifice, diligence, and devotion to socialist principles. Officially, *omul nou* was a generic identity, masking the reality that people's roles differed as a function of gender, among other identifiers. Accordingly, the state employed gender-homogenizing and gender-differentiating strategies in inscribing *omul nou*. For example, while women and men alike were expected to engage in paid labor, women were also expected to bear children and inculcate them with socialist values. However, official promotion of these roles was first and foremost a function of state expediency (i.e. for the purposes of industrialization and modernization) rather than Marxist prescriptions for gender equality. The implications for women's daily lives were often ambiguous, frustrating, demanding, and, at times, limiting and regressive—as they were for women throughout the Eastern Bloc. Indeed, in its blending of progressive and regressive policies, Romania in many ways followed the lead of the USSR under Stalin where, "the new role as worker was grafted onto her [woman's] old role of homemaker, and female identity was meant to encompass traditional male and female qualities and traits. She was glorified for her capacity to work like a man, and at the same time celebrated for her nurturance and her willingness to sacrifice herself for others."[112]

"Equality between women and men," the catchphrase for women's liberation under socialism, was codified in law and a staple of communist propaganda; yet until the last decade of socialist rule, the PCR was overwhelmingly male. This was true of the Central Committee of the Romanian Communist Party, the Grand National Assembly (Parliament), and local and regional governance. Indeed, while women constituted 12.1 percent of Central Committee members in 1948, this figure actually declined to 4.9 percent after the purging of Ana Pauker in 1952, and hovered around that number until 1979, when it reached 19.5 percent after the advent of Elena Ceaușescu to power and the implementation of a quota system.[113] From the onset of socialist rule, then, women were at a political disadvantage and thus less influential in policymaking.[114] What's more, by the time women's numbers had reached 40 percent (in 1985), the Central Committee was composed of "yes men" (and a few "yes women") who mechanically voiced support for Ceaușescu in order to maintain their privileged position.[115] Women were also underrepresented in politics on the local level, within the party, and in workers' unions and, as such, unable to significantly influence local and workplace decisions. Official fidelity to women's emancipation and political parity notwithstanding, the PCR leadership made minimal effort to share political power with women, both in the realm of high politics and on the factory floor, undermining the socialist promise to radically transform gender dynamics in society at large.

Instead, as in other socialist states (as well as liberal-democratic ones) men benefitted from patriarchal practices, be it the unpaid domestic and emotional labor performed by wives, mothers, and sisters to prevailing beliefs about men's role as breadwinner and their corresponding need for higher salaries. Lack of commitment to full gender equality was evident not only in the stark gender imbalance within the political leadership, but also in the meager funds allocated for childcare and the short maternity leave. Thus, the state did not sufficiently incentivize women's roles through policies (e.g. extensive maternity leave; adequate childcare facilities) that would have helped them reconcile workplace and family responsibilities. Similarly problematic was the fact that maternity leave was never reconfigured into "family leave," that is, an entitlement that could apply to women and men alike. Instead, socialist family policy institutionalized caregiving as a woman's responsibility, which was further reinforced by propaganda glorifying women's "noble mission as mothers." Meanwhile, efforts to "protect" women only extended to the workplace. Thus, while women were legally protected from working in environments considered potentially detrimental to their reproductive health, they were not protected from abusive husbands or the untoward advances of male coworkers and managers.

Finally, it could be argued that patriarchal practices were perpetuated—or at least tolerated—by some high-ranking members of the National Council of Women (CNF) who, especially from the late 1960s on, were seemingly concerned with maintaining privilege by demonstrating loyalty to the regime. Thus, rather than advocating for woman-friendly policies and seeking to improve women's daily lives, during the latter part of socialist rule, leading members of the CNF simply transmitted and enforced state directives. Understood in this light, the socialist regime in Romania was indeed a "state patriarchy," as feminist philosopher Mihaela Miroiu contends; however, in this respect it was not considerably different than many liberal-democratic states in which men dominate politics and implement policies that often neglect women's needs, interests, and perspectives.[116]

Although socialist rule was patriarchal in character, state prescriptions for women's full equality, including increased educational and employment opportunities, were nonetheless progressive. Indeed, despite numerous shortcomings, women's position did undergo transformation under socialism, often in positive ways. So too did notions of work, the family, and the relationship between state and citizen. As a foundation for understanding subsequent chapters, the following section examines the efforts of socialist women's organizations to mobilize women for production, demographic growth, and, more broadly, the construction of socialism. As transmission belts for the party's programs, these organizations promoted particular ideas about gender roles and social relationships. In lectures and reading circles, as well as in brochures and magazine articles, women were presented as agents who, with the help of the party, could contribute to national growth, shape their own destiny, and serve as symbols of socialist modernity. Although it is impossible to disentangle state expediency from genuine commitment to women's liberation, some of the policies implemented by these organizations were genuinely meaningful and, indeed, transformative (e.g. promotion of literacy and establishment of courses on infant health and household management, etc.). Thus, assessments of state socialist women's organizations should not lose sight of the fact that they could serve as agents of positive change, offering women valuable skills and new ways of thinking about their lives and place within society.

After the re-legalization of the PCdR in 1944, members of its women's section began agitational work with women in factories and in the countryside. In April 1945, future foreign minister Ana Pauker founded a separate communist organization for women: the Union of Antifascist Women of Romania (Uniunea Femeilor Antifasciste din România; UFAR). With local branches throughout the country, the official aim of the UFAR was to "raise women's cultural and political consciousness, improve women's health and hygiene, protect children, forge bonds with similar anti-fascist groups, and enlist women of all class, religious, and ethnic backgrounds in the fight against fascism."[117] To that end, the UFAR, like its counterparts throughout the Eastern Bloc, organized literacy and vocational training courses and founded libraries, daycare centers, and crèches.[118] As it was not the only game in town, the UFAR needed to appeal to (i.e. convert) a wide range of women to the communist cause. Thus, it did not present itself as a communist or worker's organization, but one that included women from various walks of life. To this end, it coordinated women's organizations through a larger umbrella organization, the Federation of Democratic Women of Romania (Federaţia Democrata a Femeilor din România FDFR; [established in March 1946]).[119] Accordingly, in a speech to communist women activists in February 1946, Pauker emphasized the importance of coalition building and women's essential role in shaping the nation's and, by extension, their own, future:

> We would make a huge mistake and we would not be good communists if we ever forget the immense treasure of skills, initiative and common sense that are waiting to be discovered in Romanian women. Each one of us who is here today would have a story to tell, I am sure, about the discovery of capacities she never thought she had. ... And, it is up to us women, no matter in what area we work, to mobilize other women. If we do not succeed, we will be the only ones responsible for our failure. We have to persuade women in rural and urban areas that their duty, our duty as women is to fight like mothers who are protecting their babies in order to preserve the little freedom we have gained, the rights we gained, so that we can then demand more rights for us, women, for our children and, ultimately, for our entire people. ... Comrades, the work we do now, in these several months of electoral campaigning, will raise the level of awareness and knowledge of women in our country. With their heightened will to act and confidence in their own strength, they will push our country forward through their own work, and they will then know how to redistribute the wealth from rich women to the entire people.[120]

By acknowledging women's "treasure of skills," as well as their "stories," and by emphasizing their crucial role in constructing a new social order, Pauker sought to instill confidence and social consciousness in women activists. Using maternalist metaphors, she connected safeguarding national freedoms to protecting children, underscoring the importance of gender-essentializing discourse in mobilizing women for socialism.

The UFAR's policies were shaped by an elite cadre of officials—what Alexandra Ghit refers to as "idealistic intellectuals"—some of them long-time party members who had supported women's equality during the interwar period, but many new to the organization. With the passage of universal suffrage in 1946, securing women's electoral support became particularly important for the PCdR. As such, the UFAR focused on upcoming parliamentary elections, sending teams of activists across Romania to educate women about the electoral process and urge them to vote for PCdR candidates.[121] Although activists engaged in workplace agitation, given that the majority of Romanian women worked within the larger, rural household, the UFAR also conducted door-to-door campaigning and organized housewives' and knitting circles, during which they sought to persuade women to support the PCdR. As the literacy rate of rural women remained low, these informal, verbal exchanges served as the most effective means for appealing to women.[122]

Rural women were of particular concern to the party, not only because they constituted one of the largest social groups, but also because of their lack of education and adherence to religious and traditional practices. As in the USSR and other parts of the Bloc, rural women were considered the most backward and oppressed group and, as such, most likely to be disengaged from politics or to embrace conservative parties. By forging relationships with rural women through conversations about history and politics, UFAR activists hoped to shape their political views and urge them to commit themselves to the building of socialism. They also sought to persuade them to become activists themselves so they could, in turn, persuade neighbors, relatives, and friends to join the party and support local UFAR initiatives.

While the UFAR presented work (either in the factory or on the farm) and political participation (through voting) as essential components of socialist citizenship, these were only two elements, as women were also expected to actively engage in educational, social service, and community-assistance efforts. According to Alexandra Ghit, this conceptualization of citizenship assumed not only ideological but also practical significance, compensating for the fact that Romania lacked, during the immediate postwar period, the economic conditions for solving the woman question in the Marxist sense (i.e. subsidizing an elaborate social welfare system to help women reconcile domestic and workplace responsibilities).[123] As such, the UFAR could attempt to solve—or at least deal with—the woman question by mobilizing women for the vote, activism, and relief and social service efforts. At the same time, these latter efforts were crucial given the country's devastation and impoverishment after the war and during the famine. Therefore, while ideologically inflected, these initiatives were nonetheless concrete responses to real social need.

The UFAR's initiatives varied from locality to locality and chapter to chapter; while some chapters helped evacuate children from drought-ridden areas, others founded kindergartens and crèches, and others raised funds to clothe, feed, and provide school supplies to orphans.[124] In this respect, the UFAR continued the work of prewar women's charities, even relying on membership dues and private donations rather than state funds to do so, which also provided it a degree of autonomy. The UFAR also mobilized women for public works and rebuilding efforts, including activities deemed traditionally masculine. Thus, they organized voluntary brigades to tidy up neighborhoods, build dikes, and construct tram lines, roads, and pipelines—efforts that were featured in UFAR brochures and its magazine, *Drumul Femeii* (Women's Path). Although such activities were designed to showcase "equality between women and men," they often rested on facile and androcentric notions of gender, equating women's participation in heavy labor with gender equality. For example, one brochure featured women engaged in heavy labor while a brigade of male delegates looked impressively on, sending the message that women could also "work like men" and were, as such, equal to them.[125] At the same time, the image underscored—unintentionally or not—that leadership remained a male preserve.

To spearhead local initiatives, the UFAR sought out elite women, and many articles in *Drumul Femeii* targeted well-educated and white-collar urban women, presenting activism and political education with rural women as duties they owed to their less-fortunate sisters.[126] Such articles contextualized rural women's backwardness within a history of prejudice and lack of support by elite women:

> Why is the Romanian woman uneducated? Because schools were open to her with great stinginess, because we did nothing or very little, us intellectuals, to dispel the unfortunate idea of the peasant, "What do girls need literacy for?" ... We have left women in the dark, humble and overworked, quiet and unknown. ... The Romanian woman is not stupid. ... She is just spent by work, stifled by ignorance, tired of always being considered the most patient animal of the house. The work of her reeducation has begun. Democratic organizations, led by the Union of Antifascist Women, fight with courage and energy to enlighten and inform the broad masses of women.[127]

Through their activism, then, elite women could help build a communist utopia, as well as atone for their lack of antifascist resistance during the war.

The year 1948 signified an end to pluralism in Romania both in politics and associational life. With the consolidation of communist power under Dej, the UFAR was replaced by the Union of Democratic Romanian Women (Uniunea Femeilor Democrate din România; UFDR, 1948–57). Meanwhile, all remaining women's organizations were either absorbed into the UFDR or dissolved due to their alleged "reactionary" and "bourgeois" character.[128] In comparison with its predecessor, the UFDR was an auxiliary of the PCR, with local chapters following the directives of central headquarters in Bucharest. The organization also assumed a more professional profile, employing activists trained at the "Central School of Agitation" in Bucharest.[129]

In 1948, the UFDR claimed 1.5 million members, of which 2,660 were remunerated for their efforts.[130] Having secured political power, the PCR and its affiliated organizations were no longer concerned with mobilizing women for the vote but instead for childbearing and enhancing their cultural and political education. To this end, the UFDR helped establish maternity hospitals, crèches and kindergartens, and caregiving rooms for mothers in train stations. Emphasis on women's maternal roles was rooted in concern over decreasing fertility rates, which was not limited to Romania or the Eastern Bloc, but a larger European concern due to massive population loss during the war.[131] Like women's organizations in other parts of Europe, from Stalin's Russia and Mussolini's Italy to liberal-democratic states, the UFDR was also engaged in social engineering, seeking to transform backward (e.g. peasant) populations through scientific and rational (read: modern) approaches to childrearing and homemaking. Thus, in addition to literacy campaigns and local relief and charitable activities, the UFDR sought to inculcate modern approaches to mothering and domesticity through local committee meetings, house-to-house conversations, and persuasion work. Additionally, informational brochures, articles in *Drumul Femeii*, and "Mothers' Schools" instructed women on infant health and hygiene and on how to create the conditions for raising new socialist citizens.[132]

Although well-intentioned, according to research on the UFDR's Satu Mare county chapter, strategies for incorporating rural women into the party, particularly through Mothers' Schools and workshops on hygiene, were relatively ineffective. After initial interest, attendance at these schools dropped due to the length of class meetings and activists' difficulties in establishing rapports with women whose approaches to childrearing they often discounted.[133] Although not generalizable to all chapters, such findings, along with those from communist women's organizations in other parts of the Bloc, suggest that rural women often regarded activists with indifference and even suspicion.

Concern about childrearing often extended beyond infancy to children's schooling. Thus, "parents' committees," which were organized on the local level, sought to enlighten mothers about school curricula and encourage them to be more involved in their children's education by reviewing lessons they had learned at school. Mothers were also advised to keep regular meetings with teachers and to create quiet places at home for children to study. While on the mark, such advice was often impossible to follow given the spatial constraints of peasant homes and apartments. Beyond that, due to widespread privation most families could barely afford basic necessities, let alone a bookshelf and desk for their children.

The UFDR also spearheaded food distribution initiatives, providing food to children and pregnant women in milk centers and kindergartens, planting vegetable gardens in schools, and establishing conservation centers for canning fruit and vegetables.[134] To ensure that families had sufficient sustenance for winter, the UFDR designated canning targets. Indeed, canning and preserving became part of the larger state plan, as well as a priority for the UFDR in 1949 and 1950, for which women were mobilized and featured on the pages of *Drumul Femeii*. By encouraging rational approaches to homemaking, activists sought to systematize and modernize domesticity. Such efforts also occurred in other parts of the Bloc, as well as in Western Europe and the United States, with the aim of creating modern homemakers capable of running efficient and economical households.

With the introduction of collectivization in 1949, the UFDR devoted its energies to persuading peasants to join collective farms (*Gospodăriile Agricole Colective [GAC]*) and in monitoring harvest collection—efforts that encountered substantial peasant resistance.[135] Meanwhile, to mobilize women into the labor force the UFDR sponsored job-training courses on various technical specialties.[136] As part of these efforts, the UFDR published brochures and magazine articles that contrasted women's slave-like conditions under capitalism with their manifold opportunities for advancement in the socialist workplace.

In 1957, the UFDR was disbanded and replaced by the National Council of Women (Consiliul Național al Femeilor; CNF)—a change justified on the basis of improved coordination of women and the realization of state plans. The CNF built on the UFDR's activities, defining women's citizenship with respect to the productive sphere (the factory; the collective farm) and their roles as mothers. On regional, municipal, and community levels the CNF functioned through "women's committees" under which functioned "women's commissions." These bodies were charged with organizing a host of initiatives, including mobilizing women for local voluntary work; supporting female literacy and women's technical and professional development; safeguarding women's rights in the workplace and organizing crèches and daycare centers in factories; ensuring that markets, grocery stores, and restaurants were sufficiently provisioned; organizing lecture series and conferences; and encouraging parents to help reduce the school dropout rate by sending their children to school on a regular basis.[137] For urban dwellers, the CNF promoted women's engagement in paid labor and their participation in public and community life through activism and neighborhood cleanup and beautification programs. Meanwhile, as collectivization was in full swing during the 1950s, the CNF urged rural women to join collectives, with local chapters organizing conferences on agricultural efficiency and animal husbandry. More generally, the CNF sought to wean women off religion and folk practices, raise their political consciousness, and encourage them to embrace modern forms of hygiene and domesticity to reduce disease transmission and infant mortality rates.

In the workplace, breaks provided a convenient and casual context for proselytizing, engaging women in conversation, and distributing brochures. These brochures outlined women's roles, rights, and responsibilities under the People's Republic of Romania, comparing Romanian women's superlative position to women's abysmal situation in capitalist countries. Additionally, knitting, cooking, baking, and crafting circles enabled activists to engage in political education, while also providing women with opportunities to develop skills. The CNF also organized courses and reading circles on Romanian history as well as visits to museums and historical sites. These initiatives were designed to enhance women's knowledge of history and culture while regional conferences, community lectures, brochures, and the magazine *Femeia* (the successor to *Drumul Femeii*) were designed to "enlighten" women about Marxist theory, national and international politics, and social welfare entitlements. They were also designed to inculcate women with modern values by eradicating superstitious beliefs and neutralizing religious influences.[138]

What impact did socialist women's organizations have on women's daily lives? Until recently, scholars have analyzed these organizations through the prism of the Cold War.[139] Accordingly, scholars interpret their initiatives and programs as instrumentalist: a means through which the larger goals of socialist modernization were to be achieved. As a corollary, women activists are seen as tools or willing collaborators of the regime, and, consequently, any type of liberation women experienced is understood as a byproduct of socialist modernization rather than the result of sustained efforts by female activists. This interpretation, however, not only homogenizes all organizations on the basis of their subordinate status within the party hierarchy but also fails to consider how local and contextual factors influenced their character and ability to effect change. Moreover, it fails to consider how these initiatives were implemented by the organization on the local level—and how ordinary women responded to and were affected by them.

Recent research on women's organizations in postwar Romania suggests a more complex portrait of socialist activists. For instance, activists involved in postwar relief work, literacy campaigns, and efforts to increase social welfare entitlements and ensure women's equal remuneration were genuinely devoted to improving women's status.[140]

However, given the constraints under which they operated, CNF activists enjoyed little, if any, institutional agency, particularly compared to socialist Bulgaria where the women's organization secured important provisions for women.[141] Indeed, with the centralization of power under Ceaușescu, women activists in Romania faced constraints—both budgetary and political—which generally hampered their ability to promote woman-friendly policies or to challenge policies they found detrimental to women's autonomy, such as the decree that banned abortion in 1966.[142] Additionally, appointments to the organization were increasingly based on loyalty. Thus, the CNF, like other state organizations, played an important role in sustaining the power of the leader, slavishly following regime dictates. The advent of self-seeking careerists among the CNF's ranks, who faithfully toed the party line, thus undermined much of its positive impact on women's lives. Moreover, like other state socialist organizations, exchanges with women were typically unidirectional, even if they appeared to be bi-directional in the official press. In sum, as a transmission belt for the PCR's policies, the CNF was necessarily subordinate to it, though its leading members were also in positions of power and thus enjoyed certain privileges.

Yet, such realities do not mean that all CNF members were uncaring, careerist tools of the regime—or that the CNF could not be an important engine for change. Thus, cynicism about the organization's overarching goals should not color the beneficent impact of the initiatives it undertook. Nor should it obscure the reality that opportunities did exist for activists to emphasize certain policies and initiatives over others. As Kristen Ghodsee contends with respect to socialist Bulgaria, "Unless we are willing to argue that all communist women were suffering from false consciousness, we have to accept that at least some of these women truly believed that they were best serving women by serving the Party, and that including women's issues within the broader socialist program for societal transformation was the most effective way of achieving lasting social change."[143]

Given the challenges in securing materials on the CNF's activities and members, a brief overview of its women's monthly, *Femeia*, offers insight into the party-state's construction of women and gender roles in socialist Romania.[144] The magazine was widely distributed in urban and rural areas and served as an important source for advertising national and geopolitical policies and for fashioning the new socialist woman, both explicitly through reports on party congresses and more subtly through articles, advice columns, and personal profiles.[145]

Like Soviet women, Romanian women's identities were "constructed around certain key issues such as citizenship, the welfare state, women's labor and reproductive obligations, and relations between the sexes," though the degree to which these issues were emphasized varied with respect to broader state goals.[146] Yet, while *Femeia* was an ideological tool of the regime, it should be borne in mind that the majority of its authors were women who, like women more generally, worked, raised families, and were subject to state policies and programs. As such, they were familiar with and at least somewhat sensitive to the manifold challenges women faced.

Over the course of socialist rule the magazine's subject matter varied in accordance with the state's broader ideological goals. During the early years of the Cold War, women were praised for their "struggles for peace" (*lupte pentru pace*) and "against fascist-imperialism." Accordingly, women laborers and collective farm workers were valorized for over-fullfilling the norms on the factory floor and in the fields. As a corollary, the Soviet Union was celebrated as the land of plenty, a utopian paradise of social harmony and gender equality. Moreover, the Bolshevik Revolution was celebrated annually with articles on Friedrich Engels, Lenin, Nadezhda Krupskaia, and other revolutionary figures such as Rosa Luxemburg, although Joseph Stalin received special admiration. Soviet advisers who helped Romanian women master their trade were also acknowledged. As the engineer Alexandra Constantinescu, who participated in a worker-training program at a polytechnic institute in Kiev, recalled in the "Thoughts about Friends" section of *Femeia*, "We will never forget the workers and technicians from the great factories in Kiev and Minsk, where we finished our practicum in the summer months. With what patience and affection they helped us apply our theoretical knowledge to practical matters … I learned to value work … to fall in love with it … to feel as if I can't live without it."[147] In this way, Romanian women expressed gratitude to their Soviet mentors, who nurtured their passion for their vocation and work more generally. More significantly, by personalizing its subject matter, *Femeia*'s editors sought to forge a bond between readers and the featured topic (e.g. women's productive contributions; Romanian-Soviet friendship) and, thereby, cloak the broader ideological intent of such pieces.

Meanwhile, in the column "Small Episodes from the Great Struggle," readers learned about the achievements of their socialist foremothers, who, left to fend for themselves after their male loved ones were sent to the front during World War II, participated in workplace sabotage and strikes against their "exploitative working conditions." Additionally, they read about the Romanian Women's Group for Peace, which penned a letter to Marshal Antonescu, urging him to break off Romania's alliance with the Nazis.[148] The magazine also included autobiographical pieces by women such as Paraschiva Cornea-Păunescu, who, at the mere age of fourteen, joined the Socialist Workers Party and devoted herself to her rural sisters, teaching them about basic health and hygiene, including the dangers of drinking unboiled water by having them examine well water under a microscope.[149] In this way, the party sought to forge a bond between early socialist revolutionaries and present-day socialist activists, providing the latter with an important place in the evolution of socialism. By fulfilling their manifold responsibilities, Romanian women thus honored the legacy of earlier socialist heroines.

*Femeia* also featured articles about other parts of Europe. For instance, readers learned that while East Berlin is a "city of peace," West Berlin is "the seat of imperialist occupiers," where "prostitution, corruption, and adolescent crime flourish alongside a base for atomic weapons."[150] The magazine also reported on social injustices in various parts of the globe from the mistreatment of African Americans in the Jim Crow South to the abuses faced by women in countries under colonial domination. *Femeia*'s support for civil rights and national liberation struggles in other parts of the world reflected the PCR's increasing embrace of national communism, which served as a source of regime legitimation under Dej and Ceaușescu. Thus, while articles about helpless Vietnamese women and children being apprehended by enemy soldiers were intended to appeal to women's maternal sensibilities, heroic stories about Vietnamese women fighting American aggressors were designed to foster support for national liberation struggles and against "capitalist-imperialist barbarity."[151] In this way, propagandists hoped to discredit capitalism and legitimate socialism, as well as foster an imagined community of socialist sisters. Moreover, in counterpoising images of misery and desperation to idyllic portraits of life in Romania, where "concern for women is a crucial feature," party propagandists distinguished Romania from other parts of the world, further reinforcing its allegedly beneficent program.

To familiarize women with state entitlements for mothers and workers, *Femeia* outlined family and labor codes along with other legislation (see figure 1.1). It also included reports on the annual national women's conference, as well as international women's congresses, featuring excerpts of addresses delivered by leading activists. Meanwhile, the section "The Initiatives of the Women's Commissions and Committees" kept women abreast of activities and programs undertaken on local and regional levels.

With respect to the family, the magazine stressed women's roles as mothers and educators of a new generation of healthy and socially

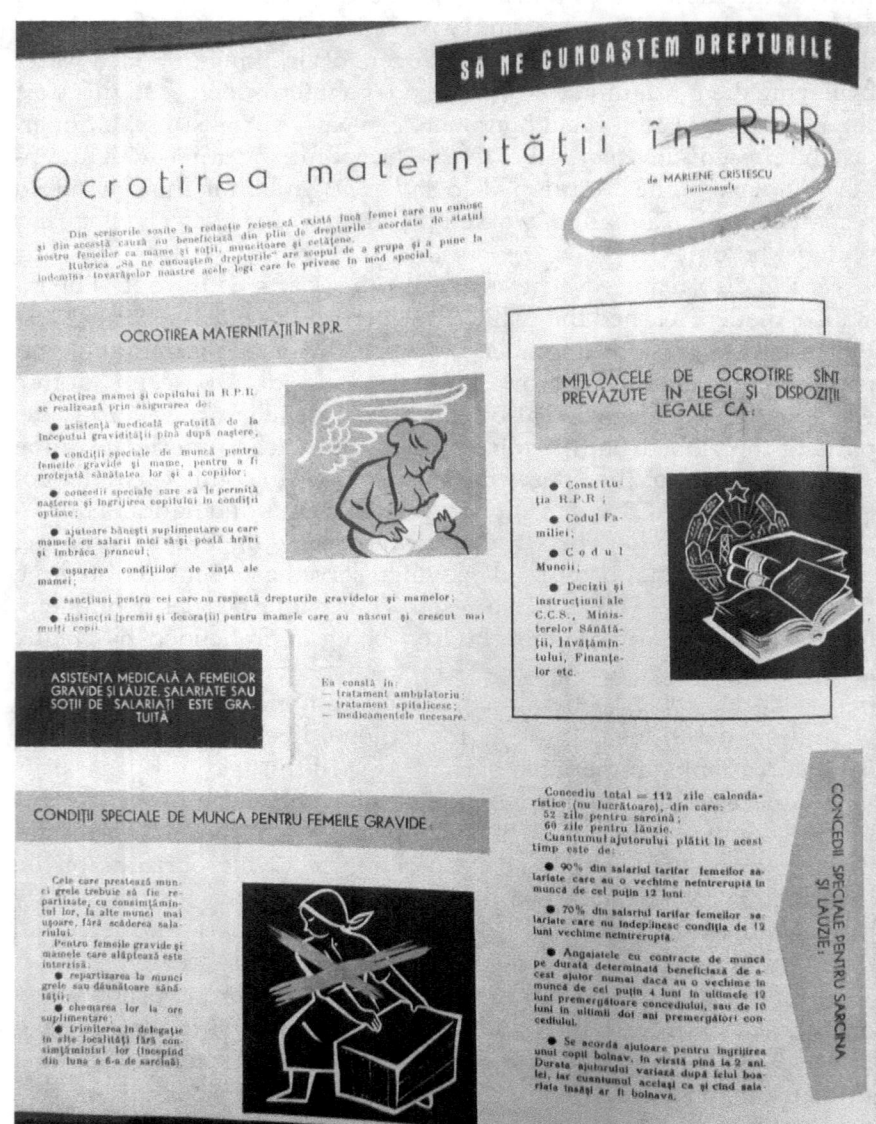

**Figure 1.1.** Knowing Our Rights, *Femeia*, March 1958

conscious youth, while also paying lip service to women's struggles in balancing workplace and domestic responsibilities. Yet, while *Femeia* echoed state commitment to ease women's burden through provision of self-service shops and household durables, it also castigated men (through published surveys and reader forums) for embracing traditional attitudes and refusing to pull their domestic weight. Thus, ordinary readers, along with experts, noted that while semi-prepared foods and all-service grocery stores might help attenuate women's burdens, at the end of the day, men needed to be more actively involved in the household. Accordingly, boys needed to be responsible for household chores and taught to regard girls as their equals. At the same time, the editors did not shy away from addressing more serious matters such as spousal abandonment and abuse. Although intended to promote family unity, such public acknowledgment of spousal abuse was novel, and these articles would have resonated with some women.

As working women, the editors of these articles were familiar with the challenges of juggling work and home and thus may have been genuinely sensitive to the plight of their readers; however, like other activists within the CNF, their ability to effect policy change was limited. Moreover, as the regime privileged industry over social services, it seems that these public, albeit controlled, forums functioned largely as safety valves, giving voice to women's frustrations, rather than as platforms for meaningful policy change.

By the mid-1960s, as the overall standard of living increased, the magazine featured more (and more colorful) advertisements of durable goods, as well as home décor and fashion spreads. It also increasingly focused on personal issues (e.g. beauty, marital relations, moral dilemmas), and advice columns, quizzes, and surveys became standard features. The advice column "Întrebări, Confesiuni, Experiențe" (Questions, Confessions, Experiences; see figure 1.2), the socialist equivalent of the "Dear Abby" column that appeared in American newspapers, is particularly insightful for understanding state conceptualizations of gender. Presented as an open forum for the exchange of ideas, the column featured letters from women seeking solutions to a broad range of problems (e.g. resolving conflicts with coworkers; dealing with insensitive husbands; raising respectful teens). Upon learning about a particular problem or concern, readers were encouraged to submit their suggestions for dealing with it, which might be published in a subsequent issue. Rather than offer simple solutions, the aim of the column was to provide a diversity of suggestions—albeit in conformity with socialist principles and values—to readers' problems. In a similar vein, in the mid-1960s a section entitled "Viața in Doi" (Life

Together) was introduced, which included relationship surveys (the results of which appeared in a subsequent issue), compatibility quizzes, and articles by psychologists and marriage experts focusing on typical problems faced by couples during the first years of marriage. Meanwhile, a section entitled "Şcoala Părinţilor" (Parents' School) advised women and men on a host of parenting issues, from disciplining unruly children to setting progressive examples of gender roles within the family. While some women may have identified with the dilemmas posed by readers in advice columns or been entertained by the relationship quizzes, these pieces were designed to promote values and behaviors that would contribute to larger state goals. Under the guise of an open exchange of ideas—a socialist version of "manufacturing consent"—the regime could thus mask the ideological purpose of the column (i.e. the promotion of diligent, [re]productive, and morally upright citizens).

**Figure 1.2.** "Questions, Confessions, Experiences," *Femeia*, 1973

The increased focus on the personal contrasted with the explicitly political articles that appeared during the early years of socialist rule. Although perhaps welcomed by some, these pieces were nonetheless political, albeit in a more insidious manner. Indeed, many were a direct outgrowth of the regime's pronatalist policies and reflected broader moralizing efforts. As such, they should be read as efforts to politicize women's reproductive lives and promote behaviors that the regime deemed befitting modern, socialist citizens. For instance, while articles on marital discord were intended to stave off divorce by suggesting ways for couples to work out their differences, articles on prenatal and maternal health were intended to promote demographic growth. In the pronatalist series "Our Specialist Consults with You," for example, health professionals advised women on diet, work, and exercise during pregnancy, urging them to visit their physicians frequently to monitor the health of both mother and fetus. At the same time, the magazine correlated reproductive output with beauty, health, and diligence, while connecting childlessness to decreased productivity, listlessness, and depression.[152] Additionally, the magazine glorified women's roles as educators and mothers of a new generation of patriotic citizens, while portraying those who didn't emphasize or sufficiently value family as negligent mothers. Thus, the magazine's focus on personal and family health underpinned Ceaușescu's draconian pronatalist policies. Glorification of large families and paeans to prolific mothers, which reached epic proportions in the 1980s, were similarly inspired by demographic concerns.

With the advent of Elena and Nicolae Ceaușescu's personality cults in the 1970s, the socialist couple was featured prominently in the magazine. Designed to encourage women to devote their energies, in various capacities, to the building of socialism, the cult of Elena was also intended to legitimize her increasing influence in politics and her scientific "career." However, as will be discussed in chapter 3, the glorification of Elena and, to a lesser extent, women scientists masked women's underrepresentation in leadership positions and the feminization of certain sectors of the workforce

While articles in *Femeia* were designed to promote particular roles, values, and behaviors it should be remembered that socialist propaganda did offer women alternative identities and new ways of thinking about themselves and their relationship to the state, the family, and the nation. Indeed, in contrast to leading American magazines of the 1950s and 1960s, which glorified women as homemakers and mothers and encouraged them to engage in activities in the public sphere only insofar as they conformed to traditional gender roles, in socialist Romania women's periodicals focused on their identities both inside and outside the home, variously representing women as laborers and professionals, agitators and political figures, writers and artists, and mothers and wives. Moreover, the magazine served as a platform for airing frustrations and inquiring about certain issues. While many of these debates and forums seemingly functioned as safety valves, it does not necessarily follow that their authors were unconcerned with the issues featured in them. Moreover, it cannot be assumed that these forums had no bearing on how ordinary women reflected on their lives and relationships. In sum, although the written and visual messages that appeared in *Femeia* were ideologically inspired and, at times, hyperbolic, women did not necessarily regard them as fabricated or wholly meaningless. This includes advice given by readers, which could be progressive (e.g. suggesting that young women postpone marriage until they received an advanced degree; advising mothers not to treat their husbands or sons indulgently). Moreover, given that *Femeia* was the only women's magazine available in Romania (outside of publications smuggled in from abroad) it is safe to say that women engaged with it in some capacity. Indeed, *Femeia* reached more than just women as it included crossword puzzles and quizzes, general articles on travel and politics, and pieces written by and for men. Thus, men also occasionally glanced over and, in some cases, even read it.[153]

According to my respondents, their engagement with the magazine was selective. As Elena, a librarian born in 1959, recalled about *Femeia*, "Of course there were articles that were propaganda, but you could skip over them. I read about how to take care of my skin and complexion, and how to decorate a corner of my house and things like that … travel, exhibitions, and history, the culture of other countries."[154] In a similar vein, D. noted, "I liked it, but only some of the features; there were good columns on the household, on cooking, there were good recipes and elegant fashions."[155] Similarly, Ildiko, who read the Hungarian version of the magazine, *Dolgozó Nö*, recalled, "it had recipes, humor, all the things that interest women, makeup. Yes [it was alright]. I didn't like the first four pages because they were with the communists [leadership], but I passed over them and read other sections."[156] The fact that respondents stressed the utility of the magazine's more practical pieces (patterns, recipes, fashion spreads) while dismissing the ideological articles and pictures of "him and her" (Nicolae and Elena Ceaușescu) suggests that people did not wholly embrace or reject socialist media but engaged with it selectively and critically. Part of this selective engagement involved interpreting the magazine's contents through their own, personal experiences, beliefs, and values which were, in turn, influenced by family practices, custom, and religion—along with other discourses. Accordingly, *Femeia* cannot simply be written off as instrumentalist propaganda, but should instead be considered a complex and polyvalent source, meriting analysis alongside women's recollections of their lived experiences.

## Conclusion

Although women did not achieve full legal equality with men until the communist consolidation of power in 1948, a range of thinkers engaged with the "woman question" from the latter half of the nineteenth century through the interwar period. Moreover, through philanthropic activities, women's organizations worked to expand girls' and women's educational and training opportunities and lobby for legal and political equality. Their work reflected similar efforts in other parts of Europe and the United States at the time and were especially impressive in light of Romania's restrictive political climate and women's subordination in the family and society more generally. During the nineteenth century, women typically argued for citizenship on the basis of their difference from or complementarity with men (e.g. contributions to the nation as mothers and moral educators); however, by the twentieth century their claims broadened to include liberal and feminist conceptions of equality and human rights. During this period, women's participation in industry, education, and various professions also increased substantially, which provided them with a degree of autonomy and a sense of accomplishment—and thus the belief that they should be entitled to such rights.

Although the interwar period was marked by economic instability, ethnic tension, and political corruption—culminating in authoritarian rule—it was also characterized by women's increased participation in industry and professions, as well as increased focus on women's issues in the public sphere. With the establishment of socialist rule after World War II, women received full political and legal equality; however, given the demands of socialist modernization and the fact that men dominated leadership positions in the labor force and the government, women's interests were subordinated to larger economic goals. Although the UFDR and the CNF sought to improve women's situation through literacy campaigns and other social service initiatives, their primary goal was to mobilize women for the purpose of socialist modernization and to foster loyalty to the state. Thus, the CNF urged women to join collective farms, take up work in industry, and serve as activists, while also stressing women's important roles as wives and mothers. Through its magazine, *Femeia*, the CNF reformulated women's roles and responsibilities, representing women as equal socialist citizens and celebrating their productive achievements in industry and farming, while at the same time presenting them in an essentialist fashion as mothers and educators of the nation. Over the course of socialist rule, the content and style of the magazine changed in accordance with the state's broader ideological goals. Articles thus went from being explicitly political and ideological to being explicitly personal and implicitly political. Although most articles, surveys, and advice columns were intended to promote particular behaviors and values, propagandists did offer women alternative roles and identities, as well as new ways of thinking about themselves and their social and family roles. Indeed, in contrast to leading American magazines of the 1950s and 1960s, which glorified women's roles as homemakers and mothers, women's magazines in socialist Romania valorized their achievements outside and inside the home, variously representing them as colleagues and agitators, writers and artists, and mothers and wives. These constructions could be descriptive, prescriptive, or a bit of both, reflecting what women encountered in factories and at community meetings, as well as their needs, goals, and aspirations. The following chapters turn to more detailed analyses of state constructions of women in law, policy, and media, considering these representations alongside women's recollections of their lives under socialism.

## Notes

1. See Friedrich Engels, *The Origin of the Family, Private Property and the State* (1884; Honolulu: University Press of the Pacific, 2001).
2. Ibid., and August Bebel, *Women and Socialism* (New York: New York Labor News, 1917).
3. Karen Offen employs the term "relational feminism" to describe feminists that emphasized the differences or complementarity between women and men to argue for women's political equality. See Karen Offen, "Contextualizing the Theory and Practice of Feminism in Nineteenth-Century Europe (1789–1914)," in *Becoming Visible Women in European History*, Third Edition, ed. Renate Bridenthal, Susan Mosher Stuard, and Merry Wiesner Hanks (Boston: Houghton Mifflin Company, 1998), 327.
4. Engels viewed domestic work as a source of oppression and believed it should be placed under state direction in the form of communal kitchens, laundries, and nurseries.
5. Prior to this, Orthodox Church services were conducted in Old Church Slavonic. See Keith Hitchins, *A Nation Affirmed: The Romanian National Movement in Transylvania, 1860–1914* (Bucharest: The Encyclopaedic Publishing House, 1999); and Peter Sugar and Ivo Lerderer, eds., *Nationalism in Eastern Europe* (Seattle: University of Washington Press, 1971).
6. The Ottomans controlled Wallachia and Moldavia from the fifteenth century to the early nineteenth century. In 1829 Moldavia fell under Russian administration.
7. Supporters of the revolution were split on the issue of social reform. While leading liberal revolutionaries tended to support land reform, the boyar class opposed it as it threatened their economic interests. The revolution in Transylvania, by comparison, was both a Romanian national effort and a peasant uprising.
8. As this applied to Romanian males living in towns, it effectively excluded the peasantry. According to the 1864 land reform, peasants received rights over the land they cultivated, but the meager plots they received were insufficient for subsistence and thus actually increased their dependence on the landowners. See William Crowther, *The Political Economy of Romanian Socialism* (New York: Praeger, 1988), 27. However, because prominent notables continued to hold political sway, newly enfranchised groups gained little, if any, political power. Keith Hitchins, *The Romanians, 1774–1886* (Oxford: Clarendon Press, 1996), chap. 6.
9. Ethnic minorities who lived in the Hungarian portion of the empire were ostensibly protected by the Nationalities Law (1868), which mandated use of local languages in schooling, public administration, and cultural affairs; however, as the government did not provide funds for schools, only a minority of Romanians had the means to attend school, one reason why the literacy rate among the ethnic-Romanian population was a mere 14 percent compared with the Hungarian population, which registered a literacy rate of 53 percent. Moreover, educational and professional opportunities were tied to language proficiency in Hungarian or German, which most

Romanians, the vast majority of them peasants, lacked. Keith Hitchins, *Rumania, 1866–1947* (Oxford: Clarendon Press, 1994), 205; and Barbara Jelavich, *History of the Balkans, Vol. 2: Twentieth Century* (Cambridge: Cambridge University Press, 1983), 73–74.

10. See Constantin Iordachi, "The Unyielding Boundaries of Citizenship: The Emancipation of 'Non-Citizens' in Romania, 1866–1918," *European Review of History* 8, no. 2 (2001): 159–63. In 1884 the franchise was extended to all male tax-paying citizens; however, because electoral colleges were weighted in favor of the landed elite, the vast majority of voters remained politically powerless. For instance, by 1911 there were only 1,077,863 male voters in Romania out of a total population of about 6.9 million. See Charles Jelavich and Barbara Jelavich, *The Establishment of the Balkan National States, 1804–1920* (Seattle: University of Washington Press, 1977), 178–79.
11. Jelavich and Jelavich, *The Establishment of the Balkan National States*, 184.
12. As M. Benjamin Thorne documents, the treatment and status of Roma was akin to African Americans in the United States under slavery. As such, they experienced physical and sexual abuse and were bought and sold at auctions. See M. Benjamin Thorne, "The Anxiety of Proximity: The 'Gypsy Question' in Romanian Society, 1934–1944 and Beyond" (PhD diss., Indiana University, 2012). 24. See also Shannon Woodcock, "'The Țigan Is Not a Man': The Țigan Other as Catalyst for Romanian Ethnonational Identity" (PhD diss., University of Sydney, 2005).
13. Iordachi, "The Unyielding Boundaries," 177–78.
14. Ibid., 178. Also, a woman who married a man of another nationality automatically lost her nationality and was forced to assume that of her spouse. See Ștefania Mihăilescu, *Din istoria feminismului românesc: Antologie de texte, 1838–1929* (Iași: Polirom, 2002), 18.
15. See Iordachi, "The Unyielding Boundaries," 178.
16. Moreover, widows in Transylvania received better benefits than women in Romania. See Maria Bucur, "The Economics of Citizenship: Gender Regimes and Property Rights in Romania in the 20th Century," in *Gender and Citizenship in Historical and Transnational Perspective: Agency, Space, Borders*, ed. Anne R. Epstein and Rachel G. Fuchs (Basingstoke: Palgrave Macmillan, 2016), 149.
17. "Statistica profesiunilor din România după recensământul general al populației din 1 ianuarie 1913," Bucharest, 1913, v–vi.
18. This is an important statistical distinction since such labor was often more arduous and demanding than tending to the garden and a few farm animals.
19. "Statistica profesiunilor din România," iv, v.
20. Mihăilescu, *Din istoria feminismului*, 15.
21. Eleonora Strătilescu, "Feminism," *Unirea Femeilor Române*, anul IV, nr. 10, 11, octombrie 1912, 503; 541–42.
22. Mihăilescu, *Din istoria feminismului*, 17.
23. Ibid.
24. Eleonora Strătilescu, "Procesul doamnei Ella Negruzzi la Casație II," *Unirea Femeilor Române*, anul VII, nr. 5 mai 1915.

25. See Maria Bucur, "Ella Negruzzi," in *A Biographical Dictionary of Women's Movements and Feminisms: Central, Eastern, and South Eastern Europe, 19th and 20th Centuries*, ed. Francisca de Haan, Krassimira Daskalova, and Anna Loutfi (Budapest: Central European University Press, 2006), 263–65.
26. Mihăilescu, *Din istoria feminismului*, 17.
27. Heliade Rădulescu, "Curier de Ambe Sexe," 1837, nr. 2, 43–48. Rădulescu stressed that the privileging of boys for schooling had not only social but familial and interpersonal ramifications, creating divisiveness within the family.
28. Bogdan Murgescu, *România și Europa: acumularea decalajelor economice, 1500–2010* (Bucharest: Polirom, 2010), 190–91.
29. See Gail Kligman, *The Wedding of the Dead: Ritual, Poetics, and Popular Culture in Transylvania* (Berkeley: University of California Press, 1988).
30. See Paul Stahl, *Sociétés Traditionnelles Balkaniques Contribution à l'étude des structures sociales* (Paris: EHESS, 1979).
31. Maiorescu presented this idea at the conference "Darwinism and Intellectual Progress" in 1882 at the Athenaeum in Bucharest.
32. Mihăilescu, *Din istoria feminismului*, 23.
33. Ibid., and Maria Bucur, "Between Liberal and Republican Citizenship: Feminism and Nationalism in Romania, 1880–1918," *Aspasia: International Yearbook of Central, Eastern, and Southeastern European Women's and Gender History* 1 (2007): 89–90.
34. Ibid., 90.
35. Mihăilescu, *Din istoria feminismului*, 21.
36. Bucur, "Between Liberal and Republican Citizenship," 90.
37. Sofia Nădejde, "Libertatea femeii în prelegerea d-lui Missir," *Contemporanul* 2, no. 18 (1882/1883): 712–17, in Ștefania Mihăilescu, *Emanciparea femeii române: Antologie de texte, Vol. 1 (1815–1918)* (Bucharest: Editură Ecumenică, 2001), 209.
38. Keith Hitchins, *A Concise History of Romania* (Cambridge: Cambridge University Press, 2014), 116.
39. Mihăilescu, *Din istoria feminismului*, 28.
40. Ibid., 30.
41. "O petiție a Ligii Femeilor Române de la Iași adresata Camerelor pe 21 aprilie 1914," *Viitorul Româncelor*, anul III, nr. 4 (aprilie 1914): 49–50.
42. Maria Bucur notes that this law was modified in September 1916 to allow women to temporarily take responsibility for a husband's property; however, in practice the ruling was full of holes and not properly enforced due to the evacuation of the government to Iași. See Bucur, "Economics of Citizenship," 145–46.
43. Ibid., 145–46.
44. See Maria Bucur, "Between the Mother of the Wounded and the Virgin of Jiu: Romanian Women and the Gender of Heroism during the Great War," *Journal of Women's History* 12, no. 2 (Summer 2000), 36.
45. Notably, the media referred to Teodoroiu as the "Virgin of Jiu" and likened her to Joan of Arc. Ibid., 46–48.
46. In 1914, the population of Romania was 7.7 million, while in 1922 it was 16.5 million, with its ethnic minorities constituting one-quarter of the

population as a result of the acquisition of Transylvania, the Banat, and Bukovina. Romania's minority population in 1920 was as follows: Hungarians (9.3 percent); Jews (5.3 percent); Ukrainians (including those self-identified as Ruthenians, 4.7 percent); and ethnic Germans (including the Saxons and Schwabs, 4.3 percent). See Sabin Manuilă, *Recensămăntul general al populaţiei României din 29 decembrie 1930, vol. II (Neam, limba maternă, religie)* (Bucharest: Institutul Central de Statistică, 1938). In addition, in 1930 the Roma population was officially registered at 1.5 percent of the population, though the actual percentage was higher as it didn't include all nomadic Roma.

47. See Irina Livezeanu, *Cultural Politics in Greater Romania: Regionalism, Nation Building, and Ethnic Struggle, 1918–1930* (Ithaca, NY: Cornell University Press, 1995), 7.
48. With respect to levels of consumption (e.g. caloric intake and meat consumption) Romania ranked among the lowest in Europe, even lower than other East European states with similar social structures. See Murgescu, *România şi Europa*, 218.
49. Ibid., 222.
50. Crowther, *Political Economy of Romanian Socialism*, 30. The reform took a particular toll on Hungarians in Transylvania who constituted the majority of large landowners.
51. Jelavich, *History of the Balkans*, 162.
52. Under the law, 1.3 million families received anywhere from 2.5 to 6 hectares of land depending on the region. However, 83 percent of holdings were 5 hectares or less. Vlad Georgescu, *The Romanians: A History*, ed. Matei Călinescu, trans. Alexandra Bley-Vroman (Columbus: Ohio State Press, 1991), 198–99.
53. Gheorghe Banu, *Mari probleme de medicină socială* (Bucharest, n.p. 1938), 100. This was down from 20.2 in 1901. The number of doctors in Romania in 1938 was 1.1 per 10,000 inhabitants. See also Andrew C. Janos, *East Central Europe in the Modern World: The Politics of the Borderlands from Pre- to Postcommunism* (Stanford, CA: Stanford University Press, 2000), 99.
54. Murgescu, *România şi Europa*, 219.
55. Maria Bucur, *Eugenics and Modernization in Interwar Romania* (Pittsburgh, PA: University of Pittsburgh Press, 2002), 193–94.
56. Primary schools increased from 7,915 before the advent of Greater Romania, to 8,081 in 1918–1919, to 17,385 in 1937–1938. See Livezeanu, *Cultural Politics in Greater Romania*, 36–38.
57. The illiteracy rate in Romania was also higher than other southeastern European states such as Bulgaria and Yugoslavia, which had literacy rates of 31.4 and 45.2 percent respectively in 1938. See Murgescu, *România şi Europa*, 219; and Gheorghe Dobre, *Economia românească în context european* (Bucharest: Editura Fundaţiei Ştiinţifice, 1996), 120, 131, 227.
58. For example, the percentage of girls enrolled in primary school in 1938 was 48 percent, secondary and technical school 41.2 percent and 16.1 percent, respectively, and university 25.9 percent. *Anuarul Statistic al României*, Comisia Naţională pentru Statistică (Bucharest, 1990), 140.
59. Mihăilescu, *Din istoria feminismului*, 36.

60. This was especially the case for women in Transylvania, as the Romanian National Party there, which was widely supported by ethnic Romanian men, supported granting women suffrage already in 1913. Oana Sînziana Păltineanu, "Converging Suffrage Politics: The Romanian Women's Movement in Hungary and Its Allies Before World War I," *Aspasia: International Yearbook of Central, Eastern, and Southeastern European Women's and Gender History* 9 (2015): 44–64.
61. Ştefania Mihăilescu, *Emanciparea femeii române: Studiu şi antologie de texte, Vol. 2 (1815–1918)* (Bucharest: Editură Ecumenică, 2002), 10.
62. Livezeanau, *Cultural Politics in Greater Romania*, 9.
63. Mihăilescu, *Emanciparea femeii române, Vol. 2*, 7; *Enciclopedia României, vol 3* (Bucharest: Imprimeria Naţională, 1939), 60.
64. Calypso Botez, "Drepturile femeii în constituţia viitoare," in *Constituţia din 1923 în dezbaterea contemporanilor*, ed., Aurel Stroe (Bucharest: Humanitas, 1990), 130.
65. Ibid., 128; and Maria Bucur, "Calypso Botez: Gender Difference and the Limits of Pluralism in Interwar Romania" *Jahrbücher für Geschichte und Kultur Südosteuropas* 3 (2001): 70–71.
66. Maria Bucur, "Ella Negruzzi," in *Biographical Dictionary of Women's Movements*, 364.
67. Maria Bucur, "Romania," in *Women, Gender, and Fascism in Europe, 1919–1945*, ed. Kevin Passmore (New Brunswick, NJ: Rutgers University Press, 2003), 65–66.
68. Roxana Cheşchebec, "Alexandrina Cantacuzino," in *Biographical Dictionary of Women's Movements*, 92.
69. For a biography of Ana Pauker, see Robert Levy, *Ana Pauker: The Rise and Fall of a Jewish Communist* (Berkeley: University of California Press, 2001). During the interwar period the acronym for the Communist Party of Romania was PCdR (Partidului Comunist din România). It was abbreviated to PCR after World War II.
70. As quoted in Luciana Jinga, *Gen şi reprezentare în România comunistă, 1944–1989* (Iaşi: Polirom, 2015), 30.
71. Luciana Marioara Jinga, "Femeile în cadrul Partidului Comunist Român, 1944–1989" (PhD diss., Universitatea A.I. Cuza, Iaşi and Université D'Angers, 2011), 17–18.
72. Similarly, Filipovici ended up in the Soviet Union, where she was executed in 1937.
73. Eligibility requirements included being a high school graduate, a war widow, a state functionary, or having been decorated for contributions to the war effort.
74. Botez also helped fund vocational training schools for women. See Maria Bucur, "Calypso Botez," in *Biographical Dictionary of Women's Movements*, 76–77.
75. "Codul de Procedură Penala din 17 martie 1936," art. 484, 89–90, *Monitorul Oficial al României*, nr. 66 din martie 1936.
76. As in other parts of the Western world, women in Romania relied on traditional methods to control their fertility (e.g. *coitus interruptus*; rhythm method).

77. Bucur, *Eugenics and Modernization*, 129, 139.
78. R. J. Crampton, *Eastern Europe in the Twentieth Century* (New York: Routledge, 1997), 112.
79. For an exemplary study of the Iron Guard and the means by which it secured widespread support among ordinary Romanians, see Roland Clark, *Holy Legionary Youth: Fascist Activism in Interwar Romania* (Ithaca, NY: Cornell University Press, 2015).
80. The Communist Party of Romania (PCdR) was legally recognized by King Ferdinand in 1922; however, it was banned in 1924, and about six hundred of its members were arrested. The party remained marginal until it emerged from the underground in 1944. Vladimir Tismăneanu, *Stalinism for All Seasons: A Political History of Romanian Communism* (Berkeley: University of California Press, 2003), 52–56.
81. Radu Ioanid, *The Holocaust in Romania: The Destruction of Jews and Gypsies under the Antonescu Regime* (Chicago: Ivan R. Dee, 2000), 19.
82. Roughly 45,000 to 60,000 Jews in Bukovina and Bessarabia alone perished in August 1941. Although Jews within the regions of Wallachia and Moldavia were spared deportation, they were nonetheless subject to Romanianization, expropriation of wealth and property, and conscription for forced labor. See "Final Report of the International Commission on the Holocaust in Romania, November 11, 2004," retrieved from http://www.ushmm.org/m/pdfs/20080226-romania-commission-iliescu-speech.pdf (accessed 16 April 2017).
83. Ibid.
84. As Holly Case demonstrates, concern over minority violence in both halves of Transylvania prompted intervention by a minorities commission under German and Italian aegis. See Holly Case, *Between States: The Transylvanian Question and the European Idea during World War II* (Stanford, CA: Stanford University Press, 2009), chap. 5.
85. For instance, women were employed in munitions production at the Malaxa factory in Bucharest during World War II. See Adrian Grama, "Laboring Along: Industrial Workers and the Making of Postwar Romania (1944–1958)" (PhD diss., Central European University, 2017), 63.
86. In sum, between 280,000 and 380,000 Jews and approximately 11,000 Roma perished during the Romanian Holocaust. See Michelle Kelso, "Gypsy Deportations from Romania to Transnistria 1942–1944," in *The Gypsies during the Second World War, Vol. II: In the Shadow of the Swastika*, ed. Donald Kenrick (Hatfield: University of Hertfordshire Press, 1999); Vladimir Solonari, *Purifying the Nation: Population Exchange and Ethnic Cleansing in Nazi-Allied Romania* (Baltimore, MD: Woodrow Wilson Center Press/Johns Hopkins University Press, 2010); Thorne, "Anxiety of Proximity"; and "Final Report of the International Commission on the Holocaust in Romania."
87. Maria F., interview with author, Brașov, 20 June 2003.
88. Case, *Between States*, 199–200.
89. Ibid., 200.
90. Tismăneanu, *Stalinism for all Seasons*, 87.

91. For a detailed examination of this unrest, see Grama, "Laboring Along," 42, 76.
92. Petru Groza was head of the Ploughman's Front.
93. Hitchins, *Concise History of Romania*, 220.
94. See Cătalin Augustin Stoica, "Once Upon a Time There Was a Big Party: The Social Bases of the Romanian Communist Party," (Part I) *East European Politics and Societies* 19, no. 4 (2005): 686–716. The PCdR also attracted support among members of the middle class, who were able to hold onto their positions in the bureaucracy after 1945.
95. See Stefano Bottoni, "Reassessing the Communist Takeover in Romania: Violence, Institutional Continuity, and Ethnic Conflict Management," *East European Politics and Societies* 24, no. 1 (2010): 59–89.
96. During her purge in 1952, Ana Pauker would be criticized for allowing many "unhealthy" elements into the party. Levy, *Rise and Fall of a Jewish Communist*, 75.
97. See Stefano Bottoni, *Long Awaited West: Eastern Europe since 1945* (Bloomington, IN: Indiana University Press, 2017), 223.
98. At the same time, Romania was required to accept the losses of Bessarabia and northern Bukovina to the USSR and southern Dobrudja to Bulgaria.
99. In 1965, upon Ceaușescu's assumption of power, the name was changed to Partidul Comunist Român (PCR).
100. Article 16, "Constituţia Republicii Populare Române din 1948," *Monitorul Oficial*, nr. 87, 13 aprilie 1948. This article also prohibited discrimination on the basis of nationality, race, religion, and cultural distinction. In none of the proposed Romanian constitutions prior to the communist takeover (1848, 1866, 1923, 1938) were women granted full political rights.
101. Elena-Simona Gheonea and Valentin Gheonea, "Statutul Femeilor," in *Femeile în România comunistă: Studii de istorie socială*, ed. Cristina Liana Olteanu, Elena-Simona Gheonea, and Valentin Gheonea (Bucharest: Editura Politeia-SNSPA, 2003), 149–50.
102. Moreover, although Article 26 enshrined special protections for women (along with children up to age eighteen), this reinforced women's difference from men, serving as a basis for excluding women from certain jobs, including those most valued by the state.
103. In 1948 the Securitate employed a staff of 4,641; by 1955 this had expanded to nearly 13,000. See Florin Abraham, *Romania Since the Second World War: A Political, Social and Economic History* (London: Bloomsbury Academic, 2017), 65.
104. "Legea nr. 13/1948 pentru modificarea unor dispoziţiuni din Codul Penal şi Codul de procedură penală," *Monitorul Oficial*, 2 februarie, 1948.
105. The Black Sea Canal was a massive project designed to link the Danube River in Romania to the Black Sea. On Stalin's orders, construction on the canal began in 1949 and was performed by forced laborers, many of them political prisoners and peasants who had resisted collectivization. Working and living conditions there were dire, with laborers using shovels and pickaxes to dig up the rocky terrain, and rations so meager that many resorted to eating snakes, mice, and grass for subsistence. Consequently,

an estimated one to two hundred thousand inmates perished there between 1949 and 1953, after which construction stopped. Construction resumed under Ceaușescu in 1973, and the canal was finally completed in 1984.
106. Mircea Stănescu, *The Reeducation Trials in Communist Romania* (Boulder, CO: East European Monographs, 2009).
107. See Smaranda Vultur, *Istorie trăită—Istorie povestită: Deportarea în Bărăgan (1951–1956)* (Timișoara: Editura Amarcord, 1997),
108. Dennis Deletant, *Ceaușescu and the Securitate: Coercion and Dissent in Romania, 1965–1989* (London: Routledge, 1995), 214–216. For a general history of the Orthodox Church in socialist Romania, see Lucian Leustean, *Orthodoxy and the Cold War: Religion and Political Power in Romania, 1947–65* (Basingstoke: Palgrave Macmillan, 2008); and Keith Hitchins, "The Romanian Orthodox Church and the State," in *Religion and Atheism in the USSR and Eastern Europe*, ed. Bohdan R. Bociurkiw, John Strong, and Jean Laux (New York: Macmillan Press, 1975).
109. See Grama, "Laboring Along," especially chap. 3.
110. G. N., interview with author, Brașov, 16 August 2003.
111. Bottoni, *Long Awaited West*, 41.
112. Lynne Attwood, *Creating the New Soviet Woman: Women's Magazines as Engineers of Female Identity, 1922–1953* (Basingstoke: Macmillan, 1999), 13.
113. See Jinga, *Gen și reprezentare*, 261–64.
114. Ibid., 260–61. After the purging of the party, women's representation on the Central Committee dropped from 12.1 percent in 1948 to 4.9 percent in 1955, a figure that did not reach double digits until the late 1970s.
115. The most well-known members were Ana Pauker, who served as secretary of agriculture during the first years of communist rule and was purged, along with other "Muscovites," in the early 1950s, and later Elena Ceaușescu, followed by Lina Ciobanu. For background on early female members of the Central Committee, see Jinga, *Gen și reprezentare*, 262–64.
116. For scholarly exchanges on gender policies in socialist states, see the forums "Is 'Communist Feminism' a *Contradictio in Terminis*?" in *Aspasia: International Yearbook of Central, Eastern, and Southeastern European Women's and Gender History* 1 (2007) 197–246; and "Ten Years After: Communism and Feminism Revisited," *Aspasia* 10 (2016), 102–168.
117. Ștefania Mihăilescu, *Din istoria feminismului românesc: Studiu și antologie de texte, 1929–1948* (Bucharest: România, 2006).
118. For a full discussion of the UFAR's structure and activities, see Jinga, *Gen și reprezentare*, 66–75. For similar efforts in Yugoslavia, see Jelena Batinić, *Women and Yugoslav Partisans: A History of World War II Resistance* (New York: Cambridge University Press, 2015).
119. Mihăilescu, *Din istoria feminismului*, 54.
120. See Maria Raluca Popa, "Raportul Tovarășei Ana Pauker, 11 februarie 1946," *Aspasia: International Yearbook of Central, Eastern, and Southeastern European Women's and Gender History* 8 (2014): 150–61.
121. Gheonea and Gheonea, "Femeile în propaganda regimului comunist," 92–93.
122. Murgescu, *România și Europa*, 386.

123. Alexandra Ghit, "Mobilizing Gender for Socialist Modernity: The Work of One Transylvanian Chapter of the Union of Anti-Fascist Women of Romania and the Union of Democratic Women in Romania, 1945–1953" (MA thesis, Central European University, 2011), 32.
124. Ibid.
125. Ibid., 48; and Gheonea and Gheonea, "Femeile în propaganda regimului comunist," 93. *Drumul Femeii* was published from 1945 to 1947.
126. Ghit, "Mobilizing Gender for Socialist Modernity," 42–43.
127. Theodosia Graur, "Femeia și dreptul de vot," *Drumul Femeii*, December 1945, 13 as quoted in Ghit, "Mobilizing Gender for Socialist Modernity," 45.
128. Virgiliu Țârău, "De la diversitate la integrare: 'Problema femeii și instaurarea comunismului în Europa Centrală și de Est: Cazul României,'" in *Condiția femeii in România în secolul XX: studii de caz*, ed. Ghizela Cosma and Virgiliu Țârău (Cluj-Napoca: Presa Universitară Clujeană, 2002): 135–59. The UFDR was established in January 1948 and was structured hierarchically, with a president, general secretary, and central and provincial administrators who coordinated and supervised local and provincial activities. Pauker served as honorary president while Constanța Craciun served as active president.
129. Party bureaucrats were trained at the A. A. Zhdanov Superior School of Social Sciences (1948–1958) and, thereafter, at the Ștefan Gheorghiu Academy.
130. Jinga, "Femeile în Cadrul Partidului Comunist Român," 42.
131. As in other parts of Europe, the state used both positive and negative incentives to promote fertility. Thus, abortion continued to be criminalized, and heroine mother awards and assistance to families with young children were established.
132. Ghit, "Mobilizing Gender for Socialist Modernity," 68.
133. Ibid., 68.
134. These canning centers excluded alleged kulaks. Ibid., 71, 74. See also *Femeia*, October 1950, 30–31.
135. For a detailed analysis of collectivization, particularly local mobilization efforts and everyday resistance to them, see Gail Kligman and Katherine Verdery, *Peasants under Siege: The Collectivization of Romanian Agriculture, 1949–1962* (Princeton, NJ: Princeton University Press, 2011); and Constantin Iordachi and Dorin Dobrincu, eds., *Transforming Peasants, Property and Power: The Collectivization of Romanian Agriculture* (Budapest: Central European University Press, 2009).
136. Ioana Cîrstocea, "La Construction Politique de L'identité Féminine pendant le Régime Communiste Roumain (1945–1965)," *Romanian Institute for Recent History*, IRIR Work in Progress Series, no. 5 (2002). For activities of the Women's Council in socialist Hungary, see Lynne Haney, *Inventing the Needy: Gender and the Politics of Welfare in Hungary* (Berkeley: University of California Press, 2002); for the GDR, see Donna Harsch, *Revenge of the Domestic: Women, the Family, and Communism in the German Democratic Republic* (Princeton, NJ: Princeton University Press, 2006); and for socialist Poland, see Malgorzata Fidelis, *Women, Communism,*

*and Industrialization in Postwar Poland* (New York: Cambridge University Press, 2010); and Basia Nowak, "Constant Conversations: Agitators in the League of Women in Poland during the Stalinist Period," *Feminist Studies* 31, no. 3 (2005): 488–518.

137. Arhivele Naționale Istorice Centrale (hereafter ANIC), fond CC al PCR, Secția Cancelarie, dosar 48/1957, f. 9. See Jinga's well-detailed study on the CNF and related bodies in *Gen și reprezentare*.
138. Jinga, "Femeile în cadrul partidului comunist Român," 69. *Femeia* was designed for a general female readership, while *Săteanca* (Peasant Woman) was designed for peasant women. *Dolgozó Nö* (Working Woman) was the Hungarian-language version of *Femeia*.
139. See Barbara Wolfe Jancar, *Women under Communism* (Baltimore, MD: Johns Hopkins University Press, 1978); and Maxine Molyneux, "Socialist Societies Old and New: Progress toward Women's Emancipation?" *Feminist Review* 8 (Summer 1981): 1–34.
140. See Raluca Maria Popa's discussion of Stana Buzatu in "Translating Equality between Women and Men across Cold War Divides: Women Activists from Hungary and Romania and the Creation of International Women's Year," in *Gender Politics and Everyday Life in State Socialist Eastern and Central Europe,* ed. Shana Penn and Jill Massino (New York: Palgrave Macmillan, 2009), 59–74.
141. The most extensive research on this topic for Eastern Europe (specifically Bulgaria) has been conducted by Kristen Ghodsee. See, in particular, *The Left Side of History: World War II and the Unfulfilled Promise of Communism in Eastern Europe* (Durham, NC: Duke University Press, 2015); and "Pressuring the Politburo: The Committee of the Bulgarian Women's Movement and State Socialist Feminism," *Slavic Review* 73, no. 3 (Fall 2014): 538–62. See also, Popa, "Translating Equality," 59–74; Barbara Nowak, "Serving Women and the State: The League of Women in Communist Poland" (PhD diss., Ohio State University, 2004); and Wang Zheng, "Creating a Socialist Feminist Cultural Front: Women of China (1949–1966)," *China Quarterly* 204 (December 2010): 827–49.
142. According to Raluca Maria Popa, select members of the CNF's leadership did offer critiques of the proposed decree, however, their perspectives were discounted by PCR leaders. See Raluca Maria Popa, "'We Opposed It': The National Council of Women and the Ban on Abortion in Romania (1966)," *Aspasia: International Yearbook of Central, Eastern, and Southeastern European Women's and Gender History* 9 (2016): 152–160.
143. See Kristen Ghodsee, "State-Socialist Women's Organizations in Cold War Perspective: Revisiting the Work of Maxine Molyneux," *Aspasia* 10 (2016): 114.
144. In contrast to the Polish and East German socialist women's organizations, there is no designated archive for the CNF in Romania; the organization's documents being dispersed through the Central Committee archive and other collections, presenting challenges in researching it. As such, Jinga's institutional history of the CNF stands as an impressive accomplishment. See Jinga, *Gen și reprezentare*.

145. *Femeia* (1948–1989) was the official publication of the CNF and was under the direction of the propaganda section of the Central Committee of the Romanian Communist Party. It should be noted that all my respondents, regardless of ethnicity, were literate in Romanian and thus would have been able to read *Femeia*, although some may have preferred to read *Dolgozó Nö*, or, if they had access to them, Hungarian or German publications from abroad.
146. For a fascinating analysis of state efforts to fashion the new Soviet woman through Bolshevik media and culture see Choi Chatterjee, *Celebrating Women: Gender, Festival Culture, and Bolshevik Ideology, 1910–1939*. (Pittsburgh, PA: University of Pittsburgh Press, 2002), 7.
147. Alexandra Constantinescu, "Recuonştinţa," *Femeia*, November 1959.
148. Maria Tălăngescu, "Mici episode din marea luptă," *Femeia*, August 1959.
149. *Femeia*, March 1952.
150. "Berlin să fie un oraş al pacii," *Femeia*, February 1959, 15.
151. See Mia Groza, "Dimensiuni actuale condiţiei femeii în lume," *Femeia*, February 1970, 7. Vietnam was frequently featured in the magazine, even as early as 1950 during the war against the French.
152. See, for example, *Femeia*, March 1967, 4.
153. Both the men and women I interviewed noted that men occasionally looked at the magazine as it was readily available in people's homes.
154. Elena, interview with author, Bucharest, 2 June 2009.
155. D., interview with author, Braşov, 23 June 2003.
156. Ildiko, interview with author, Braşov, 12 July 2003.

CHAPTER 2

# Children of the Revolution
## Gender and the (Ab)Normality of Growing Up Socialist

Youth was fundamental to both the socialist and nationalist project in Romania.[1] The party-state imbued young people with a great deal of importance since they could be molded, shaped into "new persons" who would subordinate themselves to the collective, contribute to socialist modernization, and promote social justice. Youth also served as a barometer of socialism's success: by showcasing its beneficent treatment of young people, their manifold opportunities and intellectual and physical achievements, the state advertised the system's superiority to the Romanian people and the world. Thus, youth was not simply a stage in the life cycle or a discursive construct, but the human stuff upon which socialism itself would thrive, mature, and ultimately triumph over all other political systems.

Focusing on family relations, schooling, and leisure, this chapter explores state efforts to fashion children and adolescents into socially conscious, loyal, and diligent citizens. As a corollary, it analyzes people's everyday recollections of their childhood experiences, placing them within official representations of youth and state educational and social policies. Youth served as the ideal cohort for challenging traditional beliefs and practices and for reformulating gender roles and relationships. Indeed, in comparison with other social groups, the state targeted young people more or less as a general category. Thus, education, essential for creating a socially conscious, morally upright, and productive citizenry, became compulsory for boys and girls alike. Moreover, as Romania modernized and the labor force diversified, the state increasingly encouraged young people to enter fields such as engineering, geology, and chemistry. Although rooted in economic expediency, such efforts challenged entrenched notions about gender, skill, and competence and instilled girls with the self-confidence to follow new paths of study and careers. Similarly, communist youth organizations, the Pioneers and the Union of Communist Youth, included both girls and boys among their ranks, and socialist experts promoted an egalitarian approach to leisure and sporting activities. At the same time, they cautioned against excessive forms of socializing and "asocialist" behaviors as threats to officially sanctioned values and ethics.

The state's egalitarian approach toward boys and girls, however, often conflicted with parental beliefs and practices. For example, traditional ideas about gender informed childrearing styles, as girls were often discouraged or prohibited from having boyfriends—or even socializing with boys. Moreover, parents might direct girls toward occupations or professions they considered more "appropriate" for their gender, advocating medicine and teaching over construction and engineering. Yet, while the state expanded girls' educational opportunities and promoted gender equality by targeting youth as a general category, not all young people received equal treatment. Since young people were both objects and agents of transformation, all aspects of their lives, from family to school to leisure, were to align with socialist principles. Accordingly, despite state glorification of youth and the family, during the first two decades of communist rule, children from families with "unhealthy social origins" (*origini sociale nesănătoase*) were often disfavored within the educational system for fear they would "contaminate" their classmates. Designed to inculcate Romania's version of socialism and create a new socialist person, education was thus also used as an instrument of marginalization, to punish families with "antisocialist" (e.g. bourgeois; reactionary) elements. As such, young people could be at once a source of hope and anxiety.

In addition to educational marginalization, some young people experienced economic marginalization and other difficulties in instances where a family member—especially a parent—was punished by the state. Yet, among my respondents such children were in the minority, and many recalled their childhoods fondly as parents made great efforts to shield them from difficulties and ensure their upbringing was more or less normal. Indeed, because a disproportionate number of males were imprisoned, respondents emphasized the crucial role of mothers, grandmothers, and aunts in sustaining the family and imbuing them with pride in their heritage.

Although most of my respondents recalled their younger years with fondness, emphasizing that they lived normal lives, as they entered adolescence they became increasingly cognizant of the shortcomings of socialist policy and the gulf between propaganda and everyday life. In particular, those who experienced the early or final decade of socialist rule as teens highlighted the uncertainty, fear, and poverty of the late 1940s and 1950s, and the shortages, bleakness, and sense of hopelessness of the 1980s. By comparison, those who entered adolescence in the 1960s and 1970s, during the period of liberalization, had fonder and less-critical memories of this period. That said, even during more repressive periods young people found sources of enjoyment and, according to their recollections, lived "normally," be it socializing with friends, hiking in the mountains, dancing at discos, or watching smuggled videos. However, while adolescents certainly had fun, they also needed to exercise caution, especially in public spaces. Thus, by the time children entered their teens, they developed a more nuanced understanding of how individuals operated and engaged with one another in public and private spaces, a "socialist life-skill" that would aid them as they entered adulthood. At the same time, for those who aspired to a better life, learning how to manage a repressive and morally (as well as economically) bankrupt system had its limits. With the horizon becoming increasingly dim as the 1980s wore on, in the end, young people chose not simply to manage the system, but to challenge it, and were among the principal participants of the revolution in 1989.

## All in the Family

Just as socialism proposed to fashion a new person, it proposed to fashion a new family. The more radical Bolshevik thinkers of the early 1920s, most notably Aleksandra Kollontai, regarded the traditional family as an impediment to women's full liberation and believed it would wither away once women achieved economic autonomy and childcare and domestic labor became fully socialized.[2] Lenin, by contrast, conceptualized the family in more conventional terms (i.e. as the bedrock of society), a view that was similarly adopted by the communist leadership in Romania.[3] During the early period of communist consolidation and repression, however, the family was also an object of concern and even distrust for its embrace of traditional, mystical, bourgeois, and reactionary beliefs. Consequently, families with "unhealthy social origins" and those considered threats to the establishment of the dictatorship of the proletariat (e.g. alleged or real fascists and fascist sympathizers) experienced fracturing rather than cohesion. As men and, to a much lesser extent, women were sent to labor camps and prisons, their children experienced poverty, social marginalization, and persecution.[4] Given that the majority of those imprisoned were men, many children were raised, in the words of Ruxandra, "in a world of women."[5] The reality on the ground, then, contrasted sharply with the family ideal glorified in socialist media.

Luana (b. 1945), who was raised solely by her mother, remembered the early postwar years as a time of penury since her father spent extended periods in hospital after sustaining a nervous breakdown. According to Luana, his breakdown occurred after he lost his job due to his intelligentsia status and alleged support of Romania's fascist Iron Guard during the 1930s and 1940s—a charge she claimed was wholly fabricated. As she recalled:

> For a time we lived very austerely because my mother was employed later [in life]; she came from a family of wealthy people, and when she married my father she didn't have to work. After all this [happened], she was forced to work, but she had no skills, and had only finished high school, hadn't learned a profession ... and, when my father was ill, she had to work and her earnings were very modest. We experienced a very difficult period, and only with the help of relatives were we able to make it through.[6]

As a result of her father's illness, Luana's family had no breadwinner and thus found itself in desperate circumstances, relying on relatives for support—part of the reason it was not until late in her childhood that Luana discovered "the wonders of chocolate." In addition to financial difficulties, Luana worried about her prospects for high school admittance since during that period "unhealthy social origin" typically filtered down to the next of kin, as the party believed that children would corrupt workers' and farmers' children. Fortunately, she was not only accepted into a good high school, but her experience there proved transformative, as her history teacher inspired her to become a historian.

Similarly, Tudora (b. 1941) experienced the extended absence of her father, a philosopher, who was imprisoned on "political grounds." Jailed at Aiud Prison in 1948 for having "studied in the West," he was later sent to the Black Sea Canal for forced labor. Owing to his conviction, Tudora, at the mere age of twelve, was interrogated by the Securitate. After this frightening experience, Tudora's mother instilled in her a sense of hope and dignity, ultimately helping her overcome her distress and take pride in her father. She remarked, "My mother was extraordinary ... my mother raised us to be proud of the fact that our father was in jail, because the greatest intellectuals of the country were there. She said, 'You need to be proud of the fact that your father was imprisoned.'"[7] By reconfiguring communist repression as ennobling, parents such as Tudora's taught children how to cope with personal loss and how to live in dignity, despite the inhumanity of the regime.

Tudora's mother was not alone in supporting the family without the financial or emotional resources of a spouse. Smaranda's mother similarly served as sole breadwinner and caregiver because her father's tenure as a forced laborer at the Black Sea Canal in the early 1950s blackened his work file, barring him from gainful employment upon his release. In spite of these injustices, Smaranda recalled her mother as an "exceptional woman … a source of support for her children" who "didn't get angry" and was "an optimist and a humanist."[8] Educated in mathematics and astronomy at the Sorbonne—a reflection of her family's elite status before the communist takeover—Smaranda's mother lost her teaching job upon her husband's arrest due to "guilt by association." However, she ultimately managed to secure work at a technical school and, thereafter, an all-girls school. Despite the family's hardships, according to Smaranda, her mother always tried to forgive people for the choices they made—even if they did not deserve it—since she believed that the system had forced them to act in certain ways. Her mother's efforts to maintain her faith in humanity in the face of repression underscores the essential role of parents, particularly women, in teaching their children to live ethically and cope with adversity.

During the early period of socialist rule, then, state policies often undermined family cohesion. As such, women and extended family played a crucial role in sustaining their children both financially and emotionally. Moreover, they encouraged children to retain faith in their countrymen and -women—and, in some cases, to even take pride in their imprisoned fathers. At the same time, given the stigma surrounding their fathers' status, children had to take great care to whom they spoke as this might influence how they were treated by teachers and classmates as well as relationships with neighbors and friends.[9] Such children learned early on to lead "double lives," compartmentalizing their lives into private (or family) exchanges and public ones—a practice that became commonplace over the course of socialist rule, albeit difficult for younger children to sustain. Thus, children were implored to conceal the fact that parents or relatives had been imprisoned. They were also expected to conceal the fact that family members read banned books or listened to Radio Free Europe broadcasts. As Luana recalled,

> My mother always warned me not to draw attention to myself, especially when I was younger, not to talk about what was discussed at home because there was always this danger that someone would knock at your door and arrest your parents. And I know, I lived with this fear.[10]

Family cohesion was also undermined by lack of sufficient housing and childcare, especially in newly established industrial towns. While these towns might be within daily commuting distance from the family home, in some cases they were hundreds of kilometers away. Moreover, as the factories themselves were recently constructed, adequate lodging was generally lacking or rudimentary, with shared-living style dormitories and barracks. Since these situations were not conducive to raising families, male workers and, to a lesser extent, female workers commuted to the new factory towns, leaving their children in the care of relatives, typically grandparents.[11]

Such was the case of D. and her sister C., born in 1954 and 1957 respectively. Like other families of "unhealthy social origin" (in this case belonging to the interwar elite), some of D. and C.'s relatives faced repression during the first decade of Gheorghe Gheorghiu-Dej's rule. Consequently, their parents were at the mercy of the state for securing work. Thus, when their father, a doctor, was posted to Hunedoara (an industrial town in Western Romania), he had no choice but to accept the position. However, because the couple was not assigned housing, they were forced to live in his office with the examination table doubling as a bed. Raising children under such conditions was unthinkable; therefore, rather than live with their parents, D. and C. spent their early years in Târnăveni (over 150 kilometers away) with Carla, the Austrian governess who had raised their mother and uncle. Schooled at a Catholic convent, Carla, according to D., "was like an Austrian grandmother: stern, yet loving." In addition to German, she taught the girls to be conscientious and respectful. Although the children were in good care, these extended separations were difficult for all involved, as D. and C.'s parents could only visit for a few days each month. State privileging of industry over housing and other basic necessities thus severely limited individuals' choices, in some cases forcing parents to live apart from their children. This undermined the socialist promise of improved quality of life and flew in the face of media exhortations about the primacy of the family and parents' essential role in childrearing. Such separations certainly marked children emotionally, particularly young children, though in ways that are unfortunately inaccessible to scholars. Nonetheless, these stories demonstrate the importance of considering the more subtle ways that socialist transformation affected family relationships and children's development.

After much difficulty, D. and C.'s father finally secured a position in Brașov, as well as a small apartment with one bedroom in which the entire family slept. Although cramped, D. recalled their new living situation with great fondness since it meant the family could be together again. Indeed, despite the challenges her family faced during her childhood, D. referred to it as the best period of her life:

> Although those were extremely difficult years [late 1950s to early 1960s] ... we didn't sense it. I was sheltered from worry. I knew in a way that something bad had happened to our family and that things were not normal ... [but] they never talked about the difficulties they experienced, we didn't talk much at home because such were the times. They didn't want to involve us in those problems. Not even our grandfather, who suffered very much during the communist period—he was imprisoned at Gherla. Not even our mother, who was his daughter, nor his wife, they didn't tell us at all about that period, probably because they didn't want to make us sad.[12]

D. and C.'s parents' efforts to shield them from repression can be read as both survival and protective strategies. Although people of different backgrounds and affiliations were imprisoned during this period, as previously noted, associations with such individuals could carry a stigma, as well as result in poorer treatment by teachers and others. Thus, D. and C.'s parents hoped to shield them from scorn, social marginalization, and potential exclusion from school and other opportunities. Moreover, they hoped to spare them emotionally from the injustices that had befallen their family and ensure they retained some sense of innocence, wonder, and faith in humanity. Other respondents whose family members had been imprisoned during the early communist period similarly stressed that the issue was not a topic of conversation in their family—at least not until they entered adolescence.

While a number of my respondents experienced downward mobility in the 1950s and early 1960s due to their family's "unhealthy social origins," even those not tainted with such labels struggled materially. For instance, Axinia, born in a village in Moldavia in 1953, recalled that her parents were so poorly paid on the CAP (*Cooperativele Agricole Producție*; collective farm) that the family could only eat meat once a week.[13] Although Axinia's childhood was characterized by "deprivation" and she had "neither sweets nor toys," she retained fond memories of the dolls her mother fashioned out of corn silk. Axinia's memories thus shed light on the material impact of collectivization, which for her was, at least in part, tempered by the simplicity and beauty of her pastoral surroundings.[14]

In light of the material deprivations they had experienced during the interwar, war, and immediate postwar periods, parents often made great sacrifices to ensure their children's lives were better than theirs had been. As Doina, born in 1957 and raised in rural Moldavia, emphasized, "My parents were great. They provided us with many opportunities. They offered us trips through the country. They told us about how hard their lives had been and they wanted to give us a better life."[15] In comparison with children born in the 1940s and early 1950s, "making life better" would have been easier for Doina's parents since much of her childhood coincided with the period of liberalization in the 1960s, during which wages and access to consumer goods and services increased. Moreover, opportunities for leisure expanded and were more accessible to ordinary Romanians. Meanwhile, the fear, repression, and uncertainty that had characterized the late 1940s and 1950s had subsided considerably.

While parents sought to make a better life for their children, they still expected them—in particular girls—to help with household chores. Although a historical practice, especially in rural areas where chores extended to agricultural work, children's help with chores (e.g. shopping, making meals, looking after younger siblings) was often essential for the proper functioning of the household, especially in urban areas where, by the 1960s, both parents were typically employed outside the home. Traditionally, domestic responsibilities, including ironing, cooking, washing, and looking after younger siblings, fall on girls in Romania. Although a few respondents claimed that they were solely or primarily responsible for chores, while their brothers attended school, others stressed that both boys and girls helped around the house. As Iuliana, born in 1950, recalled about her family:

> My mother worked third shift and it was very difficult for us. We [my brother and I] had to help her because to come home from third shift and begin with chores is very difficult. The routine was that you came home from school, you lit the fire, you washed the floors, you did this and that; we did all this because mom was tired and that was that.[16]

As a single parent, Iuliana's mother relied on her children's help, which, when they reached adolescence, also required working outside the home to supplement the family income.

Similarly, Maria (b. 1955) recalled that she and her brothers regularly helped around the house and, when they reached adolescence, were responsible for washing dishes and laundering their own clothing.[17] Meanwhile, Eva, who grew up in the 1970s, was assigned chores as early as first grade; indeed, she actually needed to stand on a chair to reach the sink. At the same time, she was also expected to receive high marks in school. She noted, "It would have been shameful to go home and tell my dad that I only got a four or a five. It was like this: I came home, I read the list of chores and did them quickly, after that I finished my homework and then I ran out to get sugar or oil or whatever else [was needed]."[18] Reflecting on her childhood, Eva was not resentful of her multiple responsibilities. On the contrary, she felt that it helped her later in life since housework is now "easy." Meanwhile, in D.'s family, housework was equally distributed with each family member assuming particular chores:

> It was a very good system, even my father was very hardworking and conscientious ... and from a young age I learned that each person in the family had their own job. After my father died, when I was nine and my sister was eleven, it was much more difficult, but this system that I learned when I was young, it was very good.[19]

D.'s father's contribution to the household, while perhaps exceptional, provided a progressive model to her, challenging gender stereotypes regarding the domestic division of labor. To encourage similar behaviors, the communist youth magazine, *Cutezătorii* (The Daring), along with *Femeia*, featured pictures of boys and girls helping around the house and grocery shopping.[20] The aim here was to allay any guilt mothers may have felt about soliciting help from their children with housework. Some parents, however, felt their children should devote themselves only to schoolwork. For instance, Valeria R. claimed that her chores were minimal, consisting only of picking up a few things at the market now and again and taking out the garbage. Moreover, because Valeria "didn't like the feminine stuff, cooking, making pastries," she assisted her father around the house, including "fixing a socket or changing a wire."[21] These early forays into household maintenance ultimately influenced her career path, as Valeria earned her degree in mechanical engineering.

Another reason children helped with chores, including making their own meals, was related to urban migration and the concomitant loss of extended family networks. As people left their rural environs, they also left their parents—and only source of family assistance—behind. Due to workplace demands, including working overtime and attending party meetings, parents might not return from work until late in the evening. Thus, children often took care of themselves, becoming latchkey kids (*copii cu cheia la gât*), an increasingly common phenomenon in the Eastern Bloc in the 1960s and 1970s as more women worked outside the home. Romanian latchkey kids returned to an empty home and were often expected to warm supper, tidy up, and complete their homework, an experience that my respondents, particularly those who grew up in the 1970s and 1980s, recalled as common and ordinary.

While the emergence of latchkey kids was an outgrowth of socialist modernization, which required women's full-time employment, social scientists and other "experts" expressed concern about how youth spent their free time. In particular, they worried that children who were left to their own devices might fall into the wrong crowd and begin smoking, drinking, and engaging in unsocialist behavior (e.g. delinquency, hooliganism).[22] In surveying a number of Bucharest neighborhoods in the late 1960s, sociologist Mihai Stoian found children of all ages playing and wandering about with other youth late into the evening without any adult supervision. Although Stoian noted that the young people he encountered were "not delinquents" and that some of them were "kind and respectful," in addition to being bright and well-read, he nonetheless emphasized that "the degree of independence parents grant their children is inappropriate for their age."[23] Lamenting that nobody is at home to greet children upon their arrival from school and concerned about youth lingering on the streets late into the night, Stoian stressed the need for parental supervision—or, more precisely, maternal supervision, especially in families with one child.[24] As a solution, he suggests that mothers rearrange their work schedules to ensure they are home when their children return from school. Tellingly, Stoian neglects to include fathers in his assessment, thereby presenting caregiving as a woman's responsibility. Despite women's mass influx into the labor force, including into male-dominated areas, traditional assumptions about parenting thus endured well into the 1960s.

This book was not unique for the period—or to Romania. Indeed, the 1960s and 1970s witnessed the publication of a host of works by socialist experts on parenting, childhood, and adolescence, some of which drew upon—and reflected—research by Western social scientists about the baby boomer generation then coming of age. While these experts expressed concern about the impact of socialist modernization on young people's development, at the same time, they took issue with traditional approaches to parenting. Recommending authoritative over authoritarian parenting, they emphasized the importance of open communication and affection in creating a healthy parent-child relationship. To that end, experts urged parents not to spank their children and to maintain realistic expectations of their academic achievements (i.e. to not expect a "robot-like child" who always gets perfect marks). Instead of intellectual development alone, parents were advised to focus on their child's emotional and social development as well. To cultivate closer relations, experts suggested that parents engage with their children on a daily basis, including playing with them, supervising their homework, and regularly eating meals and taking walks with them, practices, which, according to a survey featured in another book, were infrequent given the demands of parents' work schedules.[25]

State promotion of engaged parenting was designed to eradicate authoritarian parenting styles, as well as parental neglect, and to foster trusting relationships that would forestall rebellious or delinquent behavior among young people. Such advice coincided with the period of liberalization ushered in by Ceaușescu, which had provided fertile—or at least relatively tolerant—ground for the expression of alternative forms of dress, culture, and socialization among youth, manifestations that the regime viewed as unsocialist. Consequently, by the late 1960s and early 1970s, experts, along with the socialist leadership, expressed increasing concern with what they referred to as asocial activities (e.g. behaviors unbefitting a maturing socialist society) and with the impact of Western and other foreign influences on young people.[26]

## Schooling the Masses

For the party-state, public education was a vehicle for social engineering, key to fashioning *omul nou*, a conscientious and loyal citizen committed to social transformation and uncorrupted by antisocialist elements. It was also essential for creating a diverse and productive workforce—what Ceaușescu would refer to as a "multilaterally developed society." Moreover, it was essential for inculcating the population with socialist values and, as such, an antidote to religious and traditional or bourgeois forms of instruction that students had received during the interwar period. Yet, while parents may have taken issue with Marxist-influenced curricula and the compulsory homage to Stalin, Ceaușescu, and other socialist leaders, many appreciated the opportunities for upward mobility that education provided. This was especially true for families of rural origin and modest means, whose children would not have enjoyed similar opportunities during the interwar period. As historian Diana Georgescu asserts, "If the socialist state sought to instrumentalize education to create a well-trained labor force and a politically loyal citizenry, while parents (and teachers) envisioned it as a vehicle for social advance and a cultured life, they nevertheless shared the ideal of industrious youth who embraced study with passion and dedication."[27] Thus, schooling was one area where the state and parents found common cause, though for different ideological reasons.

Beginning in 1948, all Romanian citizens regardless of sex, nationality, race, and confession were legally entitled to an equal education from preschool through the postsecondary level.[28] Given the low literacy rate at the time of the communist takeover, the transformative potential of education was nothing short of revolutionary, especially for girls.[29] However, "legal education" only applied to schools under state control, as confessional and private schools and universities were disbanded. Attacks on the interwar educational system followed, with propagandists indicting it for "the illiteracy of millions" and the perpetuation of "abstract and metaphysical styles of teaching" divorced from the needs of the people, inaccessible to most young children, and detrimental to scholarly and scientific growth.[30]

Although presented as fundamental to creating an educated, highly skilled, and socially conscious citizenry, schooling in fact became a vehicle for social exclusion during the first two decades of socialist rule. Given the importance that the party attributed to social origin, the educational system was subject to cleansing, particularly the removal of "contaminating elements" (e.g. religious, bourgeois, and reactionary elements). In this repressive climate, not even children were free of contamination. Indeed, rather than blank slates upon which socially conscious, diligent, and loyal persons could be fashioned, the state viewed some children with suspicion, fearing they might infect "pure" proletarian and peasant children with reactionary beliefs. Thus, educational policies were characterized by both affirmative action and discriminatory measures, decisively affecting the educational trajectories of young people, especially during the early years of socialist rule.

Ideology, rather than merit, was a guiding principle in the selection criteria of students in the 1940s and 1950s, with restrictions beginning at the onset of communist rule and more or less remaining in force until the early 1960s. Initially, restrictions applied to higher learning: beginning in 1948, young people of "bourgeois social origin" and "capitalist exploiting elements," as well as those whose families embraced "reactionary views," were expelled or barred from attending university.[31] Additionally, starting in 1949, students whose fathers had been arrested or were identified as *chiaburi* (kulaks: "well-off" or landowning peasants) were removed from school.[32] In that same year, student hierarchies based on "social origin" and other categories were established with children of laborers, collective famers, agricultural workers, antifascist fighters and state functionaries being most favored for admission, followed by children of craftsmen, and, in the lowest category, children of industrialists, bankers, war criminals, purged individuals, and kulaks.[33]

Alongside these official hierarchies, the system was marred by corruption and favoritism, including falsifying exam results (to the benefit of the favored groups and detriment of disfavored groups), which decisively affected people's educational and, in some cases, professional futures.[34] Given that social discrimination was codified in law, teachers might privilege (or be required to privilege) workers' and peasants' children over those from the "exploiting class" or "reactionary class," regardless of academic achievement, even marginalizing or excluding the latter in the service of larger state goals. As one man recalled,

> I was a child in the fourth grade when collectivization began. For those whose parents joined the CAP, they [the teachers] displayed little flags on the children's desks as if they were heroes. They brought them sweets. For those whose parents didn't join, there were no sweets, nor little flags, nor any type of favors; instead they were terrorized so that they would go home and cry and beg their parents to join the CAP.[35]

This recollection illustrates the insidious way the regime used children as tools for socialist modernization. By playing on children's desire for candy—and attention—the regime indirectly put pressure on their parents to conform to socialist dictates, in this case joining the CAP. This subtle form of coercion was not only humiliating but also went against socialist values of kindness, equality, and community. More generally, unwillingness to acquiesce to state policies (e.g. collectivization) could be a basis for excluding children from school. Indeed, even children of impoverished peasants were not spared as officials threatened expulsion of children whose parents had refused to surrender their plots of land to the state.[36] By contrast, children of obedient peasants and workers typically benefited from affirmative action policies. Under such circumstances, parents were often forced to compromise their political convictions and economic security for their children's future.

Such treatment was not limited to resistant peasants and children with "unhealthy social origins," but also included children from minority groups. As Ruxandra, who attended primary school in the late 1950s and early 1960s, recalled:

> They seated us so that we were segregated. The good with the good, and the bad with the bad. We were the bad. And I remember that there was a Roma girl in the class. She was the daughter of a laundress. And the teacher was very nice to the daughters of the Securitate, but to the other one, she terrorized her. She brought her to the front of the class to show us how dirty she was. And one winter day she even put her head under

the faucet. There was only cold water. And my mother, I don't know why she came to school that day, but she saw it happen and took her out of there ... and she made a big deal about it because it was clearly an act of violence. And then she took her over to the brick oven [to warm her up and dry her off] but, again, it was something that I cannot forget—how differently the daughters of the Securitate were treated from her.[37]

While the teacher's privileging of Securitate children signified subservience to the political elite and was, most likely, considered a means for career advancement or receiving certain favors, the teacher's cruel treatment of the Roma girl, since it had no clear policy goal, reflected a larger intolerance toward the Roma community. It also illustrated teachers' power over students, which often went unchecked or was of minimal concern to higher-level functionaries since disciplinary measures, including mild forms of corporal punishment and shaming, far from being egregious, were simply considered a normal means for punishing students and restoring order. More generally, as historian Doru Radosav notes, such practices "created an 'us' vs. 'them' mentality," inimical to communist values of community and equality. It also contributed to vastly different lived experiences for children.[38]

Alongside marginalizing or removing potentially "contaminating" students, the state purged alleged reactionary or "unhealthy" teachers from the educational system. Consequently, during the first decade of socialist rule many university professors and secondary school teachers were fired from their jobs, often on trumped-up or flimsy evidence (e.g. alleged dishonesty, incompetence, support for the Iron Guard), and were replaced with less competent instructors of "healthy social origin," acting as tools of the regime.[39] While many teachers who had taught or been trained during the interwar period remained in the system, with the advent of the Literacy Campaign in 1948, many were assigned to schools in the countryside, usually in towns or villages with high illiteracy and poverty rates. Teachers who worked in these areas received lower salaries than their urban counterparts and typically lived in inhospitable conditions.[40] The impetus behind such efforts was both practical and ideological. On the one hand, rural areas were in desperate need of good teachers, on the other, such humbling experiences could facilitate teachers' social consciousness and neutralize or compensate for their supposed "unhealthy social origin." However, some instructors refused to relocate to the countryside and were dismissed from their jobs and dubbed "saboteurs."[41] Some of these teachers were replaced by former university professors who had been demoted to the high school level because of their social origin or political orientation—demotions that a number of my respondents praised since they recalled having "extraordinary teachers."

Primary schooling was available throughout Romania by the late 1940s, though in the countryside and in smaller towns it was often of a rudimentary nature. Those who wanted to continue their studies were thus often required to venture to the nearest town, where they stayed in dorms. For example, after attending her village school in Rădulești in Hunedoara County, Domnica commuted to a high school in a neighboring town. As the fee for room and board was considerable for parents of modest means such as her own, Domnica worked at the nearby farm during her breaks to help defray costs. Ultimately, these sacrifices paid off, as Domnica emphasized: "At that time [in the mid-1950s] a high school education was something. If you had a high school degree it was a big deal. There were very few educated children and people."[42] According to Domnica, the fact that a girl from a small village could attend high school, let alone university, and become a dentist was quite an achievement. However, of note is that Domnica, as the daughter of peasants, received preferential treatment for university admission as well as a scholarship. Indeed, the offspring of workers and peasants (excluding kulaks) were generally privileged for admission and scholarships; meanwhile, young people from other social groups were forced to compete for the few, remaining spots. Consequently, thousands of well-prepared graduates failed to make it to university.[43]

Domnica's story illustrates that already during the first decade of communist rule, female youth were enjoying the fruits of socialist modernization—in this case universal and subsidized education. This would have been much more difficult—and thus less likely—for a girl of rural origin during the interwar years, when she would have received a few years of primary schooling and then been expected to assist with the larger homestead (e.g. farming, canning, and other household chores) until she married. The expansion of girls' education under socialism, especially at secondary and university levels, was indeed impressive. For example, while in 1938 girls represented 41.2 percent of all secondary school students, by 1960 that figure was 44.6 percent, and by 1970 it had reached 51.5 percent.[44] Meanwhile, in 1938, women constituted 25.9 percent of all university students, in 1960, 33.4 percent, in 1970, 43 percent, and in 1989, 48.1 percent.[45]

During the early years of socialist rule, school curricula were purged of religious, "reactionary," and "chauvinistic" content and rewritten to reflect fidelity to Marxist-Leninist principles, the USSR, and proletarian internationalism. As a means of paying homage to Soviet achievements, classrooms included "red corners" featuring images of Soviet factories and lush, collectively labored fields, and the curriculum included readings by Lenin and his wife, Nadezhda Krupskya, as well as stories about childhood martyrs such as Pavlik Morozov.[46] Additionally, beginning with fourth grade, Russian language study was compulsory and students commonly read Soviet and Russian literature. Valeria P. (b. 1937), who attended Liceul Central in Bucharest in the early 1950s—a school that also served ambassadors' children and those of leading functionaries—thus studied Russian language, along with Russian geography, history, and literature, including classic authors such as Alexander Pushkin, Nikolai Gogol, and Ivan Turgenev.[47] However, even within this seemingly restrictive framework teachers, as well as parents, attempted to provide alternate understandings of past and present by recommending forbidden readings, especially those from the interwar period. Thus, while acknowledging that her studies of Russian were useful when she finally visited the USSR in the 1970s, Valeria also emphasized that she was fed a healthy diet of Romanian literature during her youth:

> It was a strange experience—you are born in one place, and then another country occupies you and remakes you according to its own image. But, my father, my father knew to leave the imprint of Romania on my soul, and never did my soul reorient toward the East. There was always room in my soul and my mind for Romanian education and tradition.[48]

With the shift away from the USSR in the late 1950s, school curricula assumed a more nationalist bent. Images of Stalin and references to Soviet-Romanian friendship were eclipsed by Dej and a focus on Romanian heroes of the class struggle. Moreover, after Dej's "April Declaration" in 1964, school manuals and lessons emphasized national sovereignty and Romanian roads to socialism.[49] This was accompanied by increased openness toward the West, reflected in the replacement of Russian with French, English, and German language instruction and the popularity of universal classics such as Alexander Dumas, Victor Hugo, Honoré de Balzac, Mark Twain, Rudyard Kipling, Lewis Carroll, and Jules Verne. Indeed, in recalling the books they read in the 1960s and thereafter, my respondents typically made reference to the aforementioned authors, and other classic Western texts, alongside interwar Romanian authors who had been rehabilitated in the early 1960s. For many, these books served not only as forms of entertainment but also an escape from the overly ideologized public sphere—a break from formulaic propaganda and socialist ritual. Thus, world literature provided an opportunity to experience the world outside of the homogenized new person constructed by the state. As such, it was recommended reading by parents, especially intellectuals and cultural figures.

After his assumption of power in 1965, Ceaușescu implemented a new education law with substantive reforms, including the extension of schooling to tenth grade with the option of completing an additional two years of high school (for those hoping to attend university) or enrolling in a professional or technical school.[50] Additionally, curricula followed an innovative, European-inspired pedagogical model, which involved shifting away from rote learning to more interactive class sessions that centered on problem solving and experiential learning.[51] At the same time, this modern pedagogical approach coexisted curiously with increasingly ideological, nationalistic, and isolationist content.[52]

Many of my respondents, particularly those who attended school in the early 1960s through the 1970s, boasted about their educational experience and their teachers' expertise and giftedness. They attributed this to the fact that their teachers had been trained (or educated) during the interwar period and were thus able to offer alternative interpretations of the subject matter—at times even recommending blacklisted Romanian authors.[53] Luana, who attended high school in the early 1960s when the pro-Soviet history of Mihail Roller was still required reading, recalled that her teachers "were able to go beyond the barriers in school books and teach history that was as close to the truth as possible."[54] Given the subjectivity involved in historical interpretation, the existence of censorship in Romania, and the fact that teachers were expected to toe the party line and teach history through a Marxist-Leninist frame, what Luana meant by "truth" is open to question. Nonetheless, her interpretation is important in drawing a distinction between Soviet-oriented and nationalist-oriented approaches to history, the latter of which was, for her, more authentic, though not necessarily more accurate.

Others who attended high school in urban areas during the 1960s and 1970s similarly claimed they received a high-quality education, referring to teachers as "extraordinary" and "cultured" and remarking on their dedication and exceptional pedagogical abilities. Not all instruction deviated from the official script, however. For example, C., who attended an urban middle school in the early 1970s, recalled that her *diriginte* (form teacher or headmaster) used the class period as a forum for socialist indoctrination. Yet, she also added that many children, especially those whose families had suffered repression, were adept at deciphering fact from fiction: "I think in all classes and in all schools in larger cities there was this nucleus of children that was aware of the horrible manipulation and duplicity that existed."[55] C.'s form lesson, or what she referred to as the "indoctrination hour," was common to all children who attended school during the socialist period. During such sessions, teachers typically organized debates around political, ideological, and moral issues, although some also used the period for discussing other, less-ideologically freighted issues or for focusing on academic topics, completing assignments, and organizing school-related events. More generally, C's attendance at school coincided with a political and cultural shift that began in the early 1970s, after Ceaușescu's visit to North Korea and China and the subsequent proclamation of his July Theses of 1971 (also known as the mini-cultural revolution). This period was characterized by increased embrace of nationalism and a distancing from culture deemed "cosmopolitan" or too "Western."[56] Accordingly, peace, patriotism, and struggles against capitalist-imperialism were hailed as prominent values with which students were to identify, and school manuals highlighted "decisive" events in Romania's struggle against foreign domination, from medieval battles against the Ottomans to more recent ones against the fascists during World War II. Moreover, Ceaușescu eclipsed all other socialist revolutionaries, depicted as the initiator of revolts, strikes, and other foundational events in the history of the PCR, despite his young age at the time.[57] Indeed, in the pantheon of national heroes, a direct line could be drawn between Prince Mihai Viteazul (Michael the Brave), who had united the three Romanian principalities for a few months in 1600, Prince Alexandru Cuza, who had united Wallachia and Moldavia in 1859, and Ceaușescu. Thus, Romania under Ceaușescu signified the culmination of centuries of struggle and he became the ubiquitous father figure, his image prominently featured at the front of every classroom, as well as most public places. The use of nationalism in the service of socialism, though taken to epic heights, was by no means unique to Romania as the East German and Bulgarian regimes employed a similar tack.

Upon completing tenth grade, two major tracks were open to students who wanted to continue their schooling: *real* (science/technical) or *uman* (humanities). After being "terrorized by mathematics" in the ninth grade, Florina, who attended high school in the early 1970s, opted for humanities, in which she excelled, receiving outstanding marks in literature. Although Romanian, Latin, English, and history were among Florina's favorite subjects, she especially enjoyed French because of the enthusiasm her teacher brought to the subject, which included organizing a reading circle on classic French literature. By twelfth grade, however, most of Florina's energies were devoted to preparing for the BAC (Baccalaureate exam; required for a high school diploma and progressing to the university level), which involved a great deal of late-night and early morning study. Indeed, as a result of intensive studying, Florina frequently missed first and second periods during her final year of high school and was almost required to repeat the year. Fortunately, she was spared that fate by engaging in a "very interesting conversation about philosophy" with the principal who was impressed by her knowledge and made sure she graduated on time.[58]

D., like Florina, also enjoyed the humanities; however, she ended up going the science route, noting, "I very much enjoyed chemistry. It was a job of the future. Many became engineers at the time ... it was a more reliable [career] path and after the ninth grade I decided to opt for the technical/science track."[59] Although D. initially planned on studying pharmacy at university—a field her mother had encouraged her to pursue, viewing it as "a job for women"—at the last moment, D. switched to geology, which fascinated her but for which she had not prepared. She eventually passed the exam and was accepted into the geology program at the University of Cluj, where she received a scholarship—four years she recalled as "the best time" of her life.

In discussing her fascination with the sciences, D. noted that her high school teachers had encouraged her in this area. D.'s tenure in school coincided with reforms implemented under a new education law (adopted in 1978), which promoted science, engineering, and technical fields. This was an outgrowth of a larger program, adopted at the Tenth Party Congress of the PCR, to construct a multilaterally developed society. The program involved increased investment in science and technology in an effort to compete with the West, assertions of national sovereignty, and improvement in the "spiritual level" and standard of living of the people.[60] The plan also dovetailed with efforts to encourage women in new areas of the labor force and away from physically arduous jobs. Since promoting women into fields such as physics, chemistry, and engineering could kill two birds with stone, it is unsurprising that her teacher would have encouraged D. and other girls to enter these fields.

Meanwhile, Maria, who began working as an electrical engineer in the mid-1970s, explained her attraction to the sciences in this way: "Electrical engineering is comprehensible to all children: How does a light bulb work? How does a motor work? What is a fuse? Things like this, that you encounter every day and that make you curious. I like [this kind of stuff] and I think for that reason I became an electrician."[61] Maria thus regarded her fascination with engineering not as exceptional but "normal," a subject anyone, regardless of gender, would find interesting.

While personal curiosity and teacher encouragement attracted girls to the sciences and male-dominated fields, so too might have stories in *Cutezătorii*. One article in the magazine told the story of Doina Bicazan, a chemistry student who "lost many nights of sleep" and was "plagued with self-doubt" while studying for her exams. With the support of colleagues, Doina ultimately qualified as a quality-control technician, demonstrating that through diligence, perseverance, and the support of the larger work collective, young women could achieve their goals.[62] Intended to destigmatize women's participation in male-dominated fields and instill girls with the confidence to pursue scientific careers, the article also highlights the state's central role in women's professional advancement. Alongside such articles, the magazine featured discussion forums in which ordinary teenage girls expressed their desire to study chemical engineering and work as researchers in labs. While acknowledging the rigors of studying for exams, they also highlighted girls' aptitude and ability to persevere, which may have emboldened others to pursue studies in the sciences.

By comparison, girls in the West did not receive similar encouragement in the sciences during this period (mid-1970s), as science, along with engineering, remained stubbornly male-dominated. In contrast to the West, then, gender did not decisively shape educational or professional pathways in socialist Romania. Although admirable, the promotion of women in science was not simply rooted in notions of gender equality, but also pragmatism: as the country modernized, more engineers, scientists, and other specialists were needed, regardless of gender.[63] Consequently, science and mathematics received particular attention at the high school level, with labs being set up in classrooms.[64] Emphasis on women in science also served to legitimate First Lady Elena Ceaușescu's "scientific career," for which she was honored both nationally and internationally by the 1970s, despite the fact it was wholly fabricated.

Regardless of the motivating factor, women's presence in scientific fields during the second half of socialist rule was indeed impressive, as they constituted 34.5 percent in 1967, 39.6 percent in 1976, and 44 percent in 1989.[65] Moreover, the number of women attending technical schools increased from 27.2 percent in 1960–61 to 32.7 percent in 1980–81. Socialism thus opened up new areas of study to women that would not have been available to them in societies where such fields continued to be distinctly gendered.

While personal profiles of women chemists and engineers were designed to encourage girls to study science, the vignette "Mama" was designed to disabuse boys of stereotypical attitudes regarding gender and work. The story unfolds at the breakfast table, where the youngest son, Radu, learns that his mom is rushing off to school. Perplexed, Radu laughs and exclaims, "School is for kids!" At this point, his older brother steps in to explain that their mother is learning a trade—just like their father had done years earlier. Having accepted his brother's explanation, Radu then goes on to tell his classmates that both his father and mother work as crane operators; however, because "crane operator" (*macaragiu*) is a masculine noun, one of his classmates asks, "What, do you have two fathers?," eliciting laughter among the other students.[66] The students' response was not only due to lack of a feminine term for crane operator but also the belief that it was solely a man's job, illustrating the degree to which certain jobs remained distinctly gendered in Romania—even into the 1970s. By exposing gender stereotypes, the article encouraged boys to regard women as equally capable of doing a "man's job" and attempted to make male-dominated fields more appealing to female youth. However, as the article was published the same year that the state reorganized the labor force, transferring women to less arduous jobs (including out of construction), it would seem that practice did not necessarily follow rhetoric.

Nonetheless, in challenging gender stereotypes, *Cutezătorii* was comparatively progressive for a youth magazine. Indeed, with the exception of a short section near the end of the magazine, the publication targeted youth as a general category rather than girls or boys specifically. Thus, articles promoted social responsibility, diligence, world peace and patriotism, blending socialist and nationalist values. Published on a monthly basis and required reading for all elementary and middle school students, the magazine included excerpts from recent party congresses, visits by foreign dignitaries, and reportages on major conflicts and crises such as the Vietnam War and famine in Ethiopia. Children also learned about state visits from Charles De Gaulle and Richard Nixon, among others. To personalize world events—and also arouse sympathy for the less fortunate—the magazine profiled children from different parts of the globe, from the Inuit of Alaska to children whose countries had recently thrown off the colonial yoke. During the 1960s and early 1970s, the heroic Vietnamese people were frequently featured. The article "My Friend Ly," for example, told the story of a North Vietnamese boy who, despite the threat of continued U.S. bombing, attended school, under which a network of trenches had been dug.[67] The message was that even under threat of destruction, the quest for knowledge, social justice, and national sovereignty could not be quashed.

In case there was any doubt that Romanian children enjoyed a superior standard of living, columns such as "Millions of Children without a Childhood" served as graphic reminders. Articles published under this rubric described children's deplorable living conditions in underdeveloped countries, characterized by forced labor, malnutrition, lack of potable water, and high rates of illiteracy and disease.[68] Condemning the continued existence of famine, malnutrition, and illiteracy, another article asserted, "If a fraction of the millions spent on weapons could be spent on schools and hospitals these problems could easily be eradicated."[69] Readers were also reminded of children's right to a dignified and healthy life as enshrined in the UN "Declaration of the Rights of the Child," with the authors explicitly connecting the amelioration of child hunger, disease, and labor exploitation to the installation of a new economic and political order based on equality and justice (e.g. socialism).[70] As a corollary, articles reminded readers that "through the care of the party, state and the person of Nicolae Ceaușescu, children in socialist Romania are guaranteed all conditions necessary" for a good life. As in the Soviet Union, as well as the United States, children's quality of life thus became a barometer of national achievement and humanity, sending the message that a political system was only as good as the health and happiness of its children.[71]

Readers also learned of their forefathers' and foremothers' struggles against capitalist-imperialist and fascist forces.[72] For instance, one article profiled the heroic woman soldier, Ecaterina Teodoroiu, who fought alongside the Romanian army during World War I and, when captured and subsequently tortured by the Germans, refused to betray Romanian troop movements to the enemy.[73] As Romania moved further away from World War II, peace and global cooperation replaced antifascism, and ordinary socialist heroes received increased attention. For example, in a piece that asked children to define the meaning of courage, one boy noted that while on vacation he had saved a child from drowning. However, upon further reflection the boy emphasized that such an act was not necessarily courageous, but about "doing what's right"; "doing one's duty as a human being."[74] The magazine also highlighted the defining traits of the contemporary person: diligence, responsibility, perseverance, kindness, and optimism, among other attributes. Additionally, children were lauded for their "capacity to spend long hours at [their] desk or in the library while others wasted their time at the cinema or roaming the streets."[75]

Being a good student required not only diligence and discipline but also cooperation. In an article about a group of overachieving pioneers (*pionierii fruntași*) from a primary school in Corbii Mari, readers learned not only that the group received the highest marks for semester III, but that they also helped other students receive high marks. Their slogan, "Toți pentru unu și unu pentru toți" (All for one, and one for all) was a nod to socialist collectivism as well as Alexander Dumas's classic, *The Three Musketeers*, with which many young Romanians would have been familiar.[76] Collective achievement appeared not only in the pages of *Cutezătorii*, but in actual classrooms, though it could assume more ambiguous meanings. For instance, Irina (b. 1968) recalled that during her primary school years in Bucharest in the mid-1970s, the brighter students typically helped their less-fortunate classmates:

> [During my childhood] I didn't feel oppression directly, I just saw that in my class there were children who were poorer than I was, and I had to share my food with them, and they were badly dressed and sick and they had a lot of bumps on their skin. And there were children without parents, orphans. And this was a shock for me ... I mean, seeing that we were not all equal. And the gypsy kids who were always in the last row of the class, they were separate, but we had to take care of them and make sure their homework was done ... and we did ... very rarely did students make fun of them ... we whispered the answers to them.[77]

Such a story would not have made it in the pages of *Cutezătorii*—nor any socialist media for that matter—as it would have contradicted state claims about "according great care to the children of Romania." By encountering students who were not only academically challenged, but also unhealthy and impoverished, Irina was confronted head-on with the hypocrisy of the regime, particularly its avowed commitment to social equality and the nation's youth.[78] This, in turn, prompted her to question prevailing notions of equality, which she had previously taken for granted. Yet, since her less-healthy classmates were visible reminders of social inequality, her engagement with these students reflected the socialist notion of sacrificing for the collective. Although her teacher had solicited students' help, the fact that none of her classmates complained about or mocked the less-fortunate students indicates that they felt sympathy and even a sense of responsibility for them. This suggests that school could serve as a site for teaching compassion and promoting cooperation.

Alongside moralizing pieces and personal vignettes, science and technology were common themes in *Cutezătorii*. Articles featured monumental events such as the moon landing, while "Club 2000" directed readers toward the future, particularly "Romania in the Year 2000."[79] The series, which began in 1967, focused on revolutionary changes in technology, with professors and other experts offering predictions of future discoveries. One article, titled "School of the Future," pre-

Children of the Revolution 109

Figure 2.1. Cover of *Cutezătorii*, nos. 52–53, 1976

dicted that, "computers will soon be essential to classroom learning" (see figure 2.1). Meanwhile, an article in the "Orizont Ştiinţific" section informed readers that a housecleaning robot was on the scientific horizon.[80]

The year 2000 was also celebrated in the 1970 song "We, the Children in the Year 2000" ("Noi în Anul 2000"), in which the younger generation lauded their parents' heroism and looked forward to a time when they were fully grown and to a country that would flourish like "spring," with "so many flowers, so many castles," "full of gold and bread," a time when they would "also be heroes and make their parents happy." As Diana Georgescu asserts, in socialist discourse the year 2000 was presented "as the symbolic threshold of the transition to full-fledged communism," the dawning of a new millennium and a new "political order distinguished not only by advanced technological development and egalitarianism, but also by the quality of its citizenry."[81] Thus, in addition to writing about the past and famous historical figures, students also wrote about the future, outlining what their lives might look like in the year 2000.

To both challenge and entertain children, *Cutezătorii* also included mathematical problems, puzzles, riddles, games, and short stories. Moreover, adventure and detective novels were published in serialized form, including an illustrated version of Rudyard Kipling's *The Jungle Book*. Furthermore, comic strips appeared in the magazine and were quite popular among readers. In line with Ceaușescu's increased embrace of nationalism, some featured the exploits of famous historical figures such as *Mihai Vodă Viteazul* (Michael the Brave). Hailed as a national hero in school textbooks, as well as Ceaușescu's predecessor, Michael the Brave was also the subject of the enormously popular and eponymous 1969 film that was required viewing for young people.[82] Similarly, the strip *Dan Buzdugan* (Dan Mace) featured one of Viteazul's soldiers, who wielded a mace in each hand as he fought off his enemies. Other historical figures included King Burebista, Prince Vlad Țepeș, and peasant revolt leader, Horea. Meanwhile, those interested in more recent figures could follow the journeys of Yuri Gagarin or a group of four astronauts who, in a nod to Western popular culture, were fashioned after the Beatles.[83] In a segment of the strip set in the year 2015, the team plans an expedition to Mars, which is a mere "five-week journey from earth thanks to new technologies."[84]

While certain parts of the magazine appealed more to boys than girls, on the whole, *Cutezătorii* targeted youth—particularly urban youth—as a general category. Thus, both girls and boys were featured competing in academic and sporting events. Similarly, travelogues about exotic places such as Bali and Disneyland certainly piqued most readers' curiosity regardless of gender, though they also most likely produced frustration since vacations abroad were impossible for all but the privileged few due to travel restrictions.[85] These privileged few included Eugenia Noje, who won a six-day trip to Denmark in the "Children Are Everywhere" competition.[86]

That said, the magazine was not completely devoid of gender stereotypes. For instance, activities outlined in the magazine's hobby and lifestyle section included a column for boys, "Pagina Băieților" (Boys' Page) as well as one for girls, "Pagina Fetelor" (Girls' Page), which promoted gendered leisure activities and concerns. Accordingly, girls were taught how to fashion a purse, set the table, and dress for and comport themselves at the theater.[87] Moreover, under the subsection "Help Mom at Home," girls were advised on how to prepare meals and encouraged to wake up early on a Saturday morning and make breakfast for the family so that "mother can sleep in." Additionally, "Pagina Fetelor" offered tips on health and fitness. In one issue (which included a weight and height chart), a doctor responded to readers' concerns about keeping a nice figure and suggested that girls should reduce sweets, starches, and fatty foods, never miss meals, and increase their activity level.[88] By comparison, "Pagina Băieților" focused on traditionally masculine activities such as constructing a model airplane and building a picture frame or bookshelf, and topics such as clothing, diet, and cooking were never mentioned in this section; though in other parts of the magazine boys were encouraged to help out with the shopping.

Although relegated to the latter portion of the magazine, by differentiating between hobbies for girls and boys these sections of *Cutezătorii* promoted essentialist ideas about gender and leisure. In particular, Pagina Fetelor, by suggesting that girls help their mothers around the house and concern themselves with their physical appearance, contradicted messages in other media that promoted men's contributions in the domestic sphere, encouraged women to raise their boys and girls as equals, and urged readers to regard "beauty" as more than skin-deep. Furthermore, these sections contrasted with other parts of the magazine, which targeted youth as a general category and featured boys and girls participating in academic, athletic, and leisure activities. As such, they dovetailed with initiatives, by the UTC (*Uniunea Tineretului Comunist*; Union of Communist Youth), to prepare teenage girls for marriage and motherhood through special courses (e.g. "Advice for Young Housewives" and "Mothers' Advice for Girls").[89] Such efforts, which were in line with the increased valorization of marriage and large families after the criminalization of abortion, also included documentary film screenings and presentations by gynecologists (held in high schools and boarding schools), which warned female youth about the deleterious consequences of abortion.[90] Similar courses and initiatives, meanwhile, were never organized for boys. When considered alongside the promotion of girls in the sciences and sporting events, such essentialist renderings reflect an ambiguous and, indeed, contradictory approach to female adolescent youth. However, given state expectations of women, the logic becomes clearer: these varied and multiple renderings were in fact designed to prepare girls for the numerous roles they would be expected to assume once they entered adulthood—a topic that will be explored in greater detail in subsequent chapters.

## Travel and Leisure

Children engaged in leisure activities through the official channels of school and socialist organizations, as well as in a non-official capacity with family and friends. Activities ranged from reading, viewing films, and playing with neighborhood kids to excursions in the mountains or to the Black Sea with the Pioneer group. Much of young people's leisure time was also spent in the countryside, where many were born and spent extended periods with grandparents and other relatives while they were young.

Valeria R., who grew up near Brașov in the 1960s, recalled the games she and her friends played:

> I spent a lot of time outside playing on the streets, in the trees; there was not a single character from a book or TV show that we didn't play the role of. I was Ivanhoe, I was William Tell, I was Robin Hood. We also read a lot; that's probably why I love to read. ... I think I had a very, very good childhood, very nice. Unfortunately, I look at children today, all of whom live in apartment blocks, and they have to play on the asphalt, in between cars. With so much television and computers, they don't know what it is [to play]; because of this, they don't talk to each other very much, they don't know how to be friends, to help each other.[91]

Adriana, a math teacher raised in Bucharest during the late 1960s and 1970s, echoed these sentiments, noting that her childhood was "a life without worry, without care ... parents had time for their children; there were no computers, so we read all the time."[92] Valeria and Adriana's recollections evoke nostalgia not only for youth but for childhood friendships and family relationships. Such sentiments, however, are not necessarily unique to socialism, but more broadly connected to the social anomie that often accompanies modernization, urbanization, and technological innovation, which, according to some respondents, have negatively affected childhood. Valeria and Adriana's idyllic portraits of childhood are thus not dissimilar from individuals who experienced such changes in the West, and who bemoan the alienating impact of technology, specifically computers.

In addition to playing with friends, reading ranked high on the list of many respondents' leisure activities. As D., a loyal patron of the Oradea public library, stressed, "Everyone read, to read was not noble [or something special]."[93] In addition to Romanian authors, children who, like D., came of age in the 1960s and early 1970s (during the period of cultural liberalization) could enjoy the works of Jules Verne, Mark Twain, Victor Hugo, Charles Dickens, and Honoré de Balzac, among other universal classics, along with the science fiction of Asimov. Science fiction was particularly popular during the second half of socialist rule, serving to orient youth toward the future, specifically the impending millennium.[94] *Cutezătorii* presented reading as superior to other leisure pursuits such as watching television or going to the cinema, and the magazine featured articles in which literary figures and ordinary youth discussed their favorite books and provided reading lists. Moreover, by the late 1960s, extracurricular reading and writing was promoted in schools in the form of reading circles and literary magazines. For instance, Florina fondly reflected on her participation in literary circles in high school and her work as editor of the school's *Literary Journal*. She also recalled writing poetry—some of which was published—and attended a camp where she met well-known poet Mircea Dinescu.

Participating in reading circles, editing school journals, and publishing poetry became increasingly common in the 1970s and 1980s as the regime embraced more popular forms of culture. This involved democratizing the production of art, most notably with the *Cântarea României* (Song of Romania) festival, a national event established in 1976, that featured amateur artists and was designed to promote national belonging and enrich the spiritual, cultural, and ideological life of the people.[95] It was also part of a broader anti-cosmopolitan campaign in art and culture that involved the embrace of more traditional and ordinary forms of cultural expression.

Many of my respondents from urban areas also spent weekends and, indeed, entire summers in the countryside with grandparents and other relatives. These spaces are typically represented as idyllic, a respite from the bustling city, as well as a sites of indulgence given they were in their grandparents' care. This, however, did not necessarily absolve children from work. As Elvira (b. 1948) recalled, "We went to [worked in] the fields, the vineyards, we did it all. That's how I came to know Oltenian [a region in southwestern Romania] agriculture, the culture of wool, hemp, silkworms, cereals, corn."[96] Families also took trips to the Black Sea as trade unions offered vouchers for travel and lodging, though these were limited and many families simply camped out on or near the beach. Irina, who visited the Black Sea in the late 1970s and 1980s, recalled that "the hotel was not the best, but we didn't need much. It was clean and the food was fine; it was not fancy and luxurious, but the atmosphere was more loose."[97] Like children of other cultural figures (her father was an actor at the National Theater), Irina enjoyed the relaxed atmosphere of seaside resorts. Moreover, since ration cards were not required for purchasing goods there, her family was able to acquire items otherwise inaccessible in Bucharest and other parts of the country. Given that the Black Sea was a popular destination for foreign tourists, including Western tourists, such trips also provided opportunities for meeting people from other parts of Europe and procuring goods unavailable in Romania, as well as foreign currency, which could in turn be used to purchase goods in special shops or on the black market.

Alongside family trips, school-related excursions provided youth with opportunities to see different parts of the country. Valeria R. recalled visiting resorts on the Black Sea, the monasteries of Moldavia, and salt mines and caves. A Braşov native, her class also visited the nearby town of Prejmer and the Bran and Râşnov castles. In a nod to industrialization, factories were also on the circuit, including a candy and sugar factory and a printing house. Rather than regarding these trips as ideologically freighted, Valeria remembered them as "interesting ... in addition to a piece of chocolate or candy we would see how they made nets, it was interesting, and it seemed perfectly normal to me."[98] In some cases, trips were cultural in nature, including visits to the opera and philharmonic. In other cases, they were explicitly ideological, namely visits to the museum of the Romanian Communist Party in Bucharest and the Doftana Prison, where students entered cells that had held communist leaders during World War II.[99] Such politically oriented visits, which were prefaced by lectures emphasizing the sacrifices of early communists in laying the foundations for a socialist society, typically elicited less-fond memories in my respondents.[100]

The Pioneer Organization (or Pioneers), which registered a membership of one million by 1960, also provided opportunities for exploration and physical activity.[101] Founded in 1949 for youth aged nine to fourteen (and after 1971, youth aged seven to fourteen), the Pioneers became a mass organization by the 1960s, with 60 percent of all school children enrolled as members in 1966 and over 90 percent in 1971.[102] In comparison with the Boy and Girl Scouts of America, the Pioneers were not segregated according to gender. During the first decade of socialist rule, the aim of the organization was to fashion a loyal and diligent workforce, while also encouraging children to enjoy the beauty of the countryside. Thus, trips included visits to the medieval monasteries of Bukovina or farming communities in Maramureș. By the late 1960s, however, youth expeditions became more purposeful and patriotic in character, designed to appeal to young people's sense of adventure and appreciation of the natural environment. Rather than passively observe natural surroundings, expeditions typically required a degree of endurance as students hiked through mountainous areas and difficult terrain.[103] Additionally, they conducted archaeological digs, retraced the route of the Dacian army, and visited sites of peasant rebellions.[104] Because young people were increasingly raised in towns and cities, these expeditions helped foster a sense of national pride and belonging by connecting students to their rural roots. At the same time, they were designed to highlight Romanians' historical longevity (and continuity) on Romanian soil.

Although the Pioneers was created by the state with the aim of fashioning *omul nou*, membership in the organization was nonetheless a source of enjoyment for many of my respondents who either ignored or were not bothered by its ideological character. Indeed, because membership was related to academic achievement, many took pride in this designation. Valeria R. noted that it was "a source of pride because you could only be a pioneer if you had good grades, otherwise you couldn't become one."[105] Maria similarly recalled: "I was a Pioneer. How proud I was! Do you know why I liked it? You had activities, they would give you tasks and you would need to complete them. You needed to study in order to be a Pioneer; you needed to learn. They channeled us towards good work, I can't fault them for that. It was very good, we went with pioneers on excursions, beautiful places. Very beautiful excursions."[106] Meanwhile, Angela, who became a Pioneer in the late 1970s, offered similar reasons: "Not everyone could be a Pioneer because it was based on the grades one received in school. I'm not trying to brag or anything, but I felt like I was seen differently as a student. We were involved in all these celebrations; all types of activities, all of the 'Songs of Romania.' But for us children, we enjoyed it."[107] Such perspectives reflected the basic goals of the organization: instilling youth with pride, diligence, and patriotism and forging an emotional bond between young people and the party.[108] For Ecaterina (b. 1953), who claimed, by contrast, that one had to be a pretty bad student not to become a Pioneer, it was the athletic orientation of her group that she remembered most fondly, particularly playing in volleyball, handball, and even football matches.

By contrast, Adriana's Pioneer experience was eye-opening but not in a positive way. Chosen to greet Ceaușescu at Sala Palatului in Bucharest in the mid-1970s, Adriana had initially been nervous; however, this soon turned to shock as she realized the degree to which the event, and, by extension, popular support for the regime, was orchestrated.[109] Meanwhile, by the time Alina earned her Pioneer badge—in the late 1970s—the "whole thing seemed silly." She recalled, "They [the teachers] would say, 'Wow you are a Pioneer!' but we laughed at home, we knew it wasn't a big deal. Even as children we made jokes about these things. I think because my family didn't take them seriously, I didn't take them seriously."[110] Alina's recollection supports Veronica Szabo's claim that by the 1980s "indoctrination work" with youth was done in an inept and ambivalent manner and that "whatever they [the party] accomplished in schools was further deconstructed in autonomous spaces of expression within family and friendship circles."[111]

By the teen years, leisure also included extracurricular activities such as balls and dances (organized by schools or houses of culture), hiking in the mountains, seeing films and plays, and socializing at the homes of friends. Those entering adolescence in the mid-1960s through the mid-1970s experienced the period of liberalization and opening up to the West. During this time, the regime sought to legitimate socialism by way of consumer and cultural goods, promotion of national autonomy and support of nonaligned nations, and friendly relations with the West. Thus, this cohort of young people, as well as the one that followed, recalled wearing blue jeans, listening to foreign records—especially American music—and watching American films. Indeed, Western culture, especially Western music, movies, and books, was central to many respondents' memories—not only of the 1960s and early 1970s, but also of the late 1970s and 1980s, when the regime began cracking down on Western and "cosmopolitan" culture. For instance, Elena, an avid reader, spent most of her teen years (the later 1970s) at the American and British libraries in Bucharest, "consuming" American and English literature. She was also fortunate to claim a subscription to Cinemateca, a members-only movie house in Bucharest that screened a variety of foreign and art films. Irina, who also boasted a membership, recalled seeing "old movies, all kinds of movies: American, French, Italian, Russian ... there was a lot of Fellini, a lot of New Wave films, American Westerns, stuff by Buñuel."[112] Indeed, the films on offer at Cinemateca at times subtly undermined party ideology, and flew in the face of the regime's moralizing discourses and efforts to minimize the influence of "cosmopolitan" and western culture. As such, it is unsurprising that subscriptions to it were highly-prized and people waited in line an entire night just to secure tickets for the upcoming week.[113]

In reflecting on the cultural activities on offer during the 1970s and even early 1980s, Ruxandra, an artist who attended classical concerts and also viewed films at the Cinemateca, highlighted the ambiguity of the period: "This is why I say it was very complex during that time. It wasn't only bad things and propaganda. Beneath all this, they ensured that there was some air, so that people would not suffocate and so that people would not revolt."[114] According to Ruxandra, such cultural pleasures served as safety valves that were tolerated (within reason) by the regime and, in some cases, even promoted, providing individuals with the illusion of freedom.

By the 1980s, watching foreign videos also became a popular pastime—for those who could get a hold of them. Videos were appealing not simply because of the official alternative—the short programming on Romanian television, composed of formulaic reportages, odes to the Ceaușescus, and the occasional cartoon—but also because of many Romanians' fascination with the West. As one respondent noted, "A classmate had a video player, and he was the most popular [kid in class], and everyone was so jealous because he could watch all the films that we hadn't even heard of yet ... *Rocky, Superman, Star Wars.*"[115] In Romania, videotapes and video players were highly coveted goods. Indeed, one respondent comically recalled debating if he should purchase a Dacia [a Romanian car] or a video player since the costs were equally exorbitant. While possessing foreign videos was illegal, for a time the regime assumed a surprisingly lax attitude toward video viewing, permitting—or at least tolerating—the operation of numerous "videotheques" in official spaces such as workers' clubs, student centers, and opera houses.[116] These makeshift videotheques, which served as both a safety valve and a moneymaker for the regime, functioned in a number of larger cities, screening a range of films, including martial arts, horror, and science fiction films, as well as thrillers, dramas, and romantic comedies.[117] While the films were of low quality, the characters' voices dubbed solely in the voice of Irina Margareta Nistor, and the viewing halls packed with people, these screenings elicit fond memories of this form of entertainment.[118]

In addition to cafes, cinemas, and parks, private homes were popular leisure sites. According to Simona, a teen in the 1980s, "My friends preferred to come to my house because it was always more open ... there were even friends who discussed, who confessed things to my mother ... and, in addition, my father made wine and that was a good thing."[119] Teens also held parties when their parents were away, which often involved dancing and, for those who could get their hands on them, watching videos. Others recalled going to restaurants with friends, where they might be able to order a glass of wine or beer. Meanwhile, Elena recalled skipping classes in the late 1970s, during which time she "discovered the sin of drinking Russian vodka at the flat of a friend's brother."[120]

As in other modernizing societies wherein large segments of the population retained traditional beliefs about gender, parents were generally ambivalent about—if not wholly resistant to—letting their adolescent daughters socialize, views that were frequently expressed by readers in *Femeia*, as well as my respondents' parents. As C., a teen during the mid-1970s, reflected on this period of her life, "Our father was very strict with us and we didn't really have the right to go out with friends and such."[121] Maria, a teen in the late 1960s, recalled that her parents were a bit more relaxed, but still, according to her, overly concerned:

> When we would tell them we were going to a party, our parents were very reluctant [to let us go]. They would say: "Be careful of what you do there ... don't get drunk, make sure nothing happens, don't take anyone with you." Or, when we'd go hiking through Piatra Mare: "Watch out for the bears, watch out for the snakes, be careful." But we much preferred to go [hiking] in the mountains than to a party, because with a party you needed to be home by nine, and if you weren't home, dad would wait at the window because he couldn't even sleep, [and he would wonder] "Where are they? Why are they not at home?" But in the mountains, there were no issues.[122]

While parents expressed apprehension about their children, particularly daughters, socializing with peers, beginning in the 1960s, sociologists claimed such restrictiveness was potentially detrimental to young people's development. A 1968 *Femeia* article titled "How Much Freedom Should Teens Have?" examined conflicts between adolescent girls and their parents surrounding the issue of leisure. According to a survey conducted by the author of the piece, most parents regarded socializing as a superfluous or unnecessary activity, while 30 percent of the surveyed female youth fought with their parents because they were forbidden from attending a play or engaging in extracurricular activities.[123] The featured parents offered numerous explanations for restricting their daughters' engagement in leisure activities. For example, one father claimed, "when we were her age we didn't see plays, we worked," underscoring the centrality of labor and sacrifice for this generation that had built socialism. Meanwhile, a mother criticized her daughter's apparent obsession with film, stressing, "She can go to the movies with me. One film a week is enough. The cinema is a type of psychosis."[124] The author expressed particular concern that just as girls were reaching a point in their life when they wanted to spend more time with the opposite sex (according to her, around age sixteen), parents began to restrict them from socializing with boys. Another mother, upon hearing that her tenth-grade daughter had befriended a boy at the Union of Communist Youth meeting, forbade her from even "talking to that punk," even though the mother had never met him and didn't know his name. Meanwhile, a father referred to boys as "naughty punks that want to take advantage of girls' weaknesses."[125] The author contended that, given such views, it is no wonder that girls often concealed love interests or boyfriends from parents. Thus, she concluded that parental prohibitions not only prevented young people from developing socially but, in some cases, backfired, driving girls into the arms of boys: "An adolescent [girl] seeking comfort in love is most often triggered by the family's lack of interest in her developing a close circle of friends."[126] To prevent such outcomes, the author advised parents to encourage their teenage daughters to socialize with a range of friends. Other experts suggested that mothers develop close and open relationships with their daughters and take their interests, including love interests, seriously, rather than dismissing or condemning them.[127]

When considered in the context of a modernizing society that retained traditional ideas about gender, parents' protectiveness—and their daughters' efforts to evade it—is unsurprising. Indeed, the problems outlined by the author could similarly apply to Western societies undergoing social change and characterized by tensions between those born before and after the war. Thus, the article was not simply fabrication or propaganda but genuinely reflected parental concerns regarding female youth at the time. Moreover, the article evinces a generational tension on the very necessity of leisure. The young people featured in the column were born during the early to mid-1950s and were coming of age during a period of increased standards of living and access to consumer goods and cultural pursuits. Although by no means affluent, urban Romanian youth shared with young people in other parts of the Bloc and the West a time of peace and (relative) prosperity. By contrast, their parents had grown up in the 1940s, during the tumult of war and communist consolidation. Having witnessed death, destruction, and Stalinist repression, labored long hours in the factory, and experienced prolonged material shortage, their parents thus viewed leisure as superfluous and even indulgent. In this respect, generational tension in Romania, while also apparent in the West and other societies, assumed a distinctly socialist character.[128]

While focused primarily on adolescent girls, *Femeia* also provided suggestions on rearing teen boys. Accordingly, in the article "Parents, How Are You Raising Your Boys?" the author criticized conventional views toward boys, dismissing the notion that "whoever has a boy does not have problems," and condemning the "boys will be boys" attitude embraced by many parents, which granted boys a range of liberties because "he's not a girl." The aim of the piece was to encourage parents to stop distinguishing between sons and daughters and to treat and rear them as equals. In particular, mothers were urged not to indulge or privilege boys as they would eventually become men who will have responsibilities and will need to account for their actions, including treating women as equals and with respect.[129]

Although *Femeia* stressed the importance of socializing during adolescence, it cautioned younger readers to exercise restraint in how they passed their time. The article "Where Are You Running Off to, Tina?," which appeared in the *Pagina Ta* section of *Femeia* (a section specifically designed for young female readers) in December 1970, followed the exploits of Tina, a seventeen-year-old bar-hopping girl who had grown bored of school and was in search of a bar job where she heard she could earn up to 400 lei ($22, roughly a quarter of the average monthly salary at the time) in tips a night.[130] Depicted as a lazy, self-centered girl who manipulated and stole from her parents (i.e. she attempted suicide when her mother refused to buy her new clothing and stole money from her parents' wallets) and refused to take a factory job since it would mean "waking up early," Tina is presented as the antithesis of the model socialist young person. When asked why she didn't continue her schooling, she responded, "I don't want to study anything, I don't have patience. I want to make money and have fun." Tina's story is juxtaposed against other youths who attend the theater, cinema, and dances, and only rarely go to bars because of the cost involved. The author suggests that some "parenting mistakes" may have been made, connecting Tina's self-indulgent behavior to parental and, more specifically, maternal neglect—a fact that Tina's mother acknowledges, claiming that her demanding work schedule prevented her from sufficiently supervising her daughter. However, the author places blame primarily on Tina, stressing that she is ultimately responsible for the choices she makes and the direction her life takes. The moral of the story is that, as they mature, young people need to restrain individual desire and think seriously about "what their aims and ideals are, who they are, and what they are going to do [with their lives]."[131]

As a work-shy teen who frequents bars with boys, Tina does not embrace the values of the model socialist person: sobriety, productivity, and engagement in socially acceptable leisure pursuits.[132] Instead, she exhibits "social parasitism" and "corrupted morals," designations which were outlined in a decree, issued in April 1970, designed to sanction people who were "not respecting social conventions and public order and peace."[133] Acts that fell under this designation included begging, illicit trading of goods, prostitution, unemployment, domestic violence, excessive alcohol consumption, hooliganism, and vandalism, among other morally reprehensible behaviors. Interpreted in this light, Tina's frequenting of bars with boys, as well as her desire to rapidly earn a lot of money, appears as a veiled reference to prostitution and thus a warning to parents who are not sufficiently supervising their children. At the same time, it should be noted that in practice this decree was liberally interpreted; therefore, even how one looked and dressed (e.g. donning blue jeans; scantily-clad women; long-haired men) could attract the attention of the authorities. Thus, young people that looked like hippies or did not conform to the regime's notion of sartorial propriety could fall under the designation of social parasitism or asocial behavior, even if they were not engaging in antisocialist or antistate behaviors.[134]

Individuals such as Tina were a source of concern to the regime not only for the alleged harm they brought themselves, but also because they could spread the contagion of sloth, debauchery, and immorality to their cohorts. Although the article about Tina predates the Communist Code of Ethics, a thirty-three-point document, adopted at the Eleventh Congress of the PCR in 1974, that outlined the prototypical new person, it nonetheless sets the moral and legal framework for it. Among the code's aims was the development of politically conscious, active, innovative, and morally upright citizens dedicated to work, family, and the construction of a multilaterally developed socialist society who would "manifest the highest intransigence against bourgeois life ... and the influence and mentalities of the capitalist world."[135]

On how to deal with individuals such as Tina and other young people who seemingly passed their time aimlessly loitering on city streets or drinking and smoking in bars, ordinary Romanians offered their advice in letters to the communist leadership. For instance, one man claimed that young people under eighteen should not be allowed into bars and the cost of alcoholic beverages and cigarettes should be increased to limit or deter their use. Meanwhile, another man suggested that such youth should be sent to parts of the country where workers are needed.[136] While these letters were, at least in part, influenced by socialist discourse (specifically articles and public opinion polls in *Scânteia*), they nonetheless indicate a degree of popular approval for the regime's increased focus on socialist morality and in directing youth towards productive pursuits. They also reveal that some individuals believed young people should be sanctioned for deviating from socialist ethics.

The regime did in fact take action against alleged unseemly behavior among youth, organizing, in 1974, teams composed of members of the UTC and local women's committees to combat "parasitism" and "retrograde behavior." Indeed, as a result of the teams' raids, in August of that year alone 4,250 people were identified to be without work.[137] When considered alongside the regime's active policing of young people's leisure, the article about Tina appears as a warning to other parents, specifically mothers, advising them to practice engaged parenting lest their daughters turn to asocial and amoral behavior.

In contrast, the regime supported and even praised acceptable types of leisure. In particular, sociologists believed that moderate levels of socialization, especially in larger groups, helped youth mature and develop into socially adept and culturally sophisticated individuals. That said, when it came to sexual behavior the regime was comparatively mute, and, when it did speak, conservative. Sex education was not part of the middle or high school curriculum; nor was it typically addressed within the family. As one woman reflected, "Everything about sexuality was a secret. No one talked about this normal topic. When I got my period for the first time, I thought I had to keep it a secret and would not let anyone know, not even my mother, what happened to me."[138] Of note is that sanitary products were difficult to come by in Romania during the socialist period. Thus, female youth were not only perplexed and ashamed when they began menstruating but also struggled with the practical issue of securing the necessary products for dealing with it.

Feelings of embarrassment and shame about menstruation were seemingly common among other adolescent girls, as many mothers did not educate their daughters about menses. Moreover, in most families sex was not discussed, or, if it was, premarital sex was presented as a sin and immoral, while virginity was considered a virtue. According to C., who grew up in a highly cultured and educated family and attended an urban high school from the early to mid-1970s,

> They [the teachers] didn't say a word about sexuality and relationships ... they were condemned during that period. If you had a boyfriend in high school it wasn't very socially acceptable ... Girls who had boyfriends were categorized as promiscuous ... and we [my sister and I] were not allowed. The prevailing belief was that you needed to be careful because "boys can ruin your future reputation."[139]

On the whole, then, adolescent girls were reared according to deeply ingrained beliefs that promoted sexual innocence and ignorance.[140] Consequently, adolescents made sense of the physical changes they experienced by speaking with other teens or young adults and, if they had access to them, consulting anatomy and physiology books.[141] This meant that while girls might experience untoward sexual advances (both verbal and physical) and even sexual assault, they may not have fully understood them or would have been ashamed to speak about them to family, including their mothers, let alone report such behavior to the authorities.[142] As a corollary, a general culture of homophobia—evident in jokes and religious dicta and reinforced by the criminalization of homosexuality in 1968—deterred open expression, let alone open exploration, of alternative sexual identities. In this respect, Romania was not alone as the Bulgarian state also criminalized same-sex relations. Indeed, even in East Germany, which decriminalized same-sex relations between adults in 1968, prevailing attitudes towards homosexuality remained conservative.[143]

Despite (or perhaps because of) the lack of sex education in schools, socialist propagandists encouraged mothers to be informed about female physiology and prepared to discuss issues such as puberty and relationships with the opposite sex with their daughters.[144] In the article "Intimate Dialogue with My Daughter," a physician and mother of two teen girls stressed the need for mothers to develop close and trusting relationships with their daughters. Intended for mothers and perhaps also adolescent girls, the author explains female sexual development starting with prepubescence and ending with menopause, presenting these as normal life stages and not something about which girls should be alarmed or ashamed. Moreover, the author connects intimate relations between a woman and a man to the larger comradely relationship, which, she emphasized, should be based on mutual respect and love.[145] The author concludes: "By explaining to our girls that love should not be measured by a man's burning desire for her, when the time comes we will have helped them understand and distinguish between a fling, an affair, and the profound love that they deserve."[146]

According to sociologist Radu Dimitriu, young people's ignorance about human sexuality motivated him to write the book *De vorbă cu tinerii* (Talking with Youth). Published in 1972, the book is at once an anatomy and physiology text, a primer on adolescent health and hygiene, and a guide for proper sexual behavior. Concerned that basic physiological functions such as menstruation, erection, and nocturnal emission elicit alarm and shame in young people, Dimitriu's aim was to demystify and normalize the physical changes that occur during adolescence.[147] As such, *De vorbă cu tinerii* was comparable to texts produced in Western countries during the period. At the same time, Dimitriu emphasized the book's important role in promoting socialist values and relations: "The youth of today are future spouses and parents. They must be prepared for this role, which is just as important for themselves as for the society in which they live. The foundation of the family today is love, not base material interests."[148]

While Dimitriu recommends abstinence before marriage, he does not echo Leninist rhetoric, which considered sex a frivolity and a waste of strength—a distraction from building socialism.[149] Instead, he emphasizes the risks of early sexual behavior, including venereal disease and psychological distress. Promiscuity is thus criticized on the basis of physical and psychological health and socialist morality. Furthermore, pregnancy is singled out as a particular concern for unmarried teenage girls because,

> Pregnancy cannot be avoided. No certain means to prevent fertilization of the egg exist. The famous pill is a medicine that prevents fertilization of the ova as long as it is taken regularly. However, current research is insufficient for assessing the effects of this drug. ... As for the interruption of pregnancy, this is out of the question. It is a crime punishable by law. Even if it were not forbidden, it would expose the young woman to immediate and subsequent dangers. Secondly, the psychological consequences must be taken into account.[150]

According to Dimitriu, pregnancy is practically inevitable after sexual intercourse; therefore, teenage girls needed to avoid it at all costs. While such warnings reflected conservative discourses—or, more precisely, scare tactics—designed to deter teenage girls from engaging in sexual activity, Dimitriu's warnings against contraceptive use, particularly the pill, reflected discourses by Romanian physicians and other "experts" at the time who highlighted the potentially harmful effects of hormone-based contraceptives. Accordingly, Dimitriu's denunciation of abortion, because of the legal and potential physical and psychological ramifications associated with it, is clearly designed to reinforce pronatalist policies.

Given these numerous risks, Dimitriu contends that abstinence is best prior to marriage and, echoing Lenin before him, suggests that young people redirect sexual desire toward sport, study, and other activities.[151] Indeed, Dimitriu even warns against masturbation during adolescence, claiming that it can lead to premature ejaculation during subsequent sexual activity, which can, in turn, create challenges in satisfying one's wife sexually and negatively affect spousal relations.[152] Interestingly, Dimitriu does not connect masturbation with neurosis or other psychological problems as Western doctors had previously done; instead, his concern is about managing desire and the future sexual fulfillment of one's wife. Intended as a teaching tool for parents and young couples, the book offers detailed discussions of sexuality, including sexual arousal, orgasm, frigidity, and different sexual positions, accompanied by diagrams of the female and male anatomy. While on the surface progressive and, indeed, radical considering the silence and conservatism surrounding sexuality (particularly female sexuality) in Romania, of note is that the author couches sexual relations within the context of heterosexual love, particularly within marriage. As a corollary, the emphasis on sexual fulfillment within marriage (especially on the part of women) is not simply or necessarily about personal pleasure, but is designed to promote increased sexual desire and activity—and thus increased fertility.

While state policy and propaganda reinforced cultural views about premarital sex, which promoted female virtue and chastity, in practice it often turned a blind eye toward men's sexual behavior prior to marriage. Indeed, this approach was codified in law as unmarried couples were prohibited from sharing a hotel room. In the event a *miliţia* search discovered an unmarried couple in such a circumstance, the woman would be fined and charged with prostitution, while the man received no punishment.[153] Thus, although socialist morality was represented as a value system to which all citizens were expected to adhere, its enforcement perpetuated traditional proscriptions against premarital sex for women while generally ignoring men's sexual behaviors.

Such conservatism was evident in East Germany in the 1950s and early 1960s as well; however, by the 1970s things had changed as East German sex manuals became more explicit, even featuring photos of couples having sex. That said, appropriate sexuality was still couched within the loving, monogamous, and heterosexual relationship. According to Josie McClellan, this seemingly lax approach concealed more insidious realities: "Sex was a useful way of offering young people 'a bit of freedom,' allowing the regime to appear to be on the side of the young while still pursuing its own agenda of a peaceful population and a healthy birth rate."[154] Thus, in East Germany official acceptance of youthful and premarital sex was a safety valve designed to stave off dissent, while at the same time a strategy that buttressed pronatalist policies. In the moralizing climate of Ceauşescu's Romania, which drew upon a general culture of sexual conservatism, this, however, was not an acceptable approach for placating youth.

Despite state and parental proscriptions, Romanian teens did have sex, and some adolescent girls did get pregnant. Prior to the criminalization of abortion in 1966, teen pregnancy, though considered shameful, could be quietly resolved. However, after 1966, this became increasingly difficult and dangerous. Consequently, some teen girls were forced to carry their pregnancy to term, which typically led to their expulsion from school and social stigmatization. Indeed, in some cases, students of very high academic standing and near graduation could be expelled if they became pregnant since such a fate was considered antithetical to socialist values and cultural mores. However, this was not always the case, as D. recalled: "I had a classmate in twelfth grade and she got pregnant by another classmate. It was a big deal ... a big scandal, and they wanted to kick her out of school. And with a great deal of intervention she succeeded in taking her BAC."[155] Given such conservatism, it is perhaps unsurprising that most of my respondents, regardless of generation, claimed they did not enter into serious relationships with the opposite sex until after high school.

By their later childhood years and early adolescence, young people became increasingly cognizant of the shortcomings of socialist policy and the disconnect between state rhetoric and everyday reality. This was especially glaring for youth who came of age in the 1980s and were expected to engage in a range of "patriotic work," including harvesting potatoes, tidying up their schools and neighborhoods, participating in national ceremonies and cultural performances, and supporting peace through "Training for the Defense of the Fatherland" (Pregătire pentru Apărarea Patriei) drills—a military-style training program, beginning in the ninth grade, which included firing a gun at a shooting range. After demonstrating their manifold commitments to the Romanian nation, these young people returned home to find that food, heat, and electricity were in short supply, further underscoring the enormous gulf between media glorifications of the Golden Age (*epoca de aur*) and everyday life. For Irina, these deprivations were physically palpable through heat shortages: "I noticed, when I started high school, that I was suffering from the cold ... and I remember thinking: 'It was not like this before' I remember talking about that. And this was very uncomfortable for me, to always be cold. This was a difference that I noticed [from my childhood]."[156] In her interviews with Romanians who were in middle school during the 1980s, Veronica Szabo similarly found that young people became increasingly aware that all was not right under Ceaușescu. Indeed, once parents felt confident that they could openly discuss the regime at home—as well as listen to Radio

Free Europe broadcasts—without fearing their children would share this information at school or elsewhere, young people became more attuned to the state's repressive practices. Like their elders, they could compare these broadcasts to what they learned at school, read in the newspaper, and heard on state television, and thus better understand the hypocrisy of socialist rhetoric and the widening gulf between the *nomenklatura* (administrative elites) and ordinary Romanians.[157] Considering such circumstances, it is unsurprising that young people would be at the forefront of the revolutionary barricades in 1989 and most actively involved in toppling the Ceaușescus.

## Conclusion

Young people embodied the transformative potential of socialism and were to serve as the foundation of a new society composed of new persons. Young people were also considered most receptive to new values and modes of behavior, including gender roles and relationships. In comparison with the West, socialist policymakers and propagandists typically targeted youth (at least until later adolescence) as a general category: both boys and girls enjoyed equal educational opportunities and were members of the state youth organization, the Pioneers. These educational opportunities were especially transformative for children from peasant and low-status backgrounds, facilitating upward mobility, as well as migration to urban areas. Thus, parents with no formal education might see their children earn high school and even college degrees, an accomplishment that would have been less likely under the previous system. Indeed, education proved especially transformative for girls who constituted the largest portion of the illiterate population prior to the communist takeover, and who, by the end of communist rule, attended school, including university, at the same level as boys. Significantly, girls were encouraged in areas such as science and technology and in academic and athletic competitions. Thus, the socialist educational system played an important role in challenging entrenched notions about intelligence, skill, and endurance, instilling girls with self-confidence to pursue professional and leisure pursuits in which they had been underrepresented or excluded from altogether.

That said, not all young people were considered equal as children of "unhealthy social origin," in addition to experiencing poverty, were disfavored in the educational system during the first part of socialist rule for fear they would "contaminate" their classmates. As such, education was not a universal entitlement, but a privilege bestowed upon or taken away from children based on family origin, political affiliation, or the real or alleged acts of family members. For reasons wholly out of their control, young people from such families, rather than being embraced by the collective, were often shunned from or marginalized by it. Such unequal treatment of young people reflects one of the paradoxes of "real existing socialism," and helps explain people's negative or, at best, ambiguous attitudes toward the socialist project.

With respect to leisure and sexuality during youth, state prescriptions were seemingly egalitarian as sociologists encouraged parents to allow their sons and daughters to participate in extracurricular activities and socialize with youth of the opposite sex. That said, excessive or inappropriate forms of socialization such as passing time in bars and loitering on the streets was a source of concern for the regime since such behaviors undermined the socialist code of ethics and the productivist ethos around which socialist citizenship was constituted. Meanwhile, with respect to sexual behavior, socialist experts warned against premarital sex for girls and boys alike, though girls were to exercise special caution given their reproductive capabilities. Moreover, it was girls alone who were punished for deviating from such prescriptions, facing school expulsion and stigmatization by family and the larger community if, for example, they became pregnant in high school. Additionally, in light of the sexual double standard, the general culture of silence within the family about sexuality, and the lack of legislation against sexual harassment, female youth had little recourse in the face of harassment or assault by teenage boys or adult men. Finally, non-heteronormative behavior was criminalized and medicalized, with physicians presenting same-sex relations as aberrant, a view that reinforced broader cultural attitudes. Thus, the moralizing discourse and punitive practices of the regime in matters sexual dovetailed with broader social beliefs regarding female promiscuity and homosexuality.

Despite these contradictions and ambiguities, many of my respondents recalled their childhoods fondly, stressing parents' crucial role in shielding them from difficulties to ensure their upbringing was more or less normal. Indeed, many emphasized that they lived "normally." Similarly, in her analysis of Romanians' reflections of their childhoods under late socialism, Diana Georgescu found that most stressed the normality of their lives. Such representations, she argues, are not simply or necessarily nostalgic, but, more significantly, responses to postsocialist representations that have portrayed the communist past as abnormal. Accordingly, for these individuals, presenting their lives as normal is a means of claiming personal dignity, while also presenting alternative interpretations of the past.[158] As explored in this chapter, these normal aspects of life included trips to the Black Sea and the mountains, reading, listening to music or watching videos with friends, and spending time with extended family in the countryside. While recollections of childhood as normal and enjoyable are certainly based in truth, like other life stories, these are necessarily partial, reflecting events and incidents that individuals chose to share with the researchers. Therefore, traumatic or depressing episodes may have been left out of such narratives.

As children matured and especially as they entered adolescence, their understanding of the regime and socialist society became more nuanced and critical. This stemmed from discussions with family and friends, Radio Free Europe broadcasts, personal experiences of corruption and favoritism, and, by the 1980s, the precipitous decline in the standard of living. For Irina this was most palpable in the heat shortages and frozen paintbrushes in her school's art room, as well as in her strolls through Bucharest after Ceauşescu began demolishing parts of the city to construct a new building for the Romanian Parliament, *Casa Poporului* (People's House):

> My feelings were more profound, and I resigned myself to this fate ... that we cannot do anything, that everything is very gray and there's not much hope. And when I saw the Sfânta Vineri Church being destroyed, and then, when I didn't see those other buildings ... it was shocking. And it was dark and gray, and this emptiness. It was like you used to see a whole person and now you only see their legs.[159]

Irina's recollections of the 1980s poignantly capture the despair and resignation shared by many Romanians at this time. While adulthood is usually greeted with excitement and hope, though also some trepidation, the future for many youths in late-socialist Romania appeared bleak and hopeless. Irina's recollections bear a resemblance to the melancholic portrayal of everyday life in the Romanian film *The Way I Spent the End of the World,* which depicts the final years of Ceauşescu's rule through the lives of a teenage girl and her younger brother.[160] Like the adults in her midst, Eva, the female protagonist, resigns herself to the realities of everyday life: the split between public and private life; the shortages; the bombastic rhetoric; the gray landscape, viewing them simply as normal aspects of life under socialism. That is, until she plans to escape over the Yugoslav border, a route taken, usually unsuccessfully, by other Romanians at the time and which she decides against at the eleventh hour. Yet, while it may have appeared to Irina and Eva that "everything would be forever" soon it would, in fact, "be no more," as both experienced the collapse of socialism during their youth. Indeed, youth would not only experience the revolution of 1989, but also be among its most active participants, illustrating that even resignation had its limits. Ceauşescu's children would ultimately contribute to Ceauşescu's demise.

## Notes

1. Youth is defined here as individuals from seven to eighteen years of age. As noted in the introduction, my respondents were born between 1924 and 1972; therefore, the youngest among them were adolescents during part or most of the 1980s.
2. Alexandra Kollontai, *Selected Writings of Alexandra Kollantai*. Translated and edited by Alix Holt (London: Allison and Busby, 1977), 287–88.
3. *The Woman Question: Selections from the Writings of Karl Marx, Frederick Engels, V.I. Lenin and J.V. Stalin* (New York: International Publishers, 1975), 71.
4. This was especially distressing for the imprisoned individual as they knew their families would suffer as a result of being affiliated with an "enemy of the people." See Cosmin Budeancă, "Divorțul în familiile foștilor deținuți politici," in *Stat și viață privată în regimurile comuniste*, ed. Cosmin Budeancă and Florentin Olteanu (Iași: Polirom, 2009), 161–72.
5. Ruxandra, interview with author, Bucharest, 5 June 2012. Her grandfather was sent to the Black Sea Canal, where he died in 1953.
6. Luana, interview with author, Brașov, 25 July 2003.
7. Tudora, interview with author, Bucharest, 29 May 2009.
8. Smaranda, interview with author, Bucharest, 15 June 2009.
9. Indeed, to ensure that their children's educational futures would not be jeopardized by association with their fathers, some women actually divorced their imprisoned husbands and reverted to their maiden name, which they then bestowed upon their children. Budeancă, "Divorțul în familiile foștilor deținuți politici."
10. Luana, interview with author, Brașov, 25 July 2003.
11. Commuting remained a common practice in Romania (as elsewhere in the Bloc) throughout the communist period, with commuters constituting more than one one-quarter of the labor force in 1970—a figure that continued to increase. See William Moskoff, "Sex Discrimination, Commuting and the Role of Women in Romanian Development," *Slavic Review* 37, no. 3 (1978), 443.
12. D., interview with author, Brașov, 14 July 2003.
13. CAP employees received some of the lowest wages, lower than the average income for an agricultural laborer. Consequently, they were most likely to migrate or commute to industrial towns or cities to supplement their incomes.
14. Axinia, interview with author, Râmnicu Vâlcea, 10 June 2012.
15. Doina, interview with author, Brașov, 10 June 2003.
16. Iuliana, interview with author, Brașov, 7 July 2003.
17. Maria, interview with author, Brașov, 15 June 2003.
18. Eva, interview with author, Brașov, 12 June 2003. According to the Romanian system, the highest mark one could get was a ten, with a four or five being considered mediocre at best.
19. D., interview with author, Brașov, 23 June 2003.

20. *Cutezătorii* was published from 1967 to 1989 and was preceded by *Pionierul* (The Pioneer; 1949–1953) which was renamed *Scânteia Pionierului* (The Pioneer's Spark; 1953–1967). In 1969, *Racheta Cutezătorilor*, a supplement to *Cutezătorii* that focused on technical and scientific subjects, was published on a monthly basis. Students were required to subscribe to *Cutezătorii*, which was distributed in class.
21. Valeria R., interview with author, Braşov, 2 May 2003.
22. Veronica Szabo found a report by the Center for Research on Youth titled "Delinquency among youth in the Romanian Socialist Republic of 1968," which indicated that criminal behavior among youth increased 3.8 times between 1963 and 1968. See Veronica Szabo, "Youth and Politics in Communist Romania (1980–1989)" (PhD diss., University of Pittsburgh, 2012), 102.
23. See Mihai Stoian, *Râmîn părinţii repetenţi? Dilemele adulţilor* (Bucharest: Editura Tineretului, 1968), 52–53. The book examined children in a range of living situations and provided excerpts of interviews with youth and parents.
24. Ibid.
25. The survey revealed that only 5 percent of the families ate two meals each day with their children and only 2 percent regularly went on walks with them. See Mihai Stoian, *Adolescenta: o primejdie?* (Bucharest: Editura Didactică şi Pedagogică, 1968), 34.
26. See Madigan Fichter, "Rock and Roll Nation: Counterculture and Dissent in Romania, 1965–1975," *Nationalities Papers* 39, no. 4 (2011): 567–85; and Szabo, "Youth and Politics."
27. Diana Georgescu, "Ceauşescu's Children: The Making and Unmaking of the Last Socialist Generation (1965–2010)" (PhD diss., University of Illinois, 2015), 156.
28. "Decretul nr. 175/1948 pentru reformă Învăţământului," art.1, *Monitorul Oficial al Republicii Populare Romîne*, 116, nr. 177.
29. In 1948 approximately 29 percent of the population was illiterate. See Bogdan Murgescu, *România şi Europa: Acumularea decalajelor economice, 1500–2010* (Bucharest: Polirom, 2010), 386.
30. Dinu C. Giurescu, "Învăţământul României între anii 1948 şi 1949," November 2011, retrieved from http://www.ucv.ro/pdf/international/informatii_generale/doctor_honoris/68.pdf. (accessed 28 October 2016).
31. Cristian Vasile, "Propaganda and Culture in Romania at the Beginning of the Communist Regime," in *Stalinism Revisited: The Establishment of Communist Regimes in East-Central Europe*, ed. Vladimir Tismăneanu (Budapest: Central European University Press, 2009), 374.
32. Lavinia Ivaşcu, "Noi nu am fost oameni, că am fost chiaburi: Mărturii privind colectivizarea în Maramureş," în *"Analele Sighet* 8, anii 1954–1960," (2000), 308.
33. "Directiva Biroului Politic al CC al PMR cu privire la măsurile necesare pentru îmbunătăţirea compoziţiei de clasă a elevilor şi studenţilor," nr. 36 din 4 august, 1949. Accordingly, students were given a "political certificate" (*certificat politic*), which identified their social category.

34. Vlad Pașca, "Educația în România comunistă: un joc cu sumă nulă," in *Marginalități, periferii, și frontiere simbolice identitare: Societatea comunistă și dilemele sale identitare*, ed. Luciana Jinga and Ștefan Bosomitu, *Anuarul IICCMER*, vol. IX (2014) (Iași: Polirom, 2015), 87.
35. Livia Sicoie-Coroi, ed., *Colectivizarea agriculturii în raionul Brad: mărturii*, vol. I (Cluj-Napoca: Argonat, 2010), 287–88.
36. Marius Cazan and Vlad Pașca, "Lupta de clasă la porțile facultăților: Politici de promovare socială prin învățământ în epoca Gheorghiu-Dej (1948–1965)," in *Politici culturale și modele intelectuale în România*, ed. Lucian Nastasă and Dragoș Sdrobiș (Cluj-Napoca: Editura Mega, 2013), 266–69. In order to continue schooling, some children were adopted by relatives or changed their names.
37. Ruxandra, interview with author, Bucharest, 8 June 2012.
38. Doru Radosav, "Omul nou în comunism ca istorie trăită: copilăria," in *Proiectul uman comunist: de la discursul ideologic la realitățile sociale*, ed. Vasile Boari, Alexandru Câmpeanu, and Sergiu Gherghina (Cluj: Presa Universitară Clujeană, 2011)," 273.
39. Giurescu, "Învățământul României."
40. More than ten thousand teachers were assigned to the countryside between 1948 and 1949. Vasile, "Propaganda and Culture in Romania," 377.
41. Cazan and Pașca, "Lupta de clasă," 277. This provided a pretext for the regime to initiate another purge of teachers.
42. Domnica, interview with author, Brașov, 22 June 2003.
43. This changed in 1961 when having a "good file" was no longer a determining factor for university admission.
44. See *Anuarul Statistic al Republicii Populare Romîne*; and *Anuarul Statistic al Republicii Socialiste România, 1967–1989*. Direcția Centrală de Statistică (Bucharest, 1958; 1967–1989).
45. Ibid.
46. Thirteen-year-old Pavlik Morozov became a Soviet martyr after allegedly being killed by his family for turning his father into the authorities.
47. Under the 1948 education law, beginning in the fourth grade Russian language was compulsory.
48. Valeria P., interview with author, Brașov, 5 May 2003.
49. Simona Preda, *Patrie Română, țară de eroi!* (Bucharest: Curtea Vehce, 2014), 64. Officially titled the "Declaration on the Main Problems of the World Communist Movement," the "April Declaration" challenged the USSR's privileged role in the Eastern Bloc and promoted independent paths to communism. Dej asserted: "There is not and cannot be a 'parent' party and an 'offspring' party, parties that are 'superior' and parties that are 'subordinate'; rather there is a great family of Communist and workers' parties which have equal rights." See Gheorghe Gheorghiu-Dej, *Declarație cu privire la poziția Partidului Muncitoresc Român în problemele mișcării comuniste și muncitorești internaționale, adoptată de Plenara lărgită a C.C. al P.M.R. din aprilie 1964* (Bucharest: Editura Politică, 1964), 55.
50. "Legea nr. 11/1968 privind învățămîntul în Republica Socialistă Romana," *Monitorul Oficial al României*, nr. 62, 13 mai, 1968. As a result of this law,

schooling was fully subsidized by the state, including room and board, and previously banned disciplines were reintroduced. Randolph Braham, *Education in Romania: A Decade of Change* (Washington, DC: Office of Education and Institute of International Studies, 1972), 17.

51. This approach was influenced by studies of the American and various European educational systems. Georgescu, "Ceauşescu's Children," 73; 78–80.
52. Ibid.
53. According to Vernoica Szabo's interviews with teachers, this could involve teaching Marxism by emphasizing Hegel. See Szabo "Youth and Politics," 34.
54. Luana, interview with author, Braşov, 25 July 2003. Roller's *Istoria României: Manuel unic pentru clasa a XI-a medie* (Bucharest, 1947) was introduced in 1947 and was the only official textbook of Romanian history permitted until 1965.
55. C., interview with author, Braşov, 14 July 2003.
56. The July Theses encompassed seventeen proposals, including emphasis on the leading role of the party; engagement in various types of patriotic work; the intensification of political-ideological education in schools, universities, and youth organizations; and increased propaganda efforts. It also involved the reversal of earlier liberalizations in the cultural sphere, the banning of certain authors, and a return to socialist realism. Nicolae Ceauşescu, *Propuneri de măsuri pentru îmbunătăţirea activităţii politico-ideologice, de educare marxist-leninistă a membrilor de partid, a tuturor oamenilor muncii, 6 iulie 1971* (Bucharest, 1971).
57. Preda, *Patrie Română*, 65.
58. Florina, interview with author, Braşov, 7 June 2003.
59. D., interview with author, Braşov, 23 June 2003.
60. *Programul Partidului Comunist Romậm de făurire a societăţii socialiste multilaterale dezvoltate şi înaintare a României spre comunism* (Bucharest: Editura Politică, 1975).
61. Maria, interview with author, Braşov, 15 June 2003.
62. "Combinatul Tinereţii," *Cutezătorii*, no. 9, 1974, 6–7.
63. Indeed, by 1989, one out of every two people with an advanced degree was an engineer. Paşca, "Educaţia în România comunistă," 184.
64. See Georgescu, "Ceauşescu's Children," 77–78.
65. "Scientific fields" was a collective statistic for the purposes of measurement and record keeping. Figures taken from Luciana Jinga, *Gen şi reprezentare în România comunistă, 1944–1989* (Iaşi: Polirom, 2015), 227, 232.
66. Mihai Stoian, "Mama," *Cutezătorii*, no. 46, 1974, 4.
67. Pop Simon, "Prietenul meu Ly," *Cutezătorii*, no. 1, 1967, 12.
68. See Ecaterina Roşca, "Milioane de copii fără copilărie," *Cutezătorii*, no. 7, 1976, 8. The article, "Unul din 52 milioane de copii, victime ale exploatării" (One of the 52 Million Exploited Children) profiled the difficult lives of child laborers around the world, including in Europe.
69. *Cutezătorii*, no. 27, 1971.
70. 1979 was the UN "Year of the Child."

71. On the happy, healthy, and well-educated child as a barometer of ideological superiority during the Cold War, see Margaret Peacock, *Innocent Weapons: The Soviet and American Politics of Childhood in the Cold War* (Chapel Hill: University of North Carolina Press, 2014).
72. See "Tinerețe și eroism," *Cutezătorii*, no. 12, 1974, 10–11; and "Copii și Adolescenți: participanți la războiul antihitlerist," *Cutezătorii*, no. 34, 1968, 4.
73. "Ecaterina Teodoroiu," *Cutezătorii*, no. 14, 1968, 8–9.
74. "Curajul," *Cutezătorii*, no. 1, 1967, 6.
75. Anghel Manolache, "Munca: Izvor de Bucurie și Împliniri," *Cutezătorii*, no. 2, 1977, 3.
76. Cornel Stan, "Asemeni Comuniștilor, să fim mereu în frunte," *Cutezătorii*, no. 20, 1974, 3.
77. Irina, interview with author, Bucharest, 8 June 2009.
78. Moreover, the orphans to which Irina referred might have been the offspring of women who died of botched abortions, further underscoring the hypocrisy of the regime's commitment to children and the family.
79. Nicolae Teodorescu, "România anului 2000," *Cutezătorii*, December, no. 14, 1967.
80. Dr. Prof. Univ. Edmond Nicolau, "Școala viitorului: Sub semnul ciberneticii," *Cutezătorii*, no. 37, 1968, 4–5.
81. See Georgescu, "Ceaușescu's Children," 4; 182–88.
82. According to Dragoș Petrescu, the movie was "instrumental in forging the national identity of the majority of Romanians" during this period. See Dragoș Petrescu, "Communist Legacies in the 'New Europe': History, Ethnicity, and the Creation of a 'Socialist' Nation in Romania, 1945–1989" in *Conflicted Memories: Europeanizing Contemporary Histories* ed., Konrad H. Jarausch, Thomas Lindenberger, and Annelie Ramsbrock (New York: Berghahn Books, 2007): 47–48. *Mihai Viteazul*, directed by Sergiu Nicolaescu (1969: România Film).
83. Given the fact that the Romanian leadership had begun reorienting the country toward the West, celebrating Soviet exploits in space was noteworthy as the strip on Gagarin appeared in the magazine in 1968, followed by a feature on the U.S. moon landing in 1969.
84. This comic strip was entitled *Întîlnire în Spațiu* (Encounters in Space). See *Cutezătorii*, no. 37, 1968.
85. See *Cutezătorii*, no. 40, 1970.
86. "Pe ruta: București-Copenhagen-Odense cu Eugenia Noje, cîștigătoare a concursului 'Pretutindeni trăiesc copii' Unicef-Cutezătorii," *Cutezătorii*, no. 43, 1973. The competition was sponsored by UNICEF and *Cutezătorii*.
87. "Cum sa ne Îmbrăcăm?," *Cutezătorii*, no. 5, 1971, 22.
88. "Pagina Fetelor," *Cutezătorii*, no. 9, 1971, 14.
89. See Jinga, *Gen și reprezentare*, 142; and the forum, authored by then Minister of Youth (and post-socailist president of Romania) Ion Iliescu, "Sunt pregătite pentru viață tinerele fete?" *Femeia*, May 1968, 12.
90. See Raluca Ioana Horea-Șerban and Marinela Istrate, "Rolul presei scrise în promovarea politicii pronataliste," in *După 25 de ani Comunismul în*

*Europa de Est: Statutul Femeii în România Comunistă: Politici publice și viață privată,* ed. Alina Hurubean (Iași: Institutul European, 2015), 152.
91. Valeria R., interview with author, Brașov, 2 May 2003.
92. Adriana, interview with author, Bucharest, 3 June 2012.
93. D., interview with author, Brașov, 2 July 2003.
94. See Eugen Stancu, "Engineering the Human Soul: Science Fiction in Communist Romania (1955–1989)" (PhD diss., Central European University, 2011).
95. For samples of children's poetry, see *Cutezătorii*, no. 24, 1969, 12–13; for additional poetry and graphic art, see no. 15, 1970, 8–9. For a discussion of youth's participation in these cultural practices, see Georgescu, "Ceaușescu's Children," chap. 3.
96. Elvira, interview with author, Brașov, 5 May 2003.
97. Irina, interview with author, Bucharest, 8 June 2009.
98. Valeria R., interview with author, Brașov, 2 May 2003.
99. Preda, *Patrie Română*, 271.
100. On these visits see Georgescu, "Ceaușescu's Children," chap. 4.
101. Membership in the Pioneers in 1949, the year after it was founded, was 13,500. By the 1980s that figure was 2.5 million. Preda, *Patrie Română*, 29.
102. See Virgiliu Radulian, "Raportul de activitate al Consiliului Naținoal al Organizației Pionierilor privind activitaea desfășurata in perioda noiembrie 1966—octombrie 1971," in *Educația pioniereasca* 11 November 1971, 15. As quoted in Georgescu, "Ceaușescu's Children," 65. In 1976, an organization for children aged four to six was established: Șoimii Patriei (The Motherland Falcons).
103. While structured around a national or historical theme, Pioneer expeditions, because they were not mandated by the state, offered spaces for teachers to engage students in exciting adventures in which ideology need not play a central role. Consequently, expeditions were often genuinely enjoyable for students and teachers alike. See Georgescu, "Ceaușescu's Children," chap. 4. For an early article about these expeditions in the socialist press, see "Expediția Cutezătorii Munților," *Cutezătorii*, no. 27, 1968, 4–5.
104. During these expeditions, students were assigned different tasks: diarist, photographer, ethnographer, historian, archaeologist, geologist, and botanist.
105. Valeria R., interview with author, Brașov, 2 May 2003.
106. Maria, interview with author, Brașov, 15 June 2003.
107. Angela, interview with author, Brașov, 16 June 2003.
108. According to *Femeia*, this sense of pride was shared by parents of Pioneers, who felt the organization played an important role in character formation and in children's patriotic and political education. See Eleana Alexeni, "Copilul meu a depus azi legămîntul de pionier," *Femeia*, January 1972.
109. Adriana, interview with author, Bucharest, 3 June 2012.
110. Alina, interview with author, Bucharest, 31 May 2012.
111. Szabo, "Youth and Politics," 125.
112. Irina, interview with author, Bucharest, 8 June 2009. Irina's cultural horizons were also enriched by way of her father's job as an actor at the National Theater, which enabled her to attend performances at will.

113. According to Bogdan Murgescu, subscriptions were typically acquired through connections. See the interview with Bogdan Murgescu in Ciprian Plăiaşu, "Între filmele difuzate de Cinematecă în perioada comunistă erau multe care ideologic băteau în orice alte direcţii decât ar fi bătut învăţătura de partid," *Historia*, retrieved from https://www.historia.ro/sectiune/general/articol/intre-filmele-difuzate-de-cinemateca-in-perioada-comunista-erau-multe-care-ideologic-bateau-in-orice-alte-directii-decat-ar-fi-batut-invatatura-de-partid (accessed 11 November 2017).
114. Ruxandra, interview with author, Bucharest, 8 June 2012.
115. Clara, interview with author, Bucharest, 15 June 2015.
116. Videos were smuggled into Romania by individuals who traveled abroad (e.g. pilots, foreign students, high-ranking politicians) and by those who lived near the Hungarian or Yugoslav border and engaged in cross-border trading.
117. Constantin Pârvulescu and Emanuel Copilaş, "Hollywood Peeks: The Rise and Fall of Videotheques in 1980s Romania," *East European Politics, Societies, and Cultures* 27, no. 2 (2013), 241.
118. Kit Gillet, "The voice that brought Hollywood films to communist Romania's TV screen," *The Guardian*, 25 December 2014, retrieved from https://www.theguardian.com/world/2014/dec/25/hollywood-film-communist-romania-video-dub-irina-margareta-nistor (accessed 12 June 2017).
119. Simona, interview with Ioana Manoliu, Braşov, 11 August 2003.
120. Elena, interview with author, Bucharest, 1 June 2009.
121. C., interview with author, Braşov, 14 July 2003.
122. Maria, interview with author, Braşov, 15 June 2003.
123. Cici Ioradache, "Cîtă Libertate Acordăm Adolescentelor?" *Femeia*, February 1968, 36–37. According to the author, the article was inspired by letters from youth, aged sixteen to twenty, and based on a survey conducted with teenage girls and their parents in Bucharest.
124. Ibid.
125. Ibid.
126. Ibid.
127. See "Mama, prietena cea mai apropiata," in *Femeia*, March 1964, 16–17.
128. A number of books on the topics of intergenerational relations and adolescence were published during this time. See, for example, *Adolescenta: o primejdie*; Mihai Stoian, *Generaţia '62: Reportaje* (Bucharest: Editura Militară, 1963); and Rodica Ciurea, *Conflict între generaţii?* (Bucharest: Editura Enciclopedică Română, 1969).
129. Dorel Dorian, "Părinţi, cum vă creşteţi băieţii?," *Femeia*, July 1968.
130. Gabriela Ionescu, "Unde Fugi, Tina?," *Femeia*, December 1970, 16–17. Topics in the "Pagina Ta" (Your Page) and "Pagina Tinerilor" (Youth Page) sections ranged from showcasing heroine workers and female sports champions to exploring issues that were of interest to female youth such as love, schooling, and leisure activities.
131. Ibid.
132. Similar concerns emerged during the Thaw period in the USSR. See Deborah A. Field, "Mothers and Fathers and the Problems of Selfishness

in the Khrushchev Period," *Women in the Khrushchev Era*, ed. Melanie Ilić, Susan E. Reid, and Lynne Attwood (Basingstoke: Palgrave, 2004), 98.
133. "Decret nr. 153 din 24 martie 1970 pentru stabilirea şi sancţionarea unor contravenţii privind regulile de convieţuire socială, ordinea, şi linişte publica," *Bulentinul Ofical* nr. 33, 13 aprilie 1970.
134. It should be noted, however, that students could not be charged with social parasitism.
135. *Codul principiilor şi normelor muncii şi vieţii comuniştilor, ale eticii şi echităţii socialiste* (Editura Politică, 1974).
136. ANIC, CC al PCR, Secţia Cancelarie, dosar 176/1970, f. 21, 40.
137. "Informare cu privire la acţiunile de combatere a parazitismului şi manifestărilor de încălcare a normeleror eticii şi echităţii socialiste în municipalul Bucureşti, Braşov, şi judeţul Constanţa," ANIC, CC al PCR, Secţia Organizatorică, dosar 37/1974, ff. 17–18 as cited in Mioara Anton, *"Ceauşescu şi poporul!" Scrisori către "iubitul conducător" (1965–1989)* (Târgovişte: Cetatea de Scaun, 2016), 200.
138. Quoted in Adriana Băban and Henry P. David, *Voices of Romanian Women: Perceptions of Sexuality, Reproductive Behavior, and Partner Relations During the Ceauşescu Era* (Washington, DC: Transnational Family Research Institute, 1994), 26.
139. C., interview with author, Braşov, 14 July 2003.
140. See Adriana Băban, "Women's Sexuality in Romania," in *Reproducing Gender: Politics, Publics, and Everyday Life after Socialism*, ed. Susan Gal and Gail Kligman (Princeton, NJ: Princeton University Press, 2002).
141. The only sex education adolescents received in school was "sanitary education," which focused on hygiene and physiology. Additionally, *Vita Sexualis*, a handbook on sexual life written during the interwar period, served as a medium for learning about sexuality, but the book was difficult to find. Mihaela Miroiu, conversation with author, November 2004.
142. For a discussion of the culture of shame and silence, as well as the lack of legal recourse against sexual harassment and assault in socialist Romania, see Maria Bucur, "Sex in the Time of Communism: The Ripple Effect of the #metoo Campaign," *Public Seminar*, 7 December 2017, retrieved from: http://www.publicseminar.org/2017/12/sex-in-the-time-of-communism/ (accessed 10 December 2017).
143. For example, in the 1970s, 78 percent of East German youth agreed fully or partially with the statement: "I instinctively disapprove of sexual contact between men." See Josie McLellan, *Love in the Time of Communism: Intimacy and Sexuality in the GDR* (Cambridge: Cambridge University Press, 2011), 48.
144. Elisabeta Moraru, "Falsă pudoare pseudocunostinţe," *Femeia*, August 1968.
145. Dr. M. Caza, "Dialog intim cu fiica mea," *Femeia*, December 1966, 28.
146. Ibid.
147. See Radu Dimitriu, *De vorbă cu tinerii: probleme de educaţie a sexelor* (Bucharest: Editura Tineretului, 1972), 55.
148. Ibid., 11.

149. Vladimir Il'ich Lenin *The Emancipation of Women: From the Writings of V.I. Lenin* (New York: International Publishers, 1969), 107–8.
150. Dimitriu, *De vorbă cu tinerii*, 160–61.
151. The author also asserted that engaging in sports can reduce nocturnal emissions; ibid., 145–146.
152. Ibid., 76–77.
153. Harsanyi, "Women in Romania," in Funk and Muller, eds., *Gender Politics and Post-communism*, 47.
154. McLellan, *Love in the Time of Communism*, 30–33.
155. D., interview with author, Brașov, 14 July 2003.
156. Irina, interview with author, Bucharest, 8 June 2009.
157. Szabo, "Youth and Politics," 74–78.
158. Georgescu, "Ceaușescu's Children," 339–400.
159. Irina, interview with author, Bucharest, 8 June 2009.
160. *Cum mi-am petrecut sfârșitul lumii*, directed by Cătălin Mitulescu (2006: Strada, Romania Films).

CHAPTER 3

# Career Opportunities
## Gender, Work, and Identity

> Everyone worked. In the first place, it was policy to create jobs for women to enter into the labor force, in the second place, because a man's salary was not enough to support a family, to provide the basic necessities for a family.
> 
> —Rodica, legal expert (b. 1956)

> It was like a dream. I absolutely loved it ... they [the schools] were excellent; they taught children how to respect old people, to keep things tidy, to not break things. I sat and laughed with my coworkers, told jokes about Ceaușescu.
> 
> —Maria, former primary school teacher and school inspector (b. 1932)

These quotes offer two different visions of work under socialism. According to Rodica, work was a policy initiative and propaganda tool: a medium through which the state sought to garner support by promoting women's economic autonomy. At the same time, work was a pragmatic response to economic need, underscoring the fact that wages remained low and two salaries were necessary for sustaining a family. Meanwhile, for Maria work was personally fulfilling and socially meaningful—a source of satisfaction and a site of joviality. In her view, work was much more than a paycheck; it was also a basis upon which self-identity was fashioned and a community was formed. Taken together, these quotes reflect different memories of work under socialism, demonstrating that while for some women work was simply a means to an end, a routine; for others it was transformative; a source of fulfillment and enjoyment, and a place for grousing about the regime.

This chapter explores state efforts to promote women into the labor force through policy and propaganda, placing this analysis within the larger context of socialist work cultures, labor relations, and women's everyday experiences.[1] Both a right and a duty, work was the basic determinant of socialist citizenship, a medium through which the individual and society were to be transformed. It was also the basis upon which, according to Marxist theory, women would achieve full liberation. Accordingly, it was under the universal category of worker that women and men were to become equals. However, socialist ideology diverged from practice, producing ambiguities in how women were codified and represented as workers—and in how women actually experienced this aspect of their lives. Despite being represented as equal workers, women were often treated differently, both in legislation and by male coworkers. For example, in an effort to reconcile women's roles as workers and mothers, the state instituted protective legislation and maternity leave, which, while in some respects beneficial, also limited women to certain jobs. Moreover, in the 1970s, on the heels of pronatalist policies, the state began channeling women into areas deemed more compatible with their maternal capacities, contributing further to the gendering of the labor force. As such, the workplace offered opportunities for social advancement and empowerment, but could also serve to institutionalize difference and reinforce gender hierarchies.

Just as gender influenced state directives and labor policies, so too it influenced ideas about skill and hiring and training practices. In particular, managers in male-dominated fields typically preferred hiring men, viewing them as more competent, responsible, and less beholden to household responsibilities than women. Meanwhile, those women who did make it into male-dominated fields often struggled to demonstrate their competence and maintain their dignity in hostile work environments. While some women successfully challenged workplace sexism and asserted themselves as equal laborers, they were in the minority. Consequently, labor practices reflected popular ambivalence about women's capabilities in the productive sphere. This ambivalence was directly related to traditional ideas about gender and skill and conceptions of the industrial worker.

Yet, work was characterized not only by contradictory labor codes and male prejudice; it was also a vehicle for social and personal transformation. As such, work shaped women's life trajectories, identities, and relations with men. For some women, work was burdensome and unfulfilling, especially for those unable to enter jobs of their choosing due to social origin or discrimination. Meanwhile, for others it was empowering and personally validating. Indeed, on a very basic level, work broadened women's social and cultural worlds, luring them away from the countryside and into industrial towns and cities. These realities, coupled with the monetary benefits of work, offered women alternative identities, new ways of imagining their place in society, and a sense of accomplishment. Additionally, through workplace trade unions, employees could access an array of services and benefits (e.g. free medical care, subsidized meals at canteens, low-interest loans for housing and household durables, and vouchers for travel and leisure activities), which, despite their shortcomings, improved people's quality of life.[2] In sum, women's experiences in the labor force were diverse and ambiguous, shaped by a range of factors from the nature of the job and level of remuneration to relations with coworkers and their facility in reconciling workplace and family responsibilities.

## Peasants into Workers

At the time of the communist takeover Romania was predominantly rural, with only 23.4 percent of the population officially registered as urban.[3] Moreover, in 1948 industrial workers constituted a mere 10 percent of the active population.[4] In this respect, Romania lagged not only behind the West but most of Eastern Europe as well. Thus, the development of a bona fide industrial working class was essential not only for economic modernization but for legitimating socialism. As in the USSR in the 1930s, industrialization required drawing on all able-bodied individuals; therefore, women, constituting over half the population, represented a potentially enormous labor pool.

Although women's liberation through work was, officially, a major goal of all socialist states, rapid industrial development was key to socialist progress. Women's promotion into the labor force was thus primarily instrumental; motivated by the larger goal of economic modernization. Accordingly, the degree to which state pronouncements about women's equality reflected genuine commitment to female emancipation cannot be known with certainty. Regardless, by encouraging female employment the state could, theoretically, kill two birds with one stone: advance on a path of rapid industrialization while also promoting female liberation. Moreover, by expanding women's employment opportunities, the state could showcase its progressive gender politics and, by extension, the superiority of the socialist system to the world. Yet, while women's liberation was secondary or even peripheral to the larger goal of socialist modernization, this should not obscure the positive impact of working outside the home on women's status, identity, and sense of self-worth.

Mobilizing women into the labor force, however, was easier said than done. While work was nothing new for women—women had worked for centuries in farming, crafts, and other cottage industries—these jobs occurred in the larger domestic realm and did not threaten the traditional gender order. Under such circumstances, women could combine the responsibilities of children, household, and harvest, though it should be noted that most families lived in poverty and children were also expected to work. By the late nineteenth century, women increasingly worked in industry, particularly in textiles, tailoring, and millinery, and in a professional capacity in areas such as education, medicine, and state administration. Nonetheless, by the close of World War II women still constituted 50 percent of those working in agriculture, primarily as auxiliary laborers.[5] As such, preexisting notions about gender and labor continued to shape popular attitudes well into the postwar period.

Given the rural and patriarchal character of society, during the early years of socialist rule the notion of women working in industry, especially heavy industry, was jarring, a threat to traditional values, family organization, and work cultures. Like elsewhere in the Bloc, in Romania men were known to resist women's entry into paid labor, in some cases expressing their displeasure through verbal and physical violence.[6] Moreover, parents were reticent to let their daughters venture beyond the bounds of the family farm as work outside the home was considered improper for women—in some cases even associated with promiscuity. While it is unknown how many men were opposed to their wives or daughters working outside the home—or how many women themselves were resistant to it—one of my respondents was forbidden from leaving the family home for work until she married. Similarly, some families in Poland were unwilling to "give up their daughters" to socialist industry as this was deemed inappropriate and their labor was needed to support the family.[7] Such views were rooted in cultural ideas about proper gender norms and women's sexual propriety and the pragmatic need to keep female offspring at home to tend to domestic and agricultural duties. Beyond this, some women actually preferred working on the family plot to taking up paid labor outside the home. Given these factors, as well as the distance of factories from most villages, mobilizing women into paid labor was a gradual process that did not accelerate until the late 1960s.

How to get women into the labor force then? One approach was to create or exacerbate material desperation through low wages. In the case of Romania, this was not challenging given the material insecurity of the postwar period. In particular, rising food costs, the closure of factory stores, which had subsidized consumer goods, and stagnating or declining wages placed a heavy financial burden on families, forcing women into the labor force. In this manner, the state got two workers for the price of one. Women were also compelled to take up work because they had lost the support of a male breadwinner due to abandonment, death or injury in World War II, or due to imprisonment during the early years of socialist rule.[8] Finally, collectivization, which began in 1949, drove peasants into the labor force as families lost their land—and thus their means of survival—and many preferred working in a factory to working on a state or collective farm.

Although wages and salaries increased in the 1960s, they were typically based on a two-earner family. Therefore, maintaining a decent standard of living, and, indeed, even acquiring basic necessities, required two incomes. That said, while the early years of communist consolidation were an uncertain and unstable time for many, they were also a period of social revolution that turned peasants into workers. However, given state emphasis on rapid industrialization, certain workers, particularly miners and steel workers—almost all men—were privileged by the state and treated as a rich commodity. From the onset of socialist rule, then, many women were at a disadvantage within the labor force.

In addition to keeping wages low, the regime used ideology to persuade women to take up paid labor, invoking the imminent threat of war and emphasizing women's crucial role in safeguarding their children and the nation in the larger "struggle for peace" (*lupta pentru pace*). As a textile worker commented in *Scânteia* in 1951, "I still haven't forgotten the horrible war! We will do everything we can to stop the criminal hand of the American and English imperialists who want to spread the fire of war."[9] Articles also featured stories of wives and mothers whose "tears still have not dried" from the death of their husbands and sons in the war.[10] By presenting personal losses as national tragedies, propagandists attempted to parlay women's grief into support for socialist policy and encourage them to sacrifice for the nation. The needless death from fascist and capitalist-imperialist aggression, propagandists claimed, would only end with the triumph of socialism, which, in turn, required women's full participation in paid labor. Considered from this perspective, work would not only emancipate women but also engender a more peaceful world for themselves and their children. Highlighting women's selflessness and capacity for sacrifice signified an attempt to "familialize" work and make it less jarring to the gender order—approaches that were similarly followed in Poland and Hungary during the period.[11]

By presenting productive labor as both a civic and maternal responsibility and by lauding women workers in the press, the party attempted to fashion a socialist community devoted to peace and freedom. This imagined community was further forged by contrasting women's (supposed) superior position in the socialist Bloc with women in the West who, according to an article published in *Scânteia* in 1959, "make 50% less than men and have to resort to prostitution to feed their children."[12] By graphically describing the dismal lives of women in other, nonsocialist countries, the party created a yardstick by which women could evaluate their own lives—an "at least life isn't so bad in Romania" scenario. More insidiously, by highlighting capitalist barbarity and the constant threat of war, the party sought to deflect attention away from the repression, uncertainty, and material desperation of the early Dej years.

To further encourage women's entry into the workforce, the state passed a host of laws. For instance, the 1950 Labor Code outlined work as a right and obligation of all citizens and codified women's equality with men in all spheres of life, including equal pay for equal work, provisions which were also enshrined in the Constitution of 1948.[13] At the same time, the labor code included provisions for safeguarding women as mothers, protections that Bolshevik thinker and politician, Alexandra Kollontai, had, decades before, deemed essential for balancing productive and reproductive roles. Accordingly, Article 59 exempted pregnant women, nursing mothers, and youth under eighteen from overtime work. Additionally, Article 89 mandated that pregnant women employed in heavy labor be reassigned to lighter work without a concomitant decrease in their salary, while Article 91 mandated that women who were six months pregnant, along with nursing mothers, be exempted from night work.[14] The state also granted women thirty-five days prenatal and forty-five days (with possible extension to fifty-five days) postnatal maternity leave, as well as a half-hour nursing break for every three hours they worked.[15] Finally, according to Article 93 of the code, women could extend their maternity leave to care for ill children until they reached age two (extended to age three in 1972).

Feminist scholars have criticized protective legislation for accentuating women's difference as workers and limiting their wages, occupational horizons, and individual agency.[16] While acknowledging the beneficial aspects of these protections, they argue that such gender-specific policies created a dual labor market wherein women were subordinated to men. Yet, by sparing women from arduous labor that could pose risks to their pregnancies, providing paid maternity leave, and, more importantly, protecting women's jobs while they took such leave, women were guaranteed an economic livelihood after giving birth.[17] As such, protective labor laws, in conjunction with subsidized childcare, expanded women's life choices, enabling them to combine work and family, which, in turn, enabled them to define their roles outside of the private sphere. It also allowed them to contribute to the family in a quantifiable manner, which could lead to a refashioning of spousal roles—or even provide women with the financial wherewithal to leave an unhappy marriage altogether.

In this respect, the socialist welfare state was considerably more progressive than states that were organized around the male breadwinner model and did not incentivize women's roles as workers *and* mothers. At the same time, over the course of socialist rule concern about "protecting women" restricted them from more jobs in heavy industry, including those that were the most prized by the state and garnered the highest wages. Consequently, protective labor legislation also affected women's earning power, opportunities for promotion and advancement, and, ultimately, their monthly retirement income. While restrictive labor laws were also in force in the West, in socialist states these laws coexisted with media representations emphasizing women's equality with men in all spheres. By prohibiting women from working in certain areas, then, the state compromised its commitment to women's full equality. More significantly, references to women's biological functions in early labor codes, historian Luciana Jinga argues, laid the foundation for the reorganization of the labor force under Nicolae Ceaușescu, whereby women's difference from men (i.e. reproductive capacities) determined what types of jobs they were most suited for and thus could be employed in.[18]

Despite the passage of maternity leave and other policies designed to accommodate working mothers, work schedules were not fundamentally reorganized, with the result that women did not (or could not) fully avail themselves of their rights as working mothers. For instance, while all my respondents took the designated maternity leave— in some cases substantially extending it—none took nursing breaks, either because the enterprise at which they worked did not have on-site childcare or because travel to the crèche or family home was too time-consuming. This was especially the case for women who commuted to job sites, a practice that continued until the collapse of communist rule. Prioritization of production over welfare entitlements (e.g. on-site childcare) and, until the 1970s, lack of options for part-time work thus undermined woman-friendly efforts to accommodate women's roles as workers and mothers.

More generally, women's need for workplace flexibility, because of their caregiving responsibilities, made them less attractive to bosses, not only for the purpose of promotion but also retention. While the degree to which female laborers experienced challenges reintegrating into the labor force after having children is unknown, in Romania, as in other parts of the Bloc, this transition was by no means universally smooth.[19] Indeed, a 1956 article in *Femeia* even acknowledged that factory directors had nullified women's contracts after they had returned from maternity leave, though the author also emphasized that these were "exceptional cases."[20] None of my respondents claimed to have faced such problems, however, one criticized the fact that maternity leave (which in her case amounted to two years) reduced her overall pension. Moreover, some claimed that they experienced subtle forms of discrimination upon returning from leave, such as being lower on the promotion list and even demoted to a lesser-ranking job. Thus, the socialist notion of "equality through protection" underscored another ambiguity of socialist modernization: the disparity between women's official representation as equal workers and their codification as a particular category of workers warranting special treatment, which bosses could interpret in ways that were not always favorable to women.[21]

## Constructing the Woman Worker

During the early years of regime consolidation and rapid industrialization, when all domains were open to women, articles in socialist media profiled female tractor drivers, welders, smelters, and lathe operators, presenting them as agents of modernization and symbols of female emancipation. In this capacity, the party aimed not only to increase the labor force and foster loyalty to the state, but also to challenge sexist arguments regarding women's lack of physical strength and skill. As Valeria P., a former nurse, wryly recounted about such propaganda, "There was Mița the tractor driver, there is even a song [about her] ... she was very robust: was able to work three shifts. She was also a heroine mother who had ten children. She received diplomas, medals, she probably also received money."[22]

While Mița was more fiction than fact, such heroine workers (*muncitoare fruntașe*) became yardsticks for women's productive achievements, part of the legitimating myth of both socialism and female liberation. Every March 8 (International Women's Day) heroine workers were honored in workplace celebrations during which they received the *Ordinul Muncii* (Order of Labor) medal, a modest material award, and were, in some cases, privileged for housing and other workplace entitlements. Additionally, their name, place of origin, and production levels appeared in the local, and, for the lucky few, national newspaper. Heroine workers also "wrote" short, autobiographical sketches, charting their journey from shy, illiterate peasant girl to well-read, confident, and industrious factory director. Those written during the early years of socialist rule typically connected women's exploitation within the labor force to women's general oppression under capitalist patriarchy. As Elena Chişiu, a textile worker, wrote in the party daily, *Scânteia*, in 1952, "On this day of celebration for women everywhere, I cannot help but think back on my life in the past, a life of shortages and difficulties, in which we women were humiliated and treated as inferior to men, lacking the most elementary rights. For a minuscule salary, because any type of work performed by women was "considered cheaper," I was forced to work in unspeakably difficult conditions to enrich gluttonous bosses. Only under the people's democratic regime are we women able to know liberty, to rejoice in the rights that any citizen in our country has."[23] Acknowledging the manifold opportunities the government and party have provided her, including technical training and a visit to the USSR to observe women laborers, Elena adds, "My accomplishments have increased my faith in my abilities. Last year, I was decorated with the 'Order of Labor Medal' for my productive achievements. I felt very proud when I received such an honorable distinction, which the party and government bestow on those who demonstrate their commitment to the struggle for a brighter future for our dear country. ... Today I number among those workers in our country who carry the esteemed title of Stakhanovite."[24] By drawing a sharp distinction between prewar capitalist exploitation and postwar socialist emancipation, this scripted story highlighted socialism's decisive role in facilitating women's achievement, empowerment, and fulfillment. At the same time, it reminded readers that personal skill and diligence, while important, were insufficient for realizing one's productive capacity. Rather, the proper political and social conditions were also necessary for reaching one's full potential.

Such stories not only characterized the early period of communist consolidation, but remained a central component of the party's broader narrative about women's liberation through work. For example, in a 1965 *Femeia* article, Sanda Herghelegiu described her training as an electrician during the early Dej years, an occupation, she noted, that was formerly "reserved only for men." Within a mere six months, Sanda became one of the best workers in her group, for which she thanked "the Party and the Socialist Republic."[25] Although reminiscent of the American self-made-man stories, these socialist *Bildungsromanen* were distinctly different in that it was not capitalism but socialism that was the catalyst for success. Essentially a "socialist superwoman," the heroine worker was nonetheless presented as an everywoman: her ability to exceed quotas was not due to some genetic proclivity for hyperproductivity, but rather the result of diligence, devotion, and, of course, the Party. As such, she was an inspirational figure, a model that other women could emulate and draw strength from. More broadly, the narrative of the self-made woman was designed to highlight the modernity and progressiveness of socialist Romania—a strategy similarly employed in other parts of the Bloc. This was not all fiction, however, as the state's success in transforming peasants into workers was indeed impressive, as women constituted 20.9 percent of all registered workers in 1948, 26.7 percent in 1959, 29.7 percent in 1968, 35.6 percent in 1977, and 40.4 percent in 1989, figures which were similar to other countries in Eastern Europe.[26]

Although both men and women engaged in arduous labor and were lauded for their ability to fulfill and surpass the norms, these model socialist workers garnered different awards depending on the type of labor they performed. The state's drive to rapidly industrialize meant that workers in heavy industry were privileged over all other laborers and thus received the majority of second-class medals and some of the highest wages.[27] Meanwhile, female laborers typically received third-class medals, which were relatively insignificant from a material standpoint, and were less frequently acknowledged in the press.[28] While less handsomely rewarded, heroine workers were in fact more productive than their male counterparts, as they were expected to be both workers and mothers. Indeed, after Ceaușescu criminalized abortion in 1966, women's contributions as mothers were considered equal to, and, during certain periods, more important than their contributions as workers. Additionally, these roles were presented as mutually reinforcing, with articles in *Femeia* depicting women with children as more productive than their childless counterparts.[29]

Heroine workers symbolized women's capabilities in heavy industry, an area in which women made impressive inroads during the early part of socialist rule. For example, in 1956, 32,881 women were employed in heavy industry (working as fitters, welders, smelters, and lathe and machine operators), a figure that approximated their numbers in healthcare.[30] Nonetheless, their overall proportion within heavy industry was modest, and actually began declining in the 1970s as demographic concerns influenced the organization of the labor force. Thus, while women's overall share in industry witnessed substantial growth, increasing gradually from 23.3 percent in 1948 to 28.9 percent in 1967, and then soaring during the last two decades of socialist rule from 37 percent in 1976 to 43.1 percent in 1989, women tended to be concentrated in light industry.[31] Meanwhile, jobs most valued by the state such as construction and non-ferrous metallurgy remained stubbornly male-dominated, with women representing 8.7 percent and 11.5 percent (respectively) in these areas in 1974.[32] As elsewhere in Eastern Europe (and in the West for that matter), women were employed in jobs classified as unskilled or semi-skilled (e.g. quality control sorters, assembly-line workers), which were often monotonous and poorly remunerated.

The disparity between women and men in heavy industry was partially due to the fact that women were required to "qualify" (train) for certain vocations; however, given women's domestic responsibilities, they had little time to secure additional training through supplementary (typically evening) courses. Moreover, male prejudice about women working in heavy industry perpetuated a culture wherein instructors reluctantly allowed women to enroll in training courses—or even prohibited them from doing so. Accordingly, women's representation in heavy and skilled industry remained low.

In addition to heavy industry, the percentage of women in other male-dominated sectors of the economy such as transportation remained low and, in some cases, actually declined over the course of socialist rule (in transport women's presence declined from 23 percent in 1948 to around 10 percent for most of communist rule). In fact, women were actually prohibited from becoming sailors and pilots, even though they had previously demonstrated their competence in these jobs.

By contrast, women's presence in food services, clerical work, and traditionally female-dominated areas such as medicine and education expanded. So too did women's concentration in agriculture as men increasingly commuted to industrial towns and cities, while women stayed behind to work on the CAP (*Cooperativele Agricole Producție*; collective farms) and tend to their families. Indeed, by 1975, women constituted 60 percent of all agricultural laborers, contributing to the feminization of this area by the second half of socialist rule.[33] As previously noted, work on the CAP was poorly remunerated, especially for those employed seasonally, and since the country was more than 50 percent rural in 1977, women constituted a considerable portion of the lowest-paid workers in the labor force.[34] At the same time, agricultural labor provided a degree of flexibility, enabling women to balance work with childcare, which was essential if their husbands were away for long stretches.

The gendering of the labor force increased with the implementation of the 1972 Labor Code. While reaffirming much of the 1950 code and acknowledging women's equality with men with respect to work and wages, Article 14 of the code emphasized women's difference from men by referring to their maternal roles and responsibilities.[35] Accordingly, women were granted the possibility of working part-time until their child reached age six, and protective legislation was extended to all working women.[36] This was followed by promotional measures, introduced in 1973, designed to channel women into jobs more in line with state-defined "feminine qualities" (e.g. attentiveness, patience, capacity for caregiving) and those deemed most suitable for women (read: not potentially harmful to their reproductive health).[37] At the Central Committee meeting in June 1973, Ceaușescu explained the reasoning behind this initiative:

> We need to recognize, of course, that there are some areas and activities that are better for men to work in. In place of sending men into light industry, we direct them into heavier work, which requires greater physical capacity. Conversely, we should ensure conditions in which women work in jobs, which, from a physical standpoint, don't require extraordinary effort.[38]

By the early 1970s, then, essentialist ideas about women's capacities as laborers and demographic concerns decisively influenced women's occupational opportunities.[39] At the same time, it should be noted that "less physically taxing" did not necessarily mean less-fulfilling as this promotional scheme also included targets for increasing women's presence in science, technology, and leadership positions.[40] Compared to early industrial societies in which rural and working-class women had minimal opportunities for education, particularly higher education, in socialist Romania a range of jobs in science, electronics, and engineering opened up to women in the 1970s. Indeed, women's presence in the sciences grew steadily over the course of socialist rule, from 25.7 percent in 1956 to 36.5 percent in 1968 to 39.3 percent in 1979 to 44 percent in 1989, and women scientists were featured in *Femeia* already in the 1960s (see figure 3.2). Thus, while some of the jobs associated with the promotional program were entry-level, unskilled, and monotonous, requiring only minimal training, some were prestigious and intellectually fulfilling, requiring a university degree and advanced training.

As if to prepare readers for the reorganization of the labor force, in July 1970, *Femeia* published a debate among experts to determine if women were more suited to particular types of work. On one side of the debate, an industrial psychologist claimed that "women are more emotional" than men, and, therefore, "jobs in which emotion can be a danger cannot be performed by women," adding that men perform much better in stressful situations.[41] At the same time, he emphasized that "there are a number of other professions in which women are more adept than men. The more monotonous ones such as assembly

Figure 3.1. Women's Labor Force Participation Rates in Various Sectors of the Romanian Economy, 1948–89

| Year | Women as a Percentage of the Total Labor Force | Industry | Construction | Agriculture | Transportation | Telecommunications | Commerce and Food Services | Stocking and Collection of Produce/ Administering Commune Service | Education and Culture | Scientific Fields | Healthcare | State Administration |
|---|---|---|---|---|---|---|---|---|---|---|---|---|
| 1948 | 20.9 | 23.3 | 6.6 | | 23.8 | 42.8 | 26.9 | | | | | |
| 1956 | 41.8 | 28.5 | 9.5 | 45.0 | 14.5 | | 39.2 | 16.1 | 59.2 | 25.7 | 61.3 | 25.2 |
| 1957 | 37.1 | 25.5 | 9.9 | 23.2 | 14.1 | | 40.9 | 18.2 | 54.2 | | 64.1 | 24.6 |
| 1958 | 45.3 | 25.3 | 8.6 | 23.0 | 13.5 | | 41.5 | 19.9 | 54.6 | | 77.0 | 26.7 |
| 1959 | 26.7 | 24.7 | 8.7 | 23.2 | 13.1 | | 40.1 | 19.8 | 55.4 | | 65.3 | 24.7 |
| 1960 | 27.1 | 26.3 | 6.7 | 12.7 | 7.1 | 38.1 | 34.8 | 23.5 | 55.6 | 27.7 | 65.5 | 27.6 |
| 1961 | 27.4 | 26.8 | 7.2 | 11.8 | 7.0 | 37.8 | 35.9 | 24.9 | 55.5 | 30.1 | 64.8 | 27.6 |
| 1963 | 27.5 | 26.6 | 7.1 | 10.8 | 6.8 | 39.6 | 38.8 | 27.3 | 56.4 | 29.8 | 64.2 | 28.2 |
| 1964 | 27.5 | 26.5 | 7.3 | 10.6 | 7.2 | 40.9 | 39.8 | 27.7 | 57.2 | 32.0 | 64.6 | 28.8 |
| 1965 | 27.8 | 26.8 | 7.3 | 10.8 | 7.2 | 42.2 | 40.5 | 28.7 | 57.5 | 32.6 | 64.9 | 29.8 |
| 1966 | 28.4 | 27.8 | 7.7 | 10.9 | 7.6 | 43.6 | 41.6 | 28.7 | 58.7 | 33.3 | 65.5 | 31.1 |
| 1967 | 29.0 | 28.9 | 7.7 | 10.6 | 7.4 | 44.2 | 42.1 | 28.0 | 59.7 | 34.5 | 66.4 | 31.8 |
| 1968 | 29.7 | 29.8 | 8.0 | 10.9 | 7.7 | 44.0 | 42.6 | 26.7 | 59.9 | 36.5 | 67.0 | 31.8 |
| 1969 | 29.7 | 29.9 | 7.7 | 11.2 | 7.8 | 44.1 | 44.4 | 26.2 | 64.1 | 36.5 | 69.3 | 31.6 |
| 1970 | 30.2 | 28.9 | 7.9 | 11.9 | 7.7 | 45.2 | 46.5 | 27.6 | 60.3 | 38.9 | 69.1 | 30.9 |
| 1971 | 31.7 | 32.2 | 8.3 | 14.2 | 8.2 | 44.6 | 46.9 | 26.7 | 61.1 | 39.2 | 71.3 | 31.7 |

*(continued)*

| Year | Women as a Percentage of the Total Labor Force | Industry | Construction | Agriculture | Transportation | Telecommunications | Commerce and Food Services | Stocking and Collection of Produce/Administering Commune Service | Education and Culture | Scientific Fields | Healthcare | State Administration |
|---|---|---|---|---|---|---|---|---|---|---|---|---|
| 1972 | 32.2 | 33.3 | 8.5 | 14.0 | 8.3 | 46.5 | 48.5 | 29.1 | 62.0 | 38.7 | 71.5 | 32.3 |
| 1973 | 33.0 | 34.1 | 8.5 | 17.7 | 8.7 | 46.5 | 50.7 | 31.3 | 61.7 | 39.1 | 71.7 | 32.2 |
| 1974 | 33.0 | 35.2 | 8.7 | 14.3 | 8.8 | 49.0 | 50.8 | 31.0 | 63.3 | 37.2 | 72.0 | 33.5 |
| 1975 | 34.4 | 35.7 | 8.8 | 15.0 | 9.1 | 49.7 | 53.1 | 30.8 | 62.3 | 39.0 | 73.5 | 34.4 |
| 1976 | 35.4 | 37.0 | 9.2 | 15.4 | 9.5 | 49.8 | 53.9 | 31.9 | 64.3 | 39.6 | 72.3 | 34.7 |
| 1977 | 35.6 | 37.5 | 9.3 | 16.0 | 9.3 | 50.2 | 54.7 | 31.6 | 64.3 | 39.3 | 73.9 | 34.6 |
| 1978 | 36.2 | 38.9 | 9.7 | 16.6 | 9.7 | 49.4 | 55.5 | 31.5 | 63.9 | 40.6 | 73.4 | 35.4 |
| 1979 | 36.9 | 39.5 | 11.4 | 16.4 | 10.1 | 50.0 | 57.2 | 31.8 | 64.4 | 41.9 | 74.5 | 36.1 |
| 1980 | 37.2 | 40.3 | 11.5 | 16.1 | 10.3 | 50.7 | 57.6 | 33.0 | 64.8 | 42.5 | 74.5 | 36.9 |
| 1981 | 37.7 | 40.7 | 11.6 | 17.3 | 10.5 | 51.4 | 58.5 | 32.9 | 64.6 | 42.8 | 74.4 | 37.3 |
| 1982 | 38.2 | 41.1 | 12.1 | 18.9 | 10.8 | 51.4 | 60.2 | 33.4 | 64.5 | 43.1 | 74.5 | 38.4 |
| 1983 | 38.6 | 41.5 | 12.3 | 19.2 | 11.4 | 51.9 | 61.0 | 32.8 | 65.1 | 42.8 | 75.0 | 38.9 |
| 1984 | 39.0 | 42.1 | 12.2 | 19.9 | 11.6 | 52.6 | 61.2 | 33.8 | 65.2 | 43.2 | 74.5 | 39.3 |
| 1985 | 39.4 | 42.6 | 12.3 | 20.4 | 11.8 | 53.9 | 61.8 | 35.5 | 65.3 | 43.8 | 74.7 | 39.6 |
| 1989 | 40.4 | 43.1 | 14.0 | 21.8 | 12.9 | 53.4 | 62.5 | 36.2 | 68.2 | 44.0 | 75.4 | 42.2 |

Source: Anuarul Statistic RPR/RSR, 1956–1990

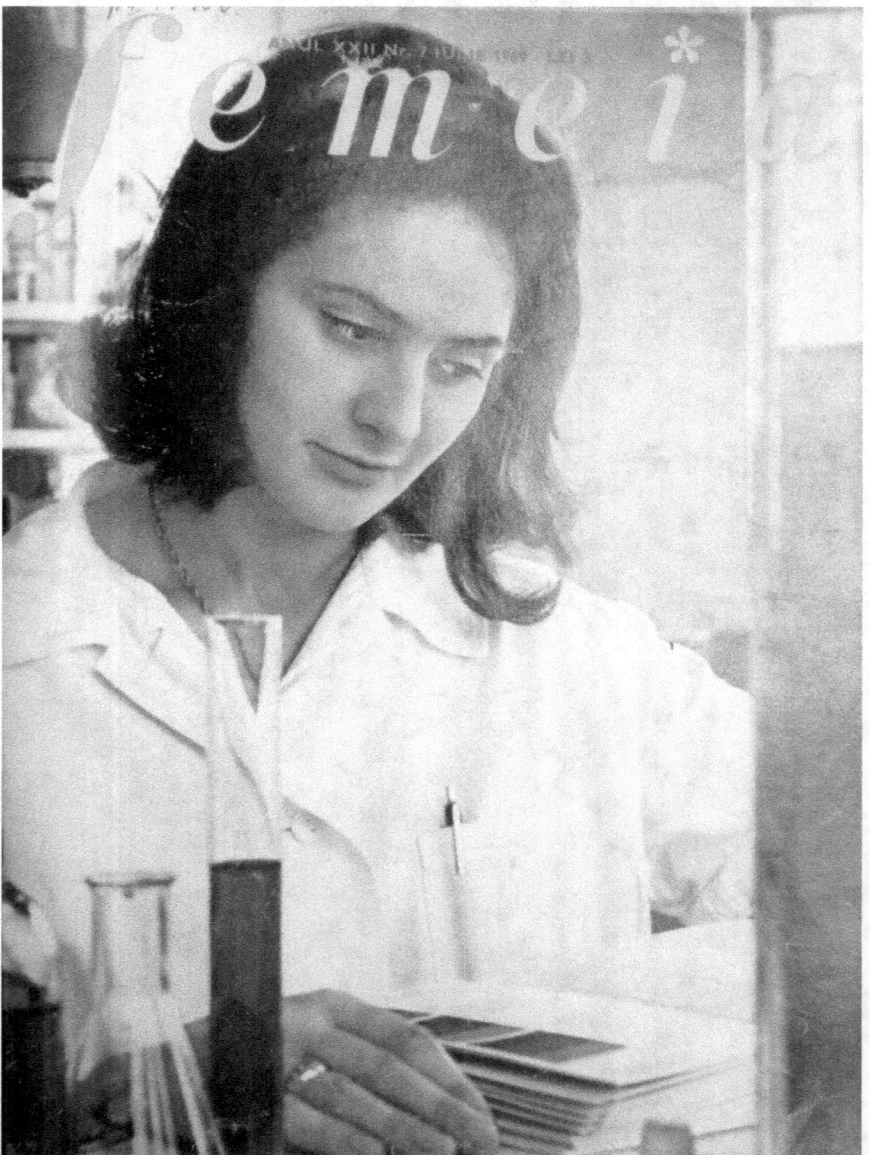

Figure 3.2. Cover of *Femeia*, July 1969

work, fine mechanics, electronics"—jobs that would, incidentally, be earmarked as "most suited" for women and in which women's presence would increase. Another psychologist, however, challenged this assessment, arguing categorically against strict demarcations of labor according to gender and asserting that women can work in almost all areas; though he also added, "further study is needed to determine which ones."[42] A professor of labor medicine elaborated, claiming that "women's nature is not as fragile as one would believe" and that when women become overly emotional at work it is not due to an innate, biological proclivity for emotionality but circumstantial; namely the combined exhaustion of workplace and household responsibilities. To facilitate women's occupational advancement, he suggested reducing their domestic responsibilities by dividing them up among family members.

While most of the featured experts argued against categorizing jobs according to sex, the article evinces a general ambivalence about women's equal participation in the labor force, evident in the concluding statement that the subject "requires further study."[43] Such forums signified a retreat from the portrait of the homogenized socialist worker, who was defined solely by his (or her) productive contributions. Additionally, they were a far cry from the autobiographical pieces written by women tractor drivers and smelters during the early Dej years, whose achievements in physically arduous jobs demonstrated their equality with their male counterparts. More generally, the article provided a discursive foundation for subsequent policy changes that differentiated jobs according to essentialized ideas about gender.

In line with the aforementioned promotional program, in 1974 the Ministries of Labor, Education, and Health and the National Council of Women (Consiliul Național al Femeilor; CNF), in cooperation with trade unions, drew up employment targets designed to increase women's presence in various productive realms and institutes.[44] Moreover, the state "scientifically" compiled a list of 640 specialized jobs (increased to 711 in 1975) in which women were to be promoted. These were presented as jobs in which women could "make the most significant contributions and perform to the best of their abilities" without negatively affecting "their health or their ability to fulfill their other social [e.g. familial] roles."[45] Areas designated for "increasing women's presence" included electronics, optics, and mechanics, as well as food industries, textiles, commerce, craft cooperatives, communications, and certain posts in transport. Thus, women's numbers were to increase not only in more modern sectors of the economy (e.g. science and technology) but also in traditionally female-dominated areas.

These targets served a number of goals and should not be considered wholly regressive. For instance, channeling women into areas that required less brawn did not necessarily mean they required less brain, as jobs in science and technology demonstrated. As such, the plan supported women's professional and educational advancement and was certainly embraced by women aspiring to enter such fields (i.e. D. from the previous chapter, who became a geologist). Indeed, efforts to promote women in these fields bore fruit as they made great strides in science and engineering during the 1970s and 1980s. For instance, while in 1973 women constituted only 11.5 percent of those employed in electrical and thermal energy, by 1980 that figure had reached 20 percent.[46] Similarly, women's presence in the chemical industry increased from 26 to 38 percent between 1973 and 1980.[47]

At the same time, efforts to spare women from "heavier work" were decisively related to Ceaușescu's drive for demographic growth, as well as a desire to retain the masculine character of heavy industry. Thus, state restructuring of the labor force enabled men to monopolize skilled jobs and contributed to the feminization of certain realms. Moreover, it restricted women from jobs that were considered dangerous to their reproductive health. Accordingly, while electronics, fine mechanics, and optics were deemed acceptable areas for women, work in the mines or slaughterhouse was not. This "regendering from above," as historian Wendy Goldman refers to it, involved recategorizing certain jobs as exclusively or primarily female (e.g. clerical and light industry) in order to channel men away from them and into heavy industry.[48] While in the case of Romania this process also opened up new or expanded existing domains to women, at the same time it closed off others. Thus, women were at once promoted and restricted as female laborers. Such "regendering from above" not only reinforced hierarchies in status and earning power, but also reversed earlier approaches to labor under Dej when all fields were open to women and female laborers were represented in a more generic fashion, hailed as Stakhanovites for their capacities in heavy labor. As such, it signified an effort, on the part of Ceaușescu, to legitimate his rule by shifting away from a Stalinist (i.e. Soviet) model of the female laborer and replace it with a more indigenous (i.e. Romanian) version that was not disruptive to conventional gender norms. However, it also signified a retreat from the state's official goal of women's full occupational equality with men. In this capacity, Romania followed its Bloc neighbors, namely the USSR, Hungary, and Poland, which had already begun transferring women out of heavy industry and into low-skilled jobs over a decade earlier.

The glaring gulf between state commitment to equality of opportunity and actual practice was even acknowledged in official media. For example, in 1973 one reader asked the editors of *Femeia* why jobs such as airline pilot or sailor were not open to her since other jobs that are open to women are just as arduous.[49] In her letter, she criticizes women's exclusion from these professions, arguing that it goes against official proclamations of equality between the sexes and makes unfounded assumptions about women's supposed lack of physical strength and stamina.[50] The reader then asks if she should petition the authorities—with the Romanian constitution in hand—to find out why such prohibitions exist and if women are in fact actually guaranteed the right to enter the profession of their own choosing. As there was no published response to her inquiry, it can be assumed that the article served as a token acknowledgment of the problem.

Beyond their pronatalist impetus, these promotional schemes served another purpose unique to the Romanian context: the legitimation of First Lady Elena Ceaușescu's scientific and political career.[51] Presented simultaneously as "comrade, academician, doctor, engineer ... and prominent personality ... with qualities as a ... scientific figure, a wife and mother," Elena became one of the new symbols of socialist womanhood during the 1970s—a source of inspiration for all women.[52] Despite the fact that she lacked both academic credentials and political experience, Elena was portrayed as part of a larger cohort of women whose professional accomplishments served to illustrate the progressiveness and superiority of Romanian socialism.[53]

## Transformative or Tedious? Women's Experiences of Work

By glorifying female workers, socialist propagandists sought to increase women's participation in paid labor, foster duty and loyalty to the state, and fashion a positive public identity for women. At the same time, they emphasized that being a diligent worker was not incompatible with being a devoted wife or a doting mother, a message that was increasingly underscored after the implementation of Ceaușescu's pronatalist policies. A piece in *Femeia* entitled "Girls of '68" is illustrative. Drawing on a survey with young women professionals, the article noted that very few of the respondents regretted the line of work they had chosen; instead, they claimed to have landed the job of their "dreams." The author asserted that these young women displayed an impressive level of maturity, foresight, and perseverance. What's more, socialist modernization had seemingly altered the very manner in which they conceived of work. Accordingly, they discounted the division of the labor force into "masculine" and "feminine" jobs and expressed confidence in women's ability to work in a wide range of professions, including those requiring high levels of skill and intelligence. Such beliefs were exemplified by a chemist who hoped to "make great discoveries." At the same time that these women expressed great satisfaction with their jobs, they also expressed a desire to retain their femininity (i.e. be "sensitive and enjoy delicate things"), to be good wives and mothers, and to help nurture a new generation of individuals for the "approaching epoch." Rather than viewing the role of mother and wife as incompatible with high rates of productivity or professional ambition, these women believed they could successfully perform all three roles. This view is further reinforced by the accompanying photo, which featured young, made-up women in miniskirts with stylish hairdos, illustrating that femininity and occupational achievement were not mutually exclusive. Thus, the author concluded that these women "embody the potential that this century has made possible: they can have their cake and eat it too!"[54]

To what degree did such depictions reflect the realities of women workers who similarly came of age in the 1960s and 1970s? Did they internalize or incorporate such constructions into their own self-identities as workers and equal socialist citizens? Were personalized stories by heroine workers and the accompanying images empowering for women, instilling them with the self-confidence to persevere through harassment by male colleagues and arduous twelve-hour shifts? Or, did women recognize their propagandistic intent and ignore or mock them? Although it is difficult to gauge the impact of socialist propaganda on women's self-perceptions, what is clear is that their experiences in the labor force affected their lives and self-identities in diverse and often ambiguous ways.

According to my respondents, women worked because "it was policy," that is, a duty expected of the state.[55] Moreover, they worked because wages remained low and two salaries were needed for supporting a family. However, a variety of other factors also facilitated women's entry into the workforce such as a desire to experience the world outside their village or town and to break free from the traditional mores (and poverty) of rural life. Related to this was a desire for economic self-sufficiency. Indeed, young women understood that without their own income they would be dependent upon family or a spouse for their livelihood. Moreover, increased educational and training opportunities enabled women to pursue areas they found interesting or fulfilling as well as expand their geographic horizons. As such, socialism provided some women with the opportunity to actively shape their lives rather than have it be determined by circumstance (i.e. family, rural life). Some women also hoped to join their fiancés in cities and new industrial towns. Additionally, despite the instrumentality of socialist propaganda, some women may have been inspired by the workers they encountered in the pages of *Femeia* or in the brochures distributed by the CNF. Also, some women were genuinely devoted to socialist principles and believed they could help fashion a new society based on equality and cooperation. Meanwhile, because productivity was the measure of civic worth in socialist Romania, some women worked to avoid being labeled a "social parasite." As C. sardonically remarked, "All women had to have jobs; if you didn't have a job you were looked down upon because you had to participate in the construction of communism."[56] Finally, for later generations, namely those that came of age in the 1970s and thereafter, working outside the home was simply viewed as a normal endeavor and not disruptive of gender norms.

Just as women's reasons for working differed, so too did their experiences. Factors such as age, occupation, educational background, family size, and relations with colleagues significantly shaped workplace experiences. As noted, women were well represented in farming and industry; yet, while a minority of women worked in heavy industry as welders, fitters, smelters, and turners, most were concentrated in light industries such as textiles, manufacturing, and food processing, often working as semi-skilled or unskilled laborers—jobs that, as in the West, garnered lower prestige and wages than skilled jobs in heavy industry. That said, universal education broadened access to professional fields in the sciences and engineering, which, alongside the promotional schemes of the mid-1970s, opened up new jobs in science and technology to women. In addition to preparing women for work in new domains, the expansion of education enabled more women to be trained in areas they had dominated prior to 1945, namely medicine, education and culture, and social services. For instance, in 1956 women constituted 59.2 percent of those employed in education and culture (a collective statistic), a figure that reached 68.2 percent by the end of socialist rule. Similarly, women's presence in healthcare increased from 61.3 percent in 1956 to 71.3 percent in 1971 to 75.4 percent in 1989.[57] Indeed, the influx of women in medicine and healthcare was so pronounced that these jobs became feminized—a phenomenon that led to their devaluation vis-à-vis male-dominated areas that did not require a university degree. Furthermore, the number of women in the rapidly expanding state administration swelled, especially during the last two decades of socialist rule, increasing from 25.2 percent in 1956 to 30.9 percent in 1970 to 42.2 percent in 1989.[58]

Although underrepresented in heavy industry, women nevertheless engaged in physically demanding labor and were subject to similar schedules, conditions, and norms as men. Training programs were supposed to prepare workers for certain jobs; however, during the early Dej years they often worked without prior training, as was the case of Regine, employed at the national railroad (*Călie Ferate Române*; CFR):

> From day one I began to work like a man because the men [on my team] said, "If a woman has the same rights as we do, they should do the same work." We worked as switchmen for the direct trains where I was a signaler for the local trains and where you had to climb in between the cars, which had to be assembled in each station, and the wagons that remained had to be taken out of the station. And these local trains were very difficult for women, but we didn't make a fuss, we had to work alongside men. One day, I was at the station in Buzău and the two male switchmen stood at the station while I, a woman, had to climb from one car into another. And the ladder was crooked, and I wanted to climb it while it [the train] was moving. ... I finally managed to grasp the ladder and climb up so the locomotive didn't run over me. This situation lasted about a year. Finally, they [her employers] noticed that regardless of what happens a woman remains a woman and a man a man. And then they withdrew the team of women from circulation.[59]

Regine began working during the first decade of socialist rule, a period characterized by mass industrialization but also repression, poverty, and uncertainty. Grateful to have survived the ordeals of forced labor in the USSR (where she had been sent under Soviet directive in 1945 as punishment for her ethnic-German heritage), Regine returned to Romania to find that she had attained full equality with men, which, in her case, meant that she had to work as hard as—if not harder than—a man. Although Regine had engaged in heavy labor alongside men in the USSR, she was nonetheless shocked by her Romanian colleagues' lack of sensitivity to the fact that performing such work was difficult for a woman. Indeed, their insistence that she "work like a man" since women and men were "equal" seems to mask a more general displeasure with being forced to work alongside women. Such treatment might also have been related to men's sense of powerlessness under the new system. Joanna Goven claims that communist constructions of masculinity were restrictive and "narrowed masculine identity, ruling out other cultural associations, such as that between masculinity and property, masculinity and religious authority, and masculinity and individual autonomy." Accordingly, women's entry into heavy industry threatened to "feminize the last remaining site of masculinity, of masculine heroism, skill, and authority."[60] The behaviors of Regine's coworkers, including standing idly at the station while she completed their share of the work, thus might be read as an effort to "break" their female colleagues' willpower and force them out of the job and, thereby, reassert this realm as exclusively male.

Although such behavior should have been brought to the attention of the trade union or resulted in a reprimand or suspension of her male coworkers, Regine's boss instead responded by disbanding the female team of switch operators and finding her a new position. This reveals that even managers lacked the will to enforce existing labor policies, belying state commitment to gender equality.

Regine's situation at the CFR was not unique. The 1957 *Femeia* article "Open Road," for example, also documented male prejudice against women railway workers; however, in comparison to Regine's real-life story, the woman featured here ultimately perseveres to stake out her place and even advance in this male-dominated realm. Narrated through the persona of Veronica, who had dreamed of working for the railroad since she was a young girl, the piece follows her trajectory from a clerk at a sugar factory during World War II to her job as a signaler under a boss who "was declared an enemy of women" to her current position as a locomotive engineer.[61] Veronica's story is accompanied by other tales of female achievement at the CFR, including promotion to supervisory posts. By hiring more women, the author of the piece claimed, the CFR not only supported women's employment in traditionally male realms, but also improved the services it offered to the public through the establishment of separate waiting rooms for mothers to care for their young children. While Veronica acknowledged that outmoded mentalities about women railway workers remained, she also emphasized the great strides women had made in this area. Despite her optimism, it seems that the article did not embolden many actual women to take up work on the railroad for statistics registered 19 women locomotive engineers in the entire country in 1956 (as opposed to 8,267 men locomotive engineers), a figure that increased by 1 (to 20 women) a decade later.[62] Such meager growth reflected women's underrepresentation in transportation more generally, which actually decreased between 1956 and 1970 (dropping from 14.5 to 7.7 percent) and only reached 12.9 percent in 1989.[63]

As previously noted, with Ceauşescu's drive for demographic growth after 1966, the state began channeling women into less physically demanding jobs. Nonetheless, women continued to work long shifts. Such was the case of Maria F. who, after being a homemaker for fifteen years, began working at a ball bearings factory in the mid-1960s. Although raised on a farm where she had been responsible for harvesting and tending to the animals, she found factory work particularly grueling. She recalled:

> Work was very difficult because we were required to meet the norms. I had no training, a seventh grade education. They put me to work sorting ball bearings. In order to meet the plan, we always worked twelve hours. That is, we worked twelve hours at night and during the day. There was [only] a first and second shift. And [we worked] Saturdays and Sundays. Not every Sunday, but on Saturday it was required.[64]

Maria F.'s job sorting ball bearings was monotonous, which, according to the industrial psychologist cited earlier in this chapter, was "more appropriate work" for women. At the same time, it was demanding, requiring long shifts, including night shifts, six days a week, thus going against the 1972 Labor Code. Therefore, unskilled jobs could be just as temporally demanding as jobs in heavy labor; however, the remuneration and status were much lower for the former.

By the 1980s, during the height of the officially proclaimed "Golden Age" (*epoca de aur*) and Ceauşescu's frantic rush to pay off the foreign debt, many people continued to work long shifts, six (and, in some cases, even seven) days a week. As Eva, who began working as an automechanic electrician at a factory at age eighteen, recalled:

> I worked about ten hours a day. Many times I came in for the first shift and returned home at one in the morning. I worked very much. I didn't really have free time. We worked on the holidays, Christmas, Easter. ... During that time I wasn't married and when I came home from work I would take a bath and sleep. That was my daily routine when I got home.[65]

In light of such grueling hours, articles such as "Women in the Fight for Peace, Equality, Rights, and Human Dignity," which appeared in *Femeia* in 1983 and detailed women's exploitation and various forms of inequity and discrimination in capitalist systems, would have appeared farcical to Eva.[66]

Eugenia, who worked as a quality control manager at a clothing factory from the 1960s through the 1980s, would have shared Eva's sentiments. Although she did not put in such hours, she expressed sympathy for workers who did, portraying them as exploited and robotic:

> You could say it was the work of animals. People didn't talk; everyone was like a robot. People came to work Saturday afternoon, second shift, and left the next day, Sunday, and [they] didn't produce much ... they were not very efficient. I wouldn't work those Saturday night shifts; I didn't follow the herd. I told them it was inefficient for people to work at that time; that they were too tired. I gave them my opinion, but I didn't get in trouble because I was very good at my job.[67]

According to Eugenia, the drive to fulfill and even surpass the plan by squeezing as much labor out of workers as possible ultimately proved unproductive. Overnight and overtime work was often necessitated by the inefficiencies of the command economy, particularly problems in the supply chain, which halted production but then required fast and furious efforts to meet the plan when supplies arrived. Therefore, workers might be idle one week and work fourteen-hour shifts the next. This, combined with the repetitive nature of assembly line and piecework, appeared mind-numbing and "robotic" to Eugenia. Even though she served in a managerial capacity, she felt that the overall atmosphere of the factory was "like being in jail."

Those employed in industry were not the only ones who felt like they were in jail. Recent university graduates, particularly teachers and doctors whose services were needed in rural areas and were posted to the countryside for their three-year *repartiție* (state-assigned first job; a type of payback to society for earning a university degree), also felt as if they had been imprisoned.[68] Theoretically, graduates were assigned jobs on the basis of family circumstance (i.e. near or in the same locale as their spouse or parental home) or academic performance; however, as most young people wanted to remain in the city they had studied, they devised ways of avoiding being sent to the countryside (i.e. through marriage or "gifts" to functionaries in charge of such appointments). As with other parts of the system, then, favoritism and bribery could help oil the wheels, enabling less meritorious individuals to remain in cities, while those of equal or greater merit headed to rural parts of the country.[69]

By the 1980s, however, increasingly more college graduates were sent to work in rural, underresourced, and remote communities.[70] For those raised in cities, the three years of *repartiție* could be humiliating. In 1984 Elena, a Bucharest native, was posted to a village thirty miles outside of Botoșani, a city in northeastern Romania. Here Elena taught

English and French to youth in grades five through ten, a period she referred to as "the most horrible time of my life," during which she experienced a mental breakdown.[71] Although guaranteed an apartment in a block of flats reserved for teachers, upon her arrival Elena was informed that it was "occupied," and she was forced to find her own lodging. To add insult to injury, her ration cards (for food and cooking gas) were not "available" since others had already "claimed" them—that is, the local authorities had taken them for themselves. As a result, Elena lost a great deal of weight and survived only by the good graces of her mother, who sent food packages from Bucharest, and the neighboring dairy farmers, who took pity on her and gave her milk and other products. Fortunately, Elena eventually made friends with a family who took her in and with whom she shared one sleeping room—the only room in the house that was heated. Indeed, the winter was so cold and wood for heating so scarce that she resorted to burning exams to keep warm. Because securing a job in one's field without completing the obligatory *repartiție* was challenging, if not impossible, my respondents who were sent to remote areas viewed this practice with disdain, presenting it as a form of coercion and oppression from which they could not escape.

While representative of some women's experiences, the aforementioned memories cannot be generalized to all women. For example, Anca (b. 1936), who began working as a technician on a construction site in the late 1950s, recalled her job fondly:

> It didn't seem difficult. You know why? Because I didn't have kids. Because I worked in construction, which was very well-paid and where one had certain advantages: a free home, free electricity, free heating .... Being young, enthusiastic, and having a disposition, as you can see now [for yourself], optimistic, happy, and in good health, I didn't sense it [the difficulties]. And don't think I came home and went to sleep. I kept a household like this [as you see here today]. I did everything at home, cooking, cleaning, ironing. My husband never did anything because that was how he was raised.[72]

Anca's recollection illustrates the influence of family size and occupational status on women's experiences of work. Because Anca was childless she could devote herself primarily to her job, which often included working overtime. Moreover, as Anca worked in a privileged industry she benefited from a host of subsidies. Therefore, even though her husband did not help around the house, she didn't experience the stress that many other working women did—a reality that, at least in part, explains her positive recollections of work and, more generally, life under socialism.

While reconciling work and family responsibilities often produced stress for women, according to Tatiana (who raised two children during the 1970s and 1980s), these roles were easily combined under socialism. Employed in a factory, she stated, "work was good," citing the short eight-hour shift, which left her time and energy for other activities:

> I was taught to work at a young age. I believe that, regardless of the regime, if you are diligent and you work, you will live well. I liked it because I worked eight hours, I came home, I put a meal on the stove, and I had time to read. I read a lot then; I led an ordered life. Yes, we worked on Saturday and sometimes Sunday, but, to be honest, that didn't disrupt anything. It was more pretense than anything else in those days.[73]

The daughter of peasants, Tatiana attributed her strong work ethic to what she learned in her youth. At the same time, her sentiments about work dovetailed with the state's "productivist ideology," which would have been omnipresent in school manuals, on workplace banners, and in newspapers and magazines. More generally, for Tatiana being productive was associated with "living well." Beyond this, the regularity of Tatiana's schedule provided her with time for cooking, cleaning, and leisure. Furthermore, work was connected to broader social and cultural changes she experienced as a result of her move from a small village in northeastern Romania to a large Transylvanian city. Thus, life in the city introduced her to new ideas, cultures, and peoples. Although Tatiana was critical of the short, three-month maternity leave and the food, electricity, and heating shortages of the 1980s, because work was inextricably connected to many positive life changes, she considered the socialist period to be the most fulfilling time of her life.

For Anca and Tatiana, both of whom were raised in rural areas, work was fulfilling, indicating that, for some women, socialism, despite its shortcomings, made good on its promise of a brighter future. Like the Polish women interviewed by Malgorzata Fidelis, for these women, "the transition from village to factory was political, ideological, and material" in nature.[74] As such, their recollections are part of the larger story of social revolution that occurred in postwar Romania and other countries in the Eastern Bloc. This social revolution turned peasants into workers, as well as city dwellers. Because many women had grown up in rural areas, work symbolized a ticket to freedom, an escape from arduous farm labor, parental restrictions, and, significantly, poverty. Thus, as it was for women in other parts of the Bloc, socialism was liberating, enabling these women to earn a living wage and define their roles outside of traditional peasant culture, though, to be sure, some of these beliefs and practices remained central to how they operated on an everyday level and related to others.[75] While work had similarly motivated women to leave farmsteads in Western Europe and the United States in the late nineteenth and early twentieth century, in these cases women headed to urban centers to face economic uncertainty.[76] By comparison, in socialist Romania this transition was eased by guaranteed employment and wages, which, while often low, were sufficient for maintaining at least a basic standard of living. Moreover, women's place within the workforce was continuously validated in socialist media, which helped make it more acceptable and, indeed, normal, while also providing women with the self-confidence to enter new vocations and professions—and perhaps even deal with male colleagues who were resistant to working alongside women.

While perhaps not as dramatic, the impact of full-time employment was also gratifying for respondents raised in urban areas. For example, Elvira's job at the research and projects office of a factory was economically and personally validating, even though she often worked six days a week:

> Saturday was a day of work during the communist period, and Sunday when there were projects and the pay was twice as much. We worked until after dinner, but we worked with pleasure because of our co-workers ... we had an extraordinary relationship. It was a collaborative effort. Everybody collaborated, and when work is like that it appears easy. [And] money had value then, things were not expensive ... you could save, I saved. There were two salaries coming in and we were able to put one salary into the bank, and off the other salary we lived very well, we went to plays and restaurants.[77]

Rather than being exhausting or burdensome, according to Elvira, the long workweeks proved not only tolerable but rewarding. This she attributed to the overtime pay she received for these shifts, which allowed her to contribute to the family's well-being in a socially recognized, quantifiable manner, as well as the atmosphere of collegiality at the office. For some women, then, the social and monetary rewards of work were as important as the job itself. These sentiments were shared by women in other parts of the Bloc, underscoring the degree to which collectivism and social relationships influenced women's experiences of work. Such recollections offer a more diverse portrait of work that goes beyond exploitation—or even productivism—to highlight the social and interpersonal aspects of work.[78]

Meanwhile, Luana's positive recollections of work were related to the intellectual fulfillment she derived from her position as a researcher at a local museum:

> It was the most beautiful period of my life. ... I researched local history, I wrote, I published articles, books ... it was very satisfying work. And what happened? They say that history under Ceaușescu was not properly researched and substantiated. I don't agree with that. I myself wrote a great deal. I verified written sources, documents. I put on beautiful exhibits on numismatics, modern history. I went around the county, I talked to people, they gave me photographs, they gave me objects [to display] and I put on expositions. ... It is true that in those years, including in the museum, you were not able to always say what you wanted to. Especially in front of people from the Regional Committee who ruled us, guided us since there was a form of control, but, I repeat, because I didn't deal with contemporary history, I did not write a book based on alternative realities.[79]

Although Luana wore coat and gloves while hanging exhibitions and conducting guided tours during the 1980s—and even moonlighted as a tutor to supplement her income—her positive memories of this job remained. Her ability to overlook the grimness of material life was certainly linked to the personal energy she devoted to her job—as well as the degree to which she was intellectually invested in her work. At the same time, Luana emphasized that she needed to be on her guard around certain colleagues:

> In my work group there were people who we knew would definitely report us. There was a colleague who, after we finished with a group of tourists, especially foreign tourists, made us tell him if we were asked questions and he jotted [them down], and we had a person from the Securitate who informed on different aspects of our work. But aspects in what sense? Those that would be a threat to our state security, our principles. It was an atmosphere in which you needed to be aware of what came out of your mouth, and you were censored. You self-censored, and the same with those around you. If an individual wanted to, they could easily take revenge on you, so you needed to be cautious.

This quote illustrates the risks of working in a surveillance-intensive society. Although Luana took great pleasure in her job, she nonetheless needed to exercise caution—both around foreigners and certain colleagues—and engage in self-censorship lest she find herself in an interrogation room at the local Securitate headquarters. As such, her experiences of work were bittersweet: personally fulfilling, but also potentially risky.

Collectively, these stories highlight the varied effects of socialist modernization on women's lives. Whether the benefits were economic self-sufficiency, freedom from patriarchal codes of behavior, intellectual fulfillment, or opportunities for social engagement, working outside the home decisively shaped many women's lives. More broadly, they demonstrate that women often supported this aspect of socialism. As such, they validate Engels's theory of female emancipation through work, as well as official representations of work as personally fulfilling and rewarding. That said, women's positive recollections of work did not reflect blind faith in or even support for the regime. Rather, women valued work for a number of reasons. These might be ideological, but they were usually practical and personal: work offered financial stability, access to social services and benefits, intellectual or creative fulfillment, and increased self-confidence and autonomy.

While work decisively shaped the course of women's lives, it was not always in a positive fashion. For example, individuals who failed to complete their *repartiție*, lacked the proper connections, and those with "unhealthy social origins" faced numerous challenges in securing work. Indeed, although the command economy depended on full employment, the state ultimately determined who could work and where. Elisabeta, for instance, struggled to find work in forestry because she did not complete her *repartiție*.[80] In sum, she was out of the workforce for five years, which, while allowing her to stay home and raise her two children, substantially reduced her retirement benefits. Meanwhile, C.'s mother, a trained pianist, was forbidden from continuing her studies at music school because of her "unhealthy social origins" and because her sister had fled the country after the communist takeover. Barred from most jobs in her field, she ultimately worked putting up lines for the state telephone company—a humiliating experience considering her educational level and talents. Such class "maladies" could even filter down to the next generation as C. was denied a position as a French translator at Radio România because of her family background.[81]

Being of "unhealthy social origin" not only prevented individuals from securing work in their field, but could prevent them from studying at university. Indeed, gaining entry into the humanities and arts faculties was nearly impossible for those who fell into such a category since, beginning in 1949, the state denied children of "capitalist-exploiting elements" admission to higher education for fear they would later work in the bureaucracy and sabotage the entire socialist project.[82] Children of such families were either prohibited from attending university or were in an unfavorable position for competing for a spot at university, forcing many into studies or jobs that did not interest them or were beneath their abilities. For instance, Cătălina, who was born into an intellectual family in 1941, faced discrimination at university because of her "unhealthy social origins." While her parents were convinced that if she worked hard she would succeed, Cătălina knew that without *un dosar bun* ("a good file," that is, of working class or modest peasant stock), she would not be accepted into the School of Architecture at the University of Bucharest. Thus, when Cătălina learned she had not been admitted into the program she was unsurprised. Her father, on the other hand, was so shocked that he sustained a minor heart attack as he believed that merit (in this case Cătălina's high academic standing in high school and BAC score) would guarantee her a place at university. In the end, Cătălina sought another route to architecture: by way of engineering and construction—jobs that were in great demand at the time. While Cătălina enjoyed the theoretical aspects of engineering, she disliked working on construction sites so much that she decided to reapply to the School of Architecture in 1961. Fortunately, by that time, the rector of the school had been replaced and the new one was, according to Cătălina, "more evolved, enlightened, and less of a Stalinist."[83] More significantly, beginning in 1961, having a "good file" was not a prerequisite for admission to university programs; therefore, Cătălina was no longer "handicapped" by her social origin and was accepted into the architecture program. Trained by a professor who had studied in Paris during the interwar period, Cătălina went on to work at the largest architectural institute in Romania and was charged with designing blocks of flats for the masses, or, in her words, "this ugly Bucharest that you see today."

Beyond possessing healthy social origins, *pile* and *relaţii* (pull and relations) were also important for securing a place at university. Stela recalled wanting to attend art school, but the stiff competition, along with her lack of connections, made it, in her words, "worthless to even think about."[84] Although friends and family encouraged her to apply, she knew her chances of being accepted were slim—at best—and thus took a supervisory position at the state telephone company.[85] For some women, then, being forced to work in an area in which they had no particular interest, inclination, or talent significantly marked lives and self-identities as workers.

## Relations with Colleagues and the Gendering of the Labor Force

Unlike capitalist economies in which employment is subject to market fluctuations, the command economies of the Eastern Bloc were centrally managed and geared toward mass production.[86] Thus, rather than serving as a "reserve labor pool," conscripted into the workforce in emergency situations such as war, women were considered essential to rapid industrialization and full employment was therefore guaranteed. As such, concern about women as "cheap laborers" competing with or displacing men from certain jobs did not emerge as it did in the context of market economies.[87] Moreover, unlike in capitalist economies, in socialist economies both men and women were represented in law and propaganda as equal workers. Since women posed no economic threat to men, it follows that they should have been fully accepted into the labor force, equally trained alongside their male counterparts and treated respectfully by them. However, given the enduring power of patriarchal mentalities, including men's resistance to women working outside the home, tensions emerged between socialist ideals and practice. Although heroine workers served to highlight women's capability in heavy industry, construction, and mechanized farming, because they were exceptional figures their symbolic capital was insufficient for overturning ingrained attitudes. Indeed, heroine workers, in their zealous devotion to overfulfill quotas, may have done more harm than good to the overall image and perception of women workers.[88] Like elsewhere in the Bloc, gender, as it turned out, did matter, both to factory bosses and male laborers, illustrating that the formation of a socialist system did not automatically mean that women would be integrated into the workforce en masse or that men's attitudes would undergo rapid transformation.

Accordingly, gender hierarchies were produced and reinforced in the labor force, with the result that women did not enjoy equal opportunities with respect to job access, job training, and promotion. This was particularly true of skilled, male-dominated jobs in heavy industry, in which women were grossly underrepresented. Moreover, in Romania, as elsewhere in the Bloc, women were underrepresented in training programs, and some specialized schools (such as those for foremen) even refused to enroll women in their courses.[89] This was not the result of state policy, but of managers and instructors who, influenced by traditional notions about gender, skill, and shop-floor culture, simply flouted or failed to fulfill state directives requiring that women also be included in training programs.

Despite this, articles in *Femeia* offered women the promise of occupational advancement through *cursuri serale* (evening classes through which a high school, university, or technical degree could be earned on an expedited basis). In a March 1966 piece entitled "Promotion," readers were informed that "promotion involves training" and that approximately half of all salaried employees with intermediate or advanced study are women.[90] The article showcased women who had availed themselves of the state's beneficent programs, including Stela Grozavescu, a factory worker who claimed: "I'm twenty-nine years old, with a family, a child. But I said [to myself]: it's a shame not to continue my studies when the state offers such opportunities." Meanwhile, Elena Ostafie, an electrician who advanced to the position of section leader, asserted she had enrolled in *cursuri serale* because she didn't "want to tread water."[91] Other women indicated they were motivated by personal ambition, the need to stay abreast of technological advances, and the desire to hone their skills. Finally, Rodica Boconcious, an engineer, added the importance of countering male prejudice, specifically the belief that women can't "handle complex technical problems." Having produced important scientific research, some of which she presented at a conference in Stockholm, Rodica claimed that, "prejudice disappears if we demonstrate our competence." Thus, she blamed not only men, but also women (and their parents) for women's lack of advancement in certain fields, particularly their resistance to working (or having their daughters work) in industry and under difficult conditions.

While parental resistance and, as we will see in the following chapter, spousal resistance, in part explained women's underrepresentation in training programs, so too did discrimination. Thus, while women did not necessarily lack the will (though they may have lacked the self-confidence), they often lacked sufficient training and were, like women in other parts of the Bloc, disadvantaged in the labor force from the get-go; placed in some of the lowest positions within the factory, including low-prestige, unfulfilling, and poorly remunerated jobs wholly unrelated to production (e.g. janitor, cook). Or, they started at the lowest level in skilled or semi-skilled jobs, advancing less rapidly than their male counterparts. Beyond this, even if women mastered the necessary skills, bosses were reluctant to hire them due to entrenched notions about gender and skill. Maria's case is illustrative. Upon applying for a job at a handicraft cooperative in the early 1970s, she recalled that when the foreman "saw I was a woman, he came closer to the window. I told him not to jump out of the window, no need for that; that it was better not to meet with me. And then I heard he was not married; it was clear he felt an aversion towards women. He just never trusted a woman doing a man's job."[92] Recognizing that he would not hire her because of her gender, Maria, rather than be angered by the foreman's sexism, responded to it comically since she was, by this point in her life, "accustomed to dealing with egotistical men who thought they were better than women."[93] By telling him not to jump out of the window—and thereby inferring that she was saving his life—Maria underscored the absurdity of the situation. Moreover, by choosing not to go ahead with the interview, Maria asserted her right to fair and respectful treatment in the workplace. Although none of my other subjects shared similar encounters with prospective bosses, Maria was certainly not alone. Research on Hungary, Poland, and East Germany reveals that male bosses were similarly reticent to hire women for skilled jobs for fear of disrupting male work cultures. They also tended to view women as liabilities, assuming they would eventually become pregnant, take maternity leave, call in sick more frequently, and even decline to work overtime by citing family responsibilities.[94] Thus, prevailing beliefs about women's reproductive and family roles often influenced male bosses' view of their capacity (or lack thereof) in production. Such beliefs translated into behaviors that undermined the socialist promise of women's full and equal participation in paid labor and Engels's prediction that once women entered the labor force en masse they would be treated as equal comrades.

While some women responded to male prejudice and discrimination by emphasizing their status as equal workers, they were not necessarily successful in changing male bosses' minds. Thus, many women certainly lost such battles, while others did not even bother waging them, resigning themselves to their subordinate status or seeking work in more woman-friendly environments. Yet, this also meant that they resigned themselves to lower wages and lower-status jobs and to the fact that women and men were not equal under socialism.

For those who did manage to enter male-dominated fields, tensions might emerge. Although it is unclear if men perceived women laborers as economic threats per se, some did view them as threats to the traditional gender order and work culture. Consequently, women who entered male-dominated realms encountered behaviors that would today be defined as harassment (e.g. criticizing the quality of women's work or sabotaging it; exchanging sexist commentary and off-color jokes; threatening female coworkers with violence, including sexual violence), but for which, at the time, no term existed in socialist Romania—or in Western countries for that matter. Such behaviors were already evident in Romania during the interwar period as women increasingly worked in industry. This reveals that some male workers (including managers) regarded their female counterparts as improper and thus deserving of disrespect or mistreatment.[95] It also indicates that state efforts to homogenize workers were resisted by male workers and managers alike. At the same time, such behaviors cannot be generalized to all men as research on the interwar period suggests that male workers also protected female coworkers from untoward advances by superiors—or at least themselves refrained from acting improperly in their presence.[96]

Harassment played out on a number of occupational levels and in various shapes and forms. In discussing promotion, one woman referred to bosses who "manipulated their positions" by granting promotions to women who "offered certain favors." Additionally, women employed in predominantly male sectors such as heavy industry, woodworking, and construction experienced harassment due to the belief that skill and brawn were the preserve of men alone. For instance, Maria, who started working in the mid-1970s, shortly after Ceauşescu began promoting women into science and engineering, recalled fighting tooth and nail to get her male colleagues to recognize her skill as an electrician:

> You know what it was like? It was a personality conflict; it was a continual battle working among men. First of all, it was very difficult until I demonstrated to them what I knew and that I knew how to do it very well ... that nobody else needed to follow me—a man for example—to correct the work once I had finished. After they got used to me, they treated me with dignity. They never talked badly to me, they never used vulgar words with me, because I would not tolerate it. Nor would I speak in a vulgar way with them. I had two choices: either to act like I didn't know anything or to be unusual. I preferred to be unusual. And I did very well.[97]

Maria's difficulty with her male colleagues, though rooted in what she refers to as a "personality conflict," was in essence a gender conflict. This conflict stemmed from her skillfulness, which her male coworkers found unsettling because they viewed skill as a masculine preserve. Although eventually accepted by her team as a competent worker, Maria never became "one of the boys." She might have been an equal from a professional standpoint, but in the end she was too sophisticated to engage in their vulgar banter. Yet, in their eyes she was also an unusual and exceptional woman, an identity she embraced rather than pretend to be a "stupid woman who needed her male colleagues' help." By assuming the identity of the unusual or oddball woman, Maria downplayed her gender, a strategy that can be read as a form of self-assertion and self-preservation—what Alf Lüdtke refers to as *Eigen-sinn* (self-will).[98] In this way, she resisted her male coworkers attempts to minimize her capabilities without threatening their sense of masculinity. Her cleverness and strength underscore women's adeptness at defusing tense situations, fostering collegiality, and staking out their place as equals in the socialist workforce. Of note, however, is that Maria acted individually, without the assistance of management or other women since she was the only woman on her team. This compares with situations in East Germany where, according to Donna Harsh, women also resisted shop-floor misogyny but did so collectively.[99]

Although Maria was apparently spared vulgarity, other women were not. My respondents did not explicitly mention being spoken to in a crude or profane manner; however, it is probable that at least some of them encountered such behaviors, but either forgot or repressed such incidents—or chose not to share them with me. Research on socialist Hungary and Poland, for example, reveals that women who worked in traditionally masculine areas might be spoken to in a vulgar manner and even labeled prostitutes by mangers and others.[100] Indeed, in some cases, the degree of vulgarity, mockery, and misogyny exhibited by male coworkers was so intense that women left their jobs altogether.[101] According to Wendy Goldman, who analyzed the experiences of women workers under Stalin, men often responded in this way because they viewed women's presence in male-dominated areas as "not only an infringement of their privileges as male workers but also a sexual transgression."[102] Consequently, their behaviors could be sexualized in nature, including the use of obscene language and sexual advances.

One of my respondents, Rodica, who was born in 1963 and worked in construction, witnessed a subtle form of such practices. Although she claimed to get on very well with her male coworkers, emphasizing that her foreman was a "very good man," she also noted that some of the other foremen had "exaggerated expectations. And, of course, they made certain propositions to the women of that age—eighteen, nineteen years old—as each one wanted to have a young woman alongside him and then, of course, other problems arose."[103] In veiled language, Rodica referred to what appears to have been sexual harassment—and perhaps even sexual assault. Given that construction work was a male-dominated field, with women's representation never surpassing 14 percent, it can safely be assumed that women, especially young women, who worked in this area encountered various types of harassment, be it in the form of indecent language, being propositioned or fondled, or being promised a promotion or other rewards in return for sexual favors.[104]

Harassment was not limited to male-dominated sectors or those with relative gender parity as women in female-dominated sectors also encountered requests for sexual favors in exchange for promotion since men held most leadership positions. Nor was harassment restricted to the industrial sphere. For instance, Viorica, who began training as a professional actress in the late 1960s, was told by her acting coach that if she, an attractive young woman, hoped to advance she would need to make certain "compromises." Viorica added that such "advice" was commonly given to young actresses—and, in some cases, followed—however, she was unwilling to compromise her moral and bodily integrity for a career in acting and thus went on to work as a high school teacher.[105] Although a few respondents claimed that their colleagues had offered up such favors in exchange for promotions, none admitted to doing so themselves.

The 1965 constitution forbade discrimination on the basis of sex, and Article 247 of the penal code made it punishable with imprisonment for six months to five years; however, it is unknown if bosses were ever fined for breaking this law.[106] Meanwhile, no prohibition or punishment existed with respect to harassment. Consequently, women lacked the legal language to identify their colleagues' and bosses' inappropriate or abusive behavior, making it difficult to articulate grievances when harassment occurred. Appeal to higher authorities (e.g. section bosses and union leaders) was theoretically possible, however, only one of my respondents mentioned this as a possible mechanism for dealing with harassment.[107] Indeed, although socialist unions had a distributive function, they did not generally have a protective one; therefore, unions were not effective channels for addressing worker complaints. Nor did they function as "participatory bodies" where workers' suggestions or appeals might be expected to result in policy change.[108] While it is unknown how many women availed themselves of this channel of complaint, given that they would have felt shock, confusion, and shame when incidents of harassment occurred, they most likely did not appeal to a boss or union leader, choosing instead to manage the situation as best as they could on their own. As a corollary, considering women's subordinate status within the workplace in particular and the lack of mobility within the socialist labor force in general, women may have feared "rocking the boat" and exacerbating an already difficult situation if they appealed to their bosses. It is also possible that women who did complain about their colleagues' unseemly behavior were themselves singled out for blame. Research on other countries in the Bloc—as well as Western countries—demonstrates that bosses often downplayed complaints of harassment, or even blamed women for these incidents, arguing that they did not occur before women entered the workforce. Finally, if the situation became unbearable, some women might have resorted to leaving their jobs altogether, though, again, this would have been challenging due to lack of workplace mobility. As such, many women repressed unpleasant or humiliating experiences—or chose not to share them with me. What is certain, however, is that Romanian women, like women elsewhere in the world, devised coping mechanisms and utilized various strategies to deal with a whole range of behaviors that made them feel unwelcome, unqualified, uncomfortable, or unsafe.

In some cases, discrimination assumed a more subtle form. As Cătălina, who, as previously noted, struggled to be admitted into the School of Architecture at the University of Bucharest because of her social origins, remarked about her job as an architect:

> I was a talented person, and my bosses recognized it. But they only admitted it verbally. I never went abroad; only men left [and with my plans]! I did work for Arab countries, for hotels, motels, and my boss left with the plans! And he came back and said, "you are so talented, he [the foreign client] liked them very much." And, as a thank you, he brought me soap.[109]

Cătălina's experiences reveal that women, even if they produced first-rate work that was highly regarded by a boss, could still be treated as subordinates by male colleagues. In this case, Cătălina did all the work, while her male colleagues took the credit—and were even able to enjoy a trip abroad. Her boss's acknowledgment of her efforts in the form of a bar of soap only added insult to injury. Essentially, she was remunerated with a personal hygiene product rather than formal recognition by peers and the chance to personally present her work abroad. Her story illustrates the enduring power of male work cultures and the subtle ways in which gender enabled access to certain privileges and opportunities.

While some women experienced subordination, discrimination, and harassment, other woman claimed to get on best with male coworkers. As Angela, who began a job as a woodworker in 1985, recalled:

> There were not very many women in my section, but I can say that in my collective women were envious of me because they saw that I was getting on better than they were and I was younger than they were and they envied me, not to my face, but you could sense it ... but I didn't let that bother me. Of the group, I got on much better with men. They were much more accepting of me than the women, and when I needed help, if I needed anything, or if I just wanted to talk, I looked to the men. In general, I have always gotten along better with men than women.[110]

A few other women also recalled getting on well with their male colleagues, including being "taken care of" by men. Eva, the only woman in a team of nine workers, remembered being treated kindly and, at times, indulgently by her male coworkers. In particular, she recalled an episode during the late 1980s when she was working third shift and her coworkers told her to "rest for a bit" and "warm up some wine" while they completed the work.[111] This exchange reveals that a good deal of camaraderie existed between male and female colleagues, and that some men retained chivalrous attitudes toward women—even within the context of male-dominated spaces. However, in this case, the combination of age and gender differences may have worked in Eva's favor. Significantly younger than many of her coworkers, Eva, as well as Angela, was most likely viewed as a type of younger sister or daughter figure. Thus, encouraging Eva to rest, along with asking her to heat up wine, reinforced traditional gender norms. Additionally, by this point life under Ceaușescu had become increasingly difficult and desperate, facilitating solidarity through shared suffering. Finally, both of these women entered the labor force during the mid-1980s when, in comparison with earlier periods, the presence of women in male-dominated realms was less novel and thus less jarring.

Taken collectively, these stories reflect a general ambivalence on the part of men towards women's participation in male-dominated areas. Propagandists occasionally paid lip service to workplace discrimination by claiming that "the history of women's evolution as workers is a history of injustice" and that "the Socialist Republic of Romania needs to do more to ensure that women are properly treated by their colleagues"; however, such proclamations were not followed by concerted efforts, by managers and bosses, to eradicate prejudice and discriminatory practices. Indeed, it is possible that behaviors we would currently consider harassment were tolerated in Romania, as they were in the Soviet Union, as a safety valve, "a culturally, if not politically acceptable target for male frustration and anger."[112]

More generally, harassment was a symptom of a larger problem: the persistence of patriarchal beliefs in the organization of the labor force and labor relations. These surfaced in exchanges between workers, especially in areas where women were in the minority, as well as in worker training and hiring practices. As Romania industrialized and the labor force diversified, women increasingly worked in electronics, engineering, and other male-dominated realms. However, since women often entered these jobs with less preparation than their male counterparts (due to lack of or insufficient training), they were the least skilled and thus at the bottom of the hierarchy for promotion.

Moreover, official claims of equality notwithstanding, the state, as previously noted, barred women from certain positions such as airline pilot, train conductor, and naval captain. Instead, women's positions in transportation were in a supportive capacity—as stewardesses, ticket sellers, controllers, and signalers—despite the fact that Article 2 of the 1972 Labor Code guaranteed all individuals the right to work in any function or area commensurate with their ability and training and the needs of socialist society.[113] Women's overrepresentation in traditionally female-dominated and unskilled or semi-skilled jobs such as cleaning and food processing also contributed to the feminization of the labor force.[114] These jobs, in turn, garnered lower wages than the heavy industry jobs dominated by men.[115]

The gendering of labor also extended to the professional realm, particularly teaching and medicine. By the second half of socialist rule, this situation did not seem to be getting better but worse. For example, an article in *Femeia* in July 1970 indicated that girls constituted over 80 percent of those enrolled in pedagogical schools. While noting that this is "not a bad thing," an expert featured in the piece also believed there should be more balance in education, asserting "just as the child needs a father and a mother, so too in school it is necessary to have the educational influences of both sexes."[116] Yet, while women made great inroads in early childhood and primary education and constituted approximately 50 percent of all high school teachers in 1960, women instructors lagged far behind their male counterparts in technical schools and higher education.[117] A similar situation was evident in healthcare. Although women increasingly trained in medicine, constituting 26 percent of all doctors in 1956, 40 percent in 1977, and 58 percent in 1992, they assumed lower-ranking and lower-paid positions, working as pediatricians, general practitioners, and dermatologists rather than as surgeons.[118] Moreover, nearly all nurses were women, and no effort was made to encourage men to enter into this area. Thus, the labor force was gendered not only horizontally, but also vertically. This vertical gendering of the labor force was especially evident in leadership positions as men were overrepresented as foremen, managers, and directors. Indeed, with the exception of the cultural domain, where women assumed one-quarter of managerial positions in 1966, women constituted an insignificant number of managers. For example, by 1966, only 5 percent of leadership positions in state administration were held by women and only 1 percent in economic units. Moreover, until 1977, the number of forewomen and women technicians did not surpass 10 percent—including in the textile industry, a female-dominated realm.[119] Indeed, even in agriculture, where women constituted 60 percent of all laborers in 1966, they assumed less than 9 percent of leadership posts.[120]

Highlighting women's varied contributions in the labor force and his commitment to equality between women and men, Ceaușescu criticized women's underrepresentation in leadership positions as unjust. Accordingly, in 1967 he instituted measures to increase the number of women promoted to managerial and directorship positions, an initiative in which the CNF assumed a principal role. The results were impressive given women's low representation in leadership prior to these efforts. For example, by 1977 women assumed 13.8 percent of leadership positions in economic institutes and centers, 27.6 percent in agricultural cooperatives, and 38.4 percent in education, art and culture, and nursing.[121] Nonetheless, of note is that women did not even come close to reaching parity with men—even in the above female-dominated areas.

Women's modest presence in management was due to male prejudice, men's desire to retain power, and workplace demands, which often required managers to log in long hours. Given their many responsibilities in the home, most women, particularly mothers, were not able to dedicate the time and effort required for advancing to managerial positions. The state, however, did not acknowledge this reality, but instead proclaimed its commitment to women's advancement. An article in a four-part series entitled "Can Women Lead?" is illustrative.[122] Written by the minister of light industry (a man, incidentally), the piece begins by acknowledging women's "impressive contributions in light industry" and the ministry's tireless efforts to promote them. It then enumerated various ways the state had improved women's everyday lives through provision of modern apartments, household appliances, nurseries and kindergartens, workplace canteens, and semi-prepared and prepared foods. Accordingly, women's comparatively slow rate of advancement was not due to lack of professional opportunities, modern conveniences, or social services, but because "motherhood, responsibilities for raising and educating children, competes with the desire to fulfill professional aspirations." The author concludes that women's inability to balance workplace and household responsibilities, along with lack of qualification, self-confidence, and initiative, are ultimately responsible for women's underrepresentation in leadership. In this way, the state targeted (and essentially blamed) individual women for their inability to reach parity with men at the managerial level.

This piece, however, provides an idealized portrait of state welfare entitlements, obscuring the fact that subsidized childcare facilities were not widely available, household appliances (e.g. washing machines, vacuum cleaners) were by no means common possessions, and men's contributions to daily household maintenance remained modest. It also fails to acknowledge another factor that decisively influenced advancement to leadership: membership in the Communist Party. Since party membership entailed staying late for meetings, women found it difficult to balance party obligations and family responsibilities, forcing them to forgo membership—although some also refused for ideological or moral reasons. As almost all of my respondents were mothers, they recognized that they could not juggle long hours at the factory and party meetings with domestic duties. Accordingly, some declined party membership.[123] As Tatiana noted, "I wanted to be a party member, but I refused, having two children at home, I categorically refused."[124] Moreover, it's possible that husbands dissuaded their wives from becoming party members since they expected them to be at home, tending to their needs.[125] Consequently, women's membership in the PCR never reached parity with men, with women constituting 9 percent of party members in 1955, 17 percent in 1960, 21 percent in 1965, 25 percent in 1973, and 34 percent in 1986.[126] Women's opportunities for promotion, then, were restricted by low party membership and challenges in balancing evening school (which was necessary for earning an advanced degree or becoming skilled) with family responsibilities. These factors, along with women's lower age for retirement (fifty-five for women and sixty for men), reinforced inequalities within the labor force, which, in turn, affected women's salaries, promotions, and pensions. As in non-socialist systems, these gender hierarchies also created a vicious cycle whereby women were unable to defend their interests due to lack of influence in the workforce.

Women's underrepresentation in the party was mirrored at the higher echelons of power, such as in the Central Committee of the PCR and in ministerial positions. For example, women constituted 4 percent of Central Committee members in 1965, 5 percent in 1974, and 20 percent in 1979, only reaching 24 percent by 1989.[127] Meanwhile, in the Political Bureau/Executive Committee, women's representation was even lower, dipping from 12.1 percent in 1948 to zero between 1955 and 1969.[128] Only after the introduction of quotas in the mid-1970s and the advent of Elena Ceauşescu to political power did women's numbers in this area increase, peaking at 17.8 percent in 1979. In contrast, women's presence in the Grand National Assembly (Parliament) witnessed impressive gains over the course of socialist rule, increasing from 7.5 percent in 1948 to 17.4 percent in 1961. Although this figure dipped down to 14.3 percent in 1975, it more than doubled by 1980 as a result of the introduction of a quota system, reaching 32.5 percent.[129] Yet with Elena and Nicolae Ceaușescu's consolidation of power, these positions were primarily token, and parliamentary members had little influence on policymaking. Therefore, women's increased, albeit comparatively low, presence in these areas did not translate into increased political influence.

## Equality, Work, and the Private Sphere

Overall, women's occupational advancement under socialism was impressive, yet it remained behind that of men. Whether due to sexist hiring practices, disparities between men's and women's wages, discrimination and harassment, or responsibilities in the home, gender equality, even by the mid-1980s, had yet to be realized in Romania. Moreover, women's increased participation in male-dominated realms did not eradicate patriarchal mentalities and behaviors, as Engels believed would happen once women entered the labor force en masse. While efforts to promote gender equality through work might be considered failures, they were not necessarily perceived as such by women. In fact, a number of my respondents asserted that women had achieved equality with men, citing women's participation in paid labor as evidence. For instance, to the question "Were women and men equal under communism?" Aneta (b. 1936) responded, "In my opinion they [women] were equal. They held leadership positions; they could work in any industry, even if it was men's work. I would say they were equal ... including the salary.[130] Similarly, Ecaterina (b. 1955) stressed equality of opportunity:

> Almost all of us were in the same boat, regardless if you were a man or woman. Sex didn't matter, that is, being a man did not mean you were privileged. Women could also achieve what they wanted, if they wanted, if they had ambitions, attended the party school, not a problem, they could make it anywhere. But from a humanitarian point of view, we were in the same boat.[131]

From Ecaterina's comment it could be inferred that Engels's formula for women's equality had proved successful in Romania. Namely, that women's full-time employment had, in fact, facilitated equality between women and men. However, this should be tempered by her assertion that women and men "were in the same boat," that is, they suffered equally under socialism. As such, women's progress in the labor force must be balanced against the deprivations and repression of living in a one-party state.

Other women viewed work more complexly. As Rodica (b. 1963) noted,

> At work, yes. Even I worked in heavy labor alongside men, in that respect you can speak of equality. But in other regards, social life or such, no. Men had more advantages, even at work. They always said, "Hey you can't earn the salary of a man," even if you worked much harder than [a man].[132]

According to Rodica, while both men and women worked arduous and demanding jobs, men retained their privileged position within society at large, which afforded them numerous advantages. Meanwhile, D. (b. 1953) claimed that women's multiple burdens placed them in a subordinate position, undermining state claims of gender equality:

> Equal? Never have women been equal to men. My opinion is that women had to work much more than men. You go to work, you have quotas ... you could be an intellectual in an office, a worker at a machine in a factory, it's all work. Then you come home and you have to take care of the family. And this was not due to the system, but family upbringing. So, it was believed that he [the husband] could read the newspaper or watch TV while the woman came home from work and set the table, took care of the house. Plus the children who, no matter how much the husband got involved, they belong to the mother, the mother tends to their needs. Equality was only formal.[133]

D.'s comments underscore the interconnection of work and family in women's conceptions of equality. For D., "work" encompassed much more than what the state and individual men were willing to acknowledge. While she admitted that women and men were, for the most part, equal on the shop floor, when it came to the kitchen, women bore the largest burden. Men's lack of participation in household duties was thus proof to her that proclamations of gender equality were purely formal. This sentiment was shared by many of my respondents, as well as women in the former GDR who, in oral histories, claimed to have received minimal help from men in domestic duties and who similarly used the phrase "formal equality" to refer to women's position vis-à-vis men.[134] As we will see in the following chapter, men's contribution to household maintenance was a frequent topic in *Femeia*, and was presented as essential to creating a more companionate and egalitarian marriage. The reality on the ground, however, often departed from the idealized portraits in socialist media as women continued to bear the brunt of household responsibilities.

## Conclusion

According to socialist theorists, women's mass employment would culminate in their emancipation and full equality with men. At the same time, employment was essential for the rapid industrialization and modernization of the country. However, because the state placed greater emphasis on the latter and only partially supported the former, as Romania industrialized women failed to achieve full equality with men. This was in part related to the enduring power of patriarchal beliefs and practices, particularly among male managers and laborers who regarded skill as a masculine preserve and were resistant to training and working alongside women. For women who did manage to secure jobs in male-dominated fields, some were subject to harassment, discrimination, and other sexist practices. While some women challenged workplace sexism and asserted themselves as equal laborers, they were in the minority.

Women's position in the labor force was also related to policy measures: the state employed both gender-homogenizing and differentiating strategies, representing women as equal socialist workers while also instituting protective legislation—and later promotional schemes—that excluded them from certain jobs and channeled them into feminized sectors. While women's presence in light industries and science and technology increased, women continued to be underrepresented in heavy industry, transport, and construction. Meanwhile, women made only modest inroads in politics, constituting a disproportionately small percentage of the Executive Committee of the PCR, as well as being grossly underrepresented in regional and local politics. As a corollary, women's manifold domestic responsibilities limited their opportunities for occupational advancement—especially to positions of leadership. Over the course of socialist rule, then, gender-homogenizing and gender-differentiating policies were not coherently configured to accommodate (and empower) women as workers and mothers. Rather, they were an outgrowth of state expediency, which required a mass labor pool and a large population, reflecting lack of commitment to women's full equality—and the ambiguities of socialist modernization.

While women's mass employment did not culminate in their full equality with men as Engels had envisaged, socialist modernization did decisively shape the course of women's lives. To be sure, some women viewed work as burdensome and unfulfilling, especially those who worked long hours and overnight shifts at the factory and who were unable to enter jobs of their choosing due to social origin or lack of connections or pull. Moreover, those who faced criticism or harassment by male colleagues struggled to demonstrate their competence and maintain their dignity and self-confidence. Yet, others found work empowering, intellectually stimulating, and personally validating. Work offered women more choices: the opportunity to leave their villages and live in new industrial towns, to earn a living wage in a socially recognized manner, and to develop new relationships. Additionally, it provided women with alternative identities, new ways of imagining their place in society, and a sense of accomplishment. Indeed, some women even claimed that work was the basis upon which they had achieved equality with men. It is, therefore, unsurprising that some women were supportive, and even enthusiastic, about this aspect of life under state socialism.

Accordingly, women's positive recollections of work are not necessarily reflective of a false consciousness or even support for the regime. Nor are they simply rooted in nostalgia for the communist past. Rather, women valued work for a number of understandable reasons. These might have been ideological, but most often they were practical and personal. Essentially, although efforts to promote women's employment were rooted more in economic expediency than in socialist principles, this does not negate the positive effect of working outside the home. This was especially true for women who had been trained in certain occupations and professions that they felt passionate about, a finding that can be extrapolated to other parts of the Eastern Bloc, and, indeed, the world. While it is impossible to know the degree to which women's perspectives were shaped by socialist propaganda, the experience of earning a living wage, or of interacting socially with men, it appears that work was one realm where the state was at least moderately successful in advancing women's status. Thus, the myopia and, indeed, sexism inherent in labor policies and programs for women must be balanced against the fact that work was meaningful for some women.

That said, although some respondents claimed that women and men were equal under socialism, citing employment opportunities as evidence, others were more nuanced in their conception of equality. According to them, full equality of the sexes was never achieved due to women's responsibilities for home and family—and men's reluctance to contribute to this realm. As will be subsequently demonstrated, reconciling household and workplace responsibilities was, at least officially, a concern for policymakers and propagandists already during the early years of socialist rule. However, as in other areas, state pronouncements were not followed by consistent or substantive policy reform, undermining state promises of gender equality and contributing to women's often ambiguous experiences of everyday life under socialism.

## Notes

1. This chapter is influenced by scholarship on gender and labor in modern Europe. See, for example, Kathleen Canning, *Languages of Labor and Gender: Female Factory Work in Germany, 1850–1914* (Ithaca, NY: Cornell University Press, 1996); Laura L. Frader and Sonya A. Rose, eds., *Gender and Class in Modern Europe* (Ithaca, NY: Cornell University Press, 1996); Eva Baron, ed. *Work Engendered: Toward a New History of American Labor* (Ithaca, NY: Cornell University Press, 1991); and Alice Kessler-Harris, *Out to Work: A History of Wage-Earning Women in the United States* (New York: Oxford University Press, 1982). On women laborers in the Eastern Bloc, see Malgorzata Fidelis, *Women, Communism, and Industrialization in Postwar Poland* (New York: Cambridge University Press, 2010); Wendy Z. Goldman, *Women at the Gates: Gender and Industry in Stalin's Russia* (New York: Cambridge University Press, 2002); Diane Koenker, "Men against Women on the Shop Floor in Early Soviet Russia: Gender and Class in the Socialist Workplace," *American Historical Review* 100, no. 5 (December 1995): 1438–1465; Martha Lampland, "Biographies of Liberation: Testimonials to Labor in Socialist Hungary," in *Promissory Notes: Women in the Transition to Socialism*, ed. Sonia Kruks et al. (New York: Monthly Review Press, 1989): 306–322; Eva Fodor, *Working Difference: Women's Working Lives in Hungary and Austria, 1945–1995* (Durham, NC: Duke University Press, 2003); Katherine Lebow, *Unfinished Utopia: Nowa Huta, Stalinism, and Polish Society, 1949–56* (Ithaca, NY: Cornell University Press, 2013); and Donna Harsch, *Revenge of the Domestic.: Women, the Family, and Communism in the German Democratic Republic* (Princeton, NJ: Princeton University Press, 2006).
2. To quote political theorist Mihaela Miroiu, "One could be born at the firm's hospital, grow up in the firm's apartment, be educated in the firm's school, sleep in its dormitories, work at the firm for a whole career, spend free time at the firm's playgrounds, resort hotels, and cultural houses, eat in its 'restaurants,' repair shoes there, be appreciated or punished there, meet colleagues, neighbors, spouses, friends and enemies in the same small world, raise children, retire, and even be buried by comrades at the firm." Mihaela Miroiu, "The Costless State Feminism in Romania," Conference paper, Women, Gender and Post-Communism, Indiana Roundtables on Post-Communism, Bloomington, Indiana, April 2005.
3. "Populaţia urbană din România socialistă,"*Anuarul Statistic Populare Romîne*, Direcţia Centrală de Statistică (Bucharest, 1958; 1967–1989), 51.
4. This figure increased over the course of communist rule, from 31.3 percent in 1956 to 38.2 percent in 1966 to 43.6 percent in 1977. See *Anuarul Statistic al Republicii Socialiste România*, 1967; and *Anuarul Statistic al României*, 1990.
5. Luciana Jinga, *Gen şi reprezentare în România comunistă, 1944–1989* (Iaşi: Polirom, 2015), 230.
6. Indeed, Laureana Urse claims that violence against women actually increased during the early years of communist rule when compared with the

interwar period. See Laureana Urse, "Populaţia feminină: modernizare şi adaptare," in *Calitatea Vieţii XVIII* nr. 1–2 (2007): 149–64.
7. Fidelis, *Women, Communism, and Industrialization*, 109.
8. Lack of a male breadwinner was a particular concern in countries such as Germany and Poland that experienced heavy casualties during the war.
9. "In ajunul lui 8 Martie printre textilistele de la F.R.B.," *Scânteia*, 8 March 1951, 1.
10. "Ziua Internaţională a Femeii," *Scânteia*, 8 March 1952, 1.
11. On the use of similar discourses in Poland and Hungary, see Fidelis, *Women, Communism, and Industrialization*, 105–6; Lebow, *Unfinished Utopia*, 100; and Joanna Goven, "Gender and Modernism in a Stalinist State," *Social Politics* 9, no. 1 (2002): 3–28.
12. "In lumea capitalistă: Victime ale mizeriei şi discriminării," *Scânteia*, 8 March 1959, 2.
13. In addition to sex, the law made no differentiation with respect to age or nationality. "Codul Muncii din 1950 (Lege nr. 3 din 30 mai 1950)" *Buletin Oficial al Republicii Populare Române* nr. 50 din 8 iunie 1950.
14. Ibid. While pregnant women assigned to lighter work were to maintain their regular salary, they were often reassigned to lower-paying positions, illustrating another way in which protective legislation undermined socialist promises of equality.
15. Ibid. In 1956 maternity leave was extended to 112 days (52 days prenatal and 60 days postnatal).
16. See, for example, Gwendolyn Mink, *The Wages of Motherhood: Inequality in the Welfare State* (Ithaca, NY: Cornell University Press, 1995); Frader and Rose, eds., *Gender and Class in Modern Europe;* Sonya Rose, *Limited Livelihoods: Gender and Class in Nineteenth-Century England* (Berkeley: University of California Press, 1992); and S. J. Kenney, *For Whose Protection? Reproductive Hazards and Exclusionary Politics in the United States and Britain* (Ann Arbor, MI: University of Michigan Press, 1992).
17. The modification of the Penal Code in 1953 outlined penalties for employers that discriminated against (1) pregnant women (2) women on maternity leave and (3) returning mothers. As such, they were comparatively progressive in upholding women's right to combine work with motherhood and be adequately remunerated while on maternity leave. The penalty for not respecting these policies could be punishment from three months to one year in correctional prison or a fine of 100 to 500 lei, however, it is unknown how many bosses were actually fined or punished for breaking this law. See "Decretul nr. 202/1953 pentru modificarea Codului Penal al Republicii Populare Române," *Monitorul Oficial al României*, 14 mai 1953.
18. Jinga, *Gen şi reprezentare*, 211.
19. Research on Poland indicates that employers did not always follow protocol with respect to reintegrating women into work after maternity leave. See Lebow, *Unfinished Utopia*, 116.
20. See, Niki Iosub, "Legislaţia socială în ajutorul femeii," *Femeia*, November 1956, 23.

21. For the Polish case, see Malgorzata Fidelis, "Equality through Protection: The Politics of Women's Employment in Postwar Poland, 1945–1956," *Slavic Review* 63, no. 2 (2004): 301–24.
22. Valeria P., interview with author, Brașov, 14 June 2003.
23. Elena Chișiu, "Bucuria muncii libere," *Scânteia*, 8 March 1952, 2.
24. Ibid.
25. Viorica Alexandru, "Comunistele la posturile lor," *Femeia*, August 1965, 5.
26. *Anuarul Statistic al Republicii Socialiste România*, 1967; and *Anuarul Statistic al României*, 1990. It should be noted that in Romania only workers officially registered with a *carte de muncă* (employment record book) were included in state statistics. Thus, agricultural laborers who worked on the CAPs (collective farms) and constituted a large portion of rural workers were not encompassed within this data since they were not registered with a *carte de muncă*. Accordingly, the overall percentage of women employed in Romania was much higher than indicated by these statistics and was similar to most countries in the Eastern Bloc. Women's percentage of the total labor force for the following countries was as follows: Hungary: 33 percent in 1955, 40 percent in 1965, and 47.9 percent in 1985; Czechoslovakia: 37 percent in 1948, 45 percent in 1979, and 47.7 percent in 1989; Bulgaria: 25 percent in 1952, 38 percent in 1962, and 49.8 percent in 1989; and Poland: 31 percent in 1950, 33 percent in 1960, and 43.2 percent in 1979. For figures, see various chapters in Barbara Lobodzinska, ed., *Family, Women, and Employment in Central Eastern Europe* (Westport, CT: Greenwood Press, 1995); and Lynne Haney, *Inventing the Needy: Gender and the Politics of Welfare in Hungary* (Berkeley: University of California Press, 2002), 33, 66.
27. First place medals were reserved for high-level functionaries, intellectuals, celebrities and sports and cultural figures.
28. This assessment is based on my own survey of the communist daily, *Scânteia*, 1947–89.
29. *Femeia*, March 1967, 4.
30. *Recensământul populației din 21 februarie 1956, Structură social-economică a populației*, Direcția Centrală de Statistică (Bucharest, 1957); Jinga, *Gen și reprezentare*, 241.
31. *Anuarul Statistic Populare Romîne*, 1958; and *Anuarul Statistic al Republicii Socialiste România*, 1965–89.
32. The respective figures for women in 1974 were: 11.5 and 13.1. See Aneta Spornic, *Utilizarea eficientă a resurselor de muncă feminine în România* (Bucharest: Editura Academiei, 1975), 82; 96.
33. See *Anuarul Statistic al Republicii Socialiste România*, 1967; and *Anuarul Statistic al României*, 1990.
34. For instance, in 1974 an industrial worker made on average 8 percent more than an agricultural laborer, though many workers made significantly more. *Anuarul Statistic al Republicii Socialiste România*, 1975, 76.
35. Article 14 read: "Women are ensured broad possibilities for self-fulfillment in conditions of full social equality with men, benefiting from equal work for equal pay and special protection. Women are guaranteed the right to occupy any position or place of employment commensurate with their

training in order to contribute to the growth of material production and spiritual creativity, while ensuring all the necessary means for raising and educating children." See "Codul Muncii (Legea nr. 10 din 25 noiembrie 1972)," *Buletinul Oficial al Republicii Socialiste România*, nr. 140 din 1 decembrie 1972.

36. Ibid.
37. "Programul de măsuri pentru creşterea participării femeilor la activitatea din întreprinderi şi instituţii," 21 august 1973.
38. "Cuvântarea tovarăşului Nicolae Ceauşescu cu privire la rolul femeii în viaţa politică, economică şi socială a ţării, Plenara CC al PCR, din 18–19 iunie 1973" in *România Libera*, 20 June 1973. In this respect, Ceauşescu echoed August Bebel decades earlier, who viewed women's work in heavy labor as potentially detrimental to women's health and reproductive capacity. Bebel also regarded heavy labor as unfeminine and unsightly, even claiming that a women's femininity would be diminished if she worked in such sectors. See Bebel, *Women under Socialism* (New York: New York Labor Press, 1904), 180.
39. Similar legislation was passed in Poland and Hungary in the late 1950s and 1960s, reversing earlier, Stalinist efforts that had integrated women into previously male-dominated realms. See Haney, *Inventing the Needy*, 104; and Fidelis, *Women, Communism, and Industrialization*.
40. "Hotărârea Plenarei Comitetului Central al Partidului Comunist Român din 18–19 iunie cu privire la creşterea rolului femeii în viaţa economică, politică, şi socială a ţării," *Buletinul Oficial al Republicii Socialiste România*, nr. 96, 4 iulie 1973.
41. Elisabeta Moraru, "Încotro ne îndreptăm fetele? (III)" *Femeia*, July 1970, 6–7. To seemingly insulate himself from charges of sexism, the psychologist added that if a woman is particularly adept at a high-stress job, she should not be prevented from doing it, thus acknowledging that in exceptional cases women may assume such work.
42. Ibid.
43. Ibid. Women's participation in the labor force was also taken up in books by socialist "experts," however, these had a limited reach in comparison with *Femeia* and brochures distributed by the CNF. See, for example, Carol Roman and Vasile Tincu, *101 interviuri cu femei* (Bucharest: Editura Politică, 1978); Ana Gluvacov, *Afirmarea femeii în viaţa societăţii: dimensiuni şi semnificaţii* (Bucharest: Editura Politică, 1975); and Aneta Spornic, *Utilizarea eficientă a resurselor de muncă feminine în România* (Bucharest: Editura Academiei Republicii Socialiste România, 1975).
44. Jinga, *Gen şi reprezentare*, 218–19. In accordance with these measures, school counselors began evaluating girls' competence in a variety of areas to determine their facility in the sciences.
45. Ibid., 247–48.
46. Ibid., 326–27.
47. Ibid.
48. See Goldman, *Women at the Gates*, 155.
49. See the reader's letter to the editor, "De ce o fata nu poate fi marinar?" in *Femeia*, September 1973, 5.

50. One justification for excluding women from the post of sailor was that they were more prone to seasickness and not as good at swimming as men were.
51. See Mary Ellen Fischer, "Women in Romanian Politics: Elena Ceauşescu, Pronatalism, and the Promotion of Women," in *Women, State, and Party in Eastern Europe*, ed. Sharon Wolchik and Alfred Meyer (Durham, NC: Duke University Press, 1985): 21–37.
52. See *Scânteia*, 8 March 1981, 1.
53. Jinga, *Gen şi reprezentare*, 220.
54. "Fetele lui '68," *Femeia*, May 1968, 6–9.
55. As previously noted, those who did not work were labeled "social parasites" under "Decret nr. 153 din 24 martie 1970 pentru stabilirea şi sancţionarea unor contravenţii privind regulile de convieţuire socială, ordinea, şi linişte publica," *Bulentinul Oficial al Republicii Socialiste România*, 33, 13 aprilie 1970. Individuals who were found guilty under this law could be placed in a correctional facility for one to six months or fined 1,000–5,000 lei.
56. C., interview with author, Braşov, 14 July 2003.
57. See *Anuarul Statistic al Republicii Populare Române*; and *Anuarul Statistic Republicii Socialiste România*, 1956–90.
58. Ibid.
59. Regine, interview with author, Braşov, 2 July 2003.
60. Goven, "Gender and Modernism," 17.
61. Ileana Luchian, "Calea libera," *Femeia*, February 1957, 12–13.
62. Jinga, *Gen şi reprezentare*, 241.
63. See *Anuarul Statistic al Republicii Populare Române*; and *Anuarul Statistic Republicii Socialiste România*, 1956–90.
64. Maria F., interview with author, Braşov, 20 June 2003.
65. Eva, interview with author, Braşov, 12 June 2003.
66. "Femeile in lupta pentru pace, egalitate, drepturi, demnitate umana," *Femeia*, March 1983, 8.
67. Eugenia, interview with author, Bucharest, 12 June 2009.
68. See "Decretul nr. 180/1950 privind reglementarea repartizării în producţie şi în instituţiile de învăţămînt superior a absolvenţilor şcolilor medii tehnice, şcolilor pedagogice şi ai instituţilor de învăţămînt superior," *Monitorul Oficial al României;* and "Decretul 158/1970 cu privire la repartizarea în productie a absolvenţilor instituţilor de învăţămînt superior de învăţămîntul de zi," *Monirotul Oficial al României*. A *repartiţie* was required for graduates of higher education institutes as well as technical schools.
69. Mirela Rotaru, "Job Assignment of Graduates of the University of Bucharest and Their Integration into the Labor System of the 1980s," *International Review of Social Research* 4, no. 2 (June 2014): 153–54.
70. In some cases, individuals actually requested to be placed in rural areas, namely their birthplaces, to be closer to families and spouses. Such requests were typically granted—regardless of merit.
71. Elena, interview with author, Bucharest, 1 June 2009. Two other teachers I interviewed, who were similarly posted to remote regions in the 1970s and 1980s, also had negative memories of their *repartiţie*.

72. Anca, interview with author, Bucharest, 12 June 2012.
73. Tatiana, interview with author, Brașov, 27 May 2003.
74. Fidelis, *Women, Communism, and Industrialization*, 99.
75. For work under socialism as liberating, see Eszter Zsófia Tóth, "'My Work, My Family, and My Car': Women's Memories of Work, Consumerism, and Leisure in Socialist Hungary," in *Gender Politics and Everyday Life in State Socialist Eastern and Central Europe*, ed. Shana Penn and Jill Massino (New York: Palgrave, 2009): 33–44.
76. See Joanne J. Meyerowitz, *Women Adrift: Independent Wage Earners in Chicago, 1880–1930* (Chicago: University of Chicago Press, 1988), 18.
77. Elvira, interview with author, Brașov, 5 May 2003.
78. On work as a site of sociability and camaraderie in East Germany, see Daphne Berdahl, *Where the World Ended: Reunification and Identity in the German Borderland* (Berkeley: University of California Press, 1999); and Toth, "My Work, My Family, and My Car."
79. Luana, interview with author, Brașov, 25 July 2003.
80. Elisabeta, interview with author, Brașov, 27 June 2003.
81. C. interview with author, Brașov, 14 July 2003.
82. As previously noted, such discrimination also applied to children whose parents had been branded *chiaburi* (kulaks) during collectivization.
83. Cătălina, interview with author, Bucharest, 18 July 2009.
84. Stela, interview with author, Brașov, 23 June 2003.
85. Ibid. Art remained Stela's life passion throughout the socialist period—when she could find paint, paper, and canvases—serving as a form of "therapy" for her.
86. Major exceptions are the Soviet Union during the NEP (New Economic Policy) period (1921–29) and Hungary after the late 1960s, when the government sought to push women, at least temporarily, out of the labor force with the Child Care Allowance Act. See Olga Toth, "No Envy, No Pity," in *Gender Politics and Post-Communism: Reflections from Eastern Europe and the Former Soviet Union*, ed. Nanette Funk and Magda Mueller (New York: Routledge, 1993), 218–19.
87. On tensions between male and female laborers in early industrial-capitalist societies see, for example, Ute Frevert, *Women in German History from Bourgeois Emancipation to Sexual Liberation*, trans. Stuart McKinnon-Evans with Terry Bond and Barbara Norden (New York: Berg, 1989), 23–24; Sonya Rose, "Gender Antagonism and Class Conflict: Exclusionary Tactics of Male Trade Unionists in Nineteenth Century Britain," *Social History* 13 (1988), 191–208; Canning, *Languages of Labor and Gender;* Rose, *Limited Livelihoods;* Frader and Rose, *Gender and Class in Modern Europe;* and Baron, *Work Engendered*.
88. According to Lynne Attwood and Diane Koenker, heroine workers in the Soviet Union often faced ridicule and psychological abuse from their male coworkers. Additionally, men were known to sabotage the machines of their female coworkers in an effort to get them demoted or fired. See Lynne Attwood, *Creating the New Soviet Woman: Women's Magazines as Engineers of Female Identity, 1922–53* (Basingstoke: Macmillan, 1999); and Koenker "Men against Women."

89. Jinga, *Gen și reprezentare*, 247. For other countries in the Bloc, see Fidelis, *Women, Communism, and Industrialization*; Harsch, *Revenge of the Domestic*, 127–29; and Donald Filtzer, "Women Workers in the Khrushchev Era," in Ilić, et al. *Women in the Khrushchev Era*, 38.
90. See "Promovarea," *Femeia*, March 1966, 2–4.
91. Ibid.
92. Maria, interview with author, Brașov, 15 June 2003.
93. Ibid.
94. See Fidelis, *Women, Communism, and Industrialization*. In the case of the Soviet Union in the 1930s, Wendy Goldman found that far from training women for skilled jobs, managers would simply put them to work as janitors and cooks. See Goldman, *Women at the Gates*, 225. Further research is needed on the Romanian case to determine how common such beliefs about hiring women skilled laborers were.
95. Adrian Grama mentions such treatment with respect to women who worked at the Malaxa factory during World War II, noting that overseers and foremen were prone to use vulgar language towards women laborers and, in some cases, even beat them. See Adrian Grama, "Laboring Along: Industrial Workers and the Making of Postwar Romania (1944–1958)" (PhD diss., Central European University, 2017), 88.
96. Ibid.
97. Maria, interview with author, Brașov, 15 June 2003.
98. Alf Lüdtke employs the term *Eigen-sinn* to illuminate the motivations behind workers' demands for increased wages and improved working conditions. See Alf Lüdtke "Organizational Order or Eigensinn? Workers' Privacy and Workers' Politics in Imperial Germany," in *Rites of Power, Symbolism, Ritual and Politics since the Middle Ages*, ed. Sean Wilentz (Philadelphia: University of Pennsylvania Press, 1990): 303–333.
99. Harsch, *Revenge of the Domestic*, 129.
100. See Sándor Hovárth, *Stalinism Reloaded: Everyday Life in Stalin-City, Hungary* (Bloomington, IN: Indiana University Press, 2017), 248; and Fidelis, *Women Communism, and Industrialization*, 127.
101. See Lebow, *Unfinished Utopia*, 113–14; Fidelis; *Women, Communism, and Industrialization*; Harsch, *Revenge of the Domestic*; and Mark Pittaway, *The Workers' State: Industrial Labor and the Making of Socialist Hungary* (Pittsburgh, PA: University of Pittsburgh Press, 2012), 267–71.
102. Goldman, *Women at the Gates*, 227.
103. Rodica M., interview with Anca Coman, Brașov, 12 August 2003. In Stalinist Poland "inappropriate behavior" on the part of male supervisors was also exhibited with the result that women either left such jobs or refused promotions. See Fidelis, *Women, Communism, and Industrialization*, 151.
104. For instance, women constituted approximately 10 percent of all construction workers until 1979, after which their presence grew slightly over the course of socialist rule, reaching 14 percent only in 1989. *Anuarul Statistic al Republicii Socialiste România*, 1965–89.
105. Viorica, interview with author, Brașov, 8 June 2003.

106. Article 17, "Constituţia Republicii Socialiste România, 1965," *Bulentinul Oficial al Republicii Socialiste România*, nr. 1 din 21 august 1965; "Codul Penal din 1968" *Monitorul Oficial al României*.
107. Aneta, interview with Anca Coman, Braşov, 25 June 2003.
108. For instance, according to a survey conducted in the mid-1970s, only one-third of workers appealed to Enterprise Workers Councils, and, of these, less than one-half believed that their proposals would result in some type of policy change. By the early 1980s, a survey with 2,500 workers at 18 enterprises revealed that only 13 percent of respondents felt they could effect policy change in the workplace. Daniel N. Nelson, "Romania: Participatory Dynamics in Developed Socialism," in *Blue Collar Workers in Eastern Europe*, ed. Jan F. Triska and Charles Gati (London: Allen and Unwin, 1981), 181 as cited in William Crowther, *The Political Economy of Romanian Socialism* (New York: Praeger, 1988), 112.
109. Cătălina, interview with author, Bucharest, 18 July 2009.
110. Angela, interview with author, Braşov, 16 June 2003.
111. Eva, interview with author, Braşov, 12 June 2003.
112. Koenker, "Men against Women," 1462.
113. "Codul Muncii (Legea nr. 10 din 25 noiembrie, 1972)," art. 157, *Buletinul Oficial al Republicii Socialiste România*, nr. 140 din 1 decembrie 1972.
114. Jinga, *Gen şi reprezentare*, 234.
115. For example, while the minimum monthly salary for a textile worker in 1974 was 1,387 lei ($116) and the maximum, 2,040 lei ($171), for miners the minimum monthly salary ranged from 1,517 lei ($127) to 1,798 lei ($151) and the maximum from 2,588 lei ($217) to 3,302 lei ($278). Both mining and textile work were defined as "skilled" jobs and, therefore, in a higher wage class (e.g. 6 and 5 respectively) than unskilled jobs. However, it should be noted that officially published wage scales did not reflect bonuses and overtime pay, from which men primarily benefited as their domestic responsibilities were minimal. These bonuses were recorded in an employee's personal employment record book (*cartea de muncă*) and are not readily accessible to scholars. Therefore, while the wage differential between a textile worker and a miner appears moderate, in reality it was often much larger than officially indicated. I thank Mia Jinga for this insight. For official wage levels and job classification information, see the tables listed under "Lege nr. 57 din 29 octombrie 1974, Legea retribuirii dupa cantitatea şi calitatea muncii," *Buletin Oficial al Republicii Populare Române* nr. 133/1 noi. 1974, retrieved from http://www.cdep.ro/pls/legis/legis_pck.htp_act_text?idt=1325 (accessed 28 November 2017). Monetary conversions based on U.S. Treasury Reporting Rates of Exchange (31 March 1974), retrieved from https://www.gpo.gov/fdsys/pkg/GOVPUB-T63_100-953ef7e79a66697c1c6e99309a5d200c/pdf/GOVPUB-T63_100-953ef7e79a66697c1c6e99309a5d200c.pdf (accessed 19 December 2017).
116. Elisabeta Moraru, "Incotro ne îndreptăm fetele? (III)," *Femeia*, July 1970. 6–7.

117. Prior to World War II, women did not surpass 40 percent of primary school teaching staff and worked exclusively in all-girls schools. By 1956 women constituted 56 percent of primary school teachers. For more detailed figures, see Jinga, *Gen şi reprezentare*, 233.
118. Jinga, *Gen şi reprezentare*, 233.
119. Similarly, while women constituted 60 percent of agricultural labors in 1966, they accounted for less than 9 percent of cooperative managers. Ibid., 237–38, 246.
120. *Recensământul populaţiei din 15 martie 1966*, vol. VII, Partea a II-a *Populaţia activă pe ramuri şi subramuri ale economiciei naţionale*, Direcţia Centrală de Statistică (Bucharest 1970), 2.
121. Ibid., 239; and *Recensământul populaţiei din 5 ianuarie 1977*, vol. VII, *Populaţie-structură socială-economică*, Direcţia Centrală de Statistică (Bucharest 1980), 600.
122. Ion Crăciun, "Pot femeile să conducă? (IV): Da! Cu condiţia să o dorească," *Femeia*, December 1969, 4. See also, "Promovarea în transfocatorul cazului concret," *Femeia*, March 1969, 3.
123. On women and party membership see William Moskoff, "Sex Discrimination, Commuting and the Role of Women in Romanian Development," *Slavic Review* 37, no. 3 (1978), 449.
124. Tatiana, interview with author, Braşov, 27 May 2003.
125. Donna Harsch found this with respect to women laborers in the GDR. See Harsch, *Revenge of the Domestic*, 130.
126. *Congresul al XI-lea al Partidului Comunist Român, 25–28 noiembrie 1974* (Bucharest: Editura Politică, 1975), 69; ANIC, CC al PCR, Secţia Cancelarie, dosar 22/1989, f. 13; and Jinga, *Gen şi reprezentare*, 257–58.
127. Ibid., 260–61.
128. Ibid., 265.
129. The quota system was implemented in 1975 and required that women constitute 25 percent or more of all communist organizations. For the next ten years, women's figures in the Central Committee stabilized (at 23 percent in 1989) but dipped down to 9.5 in the Executive Committee in 1989, falling short of Ceauşescu's goal.
130. Aneta, interview with Anca Coman, Braşov, 25 June 2003.
131. Ecaterina, interview with author, Braşov, 17 June 2003.
132. Rodica M., interview with Anca Coman, Braşov, 12 August 2003.
133. D., interview with author, Braşov, 23 June 2003.
134. See Josie McLellan, *Love in the Time of Communism: Intimacy and Sexuality in the GDR* (Cambridge: Cambridge University Press, 2011), 72.

CHAPTER 4

# Love and Marriage

## Gender and the Transformation of Marital Roles and Relations

The vast majority of men came from a tradition in which a man was not supposed to tend to the house. There were exceptions of course; there were extraordinary men who got down to business, but most of them wouldn't. And then women did all the housework, plus waiting in lines, plus waiting on their husbands who came home, watched TV, football games, and so on. ... Let me tell you, women worked harder at their jobs. Men knew how to minimize their efforts, conserve their energy, take care of themselves, but women, who are more diligent, weaker, nonconfrontational, they did it [all], while the men relaxed.
—Marcela, art teacher (b. 1942)

The burden of washing fell on Onuț. He washed; he ironed.
—Stela, artist (b. 1954)

Women's participation in the labor force often positively affected their status and self-identity and was, according to some respondents, the basis upon which they achieved equality, or at least relative equality, with men. In terms of marital relations, however, the impact of socialist transformation was more ambiguous. This was largely due to the enduring power and prevalence of patriarchal behaviors. As anthropologist Katherine Verdery asserts, "Despite reorganizations of family roles and these tendencies toward homogenization, the structure of power and the larger division of labor in the socialist family remained decidedly gendered."[1] This interpretation is underscored by Marcela's recollection, quoted above, as well as the recollections of other women I interviewed. To be sure, "decidedly gendered" roles and relations do not preclude the possibility of a loving relationship; however, they nonetheless reflect a traditional approach to marriage, which socialist experts referred to as unsocialist and which, at times, produced frustration, exhaustion, and resignation within women.

In assessing socialism's failure to transform marital roles and relations, scholars typically cite flaws in Marxist theory. In particular, they critique Engels's facile notion that with the dissolution of private property and women's wide-scale participation in the labor force, men would regard women as equals, which would, in turn, dramatically affect family roles and relations. Scholars also cite state failure to lighten women's domestic responsibilities through provision of sufficient childcare centers, labor-saving devices, and communal kitchens and laundries.[2] Finally, they target ordinary men (and, in some cases, women) for continuing to adhere to traditionally gendered family roles. As Doina Paşca Harsanyi claims, "Gender roles were modified in form not in essence. Common wisdom required that a man be also somehow superior to his wife (more education, a more lucrative workplace, a superior position, etc.) for it was widely believed that the peace in the home might suffer once the traditional patriarchal pattern was disrupted."[3]

While representative of some family dynamics, this statement fails to capture the diversity and fluidity of marital relations. This chapter provides a more complex portrait of marriage under socialism, demonstrating that spousal roles were not only shaped by tradition and upbringing but by the challenges and uncertainties of everyday life, which, at times, required men to be more flexible in their family roles. Moreover, it argues, women's ability to exercise agency in their relationships, including renegotiating and even resisting traditional roles, varied over the course of socialist rule and according to personal circumstance. While socialism by no means revolutionized marriage, family roles did undergo change. For example, expansion of educational and occupational opportunities reduced women's economic dependence on men and broadened their roles and aspirations. Although marriage continued to be a central component of many women's lives, the role of laborer or professional increasingly coexisted with—and in some cases supplanted—the role of wife. Additionally, new family codes reconfigured women's marital status from dependents to equal partners, and propagandists promoted companionate marriage, emphasizing men's need to be sensitive to women's emotional needs and engage actively in housework and parenting.

At the same time, family policies could work against egalitarian family roles. For one, the passage of maternity leave (as opposed to family leave) reinforced caregiving as primarily a woman's responsibility. Furthermore, the feminization of the labor force and women's underrepresentation in politics and leadership reinforced their subordinate status within the public sphere. Meanwhile, the criminalization of abortion in 1966 linked women's citizenship to reproductive output, defining them in essentialist and gender-differentiating terms. Religious and traditional mores and beliefs also continued to influence individuals' worldviews, including conceptions of gender, sexuality, and marital relations. Accordingly, many men retained domineering roles within the family, embracing more or less traditional beliefs whereby women were expected to assume primary responsibility for the household and children. Indeed, in some cases tradition and socialism worked in tandem.[4] For instance, the introduction of stringent divorce policy created financial barriers to dissolving marriages, which, alongside increased emphasis on socialist morality, reinforced existing stigmas surrounding divorce, essentially forcing couples to stay together. For some women, this meant enduring unhealthy relationships, including psychological and physical abuse.

That said, according to some of my respondents, marital roles did undergo change during the socialist period. This was particularly evident in men's participation in childrearing and other domestic duties. While in certain instances related to men's sensitivity to women's lot and a belief in gender equality, such helping was more often motivated by necessity: the inadequacy of state childcare facilities and, beginning in the 1980s, the time involved in food procurement required that men also contribute in the domestic realm. Thus, men's conceptions of family roles may have been less rigid than conventionally believed. As a corollary, the misapplication of Marxist theory—that is, state failure to fully socialize childcare and substantially improve the material realities of its citizens—may have inadvertently fostered more equitable marital relations. Therefore, like other aspects of life under socialism, marriage assumed diverse and ambiguous meanings, with continuities as well as changes both in how marriage was codified and represented by the state and experienced by individual women and men.

## To Create a More Equal and Permanent Union

The Civil Code of 1864 defined women as legal dependents of their husbands (or other male heads of household), prohibiting them from participating in the justice system, keeping their earnings, and withdrawing money from their own bank accounts.[5] As secondary citizens, women were also denied equal educational and employment opportunities, leaving them economically dependent on their families or, if married, their husbands. Accordingly, in Romania, as in most other parts of the globe, marriage was often essential for ensuring women's livelihood. The advent of state socialism, however, dramatically altered women's status, guaranteeing full employment and codifying equality between women and men in all spheres of life. Furthermore, the 1954 family code, modeled on the Soviet one, wholly reformulated marital rights and responsibilities.[6] In particular, the code established a minimum marriage age (eighteen for men, sixteen for women), abrogated men's status as "protector" of women, and equalized spousal roles, rights, and obligations. Additionally, with the abolition of the dowry system, men lost their proprietary status vis-à-vis their wives. The code also established equal decision-making power within marriage, including the initiation of divorce proceedings. Specifically, "reasonable grounds" (the basis upon which individuals could divorce) expanded to include a range of categories from adultery to spousal health. At the same time, marriage could only be terminated through judicial process, an interventionist measure that departed from early socialist conceptions wherein unions were to be dissolved with ease and for a host of reasons, including spousal incompatibility and cessation of affection.[7] Nonetheless, the process was simplified, a particularly important revision given the repressions of the 1950s when women (and a minority of men) sought to divorce an imprisoned spouse to avoid suffering "guilt by association."[8] Thus, divorce could be a strategic measure, at times initiated on the urging of the incarcerated spouse, to prevent job loss and restriction from employment altogether. It could also serve as a protective measure, safeguarding children's educational future, particularly at the university level. Finally, revision of divorce legislation enabled quick remarriage, which, given women's lack of professional and occupational training during the early years of socialism, was often essential for economic survival.[9]

In addition to codifying spousal rights, the family code outlined the new ideal for marriage: "Family relationships are based on friendship and mutual affection between its members" in which each provides the other with "moral and material support." Furthermore, Article 7 outlined equal responsibility for the education and care of children and the conduct of the household, though it did not detail what "conduct" entailed. Following the lead of the Soviet Union, in 1957 Romania decriminalized abortion and made it available on demand.[10] By codifying equal personhood within marriage and granting women reproductive freedom, the state signaled its commitment to women's equality and autonomy. At the same time, these measures were strategic, designed to facilitate women's mass entry into the labor force.

During the early years of socialist modernization, propagandists defined women's roles broadly, depicting women as heroine workers and socialist agitators, as well as wives, mothers, and educators of their children. Like work and education, marriage, socialist propagandists asserted, could eradicate class bias. For example, in a 1959 "Dear

Abby"–style piece titled "How Do I Convince My Parents?" a recent university graduate in education asks for advice on how to persuade her parents to accept her boyfriend—a kind, studious, and well-mannered factory worker she has known since childhood—as her future husband.[11] She notes, "We are very close and we cannot imagine anyone separating us." The crux of the problem revolves around her parents' outmoded ideas about occupational prestige, in particular their desire to see their daughter marry an engineer, doctor, or professor. Although the young woman claims to have dated professional men, she found them unsuitable, noting that a doctor she dated exhibited "unhealthy ideas" and "bad behaviors" and that an engineer who proposed to her was ten years her senior. "How," she inquires, "can I live with him if I don't like him?!" The columnist responds by praising the young woman's sound views on life and love and her ability to appreciate people's values over their status. She then advises her to have a heart-to-heart talk with her parents in an effort to convince them that people should be judged according to their personal qualities not their line of work. The author concludes that "today, unlike in the past, physical labor has the place of honor it deserves. And if your parents stand firm in their position, you must fight for your love."[12]

It is unknown if such columns emboldened women to wed outside their occupational group or socioeconomic class; however, with the introduction of universal education, women's mass entry into the labor force, and their migration to cities and industrial towns, changes in marital patterns did occur.[13] For instance, as women's participation in industry increased, more laborers married laborers (as opposed to male laborers marrying homemakers). Meanwhile, women who stayed in the countryside (working either on collective farms or as homemakers) did not necessarily marry other peasants; instead they increasingly married male laborers who commuted to industrial towns. That said, while the first two decades of socialist rule witnessed some flux in marital patterns, including an increase in inter-group marriages, during the last two decades of socialist rule marital patterns were characterized by social homogeneity. Accordingly, people married within their socio-economic group, with the vast majority of intellectuals and cultural figures marrying other intellectuals and cultural figures, functionaries marrying other functionaries or professionals, and workers marrying other workers.[14] Despite propagandists' promotion of more diverse and socially heterogeneous marital pairings, on the whole, marriage served to reinforce rather than disrupt social hierarchies.

Although propagandists encouraged women to marry men from different socioeconomic backgrounds and occupational profiles, in some cases they discouraged marriage, at least while women were young.

Instead, *Femeia* advised young people to be purposeful in choosing a mate and encouraged couples to get to know each other gradually and naturally before marriage, distinguishing between marriage for love and marriage for other, less acceptable reasons: parental pressure, to be more adult-like, and "to have a beautiful wife to display."[15] The magazine also featured case studies of failed marriages to serve as warnings to couples considering entering into hasty unions. For example, in the article "Today City Hall, Tomorrow the Courthouse," readers learn about Vasilica, a seventeen-year-old girl who had not ventured "beyond the schoolyard or factory floor," and her attraction to Nicolae, a "tall, muscular boy with blue eyes" four years her senior who "symbolized everything that life had to offer."[16] Seduced by walks in the park, movies, and dances, Vasilica marries Nicolae a mere month after meeting him only to discover that her "Adonis" doesn't really love to work, but instead prefers chasing women in the neighboring city of Târgu Mureş. As Nicolae spends increasingly more time away from home, Vasilica ultimately files for divorce—along with child support for their newborn—which the judge grants her on the basis of spousal abandonment. When asked by the judge why, given his neglect of his wife and their newborn, Nicolae married Vasilica in the first place, a nonplussed Nicolae responds that he "needed someone to look after him." The moral here is that women should not be drawn in by good looks and exciting outings but should instead get to know their suitors well, to understand their character, values, and motivations for marriage. It also illustrates that some men continued to embrace outmoded notions of marriage, viewing women first and foremost as their housemaids.

Rather than worry about finding a mate, *Femeia* encouraged young women to channel their energies into finishing technical school or university and cultivating skills. Such suggestions were often placed within the context of reader discussion forums that incorporated numerous, though typically similar, viewpoints for the purpose of arriving at a consensus. For instance, in the "Between Friends" column that appeared in the February 1959 issue of *Femeia*, a woman is encouraged to build friendships, read books, and go to plays rather than worry about finding a husband. Engaging in such activities, the editor reasoned, "will enable you to discover your true value as a person, and you will cultivate other ideas about life, love, marriage, and then it will be much easier to choose a life comrade who appreciates you."[17] Achieving one's personal and professional goals was also praised over youthful marriages. For instance, when sixteen-year-old M.N. from Piatra Neamţ shared her decision to reject a marriage proposal because she wanted "to finish coursework" and "create a future" for herself, readers universally praised her decision, claiming, "You are still too young, and one day you will certainly meet your true love who will make you happy."[18] Through such framed discussions, the magazine sought to promote particular beliefs about marriage with the aim of ultimately shaping behavior. Yet, this should not necessarily be interpreted as manipulative of or disempowering for women. Indeed, by challenging young marriage and encouraging women to focus first and foremost on their careers and personal development, the magazine promoted a progressive approach to marriage based on shared interests, values, and mutual affection, rather than economic need, tradition, or family expectations. Although the general social expectation was that women (and men) would eventually marry and have children, as depicted in official media, young women's energies were to be channeled into both personal development and building socialism. Consequently, in official media the single woman did not carry the same type of stigma that she did in Romanian society more generally.[19]

As young women increasingly left their villages and towns to work outside the home and pursue higher education, they experienced an unprecedented degree of autonomy and were more likely to postpone marriage than those who stayed in the countryside. However, this could also create problems in finding a good partner. In an anonymous letter published in 1976 titled "Where Can I Find a Man that I Want to Marry?" a young woman shared her difficulties meeting a man who will genuinely value and love her rather than a "Don Juan" who will romance her before he moves on to the next woman.[20] She wondered how, in light of so many selfish men, are girls who are "less pretty," "less bold," and who have "more serious beliefs about love" supposed to find mates, concluding her entry by asking, "What is the solution for young women who are twenty-five and unmarried?" According to this woman's experiences, while women had made great strides in Romania, men—or at least some men—had not left their womanizing ways behind. Remnants of the old, pre-socialist order, such men continued to view women as conquests rather than independent beings with their own aspirations, hopes, and passions.

Such concerns were certainly voiced by other independent and ambitious young women who struggled to find partners who would respect and appreciate them. Indeed, they were by no means unique to Romania or even the Eastern Bloc, but shared with women in other societies undergoing economic and social transformation. What was different about the Romanian case, however, is that socialism was supposed to have altered how men related to women. Accordingly, philandering men who viewed women as conquests and objects, rather than as soul mates and equals, had no place in socialist society. By publically airing a heretofore private or family issue, the magazine transformed the quest for a "life partner" into a collective concern. In response to the woman's query, readers advised her not to worry as even women aged twenty-five are far from being "old maids." Instead, they assured her that she was still "very young" and had a lot of time to find a partner.[21]

While such letters, along with women's increased participation in the labor force and post-secondary education, may have influenced some women's marital decisions, traditional ideas about marriage, which dictated women marry in their early to mid-twenties, remained powerful. Thus, progressive depictions of the new socialist woman coexisted with cultural norms and codes of behavior that reinforced gender difference. Indeed, the single woman of 1960s and 1970s Romania, like the "new woman" of 1920s America and Western Europe, had to proceed with caution as she negotiated new cultural and social spaces. On the one hand, the migration of single women from rural to urban areas and their participation in paid labor (along with their official validation as equal socialist citizens and workers) was transformative. As women left their villages, freed themselves from parental supervision, and became more or less economically independent, they experienced a different world than their mothers had. Yet, while their identity, status, and social worlds broadened, traditional behaviors and attitudes were slow to change.[22] Fearing popular responses to a radical transformation in gender roles, the state relied at once upon traditional and progressive conceptions of gender, promoting coeducation and creating opportunities for young adults of the opposite sex to interact socially, while remaining silent on or reinforcing conservative and essentialist views of sexuality. For example, the Communist Code of Ethics, which, as previously noted, outlined what constituted proper socialist behavior, prohibited premarital sex (especially on the part of women) as well as homosexual relations—behaviors that are also considered sinful in the Orthodox faith with which many Romanians identified.[23] To be sure, courtship patterns changed somewhat: work, the university, and weekend outings and summer vacations now rivaled dances and cafes as popular venues for meeting the opposite sex. However, on the whole, young women acted according to a deeply ingrained cultural code of ethics that their mothers and even grandmothers would have recognized.[24] As such, some parents, even into the 1970s and 1980s and especially in rural areas, were reluctant to let their single daughters leave home before marrying. As Tatiana, raised in a village outside of Botoşani, reflected upon her circumstances in 1973:

> I got married because my mother wouldn't have allowed me to leave home otherwise. The upbringing was that women who leave are like *that*

[promiscuous]. She said, "You'll get married, have a civil ceremony, and then you can leave." That's how it was. I didn't blame her for this. That's what they were accustomed to.[25]

Tatiana's willingness to adhere to traditional mores and marry prior to relocating was rooted in respect for her parents. Because single women were considered vulnerable and cohabitation prior to marriage was socially unacceptable, it is unsurprising that Tatiana's mother wanted her to marry before leaving home. In addition to adhering to tradition, Tatiana realized that if she respected her mother's wishes she could start a new life in a city, something that would have certainly been exciting to a nineteen-year-old who had been raised in a remote village. Recognizing that city life would offer new occupational, social, and cultural opportunities, marriage allowed Tatiana to live with the man she loved and also carve out a new life for herself. Considered from this perspective, marriage could be a form of liberation.

While marriage might liberate women from the constraints of rural life, it could also liberate them (as well as men) from communal living. Due to housing scarcity and the privileging of communist elites, the well-connected, families with children and married couples for housing, single individuals often faced years of shared-living situations in dormitories or at home with their parents. Indeed, housing remained a problem for young adults not only during the early years of socialist rule but well into the 1970s, after the boom in housing construction.[26] Thus, as in other parts of the Eastern Bloc, in Romania marriage could help people secure an apartment—a chief goal of most young people. Paradoxically, while propagandists discouraged hasty and youthful marriage, shortcomings in the command economy, particularly the privileging of industry over housing and other goods, encouraged it. More generally, Romania was comparatively stingy in supporting married couples: outside of preferential treatment for housing and low-interest loans, marriage did not confer any other substantial entitlements such as interest-free loans (for home building or purchasing needed appliances), as was the case in the GDR.[27]

While some regarded marriage as liberating, Mircea, a professor born in 1951, viewed it as a form of social control. As he reflected on his youth:

> I was a bachelor for a long time. There was this propaganda ... my opinion is that it was a system meant to trap you. You were advised to get married as you would have certain advantages; you got an apartment. Many people did this in order to get away from the dormitories. On the other hand, once you became a family man you could be manipulated. It was a form of social blackmail.[28]

According to Mircea, marriage could expedite the process of acquiring an apartment, among conferring other advantages, since family was highly valued by the state. Because owning an apartment was an aspiration for most young people, some couples, therefore, decided to marry young. At the same time, because marriage transformed bachelors into "family men," it made them more vulnerable to manipulation, essentially shackling them to the state as they were responsible for others and could not so easily flout or resist policies. Through soft power policies such as housing distribution, then, the state promoted familialism and acquiescence to state dictates.

In addition to housing, marriage could be a means of attaining residency in Bucharest (or another city) and, thereby, gain access to various services and amenities. A number of my respondents claimed that they married young in the hopes of being placed in a job in the same place as (or in the general vicinity of) their spouse during their *repartiție*. Indeed, efforts to attain urban residency in this manner were even acknowledged in socialist culture. In the romantic comedy *Buletin de București* (Bucharest Identity Card), Silvia, a recent graduate of the Agronomy Institute in Bucharest, has been posted to Dorohoi, a small town in northeast Romania, for her *repartiție*.[29] In an effort to remain in Bucharest, she appeals to her uncle, a mid-ranking functionary, who informs her that the assignment can only be transferred to Bucharest with a Bucharest identity card. Silvia subsequently seeks marriage to a Bucharest resident—in exchange for cash—in the hopes of securing an identity card, a rare commodity given that Bucharest was a closed city at the time. After a quick marriage to Radu, a taxi driver, Silvia applies for a Bucharest residency card; however, she is informed that since she has already been posted to another town for her *repartiție* she is ineligible. Frustrated by the futility of her efforts, Silvia files and eventually secures a divorce from Radu after convincing the judge he was engaged in adulterous behavior (which she "documents" by photographing Radu kissing another woman). Silvia then heads off to Dorohoi for her *repartiție*, where, in an ironic twist of fate, she runs into Radu, who, as it turns out, had only been working temporarily as a taxi driver and was, like her, a recent graduate who had been posted to the town for his *repartiție*.[30] The moral of the story is that marriage is not a tool for personal gain and when used as such will only end in disappointment. As a corollary, the film emphasized the importance of paying one's debt to society and sacrificing comfort and excitement for the common good—in this case completing one's *repartiție* in a remote, rural area of the country.

Although Silvia's efforts ended in failure, some individuals did successfully change the location of their *repartiție*, be it through marriage, connections, or bribery. In sum, while traditional beliefs led to young marriages, so too did other considerations, such as women's desire to leave the family home, eligibility for state-subsidized housing, and residence in an urban center. Given these factors, first marriages occurred between the ages of twenty and twenty-five, with women typically marrying in their early twenties and men in their mid-twenties.[31] The exception to this was the period between 1962 and 1971, which witnessed an increase in the number of women under twenty who married, a phenomenon that can in part be explained by women's inability to deal easily with unwanted pregnancy as a result of the passage of Decree 770.[32] As in other parts of the Bloc, the average age for first marriage in Romania was younger than the average age in the West (between 25 and 28 years of age).[33]

Most of my respondents married in their early to mid-twenties, typically a year after they had begun dating, and bore their first child within the first two years of marriage. Despite efforts to curtail religious worship, weddings in Romania continued to be traditional affairs. While civil ceremonies were required for legal recognition of the marriage, many individuals also had their marriages confirmed in churches. For high-ranking officials and others in publically visible positions, however, civil ceremonies were the only option. The case of Luana, a historian who worked at a municipal museum, is illustrative. Married to a journalist, she explained that a religious ceremony was impossible because "they [the authorities] would have found out, and both of us would have lost our jobs."[34] Similarly, Petre, a former *miliția* officer, asserted that despite being devoutly Orthodox, he chose not to marry in the church.[35] Meanwhile, a host of low-level party members participated in both types of ceremonies—ceremonies that occurred not only in remote, village churches, but also in urban centers—without apparently raising an official eyebrow.[36] The absence of state intervention in such matters was, at least in part, strategic. Because religion, in particular Orthodox Christianity, is a central feature of Romanian culture, punishment for transgressing such an act would have alienated (or further alienated) individuals from socialism. Turning a blind eye on religious ceremonies was thus a strategy for maintaining a modicum of support for—or at bare minimum staving off disenchantment with—the regime. More prominent party members, by contrast, were forbidden this opportunity because their symbolic capital and public visibility required that they closely follow party doctrine. Considered from this perspective, not being a privileged party member or high-level functionary could confer certain advantages.

Although young (and hasty) marriages were discouraged in state propaganda and the young, single woman was represented in a positive light, by the mid-1960s such progressive renditions existed alongside restrictive reproductive and divorce legislation. As in Poland, the Romanian state was concerned with rising divorce rates, which, by 1964, had reached one for every five marriages (with a third occurring during the first three years of marriage).[37] Thus, on the heels of the criminalization of abortion—and to encourage procreation—in 1966 the state enacted Decree 779, tightening divorce legislation.[38] Accordingly, divorce was represented as "antisocial" and deemed acceptable only when "relations between spouses are so seriously and irreparably damaged that the continuation of marriage is impossible."[39] In practice, this meant that a range of grounds that had once been acceptable for dissolving a marriage (e.g. extramarital affairs; domestic violence; spending household income on alcohol) were no longer sufficient, particularly when children under sixteen were in the picture.[40] To further discourage divorce, the associated legal fees increased dramatically, from 500 lei ($42) to between 3,000 and 6,000 lei ($252–500)—approximately three to five times the average monthly salary of 1,083 lei ($99) in 1966.[41] Finally, a six-month period of "reflection" or reconciliation (one year if the couple had children under sixteen) could be imposed and subsequently extended.[42]

In the short term, these restrictions and penalties were effective in deterring divorce. For example, the number of divorce claims decreased from 61,000 in October 1966 to 7,095 in October 1967. Indeed, by 1967 divorce had practically been eradicated as a mere 48 were registered. Furthermore, between 1960 and 1970 the number of divorces dropped from 18.7 to 5.4 (per 100 marriages).[43] By 1980, however, the number of divorces had climbed to 18.1 (per 100 marriages) and by 1989 it was at 20.2.[44] Nonetheless, even at this rate, it was substantially lower than in Western and Northern Europe, indicating that people still faced challenges, be it legal, cultural, or economic, in dissolving marriages.

The existence of progressive representations (e.g. the modern socialist woman) alongside repressive measures (restrictive divorce and reproductive laws) was a hallmark of Ceaușescu's rule, enabling the regime to present a modern and forward-looking face, while asserting ever-greater control over the population, including women's bodies. More significantly, through these regulations the state politicized both the family and the private lives of its citizens. To justify these restrictions, marriage, like reproduction, was presented as a public matter, as illustrated in Ceauşescu's speech to university students in 1972:

> We cannot be indifferent to what happens to the family, how young people marry or do not marry, believing that this pertains to their personal lives. Of course it is their personal lives, but the state has always been concerned and must always be concerned with the personal lives of its people.[45]

Morality was also a driving force behind the 1966 divorce law as Ceauşescu expressed particular concern about "blasé attitudes toward the dissolution of marriage."[46] In this capacity, not only ordinary Romanians but also high-ranking party functionaries were targeted by Ceauşescu, who claimed: "We have many comrades among us who receive divorces by telephone. We need to put an end to this state of affairs and not allow those who exhibit a lack of communist morals to occupy leadership positions in government and in the party."[47]

While morality was also mobilized by Nikita Khrushchev to dissuade couples from divorcing, especially if they had young children, in the Soviet Union official discourses did not necessarily influence legal policies and proceedings. Indeed, divorce laws were actually loosened in the USSR in the late 1950s, reflecting state efforts to rule by consent rather than coercion.[48] Thus, while Soviet sociologists and other experts promoted the preservation of marriage, at the end of the day, judges and lawyers successfully helped ease the divorce process by ignoring media proscriptions. Similarly, by the 1960s other countries in the Bloc liberalized divorce, recognizing marriage as a private matter—an emotional contract between individuals in which the state should not interfere.[49] Hungary was especially liberal in this regard, moving from "divorce as sanction" to "divorce as remedy" with the introduction of no-fault divorce under the 1952 Family Code.[50] By the 1960s, East Germany was perhaps the most progressive in the Bloc with respect to the dissolution of marriage, grating divorces on the basis of a husband's lack of respect for women's dignity and the equality of the sexes.[51] Although divorce increased dramatically (from fifteen per one hundred in 1956 to twenty-six in 1972 to forty in 1982) as a result of the new law, because the government supported single mothers, this was not followed by a marked decline in the birth rate—even though abortion was legalized in the GDR in 1972.[52] Instead, out-of-wedlock births in the GDR more than doubled between 1970 and 1985, by which time they constituted one-third of all births.[53]

In contrast, Romania continued to focus on divorce prevention, especially youthful divorce. To this end, lawyers "wrote" about cases they had counselled. For example, the cleverly titled article "Separating ... Out of Love: Or the Confessions of Lawyer, R.D.," published in *Femeia* in 1970, featured a conversation between a lawyer and a young woman who was seeking a divorce after a mere three months of marriage. During their consultation, the lawyer discovers that the woman does not want to divorce because of irreconcilable differences, but because she loves her husband too much. The message was that young people, due to immaturity, impatience, and lack of life experience, hastily give up on marriage and resort to divorce, despite the fact that they actually still care about and love each other deeply. Cautioning against letting the stresses of work intrude into the conjugal relationship—and specifically against using one's partner as a sounding board for life's troubles—the lawyer emphasized the importance of tenderness and attentiveness in sustaining a healthy relationship. In line with contemporaneous legislation, the overarching aim of the piece was to promote reconciliation and deter divorce.[54]

## Creating the New Socialist Husband and Wife

While putting women to work alongside men was a necessary condition for leveling the gender playing field, policy alone was insufficient for changing marital roles and relations. Instead, individuals needed to be persuaded that equality within marriage was essential, not only for creating a socialist utopia and crafting a modern society, but for personal happiness. Accordingly, *Femeia* published personal vignettes to demonstrate how patriarchal behaviors impeded the development of meaningful relationships. Yet, in contrast to reality, these stories typically had a "happy end," with men's gradual recognition of their outmoded ways and concerted efforts to change behavior. The 1949 article "Yes, Yes, I Must Help Her," which examined the life of Sanda, a working mother whose husband, Matei, cleverly avoids pitching in at home by sweet-talking her, is illustrative.[55] After an exhausting day at the office, which included working overtime and retrieving their daughter from her in-law's place, Sanda returns home and asks Matei, "I thought that you'd surprise me by setting the table." His response, "As a matter of principle, I don't involve myself in housework," exemplifies his insensitivity and continued embrace of traditional family roles. Relaxing in his armchair with newspaper in hand while Sanda sets the table, Matei asks, "Sanda, dearest, won't you make some French fries for your husband?," to which Sanda responds, "If you'll help me peel [the potatoes] I'll make them." His reply, "I've never peeled potatoes in my life; it's best for me not to start," is met by Sanda's sharp retort: "it's very easy to learn." Again, Matei insists that housework is "not his business" and that he could only hinder rather than help things, all the while reassuring Sanda that soon, through the aid of cooperatives and technology, housework will become easier. Sanda, however, refuses to let Matei off the hook, asserting, "That's all well and good, but until then? Until then, don't you think that in a marriage in which the husband and wife are comrades in the truest sense of the word, don't you think the husband should not leave all the housework to the wife?" After tense exchanges and a day's reflection, Matei has a change of heart and offers to pick their daughter up from school and even set the table. "As a result of our discussion yesterday?" Sanda asks him. To which Matei replies "Out of love."

Published during the early years of communist consolidation, when the country was in the throes of postwar recovery and the purging of "enemies of the people," this piece captures a society on the brink of change, illustrating that, through a bit of nudging on the part of women, men can change their behaviors and contribute to the proper functioning of the household. More importantly, it was a time of rapid industrialization, when production was prioritized over consumption and the state was not in an economic position to make good on its promise of easing women's domestic responsibilities through cooperatives and laborsaving devices. Accordingly, the piece places the onus on men to change their outmoded behavior, not simply because this aligned with socialist conceptions of marriage, but because of insufficient provision of childcare facilities and household durables.

The ability to transform marital relations was acknowledged not only in the pages of *Femeia*, but in *Scânteia*. As one factory worker reflected about his wife on the occasion of International Women's Day in 1953:

> I was also one of those who believed women are good only for the frying pan and children. However, once I began recognizing my wife's abilities and contributions a new life began in our house. We read together and discussed articles together. I realize that she understands things just as well as I do, some things even much better. Only now, after ten years of marriage, are we getting to know each other. I now know that you cannot have a happy home unless husbands and wives are comrades in life, as well as in struggle.[56]

Intended to validate Engels's claim that once women became equal partners in industry they would become equal partners at home, the piece also serves as a warning. It urges men to reassess their old-fashioned attitudes and recognize women's manifold abilities, particularly their intellectual abilities, lest they miss the joys of socialist marriage. At the same time, the man fails to acknowledge that his domestic roles were also in need of change. Thus, while he appreciates his wife's intellect, he is seemingly uninterested in more banal activities such as doing laundry or preparing the Sunday dinner.

By the 1960s, spousal relations received increased attention in socialist media. *Femeia* featured columns such as "Life Together," which included relationship surveys (the results of which were published in subsequent issues), as well as compatibility quizzes and articles by psychologists and other "marriage experts." It also featured debates, advice columns, and questionnaires that examined common problems encountered by newlyweds and suggested strategies for resolving them. In a questionnaire entitled "The First Year of Marriage," for example, couples were asked about challenges they had experienced in their relationships, from dealing with different personality types to divvying up domestic responsibilities (see figure 4.1). They were also asked to share their strategies for overcoming difficulties and resolving conflicts.[57] In line with other articles on marital relations at the time, such questionnaires encouraged readers to view the role of spouse as a learned behavior and marriages as "projects" that required kindness, cooperation, and self-reflection. Just as ordinary citizens were to engage in continuous self-improvement in the service to socialism, so too couples were to engage in continuous self-improvement in the service of marriage.

According to articles in *Femeia*, a major frustration for many women was men's reluctance to assist with domestic tasks. To better understand this problem, in 1966 the magazine surveyed male night school students about their attitudes towards women's family roles.[58] One question about housework, accompanied by an image of a man vacuuming, asked, "Do you respect your wife, the mother of your children?" While one man responded, "I help my wife [around the house] because I want a beautiful family life. We've been married for ten years and have many years ahead of us," other respondents were less concerned with and, indeed, outright dismissive of their wives' lot, claiming, "If I help her too much, she will take over," or "I won't make sacrifices for her," or "women already have enough rights."[59] Overall, most of the men surveyed justified their reluctance to help on the basis of disrupting the traditional gender order. The author concluded that despite

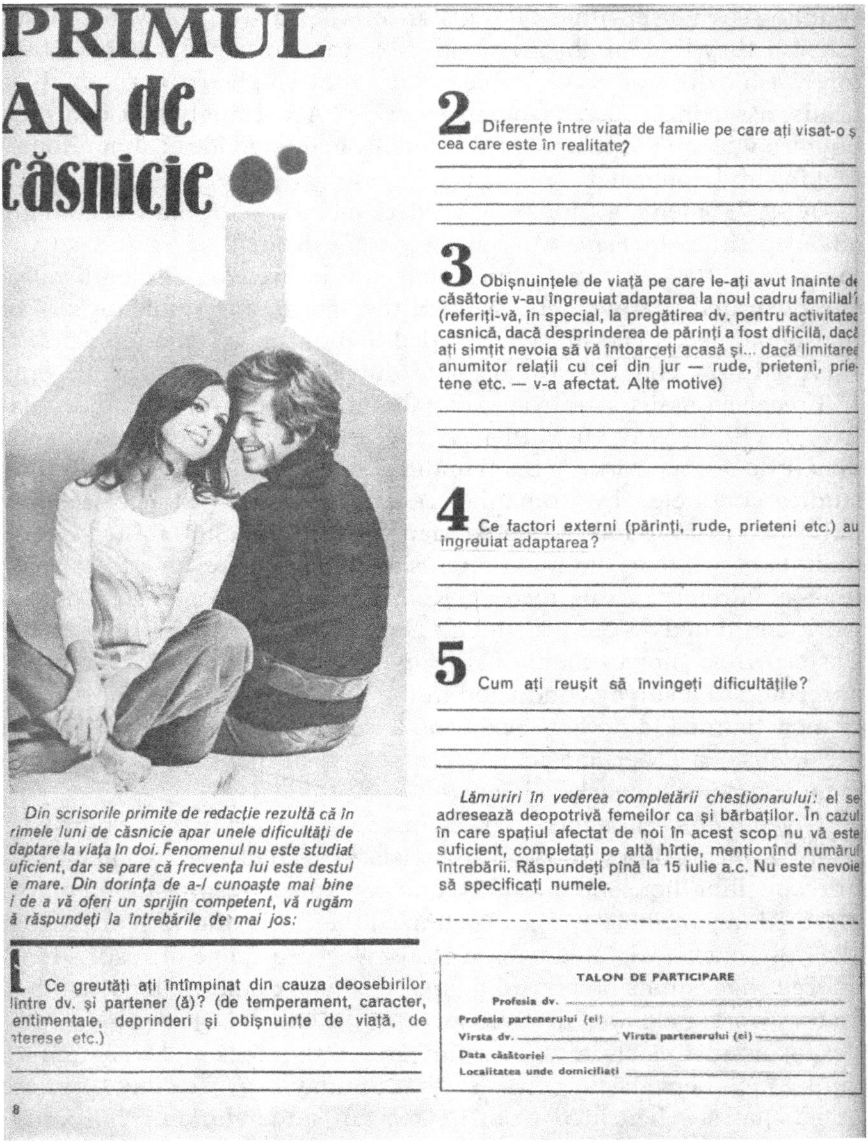

PRIMUL AN de căsnicie

*Din scrisorile primite de redacție rezultă că în rimele luni de căsnicie apar unele dificultăți de daptare la viața în doi. Fenomenul nu este studiat uficient, dar se pare că frecvența lui este destul e mare. Din dorința de a-l cunoaște mai bine i de a vă oferi un sprijin competent, vă rugăm ă răspundeți la întrebările de mai jos:*

1 Ce greutăți ați întîmpinat din cauza deosebirilor între dv. și partener (ă)? (de temperament, caracter, entimentale, deprinderi și obișnuințe de viață, de nterese etc.)

2 Diferențe între viața de familie pe care ați visat-o ș cea care este în realitate?

3 Obișnuințele de viață pe care le-ați avut înainte de căsătorie v-au îngreuiat adaptarea la noul cadru familial? (referiți-vă, în special, la pregătirea dv. pentru activitatea casnică, dacă desprinderea de părinți a fost dificilă, dacă ați simțit nevoia să vă întoarceți acasă și... dacă limitarea anumitor relații cu cei din jur — rude, prieteni, prietene etc. — v-a afectat. Alte motive)

4 Ce factori externi (părinți, rude, prieteni etc.) au îngreuiat adaptarea?

5 Cum ați reușit să învingeți dificultățile?

*Lămuriri în vederea completării chestionarului:* el se adresează deopotrivă femeilor ca și bărbaților. În cazul în care spațiul afectat de noi în acest scop nu vă este suficient, completați pe altă hîrtie, menționînd numărul întrebării. Răspundeți pînă la 15 iulie a.c. Nu este nevoie să specificați numele.

TALON DE PARTICIPARE

Profesia dv. ______

Profesia partenerului (ei) ______

Virsta dv. ______ Virsta partenerului (ei) ______

Data căsătoriei ______

Localitatea unde domiciliați ______

8

Figure 4.1. "The First Year of Marriage" *Femeia*, June 1971

state efforts to promote equality, many men "lack understanding and respect for women," adding that such attitudes could degenerate into condemnable behavior, including spousal abuse. At the same time, the survey suggested that women were, at least in part, responsible for enabling such insensitivity. For instance, when a group of women were asked if they had taught their sons how to iron pants, sew on a button, wash a dish, or even clean a potato, they laughed and shook their heads, asserting, "That's women's work."[60] Accordingly, not just men but also women perpetuated traditionally gendered ideas about homemaking and domesticity.

By 1973 men's attitudes toward domestic labor had seemingly changed little. In *Femeia*'s February issue from that year, a survey measuring the gendered dimensions of housework "scientifically" demonstrated that women assumed the vast majority—if not all—of household tasks. The study concluded that of the 582 women workers surveyed, 424 completed household duties on their own, while only 158 received assistance from a family member (e.g. a husband, relative, or child). Why, the author of the article asked, "can't husbands do a little of this work?"[61] Such findings were similarly evident in time studies conducted by Romanian researchers. For instance, a study published in 1970 found that women spent three hours more per day on housework than did men, often sacrificing leisure time to care for their children.[62] In this respect, Romania was not unique as housework continued to be a distinctly gendered practice throughout the Eastern Bloc (not to mention Europe and the world). For example, according to a survey conducted in the GDR in 1974, only 28 percent of men claimed to do housework on a regular basis.[63] Indeed, even in the 1980s, East German men expressed resentment about having to complete domestic tasks.

Given men's reluctance to participate meaningfully in the domestic realm, *Femeia* addressed the "time crisis" (i.e. challenges women faced in reconciling household, family, and workplace responsibilities), exploring how ordinary women organized their schedules. In an August 1967 piece entitled, "Readers on Housework," a range of respondents offered suggestions on how to lighten women's domestic load. While a factory worker claimed that she successfully balanced her responsibilities by organizing chores on certain days of the week and by assigning family members specific tasks so that Sunday is a "free day," a nurse noted that she benefited from having an "understanding husband," who is "always on hand to help."[64] Meanwhile, an activist had seemingly given up on the prospect of spousal assistance because "husbands don't help out at home, either because they don't want to or they don't know how to."[65] Accordingly, she emphasized the importance of assigning chores to sons and daughters alike so they would regard them as ordinary, everyday practices as they entered adulthood.[66] A school director, however, targeted actual women for blame, claiming: "First of all, we need to convince ourselves to alter our own attitude, which is profoundly wrong—that a man is a guest who doesn't have any business in the kitchen."

At the same time that readers reflected on their specific situation, they noted the state should assume greater responsibility for alleviating the "time crunch." In particular, readers suggested that seminars on "men's family duties" be organized in the workplace and that enterprises establish food delivery services whereby women could submit a shopping list at the beginning of their shift and retrieve their groceries at the end of it. Although laudable suggestions, the overarching message of the forum was that household responsibilities could best be resolved through rationalization (e.g. time management, monthly budgeting), enlisting the help of family members, and self-assertion, thus putting the onus on women to be the agents of change. To achieve optimum results, women, like factory managers, just needed to follow a "plan," efficiently organize their time, and take initiative. Such advice was not simply socialist in inspiration as experts in the United States and Western Europe similarly presented rational organization as essential to household management, albeit the sole responsibility of women.

While reconciling work and family responsibilities could be challenging and tiresome, it was nonetheless presented as evidence of modern socialist womanhood. As Ana, who responded to *Femeia*'s 1970 opinion poll "Are You a Modern Woman?" remarked:

> I am trying to be a modern woman. As an engineer, I work in the most modern technical domain—nuclear energy. As any modern woman does (and one must admit that it is not easy to be one), I carefully divide my time between work obligations, family obligations, and any other duties that the word modern implies.[67]

In comparison with industrial laborers, Ana was employed in a technologically sophisticated field—nuclear energy. Thus, her position reflects Romania's scientific progress and women's educational and professional advancement. However, what makes Ana "modern" is not only her job but her adeptness in combining it with the role of wife and mother. By featuring women who could "do it all," the state sought to normalize women's multiple burdens (or roles).[68] As such, women's ability to fulfill professional and domestic duties was an indicator of modernity—the "new normal" to which all women were to aspire. In reality, efforts to juggle duties at work (including voluntary or party-related work) and home, often with little help from a spouse, produced frustration and exhaustion for women—something that Ana subtly hints at when she notes that it is "not easy" to be a modern woman.

By acknowledging the efforts involved in being a modern woman, Ana appeared more realistic than the heroine workers of the Dej period who could work two shifts on the lathe and return home to tend to a family of nine. Thus, the article reflects a shift from exaggerated characterizations of the socialist superwoman to more realistic and sympathetic portraits of women professionals. Nonetheless, Ana's story was intended to showcase—and thus normalize—Romanian women's facility in combining the role of mother, worker, and wife.[69] Depictions of women's multiple roles (or burdens) in Polish women's magazines, by contrast, were mobilized to highlight the difficulties of combining household and workplace responsibilities. Far from encouraging men to help in the domestic sphere, these magazines promoted home-based work and a reduction in women's full-time employment so that women could dedicate more time to their family and household.[70] This was related to larger destalinization efforts, whereby the Polish leadership sought to "domesticate" socialism by pushing women out of jobs in heavy industry and encourage them to embrace traditionally gendered roles.

Attempts to eradicate patriarchal behaviors and attitudes focused not only on conscripting men to do their fair share around the house, but more serious matters such as spousal abuse. The 1973 *Femeia* article "When You Beat Your Wife, You're Hurting Yourself" took up this issue in detail. Narrated by a woman director of a textile factory, the piece tells the story of V. R., a mechanical engineer employed at the factory who is married with two children. The director claims to have once had an excellent opinion of V. R., viewing him as serious, hardworking, and ambitious, "without vice or reproach."[71] However, after discovering V. R.'s wife, Maria, in her office one day, fidgeting about in her chair and eventually breaking down into tears, her view of V. R. changed. In the ensuing exchange between the two, Maria recounted her husband's abuse toward her: "Here at the factory he's the epitome of politeness, but at home he is a tyrant. ... I am nothing but a maid. ... He swears at me, insults me in front of the kids. Do you know that one day my son called me 'stinking lazy' (*puturoasa*) because that's what he heard from his dad?"[72] Maria adds that, in addition to not helping around the house, her husband criticized her for leaving a few dirty dishes in the sink—even though her "fingertips were stinging"—and also beat her, noting that "it wasn't the first time." She then asked the director, "Tell me why I should have to endure this?" In a subtle form of victim blaming, the director then asks Maria if she might, at least in part, be at fault for her husband's abusive behavior (by nagging him, etc.). Maria acknowledges that she is frequently irritable as a result of her demanding schedule and her husband's derogatory remarks toward her, which include referring to her as a making machine, yet insists that it is his abusive behavior, not her exhaustion or irritability, that's at fault. She adds that she is not seeking a divorce for her own sake, but for the emotional health of their children.

The director concludes that V. R. is a man full of contradictions: "He adores his mother, but does not respect his wife."[73] Although initially hesitant to involve herself in the matter, the director recognizes that such behaviors are antisocialist and must be eradicated. Thus, in accordance with workplace protocol and communist ethics, she convenes a meeting with other workers (i.e. the party committee) to discuss V. R.'s behavior and "ultimately" has a heart-to-heart talk with him. By the end of the process, V. R. seemingly recognizes the error of his ways and promises to treat his wife with respect. The message was that spousal abuse is not simply a personal problem, but a larger, social one requiring mediation by the work collective.[74] In this manner, the state transformed private acts into public concerns, presenting the eradication of spousal abuse as essential to creating a modern, civilized society.

Reading between the lines of this article, however, reveals a more disturbing dynamic. Rather than advocating on behalf of (and thus protecting and empowering) the battered women, mediation through the work collective served as a coercive mechanism, a form of soft power. Since the goal was to prevent the dissolution of marriage, women were guilted—and thus essentially forced—into staying in unhealthy, and, in some cases, dangerous marriages. Meanwhile, men were shamed into admitting the error of their ways and urged to treat their wives with respect. This scenario clearly favored the perpetrator (as in this case, almost always the man) who simply needed to apologize for his misdeeds. Indeed, even the title of the article, "When you beat your wife you hurt yourself," presents the abuser as the one most harmed by his actions, effectively dismissing the longstanding psychological and physical abuse that his wife experienced. By minimizing the victim's trauma and shaming the couple into staying together, the piece reflected broader cultural views of spousal abuse, according to which women were expected to suffer in silence.

Accordingly, articles on spousal abuse (be it psychological and/or physical) and their "resolution" by the work collective or judge were designed to uphold the primacy of marriage and deter divorce, especially when minors were involved. Indeed, the courts often decided in favor of salvaging the marriage in cases when young children were in the picture, discounting battery, rape, and even threats of death on the basis of a child's right to an unbroken home.[75] Yet, while these articles were primarily strategic, inspired by the need to deter divorce, this does not necessarily mean that the authors who wrote them were unconcerned with spousal abuse. As previously noted, while some activists and propagandists were tools of the regime, others were genuinely devoted to women's equality and the transformation of gender relations. Indeed, given that domestic violence was relatively common in Romania, official acknowledgment of it may have compelled some women to discuss the issue with friends or colleagues—or even bring it to the attention of the authorities—rather than silently endure it.[76] As such, the article may have resonated with some battered women, functioning as an awareness-raising effort that helped them recognize that the abuse they suffered was neither unique nor acceptable.

At the same time, prohibition against domestic violence was not codified in law until 1960, and, even then, it was listed as one of a number of misdemeanors outlined in the Criminal Code, rather than being codified as a specific form of gendered or family violence.[77] A few of my respondents claimed that incidents of domestic violence were brought to the attention of the work collective, trade unions, and apartment block managers. This is certainly plausible given that these bodies were charged with intervening when such occurrences were reported and, in the case of communal dwellings, when it was necessary to restore peace and quiet.[78] Additionally, the *miliția* was charged with intervening when citizens perpetrated acts of violence against other citizens. Although none of my respondents mentioned the *miliția* intervening in cases of spousal abuse, one emphasized that fear of the Securitate served as a preventative measure: "Before [during the socialist period] men could not get away with being violent toward women because they feared the Securitate ... one ended up in the hands of the Securitate. In a word, she was silently protected, so the rest of us were as well."[79] The degree to which this characterization applied to men in general is doubtful given the high incidence of domestic violence reported after 1989—both in surveys and to the police. That said, given the reach of the *miliția* and Securitate, it is plausible that some men would have feared attracting their attention and thus refrained from acting violently towards their wives.[80] However, it seems that lack of legal redress was more typical. Indeed, this problem was even acknowledged in *Femeia*, indicating that it was not infrequent. For instance, in one featured story, a woman whose estranged husband takes revenge against her by cutting her electric cables claimed that she did not receive the support she needed from the police (*miliția*).[81] More problematically, since the aim of collective intervention was, by the late 1960s, reconciliation and the promotion of family stability, women who were in abusive relationships and were the subject of collective mediation would more likely than not continue to face unhealthy or dangerous situations—all in the name of morality, respectability, and demographic growth.

Although patriarchal behaviors were manifest in husbands' unwillingness to pull their domestic weight and, more tragically, in the form of spousal abuse, socialist experts nonetheless remained optimistic, believing that Romanians would "overcome patriarchy." In an article addressing the matter, philosophy professor Alexandru Tănase targeted everyday practices and selfish men who believed that "their wives should be their cooks, servants, and laundresses" and constantly at their "beck and call" for the persistence of patriarchal mentalities in Romania.[82] At the same time, he acknowledged women's "fatalistic" acceptance of such treatment, claiming to know many competent women who had refused promotions to spare their husbands' egos. However, such seemingly ingrained attitudes, Tănase argued, can be altered since "selfishness is not a masculine trait but a moral deficit." By sharing household chores, treating one another as emotional and intellectual confidantes, and developing deep and mutually rewarding relationships, Romanian couples can, the article concluded, overcome patriarchy.

Alongside articles, *Femeia* hoped to transform attitudes through images. For example, the article "The New (Kind of) Husband: A Reality, a Goal, a Trend?" was accompanied by an image of a young, attractive, and well-dressed husband—with a briefcase in one hand and a baby and duster in the other—alongside his similarly young, attractive, and fashionably clad wife.[83] Meanwhile, a photo of a column of men pushing baby carriages was featured in an article about fatherhood.[84] The message of such images was that far from being "women's work," engaging in housework and childcare were signs of modern, socialist masculinity. The magazine also featured a section titled "Only for Your Husband," with the aim of transforming behaviors and promoting socially conscious husbands and fathers. Articles that fell under this rubric critiqued traditional family roles and linked "being a man" to caring for one's wife's and one's children's needs. For instance, the piece "Be a Man!" depicted a man reading the newspaper and smoking

Figure 4.2. "Be a Man!" *Femeia*, June 1971

a cigar alongside an image of a man changing a diaper and speaking with his child (see figure 4.2).[85] According to socialist criteria, the ideal father, though a diligent and devoted worker, put family on par with his job and did not lounge about reading the paper while his wife did all the housework.

According to propagandists, men's engagement in domestic duties was not only an expression of good socialist behavior and evidence of respect towards one's wife but essential for keeping the marital spark alive. As Florica Constantinescu, a designer, asserted, "A household requires, without exception, a man's support, especially if he wants the woman to remain ... a woman (attractive, thus interesting, beautiful)."[86] In addition to urging women not to let the burdens of housework undermine their physical upkeep, the piece implores women not to give up their "free day" (*ziua liberă*), but instead use that time to cultivate their interests, which will, in turn, make them more well-rounded and more appealing wives. Thus, he suggests that women solicit their husbands' help around the house; however, he cautions that they should not expect a miraculous change. Of note is that men's contribution to household chores is directly related to women's need to retain their physical attractiveness so that men will continue to desire them. The subtext here is that men might direct their interests elsewhere if their wives failed to keep themselves up—an outcome the regime would have opposed for both moral and demographic reasons.

Indeed, while on the surface progressive, propagandists' interest in refashioning family relations was not simply rooted in a commitment to gender equality, but also concern over marital discord and rising divorce rates. This was evident in the increased attention *Femeia* devoted to marital discord beginning in the 1960s. The 1966 article "Grounds for Divorce," for instance, examined how men's adherence to traditional marital roles often conflicted with women's professional aspirations, producing resentment and marital disharmony. The piece traces Nicolae's growing frustration with his wife, Camelia, who is earning her university degree by taking evening classes.[87] To provide a "balanced" assessment, colleagues and family members weighed in on each spouse. While Camelia's colleagues describe her as a dedicated worker and morally upright individual who loves her husband, Nicolae's colleagues claim that Camelia neglects her husband's needs, leaving him to shop and prepare meals on his own. However, it is Nicolae's mother who delivers the most biting criticism, calling Camelia out for "forgetting her marital responsibilities" and urging her to "quit school if you don't want to lose him."[88] In the end, Nicolae retracts the divorce proceedings, but he does not change his views; instead, he simply resigns himself to the situation. The author concludes that as long as Nicolae maintains unrealistic expectations of Camelia (i.e. that she be an adoring wife and good housekeeper), the couple will continue to experience problems since "without mutual respect even the greatest love will fall apart."[89]

Such articles were to serve as lessons to selfish husbands: namely that expecting wives to subjugate their educational or professional ambitions in favor of domestic responsibilities was not only outmoded, but inimical to a mature, equal, and loving relationship. As such, they differed from contemporaneous Polish portrayals of marriage wherein "emancipated wives" were faulted for creating competition in their marriage through their advanced education, superior earnings, neglect of domestic duties, and lack of femininity.[90] They also differed from traditional beliefs in Romania, according to which women were to be primarily, if not fully, responsible for the household and were expected to place the needs of the family above their professional aspirations.

While propagandists hoped to reduce the divorce rate by condemning men's outmoded attitudes toward marriage and promoting progressive family roles, sexual satisfaction, particularly on the part of women, was also mobilized to keep couples together. Accordingly, the new socialist husband's concern for domestic life was to extend beyond the kitchen and into the bedroom. As Radu Dimitriu emphasized in *De vorbă cu tinerii* (Talking with Youth), "Happiness in marriage depends on many factors. Among these, the sex life of the couple is of great importance."[91] According to Dimitriu, a general lassitude sets in as the marriage progresses, and men no longer put forth the effort they once had in appealing to their wives. Women, he notes, similarly grow lax in that respect:

> The problem is, some [men] see marriage as an end of tenderness and affection, and think it is no longer necessary to court their wives. This isn't just the fault of men, but also women who don't do enough to sustain their husband's desire and affection.[92]

Dimitriu continues with a discussion of the psychological and emotional components of sex, stressing the important role of both partners in the courtship process and urging married couples to be tender and flirtatious with one another.

According to socialist experts, a tender and affectionate husband was essential for a healthy marriage because women's sexual pleasure was both physically and emotionally rooted. Thus, it followed that if married couples were to have more sex—and, thereby, fulfill their procreative role—women needed to desire sex, which meant that men needed to focus on women's emotional as well as physical needs. In broaching the issue, articles in *Femeia* focused on women's sexual satisfaction (or lack thereof) and sexual dysfunction. For instance, in the article "The Truth about Frigidity," a doctor claimed that frigidity emerges "once the luminous period of courtship is over," when

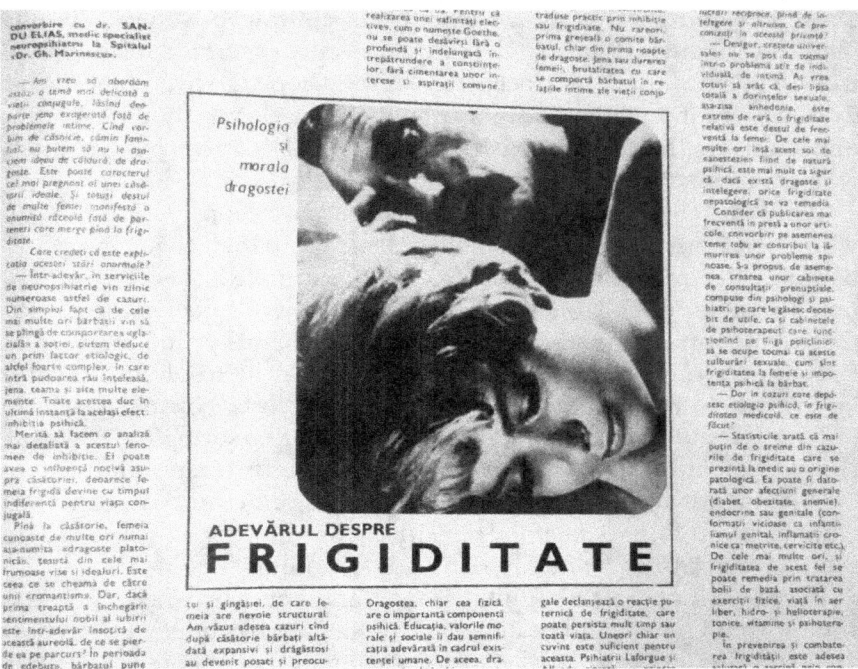

Figure 4.3. "The Truth about Frigidity," *Femeia*, October 1968

the man no longer devotes "all his spiritual resources to please the woman" and simply focuses on the physical aspect of love (making) (see figure 4.3).[93] This, he contended, produces coldness or frigidity in a woman, causing her to mechanically resign herself to her wifely duties. Arguing against the "outdated mindset" that women are sexually passive, the author emphasized that frigidity can be reversed if men exhibit greater tenderness toward their wives and devote more attention to foreplay and the emotional aspects of sex. He adds that the publication of more articles about such "taboo topics," as well as couples' counseling, would go a long way in remedying the problem.

While lack of attentiveness on the part of men was to blame for women's frigidity, in some cases women were at fault. For instance, an article published in *Femeia* in 1986, when pronatalist policies were their most draconian, claimed that frigidity could be caused by stress, trauma, glandular problems, drug and alcohol abuse, and contraceptive use.[94] By drawing a link between women's sexual fulfillment (or lack thereof) and the use of such substances, socialist propagandists sought to deter not only asocial behaviors such as alcohol and drug abuse but anti-natalist ones such as oral contraceptive use. The implicit message was that women would need to sacrifice fertility control (in this case oral contraceptives) if they hoped to overcome sexual dysfunction and achieve sexual fulfillment—a decidedly unappealing option given the anxiety surrounding sexual intercourse for many women at this time.

While articles on sex urged men to be more considerate of their wife's needs, they advised women to be more patient with their husband's performance. In an article entitled "Intimate Issues," the author noted that although women often feel sexually unsatisfied during the first year of marriage, this changes once husbands refine their skills. Drawing on a particular case study, the author explained how one wife's lack of sexual fulfillment caused her to reproach her husband, which, in turn, produced timidity and fear in him, culminating in loss of interest in sex altogether. Claiming that "sexual unity" (e.g. simultaneous climax) is rare and can often take months or even years to achieve, she emphasizes that patience and sensitivity on the part of wives are essential for attaining—and maintaining—a fulfilling sex life.[95]

By presenting sexual fulfillment as another site where women's equality with men could be achieved, propagandists hoped to promote demographic growth. In the process, they also enlightened women about their bodies and sexual pleasure, often in surprisingly explicit ways given the conservatism of Romanian society on matters sexual. For instance, the January 1969 edition of "Questions, Confessions, Experiences" acknowledged the clitoris as an important site for women's sexual fulfillment, while at the same time emphasizing the centrality of the emotional and psychological in sexual relations.[96] Like sex manuals in other parts of Europe and the United States and articles in women's magazines such as *Cosmopolitan*, publications on sexuality in Romania were intended to demystify the sexual act and help women regain—or discover—their sexual desire. However, in the Romanian context, sexual pleasure, rather than being an end in and of itself, was a catalyst for demographic growth. As such, experts suggested that couples engage in sexual activity 3–4 times per week, while also noting that excessive or infrequent sexual activity can produce nervousness, agitation, and insomnia.[97] They also warned against *coitus interruptus*, claiming it undermined spousal intimacy and could cause impotence, urethral irritation, and prostate congestion in men, and produce frigidity and pelvic congestion in women.[98]

The degree to which women experienced sexual fulfillment with their partners is unknown, however, engaging in sexual relations was a risky prospect in Romania—even prior to the banning of abortion in

1966—due to lack of access to modern contraception (condoms; birth control pills). However, once Decree 770 was in place it became even riskier, which would have compromised women's sexual agency, muted sexual desire and, more generally, compromised intimate relations. This was further complicated by men's often-dominant role within a partnership and traditional attitudes regarding sex, which considered sexual pleasure to be primarily a male preserve. As such, some women regarded sex as a routine chore, part of her wifely duties and essential for ensuring "peace at home."[99] That said, others enjoyed satisfying sex lives, although this was, at least in part, tempered by concern about unwanted pregnancy.

Although viewing sex as a routine duty was by no means unique to Romanian women, what was exceptional was the fear and anxiety that accompanied sexual encounters after the passage of Decree 770, which criminalized abortion. Thus, alongside responsibilities at work and home, after 1966, Romanian women had the added burden of dealing with unwanted pregnancy under particularly restrictive circumstances. This was similarly a concern in the United States and many European countries where abortion remained illegal; however, the anti-abortion law in Romania was particularly harsh and procuring one was not only physically risky but could also involve serious legal repercussions. Thus, women in liberal-democracies where abortion was illegal did not experience anywhere near the level of surveillance and repression as women in Romania did. Moreover, Romanian women had minimal access to modern forms of birth control and, due to travel restrictions, could not travel to other countries to procure an abortion.

Consequently, sexual activity was often accompanied by an underlying sense of anxiety. As Luana reflected "There was this fear at all times, dear God, don't let me get pregnant."[100] Or, as a woman who had procured sixteen illegal abortions emphasized, "It was enough just to see my husband appearing in the bedroom and I already felt that I was pregnant."[101] Indeed, so terrified were women of unwanted pregnancy that some couples no longer slept in the same bed. As one woman recounted, "After having given birth to two children we began to sleep apart. It was better and safer to go to sleep [that way]. We had two children to bring up; we could not afford the luxury of a normal sexual life."[102] These remarks underscore the decree's detrimental impact on intimate relations. In light of these realities, as well as the fact that many Romanians held conservative attitudes toward sex, the advice of sexologists and physicians in matters sexual (if it was even read) could have been interpreted in various ways. On the one hand, suggestions for increased tenderness might have resonated with women who did not feel physically or emotionally satisfied by sex—especially given the risks involved in having sex after 1966. On the other hand, women may have found the articles about frigidity or sexual dysfunction puzzling, insulting, and even insidious.

Although articles on spousal relations and female sexuality were more strategic than genuine, their very existence indicates that the state viewed the domestic sphere as a site for transforming not only gender roles but intimate relations. At the same time, by emphasizing that women's equality could not be achieved by policy alone, but also required transforming men's attitudes, the state placed the onus on individual men and women to change outmoded behaviors. This was underscored by an opinion poll that asked if it was possible to "mold" a husband, to which readers answered with an emphatic "yes," describing how they transformed their husbands from self-centered sloths into domestically conscientious and caring comrades.[103] In this manner, the state deflected attention away from its failure to de-gender childrearing by introducing parental leave and to lighten women's domestic burdens through labor-saving devices and communal kitchens and laundries. Beyond this, the attention *Femeia* devoted to men's roles as husbands and fathers paled in comparison to the attention it devoted to women's roles as wives and mothers. Marriage thus served as another area where the ambiguities of socialism played out as legislation codified women and men as equals, yet policy and propaganda promoted family roles that were in some cases progressive and in other cases conservative—and even regressive.

## Refashioning Roles or Reinforcing Tradition? Everyday Marital Roles

The expansion of educational and employment opportunities broadened women's social roles and facilitated their economic autonomy; meanwhile, socialist propagandists validated women's contributions as equal socialist workers. However, this process did not automatically lead to the eradication of patriarchal behaviors and a refashioning of marital roles as Engels had envisaged. As Domnica (b. 1938), a retired dentist, emphasized:

> Private life changed as a function of cultural level, and at this level there was much to be desired. They [men] understood that women had to work and that they had it hard at home, but they would come home and sit in front of the television or go out drinking and return home to find everything finished. Now [after 1989] women understand that it isn't

exactly like that ... that they also have rights ... and they have begun to realize that tasks need to be shared.[104]

In Domnica's assessment, the continuity of patriarchal behaviors was directly related to how boys had been raised. Accustomed to their mothers completing housework while their fathers read the paper or attended to other, traditionally masculine tasks, boys' understandings of family responsibilities were distinctly gendered. Other respondents also stressed the role of "culture" (i.e. upbringing) in explaining their husband's reluctance to help with the household. Accordingly, socialization during youth and traditional notions of gender proved more powerful than socialist mantras in shaping men's attitudes toward family roles.

Indeed, in some cases, policies designed to promote equality of opportunity produced tension between husbands and wives—even exacerbating patriarchal attitudes. Such was the case of T., who wanted to earn her high school diploma by attending night school but was discouraged from doing so by her husband because he didn't want her "to be smarter than him."[105] In the end, T. relented and quit night school, something she still regretted when I interviewed her, claiming that she did not feel totally fulfilled and that they should have studied together. Czech scholar Hana Havelková asserts that women's willingness to bow to their husbands' demands can be read as a strategy to boost their husbands' self-confidence and, thereby, neutralize the emasculating or disempowering effects of socialist rule.[106] Although perhaps not motivated by such reasons, T.'s acceptance of her husband's wishes contributed to the perpetuation of those very attitudes she resented, while also preventing her from realizing her educational aspirations.

Giving in to a husband's demands or being forced to contend with sexist or abusive behavior was not uncommon. As in other parts of the Bloc, a major reason for marital discord was alcohol consumption (almost always on the part of the man). According to Regine, her husband's alcoholism seriously affected their marriage and family life more generally:

> It was a struggle. A battle. He saw life as something he wanted to live, and family responsibilities did not matter to him. I ... I was raised [to believe that] if I brought these children into the world, I am obliged to be a good mother, to take care of my family. When my husband was at work, it was the most pleasant time because I was with the little ones and because he was a bit of an alcoholic ... he often didn't come home [until late] and the three of us were able to spend time together. [I was able] to raise them properly.[107]

Regine explained her husband's alcoholism with respect to his experiences as a POW during World War II, which she claimed had permanently scarred him. Because drinking and spending time with friends were his means of coping with past trauma, all household and childcare duties fell to Regine. Yet, rather than being angered by her husband's absence from home, Regine was thankful because she and the children could enjoy each other's company in peace. In contrast, when her husband returned home drunk and started fights with her "the children did not sleep and went to school tired."[108] Although her husband's behavior was clearly disruptive to family harmony, Regine minimized it, referring to him as a "bit of an alcoholic" and justifying his alcohol abuse on what seems to have been post-traumatic stress disorder. Like other women in Romania, Regine had no support network for dealing with her husband's abusive behavior. Nor did her husband have any source of support, through therapy or other means, for coping with his trauma. Thus, like other women, Regine suffered her husband's condition and her abuse in silence.

In this respect, Regine was not alone. When discussing marital relations and family life more generally, a number of my respondents emphasized problems associated with alcohol abuse. Indeed, alcohol consumption was a yardstick by which some even measured their marriages, noting that women who had husbands who drank faced the greatest challenges. For instance, one woman emphasized that her husband was "first rate" and she was lucky to have him; however, she added that she wished that "he didn't drink so much." Although alcoholism was—and continues to be—a serious problem among men in Romania, only a few respondents noted that it created problems in their own marriages, in some cases leading to divorce. That said, some respondents might have been reticent to share such matters with a stranger. Or, they may have wanted to downplay negative aspects of their relationship and present their husbands in a positive light.

In addition to alcohol abuse, spousal abuse and infidelity (or a combination of these) prompted women to sue for divorce. In the case of Valeria P., a nurse who married a doctor in 1957, it seems that abuse, at least of a psychological nature, prompted her to end the marriage:

> When a man became a husband, then he began to dominate. Even if both partners had a job, he was dominant because that's what he learned in his family and that's what he saw around him, and this type of education is contagious. When I married there was a difference of twelve years, I was twenty, he thirty-two ... I had just come from adolescence. I went into marriage straight from boarding school not knowing how to defend my

interests. When I realized that a woman could defend herself and when I realized the slogans that were being used—equality between women and men—I began to earn my rights, freedom of thought, of behavior, to rest, to take part in raising my child, to not be an obedient slave. I wouldn't take it. Especially when I saw the movie *Spartacus* ... I decided to leave because I realized I was not put on this earth to be a slave. After the divorce I decided to go to college, I wanted to change my life. I thought, if I finish university I will have more power to change my life, to change my job, and to also change my destiny.[109]

According to Valeria, gender relations were more or less equitable during adolescence; however, with adulthood and, in particular, marriage this changed as traditional norms shaped spousal relations—regardless of social or professional status. Although Valeria explained that her husband's domineering attitude was in part related to their age difference and her self-proclaimed naiveté, she emphasized that his behavior was rooted in his traditional upbringing, which socialist policy and propaganda had not altered. Rather than accept such treatment, Valeria, spurred on by socialist rhetoric and Stanley Kubrick's *Spartacus*, divorced her husband in 1963 and refashioned her life according to her own needs and hopes.

Meanwhile, Adriana (b. 1952), a philosophy teacher who had wanted to stay together for the kids, was finally driven to divorce because of her husband's continued affairs.[110] Although she divorced well after the 1966 divorce restrictions were in place, the process went quickly due to her husband's infidelities and unwillingness to reconcile, taking only three months.[111] Adriana was fortunate in this regard as others waited years before having their divorce cases finalized, even in cases of infidelity, birth of illegitimate children, and prolonged psychological and physical abuse.

Indeed, for many women divorce was simply not an option. As previously noted, divorce became more difficult—and more expensive—to obtain with the tightening of legislation in 1966.[112] Additionally, housing shortages meant that finding a separate dwelling was nearly impossible after a couple divorced. Moreover, some women were financially dependent on their husband's salary—especially in the 1980s when costs for food and other goods increased and two salaries were required to support a family. Meanwhile, some relied on their husband for childcare or wanted their children to be raised by both parents. Finally, in some cases, parents put pressure on their children to stay married. For example, although one of my respondents, Eugenia, suffered physical abuse at the hands of her husband, her mother insisted she stay married until the kids reached adulthood.

Some women also chose not to divorce because of the social stigma and personal vulnerability associated with it. As Elena emphasized:

> As a divorced woman you were looked down upon ... it was very difficult, if not impossible, to be promoted and even people around you, your family, your parents, looked down on you and condemned you—even if your husband had an affair or was drinking and abused you. The common thinking was—and I think still is in some families—that a woman should endure because we are different, we are not like men. ... You had to be married as a woman ... and women looked upon their men as gifts, as if to say, "Look at me, I'm a respectable woman, I am married." Being divorced or not married meant that you were much more vulnerable at work and in society ... any man, any colleague, any director could harass you.[113]

According to Elena, being married was in some respects a protective measure, safeguarding women from harassment. Thus, while propagandists presented the young, single woman as a symbol of socialist modernity, on an everyday level she was often defined according to traditional gender norms, which meant she was vulnerable and in need of protection (e.g. a husband). Progressive depictions of young single women also contrasted with the state's view of divorced women (and divorced individuals more generally), whom it regarded as retrograde. This was because divorce, like marriage, was a social concern, and was perceived as a moral failing that was contrary to socialist ethics. Accordingly, in addition to being the object of criticism by family and friends, divorced individuals could be subject to minor sanctions in the workplace as divorce cases were recorded in work files and used for promotion decisions.[114] In fact, Ceaușescu proposed that marital history be considered for promotion to leadership positions, stating, "I agree with the proposal to not promote those who, from a moral point of view, do not constitute an example. What type of regional secretary can one be if he changes wives every year?"[115] Thus, legal proscriptions, official condemnation, and everyday stigmatization by family, friends, and colleagues forced women to remain in unhealthy and even dangerous relationships, undermining state claims regarding concern for the welfare of women and the family. Although none of my respondents seemingly suffered professionally or experienced harassment as a result of being divorced, some noted that they were criticized by their mothers or other family members for not making the marriage work, or that they were the subject of gossip by neighbors and coworkers.

In contrast, in the GDR divorce became more socially acceptable over the course of socialist rule, with proceedings increasingly being initiated by women (for example, by 1984, 68 percent of divorces were filed by women).[116] Moreover, divorce was not economically devastating for women as the existence of child allowances and the widespread availability of childcare meant that raising children alone, without a male partner, was not only financially feasible for some women but also "emancipating," liberating them from conventional family roles.[117] In contrast, lower wages, inadequate childcare facilities, and housing shortages, combined with the social stigma surrounding divorce and restrictive divorce legislation, prevented Romanian women from experiencing similar liberation.

As demonstrated, marital relations continued to be influenced by traditional notions of gender, including the sexual double standard, women's subordination to the male head of household, and women's role as homemaker. These beliefs were manifest in instances of adultery and spousal abuse and, more generally, in men's dominance over their wives. They were also evident in men's unwillingness to contribute to the daily management of the household. In large part, men's attitudes toward housework were shaped by cultural values, which deemed housework feminine. Such attitudes were perpetuated not only by men but by women as well, especially mothers, who pampered their sons, catering to their every whim. As a result, when men married or entered into relationships with women, they often expected their partners to take care of them as their mothers had. Discussing a man she had dated in the mid-1980s, Elena recalled,

> He expected me to treat him as his mother did, but I did not do that ... and his mother told me that it was my duty to wash his trousers, to cook for him, to clean for him, and I said, "OK, is he disabled? I can help him if he's disabled ... if not, he should do these things himself." And, from that moment on, I totally refused to do these things for him. And little by little he was able to wash dishes, to cook eggs for himself, to wash his trousers, and to keep things clean.[118]

Elena's reflections are evocative of the aforementioned *Femeia* articles in which men got married in order to have "someone to take care of them" and men's mother's chided their daughters-in-law for not tending to their son's every need.

Like Elena, Corina also believed that men should contribute domestically, especially since both women and men worked full-time. Thus, when she told her husband that he needed to help around the house, she presented their marriage as a collaborative effort: "The mentality was no different: the woman at the frying pan, the man as the leader ... but I didn't accept it. ... I didn't want to accept it, I said, in the first place we are both people, we both work, we both bring in money, we will do everything together."[119] Corina's remarks underscore the degree to which working outside the home shaped women's understanding of marital relations. According to Corina, if women could work alongside men on the factory floor, then men could work alongside women on the kitchen floor.

Meanwhile, other women resorted to flattery to coax their husbands into performing household chores. As Angela, who married in the late 1980s, noted:

> In general, you need to know how to deal with men here [in Romania], to leave them to do things when they want. If you push him, "Hey, look, now I want you to do this work," and he sees that he is being pushed ... or if I say something in a certain tone ... a tone of superiority because I want something resolved immediately, well it might not be resolved. But if I leave him [alone], speak nicely to him, or say that he can do it when he wants, then he does it.[120]

While employing different strategies to get their partners to contribute domestically, these women believed that marriage should be more or less an equal partnership. For them, gender roles were not natural or immutable but the product of custom, upbringing, and habit. Because they worked as much as their partners did (and perhaps even more), their belief that men should help around the house was related to issues of justice and self-preservation.

Did the experience of working outside the home and the resultant sense of self-confidence and personal validation prompt women to renegotiate new roles vis-à-vis their husbands and demand a sharing of domestic duties? Certainly the time and energy spent at the factory, research lab, or school made housework far more burdensome for women than had they simply been housewives. Given the pressures of work and home, it is understandable that spousal cooperation was frequently referenced in women's assessments of their marriages. Rather than a source of economic security in which each person assumed distinctly gendered roles, for some women marriage was a partnership in which both spouses contributed to the proper functioning of the household.

From a practical standpoint—that of time and energy—women's requests for help can be conceptualized as a form of *Eigen-sinn*. The very act of performing socially recognizable work outside the home and earning a living wage, combined, to varying degrees, with the elevation of women's public identity via prevailing media representations, empowered some women to persuade or pressure their husbands to pitch in with the dishes or cooking. Because this entailed challenging traditional gender norms, it demonstrates that some women not only recognized the inequality of existing marital roles but also possessed the self-confidence to confront their partners about it.

In some cases, the dynamics of the marriage may have been more egalitarian or companionate from the onset, making it easier for women to request help from their partners. As Livia (b. mid-1940s) commented about her husband:

> He didn't help out as much as I wanted because he also had his work, but in general we did things together. During that period [communist period] I was responsible for the shopping ... but the rest we did together, or my husband cleaned more [than me], vacuumed. Anyway, we had our things settled and it worked pretty well, even if I usually did the cooking.[121]

Aneta (b. 1936), a retired factory worker, also shared domestic chores with her husband, a tailor:

> We split responsibilities, "You do this, I do that, I go to the market, I cook, I take care of the children." He was working two shifts, he helped with the chores when he was around; it was not hard. I was aware that I had a husband who helped; for example, if I iron today and tomorrow I wash, he did the rest. For me it seemed a very easy life.[122]

Additionally, Aneta's husband shopped for groceries and queued up for food, looked after the children, and made the family's clothing, sparing Aneta the time and energy of having to shop for these goods. Far from viewing the responsibilities of home and work as burdensome, Aneta recalled that it was "a very easy life." Women's ability to juggle work, childcare, and housework thus often depended on their husbands' ability and willingness to assist them. As Axinia, noted, "Men helped with food and looking after the kids; without them we could not have managed."[123]

In some cases, women's interpretation of "sharing" meant that men performed traditionally masculine tasks such as beating rugs and repair work, while women cooked, cleaned, and did laundry. In such instances, "sharing" was not equal since cooking could take a great deal of time, especially in the 1980s when food and cooking heat were rationed and the use of one's gas stove was dependent upon the whims of the regime, often forcing women to rise at 3 AM to make the family meal. Similarly, doing laundry was an arduous and time-consuming process, as washing machines continued to be luxury items, as was hot water, by the late 1980s. Thus, even when men did contribute domestically, they did so considerably less frequently and spent fewer hours per week than women did.

That said, in some cases women preferred that men only assume certain tasks, viewing some domains as their own. As Ecaterina emphasized, "I don't like people putting their nose in my work in the kitchen. Pure and simple. If I need help, I ask. Hey, can you do some vacuuming, can you beat a rug?"[124] However, in some instances men performed traditionally feminine tasks such as cleaning, cooking, and ironing. As Iuliana recalled about her husband's facility with housework, "He is very capable in that respect. He knows how to make anything, *cozonac* [a labor-intensive sweet bread] as well as *sarmale* [stuffed cabbage rolls]. He helped me a great deal ... he knows how to iron and make any type of food. But he doesn't know how to hammer a nail, change a pipe."[125]

More often, however, men's willingness to help around the house was related to the particular task being performed. As Mircea A. (b. 1934), a factory boss, recalled, "Naturally men waited in line, I would go and my wife would stay at home with the children."[126] Similarly, Marcela (b. 1942), an art teacher, noted about her husband:

> No, he didn't do housework. I can't even describe how clumsy he was, it was unbelievable. But he had other attributes, he could get a hold of food that you couldn't find; we never went without meat, coffee, or anything, he succeeded in finding it. He was the type who managed to make circles of friends, and one of them was a guy at a restaurant. He had many acquaintances in the area, and he bought food at cost from the restaurant.[127]

In interpreting this passage, it is important not to let Western conceptions of housework influence the analysis. Scholars of socialism argue that because men tended to assume responsibility for weekly, biweekly, or even monthly jobs—such as taking out the trash and household repairs—they spent considerably less time per week on domestic chores. However, the Romanian case complicates this claim, especially in the 1980s with the reintroduction of rationing. During this period, queuing for food became a daily activity for which many men assumed (or shared) responsibility. Marcela's husband's and Micrea's efforts were, therefore, much more significant than picking up a few items at the corner store. Indeed, in the context of the material shortages that characterized life during the 1980s, it might be more useful to think of these activities as food procurement rather than shopping. During this period, procuring food required a good deal of time, energy, and fortitude, be it going from shop to shop, negotiating deals with acquaintances at restaurants, or standing in a queue for hours on end.

Men's aforementioned contributions are not necessarily evidence of more progressive attitudes toward domestic labor—or even marital roles. Because men have traditionally been involved in food procurement in Romania, shopping and, in particular, waiting in a queue did not assume a negative stigma as was the case with other gender-specific or traditionally feminine chores such as cooking, cleaning, and ironing.[128] Indeed, the very experience of braving sub-zero temperatures in the dead of winter for a liter of milk may have been construed by some men as reflective of their physical endurance. Given state control over most aspects of life, food procurement may have thus served as a means of articulating a paternalist identity or, quite literally, the role of "breadwinner." Moreover, queues were often sites of socialization where friends and neighbors joked and shared stories. Therefore, queuing up was not a socially isolating activity—and was certainly less energy-intensive than doing laundry, cleaning, and cooking.

In addition to procuring food, Romanian men looked after the children. This was necessitated by the short maternity leave and lack of adequate state-run nurseries and kindergartens, as well as the fact that not all parents could rely on relatives as sources of childcare. Consequently, many couples resorted to the alternate shift system (whereby spouses worked opposite shifts). As Stela recalled: "We shared ... my husband organized his schedule so that his classes were mainly in the afternoon and he stayed with the kids in the mornings."[129] Similarly, Rodica noted with respect to her husband:

> Yes, when he had time he helped me, I can't say he didn't. As you can imagine [we had] a three-month old girl and no one to stay with her ... we were not in a position to pay a babysitter to look after the child. We had to work different shifts so that we could both look after her. He in the morning and me in the afternoon. Our bosses understood that we had a small child and we came to an understanding.[130]

Rodica's husband's contribution to childcare is especially noteworthy since, during this period (mid-1980s), disposable diapers were unavailable and gas heating was rationed. Thus, her husband was faced with heating milk and hot water over a minuscule flame—an activity that could take hours.[131] At the same time, it should be noted that due to women's widespread employment outside the home, such practices were not unique to Romania as men participated, albeit to varying degrees, in childcare throughout the Eastern Bloc.[132] Yet, their need to do so was related more to flawed policy than Marxist theory on women, as the short maternity leave and lack of adequate childcare facilities inadvertently encouraged shared parenting.

To be sure, not all men embraced childcare, and some women may have questioned the amount of time and energy their husbands devoted to it. However, the fact that men were taking on such duties at all lightened women's burdens at least somewhat. In addition, it meant that men were more involved as fathers, which would have benefited father and child alike. If they chose to, men could therefore play a more influential role in the education of their children—a responsibility that has historically been the preserve of women. Indeed, in comparison with socialist Hungary where, beginning in the 1970s, women were encouraged to return to the home and assume full responsibility for the household, men in Romania were more likely to be involved in childrearing.[133] Finally, men's participation in childcare may have somewhat defeminized this practice, which, in turn, would have provided a more progressive model for other fathers, as well as for young and adolescent boys.

In certain cases, men were genuinely sensitive to their wives' numerous responsibilities (or burdens) and sought to lighten them by helping with household chores. As Mircea (b. 1927), a retired pharmacist who contrasted his views of housework with those of his former colleagues, remarked:

> Women's situation was very difficult. I would characterize it in the following way: a woman is not to blame for being born a woman, for doing two shifts, one at the office, the other at home. Most men did not help around the house. When I said, at the office, that I washed dishes and did other things [around the house], a coworker jumped out of his seat and said: "How can you do such feminine work?" And I said, "But does your wife work?" "Yes," he said. And I said, "So she has to, without fail, work two jobs while you read the paper?" Many men behaved this way. I didn't understand it.[134]

Given women's full-time employment, Mircea reasoned that it was only fair that men also assume responsibility for household duties. In contrast to his coworkers, Mircea conceptualized marriage as an equal partnership based on mutual support and respect.

Finally, it should be noted that men's ability to contribute domestically was related to workplace demands. For instance, those employed in a managerial capacity typically had to put in long hours at the factory, overseeing projects and attending meetings, which often meant they returned home late in the evening. Moreover, in order to supplement family income, men picked up odd jobs in the unofficial economy (e.g.

repairing cars and other durable goods; doing carpentry work), which added to their already burdened schedules. Additionally, more men than women commuted to their jobs, leaving early in the morning and returning late—or returning only on weekends—which prevented them from contributing regularly to household management.

What were men's motivations for participating in household duties? Did men undergo transformation—as Engels envisaged—as a result of working alongside women, or did they simply recognize that traditionally gendered practices were wholly incompatible with everyday life under socialism? Did socialist propaganda facilitate men's increased participation in the domestic sphere? Or, were they compelled by more practical considerations such as maintaining a decent standard of living? As a corollary, did men's increased participation in the household reflect greater flexibility in their definitions of masculinity, a more profound recognition of gender equality and sensitivity to women's lot?

Although scholars point to patriarchal mentalities and men's reluctance to assist in the domestic realm as evidence of women's continued subordination under socialism, my respondents' recollections complicate this picture.[135] This is not to claim that men assumed half or even a quarter of the household tasks—or that they assumed them with enthusiasm. Indeed, according to Olga, women in Romania are "very hard workers ... and spend a lot of time in the kitchen, cooking and cleaning," and are thus accustomed to performing most household duties.[136] As such, respondents may have overemphasized the degree to which their husbands helped them. Or, they may have wanted to present a progressive image of their husbands and, by extension, their marriages. At the same time, it cannot be assumed that these responses are gross exaggerations or sugarcoated representations of reality. In fact, spousal cooperation was frequently referenced in women's assessments of their marriages. Rather than simply a source of economic security in which each person assumed distinctly gendered roles, for some women marriage was a partnership in which both spouses contributed to the proper functioning of the household.

As demonstrated, *Femeia* frequently reminded men, both visually and rhetorically, to treat their wives with respect, regard them as equals, and assist them with housework and childcare. Although such messages may appear hyperbolic, it should not be assumed that they had no bearing on men's and women's behaviors. Moreover, in some cases, men were genuinely sensitive to the challenges their wives faced in reconciling the dual demands of work and home. To be sure, changes in the domestic sphere were not automatic: husbands did not begin sweeping floors and baking tortes the minute their wives stepped foot on the factory floor. Also, men were often selective in deciding which chores to take up (e.g. food procurement and childcare instead of ironing and cooking). However, this seems less due to an unwillingness to help than a desire to perform masculine or gender-neutral jobs. At the same time, necessity often facilitated men's participation. In her study of married couples in the United States in the 1980s, Arlie Hochschild found that joint responsibility for housework evolved more easily when it was linked to necessity and that the sharing of household duties engendered less male-female conflict in working-class families than in more self-consciously egalitarian middle-class households.[137] Such findings suggest that material and time-management concerns play a greater role in promoting equitable marital relations than do abstract slogans of gender equality.

## Conclusion

Marriage, both as represented in policy and propaganda and experienced by women and men in their daily lives, assumed diverse and ambiguous meanings over the course of socialist rule. As they did in other spheres of life, traditional ideas about gender coexisted with modern ones. On the one hand, women's mass participation in paid labor, legal equality with men, and increased engagement in public life broadened their opportunities. Consequently, more women married out of love than economic need, in some cases postponing marriage until their mid or late twenties. On the other hand, housing shortages, traditional ideas about marriage, and, after 1966, restrictive pronatalist policies encouraged youthful marriages. Meanwhile, women's increased educational and professional opportunities could produce resentment in husbands who believed that women's responsibilities lay first and foremost in the household, tending to their needs. Traditional family roles were also reinforced in legislation, particularly maternity leave, which defined caregiving as primarily a female preserve, and with the criminalization of abortion and concomitant glorification of women's maternal roles.

At the same time, propagandists promoted progressive family roles, condemning patriarchal mentalities as antisocialist and encouraging men to assist with housework and childcare. Moreover, they promoted equal sexual relations by urging men to be more attentive to their wives' physical and emotional needs, although sexual pleasure was also instrumentalized for the purpose of demographic growth. Yet, despite such progressive depictions, many men continued to view housework as "women's work," giving rise to a double burden for women. In contrast to the precommunist period when tending to the children and household could be done in the larger, domestic realm, under socialism these roles were much more difficult to combine given women's employment outside the home. This, in turn, created significant logistical and time-management problems for women, especially if extended family did not live nearby. The state paid lip service to women's multiple responsibilities, promising labor-saving devices and one-stop grocery stores; however, provision of these goods and services did not meet demand. Accordingly, women were saddled with both workplace and domestic duties, leaving them with little time for leisure, let alone adequate sleep. In some cases, women dealt with these challenges by appealing to their husband's to pick up some of the domestic slack, particularly childcare and food procurement. Whether rooted in necessity, a belief in gender equality, or their wives' prodding, men's contribution to household maintenance could be substantial, especially in the 1980s with the onset of rationing. This is not to claim that domestic duties were divided equally between women and men or to ignore the contributions of other family members (such as parents), but rather to acknowledge that women's successful negotiation of the double burden was, in some cases, related to their husbands' contributions.

That said, state socialism by no means ushered in a period of marital bliss, as women continued to experience psychological and physical abuse. Moreover, infidelity and alcoholism clearly undermined marital harmony. However, here too women faced challenges as a result of housing shortages, social pressure, and the introduction of regressive divorce legislation in 1966, which deterred divorce. Consequently, women (as well as men) were often unable to escape unhealthy marriages. In sum, while marital relations were characterized by diversity and underwent certain changes over the course of socialist rule, continuities and traditional practices remained, including the notion that women should be primarily responsible for children and the household. To be sure, women possessed greater agency within marriage as a result of their codification as equals and contributions to the material support of the family. As a result, some women enjoyed more negotiating power within their marriages. However, early socialist thinkers' vision of marriage as a union of equal comrades, joined by mutual interests, affection, and goals, remained for some women just that—a vision.

## Notes

1. Katherine Verdery, *What Was Socialism, and What Comes Next?* (Princeton, NJ: Princeton University Press, 1996), 66.
2. For feminist critiques of Engels and Marxist theory on women, see Hilda Scott, *Does Socialism Liberate Women? Experiences from Eastern Europe* (Boston: Beacon Press, 1974); Janet Sayers, Mary Evans, and Nanecke Redclift, eds., *Engels Revisited: New Feminist Essays* (London: Tavistock, 1987); Sonia Kruks, Rayna Rapp, and Marilyn Young, eds., *Promissory Notes: Women in the Transition to Socialism* (New York: Monthly Review Press, 1989); Nanette Funk and Magda Mueller, eds., *Gender Politics and Post-Communism: Reflections from Eastern Europe and the Former Soviet Union* (New York: Routledge, 1993); Barbara Einhorn, *Cinderella Goes to Market: Citizenship, Gender and Women's Movements in East Central Europe* (London: Verso, 1993); Chris Corrin, ed., *Superwomen and the Double Burden: Women's Experience of Change in Central and Eastern Europe and the Former Soviet Union* (New York: Scarlet Press, 1993); and Sharon Wolchik and Alfred Meyer, eds., *Women, State, and Party in Eastern Europe* (Durham, NC: Duke University Press, 1985).
3. Doina Paşca Harsanyi, "Participation of Women in the Workforce: The Case of Romania," in *Family, Women, and Employment in Central-Eastern Europe*, ed. Barbara Lobodzinska (Westport, CT: Greenwood Press, 1995), 215. Also see Harsanyi, "Women in Romania," and Marianna Hausleitner, "Women in Romania before and after the Collapse," both in *Gender Politics and Post-Communism*.
4. See Verdery, *What Was Socialism?*
5. "Articolul 1224 din Codul Civil din 26 noiembrie 1864 al Principatelor Unite Române," *Monitorul Oficial*, nr. 271, 4 decembrie 1864.
6. "Codul Familiei al României din 1953," *Buletinul Oficial al Republicii Populare Române*, nr. 1, 4 ianuarie 1954. Marriage was defined as being between a man and a woman.
7. See, in particular, August Bebel, *Women and Socialism* (New York: New York Labor News, 1917), 344.
8. "Legea Nr. 18 din 12 februarie pentru modificarea codului de procedură civilă," in *Colecţiune de Legi şi Regulamente 1948* (Bucharest: Imprimeria Centrală, 1948), 82–83.
9. See Cosmin Budeancă, "Divorţul în familiile foştilor deţinuţi politici" in *Stat şi viaţă privată în regimurile comuniste*, ed. Cosmin Budeancă and Florentin Olteanu (Iaşi: Polirom, 2009), 161–72. It should be noted that some individuals remarried their divorced spouses when they returned from prison.
10. In 1948 abortion remained illegal under Article 482 of the Romanian Penal Code; however, due to the unavailability of contraception and lax enforcement of the law, women continued to procure abortions with little legal effect. "Legea Nr. 18/1948 din februarie pentru modificarea codului de procedură civilă," in *Colecţiune de Legi şi Regulamente 1948* (Bucharest: Imprimeria Centrală, 1948).

11. "Cum să ma conving părinţii?" *Femeia*, April 1959, 17.
12. Ibid.
13. That said, according to Luminiţa Dumanescu, who grew up in a small Romanian town in the 1980s, even during late socialism girls were known to run off with boys who were not accepted by their parents. Luminiţa Dumanescu, *Familia românească în comunism* (Cluj: Presa Universitară Clujeană, 2012), 114.
14. Alina Sandu Cucu and Irina Culic, "Procese de configurare a claselor sociale în România: O analiză relaţională a căsătoriilor pentru cinci generaţii," in *Înerţie şi schimbare: Dimensiuni sociale ale tranziţiei în România*, ed. Traian Rotariu and Virgiliu Voineagu (Iaşi: Polirom, 2012), 169–74; and Petru Iluţ, *Sociologia şi antropologie familiei* (Iaşi: Polirom, 2005).
15. Mihai Stoian, "Dialog cu mine însumi despre viaţa în doi: o profesiune care se învaţa," *Femeia*, April 1967, 12–13. The subject of love under socialism was also explored in a full-length book by Adriana Deculescu titled *Dragostea* (Bucharest: Editura Medicala, 1971).
16. Cici Iordache, "Azi la starea civilă, mâine la judecătorie," *Femeia*, June 1972, 34–35.
17. "Între Prietene," *Femeia*, February 1959, 17.
18. "Întrebări, Confesiuni, Experienţe," *Femeia*, February 1966, 15–16.
19. Elizabeth Heineman asserts that because single women in East Germany enjoyed legal and political equality with men and because their contributions as workers were publicly acknowledged, they had an easier time finding personal rewards in the workplace and community than did their West German counterparts who were primarily homemakers. Consequently, East German women did not view marriage as necessary—or even important. See Elizabeth Heineman, *What Difference Does a Husband Make? Women and Marital Status in Nazi and Postwar Germany* (Berkeley: University of California Press, 2003), 9.
20. Sanda Faur, "Unde găsesc bărbatul cu care vreau acum să mă căsătoresc?" *Femeia*, February 1976, 14.
21. Ibid.
22. During the socialist period, traditional and peasant values continued to shape the attitudes and behaviors of some urban dwellers. See Gail Kligman, *Căluş: Symbolic Transformation in Romanian Ritual* (Chicago: University of Chicago Press, 1981); and Gail Kligman, *The Wedding of the Dead: Ritual, Poetics, and Popular Culture in Transylvania* (Berkeley: University of California Press, 1988).
23. *Codul principiilor şi normelor muncii şi vieţii comuniştilor, ale eticii şi echităţii socialiste* (Editura Politică, 1974). Article 200 of the Penal Code, implemented in 1968, criminalized sexual relations between persons of the same sex. Punishments for transgressing these laws ranged from one to seven years imprisonment, though a person might face up to twenty-five years in prison if it was determined that relations resulted in bodily harm, death, or the suicide of one of the parties involved. See "Codul Penal al României, iunie 1968" *Buletinul Oficial al Republicii Socialiste Române* nr. 79, 21 iunie 1968.

24. Adriana Băban, "Women's Sexuality in Romania," in *Reproducing Gender: Politics, Publics, and Everyday Life after Socialism*, ed. Susan Gal and Gail Kligman (Princeton, NJ: Princeton University Press, 2000), 239.
25. Tatiana, interview with author, Brașov, 27 May 2003.
26. In the 1970s, approximately 100,000 apartments were constructed per year, up from 45,000 in the early 1960s. Despite this, the number of young workers living in urban hostels in 1978 was ten times greater than it had been in 1968, in large part due to the acceleration of industrialization in the late 1960s. See Flavius Mihalache and Alin Croitoru, "Mediul rural romanesc: evoluții și involuții. Schimbare socială și antreprenoriat" (PhD diss. University of Bucharest, 2011), 24; and William Crowther, *The Political Economy of Romanian Socialism* (New York: Praeger, 1988), 111.
27. Josie McLellan, *Love in the Time of Communism: Intimacy and Sexuality in the GDR* (Cambridge: Cambridge University Press, 2011), 42.
28. Mircea, interview with Ionuț Iuria, Brașov, 4 August 2003.
29. *Buletin de București*, directed by Virgil Calotescu (Bucharest: Casa de Filme Patru, 1982).
30. A sequel to the film, *Căsătorie cu repetiție* (1985) traces the couple's reunion during their *repartiție* and subsequent remarriage.
31. *Anuarul Statistic al Republicii Socialiste România, 1967–1989*. Georgeta Ghebrea, *Regim social-politic și viață privată: familia și politica familială în România* (Bucharest: Editura Universității din București, 2000), 29.
32. Ibid.
33. At the end of the 1970s, the mean age for first marriage in England and Spain was twenty-six while for most other Western countries this figure was twenty-seven or older. See Alain Blum, "Socialist Families," in *Family Life in the Twentieth Century*, ed. David I. Kertzer and Marzio Barbagli (New Haven, CT: Yale University Press, 2003), 323.
34. Luana, interview with author, Brașov, 25 July 2003.
35. Petre, interview with author, Bucharest, 3 June 2009.
36. The Orthodox Church allowed lower-ranking party members (as well as non-members) to hold religious wedding ceremonies. See Sabrina Ramet, *Nihil Obstat: Religion, Politics, and Social Change in East-Central Europe and Russia* (Durham, NC: Duke University Press, 1998), 191–92.
37. In Poland, divorce rates increased from 44 (for every 1,000 marriages) in 1950 to 50 by 1956. In 1963, 24 percent of couples filing for divorce did so within a year of marrying. Fidelis, *Women, Communism, and Industrialization*, 144.
38. ANIC, CC al PCR, Secția Cancelarie, dosar 101/1966, f. 109. The criminalization of abortion will be dealt with in detail in chapter 5.
39. Ministerul Justiției, "Decretul nr. 779 din 8 octombrie 1966 pentru modificarea unor dispoziții legale privitoare la divorț" in *Colecție de Legi, Decrete, Hotâriri și Alte Acte Normative* (Bucharest: Editura Științifica, 1967), 35–39.
40. In 1969, the decree was revised to include additional grounds for divorce that did not require the reconciliation period or the payment of the divorce tax: if the spouse was diagnosed with a chronic mental illness; was

officially declared as disappeared; had left the country for at least two years and abandoned the family; was sentenced for attempted murder against the plaintiff, incest, or same-sex relations; was sentenced to three years in prison for infractions against the security of the state (e.g. infanticide, prostitution, theft, deception, embezzlement). See "Decretul nr. 680/1969 pentru modificarea unor dispoziții din Codul de procedură civilă și din Decretul nr. 779/1966 pentru modificarea unor dispoziții legale privitoare la divorț," in *Buletin Oficial al Republicii Socialiste Române*, Partea I, nr. 106, 7 octombrie, 1969.

41. "Decretul 779." Monetary conversions based on U.S. Treasury Reporting Rates of Exchange (31 March 1966), retrieved from https://www.gpo.gov/fdsys/pkg/GOVPUB-T63_100-b8e9fea1b3806032f899251fd40bb96f/pdf/GOVPUB-T63_100-b8e9fea1b3806032f899251fd40bb96f.pdf (accessed 25 November 2017).
42. It should be noted that of the thirty-six thousand divorce cases filed in 1962, 62 percent were resolved through reconciliation. ANIC, CC al PCR, Secția Cancelarie, dosar 8/1968, f. 81 as quoted in Florin S. Soare, "Familia, căsătoria și divorțul între ideologia comunistă și pronatalism," in *Politică și societate în epoca Ceaușescu*, ed. Florin S. Soare (Iași: Editura Polirom, 2014), 172.
43. Ibid.
44. *Anuarul Statistic al României*, 1990, 70–73. It should be noted that from the late 1950s on, divorce rates in urban areas were typically three or more times higher than in rural areas.
45. Nicolae Ceaușescu, "Cuvîntare la festivitățile organizate la Cluj cu prilejul deschiderii noului an universitar," 2 octombrie 1972.
46. Soare, "Familia, căsătoria și divorțul," 172.
47. ANIC, CC al PCR, Secția Cancelarie, dosar 102/1966, f. 24.
48. Deborah A. Field, "Irreconcilable Differences: Divorce and Conceptions of Private Life in the Khrushchev Era," *Russian Review* 57 (October 1998): 599–602.
49. By the 1970s, the GDR claimed one of the highest divorce rates in the world. For figures, see Paul Betts, *Within Walls: Private Life in the German Democratic Republic* (Oxford: Oxford University Press, 2013), 107–9.
50. Blum, "Socialist Families," 228–29.
51. Ibid., 105.
52. *Statistisches Jahrbuch der Deutschen Demokratischen Republik, 1970–1990* (Berlin: Staatsverlag der Deutschen Demokratischen Republik) as quoted in McLellan, *Love in the Time of Communism*, 54–55.
53. That figure increased in West Germany as well but was comparatively lower, reaching only 9.4 percent in 1985. See Kertzer and Barbagli, *History of European Family, Life*.
54. Dorel Dorian, "Despărțire din dragoste sau confesiunele avocatului R.D.," *Femeia*, April 1970, 16–17.
55. Sidonia Drăgușanu, "Da, Da, trebuie s'o ajut," *Femeia*, June 1949, 10.
56. Gheorghe Turneski, "Nu numai tovărași de viața ci și tovărași de lupta," *Scânteia*, 8 March 1953, 3.

57. See "Primul an de căsnicie," *Femeia*, June 1971.
58. The survey was conducted with four hundred male and female night school students, many of whom were married with children. See Elisabeta Moraru, "Respectați-O!," *Femeia*, December 1966, 2–5.
59. Ibid.
60. Ibid.
61. *Femeia*, 1973.
62. Francisca Albert, *Dialog cu Timpul Liber* (Bucharest: Editura Politică, 1970). See also, Niki Iosub, "Legislația socială în ajutorul femeii," *Femeia*, November 1965, 2–3.
63. McLellan, *Love in the Time of Communism*, 72.
64. "Cititorii despre activitatea casnica," *Femeia*, August 1967, 13–15.
65. Ibid.
66. To foster self-sufficiency, decades earlier Nadezhda Krupskaya (Lenin's wife) had advised that both boys and girls be taught domestic tasks. See Krupskaya, *Deti-nashe budushchee* (Moscow: Proveshchenie, 1984), 207–208 as cited in Lynne Attwood, *Creating the New Soviet Woman: Women's Magazines as Engineers of Female Identity, 1922–53* (Basingstoke: Macmillan, 1999), 6.
67. Elisabeta Moraru, "Sunteți o femeie modernă? De ce?" *Femeia*, January 1970, 3–5. This piece was framed as a "passionate debate about aspirations and ideals" that went beyond a simple "yes" or "no" answer. 400 women of different age groups and backgrounds responded to the survey.
68. Further evidence that women's multiple roles had become normalized was exemplified in a collection of essays titled, *Woman: Employee, Wife, Mother*, published in 1970. See *Femeia: Salariată, Soție, Mamă* (Bucharest: Editura Politică, 1970).
69. In some cases, women's ability to reconcile these roles was presented as reinvigorating. See the interview with Ancuța Craciun in Ecaterina Oproiu, *3X8 plus infinitul: dialoguri despre condiția femeii* (Bucharest: Editura Eminescu, 1975), 34.
70. Fidelis, *Women, Communism, and Industrialization*, 212.
71. Elisabeta Moraru, "Cand îți bați nevasta, te bați pe tine însuți," *Femeia*, April 1973, 36.
72. Ibid.
73. Ibid.
74. Similarly, beginning in East Germany in the late 1950s, work collectives were encouraged to support couples in reconciling domestic problems and guide them through troubled times, which, according to Donna Harsch, was rooted in the "state's assignment of social responsibilities to the workplace," as well as concern about "socialist morality." Yet, Harsch also notes that given the general belief that relations between husbands and wives were a private matter, the collective was often reluctant to intervene in colleagues' private affairs; thus mediation via the work collective was typically deemed unsuccessful in the divorce records she surveyed. See Donna Harsch, *Revenge of the Domestic: Women, the Family, and Communism in the German Democratic Republic* (Princeton, NJ: Princeton University Press, 2006), 287.

75. "Notă în legătură cu aplicarea dispozițiilor legale privitoare la desfacerea căsătoriei," ANIC, CC al PCR, Secția Cancelarie, dosar 8/1968, f. 81–88.
76. Romania was by no means unique in this respect as articles and letters to the editor from women complaining about domestic violence appeared in Polish and Soviet magazines in the 1950s. See Fidelis, *Women, Communism, and Industrialization*; and Melanie Ilić, Susan Reid, and Lynne Attwood, eds., *Women in the Khrushchev Era* (New York: Palgrave, 2004), 13.
77. See "Codul Penal 1960" *Buletinul Oficial al Republicii Populare Romîne*, nr. 8 din 17 iunie 1960; and "Codul Penal din 1968" *Monitorul Oficial al României*, nr. 79 din 21 iunie 1968. Although no statistics were compiled on domestic violence during the communist period, given the high rate reported after 1989 it can be safely assumed that it was common prior to 1989.
78. Călin Morar-Vulcu, "Becoming Dangerous: Everyday Violence in the Industrial Milieu of Late-Socialist Romania, *European History Quarterly* 45, no. 2 (2015), 319.
79. G.N, interview with author, Brașov, 16 August 2003.
80. Data on the incidence of domestic violence during the socialist period is not available. In 1995 the first study of domestic violence was conducted in Romania. The report, which focused on the early postsocialist period, was based on qualitative research with victims, medical staff, legal professionals, and police, and included police responses to reported incidents of domestic violence. See Minnesota Advocates for Human Rights, "Lifting the Last Curtain: A Report on Domestic Violence in Romania" (1995), retrieved from http://www.theadvocatesforhumanrights.org/uploads/d_v_in_romania_1995.pdf (accessed 10 October 2015).
81. "El 'domnul și stăpînul casei!'" *Femeia*, May 1967, 13.
82. "Să depășim patriarhatul!' spune un bărbat," *Femeia*, February 1974, 24. The article was accompanied by a quiz that asked "Are you a modern husband and father?" Questions included, "Do you accept women in public life?"; "Would you be offended if your wife's job was superior to yours?"; "Do you think housework is beneath men's dignity?"; "Do you discuss issues other than the household with your wife?"; "Did you or do you care if you have a girl or a boy?"; "Do you agree that 'authority' should be used in family relationships?"
83. "Viața în doi: Noul tip de soț" *Femeia*, September 1969, 6
84. Cici Iordache, "Ce fel de tată sinteți?" July 1970, 12–13.
85. Felicia Antip, "Fii bărbat!," *Femeia*, June 1971.
86. *Femeia*, February 1966, 6.
87. Tania Tudose, "Motiv de divorț," *Femeia*, August 1966, 8.
88. Ibid.
89. Ibid.
90. Fidelis, *Women, Communism, and Industrialization*, 179.
91. Radu Dimitriu, *De vorbă cu tinerii: probleme de educație a sexelor* (Bucharest: Editura Tineretului, 1972), 11.
92. Ibid, 142.

93. Dr. E. Roşianu, "Adevărul despre frigiditate," *Femeia*, October 1968, 25. Sexual dysfunction was also attributed to "Sexual Neurosis," a complex condition examined in another article in *Femeia*. See Dr. Victor Săhleanu, "Nevroză Sexuală," *Femeia*, June 1971, 31.
94. "O problemă de comportament intim," *Femeia*, June 1986, 21. Official sexologists also warned against "anti-biological" contraceptives. See Erin Biebuyck, "The Collectivisation of Pleasure: Normative Sexuality in Post-1966 Romania," *Aspasia: International Yearbook of Central, Eastern, and Southeastern European Women's and Gender History* 4 (2010): 49–70.
95. "O problematică a vieţii intime," *Femeia*, August 1985, 21. The piece also noted that fatigue, psychological problems, and tobacco, alcohol, and drug abuse, as well as metabolic ailments (e.g. diabetes), can negatively affect men's sexual potency.
96. "Întrebări, Confesiuni, Experienţe," *Femeia*, January 1969, 17.
97. Gail Kligman, *The Politics of Duplicity: Controlling Reproduction in Ceauşescu's Romania* (Berkeley: University of California Press, 1998), 143.
98. Madeleine Maicanescu-Georgescu, "A avea sau nu avea copii," *Sănătatea*, no. 1, 184, 12.
99. For a discussion of sex as one of a number of women's domestic burdens under socialism see Mihaela Miroiu and Mircea Miclea, *R'Estul şi Vestul* (Bucharest: Polirom, 2005); and Mihaela Miroiu, "Eradicarea instinctului plăcerii," *Dilema veche*, 5, retrieved from http://dilemaveche.ro/sectiune/dileme-line/articol/eradicarea-instinctului-placerii (accessed 2 June 2016).
100. Luana, interview with author, Braşov, 25 July 2003.
101. Adriana Băban and Henry P. David, *Voices of Romanian Women: Perceptions of Sexuality, Reproductive Behavior, and Partner Relations during the Ceauşescu Era* (Bethesda, MD: Transnational Family Research Institute: 1994), 37.
102. Ibid. In some cases, wives even encouraged their husbands to take up sexual relations with other women in the hopes of sparing themselves from pregnancy.
103. "Se poate modela un soţ?" *Femeia*, February 1972, 18–19.
104. Domnica, interview with author, Braşov, 22 June 2003.
105. T. interview with author, Braşov, 27 May 2003.
106. Hana Havelková provides a nuanced analysis of marital relations in communist Czechoslovakia in "A Few Pre-feminist Thoughts," in *Gender Politics and Post-Communism*, 69.
107. Regine, interview with author, Braşov, 2 July 2003.
108. Ibid.
109. Valeria P., interview with author, Braşov, 14 June 2003.
110. Adriana, interview with author, Bucharest, 6 June 2012.
111. The regime, at least on paper, took adultery and abandonment seriously. For instance, beginning in 1968, with the adoption of a new penal code, adultery could be punished with one to six months imprisonment and abandonment with three months to three years imprisonment. While Adriana did not indicate that her former spouse received such punishment, the fact that these penalties existed for adultery may explain why she was rapidly granted a divorce at a time when it was particularly dif-

ficult to do so. See Art. 304 and 305, "Infracțiuni care aduc Atingere unor Relații Privind Conviețuirea Socială," "Lege nr. 15, din 21 iunie, Codul Penal al României, iunie 1968" *Buletinul Oficial al Republicii Socialiste Române* nr. 79, 21 iunie 1968.
112. It should be recalled that the fee for a divorce increased substantially after 1966, with costs exceeding more than three times the average monthly salary.
113. Elena, interview with author, Bucharest, 1 June 2009. Similarly, one woman interviewed by Băban and David noted, "Good or bad as he is, I have a husband of my own and wherever I go I am a married woman and not a divorced one." See Băban and David, *Voices of Romanian Women*, 59.
114. Kligman, *Politics of Duplicity*, 51.
115. See ANIC, CC al PCR, Secția Cancelarie, dosar 102/1966, f. 26.
116. McLellan, *Love in the Time of Communism*, 77.
117. See Ibid., 66–67, on single motherhood as liberating.
118. Elena, interview with author, Bucharest, 1 June 2009.
119. Corina, interview with Ioana Manoliu, Brașov, 22 July 2003.
120. Angela, interview with author, Brașov, 16 June 2003.
121. Livia, interview with Ioana Manoliu, Brașov, 11 August 2003.
122. Aneta, interview with Anca Coman, Brașov, 25 June 2003.
123. Axinia, interview with author, Râmnicu Vâlcea, 10 June 2012.
124. Ecaterina, interview with author, Brașov, 17 June 2003.
125. Iuliana, interview with author, Brașov, 7 July 2003.
126. Mircea A., interview with Ionuț Iuria, Brașov, 5 August 2003.
127. Marcela, interview with Anca Coman, Brașov, 12 August 2003.
128. See Kligman, *Wedding of the Dead*, 50–51.
129. Stela, interview with author, Brașov, 23 June 2003.
130. Rodica, M. interview with Anca Coman, Brașov, 28 June 2003.
131. Similarly, diapers needed to be washed by hand, which became increasingly difficult with the rationing of water and cooking gas.
132. For sharing of childcare and domestic duties in the GDR, see McLellan, *Love in the Time of Communism*, 71–73.
133. "Maternity leave" was in fact extended to men in Hungary after 1985; however, the vast majority of men opted not to take it. See Eva Fodor, *Working Difference: Women's Working Lives in Hungary and Austria, 1945–1995* (Durham, NC: Duke University Press, 2003). This, combined with men's widespread participation in the second economy, meant that men in Hungary were even less present in the home than their Romanian counterparts. See Olga Toth, "No Envy, No Pity," in *Gender Politics and Post-Communism*, 213–23.
134. Mircea J., interview with author, Brașov, 15 July 2003.
135. Scholarship on the gendering of housework in socialist Eastern Europe, which is based primarily on quantitative data, has demonstrated that men devoted considerably less time per week to domestic duties than women—in part because they were involved in maintenance and repair work, which was biweekly or monthly in nature. Such findings have been interpreted as evidence of continued gender inequality within the family. Although accurate, these interpretations do not address how other factors, such as

men's participation in the second economy, overtime work (especially for section bosses), commuting, and food procurement limited their ability to contribute to household chores. For data on the division of household labor, see the charts in Lobodzinska, ed., *Family, Women and Employment in Central-Eastern Europe;* Einhorn, *Cinderella Goes to Market*; and Funk and Mueller, eds. *Gender Politics and Post-Communism.*
136. Olga, interview with author, Braşov, 19 July 2003.
137. Arlie Hochschild with Anne Machung, *The Second Shift: Working Parents and the Revolution at Home* (New York: Viking-Penguin, 1989).

CHAPTER 5

# It's a Family Affair

*Parenthood, Reproductive Politics, and State "Welfare"*

Perhaps in no other area of life did Romanian women feel the impact of the state so personally and invasively as in the realm of reproduction. This was particularly the case after Ceaușescu implemented Decree 770 in 1966, which recriminalized abortion. Ceaușescu's draconian pronatalist policies affected the lives of almost everyone: the stress of an unwanted pregnancy and the health risks and potential legal consequences of obtaining a clandestine abortion placed a heavy psychological and physical burden on women. Meanwhile, the birth of additional children placed a heavy material burden on families, especially during the austerity of the 1980s. Finally, for the children left motherless and for whom other family members could not care, these policies transformed, sometimes unalterably, their physical and psychological health. The barbaric treatment of many of Romania's orphans served as a poignant testament to the inhumanity of Decree 770 and, in the popular imagination after 1989, the inhumanity of Ceaușescu's regime more generally. At the same time, the focus on orphans obscures the decree's impact on women's physical and psychological well-being, minimizing the heartrending choices and real dangers women faced in order to control their fertility.

This chapter uses reproduction and social welfare policies as frames for illuminating how women's (as well as men's) civic and parental roles were constituted, promoted, and policed under state socialism. As in many modernizing states, Romania's leadership deemed a large population essential to a strong workforce and national greatness. In particular, declining fertility rates after World War II fueled concern about population growth. In response, the state instituted a range of incentives, both positive and negative, to reverse this downward trend. These included subsidized maternity leave and childcare, family allowances, and the banning of abortion. However, as the state's demographic needs often conflicted with its productive ones, reproductive policies varied and tended to be more or less progressive during the first half of communist rule, while becoming increasingly repressive and draconian during the second half. As a corollary, the way in which motherhood and, indeed, parenthood was defined and officially represented varied. While Dej sought to promote demographic growth, he also sought to increase the industrial labor force, as well as medicalize reproduction (e.g. place it under state purview). Consequently, the prewar ban on abortion remained in force until 1957, and motherhood was encouraged and valorized. After Ceaușescu assumed power, however, pronatalist policies, along with nationalist rhetoric, was used to legitimate socialism and assert greater control over the population. Accordingly, policymakers reconfigured reproduction into a type of profession (*meserie*)—an obligation of all women of childbearing age—and reproduction, like work, became a fundamental component of women's civic worth. It also served as a basis for politicizing the family and policing women. Indeed, socialist Romania presents a rare example of a state that perpetrated gendered violence against its own citizens in the name of promoting life. Thus, unlike other modernizing states that expanded welfare entitlements to incentivize women to have children (while also often banning abortion), Ceaușescu relied primarily on punitive measures.

Alongside an analysis of pronatalist policies and propaganda, I examine women's efforts to control their fertility. Respondents emphasized the inhumanity of these policies and the anxiety, fear, and tragedy surrounding them. While an ordinary, common, and, arguably, everyday practice, procuring an illegal abortion was also potentially dangerous, carrying the risk of hemorrhage, infection, fetal deformity, arrest, and death. Although women did not actively protest the decree, given the illegality of this practice, it can be argued that women of childbearing age, as a group, were engaged in prolonged acts of resistance against the state.[1]

In addition to the anxiety and dangers associated with fertility control, women—along with their spouses—struggled to balance full-time work with parenting. With respect to reconciling the role of worker and parent, the state attempted to serve women's interests by providing maternity leave and subsidized childcare facilities; however, as there was no family leave in Romania, caregiving was codified as a woman's responsibility—media depictions of men pushing baby buggies notwithstanding. Moreover, the modest amount allocated to childcare meant that demand far outpaced supply, compelling many families to rely on informal types of childcare (e.g. family members, neighbors). These realities underscored the shortcomings of state welfare policies, which, while generous on paper, did not accommodate popular need—not to mention being at odds with state efforts to increase the birth rate. In response to these shortcomings, women devised clever strategies to maximize the time spent with their infants, drawing on maternalist discourse to persuade doctors to extend maternity leave.

Despite the challenges involved in fertility control and in securing childcare, only a minority of my respondents viewed their role as mothers as burdensome. Considering the centrality of family in Romanian society, and the fact that women's role has historically been one of sacrifice, women typically viewed maternal responsibilities as labors of love. Although some women also took great satisfaction in their jobs, far more stressed the importance of family, referring to motherhood as one of the most meaningful aspects of their lives.[2] Thus, Ceaușescu's pronatalism did not completely color women's views towards motherhood and family life. This is not to minimize the real physical danger and psychological trauma women experienced as a result of pronatalist policies, but rather to emphasize that motherhood was a source of great joy and pride for women, while the prospect of bearing an unwanted child elicited fear and anxiety.

## Creating the New Socialist Family

The gradual industrialization and urbanization of Romania from the late nineteenth century through World War II altered the country's demographic character. Rather than having four or five children, couples, particularly in urban areas, followed the West European model of the two- or three-child family.[3] Consequently, the birth rate dropped from 30.1 to 24.8 (per 1,000 women) between 1935 and 1946.[4] This decline was related to the disruption and dislocation produced by war and the political instability and economic uncertainty of the early postwar period. Romania's demographic downturn was not exceptional within the region, however. For instance, the birth rate in Hungary dropped from 21.1 in 1935 to 18.7 in 1945; and in Bulgaria from 26.4 in 1935 to 24.1 in 1945.[5] In an effort to reverse this downward trend, in postwar Romania abortion continued to be prohibited except when the health of the mother was endangered or if the child was likely to be born with a disability.[6] This measure, which was in conformity with Soviet legislation, aimed not only to reduce the abortion rate, but also the maternal mortality rate by ensuring that legal abortions were performed in hospitals by doctors, rather than by midwives or untrained individuals. However, as modern contraceptives were difficult to acquire and transgressing the law was a misdemeanor, women continued to procure abortions—both in and outside of state hospitals—practices to which the authorities turned a blind eye.[7]

Other European states also enacted or retained restrictive abortion legislation during the postwar period. Indeed, abortion was illegal or restricted throughout the Eastern Bloc well into the 1950s (and in East Germany until 1972).[8] Meanwhile, in most Western European countries, it would take until the mid-1970s for abortion to be legalized.[9] The banning (or continued banning) of abortion was thus part of a larger, European effort to increase (or replenish) the population after the war and to medicalize reproduction. However, in the socialist Bloc this restriction was accompanied by efforts to increase women's participation in paid labor and validate their public roles as equal workers and socialist citizens, whereas in many Western countries it was associated with a return to "normalcy," namely pushing women out of the labor force and into full-time homemaking.[10]

Alongside the banning of abortion, protective legislation and social welfare entitlements were implemented to encourage demographic growth and reconcile women's roles as workers and mothers. As previously noted, the Labor Code of 1950 spared pregnant women and nursing mothers from overtime and night shifts and provided mothers with nursing breaks. Moreover, mothers were granted thirty-five days prenatal and forty-five days (with possible extension to fifty-five days) postnatal maternity leave and received financial assistance during the legal period of maternity leave, 3,000 lei for infant underclothes, and subsidies for milk products for nine months.[11] Finally, to rapidly reintegrate mothers into the workforce, the state established fully subsidized (until the mid-1980s) crèches and kindergartens—though demand outpaced supply. In articles, graphs, and charts in socialist media, women were frequently reminded of the beneficence of welfare entitlements. Yet, while they welcomed paid maternity leave, nursing breaks were often impractical given the lack of crèches in or near factories. Moreover, women were hesitant to return to work a few months after giving birth; accordingly, they sought—often successfully—to extend maternity leave in order to devote more time to caring for their newborns.

As with labor productivity, women were awarded for maternal productivity. In 1952 the honorary title and medal *mama eroina* (heroine mother) was first bestowed on fecund mothers. According to official figures, twenty-five thousand maternity medals (reflecting various levels of reproductive output) were awarded in 1954 and fifty thousand in 1956.[12] In addition to medals, heroine mothers received preference for housing and other material rewards and were recognized in newspapers and magazines.[13] For example, on 8 March 1955, *Scânteia* hailed heroine mother Maria Ioniţa for "bearing and raising twelve children," some of whom were featured in the newspaper photo with her.[14] Similarly, images in *Femeia* featured women surrounded by their flock of children and grandchildren. By valorizing motherhood, Dej redefined it as an important civic role, similar to the glorified role of heroine worker and essential to socialist modernization. As such, he laid the groundwork for its increased politicization under Ceaușescu

Rewarding prolific mothers was not unique to Romania, as medals for mothers had been introduced as early as the 1920s in France and fascist Italy. Yet, whereas in liberal-democratic and fascist states women were primarily—and, in some cases, solely—defined according to their maternal role, in Romania they were defined as both mothers and workers. As such, the socialist vision of womanhood differed from that of other modernizing states. However, because childcare was not universally available and, as noted in chapter 4, men's contribution to household duties was minimal, this dual role was necessarily more demanding of women. To be sure, rural women had combined the roles of mother and laborer during the presocialist period; however, since these could be performed within the larger domestic realm, they did not present the same type of challenges as working outside the home did.[15]

While in the Eastern Bloc social welfare entitlements were motivated by state need to increase the population and expedite women's return to the labor force, as in Western democracies they were also intended to improve public health and modernize society. Feminist scholars have criticized welfare entitlements for shifting women's dependence from the family onto the state; however, in the context of the Eastern Bloc, as well as many countries in postwar Europe, such criticisms obscure the positive impact of these protections and benefits.[16] Considering the relative lack of such entitlements in Romania and the poverty and social dislocation of the 1940s and early 1950s, maternity leave, prenatal and postnatal healthcare, and state-subsidized childcare were welcomed by many women, offering families a level of security and care previously unknown to them. Moreover, in comparison with British, West German, and Italian welfare states—which were centered around distinctly gendered family roles (e.g. male breadwinner model) and allocated only limited funds for childcare, thereby reinforcing women's economic dependence on men—the Romanian welfare state, like states throughout the region, supported women's roles as workers and mothers.[17]

That said, Romanian women also acknowledged the shortcomings of state entitlements. To quote Domnica, a dentist who raised her children in the 1960s, "The state helped the family in the sense that they had a job, the majority had a home, they had the basic necessities ... places for children were substantial, that is, for that period they were substantial."[18] Other individuals echoed these sentiments, emphasizing the convenience of state childcare facilities, while also expressing criticism about overcrowding and children's increased susceptibility to illness at them. In sum, because entitlements were motivated more by economic expediency than fidelity to Marxist principles or altruistic concern for working mothers, they were characterized by numerous deficiencies. Nonetheless, many women, especially migrants who did not have family in the new industrial towns and cities, relied on these entitlements to help them reconcile work and family.

While maternity leave and subsidized childcare were designed to help women balance work and family, thereby encouraging both production and reproduction, propaganda was mobilized to promote progressive family roles—particularly men's increased engagement as fathers. As examined in previous chapters, this involved replacing authoritarian parenting styles with authoritative one's and urging men to take on various aspects of childcare, from changing diapers to supervising homework. However, first propagandists needed to convince men, or at least convince women to convince men, that their parental roles were in need of change. The 1959 article entitled "Who Is to Blame?" published under the "Parents, How Are You Raising Your Children?" section of *Femeia*, sought to do just that. In this piece, a father and mother are in the middle of a discussion when their son enters the room and mouths off to his mother—an act that earns him a slap in the face by his father. In a scolding tone, the mother tells her husband, "That's not how you raise a child," adding that he doesn't recognize how lazy he is and that he could learn a few things about fatherhood from his friends.[19] The article closes with the mother's confession that her lenient parenting is rooted in guilt that her son, for all intents and purposes, lacks a father. While demonstrating that shared parenting had yet to be realized in Romania, the piece nonetheless criticized men's privileging of work over family, as well as the use of corporal punishment as a disciplinary measure. This reflected advice of socialist experts who cautioned against authoritarian parenting and physical punishment, which they believed could permanently hamper the emotional bond between parent and child (especially father and son).

In some cases, articles on fathering were accompanied by drawings. For example, the article "Both Parents Are Responsible for Their Children's Education" included a visual representation of an exchange between a father and son in which the father reproaches his son, asking, "When will you begin to take your schoolwork seriously?" to which the son responds, "when will you begin to help me more?"[20] The author of the article, a teacher, compared educating a child to an opera performance. Accordingly, a child's education is a combined effort that requires harmonizing teachers, parents, and children lest the whole piece degenerate into discordance. By examining the link between neglectful fathers and poor academic progress, *Femeia* critiqued the male breadwinner model, especially the workaholic, type-A variety.

Neglectful fathering was not only the result of placing work above family, but of placing leisure, especially "asocial" forms of leisure such as excessive alcohol consumption, above family. Indeed, the state was particularly concerned with how parental alcoholism affected children's development. For example, the 1957 article "How Can We Combat Alcoholism?" featured a drawing of a man sitting at a table in a bar, head bowed down toward a glass of wine, while his son stares at him sadly and proclaims, "Daddy, I came to tell you that today is my birthday." Meanwhile, the mother, who stands behind her son, covers her face in shame.[21] Written by a doctor who thanks *Femeia*'s editorial board for "supporting the fight against alcoholism," the article portrays alcoholism as a self-inflicted illness and suggests medical interventions (e.g. vitamin B injections) and rest as a means of curing it; however, it also emphasizes family and community contributions to this effort. Rather than a personal sickness to be suffered in solitude, alcoholism, propagandists argued, was a social problem to be solved by the collective in the name of family unity and children's healthy development.

Alongside neglectful fathering and parental alcoholism, experts claimed that spousal abuse negatively affected children's development, as well as their performance in school. Accordingly, men were chided for acting in ways that were not only harmful to their wives' well-being, but also to their children's well-being. As one of the asocial behaviors condemned by the state, spousal abuse, as noted in chapter 4, was relatively common in Romania. Thus, by publically acknowledging its deleterious effects on children's health and academic achievement, propagandists were shining a light on a problem that was typically hidden from view. While it is doubtful that such articles convinced men to refrain from acting abusively towards their wives, by highlighting the wide-ranging effects of violence in the home, this article nonetheless presented another angle from which to address the problem.

As a means of gauging paternal competence, men were encouraged to evaluate their parenting styles through surveys published in *Femeia*. One survey, titled "What Kind of Father Are You?" revealed that three out of every five respondents were "severe," "authoritarian," or "distant" in their parenting style. These approaches to parenting, the authors argued, could impede the development of a trusting and loving relationship between father and child and also discourage adolescents—

especially male adolescents—from confiding in their fathers about serious matters. Instead, the author suggested, fathers should not fear being a "masculine mom," namely a father who plays with his child, helps her with homework, and, more generally, involves himself actively in her daily routines. By the same token, the author suggested that mothers should not shy away from disciplining their children.

Experts in child development sought not only to de-gender parenting, but also encourage all types of parents to become involved in their children's education. Thus, the magazine emphasized that any parent, regardless of intellect, can help their children with homework, create proper study conditions, and follow their children's progress at school. Unacknowledged in these articles was the fact that both parents typically worked outside the home, which significantly reduced the amount of time they could devote to their children. Beyond that, space constraints meant that creating a quiet place for study with the appropriate furnishings and aids (e.g. a desk and bookshelf) was often impossible as many children shared a room with older siblings—or simply slept on the pullout sofa in the living room.

Children's moral upbringing, by comparison, was seemingly the responsibility of mothers alone. For example, in the September 1961 *Femeia* column "Parents, How Are You Raising Your Children?" the writer expounds on women's special role as moral educators, stating, "It is the responsibility of all mothers to raise hardworking, conscientious, and patriotic children who will contribute positively to socialism."[22] To this end, propagandists urged mothers to be more engaged in their children's everyday lives, emphasizing the crucial link between maternal involvement and children's well-being. A 1964 report on the activities of a local women's commission is illustrative. Focused on a boy of divorced parents in the care of his grandmother while his mother works in a neighboring city, the report connected the boy's poor school performance to his mother's extended periods away from home. With the intervention of women activists, the mother ultimately realizes that "sending money home is not enough" and that she "should be at his side at all times."[23] The report ends on an uplifting note, with the son "finally happy because from now on he will be near his mother. His dear mother!"[24] The aim of the piece was to dissuade mothers from leaving their children with extended family while they worked in another city because this undermined their "noble mission" (i.e. educating the future generation). By linking children's educational achievement to maternal engagement, such pieces served as cautionary tales to women who put work above the role of mother.

This message would be reiterated in books by sociologists that appeared in the 1960s and early 1970s, which, as noted in chapter 2, urged mothers not to let demanding work schedules get in the way of maternal responsibilities and advised them to "rearrange" their schedules to accommodate their children. While men were also encouraged to establish a close bond with their children and not assume the role of the distant disciplinarian, it was mothers who were to be a constant presence in the family home, greeting her children when they returned from school, serving as their moral guide, and, more generally, keeping them from falling into the wrong crowd.

Similarly, family health was the preserve of women, illustrated in articles such as "The Family's Health Is in the Hands of Women," which put the onus on mothers to teach their children basic hygiene, ensure they ate a balanced diet (to prevent disease, obesity, and other disorders), and encourage them to participate in sports.[25] Accordingly, articles on family health and hygiene were not addressed to men—a pattern that remained unchanged throughout socialist rule and intensified after the advent of pronatalist policies in the mid-1960s. As will be discussed in sections that follow, from the late 1960s through the 1980s, women's maternal role was intricately bound up with demographic growth and, as such, propagandists increasingly presented mothers in their biological capacity as bearers of multiple children. Indeed, as pronatalist legislation became increasingly repressive in the 1980s, mothers were practically deified and their role as laborers was subordinated to their role as mothers. Thus, alongside personal vignettes glorifying large families, *Femeia* published poems, in some cases written by ordinary Romanians, in other cases by literary figures, extolling the virtues of their mothers.[26] In addition, "Homages" (Omagii), which celebrated women's "natural role" and "unique gift," and often assumed nationalist overtones, were published in March 8 editions of *Scânteia*. As one syrupy passage read:

> We speak from our entire heart of the special role of the woman-mother as educator of the young generation, the warmth and conviction that she transmits to children, adolescents, young people ... with the first syllable ... children learn from her [the mother] what a country is, what it means to love the country in which you were born.[27]

Such passages underscored women's roles as mothers and educators of the nation, essential for instilling their children with patriotic fervor.

Motherhood, however, was not simply about bearing children, but also modeling exemplary socialist citizenship. Mothers who did not meet the maternal ideal extolled in poetry—especially those who had spotty work records, gave birth outside of marriage, or did not sufficiently sacrifice themselves for their children—were juxtaposed against good mothers and represented as "retrograde" and publicly humiliated. For instance, an episode of the television exposé *Reflector* featured a mother who had allegedly become pregnant as a result of a one-night stand. After the reporter questioned the mother about her work history, the camera panned to a bottle of Cinzano on top of a shelf and then to her son. The reporter then asked the child why he had a bump on his head, to which he responds, "From the swing." The interview closed with the mother in tears, admitting that she is incapable of raising her son to be a useful member of society. While scripted, this reportage was not fabricated but instead based on the lives of an actual mother and son who were separated by the authorities on the basis of alleged parental neglect and immorality.[28] Despite the fact that she had been a caring mother, according to this official portrait, the woman exemplified "bad mothering" for bearing a child out of wedlock and for her alleged alcohol abuse. As a result of her "retrograde" behavior (i.e. putting herself above the needs of her child), she was morally unequipped to raise *omul nou* and lost custody of her son, who was subsequently sent to an orphanage. Such depictions reinforced prevailing cultural attitudes about women who bore children out of wedlock as dishonorable and thus might have resonated with the general populace.

## Legislating Reproduction under Dej and Ceaușescu

Despite the fact that abortion was illegal for nearly a decade under Dej, the fertility rate only increased for two years (from 2.9 children [per woman] in 1948 to 3.4 in 1950); however, by 1957 it was down to 2.73. Meanwhile the birth rate stood at 22.9 in 1957.[29] Although lower than the United States and most of Western Europe, which were experiencing baby booms at the time, these figures approximated other Eastern European countries. For example, in 1955 the fertility rate in Bulgaria was 2.26, in the GDR 2.35, in Hungary 2.68, and in Czechoslovakia 2.85. Only Albania (which already had a restrictive abortion policy in place) and Poland claimed higher birth and fertility rates in 1955.[30] The drop in Romania's fertility rate was due not only to lax enforcement of the 1948 law that banned abortion, but also to women's increased educational opportunities and mass influx into the labor force.

Recognizing the importance of industrial growth over demographic growth and the necessity of an able-bodied population for the former, Dej legalized abortion on demand in 1957.[31]

As in the Soviet Union, in Romania abortion was officially legalized in the name of women's health (i.e. to ensure that the procedure occurred in a hospital or clinic) and was interpreted by ordinary women as a progressive measure, enabling them to fully and legally reassert control over their bodies. At the same time, it served to reinforce state control over reproductive health, as abortions performed clandestinely and by those without proper medical certification (e.g. midwives) remained illegal. This followed similar measures in other Eastern Bloc countries, which had liberalized reproductive policies with the advent of Nikita Khrushchev in the USSR.[32] The exceptions were Albania, which never legalized abortion, and the GDR, which, in order to deal with massive population loss during World War II, sought to increase fertility through restrictive abortion legislation along with generous welfare entitlements.

Although it is tempting to interpret the Romanian law as part of broader de-Stalinization efforts, it is worth noting that similar liberalization was not enacted in political or economic spheres. Romania thus remained comparatively Stalinist in much of its policymaking throughout the tenure of socialist rule. Therefore, abortion legislation was motivated by economic expedience—namely encouraging more women to join the labor force. Moreover, as in Poland, it was related to housing shortages.[33] This was especially the case in new industrial towns where workers lived in barracks or dorms. Regardless of the impetus, such liberalization was welcomed by many and reveals that liberal policies often coexisted with more restrictive ones, complicating conventional interpretations of the period as uniformly repressive.

Within the broader European context this measure was comparatively progressive, as abortion was not legalized in East Germany, Denmark, Sweden, France, Italy, and the United States until the 1970s. That said, in Romania the legalization of abortion was not accompanied by concerted efforts to educate women (let alone men) about family planning. These factors, combined with the low cost of an abortion (about 30 lei or $2.00 in 1957), ensured that abortion, along with traditional methods (e.g. *coitus interruptus*; rhythm method), remained women's primary forms of fertility control. Given these realities, in 1957 Romania registered the highest abortion rate in Europe, with the number of officially recorded abortions increasing from 578,000 in 1959 to 1.115 million in 1965.[34]

By the time Ceaușescu assumed power in 1965, the fertility rate was 1.9 children (per woman), below the natural replacement level of 2.1, and the birth rate stood a 14.6 live births (per 1,000).[35] Meanwhile, according to official statistics, for every birth, four abortions were registered, illustrating continued lack of knowledge about and access to modern forms of contraception—despite the fact that physicians were charged with providing women family planning information and contraceptives were legal. The low birth rate was related to personal choice and shortcomings in social welfare services. In particular, the expansion of educational and employment opportunities for women and a desire to maintain or improve overall family well-being, along with lack of sufficient childcare facilities and inadequate housing, prompted women to limit the number of children they bore.

Within the context of Eastern Europe, Romania had one of the lowest fertility rates—ranking only ahead of Hungary. While a source of concern, this demographic trend was not unique to Romania but, as previously noted, part of a larger regional transition occurring in Eastern Europe from the late 1940s through the 1960s.[36] To tackle Romania's perceived demographic crisis, in 1966 the Ministry of Health organized a committee, composed of health specialists from various state agencies, to study natality and abortion rates in the country.[37] The committee proposed eleven measures for dealing with the declining fertility rate, including increasing production of and access to contraceptives, extending maternity leave, introducing flexible work hours for women, and expanding childcare facilities. The committee did not, however, recommend the criminalization of abortion, but rather introducing restrictions on it.[38]

For Ceaușescu, who viewed abortion as tantamount to national suicide, these proposals were overly indulgent. Rather than promote fertility through positive incentives, Ceaușescu opted for restrictive and repressive measures.[39] These measures were also more cost-effective, though this fact was shrouded in references to women's health, tradition, and morality. For example, although the committee recommended that families' material conditions be considered in determining the bases upon which abortion should be legally permissible, leading members of the Executive Committee of the PCR dismissed the idea as "foreign" and contrary to Romania's national experience. Indeed, Suzana Gâdea, president of the National Council of Women (Consiliul Național al Femeilor; CNF), made reference to traditional (e.g. peasant) family patterns—including her own and other communist elites'—to argue against such a consideration, claiming, "We all [the ruling elite] come from households with at least 5–6–7 children, from large families with modest conditions, but in which children could be raised without childcare, without subsidies."[40] This view, however, wholly ignored the realities of urban life, which differed dramatically from rural life in terms of space constraints and the role of the family as a unit of production. In addition to referencing the traditional family, the regime referenced morality and people's obligation to the socialist nation to justify demographic policies. As Ceaușescu emphasized:

> In my opinion, we have legalized prostitution through abortions and free divorces ... how is this possible that we are an institution for the encouragement of prostitution? Do we not have the responsibility to ensure the health of the people, the natural growth of the people, to defend the morality of the people? ... The problem of natality is not a problem of the desire of one to have or not have children, but a social problem, each man has obligations toward society.[41]

The resulting decree that criminalized abortion was publicized on the front page of *Scânteia* on 2 October 1966 under the title "Measures for the Regulation of the Interruption of Pregnancy."[42] Meanwhile, the details of the decree appeared on page five, including the modification of the Penal Code (Decree 771/1966) to reflect the criminalization of abortion. This page also included a preamble to the decree intended to justify the new measure: "The interruption of a pregnancy represents an act with grave consequences to the health of women, and is detrimental to the fertility and the natural growth of the population."[43] The law outlawed abortion except for "medical reasons" (if the woman was severely disabled or if the pregnancy was a threat to the mother's life) and for "medical-social reasons" (possibility of hereditary illness or congenital malformation; pregnancy due to incest or rape; if the woman was over forty-five years of age; if she had given birth to and had in her care four or more children).[44] However, abortions performed for "medical" or "medical-social" reasons required approval of the regional or local medical commission, which involved submitting a request to a medical committee.[45] Because the process was bureaucratically complex and because most abortions could only be performed during the first trimester, by the time women received approval it might be too late to legally have an abortion.[46] If a woman was denied permission, the doctor would register and closely follow her pregnancy.

Meanwhile, Article 6 of the decree stated that abortions could be performed without review by a medical commission only in cases of "extreme medical emergency" (e.g. performed immediately), though notification of the prosecutor was required either prior to or no later than twenty-four hours after the procedure, otherwise the doctor could face legal repercussions.⁴⁷ The prosecutor, in conjunction with a forensic physician, then determined if the abortion had in fact been a medical emergency, which included a "spontaneous abortion" (e.g. miscarriage) or an illegally induced abortion. If they determined that it had been a miscarriage, no further action was required, but if it had been an illegal abortion (e.g. self-induced or performed outside of a hospital or clinic), the doctor could face a fine, work without pay, or up to twelve years imprisonment and loss of medical licensure.⁴⁸ As Gail Kligman has noted, these regulations included a degree of ambiguity, which could work in a woman's favor.⁴⁹ For instance, if a woman sought care in a hospital after a botched abortion but showed no visible signs (e.g. hemorrhaging; punctured uterus), doctors, if they took pity on the woman or could profit materially, could complete the abortion (through curettage) and register it as a "spontaneous abortion" (miscarriage) versus an illegal or "provoked" (self- or otherwise-induced) abortion.

Alongside the criminalization of abortion, divorce, as outlined in chapter 4, became more expensive and difficult to obtain. Furthermore, in 1977 a law that echoed earlier ones in Nazi Germany and fascist Italy taxed all childless persons over twenty-five years of age on a monthly basis.⁵⁰ If such punitive measures were not enough to persuade couples to procreate, *Femeia* also alerted its readers to scientific studies that linked depression, exhaustion, and boredom in women to being childless.⁵¹ Meanwhile, in 1968 homosexuality had been criminalized, with those apprehended for engaging in such "nonproductive" and "anti-social" behaviors facing long prison sentences or being blackmailed into collaborating with the Securitate.⁵² Reproduction, like work, thus became a basis upon which individuals' relationship to the state was constituted and their civic worth was evaluated. It also became a basis for measuring women's psychological well-being.

What were the motivations for these policies? Scholars of gender argue that demographic growth is central to the drive to modernize and create strong nation-states.⁵³ This was especially true of Hitler's Germany where the growth of a master race, military preparedness, populating recently occupied territories, and reestablishing traditional gender roles undergirded pronatalist policies.⁵⁴ Meanwhile, pronatalism in Stalin's Soviet Union was central to building a modern socialist state, and abortion was banned on the basis of protecting the health of the mother and child. However, even liberal democracies such as Weimar Germany, Great Britain, and France implemented pronatalist policies, in large part due to demographic concerns that arose after World War I. Demographic concerns similarly undergirded pronatalist policies after

World War II; however, while most states in the Eastern Bloc decriminalized abortion in the mid-1950s and kept it legal throughout socialist rule, in the mid-1960s Romania reinstated repressive policies.

As Central Committee documents reveal, Ceaușescu, like Stalin before him, considered a large workforce essential to economic development and national sovereignty.[55] Thus, Ceaușescu's demographic policies were rooted in a desire to increase the workforce and create a vigorous, self-sufficient nation. For women this meant that their identities—and duties—were defined with respect to both productive and reproductive output. In contrast to other states where pronatalism was accompanied by efforts to return women to the home, the Romanian state, following the Stalinist model, aimed to squeeze as much productivity out of women as possible. Consequently, maternity leave was not extended and family allowances remained modest—except for those in the lowest income bracket—and typically did not outweigh the costs of having additional children.[56] Moreover, women, like the economy, became a vehicle or, more aptly, a tool for the promotion of national communism and the creation of a "multilaterally developed society."[57] Accordingly, the 1974 program of the Romanian Communist Party stipulated that to build a "multilaterally developed socialist society," greater attention should be devoted to strengthening the family because the family is "the nucleus of society." This included increasing the birth rate and educating children since "the young generation represents the future of the Romanian socialist nation."[58]

While Romania's antiabortion law was the most draconian in the Bloc, it was not the only country to restrict abortion. For example, abortion remained illegal in Albania throughout the tenure of communist rule. In addition, Bulgaria introduced moderate restrictions in 1968, which were intensified in 1973, prohibiting abortion on demand to women aged 18–45 who were married or had one or no children.[59] Moreover, Czechoslovakia restricted access to abortion between 1962 and 1972, and Hungary instituted restrictive abortion legislation in 1973, presenting women who sought abortions as "overly individualistic."[60] At the same time, the pill was legal—and available—in Czechoslovakia (beginning in the mid-1960s) and in Hungary (in the early 1970s), thus providing women with alternative options for fertility control, though traditional methods remained most common. In addition to contraception, a number of countries in the Bloc, namely Hungary, the GDR, and Poland, offered generous incentives to mothers such as long maternity leaves and family allowances.[61] Finally, because abortion was not criminalized in these countries, but only restricted, women were not subject to the same invasive and repressive measures as Romanian women were (e.g. gynecological exams in the workplace, surveillance by the *miliția* in hospitals, potential imprisonment). Compared to its neighbors, then, Romania was exceptional within the region in its use of punitive and repressive measures to encourage life.

## "One Child for Each Day of the Week": Fostering Fecundity

Ceaușescu's reproductive policies were institutionalized on all levels and disseminated through various media in the form of "scientific" studies, surveys, "personal" vignettes, symposia, and documentaries. The CNF, which had spearheaded female literacy campaigns, organized job-training programs, and established courses on health, hygiene, and child-rearing practices during the 1950s and 1960s, played a central role in this process, serving as a transmission belt for pronatalist policies. Accordingly, the CNF distributed brochures, screened short documentaries, and organized debates in factories, high schools, and vocational schools, which women and girls were required to attend. These highlighted the dangers of abortion, emphasized the importance of prenatal health, and correlated childbearing with personal well-being.[62] Ironically, as feminist philosopher Mihaela Miroiu has emphasized, the very same women spearheading these policies (e.g. leading members of the CNF) were not only postmenopausal but had also benefitted from the regime's more liberal abortion policy years earlier.[63] As such, they either did not fully understand what criminalizing abortion would entail for women of childbearing age or they were more concerned with their privileged position—and thus towing the party line—than the potential physical and psychological implications of the decree. That said, as previously noted, at least one member had spoken out against the decree when it was being drafted, and, therefore, it cannot be assumed that all CNF members agreed with it.[64]

As the CNF's mouthpiece, *Femeia* became an important conduit for disseminating pronatalist-inflected messages, featuring interviews in maternity hospitals with mothers who had recently given birth and personalized reflections from women who had bore many children. The magazine also mobilized research by medical professionals, some of it based on sound facts, some of it decidedly fabricated. While in certain cases accurate and presumably helpful, this research was motivated first and foremost by state concern with demographic growth. For instance, while advising women to consult doctors regularly during their pregnancies was justified on the basis of protecting infant and maternal health, it was also a means of ensuring women brought their pregnancies to term. An article titled "Those 280 Miraculous Days,"

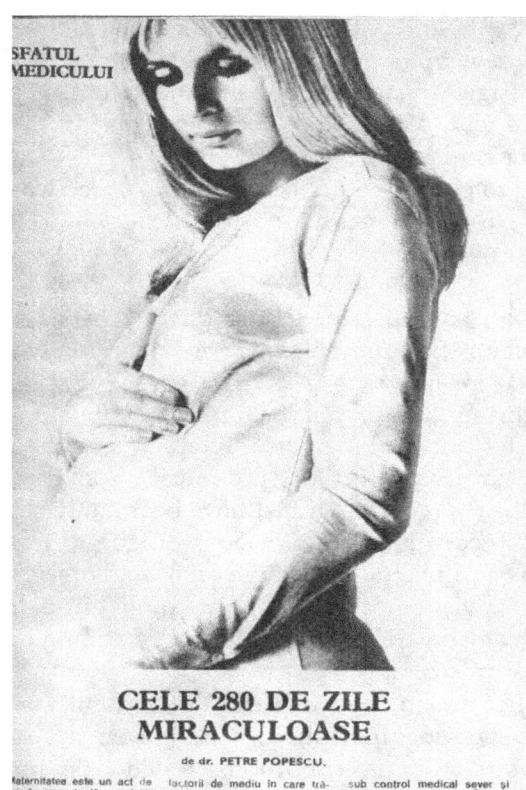
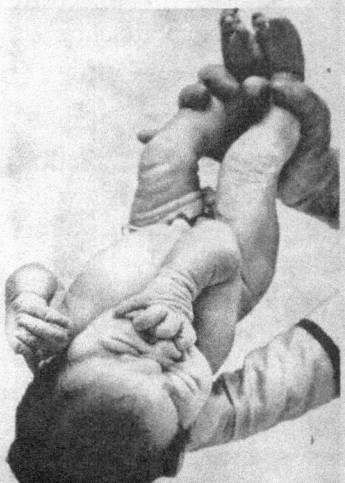

Figure 5.1. "Those 280 Miraculous Days," *Femeia* 1972

is illustrative. In it, Dr. Petre Popescu proclaimed, "motherhood is an act of maximal social importance," and provided a detailed description of the anatomical and physiological development of the fetus from conception to birth as a means of demonstrating that the fetus was not a mass of biological matter, but a human being.[65] Outlining the many maladies (pneumonia, typhoid fever, and viral infections, among others) that can affect fetal development, in some cases severely by producing deformities and triggering miscarriage, the article urges women to seek prenatal care with a trained gynecologist during the first trimester of their pregnancies.

In addition to being linked to poor prenatal health, miscarriage was closely correlated with previous abortions. In an article that featured visits to maternity hospitals, overjoyed young mothers who had recently given birth were juxtaposed against despairing women (of varying ages and professions) who had sustained their third, fourth, or fifth miscarriage. These women, the author explains, had procured abortions years earlier and were now engaged in a "fierce struggle against biological forces" to bring their pregnancies to term. Upon encountering a woman who, after numerous medical interventions, had finally managed to win this battle, the author sardonically remarks, "Congratulations, you did it!" but "wouldn't it just have been better to follow nature's intentions?"[66] According to this piece, women did not have agency when it came to bearing children but were instead objects of "nature," which they were advised not to disrupt or "fool" through unnatural interventions such as abortion—unless they were willing to pay the price (i.e. infertility or miscarriage).

Medical experts claimed that the link between abortion and miscarriage was due to the invasiveness of the former, which, even if performed by trained specialists in hygienic conditions, posed risks for bringing future pregnancies to term because of the possibility of uterine perforations, infections, and other complications that can occur during curettage (scraping the lining of the uterus). Physicians also warned that induced abortions and "spontaneous abortions" (miscarriages) can lead to a condition known as "secondary sterility," which prevented women from becoming pregnant altogether.[67] Accordingly, doctors urged young women to "bring their first pregnancy to term" and not worry about achieving a certain level of material comfort or experiencing certain pleasures (i.e. owning a house or a car; taking trips abroad) before having children.[68] At the same time, experts stressed that women were not always to blame for difficulties in conceiving as doctors identified male infertility as a major contributing factor, outlining its causes and suggesting treatments for it.[69]

Other tragic effects of botched abortion highlighted in the magazine included bearing children with deformities and disabilities. Designed to induce fear in pregnant women, such articles certainly persuaded some women to opt against having an abortion; however, on the whole, unwanted pregnancy outweighed the risks and, therefore, the impact of such scare tactics on the overall fertility rate was insignificant.

Medical discourse also offered a mantle of legitimacy around which numerous falsehoods were spread. One such falsehood was the correlation of abortion with longer menstrual periods and problems with internal organs.[70] Another was the allegedly deleterious effect of contraceptive use, which, according to one medical expert, included increased acne, diminished libido, frigidity, hair growth on atypical parts of the body, diabetes, and even cancer.[71]

Studies on women's sexual and reproductive health similarly appeared in Western magazines during this time and were part of a larger effort to medicalize sexuality and reproduction. They were also a means by which the state could use the advice of ostensibly neutral experts and professionals to promote demographic growth and particular values. In the case of Romania, the state sought to monitor women's reproductive health and ensure they did not abort by urging them to see only trained, "official" gynecologists. Meanwhile, by featuring articles on women's sexual fulfillment, *Femeia* encouraged women to have sex more frequently so they would procreate. Thus, socialist propagandists used both medicalizing and moralizing pieces, alongside more candid discussions of women's sexual pleasure, to deter abortion and promote fertility. This reflected a reliance on traditional and modern discourses to influence popular behavior, illustrating that the state was willing to draw on a range of messages, including those that might have conflicted with prevailing cultural beliefs, to achieve demographic goals.

To support mothers and prepare expectant ones, the CNF also organized "Mothers' Schools," which focused on pre- and postnatal care, including bathing and feeding infants and illness prevention. According to an article in *Femeia*, in 1967, 234 of these courses were organized in Bucharest alone; however, as none of my respondents claimed to have participated in them it is difficult to gauge their quality and impact.[72] In a nod to egalitarian caregiving, in the 1980s, "Fathers' Schools" and "Grandfathers' Schools" were also established—and advertised in *Femeia*; but, again, how popular or effective these were is not known. Due to the lack of infant formula in the 1980s, experts also increasingly urged women to breastfeed. Yet, because most women had to return to work a few months after giving birth, this was challenging, even with the officially reduced (six-hour) workday, for, as previously noted, job sites might be far away from one's crèche or home.

In the late 1960s, the magazine also began glamorizing motherhood. Whereas in the 1950s the robust peasant woman or unadorned factory manager surrounded by her flock of children exemplified the socialist mother, by the late 1960s mothers were depicted as youthful and vibrant as they cradled their newborn babies or cuddled their young daughters while donning the latest hairstyles and fashions. Indeed, even pregnancy was glamorized, with made up-women wearing maternity minis. Such images targeted a new generation of women that came of age in the mid-1960s and 1970s. Attracted to fashion and youth culture, these women needed to be persuaded that socialist Romania offered them all the goods and services of the West—or at least the promise of them. Thus, propagandists mobilized images of young, attractive women to make motherhood—and pregnancy—more appealing. Additionally, by featuring women on a relaxing stroll with their young children, the state sought to idealize the everyday experience of motherhood.

Personalized stories such as "I Am a Happy Mother" also served as testaments to the joys of motherhood. In this piece, Floarea-Doina, a geography professor and mother of four, reflected on her decision to have more than one child:

> When I felt Cosmin with his mouth glued to my breast, imbibing milk, when I felt his tiny hands touch my throat, I had the rare feeling that you are overwhelmed with love, that you're happy until it hurts. And, at this point, I decided I had to have another child; that the love for one child could be suffocating for the parents and child alike.[73]

According to Doina, the intensity of maternal love, if centered solely on one child, might prove overwhelming. Instead, a healthier approach was to share love among a number of children. Fecundity was thus encouraged on the basis of the emotional health of one's offspring. Furthermore, by featuring a university professor, *Femeia* aimed its "pro-family" message at professional women who were more likely to limit family size.[74]

The psychological and physical benefits of bearing multiple children were also emphasized by medical professionals. For example, according to the secretary of the Ministry of Health: "Women's biological and psychological fulfillment is fortified with each child she bears, raises and educates. A woman who has not experienced motherhood, has reached neither the psychic nor the emotional level of perfection, and, as the years pass, her life is characterized by a sense of unfulfillment."[75] This view was echoed in personalized articles such as "With Each Child You Live Another Life," which highlighted the rewards of raising many children—in this case seven. In this piece, Maria, a forty-three-year-old teacher of Romanian (and communist party member), explains her rationale for having a large family: "I said [to my husband]: let's have a child for each day of the week, to have somewhere to go in our old age, every day."[76] With children ranging from age five to twenty-two, Maria acknowledged that the family lives modestly—in a three-bedroom apartment—and that she and her husband can only provide the basics. However, she emphasized that they are nonetheless happy and that she does not feel overwhelmed because the children and her husband help out around the house. For readers who may have been unconvinced, she added that raising such a large family did not negatively affect her relationship with her husband, but rather that their love for one another grew. What's more, according to her, raising so many children, rather than being burdensome, was actually invigorating: "when you are surrounded by children, you always feel young, with each one you get to live life again, you do not feel the burden of the years."[77] Accordingly, fulfillment did not derive from acquiring goods or living in a large home, but by surrounding oneself with loved ones. In this manner, the state sought to encourage couples to have larger families, without providing larger dwellings for them.

The article, "Family is not an Impediment, but a Stimulant in Women's Advancement," transmitted a similar message. Portraying a day in the life Matilda Niţa, mother of four and secretary of the party committee at a buttons and plastics factory, the piece features images of her presiding over a meeting, greeting her adult son who had returned from military service, and preparing food with her daughter.[78] The final image, which depicts her husband bringing home groceries, provides the clue to Matilda's success: a partner who does all the shopping, as well as completing other household tasks. The overall message was that women need not sacrifice professional ambition for a large family or vice versa, but should instead regard the two as compatible. Yet, because her husband's domestic contributions were essential to Matilda's professional success, her story was not representative of most professional women's lives. Indeed, as noted in chapter 4, women shouldered many, and in some cases all, household duties while also working full-time and bearing children. Moreover, men often expressed resistance to women's educational and professional advancement, especially if it meant surpassing them in status and earning power. Thus, Matilda's story might have been one that Romanian women aspired to, but, on the whole, could not relate to.

Articles on large families were complemented by images in *Femeia*, which featured happy parents surrounded by their brood of four or more children (See figure 5.2).

Figure 5.2. Cover of *Femeia*, 1980

## "They Paid with Their Lives": Pronatalism as State Violence

Efforts to increase the birth rate through punitive legislation and propaganda were successful, but only in the short term. Between 1967 and 1970 the fertility rate climbed from 1.9 to 3.7 children (per woman). This surge was due to the fact that Decree 770 had been passed with no prior warning to the public. Therefore, women who were pregnant at the time of its passage—or became pregnant shortly thereafter—were caught by surprise and struggled to procure an abortion through alternative channels. Meanwhile, the number of registered or "legal" abortions plummeted from 1.115 million in 1965 to 205,783 in 1967.[79] However, women soon found ways of circumventing the decree, and the birth rate began declining in 1971.[80]

The state responded with increasingly invasive policies. In 1974, the same year that women's "right to decide freely and responsibly the number and spacing of children" was affirmed as a fundamental principle at the World Population Conference (held, incidentally, in Bucharest), work and the body intersected in a particularly invasive manner. According to new legislation, women laborers were subject to mandatory gynecological exams to be performed at workplaces on a biannual or quarterly basis.[81] Officially legitimated on the basis of women's health—specifically concern about ovarian and breast cancer—these exams were conducted on all women of childbearing age who worked in factories with a majority of female employees. In reality, however, the aim of the exams was to identify and monitor women's pregnancies and ensure they were brought to term. As Doina, a factory worker who endured the exams, explained, "They conducted checkups two times a year at the factory. It was at the factory clinic, and sometimes they did them every three months, but usually we were required to have gynecological checkups twice a year. I knew, I knew that [it would happen] ... I just didn't know the exact day."[82] By comparison, women who worked in non-factory settings claimed they were not subject to such checkups. Targeting factory workers was not only a matter of efficiency, but also due to the fact that women laborers aged twenty to thirty-five registered the highest abortion rates.[83]

The exams were typically announced the day before they were to be performed and, therefore, evasion of them was difficult, though not impossible. For instance, women might cite sickness or family emergency as a pretext for leaving work early. Although there was certainly much grousing about and, more likely, cursing of these humiliating practices, it is unknown if employees complained to union leaders or CNF representatives about them, though even if they had there was little such bodies could do. Nonetheless, some women found ways of making their voices heard, even targeting First Lady Elena Ceaușescu for criticism. Typically, this was done through the medium of letters, usually anonymous, to the communist leadership. For instance, in 1984 a group of women laborers penned a letter to Elena, which was subsequently aired on Radio Free Europe that July, in which they inquired about the impetus behind the exams:

> Whose idea was it that young women should be subject to a periodic exam to determine if we are pregnant and to be registered ... to be registered like cattle, to see, after nine months, how many children we will bring into the world for "the most beloved son of the people." I don't want to believe that if, when you were young, if someone would have come to you with such an idea, you would not have protested.[84]

The women went on to emphasize that while they opposed abortion during advanced pregnancy, they believed they should not be forced to bring children into the world when "we don't have conditions to raise them in a civilized manner." Thus, they referenced the everyday realities of 1980s Romania: protracted food shortages and lack of sufficient childcare facilities. The women noted further that while other countries also prohibit abortion, they nonetheless make contraceptives available to women. The letter closed with a threat, "If you don't rescind these obligations, we will appeal to all the young women in the world and ask them to protest against this inhumane and humiliating policy."[85] By remaining anonymous, these women felt sufficiently emboldened to publically express their hatred of the compulsory gynecological exams and encourage others to protest on their behalf, thereby bringing them to the attention of the world. They also felt emboldened to mock one of the adulatory titles bestowed upon Ceaușescu during that time (e.g. "beloved son of the people").

Although intended to monitor women's pregnancies and ensure they were brought to term, the exams could also serve as early warning signals—that is, if doctors took pity on their patients and were able to secretly notify them of their pregnancy without officially recording it.[86] As previously noted, doctors also helped women by taking advantage of loopholes in Decree 770, namely documenting an illegal abortion as a miscarriage. Sometimes this was done out of altruism, sometimes for profit. As Ecaterina stressed, "Not all gynecologists complied with the decree. And some, indeed, many of them, performed abortions for money."[87] Yet, doing so involved great risk since physicians were under the direction of head doctors, from whom they received permission to use surgical instruments.[88] Consequently, doctors might resort to desperate measures to perform an abortion. As one woman who went to the hospital after unsuccessfully self-inducing an abortion recalled, "Fortunately for me, there was a young doctor still at the hospital ... he came to the hospital at night, he knew the condition I was in, and he helped me. With his hands, pure and simple. With his hands he helped me. Without an [instrument]."[89] Such an act required a great deal of courage on the part of the doctor for, beginning in 1974, doctors were monitored by *miliţia* officers, who were stationed in hospitals and reported any wrongdoing to the prosecutor. Moreover, medical staff—physicians included—served as informers for the Securitate, further adding to the climate of fear and suspicion within hospitals. As a result, many doctors feared performing abortions—or labeling clandestine abortions as "spontaneous abortions"—unless the patient met the conditions outlined by the law.

Due to the risks associated with procuring an abortion, over the course of Ceauşescu's rule women were left with ever-fewer options for controlling their fertility. They therefore increasingly turned to untrained or poorly trained abortionists who were often motivated more by material gain than women's welfare.[90] Data on individuals who were convicted of performing illegal abortions in 1986 offer some insight into the extent to which non-medical professionals engaged in this practice. For instance, in that year only 1.5 percent of those convicted of performing an illegal abortion were actually doctors, while 8.2 percent worked in a health care facility in some capacity. The remaining convictions (the vast majority) were of individuals who held "other occupations" (74.9 percent) or were "unemployed" (15.4 percent).[91] To be sure, individuals who fell under these latter categories also included midwives, who were often skilled in performing abortions and took the necessary precautions in proper sanitary conditions. As a corollary, doctors who successfully bribed the attending *miliţia* officer and/or the prosecutor in order to evade a criminal charge (and hence potential conviction) are not captured in these statistics—but neither are non-medical professionals (e.g. those with "other occupations") who were similarly able to bribe their way out of a criminal charge. Given these possibilities, it is likely that the data are more or less accurate, and that by the mid-1980s women typically resorted to non-medical professionals to terminate their pregnancies.

Such individuals might use unsterilized instruments and dangerous methods to induce the abortion, as well as perform it in unhygienic conditions without anesthesia. In some cases, abortionists took advantage of women's desperation, extorting large sums of money from them. According to a survey conducted by political scientist Lavinia Betea, the cost of a clandestine abortion in the 1980s was around 5,000 lei ($362 in 1984)—the equivalent of approximately two months' (median) salary—an exorbitant fee for many couples, let alone single women.[92] Abortionists also exploited women's desperation by demanding additional money and other favors in exchange for performing an abortion.[93] Moreover, if something went awry during the procedure, the abortionist tried to deter the woman from seeking medical help, fearing their identity might be revealed and they would be prosecuted. The consequences for some women were dire, as Adriana recalled:

> At the university I had a good friend, my best friend, and one day I received a telephone call from a neighbor of hers asking me to come over ... and I found out my friend had died. She had been with an abortionist, and he performed an abortion and something went wrong and he let her die. This marked me horribly ... she was only eighteen.[94]

Women also resorted to various methods of self-induction, such as taking extremely hot baths, lifting weights, or using probes such as urinary catheters (some fashioned from electric cables) and knitting needles. Some women also inserted herbal infusions (e.g. lovage, wormwood), lemon juice, alcohol, and saline solutions, as well chemical substances (aluminum, potassium sulfates), into their vaginas, or swallowed a variety of substances—toxic and non-toxic alike—to end their pregnancies.[95] Like abortions performed by nonprofessionals, these interventions could lead to severe hemorrhaging and bodily injury, including punctured or infected uteruses, lesions, and sterility. As one woman claimed about her postabortion condition, "I felt very sick, trembling all over my body. I had terrible pains and a fever and I was bleeding. My husband was at work and my children, three and four years old, fetched me water and helped me change the bed sheets soaked with blood. They were crying as they caressed my head."[96] In addition to personal harm, women feared potential harm to the fetus of unsuccessful interventions. Particularly terrifying was the prospect of bearing a child with disabilities or other malformations. As one woman recalled, "[My biggest fear was] that I would somehow end up with a child with deformities; that I would not end the pregnancy and have a child with deformities and have it on my conscience. My whole life I would struggle with it."[97] This woman's fear was certainly understandable and was likely influenced by representations in *Femeia* and other media, which emphasized the tragic effects of botched abortions, including infants born with deformities and disabilities. It was also, to some extent, based on fact as the number of children born with physical and developmental disabilities did increase as the decree became more draconian and women resorted to desperate measures to end their pregnancies.[98]

In Ceaușescu's Romania, having children was presented as a "patriotic honor and debt of all families and for the entire population." Thus, while women could be fined for failing to produce offspring, termination of pregnancy through abortion incurred special penalties since "the fetus is the socialist property of the whole society [and] those who refuse to have children are deserters, escaping the law of natural continuity."[99] Consequently, women who sought abortions faced economic punishment in the form of community service work, wage garnishment of up to 80 percent, and, for repeat offenders, imprisonment in a correctional facility.[100] Like "workshy social parasites" and workers who undermined productive growth through sabotage, such women were portrayed as asocialist saboteurs, who were undermining reproductive growth. Indeed, some women charged with illicit abortion were publically shamed. As Angela recalled, "There were many people who were arrested and condemned. They publicized them in the paper and at the beginning of the news on television. It was a source of shame."[101]

Those who performed illegal abortions also faced public shame, including in the pages of *Femeia*. For example, a 1974 article examined the trial of Pascal Ionescu, "an accomplished engineer" who had been charged with performing thirty-one abortions.[102] Posing as a doctor—with actual nurses as both his accomplices and patients—Pascal performed the abortions in "primitive conditions" and ignored hygienic regulations, which put "countless young women's lives in danger" and ended the lives of "dozens of children who could have been important members of our society"[103] The article highlighted the web of individuals complicit in these acts (e.g. the nurses, the anesthesiologist, etc.), criticizing them for their greed and lack of scruples. Such greed was exemplified in Pascal's car, a Fiat 600—then a luxury item in Romania. After a 13-hour trial, Pascal admitted his wrongdoing, claiming that while he initially performed abortions out of curiosity, over time he proved too weak to refuse the women who appealed for help—nor the money they offered him. Ultimately, the court ordered Pascal to return the money—a sum totaling 9,950 lei ($837.54)—to the state and sentenced him to eight years in a correctional facility.[104] The piece ends on a redemptive note, depicting Pascal as a talented engineer, capable of "providing society with something of value," who had momentarily lost his moral compass but eventually came to recognize that "he had destroyed everything, including his own future."[105] By humanizing the perpetrator, the article served as a warning to other women who might be contemplating procuring an abortion from a seemingly upstanding professional posing as a doctor. It also served as a warning to non-medical professionals contemplating performing or otherwise assisting with abortions on the side for extra cash.

Most of my respondents did not relay their own abortion experiences to me, and I did not solicit them given the highly personal nature of the issue.[106] Similarly, Lavinia Betea found that her respondents were not forthcoming about their abortion experiences because of the trauma and guilt surrounding them.[107] In some cases, there has been a willful forgetting, mainly for the purpose of self-preservation. As one of the women interviewed by Lorena Anton noted, "I don't know if you believe me, but there are many things I don't remember. ... I have forgotten them—I had to forget."[108] Those who did reference their experiences, explained that by paying or pleading with their doctors, seeking out medical professionals or midwives, or otherwise appealing through connections with colleagues, neighbors, family, and friends, they were able to "resolve things." They also highlighted the fear and, indeed, terror surrounding the process, which they often had to face alone. As C. recalled:

> Woman was the sacrificial one during this period; all the difficulties of this period fell on her. After I got married, I got pregnant and abortions were forbidden. I found a doctor who was not a gynecologist, a medical student, and I made contact with him as if in the CIA, with a newspaper in his hand at an intersection. We met a woman that I did not know and went to a house I did not know. The abortion was done on a kitchen table, without anesthesia, with the radio turned up to the maximum volume so as not to be heard. And after that, I was bleeding but I could not call my doctor because she would have had to call the prosecutor's office. Fortunately, as the daughter of a doctor, I knew some people and got antibiotics.[109]

C.'s recollections illustrate the degree to which women often suffered abortion alone—even if they were in a partnership or marriage—due to the belief that fertility control was a "woman's concern." It also underscores the crucial role of connections, in this case being the daughter of a doctor, in potentially preventing fatality.

Because abortion was the primary form of fertility control in Romania, many viewed it simply as a normal practice. As a rural woman recalled about her abortions:

> Oh, I think [I had] about 30 something. Yes. Well, if I had three per year? That's how many, three per year. ... See, I was healthy, I was strong. For me an abortion was nothing. I did it and I left for work. My body was healthy. But not everyone is like that. And now I am very thankful to God because I did not realize how much danger I put myself in.[110]

This statement underscores how typical, indeed, "everyday" abortion was, and why this woman did not consider having one as a moral failing. In fact, she actually thanked God that she managed to survive. E., a librarian, was similarly matter-of-fact about her experiences, asserting that she had many abortions and did not feel guilty about them:

> I was aware that I didn't have the money to raise a child. ... I was not in a position to have a family at that time; I had a small flat with my parents. ... I don't know how many abortions I had but only two of them were performed by qualified doctors. ... I paid lots of money, about [a month's] salary or so. I was very much afraid. It hurt so much, and they [the doctors] tried to give you some anesthesia but it was useless. But if you wanted to have a boyfriend you could not say, "I will not sleep with you." I blamed my mom. I told her later that she should have told me about these things.[111]

Despite her fear and suffering, E. also stressed that abortion "was something very normal.... For me, it was normal, I could tell many stories and maybe I could get a Palme D'or [Prize] or I don't know. ... For me, it's normal. I mean, there are millions of stories like that."[112] By the time E. became sexually active, the decree had been in force for well over a decade. Thus for E., as for many other Romanian women, procuring a clandestine abortion was simply a normal response to living under a repressive regime that did not sufficiently incentivize motherhood by providing adequate maternity leave, childcare, and housing. It was also a normal response to living within a patriarchal society. Thus, E.'s choice to procure an abortion was related to poor material conditions and lack of access to contraceptives, as well as men's privileging of their own sexual needs above women's—not to mention above women's health.

This is not argue that women, including E., did not feel remorse or regret about procuring an abortion. As a mother of three reflected: "You know, I have thought many times during my life about the abortions. ... The ones I had. What can I say? I am very sorry. I am very sorry. But at that time, in that situation ... as I perceived it ... I didn't see any other way for me."[113] Other respondents also noted how women's lack of choice (to control their fertility) forced them into acting in ways that did not accord with their values or religious beliefs. Indeed, a number of women emphasized outright that they disapproved of abortion, but insisted that the state should not deny women options (e.g. contraception) for controlling their fertility.

Some also blamed lack of knowledge about family planning and reproductive health more generally. Indeed, girls' and women's only possible sources of information about sexuality and reproduction were female friends and relatives, *Femeia*, film and literature, and, if they had access to it, the book *Talking with Youth*. Yet, as previously noted, *Femeia* presented a number of falsehoods about reproductive health, especially contraceptive use. Additionally, traditional and highly gendered notions of sexuality characterized most families' attitudes—even in urban areas and in highly educated circles. As E. recounted, "Our parents were not willing to discuss this with us ... women didn't know much about their [reproductive] health."[114] Thus, even the daughter of progressive parents might not receive sufficient instruction on sex education or on how to negotiate sexual encounters.[115] In the belief that they were protecting their daughters' innocence and virtue, then, parents did not impart necessary information about reproductive health to their children. Regardless of the cause, responsibility for unwanted pregnancy often fell on women, who were expected to resolve the situation somehow.[116]

While only a few women shared their own abortion experiences with me, most were relatively open about others,' experiences, especially harassment by the *miliția*. As Livia recalled:

> If you went to the hospital, they [the doctors] wouldn't do anything, many times they would let them [women] suffer until they died. ... There was a man working for the Securitate, waiting there, keeping an eye on them, so the doctor would not operate to save their lives. Women were supposed to provide the names of those who had helped them, to tell them what had happened and exactly what they had done. And if they didn't, time was ticking and they lost a lot of blood ... It was inhuman to require women to have more children than they desired, and because of it, women paid a high price, including their lives.[117]

Marcela witnessed this scenario firsthand when she was in hospital recovering from surgery. At that time, she lay in a bed next to a woman who was writhing in pain and calling for help (as a result of a botched abortion), to which a *miliția* officer responded: "We can save you [if you tell us the name]." Marcela recalled, "it was terrible. ... I heard with my own ears how they pressured this woman, on the verge of death."[118] Tragically, Marcela awoke the next morning to discover the woman had died. For Corina, the decree hit even closer to home:

> My cousin had an abortion. She was pregnant with her fifth child and she died as a result of a self-induced abortion. And, one of my friends from high school also self-induced an abortion and was taken to the maternity ward, and because she didn't tell them who performed the abortion, she died. ... She died. Nobody did anything in the maternity ward. The prosecutor was called, and he told them that as long as she refused to tell them who induced it, they would not treat her.[119]

Threatening to deny a woman medical care if she refused to reveal the name of the abortionist was also referenced by women interviewed by other scholars. In addition to threats, police officers scolded, swore at, and, in some cases, beat women to force them into identifying the abortionist.[120] Although some women confessed, others remained silent and paid with their lives. Thus, the state continued to employ Stalinist forms of repression against its own citizens well into the 1980s; however, in this case, it occurred in a hospital room rather than an interrogation cell and women were the sole targets. Indeed, as Corina Doboş contends, the hospital room effectively became an "inquisitorial space."[121] Accordingly, women were required to confess their anti-socialist "sins" to the doctor or *miliția* officer and face punishment, which might involve a show trial—another continuity with Stalinist practices.[122] Meanwhile, if women did not confess, their punishment could be death. Such situations undermined the entire notion of the Hippocratic Oath, forcing doctors to choose between tending to their patients' needs (e.g. saving their lives) and sparing themselves from a potentially lengthy prison term and loss of professional credentials.

While not legally sanctioned, the practice of denying women medical treatment for refusing to reveal their abortionist's identity was common enough to constitute a systematic form of violence against women. In her analysis of the medicalization of pregnancy in postwar Europe, historian Muriel Blaive defines physical violence as "either a withholding or the overutilization of resources by an agent in a position of power leading to a physical effect such as reduced autonomy or compromised integrity of the subject's body."[123] While written with respect to the birthing process, this definition also applies to abortion in Romania since denying medical care to a woman suffering from a botched abortion clearly involved the withholding of resources by an agent of power. Moreover, the specific situation—as well as the decree more generally—sharply compromised women's autonomy and bodily integrity. This practice also functioned as a form of intimidation as women knew their lives literally hung in the balance if they did not confess, while other women (after suffering a botched abortion), refused to go to hospital for fear of the legal repercussions. On the verge of bleeding to death, Eugenia, a factory manager, claimed that she eventually convinced her doctor to come to her house and "take care of it" in exchange for money.[124] Such intervention was infrequent, however, due to legal risks; as a result, many women died.

Although a covert form of state violence compared to death by firing squad, for some women the price of "desertion" (the term Ceaușescu used to describe women who refused to have children) was not that far afield from what soldiers had faced for the same charge during World War I. In both cases, punishments were designed to deter others from engaging in similar practices by instilling terror in those who witnessed them. Moreover, because the viability of the nation was perceived to be at stake, in both cases punishment was meted out for betraying the nation. The state employed such draconian measures to reduce the abortion rate; however, since modern forms of contraception were difficult to obtain, women were left with no other choice than to engage in what was officially considered criminal behavior. Thus, "desertion" could culminate in death, as women could be denied medical treatment if they refused to identify the abortionist to the head doctor and *miliția* officer at the hospital. As such, the state was aware that women, many of them mothers, put their lives in jeopardy in order to control their fertility.

Indeed, the state betrayed its commitment to improve women's health by actually putting it at greater risk. While it is true that abortions performed prior to 1966—especially by untrained individuals—contributed significantly to maternal deaths, after 1966 abortion became the leading cause of maternal mortality in Romania. For instance, the maternal mortality rate increased from 86 deaths (per 100,000) in 1965 to 169 in 1989, of which 87 percent were abortion-related.[125] These were particularly pronounced in the 1980s, with an estimated 500 healthy women dying each year as a result of post-abortion hemorrhage, sepsis, abdominal trauma, and poisoning."[126] Paradoxically, the very law that was officially justified on the basis of improving women's health was its greatest threat.

The Romanian government also betrayed the principles outlined in the UN Convention on the Elimination of all Forms of Discrimination against Women (CEDAW) and the Helsinki Accords, to which Romania was a signatory and, as such, legally bound to respect the human rights and dignity of its citizens.[127] Finally, because those without financial means could not be selective in choosing their abortionist, the decree affected low-income women disproportionately.[128] Tragically, the very class in whose name socialism was legitimated suffered the most from these policies.

The state, however, assumed no responsibility for these deaths. Instead, the media placed blame on naïve women and opportunistic abortionists. For example, the 1974 film, *Ilustrate cu Flori de Câmp* (Postcards with Wild Flowers), which appeared briefly on cinema screens and was loosely based on real events, explored the dangers of clandestine abortions. In the film an untrained abortionist seeking material gain performs an abortion on a young, unassuming college student who subsequently dies.[129] In a similar vein, the 1987 article, "Orphans," described the fate of a thirty-five-year-old mother of three who, "in the springtime of her life," fell into the hands of an untrained abortionist—a recidivist who had been punished before—who caused her untimely death.[130] The author added that while the abortionist received 3,000 lei for his services, the woman's children—aged two, eleven, and twelve—were left motherless. "Why," the author asked, "should something so natural turn into a tragedy? As mothers and fathers, and as colleagues, it is our noble duty to protect and safeguard life. We hope that the sad story of this 35-year old woman who died and these orphans helps us to understand this truth."[131]

In other cases, maternal death was portrayed through the children who lost mothers as a result of a botched abortion. For instance, the article "Where Are You, Mommy?" was intended to pull on readers' heartstrings through its emotional title and tragic tale of a twenty-seven-year-old woman, with a young child, who died as a result of an illegal abortion.[132] So too was a *Femeia* article featuring an image of a textile worker's funeral organized by the deceased woman's coworkers and led by the four children she had left behind.[133] By highlighting the manifold and long-term effects of clandestine abortion (loss of life, orphaned children), the regime hoped to instill fear, shame, and guilt in women and, thereby, dissuade them from procuring abortions. It also sought to deter doctors and others from clandestinely performing them. Given that the birth rate did not increase, such scare tactics were clearly unsuccessful. However, such articles, combined with real-life stories, presumably prompted some women to think twice before seeking a clandestine abortion.

The dangers associated with pronatalist policies were evident by the 1980s in Romania's maternal mortality rate—the highest in Europe. Indeed, according to official statistics, 9,452 women died between 1966 and 1989 as a result of abortion-related complications.[134] The actual figure, however, is believed to be significantly higher since not all women sought medical attention after a botched or self-induced abortion and thus their deaths were not recorded under this category. Rather than being "selfish," "immoral," or "naïve," as propagandists depicted women who procured abortions, most of them were married, in their late 20s or 30s, and already had two or more children at home. Overworked and struggling to support their existing children, these women were so determined to avoid bearing another child that they were willing to risk their own health. Such desperation is reflected in the estimated ten thousand children left motherless as a result of abortion-related complications between 1966 and 1989.[135]

What the state failed to acknowledge was that by criminalizing abortion it actually contributed to the rise in infant mortality—and in the number of orphaned and abandoned children.[136] Unable to nourish an additional mouth, families left their children in state institutions. This was especially the case when a mother died from a botched abortion and remaining family was unable to care for the child. Although accurate figures for children orphaned as a result of the decree are unavailable, between 1967 and the collapse of communism, the number of children in children's homes (*caselor de copii*) increased dramatically, from 4,000 in 1967 to 11,000 in 1980 to 13,000 in 1989.[137] Meanwhile, the total number of children who had been abandoned and placed in state care (hospitals, crèches, homes for the "irrecoverables," or "partially recoverables") constituted 125,000 by 1989.[138] The conditions in the "homes for the irrecoverables" were particularly appalling, as children faced neglect and physical and psychological abuse and often did not even know their own names. Moreover, they were poorly clothed and fed—receiving porridge and scraps of food—were rarely bathed, and endured bitterly cold winters as these facilities were often unheated. To compensate for their poor diets and to boost their immune systems, some of these children were injected—via unsterilized needles—with vitamins and microtransfusions, causing some to contract HIV.[139]

Individuals who managed to survive these inhumane conditions were often diagnosed with developmental, physical, and emotional disabilities. Children with disabilities, clearly the most helpless individuals in society, were thus the most adversely affected by the decree and, as such, also objects of state violence.[140] By placing infants and children in such horrid conditions, the state not only exposed them to health dangers but also contradicted *Femeia's* authors, who expounded on "the immense care with which the country looks after its children."[141] Indeed, despite the CNF's apparent concern for abandoned children, the conditions of these institutions never entered into its local or national meeting minutes.[142] Similarly, the women's commissions and committees seemingly made no effort to organize local charitable initiatives for orphans as women's organizations had done during the immediate postwar period.

Because criminalizing abortion proved ineffective in substantially increasing the birth rate, in 1985 the state enhanced family allowances. While these allowances did not typically offset the cost of supporting additional children, they could be quite handsome for those in the lowest income bracket, supplementing household income by 70 percent (if they had 5 children). For instance, urban families with a monthly salary of 2,500 lei ($192) or less received 1,080 lei ($83) per month for three children and 1,580 lei ($121) per month for four children.[143] Also, monetary benefits were introduced to complement heroine mother awards.[144] Although presented as generous gifts of the state, such rewards did not go very far, especially in the 1980s when 1,500 lei covered only a one-month supply of powdered milk—a necessity for most mothers since they typically returned to work three months after giving birth.[145]

Due to the regime's repressiveness, it is unsurprising that individuals did not publically protest Decree 770. In fact, the mere suggestion of protest was met with a cynical laugh by many of my respondents as they emphasized the futility and potential danger associated with such an act. As Elisabeta succinctly put it, "Nobody had the courage to protest it."[146] This is not to argue that resistance did not occur. As historian Maria Bucur asserts, when women procured illegal abortions they were "acting while fully aware of the legal repressive consequences."[147] Therefore, their acts constitute a form of resistance, albeit not the visible form typically associated with the term. Nonetheless, the ramifications for transgressing the decree—wage garnishment, job loss, imprisonment, trauma, physical harm, and even death—were markedly greater than for those who engaged in other types of antistate activities such as signing petitions and writing open letters to the party leadership. Indeed, because women could be left to die if they refused to confess to doctors and *miliția* officers the name of their abortionist, a more apt comparison might be to those who attempted to flee socialist Romania or East Berlin, where the risk was also bodily injury, imprisonment, and death. Furthermore, abortion was a common, everyday occurrence and thus representative of the majority of women's experiences. As such, it was a much more ordinary, though also a much more dangerous, form of resistance than signing a petition or marching in a protest. Women's responses to Ceaușescu's pronatalism thus underscore the importance of considering how resistance was expressed in private spaces and of employing a gendered lens to historicize women's particular modes of resistance.[148]

Women also engaged in other, less dangerous forms of resistance to pronatalist policies, including surgical sterilization and the use of IUDs and birth control pills, all of which became illegal the mid-1980s.[149] With respect to surgical sterilization, only the privileged few with the financial means and connections to a courageous doctor could have this procedure performed. As Ecaterina asserted, "You had to have a doctor you trusted. But it was not only that, it was so expensive, that is, extraordinarily expensive."[150] Similarly, having a trustworthy doctor and financial means was necessary for being fitted with an IUD. In addition to the fear associated with the illegality of this procedure, women also worried about its effects on their body as they had only minimal knowledge about modern forms of contraception. As Valeria R. recalled:

> It was very risky. There weren't diverse methods [of birth control], you couldn't discuss it with a doctor. So I didn't know if it would harm me or not, if they are the best or not for me, and, in the end, through contacts, through a friend's doctor, I was fitted with an IUD. But totally illegally, trembling, anxious, because it had been banned.[151]

Beyond that, some respondents believed that contraceptives could be detected by a routine medical exam or that they were a potential health risk, a notion that was advanced by doctors and other experts, including Radu Dimitriu, author of *De vorbă cu tinerii* (Talking with Youth).[152] In light of the challenges in procuring contraception, most couples relied on traditional forms of fertility control such as *coitus interuptus*, the rhythm method, and vinegar, lemon or saline douches, as well as other herbal mixtures. In addition, individuals purchased "Vulcan" condoms and poor-quality Chinese "Butterfly" condoms in pharmacies and perfumeries.[153]

With the banning of all contraceptives—except for condoms—people acquired birth control pills at the Hungarian and Yugoslav borders (under the tacit acceptance of border guards), through contacts abroad, or when they traveled outside of Romania.[154] Privilege and location could thus facilitate access to contraceptives, with those at the western reaches of the country, as well as those whose jobs involved frequent travel abroad (e.g. the communist leadership and *nomenklaura*; airline pilots), being most poised to benefit from cross-border trading and foreign travel. So too could economic wherewithal as the black market offered access to contraceptives, including condoms, pills, spermicides, and IUDs, though the cost of these was quite high. Finally, the University of Bucharest was an important source for acquiring contraceptives since it hosted a number of foreign students who purchased them abroad or on the black market with the aim of selling them in Romania.

Although there were no public protests against the decree, some women did express disapproval and even outrage through letters to state officials. While some used a supplicating tone, praising the decree while also requesting increased material support for mothers, others were less servile, noting that they would be "forced into getting clandestine abortions."[155] Meanwhile, one woman criticized the decree by referencing men's selfishness, "I do not agree with the provisions of the decree, because some men are not interested in supporting a family, they do everything for their own self-interest and then abandon women, not recognizing that they are obligated to raise them."[156]

In September 1983, a widow identifying herself as "an unhappy mother for the rest of her life" wrote a letter to Elena Ceaușescu, which was subsequently broadcast on Radio Free Europe. In the letter, the woman, whose daughter had recently died after a botched abortion, requests an end to the "crimes" that are occurring as a result of "the Decree that bans abortion." She wrote:

> You too have been young, you are a mother, and so it's only natural that you will understand me. Since I have lost her I am no longer a person, but I don't have enough strength to end my life. If a teen or a woman risks her life for an abortion she probably has valid reasons. Why, then, are so many cases "passionately" followed by the *miliția* ... and when the unfortunate reaches the hospital they do not intervene until finding out who performed the abortion? There have been cases when the patient didn't acknowledge him and it cost her life. Afterwards, their parents are broken, destroyed for the rest of their lives, children who will be deprived of their mother's love. Unfortunately, such tragedies only happen in modest working-class families. Wives and daughters from the "bourgeois" class don't end up in these situations since it's sufficient to call and the ambulance will come and urgently intervene. ... Today, in socialist Romania, it's a tragedy to be a mother if you don't have a grandmother to take care of the young ones. Maybe it would be wise to think

about the parents who have lost daughters, the husbands who have lost wives, and the children who have become orphans because of this inhumane decree.[157]

This heartrending letter highlighted the inhumanity of legislation that coerces women to have children, yet fails to incentivize this role by reducing costs for childcare. It also exposed how status (i.e. a daughter of a high-level functionary or Securitate officer) provides immunity from the law, creating a hierarchy in which certain lives are literally deemed more worthy than others. Thus, while the state accused women of deserting or betraying the nation, according to this woman, it was the state that betrayed women through its hypocritical policies, which, in the name of protecting the lives of women and children, actually contributed to a rise in maternal deaths.

Reflecting on the decree after the collapse of socialism, my respondents referred to it as "horrible," "inhumane," and "degrading." To quote Livia, "It was inhumane to force a woman to have more kids than she desired.... Because of this [decree] many women paid a very high price ... their life."[158] Since abortion served as a primary means of fertility control in Romania and had been widely practiced prior to the communist takeover, many believed that by denying women this option, the state undermined human rights. C. (b. 1957) used particularly powerful language when denouncing the decree:

> It was purely and simply a crime! A crime ... it was one of the worst things that happened. It was political rape. We were raped, obligated at all times to do what the party wanted. We didn't have ... they didn't give us the possibility to choose. We had to go where we were assigned, we had to work where they said, we had to have children, everything was obligatory. It was horrible because many women died.[159]

In referring to the decree as political rape, C. highlighted not only its inhumanity but also the interconnection between politics and bodily control. Similarly, Doina referenced rights in discussing pronatalist policies:

> It was a very ugly thing. Now it seems degrading. To not have the right to choose [the size of] your family. But it was not a communist invention. Prohibiting abortion is a historical thing. It was [prohibited] in many countries.[160]

In conceptualizing fertility control as a human right, Doina went beyond the national particularities of the Decree to emphasize that women face challenges to their reproductive rights throughout the world. As such, the criminalization of abortion is just one of the ways women are disempowered—in democracies and communist regimes alike.

While most women placed blame on inhumane state policies, one woman claimed that women were also at fault for unwanted pregnancy. As F. claimed, "You pay for your stupidity because smart women did not suffer then. It's true, women did not have medicine for this ... but please, a man is always a brute, yes or no? Women need to be intelligent and those who were did not suffer."[161] According to F., women were ultimately to blame for their unwanted pregnancies, either because they lacked knowledge about reproductive health or they were not sufficiently assertive in dealing with men. Meanwhile, she excuses men as brutish, dominated by base instinct. However, F.'s comments wholly neglect rape (including marital rape, which was not illegal), which, among its other effects, could result in unplanned pregnancy.[162] Furthermore, as previously noted, sex remained a taboo subject in most households, leaving adolescent girls ignorant of basic human anatomy and physiology—a reality that undoubtedly contributed to countless unplanned pregnancies.

Just as women viewed Ceaușescu's regime as inhumane and criminal for banning abortion, others claimed that the officially feted heroine mothers were also inhumane. As C. asserted:

> Heroine Mother! To have so many children during this period was criminal because it was obvious that you did not have the means to raise them. This was a new form of child abuse. Gypsies were the only ones that accepted having children in any conditions. Because we tried whatever means we could to avoid having children.[163]

The perception that Roma women bore many children (four or more) during this period was common among my respondents, though it was differently understood. While some claimed that Roma women always had large families and simply continued this practice into the communist period, others argued that Roma families intentionally did so for material benefit. This they perceived as a fundamental part of Roma identity—and also evidence of bad mothering. Although determining the precise number of Roma births during this period is impossible, the increase in Roma births was a source of concern for Ceaușescu since his pronatalism was rooted in racist ideas about national value. Thus, the state relentlessly monitored Romanian women's reproductive health, while turning a blind eye to abortions performed on Roma women.[164]

Although none of my respondents donned the title of heroine mother themselves, one of their mothers did. Angela recalled that her mother, a very religious woman from rural Moldavia, took great pride in her large family: "My mother was declared a heroine mother. She was proud of it. She didn't feel insulted or bothered when they called her heroine mother because she wanted children. She was the type who wanted to have children because she was very religious."[165] The designation "heroine mother" was meaningful to Angela's mother not necessarily because she supported the regime or its pronatalist policies, but because she took great joy in having a large family and being officially acknowledged for her maternal role. Thus, while her choice to bear many children conformed to state dictates, her motivations for doing so were religious, not socialist or nationalist. This illustrates the polyvalent meanings of motherhood, underscoring the importance of acknowledging what Hana Havelková refers to as the positive aspects of the "cult of motherhood during socialism."[166]

Upon assuming power after the Romanian Revolution, the National Salvation Front government legalized abortion on demand on 26 December 1989. Despite this, fear of Ceaușescu's repressive pronatalist policies linger. After discussing the inhumanity of the decree, one of my respondents asked, "Do you think it's dangerous? It's not dangerous that I spoke the truth is it? I still relive moments of the past. I am afraid to say things."[167]

## Bringing up Baby: Parenting and State "Welfare"

Although the state glorified prolific mothers and large families, rearing children, especially during the first and final decades of communist rule, posed numerous challenges. The recollections of Regine, a railway worker who resided in a one-room apartment with her husband and newborn son in the 1950s, illustrate well the material deprivations of early socialist rule:

> I brought my child to our first place along with the suitcase that I had with me for five years [in Russia]. And I put pretty material around it and that was his cradle. When my mother visited me, she lifted up the material ... [and] I began to cry. Do you know what she said? "You don't have a better cradle for the child?" What could I do? I didn't receive anything from my parents ... I moved [into that house] with a horse, you see, a horse ... and I had a bed, a table, a dresser. That was all.[168]

Regine's shame over using a suitcase as a cradle reflects the hardships young mothers faced in the first decade of communist rule—especially former "enemies of the people" who were disadvantaged for housing and other goods.

While C. gave birth to her son in 1985—over thirty years after Regine—material difficulties also hampered her ability to properly care for him:

> It was like everything else, a mixed blessing. On the one hand, I was happy because I had him, he was a very cute baby and it was a joy for me, but from a material standpoint it was terrible. It was during the winter, there wasn't any electricity, everything was rationed, there was no clothing for children ... everything I needed was brought in somehow from contacts abroad, the same with food, through acquaintances of my father-in-law or my father. I remember they cut off the electricity and I had to carry the child and buggy up seven flights of stairs to our apartment. In order to give him a bath, I had to heat the water on the stove in a pot. I had a ten-liter pot and the flame was so small that it took two hours for the pot of ten liters to heat up. After that I put him in a plastic basin on the table in the kitchen. I would light a candle because there was no electricity, and I would give the baby a bath. It was horrible.[169]

C.'s memories of motherhood are inextricably connected to the material deprivations of the 1980s, which seriously compromised women's ability to care for their children, especially infants. Other women who raised children during this period shared similar experiences, emphasizing the difficulties in bathing and caring for them without consistently functioning heating, electricity, and hot water—and without diapers and even basic baby clothes.

Perhaps most heartrending for mothers were challenges in adequately nourishing infants. As most women returned to work after their maternity leave ran out (typically three months after they had given birth), they were dependent on infant formula. Yet, by the mid-1980s, even this legal entitlement, usually available in pharmacies, had become a scarce commodity. Valeria R. noted that after her daughter was born in 1983, she only received four boxes of powdered milk a month; however, as her daughter went through one box every three days this ration didn't come close to fulfilling her daughter's needs. Similarly, Maria recalled:

> You know why it was difficult? Because you couldn't find powdered milk, you couldn't find special food for kids. ... I had many problems with my son because my milk had run out, after three weeks I no longer had milk and I needed to supplement it. I wandered around like crazy to all the pharmacies, to all the groceries.[170]

The productive demands of the state thus undermined women's maternal capacities, as the short maternity leave prevented mothers from breastfeeding for an extended period and austerity measures hampered their ability to obtain sufficient infant formula to compensate for their inability to breastfeed. Although Maria eventually managed to acquire formula through coworkers, her struggles in acquiring even this basic necessity illustrate the hollowness of socialist rhetoric, which continually boasted of "the great care accorded to women and families in the Socialist Republic of Romania." While respondents noted that none of their children suffered significant health problems during this period, the introduction of food and heat rationing produced great distress in women, compromising their ability to fulfill their maternal role.[171] In contrast to C. and Maria, women who gave birth to their infants in the 1960s and 1970s claimed they were able to raise them with relative ease since powdered milk—as well as cow's milk—fresh produce, and clothing were widely available.

Although food was in short supply during certain periods of socialist rule, housing was always in short supply. Therefore, couples, until they became eligible for state housing, might share a small apartment (two bedrooms) with their parents and children or claim a few rooms in a larger house that the state had appropriated from pre-communist elites and subsequently divided up. Despite the massive building scheme initiated in the late 1950s, acquiring an apartment could take years, especially for those who were not part of the communist *nomenklatura* or did not have connections. This state of affairs created much disgruntlement, and many complained, often to friends and neighbors. Some also directed their concerns to local authorities, the Central Committee of the PCR, and even the Ceaușescus. For example, in 1973, Floarea Berendei penned a letter to Elena Ceaușescu, appealing for a larger dwelling for her family, which included herself, her husband, and her two daughters, aged twelve and twenty. She addressed Mrs. Ceaușescu with the "conviction of a poor mother, so you will understand the difficult situation I find myself in, and so that you can give me some comradely assistance."[172] Explaining that her retired husband has a neurological disorder and needs a quiet place to rest—lest he become abusive toward the family—and that her daughters need a decent place to study, she wrote, "With tears in my eyes, I come to you, comrade Elena Ceaușescu, as a simple, woman worker, in the hope that you'll give me some support so I can be happy too."[173] While it is unknown if Mrs. Berendei's living situation improved as a result of this letter, of note is that she used socialist parlance, along with maternal tropes, appealing to Elena as a fellow comrade and mother to issue her a larger apartment. Moreover, she referenced spousal abuse, emphasizing its deleterious effect on children. Finally, by noting that her children lacked sufficient study space, she intimated that the state had not provided her with the necessary conditions for nurturing a new generation of well-educated citizens deemed so crucial for socialist progress.

Just as women drew on their maternal role to request improved housing, so too they drew on it to extend maternity leave. As Stela explained, "There was a way to circumvent [returning to work] ... you would go to the doctor, the dispensary ... and you would invent some type of children's illness and then you could extend it [maternity leave]."[174] According to Elvira, this was because "Romanian women know how to deal with doctors."[175] Interestingly, Elvira regarded this act not only as a reasonable response to the short maternity leave but also part of the broader cultural practice of "dealing with doctors." As in other countries in the Eastern Bloc, women in Romania recognized the salience of motherhood and mobilized this role to improve their lot.[176]

Beyond citing illness, women argued that it was neither healthy nor normal to leave an infant in the care of someone other than his or her mother. Such efforts reflect what historian Donna Harsch refers to as a "female consciousness" or women's special sense of obligation to sustain gendered responsibilities.[177] Accordingly, women's conceptions of good mothering included staying at home with their infants for at least six months. In light of the cultural significance of motherhood, as well as its glorification by socialist propagandists, mothers in Romania had a good deal of bargaining power—at least in terms of prolonging their maternity leave or taking sick days. If mothers and children were indeed essential for creating a strong, healthy nation, then the state (or more specifically doctors) could not logically deny women the right to look after their young children. At the same time, women typically compensated doctors with money, food, cigarettes, and other goods in exchange for extensions (in the 1980s, for example, extensions might cost 400 lei; $30).[178] Thus, financial gain also factored into some doctors' decisions to extend maternity leave. Like the women studied by Lynne Haney in socialist Hungary, Romanian women mobilized their collective, social, and officially celebrated identity as mothers for individualistic purposes.[179] As such, maternalism could be a powerful trope, empowering women to make demands on the state. However, rather than coming together as a group (as women did in societies that guaranteed freedom of association), these women employed individualized strategies that did not challenge the more general problem of the short maternity leave or inflexible working hours.

While on medical leave, women continued to receive 50 to 80 percent of their salary and could, depending on the nature of the real or supposed illness of their child, extend the leave until the child was three years old. However, women who took such extensions were also perceived as less productive, which, in turn, affected their eligibility for promotion and the amount of their pension.[180] As Cătălina remarked, "There were a number of impediments [to advancement]. For example, when I was pregnant and after I gave birth I stayed on leave, and I was passed over for a promotion and I never made up [for that lost time]. There was a price to pay."[181]

As previously noted, propagandists paid lip service to socialist fatherhood and shared parenting, encouraging men to change diapers and develop strong bonds with their children. However, the gendered nature of family policy, men's typically larger income, and traditional ideas about family roles discouraged men from assuming equal childcare responsibilities. By failing to legislate family leave, the state reinforced men's roles as breadwinners while at the same time reinforcing women's roles as secondary earners—even though they were expected to be as productive as men. Despite the gendered nature of leave, only one respondent referred to occupational advancement as a source of concern when discussing strategies for taking extended leave; the value of staying home with their children thus seemingly counterbalanced or outweighed promotion.

Once maternity leave ran out, families were faced with finding acceptable childcare. State-subsidized childcare was a universal entitlement, with nurseries and crèches (ostensibly) provided for all infants and toddlers (up to three years old); however, according to my respondents, children were more prone to illness at the crèches. Moreover, supply usually outpaced demand. For instance, in 1966, the year Decree 770 was implemented, state childcare facilities could only accommodate 11,800 children, even though 69,000 places were needed.[182] Although provision of additional childcare facilities would have constituted a small portion of the state budget, only 6,500 more places were made available, ultimately leading to overcrowding and an increase in the child-to-caretaker ratio as existing centers simply took in more children.[183] As a result, some women were unable or unwilling to leave their children in them. Lack of sufficient and high-quality public childcare was the result of budgetary decisions and contrasted with the situation in the GDR, where such entitlements were prioritized. Meanwhile, in the 1970s and 1980s, the Polish government increased the length of maternity leave rather than expand childcare services.

In contrast to state nurseries and crèches, kindergartens were, according to a number of respondents, quite good. As Corina noted:

> There were kindergartens with normal schedules that allowed you to drop the children off in the morning and pick them up at five when you finished work ... there was much more order [back then]. I think from this perspective, things were better. Better because they had warm meals, they had a clean cot, there was a [healthy] fear of the women who worked with the children and there was discipline and care for children.[184]

Similarly, Maria stressed the convenience, cleanliness, and educational value of her son's kindergarten: "He went to kindergarten for eight hours. I took him in the morning and at three I'd pick him up. I was very satisfied: cleanliness, the child had meals, lessons, he received lunch, a dessert."[185] Indeed, some claimed that socialist kindergartens were superior to their postsocialist counterparts, not only because the state subsidized them, but also because children were disciplined.[186] Far from viewing them as sites of indoctrination, the mothers I spoke with praised kindergartens, as well as primary schools, for their educative role and for fostering interpersonal skills and social responsibility.

Initially, childcare was completely state-funded; however, beginning in 1982, the state required parental contributions toward operating costs.[187] Here again contradictions in socialist policy emerged, as class and status determined access to state childcare. Those with larger incomes were naturally better positioned to devote more money to childcare and, thereby, ensure the well-being of their children, be it by taking them to better nurseries or by hiring a nanny. To be sure, lower-income families also made the necessary sacrifices; however, with the introduction of rationing this proved difficult as the family budget was usually directed toward purchasing food and other goods, often through unofficial channels, which was considerably expensive.[188] Thus, as in other parts of the Bloc, privilege, status, and personal connections played an important role in securing benefits and entitlements—in this case, a place at good nurseries and kindergartens.[189]

If a suitable nursery or kindergarten could not be found, parents typically relied on a relative, usually a grandparent, for caregiving. Indeed, due to the early retirement age during the communist period (fifty-five for women and sixty for men), grandparents constituted the largest source of private (and free) daycare. In addition to being socialized, then, childcare became "geriatricized" in Romania.[190] By manipulating traditional family practices, the state could thus compensate for shortcomings in the "generous" benefits it offered children and families. Although not always ideal, having one's parents look after the children was preferable to transporting them to daycare in the wee hours of the morning. As Ecaterina recalled:

> In 1978 I had Linda ... I was lucky because I didn't need the nursery or kindergarten. I took her to her grandmother's, that is, I had my mother-in-law right next door and I never had problems with her. I would leave her there at quarter to six, twenty to six, in the rain, in the snow, in miserable weather. ... I saw these women with very small children in their arms and it almost brought me to tears. To wake a small child at six in the morning and take her into the cold, with that traffic, it was inhuman. You got 112 days. It's not enough for raising a child, it's not enough. A mother has to stay at home to breastfeed the child until she is one year old. When could they breastfeed if they were supposed to be at the factory?[191]

Ecaterina's comments reflect a more general dissatisfaction with the short (by non-American standards) maternity leave, which was intended first and foremost to rapidly reintegrate women into the workforce. Thus, the state's productive demands compromised women's ability to care for their infants for an extended period. To ensure her daughter didn't suffer the disruption (or what Ecaterina referred to as the "inhumanity") of being transported to childcare centers early in the morning and in the dead of winter, Ecaterina chose to leave her daughter with her mother-in-law.

In cases where retired family members moved into their children's homes, the situation was more complicated. On the one hand, living with one's parents could compromise the authority, autonomy, and intimacy of the couple. On the other hand, retired family members were a reliable, free, and typically preferred source of childcare for working families. In addition to looking after their grandchildren, grandparents played an important role in their socialization, imparting values and traditions. Moreover, grandparents often assisted with shopping, queuing for food, cooking, cleaning, and dealing with other issues, thereby lightening the domestic load. For Valeria R., whose husband died shortly after the birth of their daughter and whose job required frequent travel, her mother-in-law's contributions were essential for the proper functioning of the household. Indeed, Valeria recalled that she did not have to regularly cook until she was forty-three years old since her mother-in-law took care of practically everything in the household until her death.[192]

Leaving children with one's parents was a sensible option for Valeria, Ecaterina, and other respondents who lived near or in the same city as their parents; however, for those whose parents lived a considerable distance, it was difficult for child and parent alike. While only a few of my respondents had such an arrangement, they recalled the emotional strain of leaving their child, in some cases for weeks or months, with grandparents in the countryside. As Axinia recalled, "I sometimes didn't see him for months at a time, because it was very hard to find a good place at a crèche [where I worked]."[193] Similarly, Petre, who left his young son with his parents, emphasized, "The child felt the distance between us and him. Especially at two to three years of age when he knew that it was close to the time of our departure ... he knew and he cried."[194] These examples illustrate the shortcomings of state welfare policies and are especially ironic in light of the state's valorization of the family. While the state pushed women to bear more children, but also quickly return to the labor force, the institutional framework (e.g. onsite daycare) was insufficient for accommodating their children.

That said, those who left their toddlers with grandparents in the countryside also stressed the benefits, such as being with loved ones in the fresh, open air where they could play freely and away from the hustle and bustle of the city. Beyond that, grandparents, alongside other older relatives, played an important role in passing on traditions, often religious, to their grandchildren. Indeed, for children raised in urban areas and whose parents were not religious, grandparents—and particularly grandmothers—were often their only means of learning about religious customs and practices, including churchgoing.[195]

In some cases, women dealt with childcare challenges by "manipulating" their work schedules. As Stela recalled:

> There is a term in Romanian: "to play hooky." ... Well, I needed to be at work from seven to three ... and I was on the go a lot for work. I had to go from place to place and read [telephone meters], to interpret data. [And] in between two centers I would rush home and look after the children. ... I don't know, probably not many people were able to do that. And then there was my husband, once he got his job at the university he did his best to organize his schedule so that his classes were mainly in the afternoon, so he could stay with the kids in the morning when they had problems, were sick, and what have you.[196]

Because her daughter was often sick, Stela was unwilling to place her in a state-run nursery. Instead, she used the relative freedom of her job at the telephone company and her husband's position as a university professor to their advantage. Such behavior illustrates that individuals were willing to work the system if they felt their needs as workers, parents, and socialist citizens were not being met by state policies.

In some cases, families hired a retired woman, known as a *tanti*, or a younger nanny to look after the children. Because this practice involved an exchange of goods (usually money, though free room and board were also common), it constituted a part of the underground or second economy, though none of my respondents spoke of being secretive about such an arrangement.[197]

Mothers might also, in certain instances, leave infants at home alone to be checked on by neighbors. In other cases, they took them to work. As Eleanora, who bore her daughter in 1959 and was employed as an accountant at a state institute, recalled:

> She didn't stay at the crèche or nursery as she got sick easily, so I took her to work with me. She was very sweet and the administrative director loved her very much, he took her to his office. ... Because these were family people who had a [similar] situation, they were professors and such.[198]

Finally, a minority of families resolved the childcare dilemma by having one partner—almost always the woman—stay at home. This was especially the case during the early years of socialist rule when women's participation in paid labor was modest and the country was overwhelmingly agrarian; however, some urban women also chose to be full-time homemakers. This usually required that their husband earn a salary sufficient for supporting the entire family. Although these mothers were denied the same benefits granted to women workers, the trade-off was often worth it as they were able to devote time to their children and family, rather than to work and the attendant meetings and rallies. As Ioana recalled, "You know what was better? With one good salary it was possible for a woman to stay at home. I was able to raise the children, to shop, to prepare food, to go to the park with my family."[199]

Women's choice to stay home with their children could be interpreted as a form of resistance: by removing themselves from the productive sphere, such women were renouncing one of their state-mandated socialist identities and duties. Men, by contrast, did not have the option of taking refuge in the private sphere because there was no paternity leave and men continued to be regarded as the chief breadwinner. Although none of the stay-at-home mothers I interviewed articulated their experiences in terms of resistance, they clearly considered themselves fortunate to have been free of the demands of outside employment and thus able to devote themselves fully to their families. Moreover, rather than viewing the role of full-time homemaker as isolating or restricting—as some women in the West did during this period—they considered it liberating. Yet, because maintaining a good, or at least adequate, standard of living required two incomes (especially in the 1980s), only a minority of women were able to be stay-at-home mothers.

From a material perspective, life under socialism, especially during the first and final decade, created many difficulties for parents; however, not all mothers articulated their experiences in terms of sacrifice and frustration. Indeed, Lucia, who raised her children in the 1970s and 1980s, claimed that raising a child was easier during the communist period because she was able to take an extended maternity leave (followed by sick leave), which allowed her to stay home with her children for a few years:

> On the whole, I think it was easier than it is now for those who have young children. We managed, he [her husband] earned good money, the cost of living was good ... it didn't seem that difficult because I had him [my son] near me, I didn't have to leave him in the countryside with his grandparents like other parents did.[200]

For Tatiana, who took pride in her job at a factory, motherhood not only brought satisfaction but also a sense of accomplishment:

> I am very pleased ... how could I not be? I have nothing to reproach my children for. Even if sometimes I make fun of myself; me, who was raised in Moldavia in a poor village ... and, despite this, my kids are good ... they are well-educated. And me, coming from a small village, nevertheless I achieved something.[201]

The daughter of peasants, Tatiana measured her success as a mother through her children's educational achievements. This underscores the promise of upward mobility under socialism, whereby in a mere generation a woman could go from poor farm girl to factory worker and mother of university graduates. Ildiko similarly shared positive memories of raising her daughter in Săcele, a small town near Brașov, even though she attracted the scorn of some community members for bearing her child out of wedlock when she was twenty-four years old. Ildiko recalled:

> They looked down on me ... not my neighbors, but in general, like people from the country do. It was a small town, and in small towns everyone knows what everyone else is doing, and they talk behind your back: "And that one has a small child." But it didn't bother me because I wanted a child.[202]

As is evident from Ildiko's recollection, attitudes toward women who bore children outside of marriage remained conservative, despite the fact that the state recognized out-of-wedlock births and provided financial support for single mothers. Indeed, beginning in the early 1980s, around the time that Ildiko's daughter was born, motherhood was so highly valued by the state that teen pregnancy, traditionally a source of shame, was tolerated by the regime, and a proposal to allow pregnant teenage girls to continue high school by attending night school—rather than being expelled as stipulated in school rules—was briefly considered by the state.[203] Perhaps the regime's seeming laxity toward out-of-wedlock births and support of single mothers emboldened Ildiko to dismiss gossiping townspeople and take pride in her role as a single mother? Considering that she expressed no regrets about having borne a child out of wedlock and claimed that if she had to do things again she would still choose single motherhood, this is a distinct possibility.

## Conclusion

Reproductive and social welfare policies were used to reconstitute people's relationship to the state and nation and served to redefine both their civic and parental roles. Like other modernizing states, Romania's socialist government deemed a large population essential to a strong workforce and national greatness. Consequently, over the course of socialist rule, motherhood was transformed from a cultural practice that was encouraged and celebrated into a national duty required of all women of childbearing age. In an effort to achieve demographic goals, propagandists promoted shared parenting while also glorifying women's maternal roles. Additionally, they warned of the deleterious effects of abortion on women's reproductive health and of childlessness on women's psychological health. To promote fertility and incentivize motherhood, the state introduced a number of positive incentives, such as state-subsidized childcare and child allowances; however, as these measures did not significantly affect the birth rate, after 1966, the regime resorted to more repressive measures—the criminalization of abortion. Decree 770 served as a basis for policing women and physicians, as well as those who engaged in behaviors deemed contrary to the regime's demographic goals. Accordingly, women's civic roles were intricately bound up with producing offspring and contributing to national growth.

While the law banning abortion was easily flouted under Dej, under Ceaușescu this entailed great risk due to the intensification of surveillance and the implementation of draconian forms of punishment. Desperate to control their fertility, women self-induced or sought clandestine abortions outside of hospitals, at times from nonphysicians. In response, Romania's maternal mortality rate increased dramatically, undermining official justification of the decree, which emphasized concern about women's health and welfare. Because these practices were not arbitrary or incidental—but instead systematic—they constituted a specifically gendered form of state violence. As such, socialist Romania offers a rare example of women experiencing violence by a state during peacetime in the name of life. While women did not resist these policies in the form of public protests, by procuring an abortion (or choosing not to have children at all) they were effectively opposing the state. Given the real physical dangers and legal risks involved in this practice, women of childbearing age were thus engaged in prolonged acts of resistance against the state under Ceaușescu.

Alongside pronatalist policies, families were faced with caring for their children in often less-than-ideal circumstances. In particular, during the 1980s women had to contend with utility and food shortages, which hampered their ability to feed, clothe, and, in some cases, bathe and keep warm their infants. Moreover, many were critical of the short (from a non-U.S. perspective) maternity leave and were resistant to leaving their infants in crèches and nurseries where they were more prone to illness. In response, they devised clever strategies for maximizing the time spent with their newborns, drawing on traditional as well as socialist discourses about motherhood to persuade doctors to extend maternity leave or grant sick leave. Many families also relied on informal forms of childcare such as nannies and grandparents, traditional practices which had both advantages and disadvantages and which compensated for state failure to deliver on one of socialism's basic promises to women—provision of universal and high-quality childcare.

While women stressed the inhumanity of pronatalist policies, they did not totally color women's experiences of motherhood. Indeed, what unified most respondents was the centrality of motherhood and family in shaping their identities, experiences, and sense of self-worth under socialism. Although some women also took great satisfaction in their jobs, for the vast majority, family life was the most rewarding aspect of their lives during socialism. This is not to trivialize the stress and real physical dangers women faced as a result of Ceaușescu's policies, but to assert that the experience of motherhood and of raising a family could also be highly rewarding—and, in some cases, a type of resistance to interventionist state policies.

## Notes

1. On abortion as a form of resistance, see Maria Bucur, "Gendering Dissent: Of Bodies and Minds, Survival and Opposition under Communism," in *Beyond Little Vera: Women's Bodies, Women's Welfare in Russia and Central/Eastern Europe*, ed. Angela Brintlinger and Natasha Kolchevska, *Ohio Slavic Papers*, vol. 7 (2008): 9–26.
2. For reflections on motherhood in Romania, see Mihaela Miroiu and Otilia Dragomir, *Nașterea: Istorii trăite* (Iași: Polirom, 2010).
3. In 1900, the fertility rate stood at 5.26 children per woman. Vladimir Trebici and I. Ghinoiu, *Demografie și etnografie* (Bucharest: Editura Științifică și Enciclopedică, 1986), 78; and Jean Claude Chenais, *The Demographic Transition: Stages, Patterns, and Economic Implications: A Longitudinal Study of 67 Countries Covering the Period 1720–1984* (Oxford: Oxford University Press, 1992), 527.
4. Henry P. David and Robert J. McIntyre, *Reproductive Behavior: Central and Eastern European Experience* (New York: Springer, 1981), 178.
5. Ibid., 250; 284. Figures for fertility rates in various countries in 1950 are as follows: Bulgaria: 2.94; Czechoslovakia: 3.02; Poland: 3.71; Hungary: 2.6; and Romania 3.14.
6. This measure built on the Penal Code of 1936 by punishing women who procured and doctors who performed abortions outside of hospitals. Consiliul Legislativ, "Legea Nr. 18/1948 din februarie pentru modificarea codului de procedură civilă," in *Colecțiune de Legi și Regulamente 1948* (Bucharest: Imprimeria Centrală, 1948).
7. The law was not strictly enforced and thus punishments for transgressing it were few and not severe.
8. The exception was Albania, where it was never legalized during the socialist period.
9. Abortion was legalized in Great Britain in 1967, in Denmark in 1973, in France in 1975, and in Italy in 1978. These countries all experienced population surges (baby booms) between 1946 and the 1960s.
10. On the return to traditional gender roles in West Germany see Robert Moeller, *Protecting Motherhood: Women and the Family in the Politics of Postwar West Germany* (Berkeley: University of California Press, 1993).
11. "Codul Muncii din 1950 (Lege nr. 3 din 30 mai 1950)" *Buletin Oficial al Republicii Populare Române* nr. 50 din 8 iunie 1950. Women employed for at least 12 months of uninterrupted work prior to taking leave received 90 percent of their salary while those employed for less than 12 months prior to taking leave received 70 percent of their salary. To be eligible for maternity leave benefits, a woman had to be employed for at least 4 months of the 12 months prior to taking the leave. In cases of an ill child, mothers could take leave until the child reached 2 years of age. In 1956 maternity leave was extended to 112 days (52 days prenatal and 60 days postnatal). See "Decret pentru modificarea Codului Muncii," *Buletin Oficial al Republicii Populare Române*, nr. 20, 24 iulie 1956.

12. "Femeile—o mare forță in slujba păcii și progresului," *Scânteia*, 8 March 1957, 1. The title and award "mama eroina" was bestowed on women who bore and raised ten children, while the title "gloria materna" was for mothers who bore and raised seven to nine children (with different ranks for each). The "maternity medal" was given to women who bore and raised five or six children.
13. Beginning in 1950, a one-time payment of 20,000 lei was awarded to women for each additional child born after the tenth child (on the condition that the first eight children were still alive). See ANIC, Consiliul de Stat Decrete, dosar 3/150, vol. I, f., 142; and Decretul nr. 106/1950, "Expunere de motive." In 1950, 20,000 lei was approximately $100. After the monetary reform in 1952, 20,000 lei was equal to 1,000 lei ($89). See International Monetary Fund, *International Monetary Reform Annual Report* (IMF: Washington DC, 1952), 75, retrieved at http://www.imf.org/external/pubs/ft/ar/archive/pdf/ar1952.pdf (accessed 16 February 2018).
14. "Familie Numeroasă," *Scânteia*, 8 March 1955, 2.
15. On the historical confluence of these duties, see Maria Todorova, "Historical Tradition and Transformation in Bulgaria: Women's Issues or Feminist Issues?," *Journal of Women's History* 5, no. 3 (1994): 129–143.
16. On the gendering of family roles through welfare entitlements, see Jane Lewis, *The Politics of Motherhood: Child and Maternal Welfare in England, 1900–1939* (London: Croom Helm, 1980); and Susan Pederson, *Family, Dependence and the Origin of the Welfare State: Britain and France, 1914–1945* (Cambridge: Cambridge University Press, 1993). For feminist critiques of the welfare state in socialist Eastern Europe, see Barbara Einhorn, *Cinderella Goes to Market: Citizenship, Gender, and Women's Movements in East Central Europe* (London: Verso, 1993); and Katherine Verdery, *What Was Socialism, and What Comes Next?* (Princeton, NJ: Princeton University Press, 1996).
17. On childcare and maternity benefits in Britain and West Germany, see Jane Lewis, ed., *Women and Social Policies in Europe: Work, Family, and the State* (London: Edward Elgar, 1993), 17–19.
18. Domnica, interview with author, Brașov, 22 June 2003.
19. Prof. Ion Dragan, "Cine-i vinovatul?" *Femeia*, June 1959, 21–22.
20. Zoe Filimon, "Ambii părinți răspund de educația copiilor," *Femeia*, February 1961, 18.
21. Dr. V. Ivanov, "Cum să luptăm împotriva alcoolismului," *Femeia*, August 1957, 6.
22. "Cum vă creșteți copiii?" *Femeia*, September 1961, 16.
23. Tania Tudose, "O nobilă misiune: roadele colaborării" *Femeia*, January 1964, 20–21.
24. Ibid.
25. Elisabeta Bratescu, "Sănătatea familiei se afla in miinile femeii," *Femeia*, August 1973, 24.
26. See *Femeia*, April 1979.
27. *Scânteia*, 8 March 1981, 1.

28. As shown in the film *Născuți la comandă: Decrețeii*, directed by Florin Iepan (West End Film, 2005).
29. ANIC, CC al PCR, Secția Cancelarie, dosar 101/1966, f. 120; *Anuarul Statistic al Republicii Socialiste România*.
30. Henry P. David, ed., with the assistance of Joanna Skilogianis, *From Abortion to Contraception: A Resource to Public Policies and Reproductive Behavior in Central and Eastern Europe from 1917 to the Present* (Westport, CT: Greenwood Press, 1999), 54, 72–73, 94–95, 126–27, 148–49, 168–69.
31. "Decretul nr. 463/1957," *Buletinul Oficial al Republicii Populare Române*, din 26–30 septembrie 1957; and "Decretul nr. 469/1957 pentru modificarea Codului Penal," *Buletinul Oficial al Republicii Populare Române*, nr. 26, din 3 octombrie 1957. According to this law, a legal abortion could only be approved by a medical commission if it was performed during the first trimester by a medical professional in a state hospital or clinic. In instances where the woman could not be taken to a hospital in time, the abortion was considered legal if the doctor reported it to the authorities within twenty-four hours of the procedure.
32. A number of East European countries legalized abortion during the mid-1950s, though some restrictions remained in place. In 1955 the USSR legalized abortion on demand, followed by Bulgaria and Hungary in 1965 and Romania in 1957. Meanwhile, after much public pressure, abortion was liberalized in Poland in 1956 to include women under "exceptionally difficult life conditions," which meant that "abortion was legal only for mothers of many children who were already living in poverty." See Malgorzata Fidelis, *Women, Communism, and Industrialization in Postwar Poland* (New York: Cambridge University Press, 2010), 191. The exception here is Albania, where abortion remained illegal throughout socialist rule and could only be performed if approved by a medical committee. For a detailed discussion of abortion legislation in the Eastern Bloc, see Corina Doboș, Luciana Jinga, and Florin Soare, *Politica pronatalistă a regimului Ceaușescu: O perspectivă comparativă, vol. 1* (Bucharest: Polirom, 2010), 36–37.
33. On the lack of childcare facilities and schools in new industrial towns in Poland, see Katherine Lebow, *Unfinished Utopia: Nowa Huta, Stalinism, and Polish Society, 1949–56* (Ithaca, NY: Cornell University Press, 2013), 116.
34. The actual figure is certainly much higher since many abortions occurred outside of state clinics and hospitals and were not recorded. See Doboș et al., *Politica pronatalistă vol. 1*, 114–15.
35. See Chenais, *Demographic Transition*; and Gail Kligman, *The Politics of Duplicity: Controlling Reproduction in Ceaușescu's Romania* (Berkeley: University of California Press, 1998), 52. Indeed, at the time, Romania had the second lowest birth rate in all of Europe.
36. For example, in 1965 the fertility rate in Bulgaria was 2.08; in the GDR 2.48; in Hungary 1.81; and in Czechoslovakia 2.3, figures that continued to decline. See David and McIntyre, *Reproductive Behavior: Central and Eastern European Experience*.

37. These specialists were drawn from medicine, demography, and genetics. In addition to material conditions, the committee also proposed sex education for the population. See Raluca Maria Popa, "Corpuri femeieşti, putere bărbătească: Studiu de caz asupra adoptării reglementărilor legislative de interzicere a avortului în România comunistă (1966)," in *Gen şi putere: Partea leului în politica romanească*, ed. Oana Băluţă (Iaşi: Editura Polirom, 2006), 65–67.
38. "Studiu privind situaţiia natalatăţii din Republica Socialistă România şi propuneri de măsuri pentru redresarea natalităţii în ţara noastră," ANIC, CC al PCR, Secţia Cancelarie, dosar 101/1966, f. 102–27. See also Raluca Maria Popa, "We Opposed It: The National Council of Women and the Ban on Abortion in Romania (1966)," *Aspasia: International Yearbook of Central, Eastern, and Southeastern European Women's and Gender History* 9 (2016): 152–160.
39. It should be noted that some members of the Executive Committee argued for a more moderate approach, emphasizing that restrictions to abortion should be implemented in a "rational" way, permitting individuals to decide how large their families should be.
40. For a comprehensive discussion of the Executive Committee debates about approaches to increasing the birth rate, see Doboş et. al., *Politica pronatalistă vol. 1*, 126–29; and ANIC, CC al PCR, Secţia Administrative-Politică, dosar 102/1966, f. 31.
41. ANIC, CC al PCR, Secţia Cancelarie, dosar 102/1966, f. 23.
42. *Scânteia*, 2 October 1966, 1.
43. Ibid., 5.
44. "Decretul nr. 770 din octombrie 1966 pentru reglementarea întreruperii cursului sarcinii," *Buletinul Oficial al Republicii Socialiste România*, 1 octombrie 1966. In 1972, the minimum age eligibility for a legal abortion was lowered to 40; in 1984 it was increased to 45 again. In the case of rape or incest, the abortion could be performed only during the first trimester and the procedure had to be legally verified.
45. The medical indications were grouped into eighteen categories and included infectious diseases, tuberculosis, syphilis, heart disease, urinary and kidney disease, and blood disease, among others.
46. This period was extended to the second trimester in cases where a "pathological condition" presented a danger to the life of the woman. See Doboş et al., *Politica pronatalistă vol. 1*, 133.
47. Failure to notify the authorities could result in a fine of one to three months imprisonment for the doctor. Art. 482, "Decret pentru modificarea Codului penal," *Buletinul Oficial al Republicii Socialiste România*, 1 octombrie 1966.
48. Ibid. The sentence varied according to a number of factors, including if the woman died as a result of the procedure, which garnered the most severe sentence. If a first infraction, doctors typically did not lose their license, but were demoted to another job in medicine or were sent to work in a rural area. Given prison overcrowding, imprisonment typically referred to time in a correctional facility and was justified on the basis that all individuals could be reeducated.

49. See Kligman, *Politics of Duplicity*, 55–57.
50. "Decret privind majorarea impozitului pe veniturile persoanelor fără copii," *Buletinul Oficial al Republicii Socialiste România*, partea I, anul II, nr. 88, 31 decembrie 1966; and "Lege 1/1977 privind impozitul pe fondul total de retribuire al unităţilor de stat," 30 iunie 1977" *Buletinul Oficial al Republicii Socialiste România*, nr. 60 din 8 iunie 1977.
51. *Femeia*, March 1967, 4. This study was republished in *Femeia* in the 1980s.
52. "According to the 1968 Penal Code, same-sex relations committed in public or resulting in a public scandal were punishable by one to five years in prison. If these relations occurred with a minor, imprisonment (for the adult) could be two to seven years and include the loss of certain rights. Meanwhile, inciting or encouraging same-sex relations could lead to one to five years in prison. See "Infracţiuni Privitoare la Viaţă Sexuală" (Article 200) in "Codul Penal din 1968" *Monitorul Oficial al României*, 1 ianuarie 1969. On blackmailing homosexuals to collaborate with the Securitate and on the use of homosexuality as a charge against dissidents and others who criticized the regime, see Irina Costache, "Archiving Desire: Materiality, Sexuality, and the Secret Police in Romanian State Socialism" (PhD diss., Central European University, 2014), 166–67; and Marius Oprea, *Banalitatea răului: o istorie a Securităţii în documente 1949–1989* (Iaşi: Polirom, 2002).
53. Karen Offen, "Depopulation, Nationalism, and Feminism in Fin-de-Siecle France," *American Historical Review* 89, no. 3 (June 1984): 648–76; Atina Grossman, "Abortion and Economic Crisis: The 1931 Campaign against Paragraph 218," in *When Biology Became Destiny: Women in Weimar and Nazi Germany*, ed. Renate Bridenthal, Atina Grossman, and Marion Kaplan (New York: Monthly Review Press, 1984), 66–86; and De Grazia, *How Fascism Ruled Women*, 42.
54. See Gisela Bock, "Racism and Sexism in Nazi Germany: Motherhood, Compulsory Sterilization, and the State," in *When Biology Became Destiny*, 271–96.
55. For an analysis of the role of economic factors influencing Ceauşescu's pronatalist policies, including a breakdown of the proposed and accepted expenditures associated with them, see Florin S. Soare, "Ceauşescu's Population Policy: A Moral or an Economic Choice between Compulsory and Voluntary Incentivized Motherhood," *European Journal of Government and Economics* 2, no. 1 (2013): 59–78.
56. For instance, beginning in 1967, the one-time payment of 1,000 lei ($84), which, prior to the currency reform in 1952 was 20,000 lei, was granted to mothers upon the birth of a third child—regardless if her previous children were still alive. Moreover, beginning in 1966, modest allowances were granted to families (if one or both parents were employed) for each child until the child reached age 14 (if a child with a disability, ages 16–18). These allowances were based on family income and location (rural vs. urban) and thus urban families in the lowest wage category could ostensibly benefit most. Families that earned more than 3,500 lei ($294 in 1967) per month were not eligible for the allowance. The allowances increased slightly in 1969 and 1971, especially for families with

three or more children—a trend that continued in the years that followed. For specific details and tables see Doboş et al., *Politica pronatalistă vol. 1*, 230–238.
57. See Verdery, *What Was Socialism?*, in particular chapter 3.
58. *Programul Partidului Comunist de făurire a societăţii socialiste multilateral dezvoltate şi înaintare a României spre comunism* (Bucharest: Editura Politică, 1975), 68. This program also included birth targets.
59. Exceptions were made in case of incest, rape, or for medical reasons or other "grave circumstances." Meanwhile, those with one or two children needed permission from a medical commission in order to procure an abortion. David and McIntyre, *Reproductive Behavior*, 72.
60. In Hungary abortions were restricted to women who were unmarried, had two or more children, had housing problems, were over thirty-five, or had serious health problems. See Lynne Haney, *Inventing the Needy: Gender and the Politics of Welfare in Hungary* (Berkeley: University of California Press, 2002), 92.
61. For instance, over the course of the 1970s, paid maternity leave was extended in East Germany, reaching twenty-six weeks by 1976. In that year, the "baby year" (*Babyjahr*) was also introduced, which provided women with up to one year's paid leave for the second child and additional children. Moreover, Hungary, through universal child allowances, birth payments, extended maternity leave, and the option for part-time work, promoted conditions more conducive to child rearing; though these incentives were also a response to slowed economic growth and labor redundancy (e.g. an effort to push women out of the labor force). See Donna Harsch, *Revenge of the Domestic: Women, the Family, and Communism in the German Democratic Republic* (Princeton, NJ: Princeton University Press, 2006); and Haney, *Inventing the Needy*, 92–93.
62. Documentary films included, "Family: the basis of society," and "Intimate life." See Raluca Ioana Horea-Şerban and Marinela Istrate, "Rolul presei scrise în promovarea politicii pronataliste," in *După 25 de ani Comunismul în Europa de Est: Statutul Femeii în România Comunistă: Politici publice şi viaţă privată*, ed., Alina Hurubean (Iaşi: Institutul European, 2015), 152.
63. Luciana Jinga, Florin S. Soare, Corina Doboş, and Cristina Roman, *Politica pronatalistă a regimului Ceauşescu: Vol. 2 Instituţii şi practici* (Iaşi: Polirom, 2011), 10. It should be noted that while they were also of childbearing age when abortion was illegal from 1948–1957, due to lax enforcement of the law they would not have experienced difficulties procuring an abortion.
64. See Popa, "We Opposed It."
65. Dr. Petre Popescu, "Cele 280 de Zile Miraculoase," *Femeia*, December 1972, 33.
66. See Maria Şerban, "Copilul Meu: Cel mai frumos din lume," *Femeia*, November 1966, 1–3.
67. Dr. Petre Popescu, "Sterilitatea feminină secundară," *Femeia*, December 1966, 19. As noted in other articles, this condition was linked to curettage, which could damage the uterine wall or injure the fallopian tubes, as well

as produce cervical ruptures, which, in turn, could lead to infrequent or the total cessation of menstruation.
68. See Dr. Petre Popescu, "În atenţia tinerelor căsătorite: păstraţi primele sarcini!" *Femeia*, October 1972, 29.
69. See "Infertilitatea este şi de tip masculin?" *Femeia*, February 1985, 21. Reasons for male infertility included immunological and genetic factors, genital inflammation or abnormalities, hormonal irregularities and venereal diseases, particularly gonorrhea.
70. "Consecinţele avortului," *Femeia*, March 1983, 21.
71. "Anticoncepţionale generatoare de diabet," *Muncitorul Sanitar*, September 1966.
72. Tania Tudose, "Şcoala Mamei," *Femeia*, January 1967.
73. "Eu Sunt o mamă fericită," *Femeia*, December 1983, 12. This was similar to propaganda efforts in the GDR in the 1950s, particularly the work of social hygienist Rudolf Neubert, who presented children as the "root" of every healthy marriage while criticizing childless couples and single- and dual-child households, asserting, "Life only becomes full with three children. With four to six children it becomes really varied, cheerful, and complete." Rudolf Neubert, *Das neue Ehebuch: Die Ehe als Aufgabe der Gegenwart und Zukunft* (Rudolstadt: Greifenverlag, 1957), 270–71.
74. For example, in 1979 women who had not finished primary school bore 2.94 children on average, while those who did bore 2.58. Meanwhile, women with a high school education bore 1.58 children, and those with an advanced degree bore 1.67. Differences also existed with respect to occupational sector. While women in agriculture bore 2.9 children, unskilled workers bore 2.21, and skilled workers 1.71. Meanwhile, professional women bore 1.32. See Georgeta Ghebrea, *Regim social-politic şi viaţă privată: familia şi politica familială în România* (Bucharest: Editura Universităţii din Bucureşti, 2000), 35–36.
75. See *Femeia*, May 1985, 12.
76. Sanda Faur, "Cu fiecare copil trăieşti o viaţa în plus," *Femeia*, October 1985, 13. For a similar story, see "Ne bucurăm de ei, de copilaşii noştrii," *Femeia*, August 1989, 13.
77. Ibid.
78. Elisabeta Moraru, "Familia nu-i o piedică, ci un stimulent în ascensiunea femeii," *Femeia*, February 1980, 4.
79. Doboş et al., *Politica pronatalistă*, vol. *1*, 137.
80. By 1973 the rate stood at 2.4 children per family and ranged anywhere between 1.9 and 2.5 throughout the remainder of socialist rule.
81. Some respondents noted that the exams were performed more frequently.
82. Doina, interview with author, Braşov, 10 June 2003.
83. Factories employing more than twenty-five hundred women were obliged to have a gynecologist on staff. Jinga et al., *Politica pronatalistă vol. 2*, 42. The scale on which these exams were conducted, at least according to official data, is astounding. One report indicated that sixty-five hundred women of childbearing age had been examined in one month. See Kligman, *Politics of Duplicity*, 102, 154.

84. Letter from a group of young women to Elena Ceauşescu, Bucharest, June 1984, broadcast in Romania via Radio Free Europe on 22 July 1984, in Gabriel Andreescu and Mihnea Berindei, *Ultimul deceniu comunist: Scrisori către Radio Europa Liberă vol. I, (1979–1985)* (Iaşi: Polirom, 2010), 282–83.
85. Ibid.
86. Kligman, *Politics of Duplicity*, 153–55.
87. Ecaterina, interview with author, Braşov, 17 June 2003.
88. Unlawful use of hospital surgical instruments could lead to three months to one year in a correctional facility. Art. 482, "Decret pentru modificarea Codului penal," *Buletinul Oficial al Republicii Socialiste România*, 1 octombrie 1966.
89. Corina Doboş and Florin S. Soare, "Cei din lume fără nume: Politica pronatalistă a regimului Ceauşescu," museum exhibition brochure, retrieved from http://politicapronatalista.iiccr.ro/ 8–9 (accessed 14 May 2016).
90. In some cases these individuals were neither doctors nor midwives but mechanics and engineers.
91. "Structura persoanelor condamnate definitiv pentru săvârşirea infracţiunilor de avort (art.185, Cod penal), în anul 1986," in Luciana Jinga, Florin S. Soare, eds., *Politica pronatalistă a regimului Ceauşescu, vol. 2* (Iaşi: Polirom, 2011), 148.
92. Lavinia Betea, "Interzicerea avorturilor (1966–1989) ca fapt de memorie socială," in *Viaţa cotidiană în comunism*, ed. Adrian Neculau (Iaşi: Polirom, 2004), 252. Monetary conversions based on U.S. Treasury Reporting Rates of Exchange (31 March 1984), retrieved from https://www.gpo.gov/fdsys/pkg/GOVPUB-T63_100-82fa234e35ee5a4b0d2af3d1540a4fca/pdf/GOVPUB-T63_100-82fa234e35ee5a4b0d2af3d1540a4fca.pdf (accessed 20 November 2017).
93. See the film *Four Months, Three Weeks, and Two Days* directed by Cristian Mungiu (Bucharest: BAC Films, 2007). For the screenplay, Mungiu used women's actual abortion stories.
94. Adriana, interview with author, Bucharest, 3 June 2012.
95. See Kligman, *Politics of Duplicity*, 66; and Henry David and Adriana Băban, "Women's Health and Reproductive Rights: Romanian Experience," *Patient Education and Counseling* 28, no. 3 (1996), on the array of methods used by women to induce abortions.
96. David and Băban, "Women's Health and Reproductive Rights," 241.
97. Doboş and Soare "Cei din lume fără nume," 13.
98. Kligman, *Politics of Duplicity*, 66.
99. Nicolae Ceauşescu, "Mesajul adresat femeilor din Republica Socialistă România cu prilejul Zilei internaţionale a femeii," *Scânteia*, 8 March 1986, 1.
100. See Art. 482 "Decret pentru modificarea Codului penal," *Buletinul Oficial al Republicii Socialiste România*, 1 octombrie 1966. It should be noted that punishment for illegal abortion in Albania was also quite punitive, with women receiving "reeducation through work" or being thrown in detention centers.

101. Angela, interview with author, Braşov, 16 June 2003.
102. Sanda Faur, "În numele vieţii acuz!" *Femeia*, April 1974.
103. Ibid. According to the article, the nurses helped him identify clients, pilfer anesthesia from the hospital, and find homes in which to perform the abortions.
104. Interestingly, no mention is made of returning the funds to patients' relatives. Monetary conversions based on U.S. Treasury Reporting Rates of Exchange as of 31 March 1974, retrieved from, U.S. Treasury Reporting Rates of Exchange as of 31 March 1985 retrieved from, https://www.gpo.gov/fdsys/pkg/GOVPUB-T63_100-7eddaf4273a66e80b5be6d4909795a8e/pdf/GOVPUB-T63_100-7eddaf4273a66e80b5be6d4909795a8e.pdf (accessed: 26 November 2017).
105. Faur, "În numele vieţii acuz!"
106. Instead, I asked respondents more generally about the law banning abortion in 1966 and its effects on women and families. This provided women the opportunity to share whatever experiences they felt most comfortable with.
107. Betea, "Interzicerea avorturilor," 253.
108. Lorena Anton, "On Memory Work in Post-communist Europe: A Case Study on Romania's Ways of Remembering its Pronatalist Past," *Anthropological Journal of European Cultures* 18, no. 2 (2009): 106–22.
109. C., interview with author, Bucharest, 18 July 2009.
110. Doboş and Soare, "Cei din lume fără nume," 24.
111. E., interview with author, Bucharest, 2 June 2009.
112. Ibid. E.'s reference to the Palme D'or Prize was in relation to the film *Four Months, Three Weeks, and Two Days*, which won the award in 2007.
113. Doboş and Soare, "Cei din lume fără nume," 8.
114. E., interview with author, Bucharest, 2 June 2009.
115. Indeed, even doctors lacked knowledge about the safety and effectiveness of particular methods of contraception. For example, as late as 1990–91 some doctors promoted abortion as the safest form of birth control. Information courtesy of Maria Bucur, Spring 2007.
116. That said, there are reports of men helping their wives.
117. Livia, interview with Ioana Manoliu, Braşov, 11 August 2003.
118. Marcela, interview with Anca Coman, Braşov, 12 August 2003.
119. Corina, interview with Ioana Manoliu, Braşov, 22 July 2003.
120. See the interviews with doctors and nurses in the film *Născuţi la comandă*.
121. Doboş and Soare, "Cei din lume fără nume."
122. I thank Jan C. Behrends for the link to Stalinist confessions.
123. Muriel Blaive, "State Violence over the Female Body," 44th Annual Convention of the Association for Slavic, East European, and Eurasian Studies, New Orleans, LA, 16 November 2012.
124. Eugenia, interview with author, Bucharest, 12 June 2009.
125. Kligman, *Politics of Duplicity*, 214.
126. Ibid.
127. CEDAW was signed by Romania in 1980. According to its "General Recommendation on Women and Health," the signatory state was obligated to "respect, protect and fulfill women's rights to health care" and could not institute legal or policy barriers to healthcare access or obstruct pur-

suit of women's health goals. The state was also obligated to prevent and punish violations of this right—particularly in the form of violence against women—by private persons and organizations. "Convention on the Elimination of all Forms of Discrimination against Women," retrieved from, http://www.un.org/womenwatch/daw/cedaw/ (accessed 5 April 2016).

128. As Cristian Pop-Eleches has demonstrated, the fertility rate of less-educated women increased the most between 1966 and 1989, indicating that they were less successful in procuring abortions than professional women. See Cristian Pop-Eleches, "The Supply of Birth Control Methods, Education, and Fertility: Evidence from Romania," *Journal of Human Resources* 45, no. 4 (Fall 2010): 994–95.

129. The film was based on the death of Maria Goran and the abortionist Trandafira Popescu, the latter of whom served seven years in prison and then, upon release, went on to perform abortions for another twenty years. *Ilustrate cu Flori de Câmp*, directed by Andrei Blaier (Bucharest: România Film, 1974).

130. Vasile Tincu, "Orfanii," *Femeia*, April 1987, 12. Similarly, the article "Dincolo de lacrimi," (Beyond Tears; *Femeia*, October 1986, 11) told the story of a mother of seven who died as a result of an illegal abortion.

131. Tincu, "Orfanii."

132. "Unde eşti, mamico?" *Femeia*, July 1988, 10.

133. Luciana Jinga, *Gen şi reprezentare în România comunistă, 1944–1989* (Iaşi: Polirom, 2015), 144.

134. The number of women who officially died from abortion-related complications increased from 143 in 1967 to 545 in 1989. See Jinga et al., *vol 2, Politica pronatalistă*, 177.

135. Ibid.

136. Meanwhile, between 1967 and 1989 an estimated 327,646 children under age one died.

137. Doboş et al., *Politica pronatalistă, vol. 1*. The number of institutionalized children in Romania was about double and, in some cases, triple the rate of neighboring states.

138. Ibid.

139. The plight of Romanian orphans was brought to Americans' attention via the ABC news program *20/20*. See "Romanian Orphans," interview by Barbara Walters and Hugh Downs, aired 5 October 1990.

140. The most notorious of these orphanages, Cighid, which included physically disabled children and others deemed "non-productive members of society," was referred to as an "extermination camp" by its former director. See "Casa de Copii," Cighid, March 1990, ProTV, retrieved from http://www.youtube.com/watch?v=ILDf4r0f0gk (accessed 23 July 2013).

141. Sada Faur, "Imensa grijă cu care ţara îsi veghează copiii," *Femeia*, February 1985, 9.

142. Jinga, *Gen şi reprezentare*.

143. "Decree 410," *Buletinul Oficial*, no. 76, 26 December 1985; and Doboş et al., *Politica pronatalistă, vol. 1.*, 234. Rural families in the lowest income bracket also benefited, though less so than their urban counterparts. For instance, rural families supplemented household income by 50 percent. The average

monthly salary in 1985 was 2,872 lei ($221), *Anuarul Statistic al României*, 1990, 123. Monetary conversions based on U.S. Treasury Reporting Rates of Exchange as of 31 March 1985, retrieved from, https://www.gpo.gov/fdsys/pkg/GOVPUB-T63_100-7eddaf4273a66e80b5be6d4909795a8e/pdf/GOVPUB-T63_100-7eddaf4273a66e80b5be6d4909795a8e.pdf (accessed: 26 October 2017).

144. For example, women who bore and reared ten children received a one-time bonus of 2,000 lei, while those who bore and reared nine received a one-time bonus of 1,500 lei. Kligman, *Politics of Duplicity*, 81.
145. Personal communication with Mihaela Miroiu, March 2007. There were no breast pumps in Romania at this time, hence the high demand for infant formula.
146. Elisabeta, interview with author, Braşov, 27 June 2003.
147. See Bucur, "Gendering Dissent."
148. For an analysis of how women's experiences of Ceauşescu's pronatalism have been obscured at Romania's premier museum of communism, Sighet, see Alina Haliluic, "Who Is a Victim of Communism? Gender and Public Memory in the Sighet Museum, Romania," *Aspasia: International Yearbook of Central, Eastern, and Southeastern European Women's and Gender History* 7 (2013): 108–31.
149. In 1986 surgical sterilization and use of IUDs were prohibited "Ordinul ministrului Sănătăţii nr. 300 din 18 august 1986 privind interzicerea sterilizării chirurgicale prin ligatura trompelor şi utilizarea steriletelor," *Buletinul Ministrului Sănătăţii*, 1987.
150. Ecaterina, interview with author, Braşov, 17 June 2003.
151. Interview with Valeria R., Braşov, 2 May 2003.
152. In East Germany, by contrast, the pill was the established choice of birth control by the end of the 1970s.
153. Doboş et al., *Politica pronatalistă vol. 1*, 164.
154. As Kligman notes, condoms were still produced commercially in Romania in the 1970s; however, by the 1980s they were unavailable. Kligman, *Politics of Duplicity*, 65. Individuals also received packages of condoms and birth control pills from the West. See Thomas Keil and Viviana Andreescu, "Fertility Policy in Ceausescu's Romania," *Journal of Family History* 24, no. 4 (1999): 481.
155. ANIC, CC al PCR, Secţia Cancelarie, dosar 181/1966.
156. As quoted in Popa, "Corpuri femeieşti," 111.
157. "O mama nefericită pentru tot restul vieţii," letter, written on 21 June 1983; broadcast in Romania on Radio Free Europe 4 September 1983, in *Ultimul Deceniu Comunist*, 177–78.
158. Livia, interview with Ioana Manoliu, Braşov, 11 August 2003.
159. C., interview with author, Braşov, 14 July 2003.
160. Doina, interview with author, Braşov, 10 June 2003.
161. F., interview with author, Braşov, 9 June 2003.
162. Under article 197 of the Penal Code, rape (of a woman) was punishable with two to seven years imprisonment and three to ten years if the victim was under 14. Marital rape was not illegal.
163. C., interview with author, Braşov, 14 July 2003.

164. For a discussion of this issue, see *Născuți la comanda*.
165. Angela, interview with author, Brașov, 16 June 2003.
166. See Hana Havelková, "A Few Pre-feminist Thoughts," in *Gender Politics and Post-Communism: Reflections from Eastern Europe and the Former Soviet Union*, ed. Nanette Funk and Magda Mueller (New York: Routledge, 1993), 62–67.
167. D., interview with author, Brașov, 10 June 2003.
168. Regine, interview with author, Brașov, 2 July 2003.
169. C., interview with author, Brașov, 14 July 2003.
170. Maria, interview with author, Brașov, 15 June 2003.
171. This is not to say children and especially infants did not suffer. In addition to being malnourished, some infants actually died due to electricity cuts and lack of medicine. For instance, in the winter of 1984–85 alone, it is estimated that over 30 children died due to unannounced power cuts, which impeded the functioning of incubators. See Denis Deletant, *Ceaușescu and the Securitate: Coercion and Dissent in Romania, 1965–89* (London: Hurst and Company, 1995).
172. Floarea Berendei, "Letter to Elena Ceaușescu," ANIC, CC al PCR, Secția Organizatorică, 1921–1975, dosar 1973/213, f., 1–2.
173. Ibid.
174. Stela, interview with author, Brașov, 23 June 2003.
175. Elvira, interview with author, Brașov, 5 May 2003.
176. On the mobilization of maternal identities by women in the GDR and Hungary, see Harsch, *Revenge of the Domestic*; and Haney, *Inventing the Needy*.
177. Harsch, *Revenge of the Domestic*, 7.
178. Communication with Mihaela Miroiu, Spring 2007. This figure is for 1985. Monetary conversions based on U.S. Treasury Reporting Rates of Exchange as of 31 March 1985, retrieved from https://www.gpo.gov/fdsys/pkg/GOVPUB-T63_100-7eddaf4273a66e80b5be6d4909795a8e/pdf/GOVPUB-T63_100-7eddaf4273a66e80b5be6d4909795a8e.pdf (accessed 26 October 2017)
179. Haney, *Inventing the Needy*, 87.
180. Art. 157, "Codul Muncii (Legea nr. 10 din 25 noiembrie, 1972)," *Buletinul Oficial al Republicii Socialiste România*, nr. 140 din 1 decembrie 1972.
181. Cătălina, interview with author, Bucharest, 18 July 2009.
182. It should be recalled that during Central Committee debates (and prior to the passage of Decree 770) prolonging maternity leave was disregarded in favor of increasing the number of crèches, particularly those located in factories. Soare, "Ceaușescu's Population Policy," 73.
183. By the 1980s, the student-teacher ratio for nursery schools was roughly 26:1, and for kindergartens 27:1.
184. Corina, interview with author, Brașov, 15 July 2003.
185. Maria, interview with author, Brașov, 15 June 2003.
186. Although public primary and secondary schooling is currently free of charge in Romania, nursery schools are typically private or need-based. Consequently, childcare now constitutes a significant portion of the family budget.
187. Kligman, *Politics of Duplicity*, 83.

188. According to a World Bank Country Study, monthly expenditures on food for a family of four in Romania in 1989 (when costs were at their highest) were 2,930 lei ($325). Meanwhile the average monthly salary for those living in urban areas was 2,827 lei ($314) *World Bank Country Study: Romania*, 1990, 70. Monetary conversions based on U.S. Treasury Reporting Rates of Exchange as of 31 March 1989, retrieved from https://www.gpo.gov/fdsys/pkg/GOVPUB-T63_100-276b568c5ae9cf79608bff08c5054273/pdf/GOVPUB-T63_100-276b568c5ae9cf79608bff08c5054273.pdf (accessed 30 October 2017).
189. Haney found that status and connections played an important role in securing daycare in socialist Hungary. Haney, *Inventing the Needy*, 41.
190. See Verdery, *What Was Socialism?*, 65.
191. Ecaterina, interview with author, Braşov, 17 June 2003.
192. Valeria, interview with author, Braşov, 14 June 2003.
193. Axinia, interview with author, Râmnicu Vâlcea, 10 June 2012.
194. Petre, interview with author, Bucharest, 3 June 2009.
195. On this practice with respect to the Orthodox faith, see Maria Bucur, "Gender and Religiosity among the Orthodox Christians in Romania: Continuity and Change, 1945–1989," *Aspasia: International Yearbook of Central, Eastern, and Southeastern Women's and Gender History* 5 (2011): 28–45.
196. Stela, interview with author, Braşov, 23 June 2003.
197. Indeed, due to the dearth of public childcare facilities in Poland, "underground daycare" became commonplace and was even advertised in the classified sections of state newspapers.
198. Eleanora, interview with author, Bucharest, 17 June 2009.
199. Ioana, interview with author, Braşov, 20 June 2003.
200. Lucia, interview with author, Braşov, 17 July 2003.
201. Tatiana, interview with author, Braşov, 27 May 2003.
202. Ildiko, interview with author, Braşov, 12 July 2003.
203. Kligman, *Politics of Duplicity*, 68.

CHAPTER 6

# Good Times, Bad Times
## Gender, Consumption, and Lifestyle

We lived well enough, not that I should be nostalgic for this period, but we managed very well then. The salaries were enough for childcare, clothing, food, everything ... we went to the seaside, we organized all types of excursions; it was a different life. With the money we made back then we managed. But now the salaries are not enough for day-to-day living.
—Rodica, construction worker (b. 1963)

I was privileged, you know, I didn't experience difficulties ... of course there were people who had it much harder, who had it tough, but I didn't know difficulties. I was able to get a house, I was able to get what I needed, others didn't have housing right away, and for them it was tough ... tough times. Me, I was privileged; in our house we had gas, perhaps it was fate, destiny, or what have you.
—Domnica, dentist (b. 1938)

Some of the material problems, one now finds them humiliating, but at the time we considered them normal.
—Elena, librarian (b. 1959)

The consumption of a range of goods, as well as the enjoyment of various leisure activities, seems incompatible with conventional understandings of life in socialist Romania—especially in the 1980s. What was there to enjoy when store shelves were stocked with canned Vietnamese shrimp and fruit preserves? Where was there to travel if the borders were closed? How could one relax at home on a winter's day if the heat and electricity had been turned off? As the quotes above suggest, Romanians' conceptions of their material circumstances and overall quality of life under socialism differ, both from one another and from the conventional portrait of penury. In contrast to the narrative of "constant shortage" in which Romania, especially during late socialism, is typically placed, Rodica's recollection reveals that some families maintained a relatively decent standard of living and were able to afford not only essentials, such as clothing and food, but also nonessentials, such as cars and vacations on the Black Sea. Meanwhile, Domnica's quote illustrates that the 1980s were not dark or desperate for all, and that far from creating a more egalitarian society, socialism produced and reinforced social hierarchies. Finally, Elena's quote underscores how people normalized shortage, which to her only seems humiliating or abnormal when viewed through the prism of postsocialism. Collectively, all three quotes reflect different views of the consumer experience in socialist Romania and the ways in which memory is shaped by past and present.[1]

This chapter examines consumption both as a strategy employed by the state for securing popular legitimacy and sustaining power and as an everyday practice that shaped people's lives. During the early years of socialist rule, consumption levels in Romania were low, as they were throughout the Bloc and various parts of Europe, as countries focused on rebuilding and industrializing. In Romania, repression coexisted with austerity, both of which were justified on the basis of constructing a socialist utopia. By comparison, the 1960s ushered in a period of relative cultural and consumer liberalization during which Romania distanced itself from the USSR and individuals enjoyed increased access to a range of goods, from foods to films to furnishings. This, in turn, improved the lives of many, highlighting the modernity and progressiveness of state socialism while also garnering a modicum of popular support for the regime.

Supplying the population with a variety of goods, as well as numerous opportunities for enjoying the "good life," was a means of legitimizing socialism, a tack that was used elsewhere in the Bloc. Rather than employing the stick of coercion, socialist governments increasingly relied on the carrot of goods to placate the population and stave off dissent. Because consumption (defined broadly to include material goods and cultural activities) typically enhanced quality of life, it offers insight not only into what people ingested, imbibed, and viewed on cinema screens, but also how they constituted their identities, expressed status, and related to one another. This was especially true for those who had experienced deprivation during the interwar period, World War II, and the early years of socialist consolidation and were able to enjoy the consumer liberalization of the 1960s and early 1970s. It was also the case for individuals who lived in larger, urban areas and were thus better provisioned, especially in the 1980s, than those in small industrial towns and villages.

Provision of goods and new modes of leisure was, like education, also a tool for eradicating backwardness, promoting socialist values and behaviors, and building a modern socialist citizenry.[2] Accordingly, *Femeia* and the fashion magazine *Moda* (Fashion), through advertisements, fashion spreads, and advice columns, sought to advance modern notions of socialist womanhood, manhood, and lifestyle.[3] However, in Ceaușescu's Romania images of modern, carefree, and liberated women coexisted with repressive pronatalist policies. Considered from this perspective, consumer liberalization served to mask or counterbalance increased state control over other aspects of life.

At the same time, leisure and culture served as mediums for escaping, or at least taking brief respites from, the strictures of socialist culture, including its focus on the acquisition of material goods. Thus, some Romanians shunned or simply ignored the messages and images presented in the pages *Femeia* and other socialist media and instead embraced alternative forms of cultural expression and leisure. This was particularly true of artists and intellectuals and, increasingly in the late 1960s and early 1970, young people, who headed to remote places on the Black Sea for vacations or engaged in the fledgling countercultural movement by way of theatrical productions, concerts, art exhibitions, and film and literature.

While consumption was a long-term strategy for maintaining state power and depoliticizing the population in other parts of the Bloc, in Ceaușescu's Romania it was short-lived.[4] Faced with fiscal crisis, in the 1980s, Ceaușescu attempted to nourish the population not with healthy diets and material goods but with nationalist rhetoric and pageantry. In the context of widespread rationing, consumption elicited not pleasure but anxiety as individuals struggled to procure basic necessities for their families. In particular, the uncertainty surrounding food procurement, along with heat, electricity, and gas shortages, was a perpetual source of frustration and distress for mothers, compromising their ability to fulfill their maternal role. These realities compounded the stress and indignity women already experienced as a result of pronatalist policies and, when considered in light of official rhetoric about women's "noble roles" as mothers and state concern for families, further underscored the hypocrisy and ideological bankruptcy of the regime.

## Hard Times: The Early Years of Communist Rule

At its base, communism is a materialist ideology concerned with material conditions, material forces, and material transformations. Indeed, it was visions of crushing poverty and worker exploitation that compelled Karl Marx and Friedrich Engels to write the *Communist Manifesto*. Thus, communism was predicated on the elimination of social inequality and the fulfillment of basic material needs. Consequently, goods were defined not according to want but to need or their "use value," with anything that did not have a "use value" being deemed wasteful or superfluous.[5] While improving the proletariat's material circumstances and promoting economic equality is at the heart of Marxist theory, Marx said little about the role of the individual as a consumer under socialism. As a corollary, concerns about lifestyle were, on the whole, absent, or at least relegated to the category of "unimportant" during the early years of socialist rule. As in other parts of the Bloc, the Romanian leadership focused on production, and socialist citizens were charged with building socialism, activities that would not only forge a new system, but a new society and new persons, who, in contrast to their capitalistic counterparts, were defined by their labor and values (e.g. diligence and frugality) rather than their status and possessions.

Under state socialism, consumption levels were in large part dependent on what the regime was willing to dole out. During the early years of socialist rule this was not much as governments focused on postwar reconstruction and industrialization. So too did their Western counterparts. However, while countries in the West could rely on Marshall Plan funding to help jumpstart their economies, Eastern Europe had no economic sponsor. Indeed, Romania, as a wartime belligerent, was the provider rather than recipient of capital to the USSR. As such, austerity was rooted in the very real need to pay reparations to the USSR (totaling $300 million) and rebuild the country, though it was officially legitimated on socialist theory and the need to beat the capitalists at their own economic game (i.e. economic modernization). Consequently, the realization of a socialist utopia in the future required sacrifice of needs and desires in the present.

Upon the communist assumption of power in 1947, Romania was still reeling from the aftereffects of war and famine caused, in part, by a drought in 1946. While hundreds of thousands starved to death as a result of the famine in northeastern Romania, living standards remained low throughout the country as Soviet confiscation of food supplies, a currency reform, and land redistribution led to skyrocketing inflation. This was further exacerbated by the nationalization of virtually all sectors of the economy to the point that even by the mid-1950s food production trailed behind 1938 levels.[6] Although repression and austerity operated in tandem in postwar Eastern Europe and the Soviet Union, rationing was by no means a Romanian or even East

European phenomenon at the time as goods were rationed in Britain until 1954, and consumption levels remained low in most European countries well into the 1950s.

During the early Dej years, goods were provisioned hierarchically, with heavy laborers being the most privileged group and wages tied to production levels.[7] As Maria recalled about her and her husband's situation during the late 1940s and early 1950s:

> There was little food and it was rationed. You needed to go in the morning for meat and there was very little of it. My husband, because he was a man [and a laborer], got 700 grams [1.5 lbs] of meat per week and I, as a housewife and woman, I got 500 grams per week. That's all the meat per week. It was a big crisis.[8]

Maria added that due to the onset of collectivization and introduction of penalties for private trading, as well as the fact that she lived a considerable distance from her parent's home, she had no options for procuring food informally as many others did.

As the new privileged class, industrial laborers, specifically those working in heavy labor, were prioritized not only for food but also state-subsidized housing and other benefits. By prioritizing these workers over other segments of the population, the state was making a powerful—and, in some cases, life-threatening—statement on what constituted civic worth in the new socialist system. The state was also betraying its own ideology, veering away from Marxist principles of "from each according to his ability, to each according to his needs" to a Stalinist model in which productive output became the basis for preferential treatment (i.e. "he who doesn't work, doesn't eat"). Accordingly, people working in heavy industry (primarily men) possessed productive value, while homemakers and those employed in non-industrial and white-collar jobs did not, thus justifying their comparatively lower rations.

Until the late 1940s, about a third of the population secured food through price-controlled factory stores *(economate)*; however, provisions remained meager as Dej poured resources into industrialization and forged ahead with the forced reorganization of agriculture.[9] As a result of this brutal process, approximately eighty thousand peasants were arrested—tens of thousands of whom were imprisoned—and production was disrupted, which significantly affected agricultural output. Given the dearth of goods in state stores, people relied on the black market, despite the high costs and risks involved (e.g. jail sentences for "speculation"), informal exchanges (e.g. barter) with peasants, coworkers, and relatives, and packages from friends and family abroad to acquire necessary goods.[10] People also dealt with shortage through black humor, condemnation, and theft. For instance, a Bucharest factory worker joked that as a result of mass shortages, the socialist state had actually "transformed workers into thieves."[11]

Florina, who experienced this period as a young adult, recalled the difficulty and, indeed, absurdity of queuing up for sugar in the winter during the late 1940s:

> You would go to the market and find nothing but cabbage, zucchini, and peppers. Those years were very difficult to endure. You would stand in line for an hour and only get a little bit of sugar. Frozen, you would return home with that sugar and make a sweet cup of tea to warm yourself up to ensure you didn't get a cold from the sugar you just got.[12]

While Florina succeeded in procuring a meager amount of sugar, in wintertime this was a Sisyphean task since she used that same sugar in the tea she made to warm herself up after standing in line in the frigid temperatures. In light of such shortages, resourcefulness was essential for cooking and baking. For instance, Anda, who grew up in Bucharest in the late 1940s and 1950s, recalled that her mother made excellent pastries with oil and marmalade and used carrots as a sugar substitute to sweeten desserts and other dishes.[13]

Housing was also in short supply after the war and, unlike food and other goods, continued to be throughout socialist rule. As peasants relocated to cities and industrial towns, Romania's urban population swelled from 3.747 million in 1948 to 4.424 million in 1953.[14] However, only a modest portion of the state budget was allocated to housing construction. Thus, during the first decade of socialist rule, new migrants were housed in the homes of interwar elites, which had been expropriated and partitioned by the state, with the original tenants either being expelled altogether or assigned a single room in the house. Meanwhile, dorms, often of a rudimentary, barrack-like nature, housed workers in the new industrial towns. Although housing construction began to take off in the 1950s and experienced a boom in the 1970s, due to the continuous flow of migrants to urban areas, lodging remained insufficient—even after cities became officially "closed."[15] Moreover, dwellings were often inadequate for accommodating growing families.

Given this period of austerity, propagandists hailed the virtues of thrift and modest living. A review of advertisements published in *Femeia* and *Moda* during the first decade and a half of socialist rule yields black and white advertisements for soap, instant soups, fabric dyes and various space-saving devices (e.g. clotheslines that could be used in kitchens and easily stowed). More generally, the presentation of these goods reflected the era of scarcity and shortage characterizing Romania at the time. Alongside uninspiring and sparse advertisements, articles in *Femeia* focused on values and ideals rather than consumer goods. A two-page wish list entitled "Hello, Father New Year on the Phone," which appeared in the December 1959 issue of *Femeia*, is particularly telling in this regard. The piece features "conversations" between Moş Gerilă (Father Frost, the communist substitute for Father Christmas) and seven women. Because Christmas was replaced with New Year's Eve as the appropriate socialist holiday, Moş Gerilă asks the women what they want for New Year's. In a nod to authenticity, photographs of the women appear alongside their New Year's wishes. While Dumitrana Florea, "a diligent worker," wishes for "PEACE" and the desire to "work better than I have up until now, for our dear country, the Socialist Republic of Romania," librarian Henriette Lupescu requests "more inspiring books by our writers."[16] Meanwhile, Elena Mihăilescu, a merchant, asks for "more toys ... even nicer than the ones sold at our store 'Romarta copiilor.'" Finally, on a more serious note, Georgeta Frica, an assessor for the People's Tribunal, hopes for "fewer divorce suits and criminal cases."[17] Outside of toys for children, none of the women request material goods of any sort. Instead, they wish for peace, literary works, and a reduction in crime and divorce rates—in short, things that will enhance the moral and cultural fiber of the Romanian people. Rather than an occasion for acquiring goods, New Year's thus offered an opportunity for collective growth and betterment. By reconfiguring the New Year's wish into something nonmaterial and abstract and by mobilizing it for ideological purposes, such articles sought to imbue terms such as "wish" and "want" with entirely new meanings. They also sought to deflect attention away from the fact that consumer goods remained in short supply.

By the early 1960s, the era of austerity, uncertainty, and repression was ending, and Romania entered a period of relative liberalization. However, unlike the Thaw in the USSR, Hungary, and Poland, in Romania de-Stalinization was not a part of this process. Instead, Dej employed nationalism to legitimate socialist rule. Although Dej had demonstrated his fidelity to Marxism-Leninism and opposition to political pluralism by supporting the Warsaw Pact invasion of Hungary in 1956, this masked his larger goal of redirecting Romania away from the USSR and toward the West. This tack worked: in exchange for Dej's display of loyalty to the USSR, Khrushchev withdrew the Red Army from Romanian territory in 1958.[18]

Echoing Yugoslavia's Josip Broz Tito before him, Dej's brand of national communism culminated in the 1964 "April Declaration" in which he challenged the USSR's privileged place within the Eastern

Bloc and promoted independent paths to communism.[19] This was Dej's way of rejecting CMEA's (Council for Mutual Economic Assistance) 1962 Valev Plan, which would have relegated Romania to agricultural provider of the Bloc.[20] A firm believer in rapid industrialization as the engine of modernization, Dej viewed the Valev Plan as antithetical both to socialist progress and national autonomy. Alongside moving away from the Soviet sphere, in the early 1960s, Dej granted amnesty to political prisoners and initiated a de-Russification campaign. Accordingly, Russian-language requirements in schools and universities were abolished, Russian bookstores were closed, and streets and cities assumed their Romanian names again. Moreover, with the rehabilitation of numerous Romanian intellectuals and literary figures, Romanian authors replaced Russian and Soviet ones in classrooms and on bookstore shelves.

While welcome, cultural liberalization was in fact a substitute for genuine political liberalization. Romania's distancing from the Soviet sphere and renewal of relations with the West did not signify a departure from state socialism but was instead an effort to legitimate it according to nationalist principles. As a result, in less than ten years Romania went from being one of the USSR's staunchest allies to being the Soviet satellite most actively engaged in trade with the West.[21] The August 1959 issue of *Femeia* serves as a visual metaphor for Dej's embrace of national communism and turn westward. Published to commemorate the fifteenth anniversary of Romania's liberation from the fascist yoke, the cover features a sensuous woman in a pinup-like pose wearing a form-fitting white dress and holding the Romanian flag. Despite its socialist and nationalist overtones, the woman evokes a contemporaneous Western woman with her accentuated hourglass figure, bright red lipstick, and penciled eyebrows. Such images appeared more frequently in the magazine by the mid-1950s, replacing the earnest, generic looking women that were featured during the Stalinist period.[22] The message was clear: women no longer needed to sacrifice beauty or femininity for socialism; instead, these attributes were reflective of socialism's success in building a modern and sophisticated citizenry.

Although Romania did not experience a political thaw, it did experience a consumer and cultural thaw, albeit not as extensive and enduring as those that occurred in Hungary, Poland, and the GDR. Indeed, Romania's consumer and cultural thaw served as a substitute for genuine political thaw, a smokescreen through which the regime presented itself—both domestically and internationally—as progressive. In addition to rehabilitating Romanian intellectuals and cultural figures, Western films, publications, and exhibitions—along with Western tourists—began entering the country in the early 1960s. Furthermore, fashions and household durables appeared more frequently in the windows of state-owned shops and on the pages of magazines. Similarly, women appeared more carefree, engaging in leisure activities such as listening to records and taking short trips. An advertisement in the spring 1963 issue of *Moda* is illustrative. Featuring two women with bobbed hair ready to embark on a mountain excursion on their moped, the image conjures up visions of earlier "new women" who, during the turn of the twentieth century, were able to enjoy increased mobility, autonomy, and adventure by riding bicycles (see figure 6.1).

As in other parts of Europe by the 1960s, in Romania perfumes, cosmetics, and fashionable clothing were increasingly within reach of ordinary citizens.[23] So too were household durables such as washing machines and home furnishings. As Ivonne, a retired teacher, recalled about the later Dej period:

> I will tell you, I have never lived—nor will I ever live—like I did during the Dej period. One found everything. It was during that time that I furnished my home, that I did everything, everything, everything … it was very cheap, food was extremely cheap. You could get anything in installments. All, all, all the furniture you see, my library, everything you see in this house I got during that time. It was at that time when people who were involved in politics or I don't know, suffered, but that was their problem; but me, myself, I can tell you that things went very well for me in that period. It was probably the easiest period in my life.[24]

Born in 1934, Ivonne suffered the privation and dislocation of war as a child and postwar uncertainty as a teen. However, she did not experience repression. As such, the goods she was able to acquire after she married and received an apartment in the late 1950s were a welcome improvement to earlier economic uncertainty, which explains her positive appraisal of the Dej period. At the same time, she is seemingly uncomprehending and, indeed, dismissive of those who experienced repression during the period, noting, "people who were involved in politics at that time … suffered" and adding "that was their problem." Thus, Ivonne glibly neglects the tens of thousands who suffered simply because they were born into the wrong family, held dissenting political views, or wanted to retain the meager plot of land they owned. More generally, her story reveals that in the midst of repression, some Romanians experienced upward mobility and amassed a range of consumer goods, which, in turn, affected how they evaluated the period, underscoring the ambiguity of lived experience even during an intensely repressive period.

Figure 6.1. Traveling in Style, *Moda*, Spring 1963

Although the opening up of the consumer sphere was not synonymous with indulgence, the disjuncture between early socialism and this period of liberalization was stark. While the regime still measured success in terms of production levels, some of its citizens measured it in terms of access to material goods, as Ivonne's quote illustrates. Thus, promotion of consumerism was a strategy that enabled the regime to attract a degree of popular support without making major economic compromises or political concessions. No longer considered bourgeois frivolities, fashions and new furnishings served as symbols of socialist modernity, and consumerism became a palpable medium through which socialist leaders legitimated their rule. At the same time, socialist citizens were discouraged from consuming goods with reckless abandon as capitalist consumers did; instead, they were to engage in "managed consumption," which was predicated on rationality and needs rather than impulses and desires.[25] The promotion of moderate consumption was thus economically necessary, ideologically sound, and politically savvy. It allowed citizens to enjoy more goods and enabled the regime to secure a degree of popular support, without compromising productive goals or the leading role of the party.

## Black Caviar and the Black Sea: Consumption during Ceauşescu's Early Years

Upon assuming power in 1965, Ceauşescu built upon many of the nationalist and pro-Western tendencies of Dej, while also distancing himself from his predecessor by denouncing previous repressions. In the context of the Cold War, Romania's increased independence from Moscow was not only supported but actively encouraged by the West, with consumption serving as a powerful medium for forging diplomatic and economic ties. The broadening of the consumer sphere was facilitated by trade agreements with the European Economic Community (EEC) and loans from the United States and international lending agencies.[26] These exchanges allowed Romania to keep its debt relatively low and to modernize the economy. As a result, both exports to and imports from the West increased, the latter of which included bottles of Pepsi Cola and Hollywood films, as well technology transfers that benefitted the automobile, rail, aircraft, shipbuilding, chemical, and steel industries in Romania.[27] Indeed, it was during this time that Ceauşescu initiated a "second wave" of socialist industrialization, which entailed creating a more diversified and technologically advanced economy, what he referred to as a "multilaterally developed society."

Although the consumer and cultural thaw began during the late Dej period, liberalization is often associated with Ceaușescu since he assumed power shortly thereafter and expanded upon these measures. Respondents often interpreted these changes from the perspective of bread and butter issues and, more specifically, meat. According to one man, "When he [Ceaușescu] came to power it was good. In the first place there was enough food. I remember they made good sausages."[28] Meanwhile, Valeria, who had experienced a "life of hunger" during the early Dej years, viewed the period more broadly: "When Ceaușescu came to power all the aristocrats were freed from prison. In addition to stockings, there was chocolate and coffee. We also had foreign films. Through culture they began to promote new ideals and began to import certain things."[29] According to Valeria, political, cultural, and consumer liberalization were definitive aspects of Ceaușescu's early years in power, even though these initiatives, including amnesty of prisoners, began under Dej. Chocolate, coffee, and chewing gum not only pleased the palates of ordinary Romanians but also signaled the end of an era—and the possibility of a brighter future. While one could be modern by wearing nylon stockings and watching Westerns, the fact that the regime delivered such items meant it was, perhaps, finally making good on its promises. Moreover, as wages increased during this period, these goods were within reach of ordinary Romanians. Indeed, according to Cătălina (b. 1941), Romania was better off than some of its Bloc neighbors, most notably Czechoslovakia:

> You could find whiskey at the stores, Johnny Walker, it was a bit of an opening. I know because I was in Prague in 1966, where there was great poverty. It was before Prague Spring, and there was nothing there. And I brought cognac and cocoa with me [to Prague]. That's why there was a revolt; they couldn't handle it anymore.[30]

Like the majority of my respondents, Cătălina belonged to the cohort that was in their twenties and thirties during the period of consumer and cultural liberalization (from the early 1960s through the early 1970s). These individuals recalled the period fondly, invoking cognac, caviar, Duke Ellington, Elvis, the Beatles, and other cultural icons and goods from the West. According to Șerban, who was a university student during this time, Bucharest looked and felt vibrant: "There was nightlife in Bucharest, the city was lit up; there were bright advertisements ... restaurants, bars open until the early morning ... people were out on the streets ... it was liberal in comparison to the years of my childhood and adolescence."[31] Anthropologist Smaranda Vultur's interlocutors from Timișoara, a multiethnic city in western Romania, similarly praised the late 1960s and early 1970s as a period of cultural openness and consumer liberalization. According to one man, the period contrasted so sharply with the 1950s that it no longer seemed as if Romania was a closed society or a one-party system: "We felt the chains of socialist society less painfully, we lived, indeed, in a free society."[32]

The expansion of consumption occurred alongside criticism of Dej-era repressions, visits from Western statesmen, and Ceaușescu's bold denunciation of the Warsaw Pact invasion of Czechoslovakia in August 1968, whetting Romanians' appetite for a more liberal, anti-Soviet approach to politics, culture, and daily life.[33] When considered in the context of the immediate postwar period and much of the Dej period, the consumer thaw and (apparent) political liberalization in the form of anti-Sovietism appeared liberating for many, especially for those in their late teens and twenties.[34] As Vladimir Tismăneanu writes, "During the sixties and early seventies, large social segments found themselves stirred and exhilarated by what they saw as Romania's prospects for grandeur, the *conducător's* [leader's] defiance of the Soviet controls, and the rapprochement with Yugoslavia and the West."[35] This grandeur included not only changes in policy and proclamations of Romanian sovereignty, but also, as one woman noted, "the means to go out to dinner every two weeks and to stay at the bar all night, maybe until three in the morning."[36] It also meant greater freedom of movement, as passport regulations were relaxed between 1968 and 1971, making it easier for individuals to travel outside of Romania.[37] Moreover, in July 1967, the state authorized the opening of private shops, restaurants, and boardinghouses, and by the end of the year 183 new restaurants had opened. In this climate, communist party membership soared from 834,600 members in 1960/1961 to 2,194, 627 members in 1970/1971.[38]

Consumer goods served as important icons of Ceaușescu's liberalization, visual symbols of the achievements of Romanian-style socialism. Although the regime still measured success in terms of production levels, its citizenry increasingly began to measure it in terms of access to material goods and opportunities for leisure. While this may have restored some older people's faith in the system, it also attracted a new generation of young people who longed for modern and Western-style products and lifestyles. At the same time, it set a new standard against which the regime could be measured, raising people's expectations for the continued expansion of the consumer sphere.

As in the West, mechanization promised to liberate women from domestic drudgery. In this respect, an advertisement for the "Record" vacuum cleaner invites interesting readings of gender, consumerism, and the rationalization of housework. In the advertisement, a woman lounges in a chair reading a book while her new, cherry-red Record is prominently displayed in the foreground. The caption reads: "Do you want to complete your housework in record time? Use the Record vacuum cleaner."[39] Described as utilitarian, practical, and economical, the Record, as illustrated by the accompanying photo, provided women with *timpul liber* (free time), ultimately reducing the amount of time they devoted to housework. By delivering on the Leninist promise to liberate women from domestic servitude, the vacuum cleaner and other household devices offered time for leisure, which, according to this image, involved enlightening activities such as reading.

In addition to sparing women time, electrical appliances spared women effort. An advertisement for the "Practic" vacuum cleaner, for instance, featured a flawless woman who, much like her contemporaneous Western counterpart, dons a mini dress and kitten heels as she vacuums (see figure 6.2). As with similar advertisements in other parts of the Bloc and, indeed, throughout Europe and the United States, a woman is presented using the product, conveying the message that while modern technology could lighten domestic duties, it did not necessarily affect domestic roles. However, a closer reading offers another possible interpretation, namely that these technologies were so efficient that housework became effortless—so effortless, in fact, that it could be completed by a woman wearing the latest fashions without spoiling her makeup or clothing. Moreover, since these appliances substantially reduced the ardor and time involved in housework, there was really no need for husbands to help out around the house. Thus, the advertisement essentially gave men a free pass. The promise of being spared domestic labor and, of sparing one's wife at least some of this labor—thereby enabling her to devote more energy to her appearance and husband—may have motivated investment in such goods (or at least that's what the advertisers reasoned).[40] Although it is impossible to tap into men's mindsets at the time, as noted in chapter 4, by the mid-1960s, *Femeia* encouraged women to limit the time spent on housework so they could devote themselves to cultural enrichment and other leisure activities, as well as maintaining their femininity. Since the woman featured in this advertisement is decidedly overdressed for the task at hand, it appears that a similar message is being conveyed here. In sum, rationalizing housework through such labor-saving devices could potentially contribute to domestic harmony and spare women exhaustion. At the same time, such goods did not automatically or necessarily result in more progressive family roles.

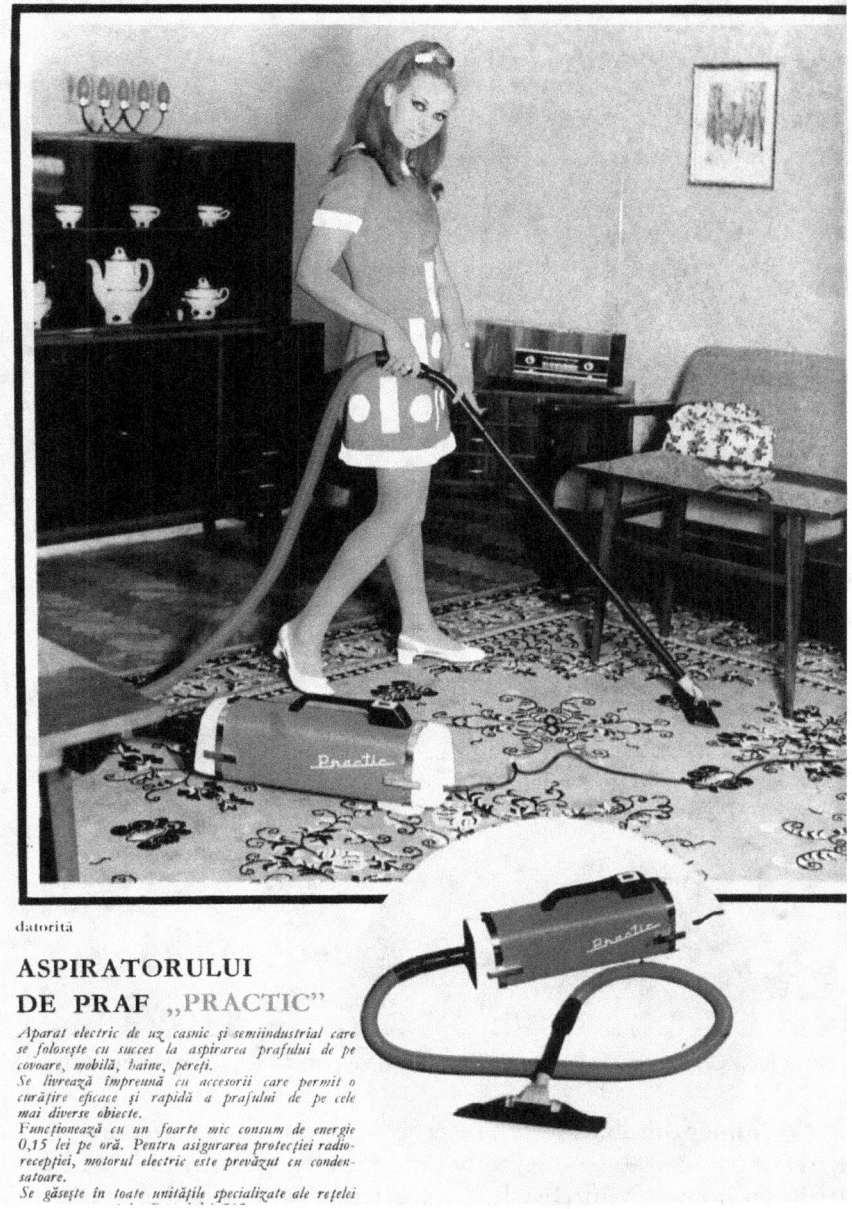

Figure 6.2. Advertisement for the "Practic" vacuum cleaner, *Moda* 97, Winter 1969–70

Figure 6.3. "Contemporary Woman: The Principal Beneficiary," *Femeia*, February 1971

Consumer durables were presented as among the many factors that had contributed to women's liberation under socialism—or at least to their development into bright, sophisticated, and confident individuals who were actively engaged in public and family life. Indeed, an infograph published in *Femeia* in 1971 identified woman as the "principal beneficiary of socialism," highlighting inroads she had made in the

labor force and consumer sphere. Alongside images of women in the workplace, the spread features photos of washing machines, refrigerators, sewing machines, furniture, and a radio. Flanked by statistics illustrating production and consumption rates, the graphic highlights women's occupational achievements and the numerous modern conveniences that have helped women reconcile work and home, as well as enjoy everyday pleasures. As such, socialism facilitated not only economic autonomy and professional fulfillment, but also a higher standard of living, making women the "principal beneficiary."

While such depictions highlighted women's "progress" under socialism, for which women were "indebted" to the state, they also masked certain realities with which all women were familiar. Among these was the fact that women were the "principal housekeepers" (if not the only housekeepers), underscoring that they had yet to benefit from socialism's promise of full equality between women and men. To this can be added a number of policies from which women did not benefit but actually suffered. These included pronatalist policies, which, after 1966, criminalized abortion and forced women to risk their lives to control their fertility, as well as lack of legal redress in matters of domestic violence and harassment. Additionally, while showcasing women's achievements in the workforce, the piece fails to mention women's near absence from leadership positions, particularly in politics, and women's concentration in low-paying and low-skilled jobs. Finally, the piece fails to acknowledge that labor-saving devices, such as vacuum cleaners and washing machines, were by no means universal possessions by this point, and that the apartments in which they were to be used remained in short supply.

Indeed, frustration with lack of housing (or lack of adequately sized housing) was pervasive under socialism, reflected in the tens of thousands of letters sent to the authorities over the course of socialist rule—including the one sent by Mrs. Berendei, referenced in chapter 5. State inability to cope with the cascade of housing requests was evident in the fact that of the 8,870 lodging-related correspondence sent to the authorities in 1966, only 182 were resolved.[41] In the years that followed, requests for housing continued pouring in and were increasingly made by women with children who referenced their maternal responsibilities and pronatalist policies to appeal to state authorities for their own apartment (rather than continuing to live with parents or in-laws) or a larger one.

For those who did manage to secure an apartment, quality was often a concern, especially since many apartment blocks were hastily and shoddily constructed, often using inferior materials. Problems included lack of or improperly functioning heating and electricity, unsafe constructions, and unfinished facades and staircases.[42] Lack of space, however, remained a perennial problem and could only be dealt with by moving into a new apartment—a virtual impossibility unless done illicitly—or making alterations to existing ones, including enclosing balconies, which, given the small size of most kitchens (typically galley-style) were used for food storage or could accommodate a small table and chairs. Accordingly, *Femeia* offered suggestions on efficient use of space and advertised space-saving furnishings such as couches that converted into beds, expandable tables, and folding chairs, items that can be found in people's homes to this day.

Alongside advertising household durables, articles in *Femeia*, as well as *Moda*, increasingly focused on beauty, health, and fashion. As an article in *Moda* asserted, "fashion is no longer considered to be a frivolous matter" but instead has "become a mandatory preoccupation for every woman."[43] While most fashions in the magazines were inspired by Western designs, some presented Romanian versions of these styles. For example, the photo essay "Fashions of Voroneț," which appeared in the spring 1970 issue of *Moda*, featured modern interpretations of traditional Romanian styles with images of Voroneț (a medieval monastery) as the backdrop. In one of the pictures, a woman models a mini-dress and vest with peasant-style detailing while wearing heels and smoking a cigarette. This blending of the traditional and modern could be read as a sartorial expression of Ceaușescu's national communism. At the same time, because peasant styles were also in vogue in the West, these fashions were considered trendy and stylish rather than simply provincial or traditional.

Versions of Western fashions appeared not only in the pages of *Moda* and *Femeia* but also in stores, such as Eva and Universal in Bucharest, as well as shops in other cities. According to my respondents, prior to the mass exports of the 1980s, many high quality and tasteful fashions were on offer at *Casa de Moda*, and fashion shows were held at Sala Palatului. When high-quality clothing was more difficult to come by or too expensive, women relied on tailors or made clothing themselves, often using patterns from *Femeia* and, if they had access to it, the West German magazine, *Burda*, or were inspired by other Western magazines. Moreover, some received packages of clothing from the West. For example, Alexandra (b. 1938), a chemist, considered herself fortunate to have had an aunt in the West who sent her Triumph bras since "Romanian bras were horrible."[44]

In addition to patterns, *Femeia* offered tips on hairstyling and applying makeup and used before and after photos to demonstrate that "there is no such thing as an ugly girl."[45] Although stylish women were visual symbols of a modern, socialist lifestyle, *Femeia*'s authors nonetheless stressed that beauty was more than skin deep: "I think that we have reached the age when one ounce of intelligence weighs more than a ton of beauty, because today even a small amount of brains can play the role of the magic wand which transforms ... whatever is ugly into its opposite."⁴⁶ Makeup and clothing might help compensate for Mother Nature's failings, the author reasoned, but, in the end, physical beauty could not compensate for inner beauty. At the same time, and, echoing contemporaneous women's magazines in the West, *Femeia* included articles on how to have the "perfect arms," as well as on exercise and dietary regimens. Moreover, many of its covers featured attractive, made-up, and well-coiffed young women, including one wearing a skimpy bikini, while sensuous celebrities such as Brigitte Bardot and Sophia Loren were repeatedly featured in the magazine in the 1960s and 1970s. Finally, in the late 1960s, the magazine launched a beauty contest whereby readers voted on contestants based on a submitted headshot, which was featured alongside their name, age, and profession. The winning candidates received not some useless medal, but a transistor radio, a twelve-day vacation on the Black Sea, or, if she won first prize, a trip abroad.⁴⁷ Such images and contests conflicted with articles that extolled the virtues of brains and inner beauty, sending women and female youth ambiguous messages about what aspects of female identity were important.

During this period, *Femeia* also increasingly focused on modern families, modern lifestyles, and modern womanhood. For instance, one of *Femeia*'s surveys asked women to answer the question, "Are You a Modern Woman?" As one woman commented:

> I live an intense and rich life, full of satisfaction ... I educate children, am the leader of a Pioneer group, instructor of dance and ballet for children, responsible for the "Friends of Film" club. I read newspapers, magazines, books, watch movies. In summer I travel through the country with my students or with my husband.⁴⁸

According to this woman, teaching young people, as well as enhancing her knowledge and cultural horizons through various cultural activities, is what made her modern. Meanwhile, another woman highlighted the importance of classical music and amateur theater performances in defining the recreational pursuits of modern women: "Being modern means listening to music (Verdi, Beethoven, Tchaikovsky) and also performing in the theater productions at the House of Culture."⁴⁹ Although still devoted to work, family, and the party, the new socialist woman was highly cultured, engaging in individual as well as collective leisure activities.

The seeming balance between political and personal issues in the pages of *Femeia*, and the increased use of color images and young, fashionably clad women and men, while perhaps a response to popular demand, was also a strategy to persuade women that the party was genuinely concerned about their needs, wants, and desires. Moreover, by focusing on fashion, home décor, and leisure, the magazine promoted interests and pleasures heretofore peripheral or unrelated to the building of socialism. Thus, propagandists attempted to make attractive and thereby legitimize the socialist project to a new generation of young women coming of age in the 1960s and 1970s. The message was that socialist states could not only emancipate women, providing them with a fulfilling job, but also offer them a host of modern goods and, indeed, a new lifestyle. However, in contrast to the West, where youth, beauty, and sex were mobilized to sell products, in socialist Romania they were strategies for selling socialism. Although these visual and written messages were ideologically inspired, it does not necessarily follow that women were manipulated by them—or that they found them useless. As previously noted, a number of my respondents stressed the utility of the magazines' practical pieces (e.g. patterns, recipes, fashion and home décor spreads, as well as articles on infant and family health) while dismissing the ideological articles and pictures of "him and her" (Nicolae and Elena Ceauşescu).

While it is difficult to know the degree to which media representations of consumer culture and modern lifestyles influenced people's attitudes, it is clear that by the mid-1960s Romanians enjoyed an improved standard of living. Praise for the period was related to the fact that since wages had increased, goods, as well as cultural pursuits, were now affordable and thus seemingly available to all. As Vali, a former postal worker remarked:

> It was a good period in that you could find everything ... there were no restrictions, people had fun. You could go to restaurants, for a beer, to the pastry shop, or the theater, films—Romanian and foreign films. Apartments were on installments, and cars—though there were only Dacias [the Romanian-brand car]—televisions, and radios.[50]

Additionally, respondents recalled purchasing home furnishings and other household durables during the 1960s and 1970s, much of which remains in their possession to this day, serving as palpable reminders of the consumer possibilities of that era. Individuals also praised the cultural activities on offer. As Alexandra, who was in her mid-twenties when Ceauşescu came to power, recalled, "From a cultural perspective things were good; theaters with excellent actors [and plays] Ibsen, Shakespeare, Beckett, Steinbeck. Once a week we saw a film. Hollywood films ... between 1965 and 1975 people lived normally."[51] Conceptualizing life as "normal" was typical in many people's recollections of the 1960s and 1970s and contrasted with their depictions of life in the 1980s, indicating that individuals—unsurprisingly—experienced these periods as distinctly different. In addition to Hollywood films, foreign films were screened, and in certain film houses such as Cinemateca in Bucharest, one could view the works of Jean-Luc Godard, François Truffaut, Federico Fellini, and Michelangelo Antonioni, though filmmakers from the Eastern Bloc, such as Andrzej Wajda, were also quite popular. For Romanians who had been fed a hearty diet of Soviet film and theater and who, according to Rodica, "didn't have great expectations," viewing a western film was indeed remarkable. So too was purchasing French perfume and Italian blouses and lingerie in Romanian shops.

Alongside purchasing goods, dining out, and attending plays, concerts, and films, reading was a major pastime as books were cheap, and, beginning in the early 1960s during the cultural thaw, a wide range of literature, including Romanian literature from the interwar period that had been banned, was available.[52] Literature could be read in serialized or abridged form in the monthly literary journals, *Secolul XX* (The Twentieth Century) and *România Literară*, as well as in other magazines and journals. Universal access to books was faciliated through lending libraries, though they could also be purchased at bookstores and kiosks in markets. In order to acquire the desired book, however, individuals often had to purchase a bundle (*pachet*) of books, which included a number of substandard books, such as propagandistic works. Of note is that the low cost of books, along with mass literacy, democratized the practice of reading. Indeed, in the 1980s, with the reduction in television programming to two hours per day, reading became an increasingly popular leisure activity. More generally, most of my respondents, regardless of educational level and occupational status, claimed to enjoy reading (evident in overflowing floor-to-ceiling bookshelves in their living rooms), though finding time to read could be challenging— especially for women—given the demands of work and family.

Another leisure activity that was democratized during this period was travel—albeit within the confines of Romania's borders. Mass travel was facilitated by workplace unions, which subsidized transport and lodging in various parts of the country. Indeed, when discussing social entitlements provided by the state, travel ranked high upon respondents' lists. As Elvira recalled:

> [We had] 15 days minimum of vacation per year. We would do a tour: "Now we'll go to Moldavia and visit all the monasteries and we'll stop at the Black Sea" ... It was very curious; we had a crazy dictator with a fourth-grade education, that is, he didn't have schooling ... but ... until 1976, you found everything in stores ... the Black Sea, the Romanian

coast was full. I can't say that this period was bad, because women had jobs, earned money; you were entitled to a ticket of rest.[53]

Like most other respondents, Elvira's memories of family vacations are among her fondest. Indeed, some women became particularly animated during our discussion of travel, pulling out albums and shoeboxes full of pictures of their annual (or nearly annual) vacations to the Black Sea and the mountains.

That said, as with other universal entitlements, rank, status, and favoritism often influenced the level of subsidy one received. As Maria, who worked as an electrical engineer in a factory, recalled about her trips: "It was cheap. I didn't even pay for the train to Mangalia [on the Black Sea Coast] … it was a very beautiful resort. You could do whatever you wanted and it didn't cost a thing. It was nice."[54] As a privileged worker, Maria was able to fully benefit from workplace travel vouchers; meanwhile, those working in other areas (e.g. light industry or commerce) did not enjoy fully subsidized holidays and might fork out anywhere between 40 to 70 percent of the total cost of lodging and train fare.[55] Beyond that, as with other workplace entitlements, favoritism was a common practice, with union leaders reserving vouchers for friends and family and privileging party members.[56] Despite these shortcomings, all of my respondents availed themselves of opportunities for travel and reduced costs by either camping or renting rooms in private homes. Respondents' recollections indicate that subsidized travel, like universal education, was among the best entitlements provided by the state—as well as among their best memories of the period.

The Black Sea not only offered Romanians respite from crowded apartment blocks, urban congestion, and stuffy factories, but also a space for alternative forms of leisure, social engagement, and creative expression. Indeed, already in the 1950s and early 1960s sites such as Doi Mai (May 2, a take on the official holiday May 1 or "Worker's Day"), a fishing village near the Bulgarian border, brought together writers, intellectuals, and other cultural figures (many of them party members who benefited from working for the regime) seeking to escape the hubbub of the city and official culture. In addition to socializing and writing, these individuals enjoyed nude sunbathing, a practice that was tacitly tolerated by Securitate agents, despite the fact that it was at variance with socialist ethics and cultural mores.

By the late 1960s, these individuals were joined by young people, many of whom could be identified as hippies, donning the requisite long hair and jeans.[57] These youths were part of a larger, vibrant counterculture that emerged in Romania in the relatively open climate of the mid-1960s and that shunned the official socialist culture featured in the pages of *Femeia* and other socialist media. While much tamer than the Western European and American variant, Romanian counterculture nonetheless reflected alternative forms of cultural expression, consumption, and dress (which might include a blending of Western-style blue jeans and Romanian folk blouses). As such, it enabled people to fashion their identities outside of the official one touted by the state (e.g. the upright, sober, and productive socialist citizen).

An urban phenomenon, youth who identified with countercultural trends typically spent time in cafes, acquired records on the black market, attended music festivals and tuned into to the highly popular radio program, *TeleMetronom*, which would have introduced them to music and youth cultures in other parts of the globe.[58] Madigan Fichter asserts that unlike countercultures in open societies, the Romanian version did not define itself in direct opposition to the existing political regime (or at least not overtly so, given the risks), and that many of its adherents in fact supported Ceaușescu's reformist policies, namely a distancing from the USSR and closer alignment with the West, criticism of Dej-era atrocities, and embrace of nationalism.[59] Nonetheless, political critique was a feature, albeit subtly and indirectly, of countercultural art, literature, theater, and film, and, more generally, in the rejection of socialist realism and embrace of experimental forms of cultural expression. Such open forms of expression, however, were short-lived, and young people who exhibited countercultural behavior or styles of dress were subject to suspicion and, increasingly by the mid-1970s, interrogation and arrest, underscoring the limits of Ceaușescu's reformism.

## Through the Golden Era, Darkly: Austerity in the '80s

Expansion of consumer and leisure opportunities in the 1960s and early 1970s, along with increased wages, generally improved people's quality of life. Moreover, the accessibility of heretofore luxury items was a symbol of the regime's modernity. As this was prefaced by a mass amnesty, a shift away from the USSR, and renewal of relations with the West, Romanians welcomed this seemingly new era of socialist rule, or were able to cope with it more easily. This was clearly a strategy to legitimate socialist rule, what political scientist Cornel Ban refers to as "remunerative legitimacy."[60] In offering up Hollywood films and Scotch whiskey and providing Romanians with affordable trips to the Black Sea and other tourist destinations (via workplace travel vouchers), the state was going beyond ideological rhetoric and actually making good on its promises of a radiant future. Thus, G., a factory worker who had been born into poverty in 1941, unquestioningly reveled in this apparent consumerist golden era:

> Until 1970–72 it was a period of blossoming. I don't know what he [Ceaușescu] wanted to do. One began to find everything ... black caviar and salmon caviar. You found them by the kilogram. One found everything that you have: whiskey, gin, bitters, everything that was over there was over here. But I didn't ask myself—people didn't ask themselves—what the use of this was, why it happened.[61]

Given the protracted period of austerity under Dej, it is unsurprising that people did not question the reasons behind the sudden availability of such goods but instead simply purchased and enjoyed them. However, by the mid-1970s, "what Ceaușescu wanted to do" became more apparent, both politically and culturally. After visiting North Korea and China in 1971, Ceaușescu initiated his *mica revoluție culturală* (mini cultural revolution), mobilizing nationalism to legitimate political and economic policies and a host of "patriotic activities" in which the population was expected to participate. These policies signified a gradual reversal from earlier liberalizations in the cultural sphere and included the denunciation of Western, cosmopolitan, and elite culture and the elevation of popular and folk art and culture.[62] It also involved the quashing of alternative forms of cultural expression (e.g. counterculture) through a decree targeting "social parasitism," a broad designation that encompassed a wide range of behaviors, styles of dress, and leisure that the regime associated with social parasitism.[63] Despite this, individuals continued to enjoy Western music and films throughout the tenure of socialist rule, practices that were tolerated by the regime as safety valves.

Ceaușescu's revolution involved further consolidation of power through the rotation of party cadres and the packing of his cabinet with relatives and other sycophants. Effectively, the Central Committee of the PCR was composed of "yes men" who simply confirmed their support for Ceaușescu's measures, rather than critique them—or even propose any on their own. This was true of political as well as economic decisions. For instance, the oil crisis of the late 1970s and the Iranian Revolution dramatically reduced Romania's access to low-cost oil. However, rather than cut productivity levels at gas-guzzling factories, Ceaușescu incurred additional loans to continue fueling them, though at the high interest rates of 1979. As a result, by 1981 the foreign debt stood at US$10.4 billion, or 28 percent of GDP (up from US$500 million in 1976, or 3 percent of GDP).[64] Fearing the harsh conditionalities imposed on Poland by the International Monetary Fund (IMF), Ceauşescu, rather than restructure the terms of Romania's loans, chose to rapidly pay them off. Thus, in contrast to other countries in the Bloc that dealt with these crises by assuming more debt—Poland being the most notorious—to appease consumer appetites, Ceauşescu took a Stalinist and autarkic approach. Asserting the need to be free from Western loans—and thus any interference in domestic affairs—Ceauşescu increased exports and decreased imports with the aim of paying off the debt.

Accordingly, imports from the industrialized West decreased by 17 percent between 1980 and 1981 and by another 45 percent in 1982, while exports rose by 12.3 percent.[65] At the same time, Romania struggled to make returns on some of its exports, as contracts with Western firms were canceled due to the shoddiness of Romanian goods, with the result that Romania lost millions of dollars in revenue.[66] Moreover, due to a drop in demand for industrial goods, the state resorted to selling them below production costs or in barter deals to least developed countries (LDCs) in Africa and the Middle East and to other countries in the Bloc, particularly the USSR.[67]

The reverberations of Ceauşescu's autonomous approach to the economy were felt in the consumer sphere already in the late 1970s, when curtailment of certain goods had begun—a rude awakening for Romanians whose hopes for a better life had been raised by the consumer liberalization of the 1960s. As one woman recounted, "After '70 the good things began to disappear, the luxury items, and after '77 much more ... and by '81 or '83 things were already unavailable."[68] In 1979, gasoline rationing was introduced, and people were allowed to drive only on certain days of the week (based on the digits of their license plate). Additionally, over the course of the 1980s, fewer trams and buses were in operation, which meant they were typically packed like tins of sardines with people hanging off the sides. For women and girls, such rides could be especially unnerving, if not wholly traumatic, since the close proximity provided opportunities for perverted men to grope fellow passengers.[69] Indeed, in some cases, people simply chose to walk—if their destination was not too far—rather than force their way onto an overcrowded tram or bus and endure such indignities.

In fall of 1981, ration cards were introduced for bread, followed by meat, milk, oil, and sugar. By the mid-1980s, queues appeared outside of stores for such basic items as oil, sugar, eggs, and, in provincial towns and villages, bread. The honeymoon between socialism and consumerism was indeed over. Rationing was justified on the basis of nutrition and personal health as well as a Ministry of Health study known as "The Program of Scientific Nourishment." The study, which was publicized in socialist media, designated a caloric intake far below the daily-recommended average.[70] Linking Romanians' high-fat diets to heart disease and high blood pressure, this "rational" approach to eating called for a reduction in starches, dairy products, and "empty calories," such as meat and refined sugar—items that were, incidentally, already being rationed by this time.

Rational eating was placed within the larger context of "rational living," which *Femeia* and other media promoted through "expert" advice, surveys, menus, and personal profiles of ordinary Romanians.[71] According to specialists, rational living included not only healthy eating but also eliminating or reducing alcohol consumption, being physically active, maintaining good hygiene, and engaging in leisure activities.[72] Those who were sedentary, ate high-fat foods, and abused alcohol, propagandists claimed, were more likely to die early than those who ate healthy foods, worked diligently, and regularly engaged in vigorous activity. At the same time, pregnant women were urged to eat well-balanced and hearty diets consisting of food items that were often difficult to procure, particularly in the quantities outlined by the state.[73]

Ceauşescu also attempted to sustain his people through a megalomaniacal form of nationalism, most visible in the growth of his and his wife Elena's cults of personality and construction—as well as destruction—projects in Bucharest. This included the building of *Casa Poporului* (the People's House), an enormous 1,100-room wedding-cake-like structure designed to house the parliament, as well as the bulldozing of various parts of Bucharest, including churches dating back to the seventeenth century, to make room for large boulevards and other thoroughfares.

In a sharp departure from socialist leaders in Hungary, Czechoslovakia, and East Germany, who placated their populations with consumer items and other trappings of the "good life," Ceauşescu offered his people neither material goods nor basic comforts. Instead, intensified nationalism, which he presented as the culminating stage of socialism, was the preferred instrument of regime legitimation and social control in Romania. As a result, Romanians never entered the consumer-oriented "post-totalitarian era" so derided by Václav Havel in Czechoslovakia.[74]

Due to the repressiveness of socialist rule in Romania, protests against shortage—such as those that occurred in Poland in the 1970s and 1980s—only surfaced during the final years of socialist rule. Thus, unlike other countries in the Bloc, people in Romania did not publically put pressure on the state for improved living conditions; rather, they expressed their disgruntlement through letters to the leadership, which often went unanswered. As a result, informal networks, the barter system, and the black market were essential for acquiring both basic and luxury items. Status, which was related to one's place in the party hierarchy and occupation, was the surest route to acquiring both types of goods. For example, party members who worked at state institutes had access to canteens that offered up food at subsidized prices. As Livia recalled, "We were privileged because we had access to a canteen ... inside this building [the Bureau of Statistics] and we found everything; goods that you would [otherwise] not have found without great difficulty."[75] Such party canteens sold not only basic foods but also "luxury" items such as citrus fruits, beer, Pepsi, and (real) coffee, among other goods.[76] Livia's case was by no means exceptional as other state functionaries also had access to a canteen and thus an additional source for securing food. Meanwhile, Anca claimed that although she queued up for food, she was nonetheless "lucky" because her husband, a local secretary, had connections, which afforded her access to certain goods. In one case, for example, he managed to procure fifteen chickens, which she stayed up all night cleaning in order to distribute to friends and family the next morning. At the same time, Anca emphasized that she didn't suffer because she didn't have high expectations in the first place. Other respondents, especially those who had experienced penury during the war and immediate postwar period, echoed these sentiments, noting that they lived "normally" and that they were more or less content during the 1960s and 1970s as they didn't have "exaggerated" or "unrealistic" expectations.

The *nomenklatura*, the group that Yugoslav politician Milovan Djilas had already identified as the "New Class" in the mid-1950s, were among the most privileged in socialist society and were assured a more or less superior, if not luxurious, standard of living. In addition to large apartments or villas, vacations abroad, and cars from the West, they had access to a range of domestic and imported goods through their travels, special restaurants, and *magazine cu circuit închis* (closed circuit stores) and *shopuri* (shops), which only accepted foreign currency.[77] The luxury items on offer at these stores included French cognac, American whiskey, blue jeans, and Kent cigarettes—the latter of which were so coveted that they constituted a form of currency in the second economy. As one respondent noted, "Kents were the best cigarettes ... the 'key' that could open doors and solve problems."[78] Accordingly, Kent cigarettes could be exchanged for a whole manner of goods and services both on the black market and in state institutions and enterprises. For instance, one respondent claimed that Kents were essential to ensuring special medical care when in hospital, noting that "for one day in hospital you'd need one pack (to give to the doctor), and for seven days you'd give him or her the entire carton."[79]

Communist elites and their families not only personally enjoyed a wide range of consumer goods, but were able to profit materially from their illicit sale. Indeed, so rife was illicit trading among elites that individuals complained to the authorities about it. For instance, in 1989 an anonymous resident of Botoşani wrote a letter to Elena Ceauşescu, condemning the former mayor for "not doing anything for the community" and for "selling refrigerators, freezers, televisions, coffee and other imported goods on the black market."[80] Since, already by the mid-1980s, these goods had become scarce commodities, the former mayor's illicit procurement and sale of them, along with her alleged "use" of local funds—a charge referenced later in the letter—was clearly a source of frustration for this individual. In other letters to the authorities, ordinary Romanians similarly expressed discontent with illicit sales and theft occurring in their locality and workplace, underscoring the sharp disconnect between the privileged few and the impoverished many, as well as the ideological bankruptcy of the regime.

Yet, while communist elites benefited most from their social position, they were not the only privileged group. Artists, literary figures, and other cultural figures and intellectuals who buttressed the regime through their work also enjoyed a superior standard of living. Moreover, individuals employed at restaurants, slaughterhouses, food-processing centers, bakeries, butcher shops, and grocery stores had special access to food, which they used for personal consumption or bartered for other goods. As Ioana noted, "My mother worked at the public grocery store and I didn't have problems."[81] The pilfering of items from work also included using factory tools, machinery, and materials to construct certain items that could be subsequently used in the barter economy. It should be noted that such practices were not conceptualized as theft but as a form of "managing" (*a se descurca*), and were justified on the basis of Romanians' low wages, long work schedules, and lack of sufficient food—a rational response to a system that was no longer functioning rationally because it was being run by an irrational dictator. Yet, while workplace theft was widespread, it was nonetheless illegal and thus subject to a fine or imprisonment.[82] Indeed, those who worked in stores, food processing plants, and the like were often checked after their shift to ensure they didn't take products with them. Given these risks, Ioana's mother would have taken great care in transporting such goods from work to home.

Others recalled how vacations at the seaside or other resorts, because they were popular destinations for foreign tourists who expected well-provisioned stores and hotels, provided opportunities for acquiring goods.[83] As Maria noted, "You found all types of produce at the ski resorts. Despite everything, tourism was greatly encouraged ... we often went to resorts to buy cheese, to buy produce, to buy ham, salami, and such, we didn't leave there empty-handed."[84] Similarly, Elena recalled, "In the women's solarium on the Black Sea they would sell things: chewing gum, sweets, condoms, whatever."[85] While ordinary Romanians could purchase food and drink—albeit at high prices—at hotels and resorts, it was the employees of these establishments who typically benefited most. In addition to having access to various foodstuffs, hotel employees received gifts from foreign tourists, as well as tips in foreign currencies, which they could use at the hotel *shop*. Such exchanges required strategic execution, however, as possession of foreign currency (as well as accepting gifts from foreigners, particularly jewelry and other precious goods) was illegal except for certain categories of state employees.[86] That said, since some tourist workers served as informers for the Securitate, the officers on duty might have turned a blind eye to such exchanges and allowed them to keep their proceeds.

Romanians came into contact with foreigners not only at tourist sites but also in large cities, which offered additional opportunities for procuring goods. For example, Romanians who attended the University of Bucharest recalled that students from Syria, Iraq, and Egypt, among other foreign countries, who came to study at the polytechnic and medical schools, sold an array of goods out of their dorm rooms, including blue jeans, bras, Western brand-name sports shoes, alcohol, cosmetics, cigarettes, condoms, VCRs, and cassette tapes. These students had typically acquired such goods on the black market and, because they were allowed to possess foreign currency, in special shops or "foreign currency stores." Those who lived near border regions, particularly the border with Yugoslavia and Hungary, also had access, through small-scale border trading, to highly coveted goods, including high-quality shoes, blue jeans, and cigarettes.[87] Yet, such exchanges involved a certain amount of risk as some guards, rather than accept a bribe in exchange for allowing the goods to cross the border, might confiscate them altogether.

Earning a good salary—and being willing to part with a chunk of it—also put people in a privileged position for accessing food. As Valeria R., a professional researcher, noted:

> I bought [food] from the restaurant; it wasn't a problem, I bought it at Aro [a hotel in Brașov]. Butter, cașcaval [cheese], whatever, because my husband and I made enough money, and my parents helped us, my in-laws helped us. ... I preferred to pay ten to twenty lei more a kilogram so I didn't have to wait in line.[88]

This, however, was not a feasible option for all families, especially those in lower income brackets who had multiple children to support.

Having a chronic illness such as diabetes was also, ironically, a form of privilege in that it entitled one to special rations of meat and other high-protein foods. As H., a diabetic, recalled, "Diabetics had a special store for meat, but you could only find chicken and beef. But you could take as much as you wanted, usually."[89] The fact that H. had seemingly unlimited access to meat, which might not be much given rationing, meant that her family, and perhaps also her friends, were better nourished than Romanians who did not know a person with a chronic illness. She also could have exchanged this precious commodity for other sought-after goods and services. Finally, individuals who provided essential or important services, such as doctors, dentists, pharmacists and teachers, were often remunerated with food.[90] Domnica, a retired dentist, explained her situation by virtue of her patients and her "connections" in the countryside:

> For me food was not a problem; on the contrary, it was abundant. I had patients who were in commerce, and so whatever I wanted they would bring to me. In addition, I had relatives in the countryside where I could go and buy a calf or a pig. Back then we ate a lot of pork, so for me it wasn't a problem; on the contrary, it was abundant. Friends, siblings, relatives came. There were always many people. The table was full, all types of food, with sweets and so on. We never went without anything. Generally speaking, people waited in line, it's true, for meat and so on, but nobody died of hunger ... they ate modestly, maybe ... but they always had something to eat.[91]

One reason why Domnica had clients in commerce was because her husband worked in commerce; thus, her access to abundant amounts of food was directly related to her marital situation. As such, she was in a particularly privileged position and did not suffer the material frustrations and deprivations that most Romanians did.

Effectively, a barter system characterized consumer practices in socialist Romania. At once traditional and modern, the socialist barter economy was multilayered and involved peasants and city dwellers, with exchanges occurring at a variety of places: the shop floor, the peasant home, the apartment block. Reinforcing existing social networks and creating new ones, the very existence of this system underscored state inability to provide materially for its citizens, illustrating the importance not of socialism but of informal networks in ensuring well-being. In contrast to East Germany and Czechoslovakia, where consumption rates were the highest in the region, not far behind Western countries, in Romania even the most basic foodstuffs were either in short supply or wholly non-existent by the mid-1980s. As such, barter and the black market were not only important for negotiating or "managing" the system, but at times essential for survival. This was evident in the many references subjects made to the parallel or underground economy and the black market.

In addition to status, connections (*relații*) were, for many, the ticket to a basic, if not superior, standard of living. Indeed, connections were such a common feature of life under socialism that some Romanians simply referred to them as "PCR," which is both the acronym for the Romanian Communist Party (Partidul Comunist Român) and the three commonly used terms for connections (*pile, cunoștințe, relații*).[92] Such connections, according to Ildiko, spared her hours upon hours of queuing up: "Honestly, we didn't really wait in line. I had acquaintances that helped me get a hold of everything and we didn't wait in line. I can't complain."[93] Many of my respondents similarly explained that they often relied on connections for securing food, goods, and services. Such connections could be complex, involving the passage of goods through numerous hands in exchange for different favors. In addition, local and high-ranking officials could be a central link in these connections, encouraging and, as previously noted, even profiting from shortage, as well as their elite status.

While connections and barter often compensated for shortage, they also perpetuated the very system that produced such stress, frustration, and uncertainty. As historian Mark Edele asserts with respect to the USSR, "social stratification engendered practices designed to get scarce information and scarce goods, and to survive in the desert of commodities and information created by totalitarian social engineering. On the level of the overall system, these same practices actually 'made the Soviet system work' despite the severe dysfunctions built into the system from the very start."[94] Thus, the relationship between the regime and its citizens was codependent: the regime's survival, like that of its citizens, depended on the continued functioning of informal networks. Indeed, the state relied on these informal practices as compensatory measures that enabled it to maintain and even intensify austerity policies, without worrying about triggering popular resistance.

Beyond local connections, most people looked to relatives in the countryside or friends and family abroad to acquire food. As Tatiana recalled:

> I would go near my village, a small town where they make cașcaval [cheese]. And there I had connections, and they would bring me a bag full, enough for two months ... my parents gave me a lot and my husband's parents ... we managed very well. ... That's when I even learned to make pizza.[95]

Utilizing one's connections to acquire goods and services, though a response to material deficiencies under communism, was presented more generally as a form of "managing," a cultural practice predating socialism. Indeed, some viewed these relationships as fundamental aspects of Romanian identity. As Luana commented, "All Romanians have connections, that is typically ours [a Romanian trait]."[96] In a similar vein, Elvira referred to the "resourcefulness of Romanians" in explaining how families, beyond simply "making do," offered up veritable feasts to their guests during the mass shortages of the 1980s:

> Romanians are very curious. When foreigners and friends would visit during the Ceaușescu period, during that crappy time when everything was rationed, food, gas and what have you ... the freezer was full of chicken, of meat, everything. It's incredible, the resourcefulness of Romanians. How did they get a hold of it [food]? I can't say. ... If you went to anyone's house, they'd put it on the table like you wouldn't believe. Everyone managed; everyone had connections.[97]

Elvira's reflection illustrates the interconnection of food and hospitality in Romania, where the well-stocked dinner table assumes both cultural and national significance and is a great source of pride for many women. Yet, while providing such feasts was a sacrifice many Romanians made to impress or demonstrate affection for friends and family, when they entertained guests from abroad, especially the West, this act was perhaps less one-sided than it appears. Indeed, these gatherings were often more akin to exchanges since Romanian families often received needed goods—as well as gifts—in return for offering their Western guests a feast. Additionally, Elvira's recollections demonstrate that shortage facilitated hoarding, which, while illegal, was a common practice at the time.[98]

Although Luana claimed that "everyone managed, everyone had relations," this was not always the case. For example, Maria, a former factory worker, recalled the injustice of real existing socialism: "It was a farce because those that had connections had [food], and those that didn't have connections had to wait in line, hours in line, and sometimes there wasn't even enough for everyone."[99] Maria's comment illustrates that connections, contrary to Elvira's claim, were not a universal phenomenon under socialism and that some Romanians were effectively helpless in the face of shortage.

Outside of privileges and connections, procuring food and other goods required a great deal of fortitude and patience. In the 1970s, *casele de comenzi* (home delivery food services) were established to deliver food to people's homes. However, because there were not enough facilities to accommodate the population, it often took two hours or more to reach an order taker by phone. This, combined with the fact that someone needed to wait at home for the delivery, meant that *casele de comenzi* were not a practical resource for most working families.[100] Therefore, queuing up became the most common means of acquiring food and other goods in the 1980s. As there was often no knowing when goods would be delivered to stores, people learned about deliveries via word of mouth (e.g. friends, neighbors, relatives, colleagues, and taxi drivers). While initially only certain items were rationed, as the 1980s wore on the list expanded, and, as goods became more scarce, people would simply get in line without inquiring about the product being distributed as one might not be able to acquire it in the near future. As Elena succinctly put it, "You joined a line, but didn't know what was being sold ... you bought what you found not what you needed."[101] Such practices reflected the uncertainty of everyday life in late-socialist Romania, and also contributed to hoarding as people stocked up on goods when they were available.

Queuing was a time-consuming practice, often involving numerous family members who took turns waiting in line. One woman recalled that her mother would get in line at 3 AM for meat and that at 7 or 8 AM her husband would take her place. In some cases, a number of family members might join the line to acquire larger quantities. As Elisabeta remarked, "I woke up at 2 at night to go to the milk [line], and because they didn't give us more than two liters a person, my father needed to come—and also my husband—so we could get six liters of milk to give to my child."[102] Queuing thus might involve the entire family, an essential practice if all family members, and especially young children, were to receive sufficient food. As such, retired family members were an invaluable resource for working parents who were unable to wait in line for milk, cheese, and other necessities. The reliance on retired family members for food procurement, like childcare, was a strategy for negotiating the system of shortage, which the regime manipulated since it compensated for insufficient provisioning of the population.

Queuing in Romania is a strategic practice, requiring alertness, assertiveness, and patience. During the socialist period, the character of the queue varied according to the neighborhood and product being sold. In some cases, the experience of everyday shortage facilitated the creation of an organized system with its own rules and codes of behavior. Indeed, according to Tatiana, this code of conduct was so ingrained that in the milk queue in her neighborhood people would simply place their empty bottles in the queue the night before delivery, go home, sleep, and return the next morning when the milk delivery arrived, bottles unmoved.[103] The fact that such trust existed reveals that society was not wholly atomized or disunited, and that a degree of communality existed. Yet, this communality was not a result of the socialist utopia envisaged by Marx and Engels but its failure in the form of the shared experience of shortage and material want.

Often queues were monitored, typically by an elderly man who assumed the role of *şef de coadă* (boss of the queue) and ensured that individuals stayed in their places. As Stela recalled:

> [It was] a bit of rugby. But usually an old man, usually retired, who had nothing to do anyway, established order. And when you'd see a crafty type weaseling his way to the front, you knew that he wouldn't be able to skip you. Because he'd [the old man] say: "Hello, mister, what are you looking for over there? To the back!"[104]

In addition to keeping order in the queue, retired individuals used their spare time by selling—often well above the official price—the goods they had procured to individuals who were unable to pass the entire day sitting in the queue.

At the same time, since there were often not enough goods for everyone, the survival instinct, rather than sentiments of communality, could guide people's behavior. For example, Adrian recalled one episode during his late teens when his father went to queue up for eggs and was engulfed by the crowd and ended up fainting.[105] Meanwhile, for others the queue was akin to hunting, requiring stealth and calculation. As Paul Cernat claimed, "It was all a sort of a 'hunt'—especially when people were queuing for meat, they would rediscover their primitive hunting instincts. This happened despite the regime's regular food policy, patented by Dr. Iulian Mincu (nicknamed Dr. Mengele), whose aim was to transform the population into a herd of domestic harmless ruminants by rationalizing deprivations and promoting vegetarianism."[106]

Sadly, in some cases, selfishness rather than communality or altruism characterized people's behaviors in the queue, as Lucia recalled:

> Once I saw a woman who came [to the front of the line] with a sick child, and she was looking for a kilogram of sugar for herself and the child and the people in the line said, "Don't give it to her" ... because she hadn't stood in line. And she showed the people her child and the injections she had gotten ... it was horrible.[107]

People also devised strategies for securing additional rations. For instance, because items were distributed according to the number of individuals per family, children were "borrowed" for the purpose of receiving larger rations. As Stela humorously recounted:

> And then you'd hear a voice: they've got *telemea* [feta cheese]! You'd rush down the stairs to be at the front of the line ... and if you had a kid next to you they'd give you two times [the regular] quantity. And kids, you'd borrow them. For example, I had a neighbor [who would ask], "Won't you lend me Nae to wait in line with?"[108]

Stela's recollection illustrates how people worked the system to ensure that they were sufficiently provisioned. While a logical response to the uncertainty associated with living in a shortage society, it also meant that goods would run out earlier, leaving some people empty-handed. Accordingly, such strategies for managing the system undermined communality and reinforced individualistic tendencies. Beyond using such strategies, as in other areas of life, status, connections, and bribery could help secure rations or a better place in line. For instance, high-ranking members of the army and *miliția* often went to the head of lines to get food, with the result that those who had waited for hours might get a few scraps—or nothing at all.

Because the queue symbolized state failure to deliver the most basic necessities, goods were often distributed from the rear of the store so as not to offend visiting party officials, foreign dignitaries, and, most importantly, the Ceaușescus. For instance, Stela recounted how stores on Brașov's main street, Bucharest Avenue, distributed goods from the rear of the shop. However, because queues became a ubiquitous feature of the Romanian landscape by the mid-1980s, attempts to shield the Ceaușescus from them were not always successful. That said, in preparation for Ceaușescu's visits, activists required that markets be filled to the brim with a wide array of foodstuffs, particularly fresh produce. Images of these visits were then featured in the press as proof that Romanians were enjoying a life of plenty and living in a "golden era," a ruse that fooled no one.[109]

By the mid-1980s, procuring food had become a daily activity, requiring considerable time and effort by various family members.[110] Along with waiting for buses and trains that were running on reduced schedules to save fuel, queuing up for food consumed a large chunk of people's time, exemplifying what Katherine Verdery refers to as the "etatization of time." This mode of state control, she notes, was a means of undermining people's sense of normality and "installing uncertainty as a rule of living."[111] Such uncertainty seized people's time, forcing them to devote hours upon hours to the mundane activity of procuring basic necessities. This, in turn, left people with less time for leisure—or even the ability to plan for leisure—since they needed to constantly be at the ready in the event certain items or goods were made available.

While the acquisition of food was not a gendered activity, its preparation was typically considered women's work. Thus, in addition to the stress of securing infant formula, women faced the daily stress of preparing meals. As in other societies, food assumes a great deal of social significance in Romania, and its proper preparation is of particular importance.[112] The rationing of food—as well as heat and electricity—however, compromised a woman's ability to properly nourish her family, compounding the guilt and stress she already felt as a mother working long hours. Accordingly, concocting a tasty torte with ersatz butter and the meager egg ration was nothing short of miraculous. Women thus relied on ingenuity and resourcefulness in crafting meals during the 1980s. As Maria stoically recalled:

> I'd come home, sit down on the chair in the kitchen, and begin to invent meals ... because I couldn't follow a cookbook. I needed to see [what could I possibly make], hmmm, what food will I make tonight? I don't have parsley... I can't make this because I need cheese. So then I prepared meals that you would not find in any recipe ... I would make the first and second course with potatoes only ... I would make potato soup and mashed potatoes. I'd add a vegetable, some eggs with flour and also make a goulash soup.[113]

Maria's three-course potato meal is reminiscent of the "hundred-ways potato party" prepared by Slavenka Drakulić's Bulgarian friend in the book *How We Survived Communism and Even Laughed*.[114] Both cases are illustrative of what Michel de Certeau has termed "the art of making do with what the system provides."[115] Although coined in reference to the capitalist system, de Certeau's notion of "making do" is also relevant for the command economies of the Eastern Bloc since individuals were often faced with shortage and shoddily produced goods. Indeed, "making do" became an art form as women concocted meals out of an odd array of seasonings, inferior meat trimmings, and ersatz and imported foods. Some of these included canned fish and Vietnamese shrimp, chicken wings, heads, and claws, "adidas" (pork hooves), and "the Petreuş brothers" (two scrawny chickens named after the Maramureş folk musicians). Other items on offer included bread made from stale flour and coffee made from chickpeas, barley, and other concoctions, colloquially known as *nechezol*—a reference to a horse's neighing because the ingredients were often akin to horse fodder. Additionally, soy was used as a substitute in salami, which, while a healthier version of the real thing (e.g. pork), many found unpalatable. Unsurprisingly, a number of my respondents noted that during the 1980s they lost their preference for certain foods and ate pretty much whatever they could get a hold of.

Scarcity also sparked a heightened appreciation for food, even if it was of substandard quality or taste, as Stela's recollection of her excitement about Pufarin (puffed rice) demonstrates: "It was puffed rice or something [like that], covered in something sweet. It was a nothing, but during that time it was something ... it was a delicacy: 'They have Pufarin!' You'd run down and grab a bag of Pufarin."[116] Stela's comical description of Pufarin as a "delicacy" and her haste to "grab a bag of it" illustrates her ability to stoically make do. Though not nourishing, such "delicacies" were, at least in the short term, psychologically nourishing.

In light of such shortages, the acquisition of certain goods was interpreted by many in fatalistic terms, as either being lucky or unlucky and as a major accomplishment, a small victory in a system where the cards are stacked against you. As Marcela recalled, "I waited in line for two hours in order to get two packets of Ness [Nescafé instant coffee]. I can't tell you, I thought that I had gotten a Porsche ... you can't imagine how proud and happy I was."[117] Moreover, scarcity forced parents to sacrifice their own nourishment for their children's, as Maria recalled: "Essentially, we sacrificed our health for our children, so that they would have all they needed."[118] Similarly, as Ivonne noted, "I don't think I ate butter for about four years so the children would have it. And when butter appeared, I think for about a month I ate only bread and butter."[119]

The consumption of food has historically been a medium for sociability in Romania and this did not change even in the context of shortage. On the contrary, according to some individuals, sharing food became the ultimate measure of friendship, with the item being shared mattering much less than the actual act of sharing. As Rodica lamented, "There were times when our friends came over and we had nothing but bread and ersatz butter. And we [drank] ersatz coffee. But people listened, we watched videos, and we got along great. Relationships were better [then]."[120] Clara echoed these sentiments: "They [people] understood each other better: 'Wait ... I managed to get two packets of butter, I'll give you one.' Or, 'Your bread ration was not enough, I'll give you ours because we don't eat that much bread.'"[121] Imbued with a host of meanings, food was at once connected to ritual and tradition, love and sacrifice, and friendship and sociability. Indeed, because the majority of the population was continuously involved in procuring food, it often served as the basis upon which friendships evolved, evoking nostalgic, or at least bittersweet, memories of the period.

As if shortages of such basic provisions as eggs, oil, and milk were not bad enough, by the early 1980s "deficit consumption" broadened to include heat, electricity, and hot water. In 1982 the state began rationing electricity, with the result that in some cities and towns the power was simply cut off after ten o'clock at night. While this affected people's ability to work or relax at home, it was particularly problematic for women, compromising nighttime safety. It also produced stress for students, who were forced to study by candlelight, and the elderly, infirm, and mothers with young infants who lived in large apartment blocks and were unable to use elevators to get to their apartment. Moreover, it proved challenging to keep perishable goods from spoiling, one reason why the balcony, at least in winter, doubled as a refrigerator.

Propagandists presented the rationing of utilities within the context of the "world energy crisis," which required a "changing of mentality" with respect to energy use. As a means of compelling people to "rationalize" (e.g. use less) electricity, *Femeia* advertised lamps that were best suited to low-wattage bulbs—which dovetailed nicely with the state's restriction to use only 40-watt bulbs.[122] In addition to cutting back on energy use, individuals were encouraged to reuse and recondition their existing goods. Accordingly, women were urged to update or refashion clothing, shoes, and leather goods either at home or at centers that provided machines and tools for doing so.[123] They could also opt to sell their clothing and shoes to these centers, which would, in turn, update, redesign, and resize them. Such messages were transmitted through a range of media: surveys in newspapers, documentaries, and public symposia.[124] Presenting energy reduction as a response to a larger, global crisis obscured the reality that these measures were rooted in a particular Romanian approach to paying off the country's massive debt. It also obscured the fact that factories continued to run at full capacity during this period (often 24/7) and that individuals' needs were being subordinated to the larger goal of continued industrialization.

As an additional cost-cutting measure, the state reduced the temperature in apartments, factories, offices, schools, and even hospitals to 57 degrees Fahrenheit—and in some cases even lower. In light of these shortages, people devised numerous means of keeping warm. Simona, who was a teenager during this time, recalled that her mother resorted to desperate measures to keep her warm: "In the last years [of Ceaușescu] everything was rationed. ... I remember that it was during the semester and my mother warmed my hands with a hairdryer so I could study. On Christmas day they finally gave us gas pressure. It was terrible, terrible."[125]

In addition to warming up with hairdryers, people wore hats and winter coats to bed and even resorted to sleeping in their kitchens and warming themselves on the burners of their stoves—that is, when gas was available. As Radu Clit notes, in comparison with food rationing, which gradually became worse, lack of heating was abrupt and shocking.[126] As A., who was born in 1968, recalled:

> I'll tell you when the difficulties arose. ... In 1984 or 1985. I was in tenth grade. We didn't have gas; we had a gas stove but no gas. This was a big problem ... because we lived near the embassies, and when they turned off ours, they turned off theirs. I remember that my dad got a hold of some wooden crates [for burning]. We had three bedrooms ... the rooms were about two degrees [Celsius; 35 degrees Fahrenheit]. We all slept in one room. We slept next to the fire with coats on. I remember I had to study for exams and I couldn't because it was so cold in the living room. My mother ironed the whole time. She didn't need to, but she did it to stay warm.[127]

Although A.'s father's position as an army officer might have helped the family secure food and other goods, it did not spare them from frigid days and nights in the 1980s when entire neighborhoods suffered after heat was simply shut off. According to Ceaușescu, such minor discomforts could be easily dealt with. As he claimed in a meeting with regional secretaries: "It is not a tragedy to wear a sweater around the house, including at night, to go to sleep in a sweater as others once did," adding "first production, then everything else.[128] While such sentiments never made it onto the pages of the communist daily, even if they had, they would have been cold comfort for the millions who did not know when and for how long the heat would be functioning. Indeed, for some, heat rationing, including of hot water, was the worst form of rationing. As Florina noted, "It was so cold and dark. That is a pain I will never forget and which seems to me the most terrible. Perhaps some people were hungry. I do not remember being hungry, but the cold and horror of darkness, yes, that was the worst."[129]

This extreme form of rationing, unprecedented in the Bloc, illustrated how steeply living standards had declined and, when combined with shortcomings in welfare entitlements (e.g. insufficient childcare facilities, substandard conditions in hospitals and orphanages, poor infrastructure and transport), further underscored the illegitimacy of the system.[130] Heating shortages also served to radicalize the population since, unlike with food and other goods, connections and bartering could not bring heating (nor electricity, for that matter) to an entire apartment block. As if these indignities were not enough, at certain points of the day the water and gas pressure was simply turned off, forcing innumerable women to cook the family meal at midnight or during the wee hours of the morning. While this was both frustrating and exhausting, further reducing many mothers' already short sleep schedules, lack of hot water for doing dishes, laundering clothing, and bathing was particularly distressing. Indeed, as related by C. in chapter 5, bathing infants during the mid-1980s (along with heating milk) was a time-consuming process, which, when combined with lack of heat, produced great distress within mothers. Because women tended to the families' nutritional needs (through food preparation and preserving) and health and hygiene needs (through cleaning, laundering clothing, and bathing infants and young children), and were even charged with such responsibilities in *Femeia*, austerity created additional burdens for them. These burdens were, one could argue, physical, mental, and psychological. Because more time, effort, and foresight were required to complete basic, domestic tasks, they needed to be carefully planned out to account for unpredictability in food delivery (to stores) and access to utilities such as gas, electricity, and hot water. Meanwhile, worry and, indeed, fear that they wouldn't be able to procure and prepare what was needed for their families was continuously at the fore of their minds.

The impact of austerity measures on families was poignantly conveyed in an anonymous letter written by a group of women to Elena Ceaușescu in spring 1984, and subsequently broadcast on Radio Free Europe:

> Mrs. Ceaușescu: You don't seem to want to understand that we have had enough of so many lies and that we wake up at 3–4 in the morning to wait in line and after that go to work, and when we leave work we try out another line, just to get a little something ... to continuously not have hot water, to not have heating in our apartments in winter, at work, to have electricity cut off in our apartments, not to be able to refill our gas canister when it's empty, to see only preserves and drinks in the stores, to procure our rationed food—especially sugar—at outrageous prices, to be required to work when ill—if we don't have a fever above 40 C— etc. etc. ... In order to personally convince us of the optimal conditions

for "The Protection of Mothers and Children" and how impressively the healthcare system has grown across the country, you make a few "unannounced" visits to hospitals, creches. ... Unfortunately, you are not at all interested in what we Romanian women endure and we ask you why. If you had been born into a palace, we would understand. Have you actually forgotten where you came from and what you fought for in your youth? If it's true that you are the dearest mother, you should understand all Romanian children, not only your own ... we also believe that our children have the right to a civilized life.[131]

Drawing on maternalist and nationalist discourse, these women underscored the hypocrisy between official pronouncements about protecting mothers and children and the everyday realities of food, heat, and electricity shortages. Moreover, by referencing Elena Ceaușescu's earlier days as a socialist revolutionary, they pointed to the gulf between the communist leadership and ordinary Romanians, rhetorically asking how a woman who had been born into such modest means could have strayed so far from earlier ideals. Finally, they address her as a mother, both to her own family and to all Romanian children, inquiring why she has neglected her maternal responsibilities to protect and care for her Romanian children and, by extension, the Romanian nation.

In the midst of such shortages, propagandists still attempted to convince the public that things were better in Romania, as C.'s recollection of the television show *The Road to Capitalism and Back*, one of the few shows to air during the 1980s when television was limited to two hours a day, illustrates:

> I remember—I will never forget—they were showing an image from France, how bad the lives of the French were and how they had to wait in line for bread. Why? Because they opened a new pastry shop in Paris—an extraordinary one—and the French were fighting to buy the first croissant from this pastry shop. But they [state television] presented it to us as if there was great penury over there, and they [the French] didn't have anything to eat and had to fight in line to get bread...but they didn't look at our lines ... people waiting in line for meat at twelve o'clock at night.[132]

For C., this particular "exposé" epitomized the absurdity of state propaganda, underscoring the enormous gulf between Ceaușescu's rhetoric and everyday Romanians' reality.

While many grumbled, cursed, and made jokes (gallows humor) about austerity measures and the disconnect between media reports and daily reality, some individuals addressed the communist leadership directly through letters, complaining about workplace injustice, graft among municipal authorities, and immorality, among other issues. Retiree and long-time party member Elena Negru penned one of the longest letters (of those archived by the Central Committee of the PCR) to the communist leadership in the 1980s. The following excerpt, from her fourteen-page letter to Elena Ceaușescu in February 1988, highlights the decline in material conditions, pervasive corruption, and Ceaușescu's tenuous hold on power:

> My son and I eat one loaf of bread a day—yet this one loaf a day seemingly is the cause for the remaining bread throughout the country to be rationed like during the war, even though "there has not been a harvest as bountiful as last year's." Well, if all these endless millions of tons of wheat have been harvested, where is the bread, in what African countries is it eaten since we are allowed only 300 grams a day, and it is mainly chaff and dirt rather than flour? ... WHO, IN REALITY, IS THE PRESIDENT OF THE SOCIALIST REPUBLIC OF ROMANIA? Comrade Nicolae Ceaușescu or the three louses in the Ministry of Justice? ... You, comrade Nicolae Ceaușescu, are the target of virulent acts of political sabotage, intended to libel you in the eyes of the people. These same people rubbed their fat bellies, grinning when, in Craiova, there was graffiti on the walls that read: DEATH TO THE TYRANT! ... Now, at the twelfth hour, ask yourself who holds the power: us, the hungry, the cold and the scared, or that gang of career-driven fat adventurers who blinded you with their flattery ... and used their demagogical speeches to sweet-talk you? Look at the photo below and ask yourselves, as we do: "how many days have the comrades' wives spent in a queue to prepare a feast while we are dying of hunger?"[133]

Accompanied by a newspaper clipping featuring the Ceaușescus and other dignitaries at a banquet, the letter functions simultaneously as a complaint and a warning. By contrasting the lavish lifestyles of the communist leadership with the privation of the people, Elena highlights the ideological bankruptcy of the regime, which celebrates "bountiful harvests" in the pages of *Scânteia* but delivers only "chaff and dirt" to stores. Moreover, she underscores the absurdity of Ceaușescu's foreign policy, which drastically limited Romanians' access to food, while funding (or, as she notes, feeding) countries in Africa—a claim that in fact reflected his economic investment in LDCs.[134] Finally, Elena seeks to alert Ceaușescu to the dangers within his midst in the form of corrupt, high-ranking functionaries who are hoodwinking him all the while encouraging his demise so they can assume power for themselves. In identifying the graft and hypocrisy of the regime, and the real suffering of ordinary Romanians, Elena's letter stands as a lone voice of courage in a time of fear and hopelessness.

Rather than read the graffiti on the wall and revamp the system, the state intensified rationing, the press emphasized the dangers of reformist movements elsewhere in the Bloc, and Ceaușescu continued to feed his personality cult, all the while praising Romanian workers for their "high rates of productivity." In April 1989, Romania's debt was finally paid off, but at an enormous cost to ordinary citizens: over the course of the 1980s, Romanians' access to food staples was reduced by nearly 50 percent.[135]

Protracted shortages and continued state repression, most evident in the bloody crackdown of the peaceful protests in Timișoara in December 1989, would ultimately lead to the collapse of the regime. In the end, Ceaușescu's version of national communism proved wholly unpalatable to the vast majority of the populace.

## Conclusion

Consumption was a constitutive element of politics, identity formation, and daily life in socialist Romania. During the early years of socialist rule, consumption levels were low as the country struggled to rebuild and rapidly industrialize after World War II. As such, the state justified material sacrifice, along with repression, on the basis of constructing a socialist utopia. By the 1960s that utopia had yet to be realized; however, life had improved considerably in the form of increased wages and access to consumer goods. This consumer and cultural liberalization highlighted the modernity and progressiveness of Romania and, when considered within the context of Ceaușescu's denunciation of the Warsaw Pact invasion of Czechoslovakia and engagement with the West, helped garner popular support for the regime. Consequently, some Romanians increasingly evaluated the regime in terms of access to consumer goods and services. As a corollary, individuals, especially those who had experienced upward mobility under socialism, increasingly constituted their identities according to consumer pleasures and leisure activities. However, as consumer liberalization was not accompanied by substantive political reform, it served more as a strategy for securing popular legitimacy than a genuine effort to loosen the political reins.

While the consumer pleasures offered new, more progressive notions of womanhood, manhood, and lifestyle, the images of carefree women found in the pages of *Femeia* or on cinema screens conflicted with restrictive pronatalist policies, which undermined women's bodily control. Therefore, consumer goods could provide people with new experiences, but also serve as a smokescreen for repressive policies. At the same time, some Romanians, most notably artists, intellectuals, and youth, shunned or simply ignored official socialist culture and embraced alternative modes of cultural expression and leisure. Be it by vacationing on the Black Sea or attending an experimental theater performance, such forms of leisure provided individuals with a respite from the formulaic, conformist, and materialist-oriented socialist culture that saturated the public sphere.

Unlike other parts of the Eastern Bloc, the opening up of the consumer sphere in Romania was short-lived. Faced with billions in foreign debt by the early 1980s and viewing foreign loans as a form of imperialism from which Romania needed to wrest itself, Ceaușescu implemented austerity measures. The regime's drive for economic autonomy was devastating for ordinary citizens, however, it was particularly distressing for mothers, as they struggled to procure food, cook nourishing meals, launder clothing and, more generally, tend to their family's basic needs in the midst of food and utility rationing. That said, women's ability to concoct meals and holiday feasts out of a limited amount of food also demonstrated their resourcefulness and ability to "make do." More generally, shortage produced a constant sense of uncertainty that hampered people's ability to organize their time, thus undermining the regime's commitment to rational and efficient living. Shortage also encouraged people to engage in illicit activities, namely trading on the black market and pilfering products from the workplace, practices that went against the values enshrined in the socialist code of ethics.

An analysis of consumption also underscores the continued salience of status and connections during late socialism. By the 1980s, much of the population was forced to queue up in the wee hours of the morning for a liter of milk or a loaf of bread; however, those in high-ranking posts could rely on the party to ensure they and their families received the French cheeses and Scottish whiskey they so enjoyed. Meanwhile, others doled out much of their monthly income to secure basic necessities (and in some cases luxury items) on the black market or through informal networks, while those who sold these good often profited handsomely. Whether a necessary strategy for survival or a means of maintaining a particular standard of living, these networks also served to sustain the very system that had produced material difficulties. Ultimately, increased penury and repression, along with the waning of socialism elsewhere in the Bloc, compelled Romanians to topple the Ceaușescu regime, illustrating the centrality of consumption in regime legitimacy and longevity.

## Notes

1. On the role of consumption on East Germans' memory of socialism, see Paul Betts, "Twilight of the Idols: East German Memory and Material Culture," *Journal of Modern History* 72, no. 3 (2000): 731–65.
2. On consumption and the promotion of modern citizens in the GDR, see Katherine Pence and Paul Betts, eds., *Socialist Modern: East German Everyday Culture and Politics* (Ann Arbor, MI: University of Michigan Press, 2008), 8–9.
3. For other countries in the Bloc, see Susan E. Reid, "Cold War in the Kitchen: Gender and the De-Stalinization of Consumer Taste in the Soviet Union under Khrushchev," *Slavic Review* 61, no. 2 (2002): 211–252; Katherine Pence, "'You as a Woman Will Understand': Consumption, Gender, and the Relationship Between State and Citizenry in the GDR's Crisis of 17 June 1953," *German History* 19, no. 2 (2001): 218–52; and Malgorzata Fidelis, "Are You a Modern Girl? Consumerism and Young Women in 1960s Poland," in *Gender Politics and Everyday Life in State Socialist Eastern and Central Europe*, ed. Shana Penn and Jill Massino (New York: Palgrave, 2009), 171–84.
4. See Susan E. Reid and David Crowley, *Style and Socialism: Modernity and Material Culture in Post-War Eastern Europe* (Oxford: Berg, 2000); David Crowley and Susan E. Reid, eds., *Socialist Spaces: Sites of Everyday Life in the Eastern Bloc* (Oxford: Berg, 2002); Julie Hessler, *A Social History of Soviet Trade: Trade Policy, Retail Practices, and Consumption, 1917–1953* (Princeton, NJ: Princeton University Press, 2004); Patrick Hyder Patterson, *Bought & Sold: Living and Losing the Good Life in Socialist Yugoslavia* (Ithaca, NY: Cornell University Press, 2011); Paulina Bren, *The Greengrocer and His TV: The Culture of Communism after the 1968 Prague Spring* (Ithaca, NY: Cornell University Press, 2010); Paulina Bren, "Mirror, Mirror, on the Wall ... Is the West the Fairest of Them All? Czechoslovak Normalization and Its (Dis)Contents," *Kritika: Explorations in Russian and Eurasian History* 9, no. 4 (Fall 2008): 831–54; and Paulina Bren and Mary Neuberger, eds. *Communism Unwrapped: Consumption in Cold War Eastern Europe* (New York: Oxford University Press, 2012).
5. Daniel Miller, *Material Culture and Mass Consumption* (Oxford: Oxford University Press, 1994), 47, 206.
6. See Daniel Chirot, "Social Change in Communist Romania," *Social Forces* 57, no. 2 (1978): 467–68. Due to lack of modern farming equipment, collectivization, which began in 1949, created food shortages and a decline in exports. As a result, the state moved, in 1951, to a policy of gradual collectivization. Moreover, despite the fact that many families boasted parents and extended family in the countryside, the disastrous impact of collectivization, combined with the harsh punishments peasants faced for distributing food to anyone other than state officials, made the procurement of food not only difficult but also dangerous.
7. At the beginning of the 1950s, ration cards were distributed according to status: red (the largest ration) for those in heavy industry; blue for workers,

primary and high school students, and officials; green for the elderly and wives of workers; orange for children up through age seven whose parents worked; and black (the smallest ration) for those who didn't work. On consumption policies in early socialist Romania, see Mara Marginean, "Minimal necesar, discreționar: Ideologizarea nevoilor ca proiect de integrare a marginalității sociale, 1945–1960," in *Marginalități, periferii și frontiere simbolice: Societatea comunistă și dilemele sale identitare*, ed. Luciana Jinga and Ștefan Bosomitu, *Anuarul IICCMER*, vol. IX (Iași: Polirom, 2014), 96.

8. Maria F., interview with author, Brașov, 20 June 2003.
9. Ion Alexandrescu, *Economia României în primii ani postbelici (1945–1947)* (Bucharest: Editura Științifică și Enciclopedică, 1986), 116.
10. "Lege nr. 5 din ianuarie, 1948 pentru modificarea unor dispozițiuni din Codul Penal" *Monitorul Oficial al Republicii Populare Române*, nr. 15 din 19 ianuarie 1948. For instance, peasants were subject to five years in prison if they were caught selling above the price fixed by the state or found with abundant (in excess of a month's) food supply.
11. Open Society Archives (HU OSA 300-60-1, box 545), as cited in Marginean, "Minimal necesar," 98.
12. Florina, interview with author, Brașov, 15 July 2003.
13. Anda, interview with author, Bucharest, 13 June 2009.
14. Chirot, "Social Change in Communist Romania," 467.
15. Between 1951 and 1955, 14,000 new apartments were built per year; between 1956 and 1960, 26,000 per year; and by the 1970s, approximately 100,000 per year. See Flavius Mihalache and Alin Croitoru, "Mediul rural romanesc: evoluții și involuții. Schimbare socială și antreprenoriat" (PhD diss. University of Bucharest, 2011), 24; and "Chirot, "Social Change in Communist Romania," 474. Cities registered as "closed" required residency permits and prohibited migration to them. In 1974, for instance, Bucharest became a closed city.
16. "Alo, la telefon Moș Gerilă!" *Femeia*, December 1959, 12.
17. Ibid.
18. The USSR retained naval and air bases on Romanian soil, as well as troops in the Soviet republic of Moldova.
19. Gheorghe Gheorghiu-Dej, *Declarație cu privire la poziția Partidului Muncitoresc Român în problemele mișcării comuniste și muncitorești internaționale, adoptată de Plenara lărgită a C.C. al P.M.R. din aprilie 1964* (Bucharest: Editura Politică, 1964), 55.
20. The Valev plan divided Eastern Europe into industrial (northern tier) and agricultural (southern tier) sectors. Unwilling to let Romania languish as an agricultural backwater, Dej refused to participate in this plan, distancing Romania from COMECON altogether.
21. In 1958, trade with the USSR constituted over 50 percent of Romania's total foreign trade and trade with other countries in the Bloc, another 20 percent. Meanwhile, trade with the West constituted less than 25 percent. Just a year later, Romania's trade with the West began increasing, and by 1965 Romania's share of foreign trade with the USSR was 38 percent and with the West 36 percent. *Anuarul Statistic al Republicii Socialiste România*,

1980, 503; and William Crowther, *The Political Economy of Romanian Socialism* (New York: Praeger, 1988), 132–33.
22. For a particularly feminine image, see the cover of the August 1956 issue of *Femeia*.
23. Judd Stitziel, *Fashioning Socialism: Clothing, Politics, and Consumer Culture in East Germany* (Oxford: Berg, 2005); Reid, "Cold War in the Kitchen"; Malgorzata Fidelis, *Women, Communism, and Industrialization in Postwar Poland* (New York: Cambridge University Press, 2010); and conversation with Eszter Zsófia Tóth, February 2010.
24. Ivonne, interview with Anca Coman, Braşov, 8 August 2003.
25. On managed consumption, see Reid, "Cold War in the Kitchen."
26. In 1971 Romania became a member of GATT (General Agreement on Trade and Tariffs) and in 1972 it was the first Eastern Bloc country to join the IMF (International Monetary Fund).
27. As Cornel Ban notes, most of these technology transfers were joint ventures between Romania and West Germany, France, and Great Britain. See Cornel Ban, "Sovereign Debt, Austerity and Regime Change: The Case of Nicolae Ceauşescu's Romania," *East European Politics and Societies* 26, no. 4 (2012), 39; and Chirot, "Social Change in Communist Romania," 474–75.
28. "The Eighties in Bucharest," *Martor: The Museum of the Romanian Peasant Anthropology Review* 7 (2002).
29. Valeria P., interview with author, Braşov, 14 June 2003.
30. Interview with Cătălina, Bucharest, 18 July 2009.
31. Şerban, interview with author, Bucharest, 20 July 2009.
32. Smaranda Vultur, "Daily Life and Constraints in Communist Romania in the Late 1980s: From the Semiotics of Food to the Semiotics of Power," in *Public and Private Recollections of Lived Experience in Southeast Europe*, ed. Maria Todorova, Augusta Dimou, and Stefan Troebst (Budapest: Central European University Press, 2014), 198.
33. Like Khrushchev had with Stalin, this included criticizing Dej's mass purges, repressions, and austerity measures.
34. See the recollections of this period in Vultur, "Daily Life and Constraints."
35. Vladimir Tismăneanu, "Understanding National Stalinism: Reflections on Ceauşescu's Socialism," *Communist and Post-Communist Studies* 32, no. 2 (June 1999) ): 155–73.
36. Ioana, interview with author, Braşov, 20 June 2003.
37. See Vlad Georgescu, *The Romanians: A History*, ed. Matei Calinescu, trans. Alexandra Bley-Vroman. (Columbus: Ohio State Press, 1991), 251.
38. Michael Shafir, *Romania: Politics, Economics, and Society: Political Stagnation and Simulated Change* (London: Pinter Publishing, 1985), 87.
39. *Femeia*, February 1967, 34.
40. In *Femeia*, reference was made to men's displeasure that, due to household duties, their wives did not devote sufficient time to them—or to maintaining their femininity. Indeed, in one instance a man filed for divorce on the basis of "spousal neglect." Such men were portrayed as "outmoded" and served as foils for the ideal socialist husband who helped around the house and viewed his wife as an equal.

41. "Informare cu privire la problemele ce s-au desprins din cercetarea sesizărilor şi propunerilor oamenilor muncii adresate conducerii partidului în trimestrul I 1966," ANIC, CC al PCR, Secţia Cancelarie, dosar 176/1966, f. 7 as cited in Mioara Anton,*"Ceauşescu şi poporul!" Scrisori către "iubitul conducător," (1965–1989)* (Târgovişte: Cetatea de Scaun, 2016), 165.
42. Anton, *"Ceauşescu şi poporul!"* 164–65.
43. "Din Paris," *Moda*, Spring 1969, 35.
44. Alexandra, interview with author, Bucharest, 13 June 2009.
45. Sanda Faur, "Nu Există Fată Urîta!" *Femeia*, January 1969, 12–13.
46. Ibid.
47. This contest was advertised in the May 1969 issue of *Femeia*. The magazine did not specify what it meant by "abroad." See "Concurs de Frumuseţe '69," *Femeia*, May 1969, 16–17.
48. Elisabeta Moraru, "Sunteţi o Femeie Modernă? De Ce?" *Femeia*, January 1970, 3–5.
49. Ibid.
50. Vali, interview with author, Bucharest, 14 June 2009. The Dacia was essentially the Romanian equivalent of the East German Trabant and was named for the region that constitutes most of present-day Romania.
51. Alexandra, interview with author, Bucharest, 16 June 2009.
52. Favorite authors among my respondents included: Marin Preda, Mihail Sadoveanu, Lucian Blaga, Liviu Rebreanu, Charles Dickens, Emily Bronte, Ernest Hemingway, Jules Verne, Honoré de Balzac, and Isaac Asimov.
53. Elvira, interview with author, Braşov, 5 May 2003.
54. Maria, interview with author, Braşov, 8 June 2003.
55. Adelina Ştefan "Where West Meets East: International Tourism and Consumerism in Socialist Romania of the 1960s–1980s," paper presented at the Association for Slavic, East European, and Eurasian Studies, Boston, MA, November 2013.
56. Ibid.
57. See Irina Costache, "From the Party to the Beach Party: Nudism and Artistic Expression in the People's Republic of Romania," in Cathleen M. Giustino, Catherine J. Plum, and Alexander Vari, eds., *Socialist Escapes: Breaking Away from Ideology and Everyday Routine in Eastern Europe, 1945–1989* (New York: Berghahn Books, 2013), 132.
58. Madigan Fichter, "Rock and Roll Nation: Counterculture and Dissent in Romania, 1965–1975," *Nationalities Papers* 39, no. 4 (2011), 571.
59. Ibid.
60. Ban, "Sovereign Debt," 746.
61. G.N., interview with author, Braşov, 16 August 2003.
62. Nicolae Ceauşescu, *Propuneri de măsuri pentru îmbunătăţirea activităţii politico-ideologice, de educare marxist-leninistă a membrilor de partid, a tuturor oamenilor muncii, 6 iulie 1971* (Bucharest, 1971).
63. "Decretul nr. 153 din 24 martie 1970 pentru stabilirea şi sancţionarea unor contravenţii privind regulile de convieţuire socială, ordinea, şi liniştea publică," *Buletinul Oficial al Republicii Socialiste România*, nr. 33, 13 aprilie 1970.
64. World Bank figures as cited in Ban, "Sovereign Debt," 746.

65. Exports of foodstuffs increased by 12.3 percent in 1982 and imports decreased by 66.8 percent. See Crowther, *Political Economy of Romanian Socialism*, 141.
66. See ANIC, CC al PCR, Secția Cancelarie, dosar 33/1982, ff. 21–22; and Anton, "*Ceaușescu și poporul!*" 153.
67. In 1981 trade with LDCs accounted for 25 percent of Romania's exports and 30 percent of its imports. See Crowther, *Political Economy of Romanian Socialism*, 142.
68. G.N., interview with author, Brașov, 16 August 2003.
69. See Maria Bucur, "Sex in the Time of Communism: The Ripple Effect of the #metoo Campaign," *Public Seminar*, 7 December 2017, retrieved from http://www.publicseminar.org/2017/12/sex-in-the-time-of-communism/ (accessed 10 December 2017).
70. See Marius Stan, "Cu sacoșa spre comunism: Programul științific de alimentație raționala în România socialistă," in *Transformarea socialistă: politici ale regimului comunist între ideologie și administrație*, ed. Ruxandra Ivan and Daniel Barbu (Iași: Polirom, 2009). The program was published in *Scânteia* on 14 July 1982, 2–3. These quantities were smaller for 1983–84.
71. See, for example, Smaranda Sburlan, "Alimentația rațională-imperativ al sănătății și longevitații," *Femeia*, January 1981, 14. See also "Alimentația și viața rațională: Meniu model pentu o săptămâna," *Femeia*, 1981, 23
72. See "Arta de a trăi rațional," *Femeia*, March 1981 and July 1981.
73. For examples of suggested menus, see Gail Kligman, *The Politics of Duplicity: Controlling Reproduction in Ceaușescu's Romania* (Berkeley: University of California Press, 1998), 140–141.
74. Václav Havel, *The Power of the Powerless: Citizens against the State in Central-Eastern Europe* (London: M. E. Sharpe, 1978), 37–40.
75. Livia, interview with Ioana Manoliu, Brașov, 11 August 2003.
76. See Vultur, "Daily Life and Constraints," 198.
77. Milovan Djilas, *The New Class: An Analysis of the Communist System* (New York: Praeger, 1957).
78. Personal communication with Adrian S., 2 March 2014.
79. Personal communication with Iulian B., 17 March 2014.
80. ANIC, CC al PCR, Secția Cancelarie, dosar 191/1972–1989, vol. 2. Anonymous letter to Elena Ceaușescu, 12 August 1989.
81. Interview with Ioana, Brașov, 20 June 2003.
82. Art. 224 "Codul Penal din 1968" *Monitorul Oficial al României*, 1 ianuarie 1969. In extreme cases, theft was liable to capital punishment.
83. Vlad Pașca, "Clienți la masa statului: Alimentația publică în România socialistă (1948–1989)," in *Între Transformare și adaptare: Avatururi ale cotidianului în regimul comunist din România*, ed., Luciana Jinga and Ștefan Bosomitu, *Anuarul IICCMER*, vol. VIII (Iași: Polirom, 2013), 82.
84. Maria, interview with author, Brașov, 15 June 2003.
85. Elena, interview with author, Bucharest, 1 June 2009.

86. "Decret nr. 210 din 14 iunie 1960 privinvd regimul mijloacelor de plată străine, metalelor prețioase și pietrelor prețioase," *Buletinul Oficial al Republicii Populare Romîne* nr. 8/17 iunie 1960. On tourist workers serving as informers, see Adelina Ștefan, "Where West Meets East."
87. On cross-border trading between Romania and Hungary, see Liviu Chelcea and Puiu Lațea, "Cultura penurei: bunuri, strategii și practici de consum in Romania in anilor '80," in *Viața cotidiană în comunism*, ed. Adrian Neculau (Iași: Polirom, 2004), 152–74.
88. Valeria R., interview with author, Brașov, 2 May 2003.
89. H., interview with author, Brașov, 4 June 2003.
90. Indeed, some Bucharest doctors received so many luxury items from their *nomenklatura* patients that they had a coffee merchant sell them in exchange for money. The *miliția* typically turned a blind eye to such illegal activities as they could also benefit from these exchanges. For one merchant's recollections of these practices, see Gheorghe Florescu, *Confesiunile unui cafegiu* (Bucharest: Humanitas, 2008).
91. Domnica, interview with author, Brașov, 22 June 2003. Although she did not explicitly mention it, Domnica was seemingly able to "live well" during late socialism because of her husband's position as the head of exports at a factory. Thus, she had access to the high-quality Romanian goods that were exported, as well as any foreign goods her husband brought into the country since he traveled widely in and outside of the Bloc.
92. PCR was also used as an acronym to refer, colloquially, to Elena and Nicolae Ceaușescu's extended family: Petrescu, Ceaușescu, și Rudele (Petrescu, Ceaușescu, and relatives). Members of both families assumed important positions in the government in the 1980s.
93. Ildiko, interview with Ioana Maoliu, Brașov, 12 July 2003.
94. Mark Edele, "Soviet Society, Social Structure, and Everyday Life: Major Frameworks Reconsidered," *Kritika* 8, no. 2 (2007), 361.
95. Tatiana, interview with author, Brașov, 27 May 2003.
96. Luana, interview with author, Brașov, 25 July 2003.
97. Elvira, interview with author, Brașov, 5 May 2003.
98. Hoarding was officially codified as "speculation" and defined as purchasing (and possessing) a quantity of food that surpassed the monthly needs of a family. See "Decretul 306/1981 privind măsuri pentru prevenirea și combaterea unor fapte care afecta buna aprovizionare a populației," *Monitorul Oficial*, 9 octombrie 1981. The punishment for specualtion could range from a prison sentence (in a correctional facility) of six months to five years.
99. Maria F., interview with author, Brașov, 20 June 2003.
100. *Femeia* tried to debunk such views. See Niki Georgescu, "Casele de comenzi," *Femeia*, April 1979.
101. Elena, interview with author, Bucharest, 1 June 2009.
102. Elisabeta, interview with author, Brașov, 27 June 2003.
103. Tatiana, interview with author, Brașov, 27 May 2003.

104. Stela, interview with author, Brașov, 23 June 2003.
105. Adrian, interview with author, Bucharest, 19 July 2009.
106. Paul Cernat, "Cozi și oameni de rând în anii 80," in *Viața cotidiană în comunism*, 192–93.
107. Lucia, interview with author, Bucharest, 20 June 2012.
108. Stela, interview with author, Brașov, 23 June 2003.
109. Anton, *"Ceaușescu și poporul!"* 180.
110. For a recollection of daily struggles in procuring goods in the 1980s, see Ciprian Plăiașu, "Țara umilinței în templele foamei: cum ne-am bătut pe un ou, pe 'Frații Petreus,' de pe cartelă sau pe o sticlă cu lapte. Lumina, butelia, și căldura la poartie," *Historia*, retrieved from https://www.historia.ro/sectiune/general/articol/tara-umilintei-in-templele-foamei-cum-ne-am-batut-pe-un-ou-pe-fratii-petreus-de-pe-cartela-sau-pe-o-sticla-cu-lapte-lumina-butelia-si-caldura-la-portie (accessed 15 March 2016).
111. Katherine Verdery, *What Was Socialism, and What Comes Next?* (Princeton, NJ: Princeton University Press, 1996), 46.
112. See Ofelia Vaduva, *Steps toward the Sacred: From the Ethnology of Romanian Food Habits* (Bucharest: Romanian Cultural Foundation, 1999).
113. Maria, interview with author, 15 June 2003.
114. Slavenka Drakulić, *How We Survived Communism and Even Laughed* (New York: Harper Perennial, 1993), 16.
115. Michel de Certeau, *The Practice of Everyday Life* (Berkeley: University of California Press, 2002), 15.
116. Stela, interview with author, Brașov, 23 June 2003.
117. Marcela, interview with Anca Coman, Brașov, 12 August 2003.
118. Maria, interview with author, Brașov, 15 June 2003.
119. Ivonne, interview with Anca Coman, Brașov, 8 August 2003.
120. Rodica, interview with Anca Coman, Brașov, 12 August 2003.
121. Clara, interview with author, Brașov, 6 July 2003.
122. Aneta Popescu, "Confort prin iluminat cu mai puțin kilowați," *Femeia*, April 1987.
123. See "Tot ce poate refolosi să refolosim!" *Femeia*, February 1983, 10. The article included addresses of places in Bucharest where such items could be "reconditioned."
124. Anton,*"Ceaușescu și poporul!"* 153.
125. Simona, interview with Ioana Manoliu, Brașov, 5 August 2003.
126. Radu Clit, "Frica de zi de zi," in *Viața cotidiană în comunism*, 60.
127. A., interview with author, Bucharest, 6 June 2012.
128. "Stenograma ședenței de lucru de la Comitetul Central al PCR cu primii secretari ai comitetelor județene de partid, secretarii cu probleme economice și alte cadre de conducere," ANIC, CC al PCR, Secția Cancelarie, dosar 5/1985, ff. 2–3; 12; in Anton,*"Ceaușescu și poporul!"* 157.
129. Florina, interview with author, Brașov, 15 June 2003.
130. Between 1980 and 1985, expenditures on health care decreased by 17 percent. See Georgescu, *The Romanians*, 271.

131. "Un grup de femei," letter broadcast in Romania on Radio Free Europe on 27 May 1984, in Gabriel Andreescu and Mihnea Berindei, *Ultimul deceniu comunist: Scrisori către radio Europa Liberă vol 1, (1979–1985)* (Iași: Polirom, 2010), 261–62.
132. C., interview with author, Brașov, 14 July 2003.
133. ANIC, CC al PCR, Secția Cancelarie, dosar 191/1972–1989, vol. 2, f., 164–178. Letter from Elena Negru to Elena Ceaușescu, 8 February 1988.
134. Despite Romanians' increasing deprivation, Ceaușescu still managed to allocate millions of dollars to support industry and infrastructure in North and Sub-Saharan Africa, Cuba, the Middle East, and the USSR. See Ban, "Sovereign Debt," 760–766.
135. When communism fell in December 1989, the Romanian government registered an impressive budget surplus. In Poland, by comparison, reduction in access to food staples never surpassed 10 percent. See Ban, "Sovereign Debt," 760.

CHAPTER 7

# Revolution Blues

### Gender and the Transformation from Socialism to Pluralism

You have the possibility to dream about something and even realize these dreams. That's the biggest gain. Not freedom of speech, that appears abstract to me. Before you didn't have a reason to dream. When you knew that everything will be the same, that nothing will change, that you are small in the face of destiny, a type of robot that functions. I think that [the freedom to do something] was a gain.
—Stela, artist and former telephone technician (b. 1954)

First of all, we have freedom of speech, which is a big deal. Economically, however, not as much has changed as I had hoped, that is, the economic situation still leaves very, very much to be desired. Unlike in '89, there is a huge gap between social strata. There is a stratum of people that is really poor and lives from one day to the next, if they don't starve, and an extremely rich stratum.
—Rodica, former construction worker (b. 1963)

I believed in communism. Not everything they did was bad.
—Adriana, retired teacher (b. 1952)

On the morning of Sunday, 15 November 1987, several thousand workers walked off their jobs at Steagul Roşu (the Red Flag) factory in Braşov to protest wage cuts.¹ On their march to Communist Party headquarters on that unseasonably warm autumn day, thousands of others joined them. Ildiko, then a twenty-eight-year-old employee of the factory, described the sense of unity born of shared discontent and immiseration: "I was not afraid. You see, when you find yourself in a group, you feel this force, it attracts you. I felt all of their dissatisfactions. They were also ours."² Such courage was especially noteworthy in Romania since, only ten years prior to the Braşov revolt, leaders of the Jiu Valley coal mining strike had been arrested and effectively disappeared after demanding wage increases and a reinstatement of disability pensions.[3]

Upon entering the city center, the marchers shouted, "Thieves ... we want our money back," "We want Sunday back," "We want food for our children," and "Down with Ceaușescu! Down with communism! Down with the Golden Era ... down with tyranny."[4] Anticommunist slogans were followed by nationalist evocations, notably the singing of the national anthem "Deșteaptă-te române!" ("Wake up, Romanian!").[5] Just as Ceaușescu had mobilized nationalism to legitimate his version of socialism, the demonstrators mobilized it to delegitimize his rule. The demonstration, which occurred on the day of local elections, was materially and existentially rooted: at its heart it was a protest against years of cold, hunger, and indignity. In the words of Livia, "They were unhappy with the daily realities, with the conditions at work. Of course they protested. It was the first really, really strong sign of collective dissatisfaction."[6] By the time the marchers reached Communist Party headquarters, the crowd numbered some twenty thousand. Once there, the marchers presented their demands, namely a retraction of wage cuts and an end to rationing, to party officials, who, in turn, refused to hear them out.[7] In response, a small group separated from the crowd and broke into party headquarters. After entering the canteen, they discovered an array of foodstuffs, from oranges and bananas to salami and cheese, which they tossed out of the windows into the cheering crowd. They also ransacked Party offices, hurling documents, paintings of the Ceaușescus, and party flags out the window, which they eventually burned in a huge bonfire.[8] Elvira, who was watching from afar, remembered thinking to herself, "This is not good ... this is not good," and left the scene. Other respondents also left around this time, mainly out of concern for their children who were at home. By nightfall the Securitate had crushed the revolt and sealed off the city. Although there were no deaths, three hundred people were arrested, sixty-two of whom were forcibly relocated to other cities and towns in Romania. As Stela recalled, "They were taken and they disappeared, pure and simple."[9]

The party justified repressive measures by portraying the demonstrators as hooligans (a term that would be used by Ceaușescu to describe peaceful protesters in Timișoara in December 1989), "vagabonds," and "vandals" who were a "stain on the collective."[10] Although the people of Brașov were punished for their disobedience through arrests, increased surveillance, and underprovisioning, the protesters' sacrifices would not be in vain as the revolt illustrated the pervasiveness of popular discontent.[11] It also emboldened others to engage in subsequent acts of opposition. As Valeria P. recalled, "It was a manifestation of great courage ... a type of desperate protest. People were desperate. So they risked their lives ... and this courage remained and ... I think it gave courage to those in Timişoara and Bucharest because they risked their lives for change."[12]

Opposition to Ceauşescu ultimately culminated in the overthrowing of the communist dictatorship and the violent revolution of 1989. Romanians greeted the collapse of socialism with relief but also hope. Democracy, they believed, would guarantee free speech, travel, and association; occupational flexibility and upward mobility; a more transparent and accountable government; and improved social entitlements. While the aforementioned political rights have been attained, most Romanians have yet to reap the economic benefits of the transformation to a market economy. Nor has the government demonstrated transparency or consistent concern for the common good. Indeed, for many, including those who were children during the late 1980s, the transformation to pluralism has turned out to be a mixed bag. This is due to a number of factors, from shifts in the global economy that began already in the 1970s to the machinations of certain political elites during the revolution and its aftermath to the influence of Western powers and international lending agencies.

While providing new rights and opportunities, the transformation to pluralism has also created uncertainties and vulnerabilities: costs for basic goods and services, as well as access to jobs and social entitlements, are subject to market forces and the whims of employers and policymakers. Moreover, the late-capitalist market is predicated on a new type of worker and, indeed, new person, who is flexible, proactive, and seamlessly negotiates economic change—characteristics alien to those accustomed to the socialist workplace. While individuals with sufficient cultural capital, much of it built up during socialism, have been able to weather these changes relatively well—and even thrive—those who lack such capital, particularly industrial workers, have discovered there is no place for them in the postsocialist labor force.

More generally, Romanians are dismayed by the high cost of food, utilities, and housing as well as the corruption that characterizes many Romanian institutions, from the parliament and judicial system to education and healthcare. While corruption was also a feature of socialist rule, most Romanians expected it would be non-existent—or at least not pervasive–under an open, democratic system. Moreover, many are angered, if not outright disgusted, by the underhanded activities of political elites and business moguls who are seemingly immune from the law. This is further exacerbated by the huge economic gulf that separates the elite from the majority of Romanians. For many Romanians, then, the belief that political pluralism, capitalism, and EU integration would usher in an era of freedom, opportunity, and social advancement has not come to fruition. As such, there is a widening social, economic, and existential gap between the losers and winners of the transformation, with the result that the transition has been characterized by hopes but also disappointments—in a word, ambiguities.

This chapter enhances understandings of the transformation to postsocialism by focusing on its gendered dimensions. The first part provides a general overview of the revolution of 1989 and the ensuing political, economic, and social changes that occurred as Romania shifted to a pluralist system and market economy. This is followed by an examination of how market forces and curtailments in the social welfare system have affected women's opportunities, perspectives on the state and democratic process, and their sense of self. As a corollary, I consider how these processes have influenced women's views of the past and of state socialism more generally.

The transformation has been particularly ambiguous for women. On the one hand, the legalization of abortion in 1989 has restored reproductive freedom.[13] Moreover, the shift to a market economy has expanded professional opportunities while the opening of borders has provided possibilities for studying and working abroad. Additionally, freedom of speech has enabled engagement in associational life, including in protests. That said, the embrace of neoliberal policies and the adoption of austerity measures in response to the global financial crisis of 2008 have exacerbated social inequality, undermining women's ability to support themselves and their families—and prompting some to forgo having children altogether.

While some women have managed to secure work and thrive professionally after 1989, others have been less successful in integrating themselves into the market economy. Indeed, already in 2003, when my first round of interviews was conducted, many were struggling to find work and lamented the loss of economic security and the sense of personal validation their jobs under socialism had provided them. Moreover, they expressed frustration over cuts in state subsidies, citing the exorbitant costs of medicine, food, and other necessities. Thus, my respondents' attitudes toward the postsocialist transformation are complex and ambiguous, shaped by their experiences of both past and present and the disconnect between expectation and reality.

## The Revolution Will be Televised: The Fall of Ceaușescu

The protest that occurred in Brașov in 1987 was both materially and morally motivated. As explored in the previous chapter, beginning in the early 1980s, basic foods such as milk, meat, eggs, and oil had been rationed; however, this eventually extended to non-foodstuffs including heat, electricity, and hot water. Indeed, by the eve of the revolution, the monthly per-person ration stood at one kilogram of flour, sugar, and meat; half a kilogram of margarine; and five eggs.[14] Meanwhile, high-ranking communists enjoyed a diverse array of goods, from Western fashions and cigarettes to caviar and exotic fruits. Moreover, while many Romanians shivered in dark apartments, the state poured millions of dollars into gas-guzzling industries and the construction of *Casa Poporului*. The massive gulf between ideology and reality and the gap between the privileged few and the impoverished many thus catalyzed ordinary Romanians to challenge Ceaușescu's rule.

Compared with other regimes in the Eastern Bloc (with the exception of Albania), Romania was the most repressive, still bound in a "rigid communist monolithism" that "displayed all the signs of arrested political development."[15] Unlike Poland, which experienced the emergence (and political triumph) of the massive Solidarity movement; Hungary, which could claim a range of nongovernmental movements and even multiple political parties by the late 1980s; and Czechoslovakia, where over a thousand individuals openly vowed to "live in truth," no bona fide dissent movement existed in Romania to challenge Ceaușescu's rule.

The absence of viable antistate organizations and dissident activity was due to the repressiveness of the regime and the seemingly omnipresent Securitate. For example, the distribution of anti-Ceaușescu leaflets could garner a ten-year prison sentence, as was the case for Radu Filipescu, an electronics engineer. Or, it could garner a somewhat lighter punishment, such as house arrest—the fate of Doina Cornea, a professor of French at the University of Cluj who, with her son, Leontin, distributed pamphlets in support of the Brașov strike of 1987.[16] Punishment for antistate activities could also be more insidious in the form of commitment to a psychiatric ward.[17] Such draconian measures, combined with the belief that one of every four Romanians was working in some capacity with the Securitate, created a general climate of fear, suspicion, and inertia within the populace. As Cornea remarked, "We are a land occupied by an invisible army of security forces under your [Ceaușescu's] guidance and leadership."[18] More generally, in an environment in which resistance could mean not only a long jail term, but also prevent one's offspring from attending university, securing a job, or even maintaining friendships, the cost of dissidence was, for many, simply too high and, in certain respects, selfish.[19]

Lack of resistance was also due to the regime's success in enticing intellectual and cultural figures to prop it up.[20] Meanwhile, writers, artists, and intellectuals who did engage in dissent typically faced house arrest or forced exile.[21] Given such risks, artists and intellectuals often engaged in more passive forms of resistance. For example, Ruxandra, an artist, noted that there were many types of resistance under socialism, and, referring to intellectuals and cultural figures, highlighted those who refused to legitimate the regime with their literary and artistic productions. The price for such non-compliance, she claimed, was felt in the material aspects of everyday life, "They refused to make propaganda. That was their resistance. And they lived poorly but truthfully. The regime no longer attacked directly. You could live in truth, but then you couldn't buy a car."[22] Thus, certain individuals not only refused to live the lie in their daily lives, but professionally as well, which meant they could live in dignity, but modestly. While this form of resistance was not public and was too diffuse to present a serious challenge to socialist rule, it nonetheless offers insight into how some individuals registered their disapproval with the regime in a manner that was explicit and that undermined their quality of life.

Efforts to reform communism from within the party, let alone critique Ceaușescu's policies, were also met with marginalization and repression.[23] For example, when veteran party leader Constantin Pârvulescu charged Ceaușescu, at the Eleventh Party Congress in November 1979, with creating a personal dictatorship and neglecting the interests of the people, the state stripped him of his position as delegate to the congress and placed him under house arrest. Meanwhile, three editors of the communist newspaper *România Liberă* were sentenced to death for attempting to publish an anti-Ceaușescu piece in the spring of 1989 (they were ultimately spared due to the revolution).[24] Although less harshly treated, the authors of the "Letter of the Six," all of them party veterans (including former Politburo members), were placed under house arrest for smuggling their "open letter to Ceaușescu" to the West in 1989.[25] The letter, which was published in Western newspapers and aired in Romania via Radio Free Europe, accused Ceaușescu of betraying principles in the Helsinki Final Act, namely denying basic civil liberties enshrined in the Romanian Constitution and violating human rights per the Vienna Conference on Human Rights. These individuals, however, represented lone voices in the wilderness of dynastic socialism, as most members of the Central Committee and other high-ranking functionaries, in order to retain their privileged status, remained slavishly loyal to Ceauşescu.

Because large and public acts of resistance proved not only futile but also risky, people engaged in everyday acts of resistance and duplicity such as reading, copying, and distributing blacklisted books, procuring foreign video cassettes and recorders, listening to Radio Free Europe and other foreign broadcasts, exchanging goods and services on the black market, and working within the second economy.[26]

Like other neo-Stalinists such as East Germany's Erich Honecker and Czechoslovakia's Gustáv Husák, Ceauşescu was wholly allergic to systemic reform. Thus, rather than follow the lead of Soviet leader Mikhail Gorbachev, he denounced him as a right-wing deviationist who was intent on destroying socialism.[27] Moreover, Ceauşescu feared foreign meddling into domestic affairs. Consequently, in 1988 he repudiated Romania's "Most Favored Nation Trading Status" with the United States out of concern the U.S. Congress would conduct investigations into human rights abuses in the country. The cost of autonomy was a $250 million loss in trade revenue for Romania, further adding to the country's mounting debt.[28] Indeed, as late as 24 November 1989, after the victory of Solidarity in Polish elections, the opening of the Berlin Wall in East Germany, and on the same day the communist leadership in Czechoslovakia resigned, Ceauşescu gave a six-hour speech at the Fourteenth Party Congress during which he castigated Romania's neighbors for betraying socialism. The response was applause, countless standing ovations, and his unanimous reelection as president of Romania. However, this was all mere spectacle as Ceauşescu's hold on power was much more tenuous than he would have the people believe.

The Romanian Revolution began on 15 December 1989, with a candlelight vigil held by Hungarian parishioners in solidarity with Reformed pastor László Tőkés of Timişoara, who had been ordered to relocate to a rural parish for criticizing Ceauşescu's systematization plan and human rights abuses.[29] By December 16, the vigil had evolved into a mass interethnic and interfaith protest that called for Ceauşescu's removal. On the following day, Tőkés was evicted from Timişoara and barricades were raised throughout the city, during which minor incidents of vandalism occurred. The *miliţia* and Securitate responded with brute force, shooting randomly into the crowd of protesters. By December 18, an estimated fifty-eight had been killed, over two hundred wounded, and seven hundred arrested (though at the time it was believed that over a thousand had been killed).[30] In the television broadcast that followed, Ceaușescu claimed to have saved the country from hooligans, fascists, and "foreign terrorists with imperialist designs on Romania."[31] This, however, did not hinder popular mobilization and the authorities ultimately lost control of the city.

On December 21, by which time protests had spread to other cities, Ceaușescu made the fateful mistake of organizing a pro-regime assembly in Bucharest. Although designed to follow the script of previous rallies wherein the crowd (particularly those in the front rows who had been cherry-picked for the purpose) chanted support for the communist leader, the event did not go as planned. After Ceaușescu condemned the Timișoara events, the crowd quickly turned volatile. The standard chant "Ceaușescu și poporul" (Ceaușescu and the people) soon morphed into "Ceaușescu dictatorul" (Ceaușescu the dictator), and the live television coverage of the event revealed a perplexed Ceaușescu, uncertain of how to restore order. Groping for a solution, Ceaușescu promised wage increases and additional subsidies for mothers and students; however, the disgruntled crowd would not be placated and the rally turned into a protest. By this point, student and worker demonstrations had broken out in the city, along with street fighting among different armed groups. Repression by state security forces and the army was brutal: on 21 December alone, 50 people were killed and 462 injured, many of them young people. Nonetheless, protests resumed again on the 22nd, and after reports that the head of the army, General Vasile Milea, had committed suicide, the army, now under new command, called back its troops. People responded by flooding into the Central Committee building, which the Ceaușescus hastily fled via helicopter.[32]

In a television broadcast that evening, a group of second-tier communists (including Ion Iliescu) army officers, and intellectuals declared the old regime defunct and asked the people to support a transitional governing body: the National Salvation Front (Frontul Salvării Naționale [FSN]). In the broadcast, Iliescu proclaimed his commitment to political pluralism, freedom of speech, and economic reform.[33] Meanwhile, the army arrested the Ceaușescus in an agricultural institute in Târgoviște, where they had hitched a ride with a bicycle repairman. On Christmas Day the couple was tried by military tribunal (essentially a kangaroo court) and found guilty of genocide and of using state money for personal purposes. That same afternoon the Ceaușescus were executed by firing squad, their hasty trial and execution justified by the FSN on the basis of saving civilian lives from assaults by "terrorists" and other pro-Ceaușescu elements and sparing the country from civil war. Like other events during the revolution, the trial and execution was televised—on Christmas day—to which Romanians responded with shock, joy, relief, and concern, among other sentiments.

Compared to other countries in the Eastern Bloc whose revolutions were relatively peaceful, the Romanian Revolution was violent. The official number of victims of the entire revolution is recorded at 1,104 dead and 3,352 wounded, many of them young adults.[34] These youths had been born after the implementation of Decree 770 and had come of age during the mass shortages of the 1980s when the future, like the landscape, looked bleak. To quote Vladimir Tismăneanu: "Romania's revolution was born out of absolute desperation: The youths who took to the streets knew that they would be murdered, but they refused to accept the prolongation of oppression."[35]

While some of my respondents joined protests in the central part of the city, others, especially those with children, stayed at home and watched the events on television. Some tuned into TVR (the state television station) and, if they got reception, Hungarian news stations, while others listened to Radio Free Europe. Reflecting on the confusion, Ecaterina noted in 2003:

> We watched television to see what was going on. We listened to Europa Liberă [Radio Free Europe]. There was such a discrepancy between TVR and what Europa Liberă was airing. It was a difference, we didn't know ... we felt that there was something [going on] but we didn't know what it was. That is, everything was a masquerade, a takeover of power, a diversion ... because they killed some innocent people and lied to the others.[36]

As with most revolutions, the Romanian Revolution was a chaotic period, as people received information from various news sources. During the final part of December, a range of information was disseminated, some of it unverified and some clearly fabricated, including news that Romania's water sources had been poisoned, that Libyans had engaged in aerial assaults on the country, and that so-called terrorists were attacking the population.[37] Ecaterina's above quote captures that confusion and offers an analysis of it. Having had over a decade to reflect on and read about those heady days, a decade characterized by corruption, economic instability, and competing representations of the revolution, Ecaterina interpreted the revolution as a masquerade wherein second-tier communists, presenting themselves as populist liberators, assumed the reins of power.

Confusion coexisted with fear as the *miliția* and other armed groups and individuals exchanged fire on the streets, in some cases entering apartment buildings. Those who stayed at home were glued to their television, while others gathered at work and marched excitedly toward the city center to celebrate. As Corina, a technician in her early twenties at the time of the revolution, recalled:

> I was in the square; it was a release, a joy, because we wanted change, liberty ... a different type of life, because by then things were already so isolated ... there was too much rigidity; we were essentially fenced in. And the pressures from the outside had a big effect on us because they were opening the borders.[38]

Fighting broke out in cities throughout the country, and, as a result of the confusion, many innocent civilians were shot or killed—in some cases friends and colleagues of my respondents. Uncertainty about the causes and nature of the revolution continue to this day. According to a number of scholars, at the time these events were "universally perceived as a revolution."[39] However, while some argue it was a spontaneous anti-regime revolt, others, including some of my respondents, believe it was a planned coup organized by the Securitate and second-tier communists who recognized the regime was on the verge of collapse and sought to maintain their privileged position—a view undoubtedly influenced by the presence of former communist elites in the government since 1989 and the various interpretations of the events that have been on offer since the early 1990s.[40] In the end, Grigore Pop-Eleches's assessment seems most appropriate: "If Romanians can agree on anything about the 1989 events, it is probably that many of the crucial details about what happened in those tumultuous days are still not known and may never be brought to light."[41]

## Postsocialism and Its Discontents

On a geopolitical level, the collapse of socialism in the Eastern Bloc signified the end of an ideological, economic, and cultural conflict that had been raging for decades. Like the revolutions themselves, the transformation to pluralism in each country varied considerably. While all countries in the former Bloc were faced with replacing an authoritarian, one-party system with democratic bodies and institutions, this was particularly challenging in Romania given the corruption that characterized the socialist bureaucracy, judiciary, and various sectors of the economy. Moreover, due to the absence of reformist elements within the PCR and lack of bona fide resistance movements prior to 1989, the incipient civil society that emerged after socialism's collapse was comparatively weaker than it was in other countries (e.g.

Poland, Czechoslovakia). Additionally, Romania could not draw on a strong democratic tradition, though in this respect it did not differ considerably from a number of its neighbors. Finally, the nature of change in Romania was decisively influenced by the presence of former communist elites in government who had reinvented themselves and were, by and large, motivated by self-interest.[42] Yet, transformation involved not only political and ideological change but also economic change. While western powers and international lending bodies such as the IMF and World Bank hoped to rapidly put Eastern Europe back on the "road to capitalism," most East Europeans had no experience with the neoliberal variant of capitalism that characterized the United States and other leading economies at the time. Nor were they aware of the degree to which globalization had reshaped trading patterns and economic competitiveness. These circumstances were further complicated by former communist elites who sought to maintain their privileged status by managing (or, depending on the perspective, mismanaging) economic change.

From the onset, postsocialist governance was beset by confusion, graft, and intimidation, with the FSN appearing more authoritarian than genuinely democratic. Although intended to be a temporary governing body, the FSN refashioned itself into a political party with Ion Iliescu as president. In response, thousands began protesting in a "communism–free zone" that had been organized at the University of Bucharest, charging the leadership with being heirs to the communist party and demanding the passage of lustration laws, the establishment of independent media, and investigations into the repression of December 1989. Their chant, "The only solution is another revolution," illustrated well early discontent with the nature of postsocialist governance. After the FSN's landslide victory in May 1990, the protests continued, and Iliescu, echoing Ceaușescu six months earlier, responded by referring to the protesters as hooligans (*golani*) and called in about 10,000 Jiu Valley miners to Bucharest to quell them. The result was the death of six demonstrators, the hospitalization of 502 more, and countless beatings—including against Roma residents unaffiliated with the demonstration.[43]

Although a new constitution in 1991 gave Romania the trappings of democracy, leadership positions were filled by second-tier communists, the parliament was fragmented, the judiciary politically compliant, and the successor to the Securitate, the SRI (Serviciul Român de Informații), loyal to Iliescu. Moreover, through its influence on the media, the FSN effectively dominated public discourse, enabling it to publicize its version of events as they unfolded.

During the first years of the transformation, unemployment soared as some industries downsized, privatized, or closed altogether. For instance, unemployment increased from 3.5 percent in 1991 to 10.9 percent in 1994, and inflation (or more aptly, hyperinflation) exceeded 200 percent in 1992 and 1993.[44] In an effort to secure the support of industrial laborers, the peasantry, and retirees and, thereby, ensure their privileged status, policymakers adopted a gradual approach to privatization, with the result that only 54 percent of large industries were privatized by 1995.[45] This approach contrasted with that of Poland, which initiated rapid and radical restructuring (e.g. shock therapy), and other former Bloc countries such as Hungary and Czechoslovakia, which demonstrated a more genuine commitment to economic reform. Gradualism benefited some Romanian workers, particularly men employed in the country's larger industries, insulating them, at least in the short term, from poverty.

Gradualism was most beneficial, however, for former communist elites, providing a socially acceptable approach to economic transformation that they manipulated to enrich themselves. Having lost political status, these elites sought to preserve as much power as possible by managing the process of economic transition, effectively transforming their political capital into economic capital.[46] Accordingly, former members of the *nomenklatura*, directors of state enterprises, and retired Securitate officers, many of whom had already participated in the market economy through secret dealings during the 1980s, profited handsomely from economic restructuring.[47] These individuals, in turn, supported politicians who turned a blind eye to and, at times, also profited from privatization.

In some cases, managers of communist-era factories purposely drove them into bankruptcy, after which they purchased and resold them at a considerably higher price, often to foreign companies. The pilfering of public property has been conceptualized by some scholars as "perverted capitalism" and as part of the "great post-communist theft," a process that deviated sharply from the "path" social scientists predicted most postsocialist societies would follow.[48] Corruption and clientism, however, were not new to the postsocialist period as they were rife during the socialist and pre-socialist periods as well. Instead, after 1989 they just assumed a new, more insidious form under the guise of political pluralism and an "open" market economy.

In 2003, Livia reflected on this state of affairs, emphasizing that privatization had not been properly implemented and that "factories were bankrupted on purpose and people, even if they worked for an entire month, were very poorly paid," concluding that "they [the managers] pretended to save the factory by taking control of it [themselves]."⁴⁹ She also noted that people of "low morals" had assumed important positions and "began to run things differently than the people had hoped for," stressing that standards of living were declining and fundamental values disappearing. In sum, she emphasized that postsocialist governance was guided more by self-interest than the common good, one reason for people's increasing disillusionment with politics over the course of the 1990s.

Disenchantment with the Iliescu government propelled university professor Emil Constantinescu and the Democratic Convention to power in 1996. As a political outsider and civil society darling, Constantinescu was greeted with great hope. However, political infighting, corruption, and bureaucratic inefficiency plagued his term. Meanwhile, his efforts at bona fide restructuring (e.g. the closure of a number of state enterprises, including coal mines) triggered protests, culminating in another mineriad—against the government—in 1999.⁵⁰ Moreover, with the lifting of price controls, inflation skyrocketed to over 150 percent in 1997.⁵¹ Nonetheless, the government did make some progress in dealing with the past, establishing the National Council for the Study of Securitate Archives (CNSAS) in 1999, which, in 2006, provided Romanians with access to their personal files and identified politicians and officials who had collaborated with the Securtiate.⁵² However, this law did not require that such individuals step down from political office. Thus, lustration, a process whereby former communist elites are barred from participating in politics, did not characterize the transformation process in Romania. Indeed, the files of high-ranking former communists (e.g. Iliescu) actually remained inaccessible.

Continued material insecurity, combined with political corruption and halting reform, polarized the electorate, forcing Iliescu into a runoff against ultranationalist (and former court poet to the Ceaușescus) Corneliu Vadim Tudor in the elections of 2000. Frustration with precipitously declining living standards and political ineffectiveness was evident in a 2001 survey that ranked the Romanian Parliament the least popular public institution, while the Orthodox Church and the army were ranked the most popular.⁵³ Moreover, a poll carried out by the Romanian Academic Society asking: "When in the last 100 years were things better in Romania?" revealed that only 8.5 percent of respondents felt that life was better after 1989.⁵⁴ Meanwhile, 18.4 percent claimed that life was better in the 1980s and 34.3 percent claimed that it was better between 1965 and 1979.

During the early 2000s, my respondents similarly expressed dissatisfaction with the nature of political and economic change. As Ecaterina remarked:

The government is not interested. Look at them, the thieves, the corruption, all the villas they built ... more and more money in foreign banks and villas on the French Riviera and other places like that. The color of the party doesn't matter. There was the PCR [under communism], at least I knew there was only one. Now, who knows how many PCRs there are? It's just old wine in new bottles.[55]

Ecaterina's comment underscores the degree to which corruption had undermined the democratic promise—and process—in Romania. Indeed, according to her, pluralism is more insidious than one-party rule because it provides a cloak of legitimacy under which self-aggrandizing politicians can hide. Similarly, Valeria R. referred to the leadership as "a disaster and nothing else," noting:

Unfortunately, policies are misguided ... and there is corruption ... because they [the politicians] lack values, principles. They only pursue their immediate interests, because if they thought a bit about others, it would be different. I don't understand how they can live off the taxes I pay, I, who work, produce things of value—they should be paying me. The way they treat us, as if we were their subjects and we ought to do something [for them]. They are not serving us, we are serving them.[56]

Olga, a former factory worker who was in the process of reinventing herself by attending university, emphasized that corruption had produced (or exacerbated existing) social inequality and insecurity:

In general, things have changed for the worse. Because some people are too rich and very many are starving. Jobs are disappearing. The factories are no longer working at the capacity they once did. I don't know, during the Ceauşescu period, even if he was stupid, as some believe, why did we have work and now we don't? Still so many years after the revolution and we are confused because nothing works well any longer. I don't know ... nothing works.[57]

Olga, like many others, had lost her job as a result of restructuring, which was inevitable if Romania was to modernize its economy and engage competitively in the global marketplace. However, because restructuring involved a good deal of corruption, she interpreted her displacement from the industrial labor force as part of a larger systemic bungling, rooted in greed.

While Olga made the above comments during Iliescu's second term (2000–2004), a period of reformism and upward mobility when Romania became a NATO member and began negotiating EU membership, many did not enjoy the economic boom. Although the middle class grew and the country witnessed an increase in homebuilding and the establishment of restaurants and shopping malls, many Romanians faced downward mobility as the economic conditions necessary for EU membership required embracing neoliberal policies. Thus, price controls were lifted, causing utility costs to skyrocket, while privatization and the closure of industries left many workers jobless. Moreover, as a result of wage freezes and curtailments in unemployment benefits many sunk deeper into poverty.[58] At the same time, Iliescu's emphasis on European integration and modernization along neoliberal lines provided a progressive facade behind which corruption and patronage could flourish.[59]

In 2004, Traian Băsescu, a former sea captain and then mayor of Bucharest, beat Prime Minister Adrian Năstase in the bid for president. Băsescu's victory was facilitated by his populist persona, anti-corruption platform, and criticism of former communists in the government.[60] Under Băsescu, the economy experienced impressive growth and control over the media was loosened. Additionally, in 2006, Băsescu established the Presidential Commission on the Study of the Communist Dictatorship, which ultimately produced the "Report on the Communist Dictatorship in Romania" and ordered the SRI to provide the CNSAS with Securitate files.[61] This was followed by Băsescu's condemnation, in parliament, of the communist regime as criminal, to which some representatives responded with physical threats against commission members. Furthermore, in 2007 the archives of the Central Committee of the Communist Party of Romania were made available to the public. Particularly significant, however, was Romania's "return to Europe" through accession to the European Union in 2007.

While from a foreign policy and macro-economic perspective Romania made impressive progress during the early 2000s, many Romanians' situation did not substantially improve and, in some cases, got worse. For instance, in 2008, prior to the global financial crisis, approximately 18 percent of employed people were defined as being poor.[62] Furthermore, in 2008, 23.4 percent of the total population was assessed to be at risk of poverty, and Romania ranked lowest among EU member states with respect to living standards and other socioeconomic indicators.[63] This was further exacerbated by the financial crisis, after which one million people were categorized as experiencing extreme poverty while nearly four million experienced relative poverty."[64]

Although policymakers sought to mitigate poverty by increasing wages and pensions and retaining welfare entitlements, this led to the devaluation of the lei and rising inflation. Those who managed to weather these economic changes were individuals who possessed capital—be it cultural or social—in particular educated individuals with foreign language and computing abilities and the well-connected. Lacking such capital, retired individuals, elderly women, single-headed households, Roma families and industrial laborers fared the worst.

In addition to economic problems, infighting continued to plague Romanian politics, culminating in two efforts to impeach Băsescu (in 2007 and 2012).[65] It is thus unsurprising that many Romanians cite political infighting, corruption, and lack of accountability among the political elite as the country's most pressing problems. As Petre, a retired police officer, stressed in 2009:

> The people should have been favored over the state given what they have been through. [Their] expectations were much higher. And this confused them. ... At the moment you assume a position of public responsibility, you need to understand the issues because you must first meet the needs of those who sent you there. They [Romanian politicians] don't do that. They realize their personal and party interests first. ... Not a single president that we've had up until now has had the backbone to sacrifice his interests for the people. Not a single one. Beginning with Iliescu. Our political class is deplorable.[66]

Petre's sentiments were echoed by Elena, a librarian:

> The politicians and people who took power after 1989 have done their best to destroy the democratic dreams and expectations. They didn't implement real democracy ... they didn't implement good Western values ... the democracy after 1989 was a very Romanian one.[67]

Although Elena had been very hopeful about her—and Romania's—future during the 1990s, by the time of our interview in 2009, she had become disillusioned with politics and only reluctantly voted. Elena's frustration about the nature of democratization resonates with many Romanians. To be sure, not all share her praise of Western values—especially when paired with neoliberalism; however, many tend to regard Western countries as models of democracy. Declining trust in government is related to corruption and opportunism in the form of party switching (to gain privileges) and political and economic scandals, of which Romanians are continuously reminded through TV news and other, often sensationalized, programs.

The prevalence of corruption and the influence of former communist elites—and their offspring—in politics and the economy were referenced by a number of my respondents in explaining why Romania was not a full democracy. A retired female engineer claimed that although Romania was attempting to establish democracy, a major problem was that "all the institutions have thus far been led by the descendants of the communist *nomenklatura* ... the fact is, we are the only [*sic*] country in the East that did not eliminate the neocommunists—the Eighth Point of the Timişoara Proclamation."[68] Drafted in March 1990 by participants of the Timişoara events of December 1989, the "Proclamation of Timişoara" was a response to the perceived illegitimacy of the communist-dominated FSN government. The declaration, which was supported by hundreds of civic groups and organizations, as well as the National Liberal Party and the National Peasant Party, demanded that former communist officials and Securitate officers be barred from running for public office for ten years because an "individual who made such a choice lacks the moral guarantees needed to be a president."[69]

Similarly, in 2012, Lidia, an artist in her late sixties, pointed to the presence of former communists—as well as their offspring—in politics to explain why, despite the adoption of basic political rights, democracy had not been fully realized in Romania: "I have the right to speak [my mind] ... but that doesn't mean things changed for the better. People who stood in the shadow of Ceauşescu, who wanted to be in power, are ... and now their sons are in power. And these kids think they deserve it ... they take advantage of their privileged position."[70] According to Lidia, the existence of basic civil rights, while necessary, is not a sufficient condition for establishing democracy as long as nepotism is a feature of politics. Essentially, democracy has been compromised by an entitled elite acting on behalf of their own economic interests rather than the common good. A sixty-year-old woman economist went further, asserting that Romanian politics is based on connections and money rather than merit and integrity: "I think Romania missed its chance. This is not democracy but anarchy. All bad habits have become unwritten rules—bribing, bargaining, and thievery—with people in high places, in political ones; all kinds of stupid, illiterate, no-good, uneducated people wanting to get rich."[71]

Although the Romanian economy experienced impressive growth during Băsescu's first term, the global financial crisis stalled or reversed much of the progress that had been made. Consequently, real estate construction and other projects screeched to a halt, while unemployment increased, though not dramatically as people traveled abroad for work. To add salt to Romanians' already painful wounds, in 2010 Băsescu implemented austerity measures, among them the slashing of state salaries by 25 percent and pensions by 15 percent.[72] Moreover, the VAT (Value Added Tax) was increased by 5 percent, significantly undermining people's purchasing power. These measures eroded Băsescu's support base, forcing more Romanians to seek work in other parts of

Europe, which further reduced the country's tax base. It also created a polarized electorate.[73]

In January 2012, discontent with neoliberal policies and austerity measures erupted in the form of protests in response to a proposed bill to privatize parts of the healthcare system, ultimately forcing the government to step down. These protests energized civic mobilization around a host of issues, from the proposed mining project in Roşia Montana in Transylvania to voting irregularities in the 2014 presidential election to the Colectiv fire in Bucharest in November 2015, which killed sixty-four people.[74] Meanwhile, January and February of 2017 witnessed the country's largest protests since 1989. Initially a response to an emergency decree decriminalizing minor corruption offenses, by public officials, in which sums do not exceed $48,000, the protests soon morphed into a larger condemnation of high-ranking corruption—what many protesters depicted as "state theft." Such large-scale mobilization illustrates not only the degree to which the principles of democracy and rights have taken root among various segments of the population, but also the degree to which democracy, especially among policymakers, is still very much a work in progress.

## The Gendered Dimensions of Transformation

Women's experiences since 1989 have varied, both in Romania and in the former Eastern Bloc. By the mid-1990s, scholars generally agreed that women had fared worse than men in the region due to economic restructuring and the apparent revival of traditional (e.g. patriarchal and religious) beliefs and practices. This, they argued, contributed to job loss, discrimination within the labor force, and the curtailment of social services, which, in turn, led to the feminization of poverty.[75] Accordingly, Barbara Einhorn claimed that "gains in civil and political rights for women are outweighed by losses of economic, social welfare, and reproductive rights."[76] Scholars also expressed concern over women's underrepresentation in politics. By the end of the 1990s and early 2000s, the picture appeared more complex and less gloomy.[77] In her study of the Bulgarian tourist industry, for instance, Kristen Ghodsee found that women had successfully adapted to market conditions by mobilizing their cultural capital (e.g. education, facility in foreign languages, and experience with Westerners).[78] A similar portrait emerged in Elaine Weiner's study of women managers in Prague, Czech Republic. In Romania as well, cultural capital has enabled some women to secure well-paying jobs and even thrive in the market economy. In contrast, many female (as well as male) laborers who had been employed in socialist industries and lost their jobs as a result of restructuring have struggled to find work commensurate with their skills. Although some have secured work in small-scale services and manufacturing, these jobs are subject to market constraints and, in light of rising inflation and scaled-back entitlements, do not pay enough to cover basic expenses.

Consequently, women's experiences of postsocialism have been ambiguous. To be sure, all individuals welcome political and civic freedoms (freedom of speech, travel, and association), the availability of consumer goods, and reproductive freedom. However, they criticize widespread corruption, rising social disparities, and the scaling back of social services. Moreover, some women, particularly former factory workers, lament the loss of security, validation, and sense of belonging that their jobs during socialism provided them with, and are frustrated that vacations are no longer financially feasible. Praise for the civic freedoms and professional opportunities after 1989 thus exists alongside more critical assessments of the postsocialist period, as well as positive appraisals of the communist period.

## Marketization: Possibilities and Limitations

With the shift to a neoliberal economy, price controls were lifted, state subsidies slashed, and work ceased to be a right guaranteed by the state. This, combined with rising inflation, produced economic insecurity for many. For example, between 1991 and 1994, the unemployment rate skyrocketed from 3 to 10.9 percent (for men) and from 4 to 12.9 percent (for women).[79] While the waning of industry had also contributed to downward mobility and job loss for laborers in the West, in that case deindustrialization was a gradual process, allowing families more time to adapt to economic change. In the former Eastern Bloc, by contrast, deindustrialization has been a rapid phenomenon as factories have virtually closed overnight. Because men represented the majority of those working in heavy industry in Romania, they were initially most affected by restructuring. That said, some men were also protected through generous leave packages for which trade unions—dominated by men—had successfully lobbied the government.[80] Meanwhile, women were encouraged to take early retirement and dedicate themselves to their families, activities presented as luxuries forbidden to them under socialism.

Yet, returning to the home has been all but impossible for most women given high rates of inflation and low wages. As a result, although women's percentage of the total employed has declined slightly since 1989, it has remained relatively high over the course of the transformation with women constituting 46.9 percent of the labor force in 2000, 45.6 percent in 2006, and 43.2 percent in 2015.[81] Meanwhile, unemployment levels have remained low, especially when compared to the EU average. Although these rates increased slightly during the economic crisis, as of 2016 they were down to 5 percent (for women) and 6.6 percent (for men).[82] Such low rates are due to the fact that some women are no longer actively looking for work and thus not registered as unemployed, because many women work in agriculture, and because millions of Romanians have migrated to other parts of Europe for work. At the same time, employment data do not capture those employed in the gray economy, a large portion of which are women. In light of these factors, women's participation in the workforce remains relatively high—a continuity with the late-socialist period.

Although employment rates in Romania are high, this does not mean individuals earn a living wage. Indeed, women's earnings are, on average, not substantially lower than men's. However, within the context of the EU, women's earnings in Romania are among the lowest since overall wages in Romania are among the lowest in the EU. For example, in 2017, women's average hourly earnings were 2.72 Euro (vs. 2.85 for men), well below the EU average earnings of 13.85 Euro (for women) and 16.73 (for men).[83] Such meager earnings, when considered with respect to the cost of housing, food, and utilities, put many workers near or at the poverty rate.

While women's presence in state industries declined with privatization, they constitute a large portion of those employed in the public sector (e.g. education, healthcare, and social work), which has not been subject to downsizing. These positions offer greater workplace flexibility than do private sector jobs, however, they are often poorly remunerated, especially when compared to male-dominated, public sector jobs.[84] Additionally, until the 2017 wage increase, public sector jobs were characterized by inequalities, including different wages for similar functions and low salaries for positions requiring an advanced degree.[85] That said, private sector jobs have also been a mixed-bag, offering higher wages for certain positions and opportunities for advancement, but also less security due to market fluctuations. Moreover, gender hierarchies are evident in the private sector. For example, although women with the requisite education, facility in foreign languages, and technological savvy have fared relatively well in IT, with foreign firms, and in the small-business sector, they are all but absent from the highest echelons of power in leading corporations.[86]

Meanwhile, women are well-represented in academia; however, they tend to be concentrated in lower-ranking positions where the pay and prestige are lower.[87] Finally, women in blue-collar, private sector jobs are concentrated in light industries (e.g. textiles and food processing), commerce, and the service industry, where they typically earn less than men in blue-collar, private sector jobs.

In addition to possessing numerous skills, employees in the neoliberal system are expected to be flexible. Thus, a sizeable portion of women (and men) employed in the private sector work on a contractual (e.g. temporary) basis or in the gray economy, where they are not protected under the law and do not contribute to the state pension fund. Finally, with the opening of borders and Romania's accession to the EU, women's (along with men's) migration to other parts of Europe has increased as individuals take up work outside of Romania. Indeed, the number of Romanians that have migrated abroad for work (be it on a temporary or permanent basis), the vast majority to Italy and Spain, has increased steadily since 2007, when Romania officially entered the EU.[88] As a result, the country has experienced a brain-drain, with doctors, professors, IT specialists, and other skilled-professionals leaving the country, along with skilled and non-skilled laborers employed in construction, agriculture, domestic service and the hospitality industry. Migration intensified with the onset of the global financial crisis as more than 10 percent of Romania's population (2.4 million people) left the country between 2009 and 2011.[89]

As a result of this process, by 2014, an estimated 350,000 children had one or both parents working abroad and were cared for by the remaining parent or, if both parents were abroad, extended family or older siblings.[90] Migration has thus undermined family cohesion by literally separating children from their parents. Although parents, particularly mothers, have been publically criticized for "leaving their children behind," such criticisms shift responsibility away from the market and state to the parent, ignoring the larger systemic roots of the problem.[91] Given the dire poverty experienced by some families, many of them headed by women living in areas with high rates of unemployment, government-imposed austerity measures and political corruption should be targeted for blame.

While the media has emphasized the negative effects of parental migration on children (e.g. increased susceptibility to depression, drug abuse, poor school performance), it has neglected the fact that material remittances sent to families are often crucial to their sustenance (e.g. covering basic necessities, including medical costs).[92] Indeed, these remittances have even enhanced children's educational prospects by covering the cost of a tutor, a computer, and university tuition.[93] Thus, parents' decision to migrate for work should be viewed as a pragmatic response to a system that has failed them and their children, as well as an effort to provide children with opportunities for educational and social advancement.

Given the instability of the labor market and the privileging of certain skills, my respondents expressed concern about their economic situation and lamented the loss of guaranteed employment, which many viewed as a basic right. Believing they would keep their jobs, or at least be gainfully employed until retirement, many women, when asked to compare their position during socialism with the post-1989 period, stressed loss of job security. According to Doina, who worked as a molder in a large factory through the early 1990s but was jobless when I interviewed her in 2003, women fared worse after 1989:

> We are no longer appreciated at the factory. The women left. I am wondering whether I should even get another job. I have another ten years until retirement and, I don't know, I wonder if I will be able to find a job. If not, I need to think about going abroad with my husband.[94]

Like other women who had been employed for a considerable time in socialist industry but lost their jobs with restructuring in the 1990s, Doina felt helpless in the new economic climate. Raised in a system where work was a right, regardless of sex and age, Doina expressed frustration that she could no longer find a job commensurate with her skills. Because Donia's self-identity is closely linked to her trade, her inability to secure work produced both financial insecurity and psychological distress. As scholars of postsocialism have demonstrated, the transformation to a market economy has not only involved the dissolution of certain industries but also the devaluation of skills. Olga (b. 1969), who similarly lost her factory job, elaborated:

> They disbanded everything. I left very disappointed. I cried very much. I was unemployed. When I realized how things stood, [that] I could not get unemployment [compensation] because of the firm, which had not paid their taxes, I was very upset. ... For some it's very good, that is, those strong women, those who knew what they wanted to do, who are bright, it's better. But not for all. There were women who learned how to work under communism; they would go to work, do their job, earn some money, come home, and tend to their own affairs, it's not like that now.[95]

Olga's comments speak to the incompatibility of socialist and postsocialist work cultures, as well as the role of cultural capital in people's adaptability to the market. According to her, many women who spent the majority of their lives working (in factories) under socialism were unable to transition smoothly from one system to another as the enterprises where they had worked had closed and there were no opportunities for using their skills elsewhere.

The sense that circumstances had changed dramatically after 1989 was not only limited to laborers. For example, D. (b. 1953), a geologist, expressed sympathy for other women in her age cohort: "After the revolution, if you want to get a job you need to be under thirty years old. ... You can be very good with lots of experience, but everybody wants young people ... because you can pay them less."[96] Thus, she contended, "My generation is the sacrificed generation. When the transition came, after the revolution, I was too old to flee the country. That is, it's very difficult to immigrate to Canada, to pick up and start again if, for ten to twenty years, you worked only within the [communist] system."[97]

Both age and family circumstance have affected women's ability to retool their skills. For example, while the closure or privatization of state enterprises left women of various ages jobless, for those who were in their forties or early fifties during privatization, retooling one's skills to suit the market was especially difficult as these women were accustomed to the rhythms of the socialist workplace and often had children (including adult offspring who were themselves struggling financially) to support. Therefore, they were not as resilient or as flexible as their younger counterparts who could attend university or acquire new skills through job-training programs. By comparison, women who had been in their twenties or early thirties when socialism collapsed possessed greater flexibility and thus resilience—especially if they did not have children. Angela's case is illustrative. Employed as a woodworker during the final years of socialist rule, she was in her early twenties and childless when the regime collapsed. Thus, Angela adapted relatively easily to economic change, earning a bachelor's degree in economics and going on to work in business. At the same time, Angela acknowledged that things became difficult for others after 1989, and expressed concern about the nature of economic change and the future of the country:

> I can say that in my life things changed for the better, including my job. Then, immediately [after the revolution], conditions were better ... I'm speaking, referring to having heating and material goods. ... As soon as Ceaușescu fell, conditions improved, but that period did not last long. Probably because they finally had paid the debt and we returned to normal. But now [in 2003] they nearly destroyed society; the factories. I can say that presently it is quite difficult. But I can also say I did better after the revolution.[98]

In addition to age, some claimed that personal appearance influenced employment opportunities. As Rodica (b. 1963), a skilled laborer employed in construction during socialism noted, "Maybe there are women who are doing well, but I think they are doing well because they make many compromises. You can't advance without making compromises or being very pretty and intelligent. But for ordinary women it's difficult, much more difficult."[99]

Although younger women (due to education, adaptability, attractiveness, or a combination of these factors) were relatively successful in navigating the uncertain economic waters of the 1990s and early 2000s, youth can also be a detriment. For example, women of childbearing age are often viewed as less productive, less reliable, and less cost-effective than male employees, as it is assumed they will eventually bear children, take family leave, and be a financial drain on the company. In fact, in the 1990s, some private-sector employers required women to sign nonpregnancy certificates whereby they agreed that in the event of pregnancy their employment could be terminated.[100] Although the passage of anti-discrimination legislation in 2000 has made such practices illegal, many women are unfamiliar with this law and employers can resort to other strategies (e.g. eliminating the position) to evade accommodating working mothers. Moreover, labor laws do not apply to jobs in the gray economy, an area that employs many women.

Fear they might lose their jobs or be passed over for promotion has prompted some women to forgo the full maternity leave—a phenomenon that has been observed in other parts of the former Eastern Bloc as well.[101] Some of my respondents understood this as one of the drawbacks of economic pluralism. For example, Rodica (b. 1956), a former legal expert, noted that with respect to work women faced more limitations than they had under socialism, "an employer is much less willing to hire a woman than a man. Because a woman gets married, has children, needs to have maternity leave."[102] When asked, in 2003, if she would change anything about her life, she stressed that if she were still young she would leave Romania so that she could "live a normal life, in a normal country, with a normal democracy. It would not matter what type of work [I would do], but I would be happy to live a normal life, in a normal democracy."[103]

Alongside youth (and beauty), success in the market economy, according to a number of my respondents, required making other compromises or sacrifices (e.g. working long hours; taking jobs outside of one's area of expertise). This has been borne out by those who work longer hours than they did under socialism, in some cases cobbling together two or three jobs just to make ends meet. Such was the case of Tatiana, who, while able to secure work after losing her factory job, found her opportunities considerably limited:

> It was not easy for me. I really struggled ... I fear being left behind. I am the kind of person who wants to have whatever she needs; to not have to rely on someone else to get it. I want to own my own things. And I worked hard to get them. That's the way things are, maybe it was easier for others to make it since they were smarter ... I hoped it would be better but, truthfully, I am not satisfied. I have the impression that they destroyed everything that was good. Everything that I have I got during Ceaușescu's time: my car, my house, my furniture. I just want to be healthy and live a decent life.[104]

Because, at the time of our interview in 2003, Tatiana did not have an advanced degree, was not proficient in a foreign language or computing, and had children at home to support, she was in a much less privileged position than Angela–as will be recalled was childless and considerably younger—for securing work. Thus, Tatiana regarded her job prospects, as well as economic conditions in the country more generally, with uncertainty and concern. Yet, she didn't aspire to wealth. She simply wanted to live decently—a sentiment echoed by other respondents, especially those who had been employed in socialist industry. Moreover, she feared losing the autonomy (or relative autonomy) that decades of work under socialism had afforded her. The general uncertainty women such as Tatiana face has been described by Susan Gal and Gail Kligman as "market coercion." In comparison with socialist systems wherein work was defined as both a right and a duty and individuals were essentially coerced, by the state, into working, market coercion is subtle and even insidious in nature as there is no bogeyman (i.e. the socialist regime) that can be targeted for imposing it. Instead, "it appears to be no one's fault, nor any part of a visible economic system—in fact not coercion at all, just what flexible workers must do to survive in a postsocialist, post-Fordist world.[105] Accordingly, Tatiana's need to cobble together various jobs or work long hours, in some cases rising at 3 or 4 AM and working until 5 PM, is simply what one does to get by in a neoliberal economy. This stands in stark contrast to her experiences before 1989, when she typically worked seven- to eight-hour shifts and had time for her children and leisure.

Meanwhile, for those who have been unable to find work, the experience of transformation has been economically and psychologically jolting. If we return to Maria's reflection, quoted at the beginning of the book, this becomes clear:

> During the communist period they guaranteed us a job, well-paid, or not so well-paid, each person was important in their own way. We led a very industrious life ... I led a very active life. Now I feel awful because it's very difficult to pass from a period full of activity to a period where time is dead. Now I'm looking for work so that I won't go crazy.[106]

For Maria, like other women who had worked a considerable time in socialist industry and lost their jobs after 1989, "liberation through work" and "productivity" were not simply ideological slogans but parts of their identities as workers. Producing goods and earning a living wage thus imbued some women with pride, a sense of accomplishment, and a strong sense of self-worth.[107] For her "work" was much more than a paycheck; rather, it was a central part of her life and identity.

Although economic instability has affected younger and middle-aged women in various capacities, it has also affected those at the other end of the age spectrum: retired and elderly individuals. Indeed, retired women are among those at greatest risk of falling into poverty as they constitute a considerable portion of the population (5.3 million retirees out of a total population of 19.8 million in 2015) and have meager pensions, primarily because the number of employed individuals who contribute to the tax base is particularly low (4.85 million in 2015).[108] Additionally, women's pensions are smaller than men's as a result of their comparatively lower salaries and earlier retirement age (under socialism) and because many women were forced into early retirement during economic restructuring.[109] Unsurprisingly, elderly women, along with single mothers, represent the largest segment of those living in poverty. As Valeria P., a retired nurse, recalled:

> Things have improved: we have heat, we have electricity, we have stores full of everything. Me, as a retired person, it does not matter that we have plenty in the stores; I cannot afford anything. As a retired woman, I must be very careful. There was no electricity before, now we have it, but I use only 40-watt light bulbs if necessary. There was no water before; nowadays hot water is so expensive that we only use cold water and we have water meters. And, if you cannot afford it, you must save. You did not have things before, now you do and you cannot afford them.[110]

Ironically—and tragically—Valeria's limited use of electricity and hot water is not due to state rationing of utilities, which had been the case in the 1980s, but inflation produced by the market economy. Valeria's situation is by no means unique as a number of older respondents claimed that they used electricity and gas heating sparingly due to their meager pensions. Although pensions increased in the early 2000s, by the time of my interview with Valeria (in 2003), the cost of food, utilities, and medications had soared, outpacing monthly pensions. Similarly, Aneta (b. 1936) bemoaned her small pension, expressing concern that she and her husband struggled to pay for necessary medications and to "live decently." She also lamented the fact that they could not afford to invite friends over for the holidays. For this she blamed those in power who seek to enrich themselves and "do not think about the people."[111]

Having enough money to cover daily expenses, from food to heating, is a constant source of worry for many retired and elderly individuals. In particular, older women and men fear falling ill since medications are cost-prohibitive. Indeed, elderly individuals begging on the street for money to cover medication is an everyday sight in Romania—and a palpable reminder of how common social vulnerability has become in postsocialist Romania.

Regine, a retired railway worker who claimed to be doing reasonably well, elaborated on such injustice, comparing Romania with Germany:

> Pensions should be enough to cover food ... this is not democracy. In Germany nobody dies of hunger. The country takes care of everyone. And things should be determined in such a manner that each person has a right to a livelihood. They [the people] are not to blame for what happened [under the previous regime]. That was the fate of the people, but we should now ensure we have true democracy.[112]

Similarly, Ivonne (b. 1934), a retired teacher, noted that she could not complain because she received help from her kids; yet she also stressed it was unfair that after "all these years of work—thirty-six years" her kids had to help support her.

For women who had been gainfully employed in now-defunct or scaled-back industries and could afford not only basic necessities but also household durables and yearly vacations, the situation is both distressing and depressing. Thus, in my interviews between 2003 and 2012, many respondents looked to the pre-1989 period fondly. To be sure, they acknowledged the difficulties of the late 1940s and 1950s, as well as the 1980s; however, they also emphasized earlier periods of financial stability and felt that parts of the system (in particular guaranteed employment and social entitlements) had significantly benefitted ordinary Romanians. As Axinia, a retired laborer, noted, "It was difficult [under communism], but today there is a lot more stress. You were secure in your job, you were given a job, they gave you an apartment."[113] Not only laborers but also professionals expressed dismay with the nature of economic change. As Adriana, a retired teacher, reflected, "I believed in communism. Not everything they did was bad; they created parks, order, provided work; they provided job training, respect for hard work ... people talked about values, principles."[114]

Although youth and beauty have helped some women secure employment, other attributes, such as initiative, education, business savvy, and personal connections have also facilitated professional success. Indeed, some women have been highly adept at retooling themselves for the market economy. Luana is a perfect example. Prior to 1989, she worked as a museum curator; however, with the fall of the regime Luana recognized she could transition into a more lucrative line of work. Thus, she founded a small printing press:

> I became an important person. I'm no longer twenty years old, but still, I am a busy person. I am an active person and I hope to be useful, that is, I feel that I am doing things that bring me satisfaction. Before, I wrote a lot, professionally I was very happy because of the things I did, research, writing, for instance, I did with passion. I thought like a specialist. Now I think like a manager. I have changed many positions, but I say that any woman and any person, if she wants to, can change their life in a positive manner and do something else.[115]

Although the cultural capital Luana and her husband acquired under socialism contributed to her successful reinvention, she also attributes this to strength of character and perseverance. A self-proclaimed feminist, Luana emphasized that the only way to change "sexist mentalities" is for women to participate actively in business, government, and the public sphere. Luana's belief that all women possess the strength to change their lives thus dovetails with her liberal feminist principles. However, this view neglects the reality that economic restructuring has benefited some groups (educated women with facility in foreign languages, business savvy, or connections) while disempowering others (industrial laborers with minimal education and training).

Similarly, Valeria R., the manager of a printing company, asserted that women had the capacity for change—if they so desired. A few years after the collapse of socialism, Valeria lost her job at a research institute and sunk into a deep depression. She recalled this as the worst period of her life, during which she often cried and didn't want to see others because, according to her, "I knew I was an intelligent woman, that I could do things, I was able to do anything, [I just] wanted to be able to do something useful." However, she managed to reinvent herself and thrive in the market economy. Thus, she interpreted women's difficulty coping with the transformation as a personal problem:

> Yes, I can say it [life] has changed for the better. If you want to you can plan things; you have many more opportunities in your life; the fact that you can travel, you have access to information, there's no basis for comparison. So, those that say it was better before have adaptation problems. Any person who has skills and know-how doesn't have a reason to be afraid of it [the transition] ... there were opportunities, there were openings during the period of transition, I'd say that '93, '94, '95 were years when things took their natural course. There was an explosion of small-sized companies.[116]

In Valeria's view, women who had not managed to secure work had "adaptation problems" and lacked initiative. In her study of Czech female managers, Elaine Weiner's respondents similarly emphasized that marketization had offered women new opportunities and that they simply needed to take advantage of them.[117] Such interpretations, however, are based on the experiences of educated, enterprising, and assertive women who had successfully negotiated the new economic climate. These women possessed the cultural capital to make the transition from one economic system to another. Their interpretations are also rooted in the "metanarrative of the market," which presupposes that the market is not only the best but the only alternative to socialism and is thus "difficult to refute and conceals patterns of domination and submission."[118] However, this narrative obscures the fact that many women (as well as men) lack the education, foreign language facility, and skills necessary for securing work in the competitive marketplace. Additionally, as entrepreneurs, Valeria and Luana participate in the small-business sector, an area that has been relatively woman-friendly.[119] Because they are part of a "new class" of entrepreneurs, they tend to see the possibilities rather than the limitations of the transformation. However, as discussed earlier, when one looks beyond small-business owners (or beyond those with the cultural capital necessary to compete in the market) to laborers whose skills are no longer in demand, the "market" is not synonymous with success but instead dashed hopes and broken promises.

## Expanding Costs, Shrinking Services

Galloping inflation and the curtailment of social entitlements have exacerbated women's and, indeed, many Romanians' economic vulnerability since 1989. As examined in previous chapters, the socialist state subsidized a range of goods and services, from food, housing, and vacations to healthcare, childcare, and education. Notwithstanding the shortcomings and favoritism associated with them, these services were a fundamental part of the social contract and improved many people's lives, eradicating illiteracy, improving public health, facilitating upward mobility, providing opportunities for leisure, and helping women balance work and caregiving. Ceaușescu's choice to pay off the debt in the early 1980s, however, caused many basic services to deteriorate. Although Romanians expected these services would be substantially enhanced and expanded after the collapse of socialism, this has not come to fruition. Indeed, as a result of budgetary decisions, decentralization, and pressure by international lending agencies (the IMF; the World Bank), on which Romania depended for loans and other forms of economic assistance and which promote a neoliberal approach to the economy, entitlements for social services were actually scaled back.

As a result, since the early 1990s, the percentage of the state budget allocated to social entitlements has been modest and is far below the EU average. For example, while in 1989, 37.4 percent of the budget went to social and cultural services (education, health, social assistance, protections for children, and art and culture) by 1996 that figure was 27.3 percent.[120] Meanwhile, in 1996 the amount of GDP allocated to "Pensions and Social Aid" was only 5.4 percent and to "Health" 8.4 percent, while to "Economic Activities" (a portion of which went toward subsidizing inefficient state-owned enterprises) it was 23.9 percent.[121] During this period, real wages declined, while the annual rate of inflation skyrocketed, exceeding 250 percent in 1993.[122] In 2004, 12.8 percent of the GDP was spent on social protection, a figure that remained stable until the onset of the financial crisis in 2009, when it increased to 16.9 percent. By 2014, the amount spent on social protection was 14.8.[123] Accordingly, among the EU 27, Romania was the stingiest in 2014 with respect to percentage of GDP allocated to social protection, ranking below Poland, the Czech Republic, and Bulgaria. Moreover, this amount was significantly lower than the EU average and nearly half the amount spent on social services in Germany, Denmark, and Belgium. Finally, most entitlements are means-tested and thus many individuals are ineligible for them. As they are no longer basic rights of all citizens, these entitlements tend to be associated with poverty (and charity) and assume a negative stigma.

The way in which funds for public services (hospitals, schools, police, etc.) are distributed also affects individuals' access to services. For instance, as a result of decentralization–a process encouraged by EU development policies–funds are allocated by local authorities who are often motivated more by political ambition and economic enrichment than the common good. Indeed, to secure additional funds from Bucharest, local authorities will support the governing national party whose priorities do not necessarily align with the needs of the community. The public health system, already in a state of crisis under Ceaușescu, was particularly hard hit by decentralization and austerity, especially after 2010 when many small and rural hospitals closed. Because of the modest funds allocated to healthcare, doctors rely on bribes or other forms of favors to compensate for their low salaries. Beyond this, finding a room or even a bed in a hospital can be challenging due to hospital mergers and closures. Thus, hospitals are overcrowded and some also lack adequate sanitary conditions. The consequences of the poor state of public health are evident in the country's high rates of maternal mortality and breast and uterine cancer, among other indicators.[124] Meanwhile, state-subsidized childcare facilities are understaffed or have been forced to close altogether, which, as will be subsequently addressed, has negatively affected women's ability to reconcile work and family.

While the scaling back of social services has affected many Romanians' standard of living, as noted, households with more than three children, Roma communities, and retired and elderly women who live alone have experienced the greatest economic difficulties.[125] Moreover, those living in rural areas or in smaller towns centered on now-defunct industries have been particularly vulnerable to poverty.[126] More generally, women tend to suffer disproportionately from budget cuts, a reality noted by my respondents. Consequently, for many, life in Romania is one of basic survival—as it had been in the 1980s—however, now a wealth of consumer goods are on constant display on store shelves, television screens, and, in some cases, in the homes of friends and family who have "made it." As such, some families suffer the reverse situation they did in the 1980s: they now have access to goods but not enough money to buy them. As Maria commented:

> Before we had money but we didn't have products. Now we have products and we don't have money. How do you think it feels for a woman to go to the market and not have enough money to buy fruit for her child? You are not able to spend money on fruit because you need to pay rent and other living expenses ... it's so expensive. The price of electricity, gas, rent—it's like in the West, but the salaries are like in Romania.[127]

As Lynne Haney found with her Hungarian subjects, neoliberalism has compromised women's "contributory identities," that is, their roles as mothers and caregivers.[128] Because many women in Maria's age cohort had lost their jobs, their biggest concern was being able to adequately support their families. Accordingly, women cobble together a number of odd jobs, some (or all) of which might be in the gray or unofficial economy, or they work outside of Romania. However, even women who are officially employed have slid into poverty, an especially problematic phenomenon since they are ineligible for most means-based subsidies.

For families with young children, declining subsidies for childcare and the high cost of private daycare has presented challenges in reconciling work and family, which, in turn, has negatively affected women's participation in paid labor. While the broadening of maternity leave to family leave is a welcome development, only a minority of men avail themselves of this option. This is due to men's proportionately higher earnings as well as traditional notions about men's roles as breadwinners. For instance, in a 2000 Gender Barometer survey conducted by the Open Society Foundation, 70 percent of respondents agreed that it was "men's duty more than women's to be the main breadwinner in the household."[129] Additionally, to the statement "Men are as capable as women in raising children," 53 percent responded "no" and only 26 percent responded "yes." Despite women's widespread participation in the labor force under socialism and the fact that many women, as single parents, serve as sole breadwinner, ideas about supporting the family and caregiving remain distinctly gendered. Because the vast majority of parents who take parental leave are women, the role of caregiver continues to be naturalized as female.[130]

Yet, here too, women and families run into challenges for although parents are technically entitled to two years family leave (three years in the case of an ill or special-needs child), job insecurity in the private sector and revisions to the family leave law have discouraged parents from taking the full two years.[131] Thus, families are faced with finding childcare before the official family leave is slated to run out. As subsidized childcare is no longer a universal right of working families, but instead means-tested, families resort to private (or fee-based) childcare facilities. However, such facilities are costly and not widely available, particularly in rural areas. Additionally, there are limited options for infant care. For instance, in 2009 Romania registered only 287 crèches in the entire country.[132] Consequently, families rely on informal arrangements (e.g. nannies, grandparents), a continuation of pre-1989 practices. Moreover, some parents (predominantly women) "opt out" of the workforce until their children reach school age (age six). Thus, the state, as Oana Băluță contends, through its lack of policies to reconcile work and family actually encourages informal caregiving.[133] In addition to insufficient daycare centers, state services for special-needs children are inadequate, forcing some parents—typically mothers—to give up work altogether.[134] As a result of these factors, the employment rate for women with one young child or more is considerably lower than for men in the same circumstance—a disparity that has increased since the global financial crisis.[135] Women's absence from the labor force, in turn, hampers their chances for economic reintegration and reduces their pensions and possibilities for promotion, further reinforcing economic inequality between men and women.

With respect to family policy, then, the postsocialist period has been characterized by continuities and discontinuities. Although caregiving is no longer gendered as female in policy, traditional ideas about caregiving remain powerful and influence how this role is assigned by partners. As all of my respondents already had children of school age—or significantly older—when the interviews were conducted, these were not issues that they had to deal with in terms of their own children. However, some were already caring for their grandchildren while their children worked.

## Family Policies and Practices: Reproduction and Domestic Violence

The collapse of socialism resulted in changes in family policy and women's reassertion of bodily control: almost immediately, with the decriminalization of abortion at the end of 1989; then the relaxation of divorce legislation; and, belatedly, the passage of long-overdue domestic violence legislation in 2003 and 2012. While in 1989 the fertility rate stood at 2.2, in 1990 it was 1.83, and by 2000 it was down to 1.31. The fertility rate has edged up slightly since, registering 1.52 in 2015; however, it remains below the natural replacement rate.[136]

Decline in family size is related not only to the legalization of abortion and increased use of contraception but is a response to rising inflation, the scaling back of childcare subsidies, workplace demands, and uncertainty about the future. This trend is by no means unique to Romania, but instead a larger trend facing postsocialist societies and, indeed, most countries in Europe. Olga's comment illustrates this uncertainty: "As I noticed I was getting older, I said, 'okay, let's have another kid,' but I don't know if I'll have a second one. I don't know because I don't know if I can offer the child more than this. Maybe, if I have a very good job."[137] Olga's sentiments are not uncommon in Romania as rising costs for housing, food, and childcare, alongside stagnating wages and job insecurity, negatively affect the overall standard of living. Indeed, the fact that apartments are no longer state subsidized and prioritized for families, as they had been during the socialist period, means that people often continue living with their parents well into their twenties and even thirties. As Corina, who was thirty-five with two children when I interviewed her in 2003, remarked, "I still live in the same apartment I've been living in with my parents for thirty-five years. I wasn't able to buy an apartment after the revolution; with the salaries, it's not possible; it's very difficult."[138] In light of such challenges, as well as the corruption characterizing Romania, Adriana, a retired teacher who raised her sons in the 1970s and 1980s, remarked, "I would not have a kid now. When I see a pregnant woman I feel sorry for her ... I don't have faith in the system."[139]

Women's reasons for limiting family size parallel their reasons during the socialist period: lack of adequate housing, financial concerns; however, there are additional factors, specific to the postsocialist context. One is a general sense of uncertainty given the unpredictability of the market economy and opportunities for gainful employment; the fear that one could lose a job at any moment and never find another. The privatization of housing and the concomitant skyrocketing costs for it further underscore this sense of uncertainty. While acquiring an apartment under socialism was a fraught process in which connections or "gifts" could help oil the wheels, families were nonetheless privileged for it and low-interest loans made it affordable. Under postsocialism, however, the market dictates housing costs, and couples who are struggling to find work or whose earnings are modest are not in a position to buy an apartment—or even rent one. Finally, with the curtailment of social benefits and closure of factories, state-subsidized daycare is virtually non-existent and has been replaced by private childcare, which, as previously noted, is often exorbitantly expensive. In light of these circumstances, couples decide not to have children or, like Olga, limit themselves to one. In a sense, this is a reversal of the situation under Ceaușescu and, more generally, points to the way in which personal choice is limited by outside forces. While reproductive freedom was undermined from the mid-1960s through 1989 and motherhood became compulsory, currently the institutional apparatus for supporting families with children no longer exists. Moreover, people experience financial uncertainty as a result of the shift to a market economy.

Thus, many couples are reticent to have children, contributing to the declining fertility rate. This underscores the ambiguity (and hidden restrictions) of living in a free, democratic society where ostensibly anything is possible.

More generally, the declining fertility rate, combined with outmigration, poses serious demographic challenges in Romania. For instance, between 1989 and 2011, Romania registered over 3 million fewer inhabitants, a decrease in the population by more than 13 percent.[140] The result is a smaller working population and, in turn, a smaller percentage of people contributing to the tax base. Although emigration is a feature of other former Eastern Bloc countries that have become EU members, in Romania it is particularly acute.[141] Indeed, as of 2018, Romania ranked just behind Syria—a country ravaged by war—in terms of emigration growth rate.[142]

While economic uncertainty has prompted some women to limit family size, it has mobilized others to protest austerity measures that target women and children. For instance, in 2010, NGOs, alongside parents with babies in strollers and sacks of diapers in hand (some of them soiled), protested in front of the Ministry of Labor, denouncing the proposed cut in the child allowance and childcare subsidies for single parents and claiming that these were not "charity" given to families by the state but instead their rights as working citizens.[143] During the protests (and in their letter to the government), they emphasized that the cuts did not make political, moral, or economic sense, citing the meager amount of the budget allotted to such entitlements. Moreover, they connected declining fertility rates to curtailment of state subsidies, underscoring that government cuts, not simply personal choice, were hampering demographic growth. Their claim that parents were, as taxpaying citizens, entitled to the aforementioned subsidies underscores how integral such subsidies have become to people's conception of citizenship. It also underscores how integral public mobilization has become to safeguarding such rights—and in challenging state curtailment of them.

Although cuts in services for families have produced—or increased—economic insecurity, the fact that women can now make their own choices about family size is a notable victory, and, indeed, perhaps one of the most positive outcomes for women of the revolution. For instance, when asked how the transformation to postsocialism had benefitted them, my respondents cited freedom of speech, travel, and association; however, many also emphasized the legalization of abortion in December 1989. As Corina claimed, "In the first place, the right to have an abortion. Each woman is free to decide what will happen to her child."¹⁴⁴ In this respect, Romania is much more woman-friendly than Poland, which bans abortion in all but exceptional cases.

That said, the Orthodox Church, the pro-life organization Pro-Vita, and some conservative politicians have sought to ban abortion. For instance, in 2012, the Draft Law on the Establishment, Operation, and Organization of Centers for Pregnancy Crisis Counseling, which would have required women to seek counseling, view stills from video clips of an abortion, and undergo a five-day period of self-reflection before having an abortion, was proposed to parliament. Although NGOs argued that the proposed law undermined women's right to privacy, health, and autonomy, and the measure ultimately failed to pass, doctors in public hospitals have refused to provide abortions to patients on "religious grounds."¹⁴⁵ Additionally, Pro-Vita holds annual "Marches for Life," condemning abortion and presenting adoption as "the noble choice."

Despite these efforts, the right to abortion on demand does not appear to be in legal jeopardy, and abortion remains an acceptable method of fertility control, particularly in rural areas where family planning counseling is limited and contraception can be difficult to acquire.¹⁴⁶ In fact, according to a 2013 survey conducted by Millward Brown, 24 percent of respondents considered abortion a contraceptive method and 62 percent believed it was necessary in some cases.¹⁴⁷ Given the influence of religion in schooling and increased rates of teen pregnancy, there is concern that youth are not being sufficiently educated about human reproduction and family planning. At the same time, the inhumane consequences of Ceaușescu's pronatalism have become part of the public memory of socialism with the films *Four Months, Three Weeks, and Two Days* and *Children of the Decree (Născuți la comandă: Decrețeii)*, public discussions and commemorations of Decree 770, including in the form of a museum exhibit in 2012, and flash mobs at the University of Bucharest¹⁴⁸

While reproductive freedom was granted in one of the first laws passed after the revolution, legal recognition of violence against women, as well as protective orders, came much later. As noted, *Femeia* occasionally paid lip service to spousal abuse during the socialist period; however, domestic violence has historically been considered a private matter that was more or less tolerated by state authorities. Accordingly, early postsocialist governments generally neglected the issue. In the 1990s, Romanian and foreign NGOs thus took the lead, establishing services for victims of domestic violence. In 1999, the first comprehensive survey on domestic violence revealed that one out of every three women in Romania had experienced domestic violence.¹⁴⁹ This finding, followed in 2000 by the Romanian *Playboy* article "How to Beat Your Wife... without Leaving Marks," which suggested that using a police rod was a way of inflicting pain on one's wife without leaving any physical traces, galvanized NGOs and ordinary individuals to protest in front of the Romanian Senate against the normalization of domestic violence and to demand legislation to protect victims and punish offenders.[150] With EU prodding and the efforts of feminist activists, NGOs, and then MP, Mona Muscă, Law 217/2003 was passed, outlawing "any physical or verbal act intentionally committed by a family member against another family member that causes physical, psychological, or sexual suffering or material damages."[151] While a step in the right direction, women generally feared pressing charges against their aggressor due to social stigma, poverty, and lack of legal protection via a restraining order. After intense protests by the women's organization FILIA and a group of feminist activists, a same-day restraining order was finally passed in 2012; however, economic insecurity, lack of sufficient shelters for women and their families, and lack of faith in the criminal justice system force many women to maintain residences with their abusers. Nonetheless, annual public commemorations of victims of domestic violence, as well as television commercials and events such as the "Violence Is Not Entertainment" protests held in Bucharest every November, continue to help raise awareness about domestic violence, transforming it from a private problem to a social concern.[152]

Promoting women's rights has been challenging given women's low representation in politics since 1989. Although men also dominated politics during socialism, since decisions were made (or mandated) by a select few at the top, most political posts were token, and policymakers were unable to effect change, including with respect to women and gender issues. Women's underrepresentation in politics since 1989 is due to a culture favoring masculine values from which women feel alienated, women candidates' lack of financial resources, and the role of political parties as gatekeepers. For most of the 1990s, women's representation in parliament was below 10 percent (dipping as low as 3.7 percent between 1992 and 1996). Moreover, women did not assume any ministerial positions until the 2000s. Although by 2018, women's share in parliament reached 19 percent, they continue to be grossly underrepresented in local politics (at the mayoral level women's presence has not exceeded 10 percent). By comparison, women's numbers are significantly higher at the EU level: in 2018 women constituted 28.13 percent of MEPs, (Members [representatives] of the European Parliament); however, this keeps women out of national and local politics by sending them off to Brussels. That said, although women are currently underrepresented in politics, compared with the socialist period they have at least a modicum of influence in the political process, as was evident in the passage of domestic violence laws in 2003 and 2012.

Outside of government, women have had more opportunities for engaging in public and civic life, leading NGOs, producing research, organizing debates and engaging in protests.[153] Women's efforts in these capacities have been instrumental in raising awareness, lobbying the government for anti-discrimination and equal-opportunity legislation, passing parental leave and anti–domestic violence policies, and promoting political parity and gender justice. Moreover, women scholars have founded programs in gender studies and have produced a wealth of research related to historical and contemporary aspects of women and gender in Romania.

## Conclusion

Although Romanians greeted the collapse of socialism with relief and hope, for some the transition to democracy and a market economy has turned out to be a mixed bag. While providing new rights and opportunities, it has also created uncertainties and vulnerabilities. On the one hand, individuals praise the existence of political and civil rights, namely freedom of speech, association, and travel. On the other hand, they criticize widespread corruption, as politicians are often guided more by self-interest and personal enrichment than the common good. A particular source of concern is downward mobility and the curtailment of social rights such as guaranteed work, high-quality education, and subsidized healthcare and childcare. This, in turn, has produced discontent about the nature of systemic change, as well as the meaning of democracy itself, causing some to look back fondly on the pre-1989 period. The 2013 "Truth about Romania Barometer" (conducted with 1,055 people) illustrates well popular ambiguity about the transformation to postsocialism. One of the survey questions asked respondents to compare Romania in 2013 to the period prior to 1989. Respondents demonstrated a preference for the pre-1989 period, with 44.4 percent indicating that they "lived better," 33.6 percent indicating that they "lived worse," and 15.6 percent indicating that they "live the same."[154] These preferences were clearly a function of age, with over 50 percent of older respondents (aged 65 and older) indicating that they had lived better before 1989.[155] While the high percentage for older cohorts is unsurprising, what is curious—and disheartening—is that of those in the 35–49 age cohort, which includes people who were involved in the revolution, more claimed to have lived better before 1989 than they did in 2013. Although rooted in frustration and disenchantment with postsocialist politics, in particular elite corruption, and a selective or nostalgic remembering of the past, this result is also related to downward mobility and the austerity measures implemented in 2010 and 2012, from which Romanians, like many others elsewhere, are still reeling and from which some will never recover. However, the younger generation and those born at the tail end of socialism and after have also been affected by austerity, as salaries remain low. Thus, there is a sense that the sacrifices made in 1989 and thereafter have been in vain. Equally interesting is that there is only a 5 percent difference between the active and inactive population (with 42.2 percent of the active and 47.1 percent of the inactive population agreeing that "life was better" prior to 1989), indicating that those with jobs do not necessarily hold more favorable views of the post-1989 period—understandable given that a large number of individuals who are employed are near or at the poverty level.

While many Romanians are disillusioned with the changes (or lack thereof) that have occurred since 1989, this has not translated into mass apathy or violence. Indeed, an important indicator of democracy in Romania is the peaceful mobilization of various groups in protests and marches, as well as people's participation in NGOs and voluntary associations to promote democratic principles. NGOs have certainly played a vital role in promoting democratic values, monitoring elections, and supporting a range of social and human rights issues. Even Elena, who, as previously noted, was critical of the political process and rarely votes, recognizes her important role in enhancing the lives of her countrymen and women. Thus, every year she coordinates a trip that provides a group of children with physical disabilities the opportunity to visit France. Although perhaps modest by Western standards, the emergence of civil society in Romania should be acknowledged as an important achievement in consolidating democracy, especially given that, unlike most countries in the former Bloc, Romania had no precedent or framework for such activities during the socialist period. However, because such engagement requires conceptualizing one's role within society as active and relational (rather than passive and individualistic), it also requires a change in thinking. According to Lidia, who was concerned that people had become too individualistic and divided—because they no longer have a common enemy—such action will not occur without strong convictions:

> I always try to see the glass as half full. I am an optimist, positive and utopian. I recognize this. I always say, if you want to do it, you can. You need to have strong convictions. If each one of us does not live truthfully,

nothing will change. But we have not been taught to live truthfully. That is, the manipulation from that period was so strong that very few still have resources and motivation. It's my belief that until you shut your eyes [die] you have a debt to pay.[156]

These remarks are evocative of Václav Havel's notion of "living in truth."[157] While coined with respect to normalized Czechoslovakia, it applies to the postsocialist period as well—indeed, perhaps more so given that the cost of living ethically is not nearly as high today as it was prior to 1989, especially in Romania, and thus should be easier for people to practice. At the same time, after forty-five years of socialist rule, there is confusion about the nature of truth and what it means to live within it, especially since there seem to be few role models in society and, in particular, politics. How does one live in truth in light of the corruption and bribery that is visible at all levels, and when the difference between life and death can depend on how much money one has in their pocket?

With respect to women's particular experiences of the transformation, some, as we have seen, have managed to retool their skills and refashion themselves—often changing occupations or professions—to integrate into the competitive marketplace. Their professional success is a measure of their abilities, initiative, and the possibilities of the market. It is also related to their cultural capital, much of which they acquired during socialism. Thus, for those who have been able to adapt to a new economic and political system, the transformation has been beneficial. Meanwhile, others, due to factors outside of their control (age or lack of education and connections), have been less successful in this endeavor. However, even for those who have managed to find work, many experience both material poverty and time poverty, working two or three part-time jobs and ten or more hours per day. This, combined with household responsibilities, has hampered their quality of life. At the same time, it should be noted that women in the West, due to the embrace of neoliberal policies and the global economic crisis, have also been struggling with economic uncertainty, including underemployment (as well as unemployment), and the scaling back of welfare entitlements. Thus, the economic uncertainties and time poverty experienced by Romanian women is not simply related to the transition to a market economy, but is part of a larger, global shift to a neoliberal paradigm that subordinates the collective to the individual and produces opportunities for some and vulnerabilities for many.

Just as some people's opportunities under the transformation have been circumscribed, so too have their identities been negated or neglected by an economic system with which they are unaccustomed and do not identify. Women lament the waning of social relationships, the dissolution of a respected value system, and their inability to adequately fulfill their maternal roles and engage in satisfying work. The tension, then, lies in the sharp disconnect between official or postsocialist identities available to women in contemporary Romania and the subjective ones as lived and experienced by women under socialism.

It is important not to write off the desire for economic stability and social entitlements as signs of dependency or nostalgia. Although paternalist and characterized by shortcomings, the social entitlements issued by the party-state, from guaranteed employment and universal healthcare and education to subsidized maternity leave, childcare, and vacations, often enhanced women's quality of life. Thus, most individuals view these entitlements not as forms of dependence, but instead as basic rights, part of the social contract. It is therefore understandable that they believe the government should play an instrumental role in guaranteeing economic security and, more generally, civic well-being. Indeed, given what has occurred since December 1989, in particular disappointments with the nature of economic and political change, it is unsurprising that some individuals exhibit positive attitudes toward certain aspects of the socialist system. Romanians' support for the maintenance and, I would add, enhancement of such benefits does not reveal a desire for a return of communist dictatorship. Rather, it illustrates that many people's—or at least many of my respondents'—conception of democracy is understood with respect to social-democratic rather than neoliberal principles. To quote Stefano Bottoni, "their frustration stems from the awareness that the golden era of the European welfare state and social inclusion is ending without their ever having enjoyed it."[158]

As a corollary, women's desire to support themselves and their families and maintain a basic standard of living is not akin to some "romantic yearning for the past or for youthfulness" but is instead a reasonable and normal human desire that Romanians share with people throughout the world, regardless of regime type. Indeed, if we adopt Svetlana Boym's multifaceted definition of nostalgia, whereby nostalgic sentiment can involve "a sense of loss and displacement" and/or "a defense mechanism to the fast-paced nature of current realities," we might interpret Romanians' apparent nostalgia for the old system as a reaction to (or defense mechanism against) the unpredictability and destabilizing effects of neoliberalism. That is, a response to a system that presents itself as democratic and according to which all people ostensibly have the opportunity to live a dignified life wherein not only basic needs are met, but opportunities for upward mobility are available to all, but in which inequality reigns and economic divergences are sharper than they had been under socialism.

\* \* \*

Historicizing women's experiences in postwar Romania offers an opportunity to reflect on state efforts to create a socialist utopia and to evaluate how these efforts shaped the lives—and memories–of a particular segment of the population. While the project of building socialism was characterized by flaws, perversions, and repressions, it was also characterized by opportunities. Opportunities for educational, professional, and social advancement and for fashioning new identities, roles, and relationships. While tens of thousands of individuals were imprisoned and perished as the state sought to punish "enemies of the people," collectivize agriculture, and promote demographic growth, millions became literate, received routine medical checkups, enjoyed indoor plumbing, and were able to take yearly trips to the Black Sea. While women's pay was lower than men's and some faced harassment by bosses or colleagues, many others experienced increased autonomy and self-confidence, as well as opportunities to develop new skills and pursue their passions. Many of these gains were, regretfully, realized under an illiberal, one-party system that subordinated individual need to the collective—and, with respect to women of childbearing age, undermined their reproductive freedom and health through draconian pronatalist measures after 1966—underscoring the ambiguities and contradictions of the socialist project. At the same time, it is important not to let the darker sides of socialist rule color the positive outcomes for certain segments of the population—women included. Moreover, it should be recalled that such contradictions and ambiguities were not unique to the socialist system or even one-party states, but part of the larger process of modernization—including in liberal democracies. By acknowledging that some women and men lived, according to them, a "normal life" does not negate the indignities and inhumanity faced by others, but instead reflects the complexity of socialist rule and the diversity of lived experience.

A focus on the gendered dimensions of socialist modernization also offers insight into state legitimacy. As examined throughout this book, the socialist regime sought to secure popular support through a number of initiatives, such as compulsory education, universal healthcare, and subsidized vacations and housing, many of which were beneficial, albeit to varying degrees, to the population. While these initiatives were in large part instrumental, rooted in efforts to modernize the country and compete with the capitalist West, this does not nullify their positive and long-term effects (e.g. a highly educated and skilled populace). State legitimacy also assumed geopolitical significance as it was intimately connected to the Cold War struggle. Thus, the promotion of egalitarian approaches to gender enabled states such as Romania to demonstrate its progress in providing women with a range of opportunities in the public sphere, including the possibility of advancing in fields that many women in the West found themselves excluded or marginalized from (e.g. science and engineering). At the same time, these opportunities coexisted with patriarchal attitudes and behaviors and, after 1966, repressive pronatalist legislation, which not only curtailed women's autonomy but, in some cases, endangered women's lives (e.g. clandestine abortion and spousal abuse). Accordingly, socialist Romania serves as a compelling case study for illuminating alternative ways that modernization was imagined and implemented, demonstrating that emancipation from above was possible, but that it was also partial, limited, and seriously compromised by traditional mentalities and repressive tendencies.

Just as socialism was a transformative process characterized by contradictions, ambiguities, and complexities so too the postsocialist period has been characterized by contradictions, ambiguities, and complexities. These ambiguities are evident at multiple levels and help explain people's critical as well as positive views of the past and present. Understanding women's complex relationship to past and present therefore requires a more nuanced appreciation of socialism and postsocialism as political, economic, and ideological systems that shaped women's lives in manifold ways but to which women also responded in manifold ways. As Titica (b. 1954), a retired employee of the CFR (state railway company), remarked in 2012:

> Life is difficult. I recognize that life is very difficult now. I recognize that life was very difficult then, too. For me they are equal ... because I know how to manage. I know how to fight. I know how to work. I don't wait for anyone to give me anything. I have a life that you could write a book about.

While Titica's reflection illustrates that women experienced difficulties and struggles during the socialist and postsocialist periods, it also illustrates that some women don't necessarily view the pre and post-1989 periods as distinct or decisively different. Thus, while the country was undergoing massive systemic change and while a longstanding geopolitical battle had finally come to an end, these transformations had only minimal impact on her life. For her, like others, life continues to be difficult. This quote underscores the importance of not overemphasizing the impact of larger political ruptures on people's everyday lives. It also underscores the fact that transformation to economic and political pluralism has not proved to be a panacea for all that ailed Romania and Romanians. On a more personal, though similarly important level, it highlights the role of human agency in dealing with such difficulties. For Titica, it was not the system that mattered as much as her ability to effectively negotiate it. Thus, she did not passively accept the challenges she faced under socialism and postsocialism but confronted them through hard work, perseverance, and self-sufficiency. Finally, she sees the value in her own life by referring to it as something one could "write a book about," illustrating the importance of life stories in understanding the complexities and ambiguities of socialism, postsocialism, and of history more generally.

## Notes

1. Steagul Roşu employed roughly twenty-two thousand people by 1987, making it one of the largest-staffed factories in the country.
2. Ildiko, interview with Ioana Manoliu, Braşov, 12 July 2003.
3. They also requested that the retirement age be changed back to 50 (from 55) and employment opportunities for their wives.
4. Ruxandra Cesereanu, "Revolta muncitorilor din Braşov, 1987," *Revista 22*, no. 14 (2 December 2003).
5. Marius Oprea and Stejărel Olaru, eds., *Ziua care nu se uită. Revolta braşovenilor din 15 noiembrie 1987* (Iaşi: Polirom, 2002).
6. Livia, interview with Ioana Manoliu, Braşov, 11 August 2003.
7. The wage cut was legitimated by the party on the basis that workers had not met production quotas, even though problems in the supply chain were the casue.
8. According to one of the participants, it was difficult to get the fire going since the matches were of such inferior quality. See Oprea and Olaru, *Ziua care nu se uită*.
9. Stela, interview with author, Braşov, 23 June 2003.
10. Cesereanu, "Revolta muncitorilor din Braşov, 1987."
11. Braşov is now referred to as "Oraşul Martir" (Martyr City), a designation in which Braşovians take great pride.
12. Valeria P., interview with author, Braşov, 14 June 2003.
13. Following Burawoy and Verdery, I employ the term "transformation" to describe the postsocialist period as it more appropriately denotes the uneven, varied, and, at times, regressive nature of change within the region than does the more teleological term "transition." See the introduction in Michael Burawoy and Katherine Verdery, eds., *Uncertain Transition: Ethnographies of Change in the Postsocialist World* (Lanham, MD: Rowman and Littlefield, 1999).
14. Dennis Deletant, *Romania under Communist Rule* (Bucharest: Center for Romanian Studies, 1998), 178.
15. Peter Siani-Davies, *The Romanian Revolution of December 1989* (Ithaca, NY: Cornell University Press, 2003), 27–28.
16. Filipescu was imprisoned in 1983 and released during the 1986 amnesty.
17. Vasile Paraschiv, a Ploieşti worker who formulated a petition, signed by thousands, to establish an independent trade union in Romania, was one of the individuals assigned to this type of punishment.
18. As quoted in Gale Stokes, *The Walls Came Tumbling Down: The Collapse of Communism in Eastern Europe* (New York: Oxford University Press, 1993), 163.
19. For a personal story on the impact of a parent's anti-regime activities on a child's everyday life in late-socialist Romania, see Carmen Bugan, *Burying the Typewriter: Childhood under the Eye of the Secret Police* (Minneapolis, MN: Graywolf Press, 2012).
20. On the relationship between nationalism, the regime, and intellectuals in Ceauşescu's Romania, see Katherine Verdery, *National Ideology under Socialism: Identity and Cultural Politics in Ceauşescu's Romania* (Berkeley: University of California Press, 1991).

21. For example, when the dissident writer Paul Goma and historian Vlad Georgescu voiced their opposition to the regime, they were forcibly exiled.
22. Ruxandra, interview with author, Bucharest, 5 June 2012.
23. For example, when veteran party leader Constantin Pârvulescu charged Ceaușescu, at the Eleventh Party Congress in November 1979, with creating a personal dictatorship and neglecting the interests of the people, the state stripped him of his position as delegate to the congress and placed him under house arrest.
24. Stokes, *The Walls Came Tumbling Down*, 162.
25. The letter was broadcast on Radio Free Europe and the BBC. See "Letter to President Nicolae Ceaușescu," in Vladimir Tismăneanu, *Reinventing Politics: Eastern Europe from Stalin to Havel* (New York: Free Press, 1992), 228–229.
26. Many of my respondents recalled listening to Radio Free Europe during the 1980s.
27. Tismăneanu, *Reinventing Politics*, 230.
28. Stokes, *Walls Came Tumbling Down*, 162.
29. Ceaușescu's systematization plan began in the mid-1980s and resulted in the razing of houses in twenty-nine towns, which were replaced by the standard, communist-style cement blocks.
30. In an effort to mask the extent of the massacre, the bodies of forty-three victims were removed from the mortuary in Timișoara and taken to Bucharest, where they were cremated on the night of December 18–19. Siani-Davies, *Romanian Revolution*, 68, 71.
31. "Foreign terrorists" referred to Hungarians from Hungary who the regime claimed had designs on the Western part of the country and Transylvania, areas with the largest Hungarian populations.
32. The army's decision to side with the people was related to its poor treatment by Ceaușescu and the rescinding, in 1989, of the promotions of a number of high-ranking army officers. Before fleeing, Ceaușescu had made one last-ditch effort, albeit failed, to appease the people in a speech on the balcony of Central Committee headquarters.
33. Ion Iliescu served as the first secretary of the Union of Communist Youth (UTC 1956–1971). In 1971 he was demoted for criticizing Ceaușescu's mini cultural revolution.
34. Siani-Davies, *The Romanian Revolution*, 97.
35. Tismăneanu, *Reinventing Politics*, 233.
36. Ecaterina, interview with author, Brașov, 17 June 2003.
37. Florin Abraham, *Romania since the Second World War: A Political, Social and Economic History* (London: Bloomsbury Press, 2017).
38. Corina, interview with Ioana Manoliu, Brașov, 17 July 2003.
39. See Richard Andrew Hall, "The Uses of Absurdity: The Staged War Theory and the Romanian Revolution of 1989," *East European Politics and Societies* 13, no. 3 (1999). Also see Katherine Verdery and Gail Kligman, "Romania after Ceaușescu: Post-Communist Communism?" in *East European Revolutions*, ed. Ivo Banac (Ithaca, NY: Cornell University Press, 1992), 117–147.
40. As Tismăneanu notes, the origins of the FSN are rather mysterious since no bona fide and popularly recognized domestic dissent movement existed

in Romania during the communist period. The fact that some of its leading members, in particular Ion Iliescu, a former Central Committee member who became leader of the FSN and served as the Romanian president for the majority of the 1990s and early 2000s, gives credence to the assertion that former party elites had prepared for the fall of the regime prior to the events of December 21–22 and manipulated the ensuing confusion. See Tismăneanu, *Reinventing Politics*, 235.

41. Grigore Pop-Eleches, "Romania Twenty Years after Communism: The Bizarre Echoes of Contested Revolution," in *Twenty Years after Communism: The Politics of Memory and Commemoration*, ed. Michael Bernhard and Jan Kubik (Oxford: Oxford University Press, 2014), 86.
42. See Michael Shafir, "The Ciorbea Government and Democratization: A Preliminary Assessment," in *Post-Communist Romania: Coming to Terms with Transition*, ed. Duncan Light and David Phinnemore (Basingstoke: Palgrave, 2001), 84–90; Frank Sellin, "Democratization in the Shadows: Post-Communist Patrimolianism," and Cătălin Augustin Stoica, "Re-Membering Romania," both in *Romania since 1989: Politics, Economics, and Society*, ed. Henry Carey (Lanham, MD: Lexington Books, 2004); Lavinia Stan, "Romania in the Shadow of the Past," in *Central and Southeast European Politics Since 1989*, ed. Sabrina Ramet (Cambridge: Cambridge University Press, 2010); and Tom Gallagher, *Romania after Ceaușescu: The Politics of Intolerance* (Edinburgh: Edinburgh University Press, 1996).
43. This is euphemistically referred to as the *mineriada* (mineriad). For a comprehensive analysis of these events, see John Gledhill, "States of Contention: State-Led Political Violence in Post-socialist Romania," *East European Politics and Societies* 19, no. 1 (2005): 76–104. There were additional mineriads in September 1991 and January 1999. On 23 December 2016, Iliescu was indicted for crimes against humanity for organizing the mineriad.
44. "Macroeconomic Indicators, 1990–2002," National Bank of Romania (2003). Although employee-buyout and mass voucher programs were introduced, they mainly benefitted former communist officials and enterprise managers "who had insider information about profitable ventures, connections to political decision-makers, raw material providers, and retailers, and previous managerial experience." See Stan, "Romania in the Shadow of the Past."
45. Tom Gallagher, *Modern Romania: The End of Communism, the Failure of Democratic Reform, and the Theft of a Nation* (New York: New York University Press, 2005), 178.
46. See Gil Eyal, Ivan Szelenyi, and Eleanor Townsley, *Making Capitalism without Capitalists: The New Ruling Elites in Eastern Europe* (London: Verso, 1998), 43–44.
47. For a discussion of how the communist *nomenklatura* was able to assume economic power after 1989, see Anneli Ute Gabanyi, "The New Business Elite: From *Nomenklatura* to Oligarchy," in *Romania since 1989*.
48. For detailed studies on the "postcommunist theft" in Romania, see Emanuel Copilaş, ed., *Marele jaf postcomunist: spectacolul mărfii şi revanşa capitalismului* (Iaşi: Editura Adenium, 2017).
49. Livia, interview with Ioana Manoliu, Braşov, 11 August 2003.

50. See Dan Daianu, "Fiscal and Monetary Policies," in *Romania since 1989*, 397–98; and Alina Mungiu-Pippidi and Sorin Ioniţa, "Interpreting an Electoral Setback—Romania 2000," *East European Constitutional Review* 10, no. 1, (Winter 2001): retrieved from http://www.law.nyu.edu/eecr/vol10num1/features/interpreting.html (accessed 12 December 2017).
51. Ibid. This was further exacerbated in 1999 when, in order to avoid bankruptcy, the Romanian government taxed working Romanians almost one-fourth of their income in order to repay foreign debts incurred by the PSDR government in 1994–95.
52. See Lavinia Stan, "Access to Securitate Files: The Trials and Tribulations of a Romanian Law," *East European Politics and Societies* 16, no. 1 (December 2002): 55–90.
53. Mungiu-Pippidi and Ioniţa, "Interpreting an Electoral Setback."
54. See "Românii se pronunţă pentru o reformă radicală a sistemului politic," and "Problema tranziţiei: o elită neperformantă," *Revista 22*, nos. 11 and 13 (March 28–30, 2000).
55. Ecaterina, interview with author, Braşov, 17 June 2003.
56. Valeria R., interview with author, Braşov, 2 May 2003.
57. Olga, interview with author, Braşov, 19 June 2003.
58. During this period, unemployment benefits were reduced to keep people off the rolls. This strategy seemingly worked as only a third of those registered as unemployed received benefits. See Cornel Ban, "Neoliberalism in Translation: Economic Ideas and Reforms in Spain and Romania" (PhD diss., University of Maryland, 2011).
59. See Tom Gallagher, *Romania and the European Union: How the Weak Vanquished the Strong* (Manchester: Manchester University Press, 2009); and Monica Ciobanu, "Travails with Democracy and Accession to the European Union," *Europe-Asia Studies* 59, no. 8 (2007), 1436.
60. In a debate with Năstase, Băsescu asserted, "You know what Romania's greatest curse is right now? It's that Romanians have to choose between two former Communist Party members."
61. The commission included well-known historians, members of civic organizations, former political prisoners and anticommunist dissidents. See the "Final Report on the Communist Dictatorship in Romania," retrieved from https://www.wilsoncenter.org/sites/default/files/RAPORT%20FINAL_%20CADCR.pdf (accessed 12 June 2015).
62. "To be poor" according to the EU definition, means having a salary below 60 percent of the median salary of the respective state. See Ministerul Muncii, Familiei şi Protecţiei Sociale, *Situaţia sărăciei în România*, retrieved from http://www.mmuncii.ro/pub/img/site/files/fb64439b129bf0910308ca2064b3707a.pdf (accessed 14 December 2017); and Oana Băluţă, ed., *Impactul crizei economice asupra femeilor* (Bucharest: Maiko, 2011), 16.
63. The at-risk-of-poverty threshold is set at 60 percent of the national median equivalized disposable income. In 2008, 16.5 percent of the EU-27 population was assessed to be at-risk-of-poverty. The at-risk-of-poverty threshold varies with respect to employment status, age, and other indicators. Thus, in 2008, the at-risk-of-poverty threshold for employed

individuals in Romania was 17.5. while for unemployed individuals it was 42.7. See Eurostat, "Living Conditions and Social Protection," *Eurostat yearbook* (2011), 270, retrieved from https://ec.europa.eu/eurostat/documents/3217494/5727941/CH_06_2011-EN.PDF/d9e58859-70cf-4864-a820-28fac72a946b (accessed 10 November 2018).

64. Cătălin Zamfir, Ion Stanescu, and Adina Mihailescu, *Raportul social al ICCV, După 20 de ani: Opțiuni pentru România* (Bucharest: Academiei Române, 2010), 18–29.
65. While the majority of Romanians who voted in 2012 supported Băsescu's dismissal, mainly because of austerity measures, because of insufficient turnout the results could not be approved by the Constitutional Court.
66. Petre, interview with author, Bucharest, 3 June 2009.
67. Elena, interview with author, Bucharest, 1 June 2009.
68. Lucia, interview with author, Bucharest, 20 June 2012.
69. "The Timișoara Declaration," *Report on Eastern Europe* (6 April 1990), 41–45. A petition, signed by over a million individuals, supported the codification of the declaration in electoral law. Although serious efforts to pass a lustration law (banning former leaders, ministers, and prosecutors of the Romanian Communist Party, as well as members of the Securitate, from public office) have been ongoing since 2005, as of February 2019 no draft has been fully adopted into law.
70. Lidia, interview with author, Bucharest, 26 May 2012.
71. S., email exchange with author, 5 March 2015.
72. "Legea 118/2010 privind unele măsuri necesare în vederea restabilirii echilibrului bugetar," *Monitorul Oficial al României*, nr. 441 din 30 iunie 2010. Later in 2010, the reduction of pensions law was declared unconstitutional; however, the majority of pensions were nonetheless reduced.
73. See Radu Cinpoes, "Political Culture and Participation: Between Enthusiasm and Indifference?" in *Post-Communist Romania at Twenty-Five: Linking Past, Present, and Future*, ed., Lavinia Stan and Diane Vancea (Lanham, MD: Lexington Books, 2015), 107–126.
74. During the first round of the presidential election of 2014 (between Klaus Iohannis, an ethnic German physics teacher, and then prime minister Victor Ponta), polling stations in European cities with large Romanian diaspora populations closed early, preventing many Romanians from voting.
75. See Mary Buckley, ed., *Post-Soviet Women from the Baltic to Central Asia* (Cambridge: Cambridge University Press, 1997); Valentine Moghadam, ed., *Democratic Reform and the Position of Women in Transitional Economies* (Oxford: Clarendon, 1993); Chris Corrin, ed., *Superwomen and the Double Burden: Women's Experience of Change in Central and Eastern Europe and the Former Soviet Union* (New York: Scarlet Press, 1993); Marilyn Rueschemeyer, ed., *Women in the Politics of Postcommunist Eastern Europe* (Armonk, NY: M.E. Sharpe, 1994); Nanette Funk and Magda Mueller, eds., *Gender Politics and Post-Communism: Reflections from Eastern Europe and the Former Soviet Union* (New York: Routledge, 1993); Barbara Einhorn, *Cinderella Goes to Market: Citizenship, Gender and Women's Movements in East Central Europe* (London: Verso, 1993); and Eva Fodor, "Gender in Transition: Unemployment in Hungary, Poland, and Slovakia," *East European Politics and Societies* 11, no. 3 (Fall 1997): 470–500.

76. Barbara Einhorn, "Gender Issues in Transition: The East Central European Experience," *European Journal of Development Research* 6, no. 2 (1994), 121.
77. See, for example, Susan Gal and Gail Kligman, eds., *The Politics of Gender after Socialism: A Comparative-Historical Essay* (Princeton, NJ: Princeton University Press, 2000); Susan Gal and Gail Kligman, eds., *Reproducing Gender: Politics, Publics, and Everyday Life after Socialism* (Princeton: Princeton University Press, 2000); and Burawoy and Verdery, *Uncertain Transition*.
78. See Kristen Ghodsee, *The Red Riviera: Gender, Tourism, and Postsocialism on the Black Sea* (Durham NC: Duke University Press, 2005).
79. The unemployed include all persons between age 15 and 74 who, during the specific period, were without work (not in paid employment or self-employment), currently available for work, and actively seeking work. Thus, the actual percentage of individuals without work is higher. See Băluță, *Impactul crizei;* and "Unemployment by sex and age," *Eurostat*, retrieved from http://ec.europa.eu/eurostat/web/lfs/data/database (accessed 27 January 2018). Yet, this was lower than other countries, namely the former GDR, which registered a female unemployment rate of 21.3 percent in 1994 (vs. male at 10.4 percent).
80. A host of unions have successfully lobbied the government for an extension of their contracts and/or leave packages—in some cases at full salary for a period of thirty-six months, a huge drain on an already strained state budget. Mihaela Miroiu refers to the protection of male workers by the government as "left conservatism." See Mihaela Miroiu, *Drumul către autonomie* (Iași: Polrom, 2004). See also Cătălin Zamfir, Elena Zamfir, and Corry Ehlen eds., *Politici sociale: România în context european* (Bucharest: Editura Alternative, 1996); and Vadimir Pasti, *Ultima inegalitate: Relațiile de gen in România* (Iași: Polrom, 2003).
81. Eurostat, "The Life of Women and Men in Europe: A Statistical Portrait," (2008) retrieved from https://ec.europa.eu/eurostat/documents/3217494/5698400/KS-80-07-135-EN.PDF/101b2bc8-03f8-4f49-b4e4-811fff81b174 (accessed 20 December 2018), 169; "Forța de Munca în România: Ocupare și Somaj" (Anul 2015), Institutul Național de Statistică (2016), retrieved from http://www.insse.ro/cms/sites/default/files/field/publicatii/forta_de_munca_in_romania_ocupare_si_somaj_in_anul_2015_0.pdf (accessed November 2016). In 1989 women constituted 47.1 percent of the total employed.
82. As a result of the economic crisis, unemployment rates increased from 6.5 to 7.7 percent (for men) and 4.4 to 6.5 percent (for women) between 2008 and 2011. Meanwhile, the EU average for those years was 9.3 and 8.4 (for men) and 9.5 and 8.8 (for women). See Băluță, ed., *Impactul crizei*.
83. Accordingly, the unadjusted gender pay gap—the difference between the average gross hourly earnings of male and female employees as a percentage of male gross earnings—is smaller in Romania than the EU average (Romania 26.8 vs. EU average of 39.7). It should be noted that the unadjusted gender pay gap does not take into account differences in educational level and job type or undocumented work. See "Gender Statistics," *Eurostat*, retrieved from http://ec.europa.eu/eurostat/statistics-explained/index.php/File:Gender_statistics_Table1.PNG (accessed 17 December 2017).

84. Men tend to dominate such public sector jobs as transport, the police and army, oil industries, and utilities.
85. "Legea-cadru nr. 153/2017 privind salarizarea personalului plătit din fonduri publice," *Monitorul Oficial al României*, nr. 492 din 28 iunie 2017.
86. "The Life of Women and Men in Europe," 182.
87. Ibid., 196.
88. See Institutul Național de Statistică, "Migrația internațională a României" (2014), retrieved from http://www.insse.ro/cms/files/publicatii/pliante%20statistice/Migratia_internationala_a_Romaniei_n.pdf. (accessed 12 September 2015).
89. WIW Handbook, 2012, Countries by indicator as referenced by Philipp Ther, *Europe Since 1989: A History* (Princeton, NJ: Princeton University Press, 2016), 228.
90. According to state statistics, this figure was 84,000 in 2014; however, because not all parents notify the authorities before migrating—even though required to do so by law—the figure is believed to be substantially higher. The law includes a 500–1,000 lei fine for parents who do not notify the authorities about their intention to work abroad and do not receive judiciary approval of a guardian for their children at least forty days before their departure. "Lege nr. 272 din 21 iunie 2004 (**republicată**) privind protecția și promovarea drepturilor copilului," *Monitorul Oficial al României*, nr. 159 din 5 martie 2014.
91. See Cristina Bezzi, "Romanian 'Left Behind' Children? Experiences of Transnational Childhood and Families in Europe," *Martor: Journal of the Museum of the Romanian Peasant* 18 (2013), 66. For a personalized portrait of the separation between mothers and children, see Liliana Nechita, *Exodul Mamelor* (Bucharest: Editura SC Ringier Romania, 2014).
92. According to Stefano Bottoni, between 2005 and 2010, remittances from Romanians working abroad exceeded 30 billion Euros. Stefano Bottoni, *Long Awaited West: Eastern Europe since 1944* (Bloomington, IN, Indiana University Press, 2017), 230.
93. See Lina Vdovii, "Romania's Resilient Generation: The Kids 'Left Behind' Who Get Ahead," *Balkan Insight*, 29 December 2014, retrieved from http://www.balkaninsight.com/en/article/romania-s-resilient-generation-the-kids-left-behind-who-get-ahead. (accessed 7 March 2016). For a critique of prevailing discourses on "children left behind," "abandoned children," and "heartless mothers" see Bezzi, "Romanian 'Left Behind.'"
94. Doina, interview with author, Brașov, 10 June 2003.
95. Olga, interview with author, Brașov, 19 July 2003.
96. D., interview with author, Brașov, 23 June 2003.
97. Ibid.
98. Angela, interview with author, Brașov, 16 June 2003.
99. Rodica M., interview with Anca Coman, Brașov, 12 August 2003.
100. With the passage of anti-discrimination legislation in 2000, such practices are now illegal; however, reconciling work with children remains a major concern for many women due to the competitiveness of the labor market, the closure of state-subsidized childcare, and the high cost of private daycare.

101. See Georgeta Ghebrea, "Gender Politics in Romania: From Infrastructure to Action," *Journal for the Study of Religions and Ideologies* 5, no. 14 (Summer 2006), 19; Barbara Einhorn, *Citizenship in an Enlarging Europe: From Dream to Awakening* (Basingstoke: Palgrave Macmillan, 2006), 153; Elaine Weiner, *Market Dreams: Gender, Class, and Capitalism in the Czech Republic* (Ann Arbor, MI: University of Michigan Press, 2007); and Elizabeth Dunn, *Privatizing Poland: Baby Food, Big Business, and the Remaking of Labor* (Ithaca, NY: Cornell University Press, 2004), 149–150.
102. Rodica, interview with Anca Coman, Brașov, 12 August 2003.
103. Ibid.
104. Tatiana, interview with author, Brașov, 27 May 2003.
105. Gal and Kligman, *The Politics of Gender after Socialism*, 76.
106. Maria, interview with author, Brașov, 15 June 2003.
107. On how job loss affected women in the former GDR, see Daphne Berdahl, *Where the World Ended: Re-Unification and Identity in the German Borderland* (Berkeley, CA: University of California Press, 1999); and Weiner, *Market Dreams*; and Dunn, *Privatizing Poland*.
108. In 1990 these figures were 3.58 million (pensioners) versus 8.15 million (employees). See Florin, *Romania since the Second World War*, 176. The decline in employed individuals is due to the early retirement age in Romania and outmigration.
109. Those with fewer than fifteen documented years in the labor force do not qualify for a pension in Romania, and those with fewer than thirty-five years in the labor force receive a lower than average pension—often well below subsistence level. This is especially problematic for peasants, particularly peasant women, who did not have an employment contract (*carte de munca*) and thus cannot prove how long they worked during the socialist period.
110. Valeria P., interview with author, Brașov, 14 June 2003.
111. Aneta, interview with Anca Coman, Brașov, 25 June 2003.
112. Regine, interview with author, Brașov, 2 July 2003.
113. Axinia, interview with author, Râmnicu Vâlcea, 10 June 2012.
114. Adriana, interview with author, Bucharest, 6 June 2012.
115. Luana, interview with author, Brașov, 25 July 2003.
116. Valeria R., interview with author, Brașov, 2 May 2003.
117. See Weiner, *Market Dreams*, chap. 4.
118. Ibid.
119. See Miroiu, "State Men, Market Women."
120. *Anuarul Statistic al României*, 1990; 1997.
121. Traian Rotariu and Livia Popescu, "Poverty in Romania," in *Poverty in Transition and Transition in Poverty: Recent Developments in Hungary, Bulgaria, Romania, Georgia, Russia, and Mongolia*, ed. Yogesh Atal (Oxford: Berghahn Books, 1998), 116–117.
122. The annual rate of inflation went from 5.1 percent in 1990 to 256 percent in 1993. It began declining in 1994 and in 2001 stood at 34.5 percent. See United Nations Development Programme, "A Decade Later: Understanding the Transition Process in Romania"; "National Human Development

Report Romania 2001–2002," 89, retrieved from http://hdr.undp.org/sites/default/files/romania_2001_en.pdf (accessed 13 January 2014).
123. "Expenditure on social protection, 2004–2014 (% of GDP)" *Eurostat*, retrieved from http://ec.europa.eu/eurostat/statistics-explained/index.php/File:Expenditure_on_social_protection,_2004-2014_(%25_of_GDP)_YB17.png (accessed 15 April 2017). Social protection, as defined by the EU, "encompasses interventions from public or private bodies intended to relieve households and individuals of the burden of a defined set of risks or needs, provided that there is neither a simultaneous reciprocal nor an individual arrangement involved."
124. See Băluţă, *Impactul crizei*, 23.
125. Ibid.
126. On these dying industrial towns, see Lucian Davidescu, "10% dintre români locuiesc în oraşe pe cale de dispariţie: Vezi care sunt localităţile în pericol," *România Liberă*, 24 May 2011, retrieved from http://www.romanialibera.ro/bani-afaceri/economie/10-dintre-romani-locuiesc-in-orase-pe-cale-de-disparitie-vezi-care-sunt-localitatile-in-pericol-226239.html (accessed 1 March 2014).
127. Maria, interview with author, Braşov, 15 June 2003.
128. Lynne Haney, *Inventing the Needy: Gender and the Politics of Welfare in Hungary* (Berkeley: University of California Press, 2002), 223.
129. Interestingly, educational status more so than age shaped respondents' perceptions, with only 44 percent of those with higher education claiming that men should be the main breadwinner in the household. The survey was conducted with 1,839 men and women over age eighteen from both urban and rural areas throughout Romania. See "Barometrul de gen România, August 2000" (Bucharest: Open Society Foundation, 2000), retrieved from http://www.fundatia.ro/barometrul-de-gen-2000 (accessed 11 August 2015).
130. For instance, during the period from July 2004 to April 2005, 92.2 percent of those who took parental leave were women. See *Reconcilierea vieţii profesionale cu cea familia*, trimestrul II, 2005, Institutul Naţional de Statistică, 61.
131. Revisions enacted as part of larger austerity measures in 2010 encourage parents to take shorter leaves by reducing their remuneration for the second year if they choose to take two years. Meanwhile, those who limit their leave to one year enjoy an increased remittance for that year.
132. "Activitatea unităţilor sanitare, 2010," (Institutul Naţional de Statistică, 2011). Of note is that while the number of state-subsidized childcare facilities has declined, the number of children attending them has not. Therefore, the demand is there but the supply is not.
133. Băluţă, *Impactul crizei*, 64.
134. See Alice Iancu, Oana Băluţă, Alina Dragolea, and Bogdan Florian, "Women's Social Exclusion and Feminists: Living Parallel Worlds? The Romanian Case," in *Gendering Post-Socialist Transition: Studies of Changing Gender Perspectives*, ERSTE Foundation Series, vol. 1, ed. Krassimira Daskalova, Caroline Hornstein Tomic, Karl Kaser, and Filip Radunović (Berlin and Vienna: LIT Verlag, 2012), 195, 198.

135. In 2006, the employment rate for married women (aged 25–49) with one child younger than 6 years of age was 73.7 percent, and for those with two children it was 66 percent. Meanwhile, for men it was 87.7 percent and 85.1 percent, respectively. By 2011, those figures stood at 69.9 percent (one child) and 64 percent (two children) for women, and 87.3 percent (one child) and 86.1 percent (two children) for men. For an excellent discussion of how the crisis has affected women's ability to reconcile work and family, see Băluță, *Impactul crizei*, chap. 2.
136. The EU average in 2014 was 1.58. See "Total Fertility Rate, 1960–2015," *Eurostat*, retrieved from http://ec.europa.eu/eurostat/statistics-explained/index.php/File:Total_fertility_rate,_1960%E2%80%932015_(live_births_per_woman)_YB17.png (accessed 7 March 2016).
137. Olga, interview with author, Brașov, 19 June 2003. She also added that if she could move abroad she would have another child.
138. Corina L., interview with Ioana Manoliu, Brașov, 17 July 2003.
139. Adriana, interview with author, Bucharest, 6 June 2012.
140. *Anuarul Statistic al României*, 2011.
141. For instance, according to Eurostat projections, the population of Romania could decrease by 20 percent between 2010 and 2060. "Population Projections 2010–2060"; "Demography Report 2010"; and "Staff Working Document, European Commission Directorate-General for Employment, Social Affairs and Inclusion," *Eurostat*, retrieved from http://epp.eurostat.ec.europa.eu/portal/page/portal/population/…/report.pdf. (accessed 7 March 2016).
142. "Situația populației plecate din România," *Monitor Social*, retrieved from: https://monitorsocial.ro/indicator/situatia-populatiei-plecate-din-romania/ (accessed 12 February 2018).
143. The childcare allowance is a universal entitlement. The amount as of June 2018 was 84 lei per month for children age 2 to 18 and 200 lei for children with disabilities.
144. Corina M. interview with author, Brașov, 6 August 2003.
145. See Adrian Panduru, "Unul dintre medicii din Timișoara care refuza să facă avorturi la cerere: Trebuie să extragi fatul bucați," *Timis Online* (31 ianuarie 2016) retrieved from http://www.tion.ro/unul-dintre-medicii-din-timisoara-care-refuza-sa-faca-avorturi-la-cerere-trebuie-sa-extragi-fatul-bucati/1612387"; "Marturia un ginecolog care refuza sa mai faca avorturi și lupta pentru viața: Doctorul Ionel Cioata din Timișoara," retrieved from http://www.cuvantul-ortodox.ro/recomandari/2013/04/18/dr-ionel-cioata-ginecolog-anti-avort/ *Cuvântul Ortodox*; and "Rapoarte: Refuzul la efecuarea avortului cerere în România," *Euroregional Center for Public Initiatives* (19 March 2015) retrieved from http://www.ecpi.ro/rapoarte-refuzul-la-efectuarea-avortului-la-cerere-in-romania/ (all accessed 17 December 2017).
146. By law, doctors are required to provide sex education and contraception to all women of fertility age.
147. Andrada Floria, "24% din românce cred că avortul este o metodă contraceptivă și numai 1% folosesc pilula de a doua zi," 2 October 2013, retrieved from http://adevarul.ro/sanatate/medicina/24-romance-cred-

avortul-metodacontraceptiva-numai-1-folosesc-pilula-doua-zi-1_524d51c8c7b855ff56f4c3dd/index.html (accessed 3 March 2014).

148. That said, the violation of women's reproductive rights tends to be neglected in institutional representations of communist repression and suffering. See Alina Haliliuc, "Who Is a Victim of Communism? Gender and Public Memory in the Sighet Museum, Romania," *Aspasia: International Yearbook of Central, Eastern, and Southeastern European Women's and Gender History* 7 (2013): 108–31.

149. The survey was conducted by the U.S. Department for Health and Human Services and was financed by international organizations, among them the UN and World Bank.

150. *Playboy* (Romanian) April 2000, Anul 2, no. 4. For a translation of the article see: http://www.eurowrc.org/00.news/10.news.htm. The article claimed the Romanian police had developed the technique. Local editors of the magazine claimed it was an "April Fool's Day" joke.

151. "Legea 217/2003 pentru prevenirea şi combaterea violenţei în familie," *Monitorul Oficial al României* nr. 367 din 29 mai 2003. In this case, "family member" was defined broadly to include a spouse, close relative, or person who established a relationship similar to a spouse or parent. While not a conditionality for EU membership, the passage of anti–domestic violence legislation was strongly encouraged by the EU. See Andrea Krizsan and Raluca Popa, "Europeanization and Making Policies against Domestic Violence in Central and Eastern Europe," *Social Politics* 17, no. 3 (Fall 2010): 379–406.

152. The first "Violence Is Not Entertainment" protest was held in November 2011 and was centered not only around raising awareness but the passage of a restraining order for perpetrators, which the 2003 law had excluded. See also the article "Inegalitatea de acasă" by Ana Maria Ciobanu and Oana Sandu in *Decât o Revista* 24 (June 2016).

153. For a detailed discussion of women's and feminist groups in post-1989 Romania, see Mihaela Miroiu, "On Women, Feminism, and Democracy," in *Post-Communist Romania at Twenty-Five Years*, 93.

154. The survey was administered to people eighteen years of age and older in thirty-seven counties (including Bucharest) and eighty localities (large, medium, and small-sized cities, towns, and villages). "Barometrul, Adevărul despre România (2013)," retrieved from http://www.inscop.ro/wp-content/uploads/2014/01/INSCOP-noiembrie-ISTORIE.pdf (accessed 15 February 2015).

155. Ibid.

156. Lidia, interview with author, Bucharest, 28–30 May 2012.

157. Václav Havel, *The Power of the Powerless: Citizens against the State in Central-Eastern Europe* (London: M. E. Sharpe, 1978).

158. Bottoni, *Long Awaited West*, 251–252.

# Bibliography

## Archives

Arhivele Naţionale Istorice Centrale (Bucharest) (ANIC)
Comitetul Central (C.C.) al Partidului Comunist Român (PCR):
  Secţia Administrativ-Politică
  Secţia Cancelarie
  Secţia Organizatorică
  Secţia Propagandă

## Interviews

### Interviews conducted by Jill Massino

Interview with Valeria R., Braşov, 2 May 2003.
Interview with V., Braşov, 5 May 2003.
Interview with Elvira, Braşov, 5 May 2003.
Interview with Tatiana, Braşov, 27 May 2003.
Interview with Florina, Braşov, 7 June 2003.
Interview with Maria, Braşov, 8 June 2003.
Interview with Viorica, Braşov, 8 June 2003.
Interview with Doina, Braşov, 10 June 2003.
Interview with Eva, Braşov, 12 June 2003.
Interview with Valeria P., Braşov, 14 June 2003.
Interview with Maria, Braşov, 15 June 2003.
Interview with Angela, Braşov, 16 June 2003.
Interview with Ecaterina, Braşov, 17 June 2003.
Interview with Olga T., Braşov, 19 June 2003.
Interview with Maria F., Braşov, 20 June 2003.
Interview with Ioana, Braşov, 20 June 2003.
Interview with Domnica, Braşov, 22 June 2003.
Interview with Stela, Braşov, 23 June 2003.
Interview with D., Braşov, 23 June 2003.
Interview with Maria C., Braşov, 24 June 2003.
Interview with Doina, Braşov, 25 June 2003.
Interview with Elisabeta, Braşov, 27 June 2003.
Interview with Ileana, Braşov, 30 June 2003.
Interview with Regine, Braşov, 2 July 2003.

Interview with Rodica, Braşov, 3 July 2003.
Interview with Alexandra, Braşov, 4 July 2003.
Interview with Hilde, Braşov, 5 July 2003.
Interview with Margarita, Braşov, 5 July 2003.
Interview with Iuliana, Braşov, 7 July 2003.
Interview with Mariana, Braşov, 7 July 2003.
Interview with Daniela, Braşov, 9 July 2003.
Interview with Viorica Z., Braşov, 10 July 2003.
Interview with Florica, Braşov, 12 July 2003.
Interview with D., Braşov, 14 July 2003.
Interview with C., Braşov, 14 July 2003.
Interview with Florina J., Braşov, 15 July 2003.
Interview with Mircea J., Braşov, 15 July 2003.
Interview with Olga, Braşov, 19 July 2003.
Interview with Oana, Braşov, 24 July 2003.
Interview with Luana, Braşov, 25 July 2003.
Interview with Ruxandra, Braşov, 27 July 2003.
Interview with Margareta, Braşov, 27 July 2003.
Interview with Aurelia. S., Braşov, 29 July 2003.
Interview with C.C., Braşov, 30 July 2003.
Interview with Malina, Braşov, 1 August 2003.
Interview with Aurelia, Braşov, 2 August 2003.
Interview with Elena, Braşov, 4 August 2003.
Interview with M., Braşov, 5 August 2003.
Interview with Lena, Braşov, 6 August 2003.
Interview with G.N., Braşov, 16 August 2003.
Interview with Tudora, Bucharest, 29 May 2009.
Interview with Elena, Bucharest, 1 June 2009.
Interview with Pavel, Bucharest, 2 June 2009.
Interview with Petre, Bucharest, 3 June 2009.
Interview with Irina, Bucharest, 8 June 2009.
Interview with Traian, Bucharest, 9 June 2009.
Interview with Mirel, Bucharest, 11 June 2009.
Interview with Alexandra, Bucharest, 13 June 2009.
Interview with Aurel, Bucharest, 13 June 2009.
Interview with Vali, Bucharest, 14 June 2009.
Interview with Smaranda, Bucharest, 15 June 2009.
Interview with Doina, Bucharest, 16 June 2009.
Interview with Alexandra P., Bucharest, 16 June 2009.
Interview with Eleanora, Bucharest, 17 June 2009.
Interview with Carmen, Bucharest, 18 June 2009.
Interview with Constantina, Bucharest, 5 July 2009.
Interview with Zoe, Bucharest, 7 July 2009.
Interview with Maria, Bucharest, 12 July 2009.
Interview with Eugenia, Bucharest, 12 July 2009.
Interview with C., Bucharest, 18 July 2009.
Interview with Cătălina, Bucharest, 18 July 2009.
Interview with Adrian, Bucharest, 19 July 2009.

Interview with Șerban, Bucharest, 20 July 2009.
Interview with Rodica, Bucharest, 21 July 2009.
Interview with Lidia, Bucharest, May 28–30, 2012.
Interview with Alina, Bucharest, 31 May 2012.
Interview with Adriana, Bucharest, 3 June 2012.
Interview with Ruxandra, Bucharest, 5 June 2012.
Interview with A., Bucharest, 6 June 2012.
Interview with Adriana, Bucharest, 6 June 2012.
Interview with Axinia, Râmnicu Vâlcea, 10 June 2012.
Interview with Anca, Bucharest, 12 June 2012.
Interview with Paul, Bucharest, 14 June 2012.
Interview with Titica, Bucharest, 14 June 2012.
Interview with Alexandra, Bucharest, 18 June 2012.
Interview with Lucia, Bucharest, 20 June 2012.

## Interviews conducted by Ioana Manoliu

Interview with Ildiko, Brașov, 12 July 2003.
Interview with Elena, Brașov, 13 July 2003.
Interview with Corina L., Brașov, 17 July 2003.
Interview with Corina, M., Brașov, 22 July 2003.
Interview with Maria C., Brașov, 11 August 2003.
Interview with Livia, Brașov, 11 August 2003.
Interview with Simona, Brașov, 11 August 2003.

## Interviews conducted by Anca Coman

Interview with Aneta, Brașov, 25 June 2003.
Interview with R., Brașov, 28 June 2003.
Interview with Maria S., Brașov, 30 June 2003.
Interview with I., Brașov, 6 July 2003.
Interview with H., Brașov, 5 August 2003.
Interview with G., Brașov, 7 August 2003.
Interview with Ivonne, Brașov, 8 August 2003.
Interview with C., Brașov, 8 August 2003.
Interview with V.M. Brașov, 9 August 2003.
Interview with Marcela, Brașov, 12 August 2003.
Interview with Rodica, Brașov, 12 August 2003.

## Interviews conducted by Ionuț Iuria

Interview with Mircea I., Brașov, 4 August 2003.
Interview with Mircea A., Brașov, 5 August 2003.

## Periodicals and Government Documents

*Anuarul Statistic al Românii*
*Anuarul Statistic al Republicii Populare Romîne*
*Anuarul Statistic al Republicii Socialiste România*
*Balkan Insight*
*Buletinul Oficial al Republicii Populare Române*
*Buletinul Oficial al Republicii Socialiste România*
*Colecție de Legi, Decrete, Hotâriri și Alte Acte Normative*
*Cutezătorii*
*Drumul Femeii*
*Eurostat*
*Femeia*
*The Guardian*
*Historia*
*Martor: Journal of the Museum of the Romanian Peasant*
*Moda*
*Monitorul Oficial al României*
*Revista 22*
*România Liberă*
*Scânteia*

## Films

*Buletin de București,* directed by Virgil Calotescu (Bucharest: Casa de Filme Patru, 1982).
*Căsătorie cu repetiție,* directed by Virgil Calotescu (Bucharest: Casa de Filme Patru, 1985).
*Cum mi-am petrecut sfârșitul lumii,* directed by Cătălin Mitulescu (Bucharest: Strada România Films, 2006).
*Four Months, Three Weeks, and Two Days,* directed by Cristian Mungiu (Bucharest, BAC Films, 2007).
*Ilustrate cu flori de câmp,* directed by Andrei Blaier (Bucharest: România Film, 1974).
*Născuți la comandă: Decrețeii,* directed by Florian Iepan (Westend Film, 2005).
*Mihai Viteazul,* directed by Sergiu Nicolaescu (Bucharest: România Film, 1969).

## Published Primary and Secondary Sources

Abraham, Florin. *Romania since the Second World War: A Political, Social, and Economic History*. London: Bloomsbury Press, 2017.
Albert, Francisca. *Dialog cu Timpul Liber*. Bucharest: Editura Politică, 1970.
Alexandrescu, Ion. *Economia României în primii ani postbelici (1945–1947)*. Bucharest: Editura Științifică și Enciclopedică, 1986.
Alexopoulos, Golfo. "Soviet Citizenship, More or Less: Rights, Emotions, and States of Civic Belonging." *Kritika: Explorations in Russian and Eurasian History* 7, no. 3 (2006): 487–528.
Andreescu, Gabriel, and Mihnea Berindei, eds. *Ultimul deceniu comunist: Scrisori către Radio Europa Liberă vol. 1 (1979–1985)*. Iași: Polirom, 2010.
Antohi, Sorin, and Vladimir Tismăneanu, eds. *Between Past and Future: The Revolutions of 1989 and Their Aftermath*. Budapest: Central European University Press, 2000.
Anton, Lorena. "On Memory Work in Post-communist Europe: A Case Study on Romania's Ways of Remembering Its Pronatalist Past." *Anthropological Journal of European Cultures* 18, no. 2 (2009): 106–122.
Anton, Mioara. *'Ceaușescu și poporul!' Scrisori către 'iubitul conducător' (1965–1989)*. Târgoviște: Cetatea de Scaun, 2016.
Anton, Mioara, and Laurențiu Constantiniu, eds. *Guvernați și guvernanți: Scrisori către putere, 1945–1965*. Iași: Polirom, 2013.
Attwood, Lynne. *Creating the New Soviet Woman: Women's Magazines as Engineers of Female Identity, 1922–53*. Basingstoke: Macmillan, 1999.
Băban, Adriana, and Henry P. David. *Voices of Romanian Women: Perceptions of Sexuality, Reproductive Behavior, and Partner Relations during the Ceaușescu Era*. Bethesda, MD: Transnational Family Research Institute: 1994.
Baker, Catherine, ed. *Gender in Twentieth-Century Europe and the USSR*. London: Palgrave Macmillan, 2017.
Băluță, Oana, ed. *Impactul crizei economice asupra femeilor*. Bucharest: Maiko, 2011.
———, ed. *Gen și putere: Partea leului în politica românească*. Iași: Editura Polirom, 2006.
Ban, Cornel. "Sovereign Debt, Austerity, and Regime Change: The Case of Nicolae Ceaușescu's Romania." *East European Politics and Societies* 26, no. 4 (2012): 743–76.
———. "Neoliberalism in Translation: Economic Ideas and Reforms in Spain and Romania." PhD diss., University of Maryland, 2011.
Banac, Ivo, ed. *Eastern Europe in Revolution*. Ithaca, NY: Cornell University Press, 1992.
Banu, Gheorghe. *Mari probleme de medicină socială*. Bucharest, n.p. 1938.
Baron, Eva, ed. *Work Engendered: Toward a New History of American Labor*. Ithaca, NY: Cornell University Press, 1991.
Batinić, Jelena. *Women and Yugoslav Partisans: A History of World War II Resistance*. New York: Cambridge University Press, 2015.
Bebel, August. *Women and Socialism*. New York: Labor Press, 1904.

Berdahl, Daphne. *Where the World Ended: Re-Unification and Identity in the German Borderland.* Berkeley: University of California Press, 1999.
Berdahl, Daphne, Matti Bunzl, and Martha Lampland. *Altering States: Ethnographies of Transition in Eastern Europe and the Former Soviet Union.* Ann Arbor, MI: University of Michigan Press, 2000.
Bernhard, Michael, and Jan Kubik, eds. *Twenty Years after Communism: The Politics of Memory and Commemoration.* Oxford: Oxford University Press, 2014.
Betts, Paul. "The Twilight of the Idols: East German Memory and Material Culture." *Journal of Modern History* 72, no. 3 (2000): 731–65.
———. *Within Walls: Private Life in the German Democratic Republic.* Oxford: Oxford University Press, 2010.
Bezzi, Cristina. "Romanian 'Left Behind Children?' Experiences of Transnational Childhood and Families in Europe." *Martor: Journal of the Museum of the Romanian Peasant* 18 (2013): 57–74.
Biebuyck, Erin. "The Collectivisation of Pleasure: Normative Sexuality in Post-1966 Romania." *Aspasia: International Yearbook of Central, Eastern, and Southeastern European Women's and Gender History* 4 (2010): 49–70.
Blaive, Muriel. "State Violence over the Female Body: Giving Birth in Czechoslovakia and in the US from the 1950s to the 1970s." Paper presented at the Association for Slavic, East European, and Eurasian Studies, New Orleans, Louisiana, 20 November 2012.
Bonnell, Victoria, ed. *Identities in Transition: Eastern Europe and Russia after the Collapse of Communism.* Berkeley: University of California Press, 1996.
———. *Iconography of Power: Soviet Political Posters under Lenin and Stalin.* Berkeley: University of California Press, 1997.
Borovoy, Amy, and Kristen Ghodsee. "Decentering Agency in Feminist Theory: Social Democracy, Postsocialism, and the Re-engagement of the Social Good." *Women's Studies International Forum* 35 (2012): 153–165.
Botez, Calypso. "Drepturile femeii în constituţia viitoare." In *Constituţia din 1923 în dezbaterea contemporanilor,* edited by Aurel Stroe, 124–142. Bucharest: Humanitas, 1990.
Bottoni, Stefano. "Reassessing the Communist Takeover in Romania: Violence, Institutional Continuity, and Ethnic Conflict Management." *East European Politics and Societies* 24, no. 1 (2010): 59–89.
———. *Long Awaited West: Eastern Europe since 1944.* Bloomington, IN: Indiana University Press, 2017.
Bourdieu, Pierre. *Distinction: A Social Critique of the Judgment of Taste.* Translated by Richard Nice. Cambridge, MA: Harvard University Press, 1984.
Boym, Svetlana. *Common Places: Mythologies of Everyday Life in Russia.* Cambridge, MA: Harvard University Press, 1995.
Braham, Randolph. *Education in Romania: A Decade of Change.* Washington, DC: Office of Education and Institute of International Studies, 1972.
*Braşovul în cincisprezece dimensiuni.* Braşov: Comitetul Judeţean de Cultură şi Artă, 1969.
Bren, Paulina. "Mirror, Mirror, on the Wall ... Is the West the Fairest of Them All? Czechoslovak Normalization and Its (Dis)Contents." *Kritika: Explorations in Russian and Eurasian History* 9, no. 4 (Fall 2008): 831–54.

———. *The Greengrocer and His TV: The Culture of Communism after the 1968 Prague Spring*. Ithaca, NY: Cornell University Press, 2010.

Bren, Paulina and Mary Neuberger, eds. *Communism Unwrapped: Consumption in Cold War Eastern Europe*. New York: Oxford University Press, 2012.

Bridenthal, Renate, Atina Grossman, and Marion Kaplan, eds. *When Biology Became Destiny: Women in Weimar and Nazi Germany*. New York: Monthly Review Press, 1984.

Bridenthal, Renate, Susan Mosher Stuard, and Merry Wiesner Hanks. *Becoming Visible Women in European History*, Third Edition. Boston: Houghton Mifflin Company, 1998.

Brunnbauer, Ulf. *Die sozialistische Lebensweise: Ideologie, Gesellschaft, Familie und Politik in Bulgarien (1944–1989)*. Vienna: Böhlau Verlag, 2007.

Buckley, Mary, ed. *Post-Soviet Women from the Baltic to Central Asia*. Cambridge: Cambridge University Press, 1997.

Bucur, Maria. "Sex in the Time of Communism: The Ripple Effect of the #metoo Campaign." *Public Seminar*. 7 December 2017. Retrieved from: http://www.publicseminar.org/2017/12/sex-in-the-time-of-communism/ (accessed 10 December 2017).

———. "Between the Mother of the Wounded and the Virgin of Jiu: Romanian Women and the Gender of Heroism during the Great War." *Journal of Women's History* 12, no. 2 (Summer 2000): 30–56.

———. "Calypso Botez: Gender Difference and the Limits of Pluralism in Interwar Romania." *Jahrbücher für Geschichte und Kultur Südosteuropas* 3 (2001): 63–78.

———. *Eugenics and Modernization in Interwar Romania*. Pittsburgh, PA: University of Pittsburgh Press, 2002.

———. "Between Liberal and Republican Citizenship: Feminism and Nationalism in Romania, 1880–1918." *Aspasia: International Yearbook of Central, Eastern, and Southeastern European Women's and Gender History* 1 (2007): 84–102.

———. "Gendering Dissent: Of Bodies and Minds, Survival and Opposition under Communism." In *Beyond Little Vera: Women's Bodies, Women's Welfare in Russia and Central/Eastern Europe*, edited by Angela Brintlinger and Natasha Kolchevska. *Ohio Slavic Papers* 7 (2008): 131–52.

———. "Gender and Religiosity among the Orthodox Christians in Romania: Continuity and Change, 1945–1989." *Aspasia: International Yearbook of Central, Eastern, and Southeastern Women's and Gender History* 5 (2011): 28–45.

———. "The Economics of Citizenship: Gender Regimes and Property Rights in Romania in the Twentieth Century." In *Gender and Citizenship in Historical and Transnational Perspective: Agency, Space, Borders*, edited by Anne R. Epstein and Rachel G. Fuchs, 143–65. Basingstoke: Palgrave Macmillan, 2016.

Bucur, Maria, Rayna Gavrilova, Wendy Goldman, Maureen Healy, Kate Lebow, and Mark Pittaway, "Six Historians in Search of Alltagsgeschichte," in *Aspasia: International Yearbook of Central, Eastern, and Southeastern European Women's and Gender History* 3 (2008): 189–212.

Budeancă, Cosmin. "Divorțul în familiile foștilor deținuți politici." In *Stat și viață privată în regimurile comuniste,* edited by Cosmin Budeancă and Florentin Olteanu, 161–176. Iași: Polirom, 2009.

Burawoy, Michael, and Katherine Verdery, eds. *Uncertain Transition: Ethnographies of Change in the Postsocialist World.* Lanham, MD: Rowman and Littlefield, 1999.

Canning, Kathleen. "Feminist History after the Linguistic Turn: Historicizing Discourse and Experience." *Signs* 19, no. 2 (1994): 368–404.

———. *Languages of Labor and Gender: Female Factory Work in Germany, 1850–1914.* Ithaca, NY: Cornell University Press, 1996.

———. *Gender History in Practice: Historical Perspectives on Bodies, Class, and Citizenship.* Ithaca, NY: Cornell University Press, 2006.

Case, Holly. *Between States: The Transylvanian Question and the European Idea during World War II.* Stanford, CA: Stanford University Press, 2009.

Cazan, Marius, and Vlad Pașca. "'Lupta de clasă' la porțile facultăților: Politici de promovare socială prin învățământul superior în epoca Gheorghiu-Dej (1948–1965)." In *Politici culturale și modele intelectuale în România,* edited by Lucian Nastasă and Dragoș Sdrobiș, 251–279. Cluj-Napoca: Editura Mega, 2013.

Ceaușescu, Nicolae. *Propuneri de măsuri pentru îmbunătățirea activității politico-ideologice, de educare marxist-leninistă a membrilor de partid, a tuturor oamenilor muncii, 6, iulie 1971.* Bucharest, 1971.

———. "Cuvîntare la festivitățile organizate la Cluj cu prilejul deschiderii noului an universitar, 2 octombrie, 1972."

Cernat, Paul, Ion Manolescu, Angelo Mitchievici, and Ioan Stanomir. *Explorări în comunismul românesc, vol. 1.* Iași: Polirom, 2004.

———. *Explorări în comunismul românesc, vol. 2.* Iași: Polirom, 2005.

———. *Explorări în comunismul românesc, vol. 3.* Iași: Polirom, 2008.

Cesereanu, Ruxandra. "Revolta muncitorilor din Brașov, 1987." *Revista* 22, no. 14 (2003).

Chakrabarty, Dipesh. "Postcoloniality and the Artifice of History: Who Speaks for 'Indian' Pasts." *Representations* 37 (1992): 1–26.

Chatterjee, Choi. *Celebrating Women: Gender, Festival Culture, and Bolshevik Ideology, 1910–1939.* Pittsburgh, PA: University of Pittsburgh Press, 2002.

Chelcea, Liviu and Puiu Lațea. "Cultura penurei: bunuri, strategii și practici de consum în Romania in anilor '80." In *Viața cotidiană în comunism,* edited by Adrian Neculau, 152–74. Iași: Polirom, 2004.

Chenais, Jean Claude. *The Demographic Transition: Stages, Patterns, and Economic Implications: A Longitudinal Study of 67 Countries Covering the Period 1720–1984.* Oxford: Oxford University Press, 1992.

Chirot, Daniel. "Social Change in Communist Romania." *Social Forces* 57, no. 2 (1978): 467–99.

Ciobanu, Monica. "Romania's Travails with Democracy and Accession to the European Union." *Europe-Asia Studies* 59, no. 8 (2007): 1429–50.

Cîrstocea, Ioana. "La Construction Politique de L'identité Féminine pendant le Régime Communiste Roumain (1945–1965)." Romanian Institute for Recent History: IRIR Work in Progress Series, no. 5 (2002).

Ciurea, Rodica. *Conflict între generații?* Bucharest: Editura Enciclopedică Română, 1969.
Clark, Roland. *Holy Legionary Youth: Fascist Activism in Interwar Romania.* Ithaca, NY: Cornell University Press, 2015.
*Codul principiilor și normelor muncii și vieții comuniștilor, ale eticii și echității socialiste.* Editura Politică, 1974.
*Congresul al XI-lea al Partidului Comunist Român, 25–28 noiembrie 1974.* Bucharest: Editura Politică, 1975.
Copilaș, Emanuel, ed. *Marele jaf postcomunist: spectacolul mărfii și revanșa capitalismului* Iași: Editura Adenium, 2017.
Corner, Paul, ed. *Popular Opinion in Totalitarian Regimes: Fascism, Nazism, Communism.* Oxford: Oxford University Press, 2009.
Corrin, Chris, ed. *Superwomen and the Double Burden: Women's Experience of Change in Central and Eastern Europe and the Former Soviet Union.* New York: Scarlet Press, 1993.
Costache, Irina. "From the Party to the Beach Party: Nudism and Artistic Expression in the People's Republic of Romania." In *Socialist Escapes: Breaking Away from Ideology and Everyday Routine in Eastern Europe, 1945–1989,* edited by Cathleen M. Giustino, Catherine J. Plum, and Alexander Vari, 127–144. New York: Berghahn Books, 2013.
———. "Archiving Desire: Materiality, Sexuality, and the Secret Police in Romanian State Socialism." PhD diss., Central European University, 2014.
Cott, Nancy F. *The Bonds of Womanhood: "Woman's Sphere" in New England, 1780 – 1835.* New Haven, CT: Yale University Press, 1997.
Crampton, R. J. *Eastern Europe in the Twentieth Century.* New York: Routledge, 1997.
Crowley, David, and Susan E. Reid, eds. *Socialist Spaces: Sites of Everyday Life in the Eastern Bloc.* Oxford: Berg, 2002.
Crowther, William. *The Political Economy of Romanian Socialism.* New York: Praeger, 1988.
David, Henry P., and Robert J. McIntyre. *Reproductive Behavior: Central and Eastern European Experience.* New York: Springer, 1981.
David, Henry P., ed. with the assistance of Joanna Skilogianis. *From Abortion to Contraception: A Resource to Public Policies and Reproductive Behavior in Central and Eastern Europe from 1917 to the Present.* Westport, CT: Greenwood Press, 1999.
David, Henry P. and Adriana Băban. "Women's Health and Reproductive Rights: Romanian Experience." *Patient Education and Counseling* 28, no. 3 (1996): 235–45.
Davies, Sarah. *Popular Opinion in Stalin's Russia: Terror, Propaganda, and Dissent, 1934–1941.* New York: Cambridge University Press, 1997.
Davis, Belinda. *Home Fires Burning: Food, Politics, and Everyday Life in World War I Berlin.* Chapel Hill, NC: University of North Carolina Press, 2000.
De Certeau, Michel. *The Practice of Everyday Life.* Berkeley: University of California Press, 2002.
Decuble, Gabriel H., ed. *Cartea roz a comunismului,* vol. 1. Iași: Versus 2004.
Deculescu, Adriana. *Scrisoare către o tînără căsătorită.* Bucharest: Editura Medicală, 1967.

———. *Viaţa şi Dragostea*. Bucharest: Editura Medicală, 1968.
De Grazia, Victoria. *How Fascism Ruled Women, Italy, 1922–1945*. Berkeley: University of California Press, 1992.
De Haan, Francisca, Krassimira Daskalova, and Anna Loutfi, eds. *A Biographical Dictionary of Women's Movements and Feminisms: Central, Eastern, and South Eastern Europe, 19th and 20th Centuries*. Budapest: Central European University Press, 2006.
Deletant, Dennis. *Ceauşescu and the Securitate: Coercion and Dissent in Romania, 1965–89*. London: Hurst and Company, 1995.
———. *Romania under Communist Rule*. Bucharest: Center for Romanian Studies, 1998.
Dimitriu, Radu. *De vorbă cu tinerii: probleme de educaţie a sexelor*. Bucharest: Albatros, 1972.
Dimitrov, Martin K. "What the Party Wanted to Know: Citizen Complaints as a 'Barometer of Public Opinion' in Communist Bulgaria." *East European Politics and Societies* 28, no. 2 (2014): 271–295.
Djilas, Milovan. *The New Class: An Analysis of the Communist System*. New York: Praeger, 1957.
Doboş, Corina, Luciana Jinga, and Florin Soare. *Politica pronatalistă a regimului Ceauşescu: Vol. 1: O perspectivă comparativă*. Iaşi: Polirom, 2010.
Doboş, Corina, and Florin S. Soare. "Cei din lume fără nume: Politica pronatalistă a regimului Ceauşescu." Museum exhibition brochure. Retrieved from http://politicapronatalista.iiccr.ro/ (accessed 14 May 2017).
Dobre, Gheorghe, ed. *Economia României în context European-1938*. Bucharest: Editura Fundaţiei Ştiinţifice, 1996.
Drakulić, Slavenka. *How We Survived Communism and Even Laughed*. New York: Harper Perennial, 1993.
Dumanescu, Luminiţa. *Familia românească în comunism*. Cluj: Presa Universitară Clujeană, 2012.
Dunn, Elizabeth C. *Privatizing Poland: Baby Food, Big Business, and the Remaking of Labor*. Ithaca, NY: Cornell University Press, 2004.
Edele, Mark. "Soviet Society, Social Structure, and Everyday Life: Major Frameworks Reconsidered." *Kritika* 8, no. 2 (2007): 349–73.
Einhorn, Barbara. *Cinderella Goes to Market: Citizenship, Gender and Women's Movements in East Central Europe*. London: Verso, 1993.
———. "Gender Issues in Transition: The East Central European Experience." *European Journal of Development Research* 6, no. 2 (1994): 119–40.
———. *Citizenship in an Enlarging Europe: From Dream to Awakening*. Basingstoke: Palgrave Macmillan, 2010.
Einhorn, Barbara, and Swasri Mitter. "A Comparative Analysis of Women's Industrial Participation during the Transition from Centrally Planned to Market Economies in East Central Europe." In *The Impact of Economic and Political Reform on the Status of Women in Eastern Europe*. Proceedings of a UN Regional Seminar, Vienna, April 8–12, 1991.
Ekman, Joakim, and Jonas Linde. "Communist Nostalgia in Central and Eastern Europe: A Matter of Principle or Performance?" Paper presented at the Nordic Political Science Association's Annual Meeting, Aalborg, Denmark, 2002.

Eley, Geoff, and Jan Palmowski, eds. *Citizenship and National Identity in Twentieth-Century Germany*. Stanford, CA: Stanford University Press, 2008.
Ely, John F., and Cătălin Augustin Stoica. "Re-Membering Romania." In *Romania since 1989: Politics, Economics, and Society*, edited by Henry F. Carey, 97–115. Lanham, MD: Lexington Books, 2004.
Engels, Friedrich. *The Origin of the Family, Private Property and the State*. Honolulu: University Press of the Pacific, 2001.
Eyal, Gil, Ivan Szelenyi, and Eleanor Townsley. *Making Capitalism without Capitalists: The New Ruling Elites in Eastern Europe*. London: Verso, 1998.
Fejtő, Francois. *A History of the People's Democracies: Eastern Europe since Stalin*. New York: Praeger, 1971.
Fichter, Madigan. "Rock and Roll Nation: Counterculture and Dissent in Romania, 1965–1975." *Nationalities Papers* 39, no. 4 (2011): 567–585.
Fidelis, Malgorzata. *Women, Communism, and Industrialization in Postwar Poland*. New York: Cambridge University Press, 2010.
———. "Are You a Modern Girl? Consumerism and Young Women in 1960s Poland." In *Gender Politics and Everyday Life in State Socialist Eastern and Central Europe*, edited by Shana Penn and Jill Massino, 171–184. New York: Palgrave Macmillan, 2009.
———. "Equality through Protection: The Politics of Women's Employment in Postwar Poland, 1945–1956." *Slavic Review* 63, no. 2 (2004): 301–24.
Field, Deborah A. "Irreconcilable Differences: Divorce and Conceptions of Private Life in the Khrushchev Era." *Russian Review* 57, no. 4 (October 1998): 599–613.
"Final Report of the International Commission on the Holocaust in Romania, November 11, 2004." Retrieved from http://www.ushmm.org/m/pdfs/20080226-romania-commission-iliescu-speech.pdf (accessed 16 April 2015).
Fischer, Mary Ellen. "Women in Romanian Politics: Elena Ceaușescu, Pronatalism, and the Promotion of Women." In *Women, State, and Party in Eastern Europe*, edited by Sharon L. Wolchik and Alfred G. Meyer, 121–137. Durham, NC: Duke University Press, 1985.
Fitzpatrick, Sheila. *Everyday Stalinism: Ordinary Life in Extraordinary Times. Soviet Russia in the 1930s*. New York: Oxford University Press, 1999.
———. "Supplicants and Citizens: Public Letter-Writing in Soviet Russia in the 1930s." *Slavic Review* 55, no. 1 (1966): 78–105.
Florescu, Gheorghe. *Confesiunile unui cafegiu*. Bucharest: Humanitas, 2008.
Fodor, Eva. "Gender in Transition: Unemployment in Hungary, Poland, and Slovakia." *East European Politics and Societies* 11, no. 3 (1997): 470–501.
———. "Family Policies and Gender in Hungary, Poland, and Romania." *Communist and Post-Communist Studies* 35, no. 4 (2002): 475–90.
———. *Working Difference: Women's Working Lives in Hungary and Austria, 1945–1995*. Durham, NC: Duke University Press, 2003.
Frader, Laura L., and Sonya A. Rose, eds. *Gender and Class in Modern Europe*. Ithaca, NY: Cornell University Press, 1996.
Frevert, Ute. *Women in German History from Bourgeois Emancipation to Sexual Liberation*. Translated by Stuart McKinnon-Evans with Terry Bond and Barbara Norden. New York: Berg, 1989.

Friedrich, Carl and Zbigniew Brzezinski. *Totalitarian Dictatorship and Autocracy*. Cambridge, MA: Harvard University Press, 1956.
Fukuyama, Francis. *The End of History and the Last Man*. New York: Free Press, 1992.
Funk, Nanette, and Magda Mueller, eds. *Gender Politics and Post-Communism: Reflections from Eastern Europe and the Former Soviet Union*. New York: Routledge, 1993.
Furet, François. *The Passing of an Illusion: The Idea of Communism in the Twentieth Century*. Chicago: University of Chicago Press, 1995.
Gal, Susan, and Gail Kligman, eds. *Reproducing Gender: Politics, Publics, and Everyday Life after Socialism*. Princeton, NJ: Princeton University Press, 2000.
———. *The Politics of Gender after Socialism: A Comparative Historical Essay*. Princeton, NJ: Princeton University Press, 2000.
Gallagher, Tom. *Romania after Ceauşescu: The Politics of Intolerance*. Edinburgh: Edinburgh University Press, 1995.
———. *Modern Romania: The End of Communism, the Failure of Democratic Reform, and the Theft of a Nation*. New York: New York University Press, 2008.
———. *Romania and the European Union: How the Weak Vanquished the Strong*. Manchester: Manchester University Press, 2009.
Gapova, Elena. "Writing Women's and Gender History in Countries of Transition." American Association for the Advancement of Slavic Studies Conference, Toronto, Canada, December 2003.
Georgescu, Diana. "'Ceauşescu's Children': The Making and 'Unmaking' of the Last Socialist Generation (1965–2010)." PhD diss., University of Illinois, 2015.
Georgescu, Vlad. *The Romanians: A History*. Edited by Matei Calinescu. Translated by Alexandra Bley-Vroman. Columbus: Ohio State Press, 1991.
Ghebrea, Georgeta. *Regim social-politic şi viaţă privată: familiă şi politica familială în România*. Bucharest: Editura Universităţii din Bucureşti, 2000.
———. "Gender Policies in Romania: From Infrastructure to Action." *Journal for the Study of Religions and Ideologies* 5, no. 14 (2006): 5–30.
Gheo, Radu Pavel, and Dan Lungu. *Tovarăşe de drum: Experienţa feminină în comunism*. Iaşi: Polirom, 2008.
Gheorghiu-Dej, Gheorghe. *Declaraţie cu privire la poziţia Partidului Muncitoresc Român în problemele mişcării comuniste şi muncitoreşti internaţionale, adoptată de Plenara lărgită a C.C. al P.M.R. din aprilie 1964*. Bucharest: Editura Politică, 1964.
Ghit, Alexandra. "Mobilizing Gender for Socialist Modernity: The Work of One Transylvanian Chapter of the Union of Anti-Fascist Women of Romania and the Union of Democratic Women in Romania, 1945–1953." Master's thesis, Central European University, 2011.
Ghodsee, Kristen. *The Red Riviera: Gender, Tourism, and Postsocialism on the Black Sea*. Durham, NC: Duke University Press, 2005.
———. "Pressuring the Politburo: The Committee of the Bulgarian Women's Movement and State Socialist Feminism." *Slavic Review* 73, no. 3 (Fall 2014): 538–62.

———. *The Left Side of History: World War II and the Unfulfilled Promise of Communism in Eastern Europe.* Durham, NC: Duke University Press, 2015.

———. "State-Socialist Women's Organizations in Cold War Perspective: Revisiting the Work of Maxine Molyneux." *Aspasia: International Yearbook of Central, Eastern, and Southeastern European Women's and Gender History* 10 (2016): 111–21.

Giurescu, Dinu C. "Învățământul României între anii 1948 și 1949." November 2011. Retrieved from http://www.ucv.ro/pdf/international/informatii_generale/doctor_honoris/68.pdf (accessed 28 October 2016).

Gledhill, John. "States of Contention: State-Led Political Violence in Post-socialist Romania." *East European Politics and Societies* 19, no. 1 (2005): 76–104.

Gluck, Sherna Berger, and Daphne Patai, eds. *Women's Words: The Feminist Practice in Oral History.* New York: Routledge, 1991.

Gluvacov, Ana. *Afirmarea femeii în viața societății: dimensiuni și semnificați în România.* Bucharest: Editura Politică, 1975.

Goldman, Wendy Z. *Women, the State and Revolution: Soviet Family Policy and Social Life, 1917–1936.* New York: Cambridge University Press, 1993.

———. *Women at the Gates: Gender and Industry in Stalin's Russia.* New York: Cambridge University Press, 2002.

Goven, Joanna. "Gender and Modernism in a Stalinist State." *Social Politics* 9, no. 1 (2002): 3–28.

Grama, Adrian. "Laboring Along: Industrial Workers and the Making of Postwar Romania (1944–1958)." PhD diss., Central European University, 2017.

Grossmann, Atina. *Reforming Sex: The German Movement for Birth Control and Abortion Reform, 1920–1950.* New York: Oxford University Press, 1995.

Haliliuc, Alina. "Who Is a Victim of Communism? Gender and Public Memory in the Sighet Museum, Romania." *Aspasia: International Yearbook of Central, Eastern, and Southeastern European Women's and Gender History* 7 (2013): 108–31.

Hall, Richard Andrew. "The Uses of Absurdity: The Staged War Theory and the Romanian Revolution of 1989." *East European Politics and Societies* 13, no. 3 (1999): 501–42.

Haney, Lynne. *Inventing the Needy: Gender and the Politics of Welfare in Hungary.* Berkeley: University of California Press, 2002.

Harsanyi, Doina Pasca. "Participation of Women in the Workforce: The Case of Romania." In *Family, Women, and Employment in Central Eastern Europe,* edited by Barbara Lobodzinska, 213–17. Westport, CT: Greenwood Press, 1995.

Harsch, Donna. *Revenge of the Domestic: Women, the Family, and Communism in the German Democratic Republic.* Princeton, NJ: Princeton University Press, 2006.

Havel, Václav. *The Power of the Powerless Citizens against the State in Central-Eastern Europe.* London: M. E. Sharpe, 1978.

Healy, Maureen. *Vienna and the Fall of the Habsburg Empire: Total War and Everyday Life in World War I.* Cambridge: Cambridge University Press, 2004.

Heineman, Elizabeth. *What Difference Does a Husband Make? Women and Marital Status in Nazi and Postwar Germany.* Berkeley: University of California Press, 1999.

Hessler, Julie. *A Social History of Soviet Trade: Trade Policy, Retail Practices, and Consumption, 1917–1953.* Princeton, NJ: Princeton University Press, 2004.
Higonnet, Margaret R., Jane Jenson, Sonya Michel, and Margaret Collins Weitz, eds. *Behind the Lines: Gender and the Two World Wars.* New Haven, CT: Yale University Press, 1987.
Hitchins, Keith. "The Romanian Orthodox Church and the State." In *Religion and Atheism in the USSR and Eastern Europe,* edited by Bohdan R. Bociurkiw, John Strong, and Jean Laux, 314–27. New York: Macmillan Press, 1975.
———. *Rumania, 1866–1947.* Oxford: Clarendon Press, 1994.
———. *The Romanians, 1774–1886.* Oxford: Clarendon Press, 1996.
———. *A Nation Affirmed: The Romanian National Movement in Transylvania, 1860–1914.* Bucharest: The Encyclopaedic Publishing House, 1999.
———. *A Concise History of Romania.* Cambridge: Cambridge University Press, 2014.
Hochschild, Arlie, with Anne Machung. *The Second Shift: Working Parents and the Revolution at Home.* New York: Viking-Penguin, 1989.
Hoffmann, David. *Stalinist Values: The Cultural Norms of Soviet Modernity, 1917–1941.* Ithaca, NY: Cornell University Press, 2003.
Horea-Șerban, Raluca Ioana and Marinela Istrate. "Rolul presei scrise în promovarea politicii pronataliste," in *După 25 de ani Comunismul în Europa de Est: Statutul Femeii în România Comunistă: Politici publice și viață privată,* ed. Alina Hurubean. Iași: Institutul European, 2015.
Hovárth, Sándor. *Stalinism Reloaded: Everyday Life in Stalin-City, Hungary.* Bloomington, IN: Indiana University Press, 2017.
Huntington, Samuel P., and Clement H. Moore, eds. *Authoritarian Politics in Modern Society: The Dynamics of Established One-Party Systems.* New York: Basic Books, 1970.
Iancu, Alice, Oana Băluță, Alina Dragolea, and Bogdan Florian. "Women's Social Exclusion and Feminists: Living Parallel Worlds." In *Gendering Post-Socialist Transition: Studies of Changing Gender Perspectives,* edited by Krassimira Daskalova, Caroline Hornstein Tomic, Karl Kaser, and Filip Radunović: 183–216. ERSTE Foundation Series, vol. 1. Berlin and Vienna: LIT Verlag, 2012.
Ilić, Melanie, ed. *Women in the Stalin Era.* New York: Palgrave Macmillan, 2002.
Ilić, Melanie, Susan E. Reid, and Lynne Atwood, eds. *Women in the Khrushchev Era.* Basingstoke: Palgrave, 2004.
Ilić, Melanie, and Dalia Leinarte, eds. *The Soviet Past in the Post-Socialist Present: Methodology and Ethics in Russian, Baltic and Central European Oral History and Memory Studies.* New York: Routledge, 2016.
Iluț, Petru. *Sociopsihologia și antropologia familiei.* Iași: Polirom, 2005.
Ioanid, Radu. *The Holocaust in Romania: The Destruction of Jews and Gypsies under the Antonescu Regime, 1940–1944.* Chicago: Ivan R. Dee, 2000.
Iordachi, Constantin. "The Unyielding Boundaries of Citizenship: The Emancipation of 'Non-Citizens' in Romania, 1866–1918." *European Review of History* 8, no. 2 (2001): 157–86.

Iordachi, Constantin, and Dorin Dobrincu, eds. *Transforming Peasants, Property and Power: The Collectivization of Romanian Agriculture.* Budapest: Central European University Press, 2009.
Ivan, Ruxandra, ed. *Transformarea socialistă: Politici ale regimului comunist între ideologie și administrație.* Iași: Polirom, 2009.
Ivașcu, Lavinia. "'Noi nu am fost oameni, că am fost chiaburi:' Mărturii privind colectivizarea în Maramureș." *Analele Sighet* 8, anii 1954–1960 (2000): 305–308.
James, Daniel. *Dona Maria's Story: Life, History, Memory, and Political Identity.* Durham, NC: Duke University Press, 2000.
Jancar, Barbara Wolfe. *Women under Communism.* Baltimore, MD: Johns Hopkins University Press, 1978.
Janos, Andrew C. *East Central Europe in the Modern World: The Politics of the Borderlands from Pre- to Postcommunism.* Stanford, CA: Stanford University Press, 2000.
Jarausch, Konrad, H. ed. *Dictatorship as Experience: Towards a Socio-Cultural History of the GDR.* New York: Berghahn Books, 1999.
Jelavich, Barbara. *History of the Balkans, Vol. 2: Twentieth Century.* Cambridge: Cambridge University Press, 1983.
Jelavich, Charles, and Barbara Jelavich. *The Establishment of the Balkan National States, 1804–1920.* Seattle: University of Washington Press, 1977.
Jinga, Luciana, Florin S. Soare, Corina Doboș, and Cristina Roman. *Politica pronatalistă a regimului Ceaușescu, Vol. 2: Instituții și practici.* Iași: Polirom, 2011.
Jinga, Luciana-Marioara. "Forme de organizare ale muncii cu femeile în cadrul PCR (1944–1954)." In *Structuri de partid și de stat in timpul regimului comunist,* edited by Luciana Jinga and Ștefan Bosomitu, 53–96. *Anuarul IICCMER,* vol. III. Iași: Polirom, 2008.
———. Femeile în Cadrul Partidului Comunist Român, 1944–1989." PhD diss., Universitatea A. I. Cuza, Iași and Universite D'Angers, 2011
———. *Gen și reprezentare în România comunistă, 1944–1989.* Iași: Polirom, 2015.
Keil, Thomas, and Viviana Andreescu. "Fertility Policy in Ceaușescu's Romania." *Journal of Family History* 24, no. 4 (1999): 478–92.
Kelso, Michelle. "Gypsy Deportations from Romania to Transnistria, 1942–1944." In *The Gypsies during the Second World War, Vol. II: In the Shadow of the Swastika,* edited by Donald Kenrick, 95–130. Hatfield: University of Hertfordshire Press, 1999.
Kenney, Padraic. *Rebuilding Poland: Workers and Communists, 1945–1950.* Ithaca, NY: Cornell University Press, 1997.
———. *A Carnival of Revolution: Central Europe 1989.* Princeton, NJ: Princeton University Press, 2002.
Kertzer, David I., and Marzio Barbagli, eds. *Family Life in the Twentieth Century.* New Haven, CT: Yale University Press, 2003.
Kessler-Harris, Alice. *Out to Work: A History of Wage-Earning Women in the United States.* New York: Oxford University Press, 1982.
Kligman, Gail. *Căluș: Symbolic Transformation in Romanian Ritual.* Chicago: University of Chicago Press, 1981.

———. *The Wedding of the Dead: Ritual, Poetics, and Popular Culture in Transylvania*. Berkeley: University of California Press, 1988.

———. *The Politics of Duplicity: Controlling Reproduction in Ceaușescu's Romania*. Berkeley: University of California Press, 1998.

Kligman, Gail, and Katherine Verdery. *Peasants under Siege: The Collectivization of Romanian Agriculture, 1949–1962*. Princeton, NJ: Princeton University Press, 2011.

Koenker, Diane P. "Men against Women on the Shop Floor in Early Soviet Russia: Gender and Class in the Socialist Workplace." *American Historical Review* 100, no. 5 (1995): 1438–64.

Koleva, Daniela, ed. *Negotiating Normality: Everyday Lives in Socialist Institutions*. New Brunswick, NJ: Transaction Publishers, 2012.

Kollantai, Alexandra. *Selected Writings of Alexandra Kollontai*. Translated and edited by Alix Holt: London: Allison and Busby, 1977.

Koonz, Claudia. *Mothers in the Fatherland: Women, the Family and Nazi Politics*. London: St. Martin's, 1987.

Kotkin, Stephen. *Magnetic Mountain: Stalinism as a Civilization*. Berkeley: University of California Press, 1995.

Krizsan, Andrea, and Raluca Popa. "Europeanization in Making Policies against Domestic Violence in Central and Eastern Europe." *Social Politics* 17, no. 3 (Fall 2010): 379–406.

Kruks, Sonia, Rayna Rapp, and Marilyn B. Young, eds. *Promissory Notes: Women in the Transition to Socialism*. New York: Monthly Review Press, 1989. Lanham, MD: Lexington Books, 2015.

Lapidus, Gail Warshofsky. *Women in Soviet Society: Equality, Development, and Social Change*. Berkeley: University of California Press, 1978.

Lavigne, Marie. *International Political Economy and Socialism*. Cambridge: Cambridge University Press 1991.

Lebow, Katherine. *Unfinished Utopia: Nowa Huta, Stalinism, and Polish Society, 1949–56*. Ithaca, NY: Cornell University Press, 2013.

Lenin, Vladimir Il'ich. *The Emancipation of Women: From the Writings of V.I. Lenin*. New York: International Publishers, 1969.

Levy, Robert. *Ana Pauker: The Rise and Fall of a Jewish Communist*. Berkeley: University of California Press, 2001.

Lewis, Jane. *The Politics of Motherhood: Child and Maternal Welfare in England, 1900–1939*. London: Croom Helm, 1980.

Lewis, Jane, ed. *Women and Social Policies in Europe: Work, Family, and the State*. London: Edward Elgar, 1993.

Light, Duncan, and David Phinnemore, eds. *Post-Communist Romania: Coming to Terms with Transition*. Basingstoke: Palgrave Macmillan, 2001.

Lindenberger, Thomas, ed. *Herrschaft und Eigen-sinn in der Diktatur: Studien zur Gesellschaftsgeschichte der DDR*. Cologne: Böhlau, 1999.

Livezeanu, Irina. *Cultural Politics in Greater Romania: Regionalism, Nation Building, and Ethnic Struggle, 1918–1930*. Ithaca, NY: Cornell University Press, 1995.

Lobodzinska, Barbara, ed. *Family, Women, and Employment in Central-Eastern Europe*. Westport, CT: Greenwood Press, 1995.

Lüdtke, Alf, ed. *The History of Everyday Life: Reconnecting Historical Experience and Ways of Life*. Princeton, NJ: Princeton University Press, 1995.
———. Organizational Order or *Eigensinn*? Workers' Privacy and Workers' Politics in Imperial Germany." In *Rites of Power: Symbolism, Ritual and Politics since the Middle Ages*, edited by Sean Wilentz, 303-33. Philadelphia: University of Pennsylvania Press, 1985.
Lukić, Jasmina, Joanna Regulska, and Darja Zaviršek, eds. *Women and Citizenship in Central and Eastern Europe*. Aldershot: Ashgate, 2006.
Magheru, Mihai. "Decentralization of Social Protection System in Romania: An Analysis Focused on Social Assistance in the Benefit of the Most Vulnerable Children and Their Families." UNIFECF (2010). Retrieved from http://www.unicef.org/romania/Decentralization_of_Social_Protection_In_Romania_(EN).pdf (accessed 17 November 2016).
Manuilă, Sabin. *Recensământul general al populaţiei României din 29 decembrie 1930, vol. II (Neam, limba maternă, religie)*. Bucharest: Institutul Central de Statistică, 1938.
Marginean, Mara. "Minimal necesar, discreţionar: Ideologizarea nevoilor ca proiect de integrare a marginalităţii sociale, 1945-1960." In *Marginalităţi, periferii şi frontiere simbolice: Societatea comunistă şi dilemele sale identitare*, edited by Luciana Jinga and Ştefan Bosomitu, 87-109. Anuarul IICCMER, vol. IX (2014). Iaşi: Polirom, 2015.
Marin, Manuela. *Între prezent şi trecut: cultul personalităţii lui Nicolae Ceauşescu şi opinia publica româneasca*. Cluj-Napoca: Editura MEGA, 2014.
Marshall, T. H. *Class, Citizenship, and Social Development*. New York: Doubleday, 1964.
May, Elaine Tyler. *Homeward Bound: American Families in the Cold War Era*. New York: Basic Books, 1988.
McLellan, Josie. *Love in the Time of Communism: Intimacy and Sexuality in the GDR*. Cambridge: Cambridge University Press, 2011.
Meyerowitz, Joanne J. *Women Adrift: Independent Wage Earners in Chicago, 1880-1930*. Chicago: University of Chicago Press, 1988.
Mihăilescu, Ştefania. *Din istoria feminismului românesc: Antologie de texte, 1838-1929*. Iaşi: Polirom, 2002
———. *Emanciparea femeii române: Antologie de texte, Vol. 1 (1815-1918)*. Bucharest: Editura Ecumenică, 2001.
———. *Emanciparea femeii române: Studiu şi antologie de texte, 1929 – 1948*. Iaşi: Polirom, 2006.
Mihalache Flavius and Alin Croitoru. "Mediul rural românesc: evoluţii şi involuţii: Schimbare socială şi antreprenoriat." PhD diss. University of Bucharest, 2011.
Miller, Daniel. *Material Culture and Mass Consumption*. Oxford: Blackwell, 1987.
Mink, Gwendolyn. *The Wages of Motherhood: Inequality in the Welfare State*. Ithaca NY: Cornell University Press, 1995.
Miroiu, Mihaela. "State Men, Market Women: The Effects of the Left Conservatism on Gender Politics in Romanian Transition." Presentation, Indiana University, April 2004.

———. "The Costless State Feminism in Romania." Conference paper, Women, Gender and Post-Communism, Indiana Roundtables on Post-Communism, Bloomington, Indiana, April 2005.

———. "Eradicarea instinctului plăcerii," *Dilema veche*, 5. Retrieved from http://dilemaveche.ro/sectiune/dileme-line/articol/eradicarea-instinctului-placerii (accessed 13 March 2017).

———. "On Women, Feminism, and Democracy," in *Post-Communist Romania at Twenty-Five Years: Linking Past, Present, and Future*. Edited by Lavinia Stan and Diane Vancea. Lanham, MD: Lexington Books, 2015.

Miroiu, Mihaela, and Mircea Miclea. *R'Estul și Vestul*. Bucharest: Polirom, 2005.

Miroiu, Mihaela, and Otilia Dragomir, eds. *Nașterea: Istorii trăite*. Iași: Polirom, 2010.

Mitu, Sorin. *National Identity of Romanians in Transylvania*. Budapest: Central European Press, 2001.

Moeller, Robert G. *Protecting Motherhood: Women and the Family in the Politics of Postwar West Germany*. Berkeley: University of California Press, 1993.

Moghadam, Valentine, ed. *Democratic Reform and the Position of Women in Transitional Economies*. Oxford: Clarendon, 1993.

Mohanty, Chandra Talpade, Ann Russo, Lourdes Torres, eds. *Third World Women and the Politics of Feminism*. Bloomington, IN: Indiana University Press, 1991.

Molyneux, Maxine. "Socialist Societies Old and New: Progress toward Women's Emancipation?" *Feminist Review* no. 8 (Summer 1981): 1–34.

Morar-Vulcu, Călin. "Becoming Dangerous: Everyday Violence in the Industrial Milieu of Late-Socialist Romania. *European History Quarterly* 45, no. 2 (2015): 315–335.

Moskoff, William. "Sex Discrimination, Commuting, and the Role of Women in Rumanian Development." *Slavic Review* 37, no. 3 (1978): 449–56.

Mungiu-Pippidi, Alina, and Sorin Ioniţa. "Interpreting an Electoral Setback—Romania 2000." *East European Constitutional Review* 10, no. 1 (2001).

Murgescu, Bogdan. *România și Europa: Acumularea decalajelor economice, 1500–2010*. Bucharest: Polirom, 2010.

Muzeul Ţăranului Român. *Mărturii orale: Anii '80 și bucureștenii*. Bucharest: Paeida, 2003.

Naimark, Norman, and Leonid Gibianskii, eds. *The Establishment of Communist Regimes in Eastern Europe, 1944–1949*. Boulder, CO: Westview Press, 1997.

Nastasă, Lucian, and Dragoș Sdrobiș, eds. *Politici culturale și modele intelectuale în România*. Cluj-Napoca: Editura Mega, 2013.

Nechita, Liliana. *Exodul Mamelor*. Bucharest: Editura SC Ringier Romania, 2014.

Neculau, Adrian, ed. *Viața cotidiană în comunism*. Iași: Polirom, 2004.

Neubert, Rudolf. *Das neue Ehebuch: Die Ehe als Aufgabe der Gegenwart und Zukunft*. Rudolstadt: Greifenverlag, 1957.

Nowak, Basia A. "Constant Conversations: Agitators in the League of Women in Poland during the Stalinist Period." *Feminist Studies* 31, no. 3 (2005): 488–518.

———. "Serving Women and the State: The League of Women in Communist Poland." PhD diss., Ohio State University, 2004.
Oakley, Ann. "Interviewing Women: A Contradiction in Terms." In *Doing Feminist Research*, edited by Helen Roberts, 30–61. London: Routledge, 1981.
Offen, Karen. "Depopulation, Nationalism, and Feminism in Fin-de-Siècle France." *American Historical Review* 89, no. 3 (1984): 648–76.
———. *European Feminisms, 1700–1950: A Political History.* Stanford, CA: Stanford University Press, 2000.
Olteanu, Cristina Liana, Elena-Simona Gheonea, and Valentin Gheonea. *Femeile în România comunistă: Studii de istorie socială.* Bucharest: Editura Politeia-SNSPA, 2003.
Oprea, Marius. *Banalitatea răului: o istorie a Securității în documente 1949–1989.* Iași: Polirom, 2002.
Oprea, Marius, Flori Bălănescu, and Stejărel Olaru. *Ziua care nu se uită: Revolta brașovenilor din 15 noiembrie 1987.* Iași: Polirom, 2002.
Oproiu, Ecaterina. *3X8 plus infinitul: dialoguri despre condiția femeii.* Bucharest: Editura Eminescu, 1975.
Osokina, Elena. *Our Daily Bread: Socialist Distribution and the Art of Survival in Stalin's Russia, 1927–1941.* Edited and translated by Kate Transchel. New York: M. E. Sharpe, 2001.
Pârvulescu, Constantin, and Emanuel Copilaș. "Hollywood Peeks: The Rise and Fall of Videotheques in 1980s Romania." *East European Politics, Societies, and Cultures* 27, no. 2 (2013): 241–59.
Pașca, Vlad. "Clienți la masa statului: Alimentația publică în România socialistă (1948–1989)." In *Între transformare și adaptare: Avataruri ale cotidianului în regimul comunist din România,* edited by Luciana Jinga and Ștefan Bosomitu, 75–95. *Anuarul IICCMER*, vol. VIII (2013). Iași: Polirom, 2014.
———. "Educația în România comunistă: un joc cu sumă nulă." In *Marginalități, periferii și frontiere simbolice: Societatea comunistă și dilemele sale identitare,* edited by Luciana Jinga and Ștefan Bosomitu, 181–195. *Anuarul IICCMER*, vol. IX (2014). Iași: Polirom, 2015.
Pascall, Gillian, and Nick Manning. "Gender and Social Policy: Comparing Welfare States in Central and Eastern Europe and the Former Soviet Union." *Journal of European Social Policy* 10, no. 3 (2000): 240–266.
Passerini, Luisa, ed. *International Yearbook of Oral History and Life Stories: Volume I: Memory and Totalitarianism.* New York: Oxford University Press, 1992.
Passmore, Kevin, ed. *Women, Gender and Fascism in Europe, 1919–1945.* New Brunswick, NJ: Rutgers University Press, 2003.
Pasti, Vladimir. *Ultima inegalitate: Relațiile de gen în România.* Iași: Polirom, 2003.
Pateman, Carole. *The Sexual Contract.* Stanford, CA: Stanford University Press, 1998.
Patterson, Patrick Hyder. *Bought and Sold: Living and Losing the Good Life in Socialist Yugoslavia.* Ithaca, NY: Cornell University Press, 2011.
Peacock, Margaret. *Innocent Weapons: The Soviet and American Politics of Childhood in the Cold War.* Chapel Hill, NC: University of North Carolina Press, 2014.

Pederson, Susan. *Family, Dependence, and the Origins of the Welfare State: Britain and France 1914–1945.* Cambridge: Cambridge University Press, 1993.

Pence, Katherine. "'You as a Woman Will Understand': Consumption, Gender, and the Relationship between State and Citizenry in the GDR's Crisis of 17 June 1953." *German History* 19, no. 2 (2001): 218–52.

Pence, Katherine, and Paul Betts, eds. *Socialist Modern: East German Everyday Culture and Politics.* Ann Arbor, MI: University of Michigan Press, 2008.

Penn, Shana. *Solidarity's Secret: The Women Who Defeated Communism in Poland.* Ann Arbor, MI: University of Michigan Press, 2005.

Penn, Shana and Jill Massino, eds. *Gender Politics and Everyday Life in State Socialist Eastern and Central Europe.* New York: Palgrave, 2009.

Petrescu, Cristina. "A Genderless Protest: Women Confronting Romanian Communism." *Annals of the University of Bucharest, Political Science Series* 16 (2014). Retrieved from http://nbn-resolving.de/urn:nbn:de:0168-ssoar-411792 (accessed 2 December 2016).

Petrescu, Dragoş. "Communist Legacies in the 'New Europe': History, Ethnicity, and the Creation of a 'Socialist' Nation in Romania, 1945–1989." In *Conflicted Memories: Europeanizing Contemporary Histories,* edited by Konrad H. Jarausch and Thomas Lindenberger with the collaboration of Annelie Ramsbrock, 37–54. New York: Berghan Books, 2007.

Pittaway, Mark. *Eastern Europe, 1939–2000.* London: Arnold, 2004.

———. *The Workers' State: Industrial Labor and the Making of Socialist Hungary, 1944–1958.* Pittsburgh, PA: University of Pittsburgh Press, 2012.

Popa, Maria Raluca. "Corpuri femeieşti, putere bărbătească: Studiu de caz asupra adoptării reglementărilor legislative de interzicere a avortului în România comunistă (1966)." In *Gen şi putere: Partea leului în politica românească,* edited by Oana Băluţă, 93–116. Iaşi: Polirom: 2006.

———. "Translating Equality between Women and Men across Cold War Divides: Women Activists from Hungary and Romania and the Creation of International Women's Year." In *Gender Politics and Everyday Life in State Socialist Eastern and Central Europe,* edited by Shana Penn and Jill Massino, 59–74. New York: Palgrave Macmillan, 2009.

———. "Raportul Tovarăşei Ana Pauker, 11 februarie 1946." *Aspasia: International Yearbook of Central, Eastern, and Southeastern European Women's and Gender History* 8 (2014): 150–61.

———. "'We Opposed It': The National Council of Women and the Ban on Abortion in Romania (1966)." *Aspasia: International Yearbook of Central, Eastern, and Southeastern European Women's and Gender History* 9 (2016): 152–160.

Pop-Eleches, Cristian. "The Supply of Birth Control Methods, Education, and Fertility: Evidence from Romania." *Journal of Human Resources* 45, no. 4 (2010): 971–97.

Pop-Eleches, Grigore. "Romania Twenty Years after Communism: The Bizarre Echoes of Contested Revolution." In *Twenty Years after Communism: The Politics of Memory and Commemoration,* edited by Michael Bernhard and Jan Kubik, 85–103. New York: Oxford University Press, 2014.

Portelli, Alessandro. *The Death of Luigi Trastulli and Other Stories: Form and Meaning in Oral History.* Albany, NY: State University of New York Press, 1991.
Preda, Simona. *Patrie Română, țară de eroi!* Bucharest: Curtea Veche, 2014.
*Prima Conferinţa sindicală a femeilor din Republica Română.* Bucharest: Editura Confederaţiei Generale Muncii, 1945.
*Programul Partidului Comunist Român de făurire a societăţii socialiste multilateral dezvoltate şi înaintare a României spre comunism.* Bucharest: Editura Politică, 1975.
Radosav, Doru. "Omul nou în comunism ca istorie trăită: copilăria." In *Proiectul uman comunist: de la discursul ideologic la realităţile sociale*, edited by Vasile Boari, Alexandru Câmpeanu, and Sergiu Gherghina. Cluj: Presa Universitară Clujeană, 2011.
Raleigh, Donald J. *Soviet Baby Boomers: An Oral History of Russia's Cold War Generation.* Oxford: Oxford University Press, 2012.
Ramet, Sabrina. *Nihil Obstat: Religion, Politics, and Social Change in East-Central Europe and Russia.* Durham, NC: Duke University Press, 1998.
Ratesh, Nestor. *Romania: The Entangled Revolution.* New York: Praeger, 1991.
Reid, Susan. "Cold War in the Kitchen: Gender and the De-Stalinization of Consumer Taste in the Soviet Union under Khrushchev." *Slavic Review* 61, no. 2 (2002): 211–52.
Reid, Susan E., and David Crowley, eds. *Style and Socialism: Modernity and Material Culture in Post-War Eastern Europe.* Oxford: Berg, 2000.
Roberts, Mary Louise. *Civilization without Sexes: Reconstructing Gender in Postwar France, 1917–1927.* Chicago: Chicago University Press, 1994.
Roman, Carol, and Vasile Tincu, eds. *101 interviuri cu femei: împliniri, opţiuni, responsabilităţi, temeri.* Bucharest: Editura Politică, 1978.
Rose, Sonya O. "Gender Antagonism and Class Conflict: Exclusionary Strategies of Male Trade Unionists in Nineteenth-Century Britain." *Social History* 13, no. 2 (1988): 191–208.
———. *Limited Livelihoods: Gender and Class in Nineteenth-Century England.* Berkeley: University of California Press, 1992.
Rostás, Zoltán, and Sorin Stoica, eds. *Istorie la firul ierbii: Documente sociale orale.* Bucharest: Tritonic, 2003.
Rostás, Zoltán and Theodora Eliza Văcăresu, eds. *Cealaltă jumătate a istoriei: Femei povestind.* Bucharest: Curtea Veche, 2008.
Rotaru, Mirela. "Job Assignment of Graduates of the University of Bucharest and Their Integration into the Labor System of the 1980s." *International Review of Social Research* 4, no. 2 (June 2014): 153–62.
Rotariu, Traian, and Livia Popescu, "Poverty in Romania." In *Poverty in Transition and Transition in Poverty: Recent Developments in Hungary, Bulgaria, Romania, Georgia, Russia, Mongolia*, edited by Yogesh Atal, 102–129. New York: Berghahn Books, 1998.
Rotariu, Traian, and Virgiliu Voineagu, eds. *Inerţie şi schimbare: Dimensiuni sociale ale tranziţiei în România.* Iaşi: Polirom, 2012.
Rothschild, Joseph, and Nancy M. Wingfield. *Return to Diversity: A Political History of East Central Europe since World War II.* 3rd ed. New York: Oxford University Press, 2000.

Rueschemeyer, Marilyn, ed. *Women in the Politics of Postcommunist Eastern Europe*. Armonk, NY: M. E. Sharpe, 1994.
Sachse, Carola. *Der Hausarbeitstag: Gerechtigkeit und Gleichberechtigung in Ost und West, 1939–1994*. Gottingen: Wallstein Verlag, 2002.
Sainsbury, Diane. *Gender, Equality and Welfare States*. Cambridge: Cambridge University Press, 1996.
Sampson, Steven L. "Regime and Society in Rumania." *International Journal of Rumanian Studies* 4, no. 1 (1984–86): 41–51.
Sandoval, Chela. *Methodology of the Oppressed*. Minneapolis: University of Minnesota Press, 2000.
Sayers, Janet, Mary Evans, and Nannecke Redclift, eds. *Engels Revisited: New Feminist Essays*. London: Tavistock, 1987.
Scott, Hilda. *Does Socialism Liberate Women? Experiences from Eastern Europe*. Boston: Beacon Press, 1974.
Scott, James C. *Seeing Like a State: How Certain Schemes to Improve the Human Condition Have Failed*. New Haven, CT: Yale University Press, 1998.
Scott, Joan Wallach. "Gender: A Useful Category of Historical Analysis." *American Historical Review* 91, no. 5 (December 1986): 1053–75.
———. "The Evidence of Experience." *Critical Inquiry* 17, no. 4 (1991): 773–797.
Seton-Watson, Hugh. *The East European Revolution*. New York: Praeger, 1951.
Shafir, Michael. *Romania: Politics, Economics, and Society: Political Stagnation and Simulated Change*. London: Frances Pinter, 1985.
———. "Ceauşescu's Overthrow: Popular Uprising or Moscow-Guided Conspiracy?" *Radio Free Europe: Report on Eastern Europe* 1, no. 3 (13 January 1990): 15–19.
Siani-Davies, Peter. *The Romanian Revolution of December 1989*. Ithaca, NY: Cornell University Press, 2005.
Sicoie-Coroi, Livia ed. *Colectivizarea agriculturii în raionul Brad: regiunea Hunedoara: Mărturii*, vol. I. Cluj-Napoca: Argonat, 2010.
Siegelbaum, Lewis. *Stakhanovism and the Politics of Productivity in the USSR, 1935–1941*. Cambridge: Cambridge University Press, 1988.
Soare, Florin S. "Ceauşescu's Population Policy: A Moral or an Economic Choice between Compulsory and Voluntary Incentivized Motherhood?" *European Journal of Government and Economics* 2, no. 1 (2013): 59–78.
———, ed. *Politică şi societate în epoca Ceauşescu*. Iaşi: Polirom, 2014.
Solonari, Vladimir. *Purifying the Nation: Population Exchange and Ethnic Cleansing in Nazi-Allied Romania*. Baltimore, MD: Woodrow Wilson Center Press/Johns Hopkins University Press, 2010.
Spornic, Aneta. *Utilizarea eficientă a resurselor de muncă feminine în România*. Bucharest: Editura Academiei, 1975.
Stahl, Paul. *Sociétés Traditionnelles Balkaniques: Contribution à l'étude des structures sociales*. Paris: EHESS, 1979.
Stan, Lavinia. "Access to Securitate Files: The Trials and Tribulations of a Romanian Law," *East European Politics and Societies* 16, no. 1 (December 2002): 145–81.
———. "Romania: In the Shadow of the Past," in *Central and Southeast European Politics since 1989*, edited by Sabrina Ramet, 379–400. Cambridge: Cambridge University Press, 2010.

Stan, Lavinia, and Diane Vancea. *Post-Communist Romania at Twenty-Five: Linking Past, Present, and Future.* Lanham, MD: Lexington Books, 2015.
Stancu, Eugen. "Engineering the Human Soul: Science Fiction in Communist Romania (1955–1989)." PhD diss., Central European University, 2011.
Ștefan, Adelina. "Where West Meets East: International Tourism and Consumerism in Socialist Romania of the 1960s–1980s," paper presented at the Association for Slavic, East European, and Eurasian Studies, Boston, Massachusetts, November 2013.
Stites, Richard. *The Women's Liberation Movement in Russia: Feminism, Nihilism, and Bolshevism, 1860–1930.* Princeton, NJ: Princeton University Press, 1978.
Stitziel, Judd. *Fashioning Socialism: Clothing, Politics and Consumer Culture in East Germany.* London: Berg, 2005.
Stoian, Mihai. *Generația '62: Reportaje.* Bucharest: Editura Militară, 1963.
———. *Rămin părinții repetenți? Dilemele adulților.* Bucharest: Editura Tineretului, 1968.
Stoica, Cătălin Augustin. "Once Upon a Time There Was a Big Party: The Social Bases of the Romanian Communist Party (Part I)." *East European Politics and Societies* 19, no. 4 (2005): 686–716.
Stokes, Gale. *The Walls Came Tumbling Down: The Collapse of Communism in Eastern Europe.* New York: Oxford: 1993.
Strătilescu, Elenora. "Feminism," *Unirea Femeilor Române,* anul IV, nr. 10, 11, octombrie 1912.
Sugar, Peter and Ivo Lederer, eds. *Nationalism in Eastern Europe.* Seattle: University of Washington Press, 1971.
Szabo, Veronica. "Youth and Politics in Communist Romania (1980–1989)." PhD diss., University of Pittsburgh, 2012.
Țârău, Virgiliu. "De la diversitate la integrare: 'Problema femeii' și instaurarea comunismului în Europa Centrală și de Est: Cazul României." In *Condiția femeii în România în secolul XX: studii de caz,* edited by Ghizela Cosma and Virgiliu Țârău, 135–59. Cluj-Napoca: Presa Universitară Clujeană, 2002.
Ther, Philipp. *Europe Since 1989: A History.* Princeton: Princeton University Press, 2016.
*The Woman Question: Selections from the Writings of Karl Marx, Frederick Engels, V.I. Lenin and J.V. Stalin.* New York: International Publishers, 1975.
Thompson, Paul. *The Voice of the Past: Oral History.* Oxford: Oxford University Press, 2000.
Thorne, M. Benjamin. The Anxiety of Proximity: The "Gypsy Question" in Romanian Society, 1934–1944. PhD diss. Indiana University, 2012.
Tismăneanu, Vladimir. *Reinventing Politics: Eastern Europe from Stalin to Havel.* New York: Free Press, 1993.
———. "Understanding National Stalinism: Reflections on Ceaușescu's Socialism." *Communist and Post-Communist Studies* 32, no. 2 (1999): 155–73.
———. *Stalinism for All Seasons: A Political History of Romanian Communism.* Berkeley: University of California Press, 2003.
———, ed. *Stalinism Revisited: The Establishment of Communist Regimes in East-Central Europe.* Budapest: Central European University Press, 2009.

Tismăneanu, Vladimir, and Gail Kligman. "Romania's First Postcommunist Decade: From Iliescu to Iliescu." *East European Constitutional Review* 10, no. 1 (2001): 78–85.

Todorova, Maria. "Historical Tradition and Transformation in Bulgaria: Women's Issues or Feminist Issues?" *Journal of Women's History* 5, no. 3 (1994): 129–43.

Todorova, Maria, Augusta Dimou, and Stefan Troebst, eds. *Remembering Communism: Private and Public Recollections of Lived Experience in Southeast Europe*. Budapest: Central European University Press, 2014.

Tóth, Eszter Zsófia "'My Work, My Family, and My Car': Women's Memories of Work, Consumerism, and Leisure in Socialist Hungary." In *Gender Politics and Everyday Life in State Socialist Eastern and Central Europe*, ed. Shana Penn and Jill Massino, 33–44. New York: Palgrave, 2009.

Tóth, Olga. "No Envy, No Pity." In *Gender Politics and Post-Communism: Reflections from Eastern Europe and the Former Soviet Union*, ed. Nanette Funk and Magda Mueller, 213–223. New York: Routledge, 1993.

Trebici, Vladimir, and Ion Ghinoiu. *Demografie și etnografie*. Bucharest: Editura Științifică și Enciclopedică, 1986.

Triska, Jan F. and Charles Gati, eds. *Blue-Collar Workers in Eastern Europe*. London: George Allen and Unwin, 1981.

Urse, Laureana. "Populația feminină: modernizare și adaptare." *Calitatea Vieții*, XVIII nr. 1–2 (2007): 149–64.

Văduva, Ofelia. *Steps toward the Sacred: From the Ethnology of Romanian Food Habits*. Bucharest: Romanian Cultural Foundation, 1999.

Vasile, Cristian. "Propaganda and Culture in Romania at the Beginning of the Communist Regime." In *Stalinism Revisited: The Establishment of Communist Regimes in East-Central Europe*, edited by Vladimir Tismăneanu, 367–386. Budapest: Central European University Press, 2009.

Verdery, Katherine. *Transylvanian Villagers: Three Centuries of Political, Economic, and Ethnic Change*. Berkeley: University of California Press, 1983.

———. *National Ideology under Socialism: Identity and Cultural Politics in Ceaușescu's Romania*. Berkeley: University of California Press, 1995.

———. *What Was Socialism, and What Comes Next?* Princeton, NJ: Princeton University Press, 1996.

Vogel, Lise. *Marxism and the Oppression of Women: Toward a Unitary Theory*. New Brunswick, N.J: Rutgers University Press 1983.

Vultur, Smaranda, ed. *Istorie trăită—Istorie povestită: Deportarea în Bărăgan (1951–1956)*. Timișoara: Editura Amarcord, 1997.

———. *Germanii din Banat prin povestirile lor*. Bucharest: Paideia, 2000.

———. "Daily Life and Constraints in Communist Romania in the Late 1980s: From the Semiotics of Food to the Semiotics of Power." In *Public and Private Recollections of Lived Experience in Southeast Europe*, edited by Maria Todorova, Augusta Dimou, and Stefan Troebst, 175–200. Budapest: Central European University Press, 2014.

Watson, Rubie, ed. *Memory, History, and Opposition under State Socialism*. Santa Fe, NM: School of American Research Press, 1994.

Weiner, Elaine. *Market Dreams: Gender, Class, and Capitalism in the Czech Republic*. Ann Arbor, MI: University of Michigan Press, 2007.

Wingfield, Nancy, and Maria Bucur, eds. *Gender and War in Twentieth-Century Eastern Europe*. Bloomington, IN: Indiana University Press, 2006.
Wolchik, Sharon, and Alfred Meyer, eds. *Women, State, and Party in Eastern Europe*. Durham, NC: Duke University Press, 1985.
Wollstonecraft, Mary. *A Vindication of the Rights of Men and a Vindication of the Rights of Women*. Cambridge: Cambridge University Press, 1995.
Wood, Elizabeth A. *The Baba and the Comrade: Gender and Politics in Revolutionary Russia*. Bloomington, IN: Indiana University Press, 1997.
Woodcock, Shannon. "'The Țigan Is Not a Man': The Țigan Other as Catalyst for Romanian Ethnonational Identity." PhD diss., University of Sydney, 2005.
Yurchak, Alexi. *Everything Was Forever until It Was No More: The Last Soviet Generation*. Princeton, NJ: Princeton University Press, 2005.
Zamfir, Cătălin, Elena Zamfir, and Corry Ehlen, eds. *Politici sociale: România în context European*. Bucharest: Editura Alternative, 1995.
Zheng, Wang. "Creating a Socialist Feminist Cultural Front: Women of China (1949–1966)." *China Quarterly*. December 2010: 827–849.

# Index

Note: Page references with an *f* are figures.

abortion, 46, 65, 124, 126, 247, 248, 250, 258, 262, 264, 265, 271, 272, 399; clandestine, 271–274, 283; complications from, 280, 283–284; criminalization of, 22, 23, 111, 149, 196, 206, 222, 223, 236, 249, 256, 259–260, 281; legalization (decriminalization) of, 198, 250, 257, 261, 286, 396, 398–399; link to maternal death, 278–280; providers of (abortionists), 260, 270–272, 274, 277, 279; punishments for having, 273, 277–278; spontaneous (miscarriage), 260, 264, 270, 271; women's experience of, 272, 274–277, 279
abuse: alcohol, 121, 221, 225–226, 237, 253, 256, 337; spousal, 19, 69, 197, 211, 214–217, 227, 229, 237, 254, 399–400, 401. *See also* domestic violence
activism and activists, 39, 46, 59, 60, 61, 64–65, 400
adultery, 206, 227, 229
agency (individual), 4, 6, 7, 145, 196, 223, 237, 264, 407
Agrarian Law of 1918–1921, 42
agriculture, 36, 44, 152–153*f*, 179, 384; collectivization of, 63, 92, 144, 315; women in, 36, 143, 150, 179, 315, 383
Albania, 256, 257, 261
Allied Control Commission, 51
Allies, 49
anti-discrimination legislation, 387, 401

anti-domestic violence policies, 401
Antonescu, Ion (Marshal), 48, 50, 66
April Declaration (1964), 101
Arrow Cross, 49
Association for the Political and Civic Emancipation of Romanian Women, 44
austerity, 23, 55, 314, 316, 317, 335; in the 1980s, 336–337, 351–352, 355; postsocialism, 367, 380–381, 384, 394, 398, 402
Axis powers, 49
BAC (Baccalaureate exam), 103
Băsescu, Traian, 378, 379, 380
birth (fertility) control, 222, 223, 249, 275; *coitus interruptus*, 222, 257, 282; condoms, 282, 283; IUDs, 282, 283; pills, 282, 283; rhythm method, 257, 282
birth rates, 22, 249, 256, 258, 261, 269, 279, 281
black market, 114, 283, 315, 334, 338–339, 340, 342, 355, 370
Black Sea, 112, 114, 312, 313, 332–333, 340, 355, 405
Black Sea Canal, 53, 89, 90
Bolshevik Revolution, 42, 66
Botez, Calypso, 44, 46
boys: household chores, 93, 94; in relationships, 119; secondary school, 100
Brașov strike of 1987, 368
breadwinner, 42, 57, 89, 90, 144, 146, 233, 253, 290, 294, 395
Bulgaria, 48, 65, 393; birth and fertility rates, 249, 256; abortion restriction, 261

Cantacuzino, Alexandrina, 44, 45, 46

CAP (*Cooperativele Agricole Producție* [state farms]), 92, 98, 150; collective farms (*Gospodăriile Agricole Colective*), 63
Ceaușescu, Elena, 56, 71, 72, 105, 157, 180, 181, 270, 283, 288, 331, 339, 351, 352, 353; political power, 180
Ceaușescu, Nicolae, 11, 12, 15, 18, 21, 22, 71, 72, 96, 102, 103, 110, 116, 127, 129, 146, 149, 151, 156, 157, 162, 173, 177, 179, 181, 206, 251, 258, 331, 335–336, 337, 346, 350, 351, 352, 353–354, 365, 368, 369–370, 371, 374, 393, 397; consumption during early years of, 313, 321–323, 331–332; criminalization of abortion, 149, 247; fall of, 368–373; July Theses (1971), 103; on marriage, 107, 207, 228; pronatalism, 249, 259–261, 262, 282, 286, 399; reformist policies, 334; systematization plan, 370
Central Committee of the Romanian Communist Party (Comitetul Central al Partidul Comunist Român, PCR), 13, 56, 151, 180, 261, 288, 335, 342, 353, 378
Central Powers, 40–41
Central School of Agitation, 61
Charles II (King Carol II), 47, 48
Charles of Hohenzollern-Sigmaringen (King Carol I), 34
childcare: crèches, 146, 250, 265, 290, 293, 395; facilities, 22, 57, 180, 197, 209, 234, 248, 252, 258, 270, 290, 394, 395; kindergartens, 45, 233, 250, 291; men's contributions to, 217–218, 231, 233, 234, 236, 252, 290, 293; nannies, 294; relatives, 291–293; subsidies, 395, 396, 398
children: development, 22, 253–255; with disabilities, 264, 272–273, 280; household chores, 93–94; and morality, 103, 121–122, 254–255; orphaned, 41, 279, 280, 281; rearing, 70, 87, 95–96, 118–120, 123, 253–255, 286–288, 289–290 (*see also* parenting); Roma, 98–99; sex education, 122
children's homes (*caselor de copii*), 280
Chrisoscoleu, Sofia, 39
citizenship, 6, 39, 65, 196; Jews, 34, 47; socialist, 9–10, 14, 60, 63, 128, 140, 196, 255; postsocialist, 398; women's, 32, 35, 63
Civil Code (1856), 41
Civil Code (1864), 197
Civil Code (1865), 35
closed circuit stores (*magazine cu circuit închis*), 338
CMEA (Council for Mutual Economic Assistance), 318
Cold War, 9, 11, 53, 64, 66, 321, 406
command economy, 163, 168, 203
Communist Code of Ethics (Codul principiilor și normelor muncii și vieții comuniștilor, ale eticii și echității socialiste), 121, 202
Communist Party of Romania (Partidul Comunist Român [PCR]; Partidul Comunist din România [PCdR]), 45, 47, 50–52, 58, 59–60, 67, 104, 121, 258, 288, 335, 342, 353, 373; membership in, 47, 52, 180, 323
commuting, 146, 150, 199, 235; and family cohesion, 91
connections/relations (*relații*), 8, 23, 168, 169, 205, 274, 291, 338, 341–344, 346, 351, 380, 391, 403
Conservative Party, 34, 35
Constantinescu, Emil, 376
Constitution of 1866, 34, 37
Constitution of 1923, 43, 53
Constitution of 1948, 145
Constitution of 1991, 374
consumption, 23; austerity in the 1980s, 336–347, 349–354; Ceaușescu's early years, 321–323, 331–332; under Dej, 315–316; managed, 321. *See also* shortages
contraception, 222, 223, 249, 258, 278, 282, 283, 396, 399. *See also* birth control

Cornea, Doina, 368
corruption, 2, 16, 35, 47, 52, 98, 353, 366, 372, 373 375, 376, 377–378, 379, 381, 382, 384, 397, 401, 402, 403
cultural capital, 366, 381, 385, 391–392, 403
cultural liberalization, 113, 318, 322
Cuza, Alexandru Ioan (Prince), 34, 103
Czechoslovakia, 256, 261, 322, 337, 354, 368, 370, 375, 403; consumption rates, 342; Warsaw Pact invasion of (1968), 323

debt, 321, 335, 336, 354, 355, 370, 393; annulment of peasant, 51
Declaration of the Rights of the Child (UN), 107
Decree 770, 205, 223, 247, 269, 270, 281, 290, 372. *See also* abortion
Decree 779 (divorce law of 1966), 206, 207
deindustrialization, 382
democracy, 2, 3, 15, 44, 50, 366, 374, 379, 380, 381, 401, 402, 404
Democratic Convention (1996), 376
demographic policies, 156, 162, 259, 260–262. *See also* pronatalism; reproductive policies
demonstrations, 51, 364–366, 368, 371, 374, 400
dictatorship, 47, 48, 88, 369; communist, 366, 404; welfare, 9
discrimination, 10, 12, 17, 18, 43, 44, 49, 98, 169; workplace, 147, 171, 172, 175–176, 177, 381
dissent, 368–369; dissidents, 14, 18
divorce, 43, 197, 198, 206–208, 219, 220, 226–229, 237, 260; policies, 206, 207, 396; prevention, 208
Djilas, Milovan, 338
domestic responsibilities (household chores), 10, 93, 143, 150, 155, 180, 210, 212–213, 214, 219, 220, 225, 229–236, 324, 351. *See also* housework

domestic violence, 38, 121, 206, 216, 253, 396, 399–400. *See also* spousal abuse
dowry system, 198
Dunca, Constanța, 39

Eastern Bloc, 2, 9, 11, 23, 55, 56, 58, 60, 62, 63, 94, 119, 143, 145, 147, 149, 156, 165, 166, 170, 171, 184, 201, 203, 205, 207, 212, 225, 233, 250, 251, 257, 261, 289, 291, 313, 314, 318, 324, 332, 336, 347, 355, 368, 372, 373, 375, 381, 382, 387, 398, 402
East Germany/German Democratic Republic (GDR), 5, 125, 172, 174, 203, 318, 337, 342, 370; abortion, 250, 257; divorce, 207, 228–229; fertility rate, 256; harassment, 174
economic restructuring, 375–376, 377, 381–382, 385, 389, 391
education: and class, 96–99; communist period, 151, 159; girls/women's, 36, 37, 38, 39, 43, 44, 86, 100, 156, 159, 178; interwar period, 42–43; peasants, 97–98; political, 61, 62, 64; postsecondary, 36, 38; reform under Ceaușescu, 102–104; sex, 122–124. *See also* schools
*Eigen-sinn* (self-will), 8, 173–174, 230
Elimination of all Forms of Discrimination against Women (CEDAW), 278–279
Engels, Friedrich, 31–33, 66, 168, 172, 181, 184, 196, 210, 224, 235, 314, 345
entitlements: welfare, 10, 64, 67, 146, 180, 248, 250, 251–252, 257, 291, 332, 351, 366, 378, 390, 392, 393, 398, 403, 404; workplace, 147, 332–333
European Economic Community (EEC), 321
European Union (EU), 2, 16, 367, 377, 378, 383, 384, 393, 398
everyday life history (*Alltagsgeschichte*), 7–8

factory: contracts, 147; jobs, 36, 49, 58, 162–163, 165; stores (*economate*), 143, 315
family: allowances, 281; leave, 57; planning, 258, 276, 399 (*see also* contraception); policy, 396–401
Family Code (1952), 207; (1954), 197–198
famine of 1946–1947, 54, 55
fatherhood, 217–218
Federation of Democratic Women of Romania (Federaţia Democrata a Femeilor din România [FDFR]), 59
Female Front, 45
Ferdinand (King), 40
fertility: control, 248–249, 257, 261, 271, 274–276, 278, 282–284, 297, 399; rate, 42, 62, 256, 258, 269, 396, 398
Filipescu, Radu, 368
food: rationing, 288, 313, 315, 336, 341–343, 347, 355, 365, 389; ersatz, 348
foreign currency stores, 338, 340
France, 43, 251, 257, 260
free time (*timpul liber*), 324
frigidity, 220–222
Front of National Rebirth, 47

Gâdea, Suzana, 258
Germany, 1, 41, 47, 55, 260
Gheorghiu-Dej, Gheorghe, 11, 53, 61, 91, 101, 148, 156, 160, 248, 249, 251, 257, 296, 315, 317, 318, 319, 321, 322, 335
girls: autonomy, 118–119; household chores, 93–94; in relationships, 119; in sciences, 105
Golden Age (*epoca de aur*), 126, 162
good file (*un dosar bun*), 169
Gorbachev, Mikhail, 370
gradualism (economic), 375
Grand National Assembly (Parliament), 56, 180
gray economy, 383, 384, 387
Groza, Petru, 51
gynecological exams (forced), 269–270

harassment (workplace), 172–176
Havel, Václav, 337, 403
health care, privatization of, 381
Helsinki Accords (Final Act), 279, 369
heroine mother (*mama eroina*), 250–251, 281, 285–286
heroine workers (*muncitoare fruntaşe*), 147–149, 158, 170
hierarchies: gender, 6, 21, 141, 170, 180, 383; social, 23, 97, 199, 312
HIV, 280
home delivery food services (*casele de comenzi*), 344
homogenization, 195
homophobia, 123
homosexuality (homosexual relations), 10, 19, 123, 128, 202, 260
Honecker, Erich, 370
hooliganism, 95, 121; hooligans (*golani*), 365, 371, 374
housework, 93–94, 210, 212–213, 225, 235–236, 324; and men, 217–219, 229–234. *See also* domestic responsibilities
housing: marriage, 203–204; supply of, 91, 229, 257, 275, 288, 316, 328–329, 366, 397
human rights, 73, 279, 284, 369, 370, 402
Hungary, 5, 47, 50, 144, 156, 174, 234, 289, 317, 318, 337, 340, 368, 375; abortion, 261; birth rates, 249; divorce, 207; fertility rates, 256, 258; reluctance to hire women, 172
Husák, Gustáv, 370

Iliescu, Ion, 371, 374, 376, 377, 378
illiteracy, 37, 43, 97, 99, 107
immigration, 384–385
indoctrination hour, 103
industrialization, 10, 56, 142, 144, 147, 160, 170, 209, 249, 314, 315, 318, 321, 349
infant formula, 265, 287, 288, 347
infant mortality, 42, 64, 280
inflation, 42, 314, 375, 376, 382, 392–396

informers, 271, 340
intellectuals (discrimination against), 89, 168, 169
International Monetary Fund (IMF), 336, 374, 393
International Women's Day, 147, 209
Iron Guard, 15, 47, 48, 52, 89, 99
Italy, 18, 43, 47, 54, 257, 260, 384

Jews: and citizenship, 34, 43, 47, 52; and World War II, 48–49
Jiu Valley miners, 374
July Theses of 1971, 103

Kent cigarettes, 338, 339
Khrushchev, Nikita, 207, 257
Kollontai, Aleksandra (Alexandra), 32, 88, 145
Krupskaia (Krupskya), Nadezhda, 66, 101
kulaks (*chiaburi* [well-off peasants]), 10, 97, 100

Labor Code (1950), 145, 250
Labor Code (1972), 150, 162, 178
labor force: effect on women's status, 195; feminine jobs, 158; gendering of, 21, 141, 150, 170–181; laws, 145, 146; masculine jobs, 158; mobilizing women into, 63, 142, 143; reorganization of, 146, 149, 151, 156
labor force participation rates: women, 152–153f
latchkey kids (*copii cu cheia la gât*), 94–95
leadership positions, women in, 37, 71, 151, 178–181, 183, 328
legitimacy, 9, 14, 23, 312, 334, 354, 377, 405–406
leisure, 87, 93, 111, 112–113, 116–119, 121, 122, 165, 212, 237, 311, 313, 319, 323, 324, 331, 332, 333, 335, 347, 354, 355
Lenin, Vladimir, 66, 88, 101, 124
LGBT individuals, 19. *See also* homosexuality

liberalization, 11, 12, 88, 93, 96, 113, 116, 257, 354; consumer, 312–313, 321–323, 336; cultural, 318, 331–334
Liberal Party, 34–35, 42
liberation, women's, 32, 33, 45, 56, 58, 64, 141, 142, 148, 203, 326, 389
life expectancy, 42
Literacy Campaign (1948), 99; literacy campaigns, 62, 64, 73; literacy rates, 37, 43
Luxemburg, Rosa, 66
luxury items, 334, 336, 338, 355

Maiorescu, Titu, 38, 39
managing (*a se descurca*), 339, 343, 346; (making do), 343, 347
Maniu, Iuliu, 52
Marie (Queen), 41
marriage: average age, 205; and class, 199; dowry system, 198; first marriage, 205; remarriage, 198; and spousal abuse, 197, 211, 214–217, 229, 253, 288; traditional marriages, 37, 195, 196, 202, 203, 219–220
Marshall Plan (European Recovery Program), 55, 314
Marx, Karl, 314, 345
Marxism (Marxist-Leninism), 53, 56, 60, 64, 96, 100, 196, 233, 252, 314, 315, 317
maternal mortality rate, 249, 278, 280, 297
maternity leave, 57, 141, 145, 146, 147, 165, 172, 196, 233, 234, 250, 251, 252, 258, 261, 275, 287, 289, 290, 292, 295, 297, 387, 395
Michael (King Mihai), 48, 50–51, 53
midwives, 56, 249, 257, 271, 274
Mihai Viteazul (Michael the Brave [Prince]), 103, 110
*miliția* (police), 125, 205, 216, 217, 262, 271, 276, 277, 278, 281, 346, 370, 372
mini cultural revolution (*mica revoluție culturală*), 103, 335

Ministry of Health, 258, 266, 336
minorities, 43; (ethnic), 49, 50, 52–53
miscarriages/spontaneous abortion, 260, 264, 270, 271
modernity, 11–12, 23, 58, 149, 213, 312, 321, 334, 354
modernization, 4, 36, 112, 318, 378, 405, 406; economic, 46, 47, 52, 142, 314, 378; socialist, 10–12, 20, 32, 33, 64, 73, 95, 98, 100, 147, 158, 168, 198, 228, 251
morality, 8, 13, 122, 124, 125, 197, 207, 217, 256, 258, 259
motherhood, 111, 250–251, 255–256, 263, 265–266, 275, 286–287, 289, 295–296, 297; responsibilities and work schedules, 255, 256. *See also* parenting

Nădejde, Sofia, 39–40
nannies (*tante*), 294, 297
Năstase, Adrian, 378
National Council for the Study of Securitate Archives (CNSAS), 376, 378
nationalism, 12, 33–34, 43, 47, 103, 110, 317, 334, 335, 337, 365
National Council of Women (Consiliul Naţional al Femeilor [CNF]), 20, 33, 57, 63, 64, 65, 69, 73, 74, 155, 159, 179, 258, 262, 265, 269, 281
National Legionary State, 48
National Liberal Party: interwar, 42; postsocialist, 380
National Peasant Party (NPP), 46, 50, 52, 380
National Salvation Front (Frontul Salvării Naţionale [FSN]), 286, 371, 374, 380
National Society for Romanian Orthodox Women (SONFR), 44
Nazi Germany, 47, 54
Nazis, 50, 66
*nechezol*, 348
Negruzzi, Ella, 36, 37, 44, 46
neoliberalism, 379, 394, 403, 404

new man (*omul nou*), 56, 96, 115, 256
*nomenklatura* (administrative elites), 127, 283, 288, 338, 375, 380
non-governmental organizations (NGOs), 398, 399, 400, 401
nostalgia, 16, 24, 112, 184, 404

Order of Labor medal (*Ordinul Muncii*), 147, 148
orphans, 54, 60, 247, 279, 281
Orthodox Church (faith), 12, 15, 33, 38, 54, 202, 205, 376, 399

parenting, 95–96; authoritarian, 252; fathers, 253–254, 290; mothers, 254–256; parental neglect, 253, 256; shared, 233–234
patriarchy: behaviors/attitudes, 12, 21, 31, 37, 168, 170, 177, 181, 183, 195, 208–209, 214, 217, 224–225, 235, 236; and socialist rule, 58; society, 143, 275; state patriarchy, 57
Pauker, Ana, 45, 56, 58, 59
Pârvulescu, Constantin, 369
peasants, 3, 4, 10, 35, 42, 46, 47, 51, 52, 56, 149, 165, 199, 295, 316, 341; collectivization, 63, 144, 315; education, 98, 100; repression of, 53, 97, 315
Penal Code, 259
pensions, 147, 180, 378, 380, 389, 390, 396. *See also* retirement
People's House (*Casa Poporului*), 129, 337, 368
Pioneer Organization (Pioneers), 86, 107, 114, 115, 116
Poland, 47, 55, 143, 144, 156, 206, 214, 257, 290, 317, 318, 336, 337, 368, 375, 393, 399; fertility rate, 256; harassment, 174; reluctance to hire women, 172; social entitlements, 261
police (see *miliţia*)
poverty (poverty level), 35, 37, 42, 54, 88, 143, 165, 251, 313, 375, 378, 381, 383, 384, 389, 393, 394, 395, 402, 403

POW camps, 41, 49
pregnancy, 71, 124, 126, 145, 205, 223, 262–264, 266, 272, 277, 387, 399; fear of, 223; monitoring, 269–270; unwanted, 46, 276, 285. *See also* sex; abortion
premarital sex, 122, 124–125, 128, 202
Presidential Commission for the Study of the Communist Dictatorship in Romania, 378
primary schooling, 37, 43, 98, 100
private: childcare, 395, 397; life 8, 90, 129, 207; property, 32, 196; sector, 383–384, 387; sphere/spaces, 45, 88, 146, 282, 294; trading, 315
privatization, 375, 378, 381, 383, 386, 397
privileges, 10, 65, 174, 344
Proclamation of Timişoara, 380
Program of Scientific Nourishment, 337
pronatalism (pronatalist policies) 6, 9, 11, 71, 124, 221, 247–249, 255, 259–264, 280, 282, 286, 313, 328, 399; as state violence, 269, 273, 277–280, 297. *See also* demographic policies; reproductive: policies
prostitution, 121, 125
protective legislation, 141, 145, 151
protest, 9, 22, 24, 47, 48, 51, 337, 354, 364, 365, 371, 374, 376, 381, 398, 400
pull (*pile*), 169

queues (queuing up), 231, 233, 336, 338, 344–346, 355
quotas, 56, 148, 170, 180–181

Radio Free Europe, 14, 90, 129, 270, 283, 351, 369, 370, 372
rationing, 232, 237, 313, 314; food, 336, 338, 340, 341–343, 347, 365, 389; gasoline, 336; heating, 350, 351; strategies, 345, 346. *See also* queues; shortages

Red Army, 49, 50, 51, 317
religion, 54, 64, 205, 399
reproductive: legislation, 206, 257–262; policies, 248, 262–267; politics, 247; *See also* demographic policies; pronatalism
residency cards, 204
resistance, 7, 8, 12, 14, 22, 35, 63, 170, 171, 281, 282, 294, 297, 342, 368–370, 373
retirement, 146, 168, 180, 382
Reunion of Romanian Women for the Assistance of the Poorest Romanian Orphans, 38
Reunion of Romanian Women of Iaşi, 38
Revolution of 1989, 130, 366, 367; fall of Ceauşescu, 368–73; violence, 372–373
rights: civil, political, social, economic, 9, 10, 16, 24, 39, 40, 44, 46, 53, 67, 366, 380, 381, 401; human (*see* human rights); reproductive, 198, 284; spousal, 197–198
Roma (Gypsies), 14–15, 35, 48, 98–99, 285, 379, 394
Romanian Chamber of Deputies (Parliament), 39
Romanian Kingdom, 36
Romanian National Party, 43
Romanian Revolution, 15, 286, 370–373. *See also* Revolution of 1989
Rosetti, C. A., 40

Sănătescu, Constantin, 50
schools: confessional, 54, 97; evening (*cursuri serale*), 171, 180; exclusion from, 96–99; Fathers', 265; Grandfathers', 265; Mothers', 62, 265; primary, 100; public, 42, 96; secondary, 43, 100; trade/vocational, 38, 44. *See also* education
scientific fields: promotion of girls in, 105; women in, 151, 152–153f
Securitate, 53, 54, 89, 98–99, 167, 216, 260, 271, 276, 284, 333, 340, 365, 368, 370, 373, 374, 375, 376, 380

semi-skilled jobs, 150, 159, 171, 178
Serviciul Român de Informații (SRI), 374, 378
sex: contraception for, 124, 222, 249, 258, 270, 275, 282–283; education, 122–123; male sexual performance, 222; premarital, 122, 125, 128, 202; traditional attitudes toward, 223; women's sexual satisfaction, 220–223, 224
sexuality, 19, 122, 125, 128, 197, 202, 222; homosexuality, 123, 125, 260; sources of information about, 276
shortages, 87, 126, 129, 229, 232, 237, 312, 316–317, 337, 342–343, 348, 349–352, 354, 372; food, 55, 288, 297, 348, 349, 355; heating, 165, 350–351
Social Democratic Party, 53
Socialist Party, 43
Socialist Workers Party, 67
social parasitism, 121, 122, 159, 335
social vulnerability, 390
Society for the Protection of Mothers and Children, 45
Solidarity movement (Poland), 368
Song of Romania (*Cântarea României*), 113, 115
Soviet Union/USSR, 1, 17, 49, 51, 52, 54, 56, 60, 66, 107, 142, 156, 177, 198, 312, 318, 334, 336; capital to, 314; divorce laws, 207; forced labor in, 160; as liberators, 50; Nazi invasion of, 48; reproductive politics, 249, 257, 260
Sovroms, 52
special shops (*shopuri*), 338
spousal abuse. *See* abuse; domestic violence
Stakhanovites, 148, 156
Stalin, Joseph, 55, 66, 96, 101, 261, 318; Stalinism, 17, 261, 277, 315
standard of living, 69, 104, 106, 119, 129, 144, 166, 235, 294, 311, 314, 328, 331, 338, 339, 342, 351, 355, 376, 378, 394, 397, 404

state-assigned first job (*repartiție*), 163–164, 168, 204, 205
Steagul Roșu (the Red Flag) factory, 364; workers' strike (1987), 17
sterilization, 282
struggle for peace (*lupta pentru pace*), 15, 66, 144
subsidies, 164, 250, 367, 371, 382; childcare, 396, 398; means-based, 395
suffrage (female), 39, 43, 44
surveillance, 8, 45, 167, 223, 262, 365
systematization plan, 370

Teodoroiu, Ecaterina, 41, 107
theater, 114, 120, 330, 332, 334, 335
Third Reich, 48. *See* Nazis
Timișoara, events of December 1989, 370–371
Tito, Josip Broz, 317
totalitarianism, 337, 342; interpretation/model, 3
tourism, 340. *See also* vacations
trade unions, 50–51, 114, 142, 155, 216, 382
Transylvania, 33, 34, 35, 36, 40, 41, 43, 48, 50, 165; Jews killed in, 49

unemployment rates, 47, 382, 383
unhealthy social origins (*origini sociale nesănătoase*), 10, 17, 54, 87–89, 98–99, 127, 168, 169
Uniate (Greek Catholic) Church, 54
Union of Antifascist Women of Romania (Uniunea Femeilor Antifasciste din România [UFAR]), 58–61
Union of Communist Youth (Uniunea Tineretului Comunist [UTC]), 86, 111, 119
Union of Democratic Romanian Women (Uniunea Femeilor Democrate din România [UFDR]), 61–63
United States, 1, 63, 87, 166, 222, 223, 236, 321, 324, 374; abortion, 46, 223, 257; films, 116; music, 116; marriage, 236

university, 38, 43, 100; admission to, 97, 169
urban population, 142, 316

vacations, 312, 313, 333, 338, 340, 382, 390, 393
victims, 3, 16, 41, 372; of domestic violence, 399–400
Vietnam War, 106
violence, 41, 52, 54, 172, 402; domestic, 19, 38, 121, 206, 216, 253, 396, 399–400, 401 (*see also* spousal abuse); pronatalism as state violence, 248, 276–281, 297; Revolution of 1989, 370, 373

wages, 143, 144, 146, 149, 150, 158, 159, 166, 172, 178, 181, 281, 351, 339; increase (during 1960s), 144, 322, 354; postsocialism, 378, 382–383, 393, 397
Wałęsa, Lech, 1
Wallachia, 33, 34, 35, 42
weddings, 205. *See also* marriage
welfare, 247; dictatorship, 9; entitlements, 10, 64, 146, 180, 248, 250, 251, 257, 291, 332, 351, 366, 378, 390, 392, 393, 398, 403, 404
Western Europe, 63, 166, 202, 206, 213, 256, 314, 334; immigration to, 24, 380–381
woman question, 32, 39–40, 60
Woman's House (*Casa Femeii*), 45
Women's Emancipation, 43
Women's League of Romania, 40
Women's Rights (Drepturile Femeii), 40
Women's Society of Bukovina, 38
work schedules: conditions, 95, 255, 293
World Bank, 374, 393
World Population Conference, 269
World War I, 35, 40, 278; Romania in, 40–48
World War II, 15, 19, 43, 48–50, 103, 247, 249, 257, 261, 312, 354; Jews and Roma killed in, 48

Yugoslavia, 55, 282, 323, 340

Zetkin, Clara, 32
*Zhenotdel*, 32